Conflicting Paths

HARVEY J. GRAFF

Conflicting Paths

Growing Up in America

Harvard University Press
Cambridge, Massachusetts
London, England
1995

30780010
DLC

4-21-95

This book is printed on acid-free paper, and its binding
materials have been chosen for strength and durability.

Library of Congress Cataloging-in-Publication Data

Graff, Harvey J.
Conflicting paths: growing up in America / Harvey J. Graff.
p. cm.
Includes bibliographical references and index.
ISBN 0-674-16066-5
1. United States—Social conditions.
2. Adolescence—History.
3. Children—United States—History.
I. Title.
HN57.G64 1995
305.2'35'0973—dc20   94-28404
CIP

Designed by Gwen Frankfeldt

For lives past
Carolyn L. Galerstein: friend and colleague
Sally Ramsey: student, friend, and colleague

For lives present
Ben, Hannah, Josh, Ryan, and Taylor

And for young lives future

Contents

Preface

ALTHOUGH it sometimes seems a major industry inside the academy as well as outside, reading "signs of the times" can be as hazardous as it is compelling. Signs may be misleading, ambiguous, contradictory, and fragile. With respect to the young—children, adolescents, youth—this is unmistakable. It marks the modern era. Consider some indicators.

"Ah!" said an old lady, "there are no girls or boys now-a-days as there were when I was young; they are all little men and women now." Perhaps our venerable friend whose sigh over the *degeneracy* of the present generation of children yet rings in our ears, may have been influenced by the feeling not uncommon to the age. We are quite apt, as we advance in years, to forget the feelings of youth; and as we compare what is passing under our eyes with the indistinct and imperfect recollections of childhood, every thing seems changed, and it is difficult for us to believe that children now feel, act and speak as we and our childish companions did. How much of what is at present said on this subject may be explained in this way, we know not. We think, however, that the complaint of our friend is not entirely without reason. At all events she is not alone in her way of thinking, that a great degree of precociousness is observable among the young of the present age. Numbers may be no test of truth; and yet in this matter, we are inclined to look upon the frequency of the complaint with regard to the children of this day as an indication that it has some justification in the actual state of things. We have often heard the remark made, and our experience and observation have—we think—verified it, that there prevails now among the young a spirit of insubordination which leads them to look upon age as possessing no claims for deference and respect,—to push forward into places belonging to those of more years and experiences, and in all practicable ways, ape the dress, the fashions and manners of the grown up men and women of society.[1]

If the slightly archaic rhetoric of this statement did not suggest its nineteenth-century origin, its substance might be confused with many more recent observations, whether from the shrill editorial pages of magazines and newspapers or worried sermons or tracts with titles such as *Children without Childhood; Our Endangered Children*: childhood as "lost," "disappearing," or "eroding."[2] This passage, from an 1847 issue of *The Child's Friend*, is reminiscent of sentiments expressed over many centuries, regardless of its seeming affinity with our own. When the English translator of Philippe Ariès's seminal but misleading work *L'enfant et la vie familiale sous l'ancien régime* (1960) transformed the original French title into *Centuries of Childhood* (1962), he likely had little notion of the multiple ironies this evoked.[3] That the book which stimulated the still young field of the history of children might as easily have been titled "centuries *without* childhood" underscores the timelessness of the issues.

Despite the singularity presumed by many generations of adults in their complaints about the precocious or other unchildlike behavior of the young, none of them, whether in the 1840s or the 1990s, can claim uniqueness. That is a first point to grasp in the history of growing up: the young have always and everywhere been condemned for presuming to transcend their expected place—expected, that is, in the eyes of at least some of the unyoung. From classical civilizations through the medieval era to modern times, the young have reaped the consequences of offending against their status. Only since the nineteenth century have such offenses been accorded legal provenance and institutional certification. The mode of discourse, necessarily a selective one, long predated its institutionalization in law and policy. It marked a struggle for control which included the power of definition and language within its authority.[4]

The report from *The Child's Friend* raises another point: the easy confusion and ready substitution of adult opinion for evidence of youthful misdeeds. The editor is exceptional in being willing at least to admit that the frequency of complaint is taken as "indication" that there is something to complain about. It is much more common to accept the "evidence" of adult comment as reason to indict the dress, manners, insubordination, and precociousness of the young, among the countless charges that assume legitimacy. Whether from Tocqueville's observations or many others', that view echoes through the ages. The inescapably biased nature of generational complaint and the inherent problem of evidence, as well as the confusion and substitution of elders' views for the actions of the young, complicate efforts to apprehend and comprehend. How seldom even serious students of these subjects note the contradictions.[5] Balanced judgments become harder to make, as easy condemnation of the young takes their place. In the late twentieth century, an era once deemed that of the child, we have unfortunately become heirs to this legacy. The young deserve better.

The images of the past on which we base our judgments of the present are seldom the kinds of useful guides we need. Always emotionally powerful, they are often surprisingly fragile when examined closely. Images of and ideologies about the young intertwine in complex and inseparable ways.[6] Notions deriving from sources such as *The Child's Friend*, child-rearing advice, the observations of foreign visitors, "realistic" art or fiction, and the work of social reformers and others run, on the one hand, to dark pictures of unchildlike young persons, abused, neglected, and bad. Or, on the other hand, they turn on brilliant images of innocent, angelic youngsters in some vaguely dated "golden era." The first set of pictures provides rhetorical grist for progressives who wish to applaud recent advances and promote further reform and change; the dark images are aimed at persons found lagging behind. That conception of the past is a tool for approving and molding the present.[7] In sharp contrast, the second set of pictures serves as a cudgel to beat contemporary young persons, as well as adults, for their supposed fall from past perfection, their loss of elevated status, their threat to the social order present and future.[8]

Rhetorical images of the young prove powerful indicators for conflicting trends, and the uses to which they typically are put often bear little relation to their accuracy. Nevertheless, policy, parental advice, institutional arrangements, dicta to and for the young, and definitions of both normative behavior and deviance all follow, however contradictorily or illogically from simple presumptions of progress or decline. Large-scale theories and explanations, ringing with a rhetoric of the rise and/or fall of childhood, or adolescence, follow.[9]

In this context other signs of our own times sound loudly if not always clearly. They dance in their delicious ambiguity and expression of contemporary ambivalence and confusion. One such sign is the automobile bumper sticker I first spied in 1984 in Dallas: "Live a long time and become a burden to your children." A second sign is a cartoon, printed in *Harper's* (March 1989), that depicts a man in earnest conversation with his spouse. Looking into her eyes he says, "Let's get rid of the kids. The animals are allergic to them."[10] Hardly "child-centered," this message goes beyond ambivalence. A third sign, a cartoon from the *Wall Street Journal* of the mid-1980s, depicts an executive- or professional-class father advising his young son: "Never mind the facts of life! Learn all you can about the myths of life." That advice might prove useful in a society proclaimed "postmodern," more useful than the cartoonist may know, given the presence and power of myths about growing up. A fourth sign, a cartoon from the *New Yorker* of the mid-1980s, shows another executive-class father, seated in a modern armchair, announcing to a scruffy little boy: "Now that you're six, son, I'm putting you in charge of your own childhood."[11] This suggests a new stage in the division of labor and delegation of generational authority, one that gives pause to proponents of increasing children's responsibilities and safeguarding their rights. A final indicator comes from *Z Magazine* (November 1990) in the form of a cartoon that depicts a middle-class family—father, mother, and four young children—seated around the kitchen table. Father figure says: "I've called the family together to announce that, because of inflation, I'm going to have to let two of you go."[12] This suggests a novel route to homelessness, whose rise (especially among the young, and among families) sparks so much handwringing today.

These indicators transcend the common simplistic or reflexive explanations that feature "broken" families; failing parents; immature, selfish, narcissistic, or antichild "yuppies"; and other deviants from traditions long presumed American. They are complex, ambiguous, difficult texts, which encapsulate, however awkwardly or tellingly, the culmination of a lengthy historical process. They must be read with explicit reference to their layers of embedded meanings rather than simply decoded. Only at the high costs we now pay can they be taken at face value, as the history of the aged and their images also remind us.

In the history and historiography of children, adolescents, and youths— including present-day lives and understandings—myths are astonishingly powerful. Those that relate to public attitudes toward the young only suggest the difficult terrain. Combined with striking images, they provide their own discourse and means of legitimation.[13] The view associated with Ariès, for example, that there was no recognizable or recognized stage of childhood before the onset of modernization in the Western world, is but one case in point. Despite its frequent refutation, it remains endlessly repeated. Yet it also provides useful grist for two diametrically opposed interpretations: of both the "rise" and the "fall" of the young. And it suggests the costs of protecting and segregating young persons.[14]

As this book illustrates for the history of growing up—a phrase I use to integrate childhood, adolescence, and youth—such evidence begins to suggest that there are no satisfactory easy answers or linear interpretations. This history is a blurred canvas, one that obstructs vision. The task of seeing it clearly is difficult, just as growing up itself is and always has been difficult. Expectations and social policies, parent-child relations, and the role of the young in shaping their own development derive from the same messages and myths hinted at in the cartoons. There is no golden age to which we may return. Similarly, my reading of the more than five hundred first-person accounts relating to growing up from the middle of the eighteenth through the early twentieth centuries presented in this book finds no great age of youthful orthography, despite recent cavils.

Nor is the chronological march to the present a resolute advance in the conditions and lives of the young. Contrary to the psychohistorian Lloyd DeMause, as well as Philippe Ariès and J. H. Plumb, the past is far more than a nightmare from which liberated twentieth-century persons have awakened. As each day's news reminds us, the present is no panacea, no utopia for the young, regardless of adult claims to the contrary. In many ways lives have improved; in others they have not. Comparisons can be misleading.

Enormous and consequential transformations remade growing up during the two-century span covered by this book. Continuities and contradictions marked the transitions. Conflict, a key concept in this volume, typifies all phases of growing up among diverse youths who took different paths toward adulthood. This conflict ranges from the personal and psychological to overt breaks with authority. Despite striking legacies, images, and myths to the contrary, transformations of growing up neither homogenize and simplify nor hopelessly complicate the passages of childhood, adolescence, and youth on the march toward adult competence and maturity. Never has there been one common path—and this is another key point. There has always been a number of paths, although they were transformed during the seminal period described in this volume. In this history of growing up, gender, race, and social class, along with ethnicity, place of residence, and age itself—as well as time and fortune—emerge as especially powerful factors determining the different paths.

That the transformation of conflict-laden paths toward growing up occurred at the same historical moment when modern forms were taking shape is no accident. Each impinged on the other, often unevenly, always in complex and contradictory ways. That late in this history, on the eve of the twenty-first century, conflicts continue to erupt and problems appear should not surprise us. That young persons today are simultaneously branded endangered, children without childhood, yet also a postponed generation, late to mature, perpetually in search of adulthood, marks a fitting if discomfiting moment in the history of growing up. *Conflicting Paths* confronts that history in a fresh way and traces alternative paths and alternative understandings.[15]

Conflicting Paths

CHAPTER ONE

Growing Up in History: Conflicts, Paths, and Experiences

WE KNOW children past and children present through images we develop throughout our lives. Some images are richly nuanced; others are crude. They govern our understanding regardless of their accuracy.[1] Often diffuse, sometimes obtuse, images of children are powerful. Shakespeare's characters shape our images of adolescents, Dickens's those of poor children, the mass media those of mid- to late twentieth-century youth. To a considerable extent children of the past appear to us in terms of difference from children of the present. They also appear in terms of similarity to adults of the past, whereas modern children are more likely to be seen as different from adult contemporaries.

In addition, these images of difference tend to be contradictory. They can suggest a positive difference: the superiority of past to present children, the story of decline and fall. Or they can suggest a negative difference: the superiority of present or recent children to those in the past, a story of their rise. The historian John Sommerville writes of "the rise and fall of childhood" and John Demos of "the rise and fall of adolescence." The cultural critic Neil Postman writes of "the disappearance of childhood"; others speak of the "end of adolescence." Simple images and simple evaluations are a poor substitute for complicated stories with complicated consequences.[2] Inseparably intertwined with these images of the young are what I call the myths of growing up. They provide a language and a moral, a discourse of childhood, adolescence, and youth. As W. Norton Grubb and Marvin Lazerson's *Broken Promises* illustrates for the United States, such myths shape popular attitudes and public policies. The notion that children and youth constitute "private" matters for families rather than "public" concerns, misleading at best, precludes satisfactory policies. Only "other people's children" progressively encounter extrafamilial intervention. The myth that Americans are a child-loving culture obscures our niggardly and contradictory treatment of the young.[3]

Myths of growing up begin with an "origin myth"—often derived from Ariès's *Centuries of Childhood*—of the "invention" or "emergence" of childhood and adolescence in which early modern, specialized, and segregated elite boys supposedly came first. Prior to that time, according to this myth, in a world lacking a concept of childhood, the young resembled "little adults." In the nineteenth century notions of adolescence as "crisis" took shape. They were joined in the twentieth century by a picture of homogeneous, "spoiled" youngsters whose turf is consumption rather than production and for whom the travails of growing up have supposedly eased. Owing to biological and social immaturity, children and adolescents are thought to be inherently incompetent and dependent, more like infants than adults, and best served by compulsory segregation from the business of life and responsibility.[4]

Myth thus takes the place of history. It provides story, chronology, lessons, even a lexicon from the discourse of age relations. The father in the *Wall Street Journal* cartoon mentioned in the preface knew well of what he spoke! Myth embraces major contradictions. The lessons are sometimes dangerous. Innocent children do not need to know how to protect themselves from victimization and abuse. Those who do are no longer innocent. The borders that distinguish expected, acceptable difference and deviance from the unacceptable and the delinquent blur.[5]

The notion of the young as different is a striking and powerful thread woven through our images of past lives. It stitches these images together into a full "historical" narrative: (1) in the past life was nasty, brutish, and short; (2) parent-child relations were indifferent or abusive owing to life's uncertainties or psychological immaturity and selfishness; (3) familial strategies involved a rigid emphasis on the present and on the family unit rather than on individuals or on "investing" in the children's future; (4) the stability of the primary residential unit was also short-lived because dependent children left home early, often to reside in the homes of others. Early independence, at least from one's own family (if not others), accompanied this movement. The departure of children stemmed from various causes including physical exploitation of the young for labor or service, but also in some versions of the narrative from parents' fears that their love for their offspring interfered with necessary discipline.[6]

In the face of these familiar, useful, powerful, and comforting images, contrary evidence or complications in logic typically pale. When Linda Pollock fashioned her assault on the "Ariès thesis" in *Forgotten Children*, she replaced one set of images with another, a portrait of parental affection unvarying over time, to which she added a sociobiological twist. Other revisionists place the onset of "modern," "enlightened" child rearing progressively earlier.[7] Tellingly, recent studies that refute key elements of the dominant image have had little impact on its hegemony.[8] Among historians today there is no consensus in support of what we might call, after Ariès, a normative or traditional view of the histories of children, adolescents, and youths. Many of the threads that combined to form that composite interpretation no longer hold. The weight of evidence and argument now supports a number of conclusions, each a reversal of earlier arguments.

1. Though they are not synonymous with the late twentieth-century notions, there is no longer serious debate that concepts of childhood and adolescence antedate origins variously proclaimed in the thirteenth, seventeenth, nineteenth, or twentieth centuries.[9] Despite some persisting controversy, most students now agree that no era in recorded Western history lacked a concept of childhood or children and adolescents. Parents "loved" their offspring irrespective of life expectancy or presumptions about their inherent nature. Neither high mortality rates nor harsh discipline precluded affection.[10] Parental and filial love takes many forms, changing its manifestation and meaning over time.[11]

2. Reliable age-specific mortality rates are hard to calculate. It is clear that early death wasted countless human lives and that the very young are always at risk, especially at times of episodic crises of subsistence and disease. Nevertheless, mortality at birth and in infancy and childhood has often been exaggerated, sometimes intentionally. Extremely variable over time and space, early mortality levels seldom correspond sufficiently closely to other economic, demographic, and cultural indicators to underwrite claims about the close connections tying love to "investment" or its absence to low expectations of survival.[12]

3. In eras in which families formed society's fundamental units of production as well as consumption and residence, the practice of expecting and extracting useful contributions from all, including the young, to the best of their ability does not by itself constitute what modern societies condemn as exploitative "child labor." Similarly, efforts to romanticize familial communalism which applaud early work as a fundamental form of childhood socialization or presume equality in the household distract attention from gender-biased patriarchal hierarchies. Age, in combination with gender and social standing, contributed to power.[13] All comparisons over long spans of historical time run the risk of anachronism; and in the history of growing up the dangers are especially pronounced. The argument, advanced by Hugh Cunningham for England from 1680 to 1850, that the extent of child labor outside the home has been exaggerated is telling.[14]

4. The view that in preindustrial and even commercial and early indus-

trial society young persons left the homes of their families of origin, by their early teen years if not sooner, to live and labor in other households constitutes another part of the dominant image.[15] Recent research qualifies these notions. We now have a clearer sense of the wide variety of reasons, destinations, and expectations for young persons who left home early. Ground-breaking studies by Richard Wall and Michael Mitterauer confirm that the youthfulness of transients has been exaggerated. This research encourages us to uncouple the phenomenon of leaving home from that of assuming the status of servant in another household. Leaving home before the mid- to late teen years may well have been less common than has long been presumed. Thus, the reasons for doing so take on a different set of meanings.[16]

The history of growing up is deeply fragmented in its definition and delineation and in the approaches to it.[17] Advances within various areas of specialization deepen the problem. Despite the ring of a sad joke, the divisions are so great that students of children/childhood, adolescents/adolescence, and youth rarely consider others' subjects properly part of their own. Slip-sliding over "boundary" issues promotes confusion and distortion, especially when so much weight is attached to the precise demarcation of childhood from adolescence by age. That, however, can be less harmful than the consequences of segregating and fragmenting the principal components of the life course. Relationships to prior or subsequent stages and ages and historical eras seldom receive their due, and transitions between them, a subject of great import and much speculation, have had scant attention until relatively recently.

Mistaken dichotomies rank high among the overarching problems. More than most subjects in social history, the history of growing up is plagued by this error. In part a problem of definitions, but with disturbing implications, distorting dichotomies parallel the major mythologies in the history of growing up. Insistently asked are questions such as: When did parents love (or not love) their children? When was childhood or adolescence discovered or invented? When were children or adolescents treated specially, as other than "little adults"? When did their status "rise" or "fall"? The last is the ultimate dichotomy: along with literacy levels and the status of "the family" or religion, children and adolescents seem to decline at least once per generation!

In addition to fragmentation and segregation, there are problems of exclusion. First, in privileging the words of adults, many studies simultaneously silence and denigrate the voices of the young. Second, most histories framed within the boundaries of childhood, adolescence, and youth focus on middle-class Anglo-Saxon males. Other persons, especially girls, the poor, the working class, and ethnic and racial minorities, receive scant attention and are often completely ignored, if not derogated for their presumed lack of special age-graded status. Their relationship to the discourse of growing up differs sharply from that of those youngsters who occupy center stage in most studies.[18] The reasons advanced for this discrepancy range from the inadequacy of primary sources to the irrelevance of certain life stages given the presumed material, cultural, and/or cognitive conditions of the class, race, ethnic, gender, or geographic group in question. For girls, sociobiological differences from boys with respect to, say, puberty supply one rationale.[19] In practice, as often in theory, prior to the twentieth century growing up, it seems, was an advantaged minority group experience! Thus, another dichotomy rears its head in the discourse of age and authority. Large numbers of the young along with whole historical eras lacked, or were excluded from, common concepts and/or experiences of growing up.

The approach and design of the research reported in this volume developed from my sense of the strengths and limitations of previous works and the needs of the field. My signposts along the paths of growing up emphasize the importance of integration, inclusion, conflict (along with the enduring characteristics of dependence and difficulty), and historicity.

By "integration" I mean several closely related elements critical to a new history of growing up. First is the need to recombine the fragmented early stages of the life course in order to construe growing up as an integrated human developmental process. This encompasses transitions and passages through and between the formative stages of childhood, adolescence, and youth. We can delineate distinct patterns across space and time as paths of growing up. The notion of paths, discussed later on, serves as analytical tool, metaphor for passage through the life course, and heuristic.

The second is the need to pay close attention to the distinctions, as well as the connections, between childhood/children and adolescence/adolescents. More than semantics is at stake when students substitute or confuse one part of each pair for the other. This common fallacy often helps to explain major discrepancies between the title and stated goal of a study and its substance. Although one cannot study children or adolescents seriously without recognizing and understanding the concepts and constructs, the expectations, sentiments, and policies about both childhood and adolescence, the two are neither the same nor easily interchangeable.

A third aspect of integration is reflected in the focus of this book, which falls principally on the history of children, adolescents, and youth and the range of human developmental experiences that constitute, as they shift during the period under study, different paths of growing up. The young themselves, their voices, are central to this history, although they are not the only characters on the stage.

Fourth, neither crude nor deterministic, an integrated approach to growing up must be sensitive to the psychological and physiological aspects of development. Recent research in cognitive, developmental, life course, and conflict psychology and social psychology, discussed later, is useful in interpreting the sources used here and in linking experience with the social and cultural constructions that historically have shaped and reshaped growing up.

A fifth aspect of integration is that children, adolescents, and youth never exist—outside discourse, that is—as singular, unitary, homogeneous populations. There is no "child," no "adolescent," no one "childhood" or "adolescence," nor is there a "family." Despite the ways in which students of past and present discuss the young as largely undifferentiated, constructing theories about their convergence, the young are always diverse. Differences are multiple, and they are not random. Central to this book is the task of delineating the principal paths (note the plural) of growing up and the changes that shaped them from the eighteenth to the twentieth centuries.

Inclusion, the second area of emphasis after integration, calls for attending closely to the identity, origin, and provenance of all voices in the sources of growing up. Constituting a crucial corollary to integration, the goal of inclusion overlaps integration, especially with respect to the multiplicity of paths and experiences. The voices and actions of those growing up are a major element in this history, one that is ignored at great peril. To the extent that the young are active agents in making their own history, as John Gillis put it, and to the extent that these subjects are more than histories of ideas, their presence must be significant and direct. Many useful sources await the reader's attention.

This book seeks in part to deal with the problem of inclusion. It, too, is limited by what I term the problem of "missing paths," especially by race, but also by class and ethnicity.[20] Despite my intentions and efforts to the contrary, those paths marked especially by race—including African Americans (slave and free) but also Native, Hispanic, and Asian Americans—as well as by foreign-born and immigrant status or poverty and lower-class position could not fairly be considered in the same manner and terms as the history of other major groups and classes. For practical and other reasons, racial minorities are not included as such in these pages; the poor and immigrants appear but are underrepresented. Women, working-class and upper-class youth, and ethnics, however, achieve a new level of inclusion and attention.

Conflict and the related elements of dependency and the difficulty of growing up constitute three extremely important enduring or defining characteristics of the process. This third key element, conflict broadly conceived, is also discussed later in this chapter. From the psychological processes of growth toward competence, maturity, and autonomy to interactions along the path of age with parents, institutions, civil authorities, social expectations, and the like, conflict takes innumerable forms and produces diverse effects. Its forms and meanings often vary according to class, gender, race, ethnicity, location, age, and time. Necessarily at the core of growing up, conflicts are historical and variable dimensions of the process and its transformations. To a large extent conflict defines growing up and its contradictions: as experience and as concepts, theories, and expectations. The discourse and ideologies of growing up in turn constitute key elements of these contests for power.

Intrinsic to and inseparable from conflict is the issue of dependency. A crucial relationship that defines growing up, dependency varies historically, psychologically, socially, legally, and economically across the paths of individuals. It encompasses status, relationships, aspects of the self, social and legal definitions, metaphors of youth, and processes of growth. To evoke these relationships, historians use useful but incomplete terms such as *semidependent* and *semiautonomous*. Normative theories' notions of a relatively linear progression from total dependency to full autonomy seldom approximate the actual paths taken by persons in growing up. Nevertheless, legal concepts including the "emancipation" of minors, social policies, institutions, adult expectations, norms, and theories seldom deviate from an at least implicit linearity and consistency. No less consequential are the interactions of dependency with the main influence on growing up: age, class, sex, race, ethnicity, location, and time. In one sense a foundation of paths of growing up, dependency spans the distinct domains of experience, expectations, and evaluations, often with contradiction and conflict. It marks the efforts of the sometimes vulnerable young to negotiate their way, as well as their elders' controls and concepts. Dependency emerges among the complex characteristics not only of growing up but also of the struggle to define, control, and complete the process.

Almost always overlooked or denigrated by adults, including many who study children, is another factor, the inescapable truth that growing up is hard to do. Meeting the multiple, contradictory challenges of biology, physiology, culture, and society is never an easy task. Powerful images allow little leeway for complexity and variation. Instead they encourage summary judgments about the long-term decline or improvement of the young. Ambivalence or insufficient sympathy toward those in the snares of growing up among persons who nominally have already done so gives rise, on the one hand, to grand notions of "rise and fall" or "fall and rise," and, on the other hand, to quick condemnation of the young, at least other people's children, for offending against their status, regardless of their own actions.[21]

The historicity or historical constructedness of growing up forms the final area of emphasis. Just as the images that typically govern our understanding of the young derive from notions that are at least implicitly historical, more formal conventions, concepts, policies, even definitions of life's stages are made with reference to what is usually an imputed or implicit past. The young, their experiences, and the ways we come to terms with them stand as culminations of the historical course of growing up. History, myth, and image inseparably intertwine in complex cultural process, from whose neglect we suffer today.

Historians of growing up need to contribute to all these areas, providing new responses to today's pressing questions. What gives rise to shrill, confused outcries about "endangered children," "children without childhood," "adultlike children" (and "childlike adults"), or a "postponed generation" that can't or won't grow up? Is there "a new politics of age," a "war in the nursery"? How can we understand difficult issues that intertwine inseparably the personal, political, and cultural, that overtax the power of images and myths to organize and interpret seemingly unprecedented realities?

By itself that historical recognition need not prove helpful. At least from the time that Ariès located the "invention" or "discovery" of childhood and adolescence in the early modern West, the search for origins risked anarchism as well as anachronism; it became a form of the infinite regress, the historians' self-parody. No more encouraging is the persistence in numerous corners—among historians as well as others—of versions of Ariès's view despite its general repudiation. Newer claims relegate the very historicity of our subject to the past, to the great dung heap of the ages before the postmodern or "posthistorical" era. To say "that's history now" is a sharp slap. To those for whom adolescence has "ended" and childhood and children have "disappeared," the provenance of history becomes at best a cudgel to beat the present. At worst it is irrelevant, dead and gone.

An additional view also rejects or reduces the significance of history. In contrast with those who stress the power of the past in shaping, at least in part, the present are those who argue for a "universality" of childhood and adolescence, based on biological, physiological, psychological, anthropological, and more recently sociobiological perspectives. Linda Pollock offers one view in *Forgotten Children*: "stages" of development and their psychological correlates appear to be so persistent and pervasive that they constitute a "universal experience of adolescence."[22]

There are some impressive continuities in human development. Historians' expectations about human behavior or attitudes and possibilities of change can benefit from perspectives that include physiological influences and effects. Ground-breaking studies of height and weight, nutrition, age at menarche, and the like, for example, by J. M. Tanner, Peter Laslett, and Robert Fogel and his colleagues can be enormously helpful.[23] Apparently "universal" are general forms of early childhood sheltering; gerontological symbolism; age-related hierarchies of tasks, responsibilities, and power; individual and collective responses to certain kinds of challenge or crisis; patterns of adaptation; and rites of initiation and passage.[24] Some general relationships connect the biological with the physiological and the social with the cultural and psychological.

Despite the benefits derived from such views, the risks of confusion, distortion, and reductionism can be great. Again, we confront obstructing dichotomies: the putatively change-prone "historical" stands against the unvarying "universal" as opposed rather than interacting universes. When data improve during the last few centuries, evidence of change seems to become more constant. This is true, for example, with respect to height, weight, and age at sexual maturity in relation to nutrition, sanitation, and demographic factors. Some scholars argue that in the past 150 years average age at first menstruation for girls fell approximately one month per decade. When change is so dramatic, there often is little interest in continuities.

Such research begins to stimulate historians to probe the evidence of biological and physiological history. Data concerning variations in physical development across populations and over time are certainly relevant to paths of growing up. Evidence of shifts in onset of sexual and other forms of maturity raises large questions. When these data are used, it is mostly to repudiate approaches that relate to "universals" or to underscore modern progress. The experiences and meanings that human physiology and biology derive from culture and history—major elements of the structure of growing up—are ignored.

When personal accounts allow it, this book attends to biology and physiology, and considers their effects within specific historical contexts. Any useful definition or conceptualization of growing up as a human developmental process and its component life course stages necessarily integrates the biological, physiological, psychological, and anthropological—the biocultural—with more time-specific and historically contextual factors: the historical-sociocultural. This book embraces the conflicts, contradictions, and ideological appropriations of these fundamental intersections and incorporations. Each stage of the life course includes "universal" dimensions (and their historical variations) and the shifting or conflicting meanings taken from and given to them. No wonder we stumble and stutter when asked what we mean by "adolescence" or "childhood," and often retreat into moralisms, legalisms, psychologisms, or "refinements" of each stage into its own fragments of "early," "middle," and "late."

The historical constructedness of childhood/children, adolescence/adolescents, and youth cuts deeply in different directions. Some of them are semantic; some are ideological; others are conceptual or substantive; many pertain to power and authority. None stand uncritically alone except as unhelpful, sometimes dangerous abstractions. In his history of abandoned children, *The Kindness of Strangers,* the medievalist John Boswell writes: "'Child' is itself not an uncomplicated term." Close attention to language usage and connotations, the trusty test of historians, is an uncertain safeguard: "Among ancient and modern writers, conceptions of 'childhood' have varied widely, posing considerable lexical problems for investigators. Even the bases of distinction change." Scholarly and legal discussions of age classification bear no necessary relation to social attitudes or experiences. Although Boswell deems the complications greater for students of early societies, they remain obstacles for all.[25]

For modern historians, prescriptions and descriptions are confusingly intertwined. The nineteenth- and twentieth-century explosions in advice literature camouflage and complicate the problem.[26] The blessings of popular literacy, print, and other mass media—which in time all aim at the young—are not unmixed. Distorting rhetoric and discourse persist to plague students. Discourses of hierarchy and authority, as well as of romance and gender, continue to overlap misleadingly with those of age relations.[27] Class, race, gender, and age come to take the place of legal servility for Boswell's era, a transformation wrought with irony and contradiction in the century of the child and age of the adolescent, and no boon to its students.[28]

That "no analytical apparatus can clear away entirely the layers of conceptual and historical debris covering and complicating the recovery of 'childhood' as an idea or a phenomenon"[29] is indisputable. Only in those "layers of conceptual and historical debris" are childhood and children, adolescence and adolescents, and youth located: in the discourse and the experience of growing up. The paleontologist holds an advantage over the miner and the archaeologist. The historian of growing up refuses no offers of assistance. In pursuit of those historical experiences and their transformation, let us turn to our principal metaphorical, conceptual, and analytical tools: paths, conflicts, experiences.

Conflicts

Exaggerated in contrast with their modern counterparts, images of the young in traditional societies lean toward the idyllic. In contrast, modern times mark adolescence, even more than childhood, with conflicts both manifest and defining.[30] So familiar to us that they are hard to question, these partial truths and dominant images obscure a great deal. They remind us that conflict is important and variable throughout the history of growing up. The received wisdom minimizes the centrality of conflict in growing up in times past in contrast to the present.

The consequences are of more than historical interest. Ironically and tragically, presumptions about children's "natural" innocence prevent them from gaining the knowledge they need to protect themselves. Children are supposedly weak; they require protection. This "vulnerability" forms an ideological barrier against efforts to increase their knowledge, assertiveness, self-determination, and self-protection. Those qualities stand in opposition to, negating the very notion of, the child.[31] Class, gender, and race add their contradictory, conflicting influences. Linda Gordon's history of family violence, Viviana Zelizer's study of the "value" of children, W. Norton Grubb and Marvin Lazerson's account of failings in family and child policy, and Hugh Cunningham's story of shifting representations testify powerfully to the historical roots and dimensions of these problems.

The history of growing up is a history of conflicts, of conflicting paths, as myriad indicators, including first-person testimonies, richly demonstrate. Conflicts exist within the developing self in pursuit of the maturity and competence appropriate to its era and station; the dialectical dance of generations within and without the family; tradition and change. They confront developing institutions and expectations, as well as class, gender, race, geography, ethnicity, and age itself. They criss-cross and overlay other conflicts that stem from socialization, authority, morality, ideology, and historical circumstances. In personal as in social, cultural, economic, and political terms, growing up is a conflict-defined, conflict-ridden, and conflict-bound historical process.

Easily distorted and confused, the place of conflict in human development includes but is not limited to the psychological domain. Within specific historical contexts we recognize the omnipresence of conflict in experiencing socialization, developing character, adapting to environments, gaining competence in various domains, mediating internal with external discipline, accepting dependence and balancing later autonomy (within their limits), forming one's self and developing appropriate identity, and maturing. The contradictions of dependency and its relation to the varied defining qualities of the young embody conflict to perhaps its greatest extent.

Among images of the young and their spheres, the diffuseness and ubiquity of conflict, its very mundaneness, camouflage its presence and import, except in the notorious case of modern adolescents and other "problem," or more than normally "deviant," young persons.[32] In some views excessive conflict mars modern or contemporary growing up in contrast to images of "the good old days."[33] Ironically, the prevalence of adolescent maladjustment, rebelliousness, and alienation is greatly exaggerated, as studies repeatedly reveal. That does not lessen the power of the presumption. Some sympathetic "experts" on the young celebrate their overt (rebellious) conflict while many others decry it. Nonetheless, the centrality of conflict itself is distorted.

This situation is striking. So many signs of conflict in growing up, past and present, surround us. The mass media deluge us with them. Social science and public service careers are built on them. The young, their parents, and other adults who supervise them cry out for help. This is not a uniquely contemporary phenomenon. Literary studies such as Richard N. Coe's *When the Grass Was Taller* and Patricia Meyer Spacks's *Adolescent Idea* richly evoke the common theme of conflict that runs through writings about one's own and others' growing up since at least the sixteenth century. Spacks stresses conflict between the generations as well as conflicting representations of youth. Coe concentrates on "the conflict between an acute sense of individuality . . . on the one hand, and on the other, the unalterable, and therefore 'fatal' evidence of a factual past." Literature and other art forms provide venues for expressing and exploring these conflicts. It is hard to imagine fiction or films without them.[34]

Regardless of the dominant culture's distaste for conflict, and the clichés, excesses, and fallacies of pseudoscientific, seemingly universal schema, psychologists and other students do not fail to grasp, if often awkwardly, its central, necessary place for the developing self, from the classical philosophers through Rousseau to Freud and Erikson. A central conflict characterizes each of Erik Erikson's "eight stages of man," from trust versus mistrust to identity versus role confusion, generativity versus stagnation, and ego integrity versus despair.[35] Writing from a psychoanalytic perspective, the historian Ludmilla Jordanova emphasizes deep-seated conflicts: "The feelings we call our emotions also contain their opposites, and all the shades of feeling in between, so that notions like 'love' should be used with the greatest of care."[36]

Conflict serves many purposes. In children's linguistic expression the sociologist Douglas Maynard locates social conflict whose "manifest function" appears as the young reproduce the social structure of small-group society. In arguing and disputing, children create their own social organization, political alignment, and means of resolving disagreements.[37] Within formal classroom settings among older children, Valerie Walkerdine identifies the underlying conflict that is essential to learning "rational" argument, which she deems "the pinnacle of intellectual achievement."[38]

Conflict clearly shapes growing up at countless points. Many conflicts are formative. Conflicts are at once historical causes or consequences and historical legacies. Conflict in these pages covers a multitude of domains and dimensions, with special regard to the formative aspects of social class and gender.[39]

In *Being Adolescent* the psychologists Mihaly Csikszentmihalyi and Reed Larsen explore the developmental conflicts of growing up. They combine insights from new work in developmental and cognitive psychology with an awareness of life span or life course perspectives.[40] Csikszentmihalyi and Larsen convey the mundaneness, ubiquity, and inescapability of conflict in one form or another, writing: "The simplest task of adolescence is to learn the patterns of action required for participation in society. Teenagers must acquire habits to live by . . . Hence much of the conflict between parents and their adolescent children revolves around simple issues such as getting up in the morning, cleaning their rooms, and going to bed at night, as well as more central issues such as how much to study and how much time to spend with friends."[41] They note, further, that "A young person has to learn habits of thought, action, and feeling that are often difficult and unnatural. This is a process which, not surprisingly, is cause for much tension and conflict." The conflict of socialization—that is, the tension between internal and external goals—as well as conflicts involving consciousness, growth, solitude, families, peers, and school permeate these difficult, "unnatural" tasks. Contemporary conditions, the authors assert, exacerbate "universal tensions" and increase stress.[42] Chronology and context demand closer attention. "Our culture," as they term it, holds no monopoly on these conflicts.

Conceptualizing conflict as central to growing up can be fundamentally historical and contextual. Formative conflicts lie beneath sentimental glosses of past family life. The sociologist Anne Foner notes that conflict "as a basic ingredient of family life" attracts less notice than family cohesion, "and where conflict is dealt with, it is too often viewed as a form of deviance or a social problem." In contrast, Foner emphasizes: "Not only do family members of different ages have diverse functions, but they also receive unequal rewards. There are age differences in power, privilege, and prestige . . . These inequalities can generate age-related dissension."[43]

For Foner, studies of nineteenth-century families show the historicity of conflicts in age relations, which stand among the most consistent characteristics of growing up over the centuries. She points to "the anomalous position of the young people over 17 and 18 who remained at home. On the one hand, they had adult responsibilities in their work roles. On the other hand, they were in a position of at least partial subordination at home since they did not head their own households . . . To be treated like an adult for most of the day only to resume a subordinate role when in the parental home could not but create frustrations among the young."[44] Intergenerational antagonisms erupted over many things, including what Foner terms "the indeterminacy of the timing of the transition to full adulthood." During periods of great change, "differing outlooks of parents and children [and siblings] might easily lead to conflicts."[45]

Families are only one site in which age-related differences (as well as differences of class, gender, race, ethnicity, and so on) commonly sparked significant conflicts for young people growing up.[46] In a study of English children's magazines, the cultural sociologist Kirsten Drotner identifies another major source of conflicting and contradictory experiences since the mid-eighteenth century: "Childhood and youth as the phases of life we know today are based on a structural paradox: the young are brought up to adulthood at a remove from the social experiences of their elders . . . The contradictory needs and experiences of the young are felt consciously and unconsciously, and their modes of expression, dependent on class and gender, change over time."[47]

Varying by time, class and gender, multiple grounds for conflict emanated from the "structural paradox." They included age, norms of conduct, sources and substance of knowledge, innocence versus experience (including sexual), learning versus doing, internalization versus resistance, dependence versus autonomy, freedom versus restraint, obedience versus disobedience, home and family versus school and other realms, and so on.

Gender was part of this epochal transformation along with class and family.[48] Conflicts in growing up were inextricably linked to social formation. Drotner observes:

> The differences of experience indicate the contradictory possibilities that were engendered through the historical development of childhood and youth as distinct age categories and as a social space of subordination. As childrearing became domesticated and personalized, social contradictions would be perceived by the young as individual conflicts. Thus, the closer family ties that this form of socialization facilitated offered new means of parental supervision and adult repression, but the strengthening of personal bonds equally enhanced the possibilities of intimate emotional attachments.

The control and repression of socialization by anxious parents, prompted by their advisers, confronted contradictorily the tasks and challenges of growing up in changing circumstances.[49]

According to Drotner, juvenile reading contributed to escape and to action, the imagination's anticipation of alternatives.[50] Deemed idle on account of their status, the middle-class young might find resolution there for their conflicts of identity and self. Similarly double-edged were young people's responses to issues of mortality, religion, self-determination, and innocence.[51] Conflicts faced by working-class children were more often overt and explicit, involving authority and control, school conduct and learning, in contrast with street experience, work preparation, and actual labor.

For all classes, Drotner concludes, the late nineteenth and early twentieth centuries brought more, and more tangible, contradictions.[52] Increasing conflict over dependency and autonomy heightened the pain of confronting one's emerging sexuality, a process shared, if differentially, by girls and boys. Conflict and contradiction characterized the complex process as they scarred, both consciously and unconsciously, the growing person.

Many, though certainly not all, central conflicts in growing up relate closely to differences in social class, gender, race, ethnicity, and similar "ascriptive" factors. Experiential and structural differences relating to these defining and differentiating characteristics criss-cross virtually all other categories in this history. Their weight is felt in interactions with shifting social attitudes and values (sometimes elevated to the status of "theories" or "laws of nature"), which they also play a part in shaping. Notions of normality versus deviance and delinquency developed together, images of one reciprocally shaping the others. As they developed, in turn, they shaped schools, reformatories, and juvenile courts, as well as "normative" expectations.[53] Over the principal period of this study the impact of class, gender, race, and ethnicity increased sharply, influencing not only the experiences of the young themselves but also the responses of others to them. Those responses included changing expectations, developing laws and institutions, emerging professions and intellectual disciplines, and rhetorical discourses.

Michel Foucault taught us to search out and listen to discourses and rhetorics of power, with their enormous effects in transforming worldviews and worlds. Deconstruction and feminism, separately and together, put "difference" high on the agenda. With respect to growing up, groundbreaking studies of working-class women and children by Christine Stansell, the Children's Aid Society by Bruce Bellingham, and, more generally, policies and institutions aimed at "other peoples' children" highlight major conflicts of a developing America. Grubb and Lazerson's *Broken Promises* identifies the gaping contradictions that cut through American family and children's policies as a result of social inequality, discrimination, unexamined myths and assumptions, cheapness and meanness. Dual notions of responsibility accompany dichotomous notions of families and children: our own, for whom no exception or expense is too much, and other people's, about whom our anxieties, fears, and blame lead to demeaning, punitive, or inadequate responses that smash clichéd notions of the public love of children. Our families are private and sacred; other people's are exposed to public (and sometimes private) scrutiny and intervention. At best, ambivalence characterizes our attitudes and actions. A crescendo of conflicts echoes throughout the great chasm.

Conflicts continue to characterize the process of growing up. Fragile understanding combines confusingly with the shrill pitch of voices in a historical moment far from complete. The sea of contradictions ebbs and flows with "disappearing" children on the one hand and, on the other, young persons who "won't grow up." Regardless of the accuracy of such signs, they are better indicators of other crises of late modernity than of growing up per se. But they do complicate the already difficult tasks facing the young.

In *The Script of Life in Modern Society*, the Swiss sociologist Marlis Buchmann compares survey data from U.S. high school classes of 1960 and 1980. Based on structural and life course approaches, her conclusions center on conflict. Despite the language of social science, her point is plain: "Overall, the life course regime in advanced industrial society is characterized by tensions inherent in the relationship between standardization and destandardization of the life course: Increasing bureaucratically determined status allocation coexists with growing discontinuity/flexibility and diversification of life course patterns supported by the shifting cultural imagery of the private and public spheres." Individuals face these contradictions as they determine their paths toward adulthood. "Current transformations of the life course regime thus highlight the dialectics between action autonomy and action constraint."[54]

Here lies the culmination of "centuries of childhood," the transformations of growing up, in its latest chapter. Buchmann locates a complicated pattern of choices and challenges for negotiating paths toward adulthood. Those growing up face diversity, flexibility, and alternative identities. Yet the "multidimensional" identities constructed in such settings lack "a clear hierarchic ordering of elements" which "tends to reduce the likelihood of building up long-term, stable expectations." With structural support for action directed more toward present than future, these contradictions clash: "Discrepancies between expected and realized career paths may give rise, on the one hand, to increased psychological problems as a result of self-blame and, on the other hand, to social conflicts (in instances where the unfulfilled projects are interpreted as problems of the social structure, i.e., structural blame)."[55]

Is this society's revenge on the young in what was once proclaimed their century? In stressing the historicity and centrality of conflicts, this volume's approach better accords with evidence of these transformations than views that portend the "end" of children, adolescents, or youth. The hand of the past on the present, if gnarled and distorted, still pulses with life.

Paths

Images of children, adolescents, and youth are typically binary: good-bad, ours-theirs, male-female, white-black, past-present. They are also flat, one- or two-dimensional. When we consider how young persons move from childhood toward adulthood, our notions are no more flexible. The young may be well-adjusted or maladjusted, conformist or rebellious, and so on. These conceptions allow little room for diversity among either the young themselves or the ways in which they grow, the lines they follow in their transitions through childhood, adolescence, and youth to maturity. Regardless, powerful expectations, theories, laws, and policies are constructed around them, sometimes with high human and social costs.

Concluding a study of ten communities, the psychologist Francis Ianni emphasizes systematic, patterned variations among the young. First, he notes: "While most people tend to talk about adolescence as if it were one unified period in the life course, teenagers more often experience it as a number of more or less synchronized periods, each structured by the various socializing environments."[56] Second, Ianni observes that patterns of variation or difference cut deeply across and divide the experiences of each life stage: "All American adolescents are not alike, different communities can and do develop different kinds of adolescents, and diversity among adolescents—even within the same community—can be as great as it is among adults."[57] Across formative early developmental stages children and youth in fact demonstrate an unmistakable heterogeneity: "Other unique experiences and characteristics, chance events and life contingencies . . . combine with the various differences among adolescents to insure that there is no universal developmental path into and throughout adolescence."[58] Also true for children and youth, this observation characterizes growing up writ large.

This recognition is fundamental, its implications many. The sociocultural historical construction of the life course lies in the interactions of young persons with identifiable characteristics and from different origins with biology and physiology, norms and expectations, socializing environments and institutions, and historical time and place, what Tamara Hareven, following Glen Elder, terms "family time" and "historical time."[59] Conflict marks these intersections.

Common assumptions tend to stress an almost linear increase over time in the complexity and difficulty of growing up, while some "experts" proclaim the ease of growing up, sometimes to decry, sometimes to applaud it. Whereas change stands as a constant challenge to those who are negotiating their way toward adulthood—and those who attempt to influence them—at no time during the two centuries this book examines did growing up consist of a progressive increase in the number and complexity of paths. That is a major modern myth. Growing up has never been anything other than difficult and complicated.

The major focus of this book is on the formation, experience, and transformation of the principal paths of growing up from about the mid-eighteenth century to the twentieth century. The concept of paths is a useful one for organizing and probing the mass of evidence provided by the testimonies. The term is employed in these pages in several ways: as an analytical instrument, an organizing device, and an evocative, discursive metaphor. I attempt, at least in part, to substitute a new set of images for the old, images that are more accurate but also more appropriate, practical, and flexible.

In contrast to other views, this approach recognizes and emphasizes that paths of growing up are socioculturally constructed, variable, multiple, and heterogeneous. They are historically defined and characterized by central conflicts. Paths are contingent, structured across a population. Regardless of images and expectations, neither single factors nor unitary routes characterize the means and the ways that young persons follow in growing up. Some variables can make an enormous difference. Neither all young persons nor all paths are created equal.

Recent developments in the social and human sciences have influenced my approach. As leading students of human development such as Paul Baltes, John Clausen, Matilda White Riley, David Featherman, and Glen Elder write, various traditions in psychology, sociology, anthropology, demography, and history address the problems of studying human lives developmentally and dynamically over time. From the collection of life histories early in this century, efforts have advanced from conceptions and tests of notions running from generation, cohort, and cycle, to life span and life course.[60]

New interest in the sociology and anthropology of age, gerontological sociology and demography, and transitions studies complements these emphases. Increasingly sophisticated conceptualizations, methodologies, measures, and data sometimes outrun theories and conclusions. Nevertheless, interest in and research on the life course and life span impressively cross disciplinary divides and stimulate exciting collaborations.[61] Such research also reinforces the need to link life course approaches with emphases on cognitive and developmental psychology and their novel, expansive conceptions of learning and development. Without recasting concepts of human development, we cannot begin to reconsider growing up in terms of the central but difficult themes of dependency, growth, maturation, competence, and autonomy as they differ across populations and over time. Richer concepts of development across life's span; learning as diverse and practical; growth, maturity, and autonomy as flexible, varied, and connected with competence: together these themes revise the "script of life," to borrow Buchmann's phrase.

In his introduction to *Transitions: The Family and the Life Course in Historical Perspective,* the sociologist Glen Elder writes: "The life course refers to *pathways* through the age-differentiated life span."[62] Another sociologist, David Featherman, wisely notes: "Life-span thinking represents a *metatheoretical* approach rather than an explicit set of grounded concepts and hypothetical relationships."[63] Because of my sense of the primary needs and questions of research, I did not write a history in explicit reference to the life course or life span. And because of the nature of the major primary sources and my approach to historical expression in this volume, I make no effort to quantify or model the data or similarly structure the text. That is not appropriate to my conception of the task at hand or my idea of the best use of this source material. Historical efforts along such lines have influenced my understanding of the relations between life course patterns and historical contexts. Among the most important are studies by John Modell and others, Michael B. Katz, Glen Elder, Tamara Hareven, Avery Guest, Laurence Glasco, Peter Uhlenberg, and Robert Wells. Stimulating comparisons come from Michael Anderson, Peter Laslett, Richard Smith, and Richard Wall for England, and Michael Mitterauer among others on the Continent.

In concentrating on what I consider the principal paths of growing up in any given era, I focus on a relatively small number. Significance is interpretive, not statistical, although the greatest number of lives at any time surely falls within the net. Parsimoniousness is a sound strategy, especially in guarding against the dangers of proliferating paths.[64] For several important paths, as I have noted, personal accounts are frustratingly rare; this is especially true of racial minorities, the poor, and the working class.

Despite differences in emphasis and expression, *Conflicting Paths* shares much with life course studies. This includes a focus on transitions or turning points, particularly as they surround entries and exits from distinct life course stages such as school, work, leaving home, migration, marriage, and so on. As Buchmann expresses them, other points of agreement are: (1) that neither life stages nor transitions can be understood independently from the life course as a whole (this is in part a question of conceptualization, in part an empirical issue about which personal accounts are quite useful); (2) that broad social changes "provide the appropriate frame of reference for assessing the significance of changes in the patterns associated with particular life stages and in the life course as a whole" (a task for which historians are well placed); and (3) that "understanding how society organizes individual life courses and how people direct and give meaning to their own biographies requires an approach that integrates a macrosociological perspective with an actor-oriented one" (the design of my research meets this demand).[65]

Both paths and periods are metaphorical concepts, and necessarily somewhat arbitrary ones. In this study overlapping periods of approximately a half century in length meaningfully define both "historical time" and "growing-up time." Overlapping chronological boundaries—the mid-eighteenth to the early nineteenth century, the late eighteenth to the mid-nineteenth century, the mid-nineteenth to the early twentieth century, and the late nineteenth century to the 1920s—appropriately allow for the unevenness and irregularity of historical development just as they caution against false precision. At the same time, this flexible periodization approximates historians' recent revision of the chronology of American social history with its emphasis on the changes in the second half of the eighteenth century, before and after the Revolution; in the first half of the nineteenth century, including the impact of immigration and migration, commercialization, urbanization, and industrialization; and in the late nineteenth and early twentieth centuries, where we see the foundations of modern America.

My focus, I have said, falls on a limited number of principal paths. Each path, as I explain in the chapters that follow, combines social-historical description, interpretation, and metaphor. The names given to the paths are evocative as well as descriptive. Scanned either synchronically or diachronically, they offer a summary survey of the course of growing up in its variations and transitions. Each path is rooted in the evidence and events of its own time and place.[66] The paths deemed dominant in each period derive from my understanding of demographic, social, economic, geographic, and cultural structures and trends; patterns of uneven social change; and major social differences and variations, all in conjunction with my reading of the personal accounts. Each of these elements reciprocally supports the others. Chapters 2 through 5 present periods and paths through an interpretive choreography of testimonies from hundreds of personal accounts. Chapter 6 selectively and briefly surveys the recent past and present. The period from about 1750 to about 1920 receives the greatest attention and emphasis.

The contrapuntal connections between change and continuity that comprise the historical transformation of growing up have a lengthier, more complex and varied, and richer historical span than most accounts allow. For obvious reasons, the years from the late nineteenth and early twentieth centuries and those following the Second World War have attracted a disproportionate amount of attention. This history is sometimes traced back to G. Stanley Hall's fin-de-siècle writings, and sometimes even earlier in the nineteenth century. Regardless, "modern" history usually begins with the present century.[67] We thus miss the enormous significance of the earlier formative eras in which the remaking of growing up fundamentally commenced and in which the course and contradictions of its more familiar recent history experienced their own early shaping.

In the rhetoric of their nomenclature, the principal paths of growing up outline, discursively if simply, the historical transformation, its nature and timing. The eighteenth-century beginning (cutting into the continuing historical process) finds an early modern mix of paths. Termed "traditional," "transitional," and "female," these paths share the ground with "emergent paths." The strong hand of tradition weighs heavily and influentially but also dynamically. The "separate" sphere of varied female experiences is present more or less at the creation of our tableau. The dynamism, precocity, and contradictoriness of components within the evocative path of transition foretell not only future routes but the complications of countless individual experiences of change.[68] These paths are complicated by multiple components. Over time, the transitional path unevenly supplants the traditional. The former overlaps and is joined by emerging class (and racial) paths. The female path also develops in relation to the long, uneven transition to modern social forms and relations. Major paths revealingly overlap and cross one another.

The century and two thirds that begins in the middle decades of the 1700s serves as cradle and nourishment for the conception, birth, and maturing of "modern" growing up. Growing up was recreated amidst the massive changes that wrought the modern United States (and much of the West). Growing up reflected the consequences of that world-making history in all its human richness and its human costs.[69] These are neither the terms nor the images with which this great story of transformation is usually told. They will strike as odd, perhaps anachronistic, readers who anticipate the withering away of great social divisions and their replacement with homogeneous children, adolescents, and youth, whether for better or for worse. Personal testimonies tell this powerful story clearly and forcefully. Before I studied them, I did not anticipate the extent to which they would so compellingly describe the great transformation that modern growing up represents. The story gains coherence from that telling.

Experiences

Throughout this study, I refer to "experiences" of growing up. I use this term advisedly and recognize its problematic status both conceptually and theoretically.[70] I also employ it in a double sense. On the one hand, experience refers to paths of growing up in the explicit sense of description, including reconstructions of the life course of individuals singly and collectively in a historical and comparative context. On the other hand, experience also refers to individuals' efforts to grasp, express rhetorically, and make meaning of their growing up in their own words, including appropriation of cultural terms and mythologies in varying degrees of explicitness. These are not synonymous usages; potentially they are contradictory. I take pains to keep my meaning clear. Nevertheless, in this book individuals' expressions of their constructed experience are connected closely with my own historian's constructions.

Not only are notions of experience problematic, as William Sewell, Jr.'s, brilliant critique of E. P. Thompson's use and privileging of the word in his seminal *Making of the English Working Class* illustrates. Experience, as lived and/or recorded, is never "pure" or unmediated. Neither is it nonmaterial nor transparent. Nevertheless, as Sewell writes, "restored to something like its usage in ordinary language, experience has a place in the theory of class formation—and in the theory of historical change more generally." Although the tasks of this book differ from Thompson's, Sewell's clarification merits attention:

> The first step is to disengage the notion of experience from the quite distinct problem of multiple causation. Deviations of historical events from a strict economic determinist model should not automatically be assigned to "experience" . . . Experience should be conceptualized much more narrowly, in line with *Webster's,* as "the actual living through an event or events . . . ; actual enjoyment or suffering; hence, the effect upon the judgment or feelings," with knowledge as a result. When we call an event an experience, we usually mean that the person who has enjoyed or suffered the event has reflected upon it. Experience, as Clifford Geertz puts it, is something "construed." Thompson himself, in *The Poverty of Theory,* at one point gives a definition of experience very similar to that in *Webster's* . . . "*Experience,*" he says, "comprises the mental and emotional response, whether of an individual or of a social group, to many interrelated events or to many repetitions of the same kind of events."[71]

This perspective accords nicely with my intentions. As Sewell notes: "This definition is reasonably clear and specific. It indicates something important but not very mysterious—that people respond mentally and emotionally, both individually and in groups, to what happens to them."[72] That includes growing up. Our task is to listen, and to hear.

Voices from the Past

Through the lens of about five hundred first-person narrative accounts, distinct patterns of growing up in specific historical circumstances come into focus.[73] Among the literary genres that constitute this collection, diaries, memoirs, and autobiographies are most numerous, followed by letters and other forms. This is no "random" or "representative" sample. Its range, nevertheless, is wide as well as deep.

This collection has its biases. Some stem from the genre of first-person narration; the reasons for others are more diffuse.[74] None of them precludes careful reading and cautious exploitation within clear historical contexts. Indeed, some biases may be construed as useful. Whether created contemporaneously with growing up or written later, these accounts have a rhetoric all their own, as students of these works as literature note.[75] Biases—challenges to readers—range from the motives and means of a record's creation and the chances of its survival, to the circumstances of its composition, to the breadth of a writer's vision and understanding, sharpness of memory, completeness of account, and literary ability. They include questions of time and process or mode of composition. Each form has disadvantages as well as advantages. Comparing the paths of growing up across individual accounts is complicated by missing variables and variations. These limit the usefulness of a source for certain analyses; at the same time, they promote other rhetorical strategies for historical inquiry and expression.

Another challenging element of these forms of writing is the unacknowledged but inescapable presence of cultural forces, from nostalgia to novel cultural notions, for example, about child rearing or adolescence; or explicit and implicit reflections or reactions as a result of an author's class, race, gender, ethnicity, geographic location, age, later experience, and so on. There is no unmediated or uninterpreted testimony of life history. "Fact" and "fiction" must always be construed in their interrelationships and interactions, not as ideal-typical oppositions. Potential problems, some of them severe, can be turned into sensitive indicators of change, interactions of individuals with shifting cultural influences, struggles for competence and autonomy. Pioneering studies of working-class women's and men's autobiographies and memoirs, women's narratives, and African Americans' personal writings have prepared us to appreciate the special qualities and rich repositories of knowledge "hidden" in the resources of personal narrative that historians and critics have long ignored.[76]

The difficult task of writing about, re-presenting, and expressing one's own self in a relatively explicit way cuts across all other variations in the population this or any comparable collection comprises. These first-person accounts are efforts to present personal experience in terms of a description of one's life, and to express that experience discursively and appropriately. They can also be read as efforts to communicate within a culture or subculture, with varying degrees of explicitness and consciousness of self and others. Cultural products themselves, they reflect cultural mythologies and metaphors that can be particularly telling. (Of the many we see here, the "frontier origins" and "Ben Franklin" paths are common examples.) Retrospective examinations and expositions differ from contemporaneous accounts and earlier recollections. Memory plays its part in relation to immediacy and freshness, on the one hand, and lack of distance, on the other.[77]

Forms of expression and their contents follow in part from the historical moments and locations that shape not only each life but also the writing about it. Both reflect major influences on the life course. These influences emerge perhaps more visibly and usefully in the writings of nonliterary and nonelite persons. Because of that bias (among others) and my own overarching interest in "ordinary" persons, literary accounts and accounts of literary persons receive little attention here.

Personal narratives of growing up constitute one cluster among the life histories that sociologists, anthropologists, and psychologists, have long studied, especially in Europe.[78] Newer to historians, they are construed simultaneously as stories and as histories. Considering "On the Analysis of Life Accounts" in the important collection *Biography and Society*, Nicole Gagnon probes such writing for the presence of historical consciousness. "In practice," she notes, "this amounted to examining how social change had been experienced and understood."[79] Although her notion of history is conventionally "great event"–oriented, her conclusion corresponds with my own: personal testimonies are sources of individuals' historical place and their struggle to make sense of them.[80]

Despite the complications, sources such as diaries, memoirs, autobiographies, letters, and the like provide direct (although not unmediated) access both to the experience of growing up and to the tasks of expressing and creating meaning out of it.[81] No other kind of historical evidence provides this access for substantial numbers of persons. Comparing and building from contrasting observations from various points across the life course, personal testimony captures the rich diversity of human experience in growing up as well as the unevenness, contradictions, conflicts, and consequences of the epochal transformations of the early life course in this period. These sources also heighten awareness of their creators as active agents in their own, and their society's, history. Their absence contradicts and weakens many related studies.

No evidence, whatever its origin or provenance, speaks for itself. This history of growing up experiments in the interpretive construction and rhetorical presentation of its life stories. *Conflicting Paths* attempts a textual organization and presentation that privileges and gives priority to the voices and the experiences of growing up rather than to my own visible presence as author. I offer no false claims for this experiment. My selections of the lives and voices that testify are self-evident interpretive acts of authorial intervention. They represent the results of my questions, readings, interpretations, and historical assumptions. Based on my encounters with the literatures of the relevant fields, they unavoidably reflect my own views of historical development. Unavoidably I "read" first-person materials within an explicit critical, theoretical, and historical perspective detailed here. Central to it are the notions of paths, conflicts, and experience and their roles in the making and remaking of growing up.

Influenced in part by the so-called new narrative, this work stands apart from other histories constructed from first-person sources. I draw inspiration from the brilliant scholarly examples of Carlo Ginsberg, Natalie Zemon Davis, Robert Darnton, and Jonathan Spence, among others, and from authors of pioneering works representing the collective biographies of nonelites.[82] In addition, Linda Pollock and Philip Greven, Jr., showed the potential (and limits) of child-rearing narratives taken in large numbers.

Recent historical writing underscores the rich potential of personal sources to demonstrate the dialectical relationships between individuals and changing societies, as producer and product, subject and object, of historical currents. Discussing black South African oral histories, Tim Keegan puts the point forcefully:

> What the oral record makes clear is the futility of schematic, unilinear, homogeneous images of social change. Transformations are seldom as complete as they seem superficially, and social revolutions often appear in larger perspective to be strangely inconclusive. The same morbid symptoms of the old order reassert themselves long after they are supposed to have been buried in the dust of a previous epoch. Historical change tends to be cyclical, repetitive and cumulative. The "view from below" alerts us to unexpected dimensions of social change, and reveals some of the contradictions and complexities and local variations of the processes involved.[83]

First-person testimonies tell their tales of growing up with power and sometimes with surprising clarity and insight as well as contradiction, complexity, and variation.

CHAPTER TWO

First Steps in the Eighteenth Century

PERSONAL testimonies give voice to a surprising variety and complexity in ways of growing up for young people born in the second half of the eighteenth century. No single image can accommodate the diversity of journeys through childhood, adolescence, and youth at this relatively early point in modern history, for there was no one path of growing up. Separate developmental stages of childhood and adolescence were recognized even then; this was no homogeneous world of "little adults."[1] Not only was there a variety of paths, but also they cut across most lines of social difference. No scholarly squabbles or simple images can alter this fact.

Changing social, cultural, and economic relations reshaped the paths of the young toward adulthood. These transformations were often ambiguous and contradictory. The process of growing up was in transition, although the results were hardly apparent at the time.[2] Nonetheless, an ongoing if accelerating process of change was already under way in the eighteenth century. Threads of tradition and change often overlapped, sometimes intertwining intricately and blurring the lines between paths of growing up. In various forms conflicts were experienced by many of the young, and these constituted important aspects of growing up. Together the principal paths show how young people came of age in the late colonial and early republican eras and what problems or advantages they faced. They also constitute a baseline from which we may assess the ways in which paths persisted or deviated.

The dynamism of this period in American social development is central to the story. By beginning at this point we frame a larger canvas which in turn captures developments often slighted by images and assumptions of "traditional" or "colonial" stability or immobility. American social and economic development in the second half of the eighteenth century blended tradition and change, family orientation and individual market relationships, threats to independence and opportunities, and striving for autonomy. The evocative phrase "transition to capitalism" barely hints at the complexity, instability, and irregularity of the transformations and their implications for growing up.

In the 1950s and 1960s historical interpretations stressed the precocious capitalist modernity of this period over earlier views of the period as one of traditional self-sufficiency. Today, more complicated approaches attempt to incorporate both social and market perspectives. "The dimensions of economic existence had changed," James Henretta comments. "Thousands of farm families and artisan households were now more deeply embedded in profit-oriented exchange relationships . . . Many thousands more, a full tenth of the free labor force, worked for wages . . . Thousands of enslaved southern blacks experienced new capitalist intrusions into their lives." Four interrelated developments propelled this transition: the growth of farm production and sales to markets to meet the trans-Atlantic demand for agricultural produce; the spread of wage laboring stemming from surplus population owing to rapid growth from natural increase and migration; the reorganization of production resulting in the exploitation of new market opportunities and labor supply by entrepreneurial merchants, landowners, and artisans; and the political responses of newly independent states to the needs and interests of "monied men."[3]

Families and individual family members neither welcomed nor sought these disorienting, potentially disruptive transformations. Changes affected them—often unevenly—and factors such as geography, status and wealth, family circumstances and desires, gender, age, chance, and the place of the market in their lives affected and were affected by those shifts. As Daniel Vickers concludes: "In an age of nascent capitalism, when family producers had to confront ever more constantly the possibilities of hiring their neighbors or working for them, and of marketing produce or buying their own bread, it was the worry over whatever level of independence and material well-being they possessed that occupied their minds. For some, the rising winds of the market economy blew fair, full of promise for prosperity and control over their own affairs; for others, they whispered of poverty and dispossession."[4]

For young people growing up, Allan Kulikoff adds, "the sexual and age division of labor within households was profoundly influenced."[5] For them to achieve independence, their families had to protect and transmit, or the individuals had to obtain (alone or with aid), an adequate degree of competence. In times of sweeping transformation, means of protecting and transmitting as well as obtaining the skills and abilities that constituted competence shifted too. Where one started with respect to geography, wealth, family, gender, and age mattered a great deal. When Henretta states that "autonomy required increasing ingenuity," he merely hints at the challenges faced, and in part fashioned, by young persons growing up.[6] In their efforts to mediate change, a great many families and individuals, however ironically, advanced the social and economic transformations they sought to limit or accommodate only partially. "In time," Vickers writes, "the very term *competency* would come to denote a degree of skill or capacity (sufficient to survive in an industrializing world) and lose its traditional meaning, which had hinged on property ownership. But these developments were never anticipated." Young people cast the seeds of change themselves, whether anticipated or unanticipated.[7]

Not all young persons had that chance. To an extent unimaginable today, early death (whether at birth or in childhood) was a common presence.[8] Despite a dramatic increase in historical demographic research, we have no satisfactory estimates of age-specific mortality and life expectancy, especially for the young, for the second half of the eighteenth century. Mortality and morbidity levels varied greatly from place to place and year to year. Infant mortality in Andover, Massachusetts, from 1730 to 1759 stood at 156 per 1,000; in late eighteenth-century Philadelphia it ranged from 187 per 1,000 for the entire population to 146 for Quaker children and 254 for infants of unskilled laborers. Infant and child mortality rates were even higher in the South. Early in the century more than one third of Chesapeake children died in their first year, while more than half died before age twenty.

Infant mortality improved in some areas, such as the Philadelphia region, during this period. In others it remained virtually unchanged or even worsened. Mortality in the aggregate likely did not decline irrevocably until the second half of the nineteenth century. As late as 1900–1902 (a period for which data are far more readily available), more than 12 percent of infants died before reaching one year; more than 18 percent died before their fifth birthday. Despite these high levels of early loss, exaggeration remains a risk. Persons who lived to, say, age ten or twenty had a very good chance for life expectancy well into their forties, fifties, and even sixties. And there is no evidence that the danger of infant or child death prevented parents from loving their children.[9]

The impact of child mortality on family, friends, neighbors, and other young persons is harder to gauge than its frequency. Likewise, we can estimate how many children lost their parents but can do little more than speculate about the overall effect. Few young people were untouched by encounters with death, early and close by. Orphanhood was common, especially in the South, and few reached adulthood without losing at least one parent. At the end of the seventeenth century, two thirds of children in the Chesapeake had lost at least one parent. Mortality arises in the stories and transformations of growing up in many ways: parental death, the care of legal guardians and trustees, stepparents, orphanhood.

The uses—emotional, spiritual, exemplary—to which the image of morbidity was put were many. Those who died young gained a certain power as positive or negative models for others to emulate or reject. Evangelical religious literature in particular seized on the notion of the premature death of the saved and made it into an inspirational literary genre with implications for gender and status differences.[10]

Four major paths of growing up stand out in life accounts dating from the 1740s to the early 1800s: traditional, transitional, female, and emergent. Other common paths are missing from the account because of biases in creating, preserving, or locating first-person sources. These include accounts by and about servants, especially women; poor and working people, both rural and urban; African Americans; and native peoples.[11]

I have included a female path for each period, despite substantive and rhetorical problems. The issues are complicated, and resolution is difficult. A strategy of placing women on a path of their own rather than alongside their brothers, thus emphasizing commonalities, might be construed as assigning them a minority status by reification of a separate sphere.[12] The dangers of marginalization are greater, however, when young women are included within paths of growing up that are defined primarily by male experience. Women also fall prey to male numerical domination of available first-person sources. Any recognition of similarity and shared experience, a laudable if misplaced effort at democraticization, detracts from an appreciation of the seminally shaping contribution of gender.

Recognition of the differences, nevertheless, in no way diminishes the importance of similarities. Any useful approach must embrace both. When I write that traditional, transitional, and emergent paths of growing up stand out among both young women's and young men's accounts in the late colonial and early republican years, I do not mean that these paths were identical for them, nor do I neglect the interplay of similarity and difference crucial to a gendered perspective. By privileging gender I advance the story of the rise of gender along with social class and race in the historical reconstruction of growing up.

For men and women both the *traditional* path is the most familiar. Stereotypes and images combine to form our common presumption of the normative path for the time, our assumptions about how "traditional" society reproduced itself. Sons followed in the footsteps of their fathers, within the bonds and bounds of family, typically in settled farming areas but also in migrations to the frontier and in artisanal or professional work.

Traditional standards for adulthood were marked by ownership of land or acquisition of skills, followed by marriage and the establishment of an independent household. Inheritance could be direct or indirect. Frequency and extent of schooling were varied. In a word, notions of stability and continuity define, if sometimes misleadingly, the traditional path.

But our images of the "traditional," as we shall see, are too narrow and inflexible. Traditional paths of growing up span a considerable social distance, from the very wealthy to the very poor, as well as geographic space. This mode of growing up thus encompassed a variety of institutional relations, especially in terms of schooling and leaving home. With help from anthropologists, historians have learned that even efforts to establish and maintain traditions can contribute to change. Traditional paths may involve a great deal of movement, from mobility of the young for purposes of work, training, or study, to migration to frontier areas to acquire farmland no longer available in settled areas or depleted patrimonies. Forms of education or vocational training deemed traditional may open up new opportunities and perspectives. Various routes go toward making up traditional paths.

The second major path of growing up I call *transitional*. Discontinuity, uncertainty, shifting expectations, and shifting locations mark experiences of growing up along this path.[13] Transitional paths occupy the ground that lies, materially and metaphorically, between traditional and newly emergent paths, between apparent stability and continuity on the one hand and manifest opportunities and new rhythms or schedules on the other.

Because of frequent discontinuities—in place of residence, family relations, education and training, work, dependent or independent status—a sense of uncertainty, of encountering obstacles, often characterizes this path. Obstructions, frequently to reaching traditional destinations, may be both internal and external. Although education and at least temporary absence from home for schooling, apprenticeship, or work are increasingly common along this path, there is little of the conscious choice of route and destination that helps to define emergent paths. But even though education beyond the basics was becoming more common for those who took transitional paths, their schooling often occurred discontinuously and late, as did their choice of career. These career quandaries, as I term them, are not to be confused with modern notions of choice and opportunity. A pronounced uncertainty and difficulty in making decisions or taking action distinguished youths facing such quandaries from their peers even among those taking discontinuous paths.

For some young men on transitional paths, opportunities especially for further schooling or professional training came precociously early, leading to career or other advancement. Over time, age-grading worked its transformations by limiting the number of exceptionally young as well as older students. New norms were created as expectations, patterns of socialization, and family and institutional relationships were reconstructed. Precocity, once applauded and promoted, became a danger, something to be avoided.[14]

For other young men religion paved a path to opportunity in the wake of evangelical conversion or similar spiritual episodes. Intense introspection following early life crises could produce severe discontinuities along the paths of growing up—or it could provide their resolution as well. Transitional eras, not surprisingly, are characterized by major religious revivals or awakenings.

Owing to the complex contribution of gender and the common neglect of young women in histories of children and adolescents, growing up female calls out for special attention. My recognition of *female* paths allows us to grasp that women's experiences simultaneously shared a great deal with those of their brothers—they too followed paths marked by tradition, transition, and emergence—but also that their journeys differed critically. Gender clearly played the part of an independent variable. Following the well-trodden paths of tradition (given regional, wealth, and other variations) are the women who left the family setting in their early twenties in order to marry a suitable spouse. The meaning of maturity and independence as signs of their having completed the process of growing up thus differs sharply from the meaning of those qualities for their husbands and brothers. But for them growing up in what we consider the traditional way also included the death of parents, siblings, or others close to them, some schooling or domestic training, family migration, and other shifts. Typical everyday experiences featured the society of other women, peers as well as more mixed company. Widowhood, sometimes quite early, was common, followed for many by remarriage.

For other women, as for men, transitional paths reigned. Changes in family circumstances—owing to illness or death, economics, domestic or familial responsibilities and demands that fell differently on young women than on men, and other discontinuities—led to uncertainties, anxieties, and unanticipated departures and destinations. Evangelical conversion and exceptional religiosity stimulated change for women as well as for men. Marriage transformed life for some more than for others, combining, for example, with migration or relocation or abrupt shifts in status resulting from a husband's social position or a sudden change in his affairs.

For other young women the transitional path resulted from intellectual precocity, unusual opportunities for education, and literary or other achievements. Sometimes family circumstances contributed, sometimes not. For some precocity and achievement led to pursuit of a career; many of these women grew up to live their adult lives in spinsterhood.[15] We may also characterize as transitional the journeys of young women influenced by new currents of romanticism, a path that also led some to spinsterhood.

Echoing the similarities and the differences between the male and female experiences of growing up are the increasing numbers of young women, exceptional according to our narrow images, who for whatever reasons of choice and need performed paid work prior to marriage, sometimes combining working with leaving home. An underlying factor for women is the difference in opportunity and in the meaning of dependence and independence between the sexes.[16]

The fourth major path I call *emergent.* In this period we begin to see the lines leading toward the modern understanding of growing up, a picture blurring at its edges with the transitional path. Hallmarks of the emergent path include conscious choice and self-direction, a search for opportunities including social mobility, the instrumental use of further (especially higher) education, and risk-taking in the commercial marketplace. None of these characteristics is unprecedented. Nevertheless, they remained atypical before the nineteenth century, although they were becoming more common. These behaviors look more to the future of growing up than to its past.

One route lay in conscious self-making through calculated life planning and the careful use of all available resources without waste or loss, from schooling to saving pennies to living by maxims. In some accounts this attitude is expressed in explicit emulation of the exemplary autobiography of Benjamin Franklin. Before long his model and moral came to mark the larger culture as icons, myths to live by, influencing the life paths and expectations of future generations. Other young people concentrated specifically on education beyond the norm. Attendance at college, though not yet expected, began to take on a closer relationship to professional preparation and particular career opportunities, especially when combined with a willingness to migrate or to make other sacrifices to enhance one's chances of success. In either case the lines of growing up were changing into paths familiar to us today.

Other forms of the emergent path were shaped by commercial capitalism and the spreading marketplace. For some young men on traditional as well as more clearly transitional or emergent journeys, the opportunities and risks of commercial exchange transformed their paths and reoriented their destination. As the world in which they were to make their way was redefined by cash markets, wages, long-distance trade and communication, greater gains and larger losses, and novel requirements for participation, growing up for increasing numbers of young persons was transformed.[17] The fit between paths, opportunities, and young persons seeking autonomy was seldom perfect, as the often difficult and conflicting transitions tell us.

The stories of growing up told in this chapter reflect the era's turbulent history. Flexibility seems to mark age and life course relationships and expectations and their connections to family, community, school, work, migration, and the meaning of growing up itself. At the same time, new paths take shape within our view. During the century to come, growing up would be fundamentally transformed.[18]

Traditional Paths

The experience of Samuel West (1738–1808) illustrates one especially common male pattern of growing up: following in his father's footsteps, he became a minister. Samuel tells his story in a manuscript memoir of 1807 that rings with the values and conventions of his path to maturity.[19] He saw himself as the fortunate son of a venerable father, a fifth-generation Massachusetts settler "destined" for a liberal education at Harvard, who had provided for himself with little financial aid from his parents.

"My worthy parents gave an excellent specimen of what may be effected by prudence and industry," Samuel recalls (17). They raised nine children (three more died in infancy), and despite his mother's feeble "habit," family life offered comfort, satisfaction, and opportunities: "In my father's family every member who was capable of it had some useful service to perform; and even the children who attended school were previous to their going and immediately on their return busily employed." Samuel worked at home when he was not in school. "Our manner of living," he writes "tho' wholesome and comfortable, was of the cheapest and coarsest kind, and I feel the good effects of it, and have through life. Instead of all that fastidious taste which many contract from a different mode of education all kinds of food are agreeable to me, and I would not cross the street to exchange one dinner for an other" (18).

The family regimen formed Samuel's character—his "willowness" or control over his passions—"evidence of what may be effected in the way of self-government if the business is begun at an early period" (19). In his memoir Samuel stresses that establishing right self-government, central to proper child rearing, lay in "a control over our feelings or passions, so as to prevent their ever betraying us into an impropriety either in words or actions" (19).[20]

West's upbringing reflects the persistence of traditional Calvinism.[21] As an adult he recognized the costs: "The piety of my parents and the consequences of a serious, not to say superstitious manner in which I was educated gave rather a gloomy cast to my mind, and being early initiated in all the horrors of Calvinism, I became a zealous defender of all the dogmas of that absurd system of divinity." Young Samuel suffered from his failure to experience "that strange and unnatural kind of conversion or regeneration of which I so often heard" (20). Only as his religious education advanced was Samuel able to come to terms with this inheritance and make his own compromises with tradition. His partial and indirect rejection of his father's faith did not lead Samuel to examine more deeply the conflicts of his early life or to criticize his parents openly. Indeed, he resisted more "modern" ideas about child rearing: "It may not be improper here to correct an opinion with respect to the education of sons which from my own experience and observation I have found both false and dangerous viz. that the inclinations of children are to be consulted in the choice of a profession, or the business for which they are educated." To his mind, both parents and children were harmed when "caprice or accident" was heeded in such matters (23). His own experience may have contributed to this view: when young West showed an interest in the work of an itinerant shoemaker who annually visited the family, his parents sought to please their son by seeking an apprenticeship for him. But by the time the journeyman had completed his labors, Samuel's interest was also gone.

Despite their relative poverty, the Wests encouraged Samuel to seek an education at Harvard in preparation for the ministry.[22] When Samuel was seventeen, his father began to teach him the learned languages, a late beginning in Samuel's opinion. His experience reflects the lack of age-grading in education at the time as well as the interruptions caused by the demands of farming. Nonetheless, he reports: "I made such progress as to be pretty well fitted for the University in almost two years from the time of my commencing my studies. With the very great exertions of my Parents I was furnished with what was essentially necessary for entering and residing at College . . . I looked forward to it with a mixture of pleasure and painful apprehension. It was indeed opening a new world to my view" (27). In Samuel West's case, at least, parental poverty had its rewards: President Edward Holyoke of Harvard offered to pay for his chambers.

Leaving home at nineteen was a wrenching experience: "Old as I was when I entered College so little have I been accustomed to any other place or persons than my Fathers family that it gave me some painful sensations to leave them, and I experienced something of what is called homesickness during my first term" (28). Bible reading provided consolation and solace: "It revived in my mind all the pleasures of my early years which had always been of the serious kind" (29). Before the first vacation Samuel received the president's permission to visit his parents. During part of his extended vacation Samuel kept school, a tradition among college students for earning money to pay for higher education.

Also during this holiday Samuel West confronted for the first time the lure of marriage. Visiting relatives on Nantucket, he was taken with the residents' virtues and simplicity of manner: "Two of my companions in this visit found wives on the Island . . . Had I indulged the fascination I could very soon have been as enraptured as those who . . . sacrificed every dictate of prudence at the Altar of Hymen . . . I left the Island although with some reluctance, yet without any improper engagement" (30–31). Returning to Harvard, Samuel "obliterated" from his mind "the impression of the Island beauties" with diligent attention to his studies: "If my heart had been fluttered it now regained its usual peace" (31). Divinity was his calling, and on it he concentrated. With no professor or tutor to guide him—a lamentable trait of Harvard, he found—Samuel lost much time. Through "studious inactivity" he neglected his health; by "feeding freely and smoking tobacco," common habits, he did lasting damage to his digestive and nervous systems (34–35). Samuel nevertheless renewed his studies "with a degree of ardour greatly encouraged by the flattering distinctions conferred upon me by the Governors of the College and by my Class." The governors rewarded his performance in public examination by the Overseers, and his classmates designated him Thesis Collector and Respondent at commencement (36–37).

Neither academic honors nor family tradition helped Samuel in taking the next step: "I had in short my full share of the honors of the University. I left the University therefore with expectations too sanguine, the disappointment of which was inevitable, and altho' I trust I have in a great measure risen above such vain ambition, it has in some periods of my life been painful to me" (36–37).

Leaving college "perfectly poor," he received no further support from home, for his father already had debts to repay on Samuel's account. Yet Samuel "felt at that period not the least concern with respect to subsistence. 'The world was all before me and Providence my guide' and although it . . . sets in a strong light my want to prudence . . . the evening after taking my degree, I purchased a horse and in a few days a watch for each of which I engaged to give considerable more than they were worth" (38)—no small contradiction to the self-effacing piety of his Calvinist upbringing.

In 1761 West was offered the post of chaplain of Fort Townal at Penobscot. Samuel much preferred this opportunity to the typical alternative of keeping a school while awaiting a call to the pulpit, since his early experience of teaching had not been to his liking. West went on to serve congregations in Needham and Boston.[23]

Following the path of inheriting a father's position was common outside the ministry as well. There were professions, such as law and medicine, for which apprenticeship was customary. Also taking traditional routes were countless sons of landowners, artisans, laborers, and merchants, among others.

Some young men followed the paths of relatives other than their fathers. Alexander Graydon published his memoirs when he was nearly sixty.[24] He was born near Philadelphia in 1752, the child of a prosperous commercial family. Sent away to Philadelphia for schooling at age six or seven, he lost his father by the age of nine. When Alexander tired of schooling by his teens, he precipitated a family crisis over his future: "The choice of vocation for me, had for some time engaged the attention of my near connections. The question was, whether I should be a merchant, a physician, or a lawyer. My inclinations were duly consulted. I had no predilection for either, though I liked the law the least of the three, being sensible that my talents were not of the cast which would enable me to succeed in that profession" (72, 74).

Alexander finally opted for medicine, but when no place was found, "it was deemed inexpedient any longer to defer placing me somewhere." The final choice was made by his uncle, "who had all along been desirous that I should go to the bar, his own profession." Into the uncle's family as well as his practice the teenager went. Alexander differed from his contemporary Samuel West on the importance of a young person's own inclinations: "As to the sober part of the calculation, whether the occupation I was about to embrace was adapted to my talents, would command my application, and be likely to afford me the means of future subsistence, it was put aside for the more immediately grateful considerations already mentioned." In the end Alexander hedged: "I cannot venture to pronounce, however, that the medical profession would have suited me much better. In truth, I was indolent to a great degree; and with respect to that heroic fortitude which subdues the mind to its purposes, withdraws it at will from the flowery paths of pleasure, and forces it into the thorny road of utility, the distinguishing trait . . . I have very little to boast of" (74–75).[25]

The traditional path for sons could be disrupted by deaths in the family, scarcity of land, or opportunities for economic development. Some sons who did not wish to fill their father's shoes struggled along other paths, with or without patrimonies. For sons of the rich, a father's wealth paved traditional paths.[26] Seldom seen as a factor among many routes of growing up, in biographies and histories inheritance nonetheless plays a frequent part.[27] Edward and John Ambler were the sons of Richard Ambler of Yorktown, Virginia, an English-born merchant who had migrated to America and married into a wealthy aristocratic family.[28] By sending his sons abroad, Richard sought to provide them with the fine education he felt he lacked, and to confirm and enhance their status.

Eschewing limited opportunities in the colonies, and leaving just prior to or in their early teens, the boys attended Leeds Academy under the supervision of an aunt and uncle. Edward completed his schooling and returned to Virginia in 1752, settling in Jamestown as a merchant, planter, and public servant. John became the family scholar. After Leeds he attended several schools in Wakefield, and had a year at Edinburgh University. Choosing to study the law, he went to Trinity College, Cambridge, and the Temple in London. On his return to Virginia in 1757 or 1758, he established an office in Williamsburg and began a promising career.[29]

Another traditional path for young men combined rural origins with a migratory search for a career or a place to settle.[30] This route followed the course of settlement and development of the continent. James P. Collins, born in 1763 in South Carolina, recounts this path—later the stuff of frontier lore—in his autobiography.[31] James's Irish-born father had worked as a clerk and a teacher before moving his family to the Carolinas, where he farmed and also served as county clerk. The fourth of seven children, James forever felt the loss of his mother, who died giving birth to her last child. That death transformed the family. Three sisters were sent out to neighboring women; the boys remained at home with their father, who quickly remarried a young widow with eight children of her own. James's father was a disciplinarian who demanded strict morality. For the children of his first marriage, having a stepmother added to family pressures.

James attended school until he was twelve. He learned to read and to write a fair hand, and he gained a moderate knowledge of arithmetic. To his surprise his father proposed that he attend an academy to prepare to study divinity. Neither willing nor interested, James objected. Straitened family circumstances suggested that he learn a trade. His father then proposed binding him to a tailor, but James preferred woodworking. The father prevailed. James was bound to a tailor for five years. Because it meant leaving his stepmother, he deemed this move "agreeable." James had served just over two years of his apprenticeship when the Revolutionary War erupted. He was then placed with a shoemaker, but this was a trade the teenager did not like. He was subsequently put to weaving, moving from apprenticeship to wage work. With the incentive of work for pay, James at last gained some proficiency.

Craft training and work accompanied James's labor on the family farm. He also had time to play games with other boys. When the Revolution broke out, James's father tried to keep his sons out of the conflict. In his mid-teens James served as "collector of news" for the militia captain, reporting what he saw or heard among the Tories. With his father he joined the local "minutemen," guarding the home front and experiencing the excitement of wartime.

The cessation of hostilities found James at home. His father fell even further behind in the struggle to maintain his large family. James was growing up, and it was clear "that I had not the best feeling for my step-mother; although a fine woman, in many respects . . . she did not treat me with motherly affection and kindness, which she ought to have done." Just shy of twenty years of age, James writes: "There being no great prospect of making anything for myself, by remaining with my father, he advised me to turn out into the world, and do the best I could, at the same time, giving me good advice as to the course I should pursue" (68).

That course led to Georgia, where land was available at a good price. But first James needed money. Having "no way to get it without labor" (68), he hired himself out to a succession of neighbors, though he was not always paid as promised. Finally, in January 1785 James left for Georgia with his sisters and a brother-in-law.

For three months he taught at a country school of twenty-five pupils for a dollar per pupil plus board. He next began surveying, continuing to shift jobs and residences. This work helped him to locate land, secure a warrant for two hundred acres, and begin to hunt game in his woods. The early period of colonial settlement offered wide opportunities for labor and civic participation. James worked as a journeyman tailor and a horse trader, served in the militia, and engaged in war and sat on councils with native peoples. With settlement came schools and churches and social life. James "was immoderately fond of music and dancing," often attending dancing schools and sometimes singing schools (95). When not attending meetings and schools, he farmed, hunted, wove cloth or made shoes, coopered or tailored, gaining some benefits from his fitful early training.

One major step on his path toward growing up remained unfulfilled: marriage.[32] "Like the most of men," he writes, "by mixing so often in company, I fell into many little courting scrapes . . . I was by nature an admirer of the fair sex; indeed, I had almost a superstitious veneration for them, for I thought a handsome neat looking female almost incapable of doing wrong; and to this day I can not avoid feeling a kind of veneration for a modest looking female" (98).

Marriage was fashionable, James observes, and it is clear that he wished to end his bachelor status. But he was troubled by his lack of property with which to attract a wife; and courting was not his forte. He was well received by young women and their families, but for one reason or another, matrimony did not ensue. James's less than confident search for a mate occupied his late twenties. Then, in his thirtieth year, he found a partner. On March 22, 1793, James Collins took a Miss Neil as his wife, formally concluding his growing up.

Ephraim Bacon, born in 1780 in Sturbridge, Massachusetts, journeyed along a similar winding path.[33] With his two brothers, Ephraim was educated in the common free schools of the county "where the rudiments are taught; that is—to read, write and cypher sufficiently to transact the general business of the farmers and mechanics" (1). No more was deemed necessary, unless a young man hoped to go to college.

Ephraim's childhood was marked by the death of his mother after a five-year struggle with consumption, when he was ten, and by his father's remarriage, by which "the happiness of the family was not promoted" (2). He recalls his mother's kindness, piety, charity, and humility—and her prayers for her children. Feuding with his stepmother drove him out of the house at nineteen.[34] Ephraim moved to Vermont, where two of his sisters lived, and hired on as a laborer for a farmer for $100. A great personal conflict with tradition ensued: "I had put into my hands TOM PAINE'S AGE OF REASON, which seemed to coincide with my natural heart. Yet often, thoughts of my dear mother's advice seemed to check the thought of adopting TOM PAINE as my guide. My employer and his lady were both very kind to me, but were very liberal in their views of religion. I soon began to express my infidel principles" (2).

After eighteen months Ephraim's father asked him to return home. He found that "the family difficulties were considerably mitigated in the paternal domain," but his religious conflict remained: "I sometimes advocated Infidelity in the presence of my father. Yet the thoughts of my mother often seemed to check my views, and cause some doubts in my mind on the subject; yet those impressions soon subsided. I embraced every opportunity to hear skeptical preaching, and often endeavored to influence others, notwithstanding my secret doubts" (2–3).

Ephraim met and married Lucy Chamberlain. This happy union lasted fourteen years, until her death left him a "poor infidel" with four children to raise and no religious consolation to lessen his distress. His renewed search for spiritual comfort and stability took him to New York, Pennsylvania, and family home. He then converted to the faith of his mother. As we see from these examples, the migrations of young men in adolescence or early youth helped the new nation to fill in its boundaries and design its future as they sought a future of their own.[35]

Transitional Paths

During the early modern period increasingly more young men followed the path I call transitional. Such paths characterized the era, mixing tradition and change, as young men responded to new opportunities and obstacles. These routes led toward the next century. Discontinuities, involving education and careers in particular, marked this path. Precocity and religiosity are also prominent along its way.

Discontinuities

Born in Newcastle, Maine, in 1779, Ephraim Abbott took a transitional path of growing up that was punctuated by movement. His autobiography, written in his late forties, tells that story.[36] His father, a cabinetmaker who fought in the Revolution, moved the family several times during the boy's childhood. Ephraim encountered a variety of schools and instructors.[37]

When Ephraim was old enough to assist in family farm work, his schooling was restricted to the winter, alternating seasonally with working. Frequent accidents and poor health weigh heavily in his memories about growing up. Ephraim matter-of-factly recounts that as a teenager he "relinquished the idea of becoming a joiner" like his father. "My mind was considerably exercised on the subject of religion, and I became desirous of obtaining a public education, and becoming a minister. Like many other young men, I thought I should preach the Gospel more earnestly, and more successfully, than some aged ministers, that I then heard preach."

Given family circumstances, this was no easy path. More schooling was the first step. The summers of 1797–1799 he spent at farm work and the winter of 1797–98 in the district school. He also studied English grammar with a local clergyman. During the winters of 1798–99 and 1799–1800, Ephraim taught school.

In 1800 his uncle surprised him with a proposal: he offered the twenty-one-year-old his estate if the lad would marry a woman the uncle named and move in with him. Ephraim "told him, that if he would give me the whole town of Concord, and require me to relinquish the idea of obtaining a public education, I could not accept it. He then said, 'As you are so desirous of obtaining an education, I will assist you.'" Ephraim continued his education locally. Despite his lack of funds, young Abbott's will and desire increased. He was accepted as a beneficiary of the trustees of Phillips Exeter Academy and thus resolved both his financial and his educational needs.

Entering in 1800, he rededicated himself to his goals. His advanced age was not then unusual.[38] Ephraim pursued the task of learning Latin with a youthful single-mindedness that allowed him but five hours' sleep each night for two years and took its toll on his health. On September 28, 1800, he signed his covenant of religion, his faith having been reinforced by the school's exercises and the principal's warnings against temptation. He also found time for walks and outdoor sports.

In 1802 Ephraim Abbott progressed to Harvard. He was still struggling to make ends meet and to accomplish his goals. His resolve to sleep six hours a night quickly collapsed in the press of monetary needs and the many activities he had undertaken. Some aid came from Harvard in return for cleaning recitation rooms. Like many of his peers Ephraim spent time away from college teaching winter school in each of his first three years, although this was against college rules.

His severe regimen did not preclude other activities. Ephraim was class president and gave himself credit for his classmates' proper, conservative conduct. He assisted in forming a secret society for religious improvement, the Saturday-Evening Religious Society, among his many peer activities.[39] He was also engaged during his senior year in private tutoring by subscription at Charlestown Academy for eight hours a day. After his graduation Abbott tutored at the academy for two years. In 1808, almost thirty years old, he finally began his formal theological training at the new theological academy at Andover, graduating with the first class in 1810. In 1813, at thirty-four, he took a post in New Hampshire as minister and preceptor of the newly established Brackett Academy. Ephraim married a year later.[40]

In his lengthy transitional path of growing up, Ephraim Abbott was in many ways typical of his time. He did not leave home as early as some of his peers (though our impression of widespread early home leaving is exaggerated).[41] He decided against a craft apprenticeship, a path that likely would have taken him from home earlier, nor did he lose a parent. Nevertheless, his relocations and shifts in status, as well as his teaching stints, are common characteristics of the transitional path. Marked by obstacles and discontinuities, this route could be a difficult one to travel. It cut across social divisions and took young men to various destinations, not only in the professions but also in commerce, trades, agriculture, labor, and public life. And it took them from country to city and back again, as Ephraim's journey illustrates.[42]

For some young men the route to a career was determined by personal inclination as well as changing conditions and opportunities. This phenomenon caused serious concern and stimulated a variety of efforts to assist the young in making their decisions.

Born in 1787 in New Mills (later Danversport), Massachusetts, Archelaus Putnam followed such a path. His diary, kept from his eighteenth to his thirtieth years with a resolve that he did not exhibit elsewhere, reveals a mundane, conventional life plagued by fundamental questions about what he should do with himself as his period of growing up dragged on.[43]

Archelaus's mother died when he was a few months old, and his father, Nathaniel, quickly remarried. He expired in 1800 when Archelaus was thirteen. At the time he began the diary at age eighteen, Archelaus worked in his older brother's general store. His dilemmas surrounding his future work and life stemmed neither from a lack nor from an excess of resources. The onset of the "commercial revolution" made for increased opportunities as well as risks.

Archelaus's activities in his late teens included the volunteer fire company, the militia, evening school, religious meeting, and young people's gatherings—a range of associations and other social events involving many friends and acquaintances. Yet, as he notes sadly, "I am 18 years old today, told nobody & got less stripes" (June 19, 1805).

Dissatisfied working for his brother, Archelaus considered other options. On July 8, 1805, he speaks of going to sea; two weeks later, on July 25, he wonders about learning the printing trade. After seeking advice, he concludes: "I find I was wrong in being so discontented. I have concluded trusting in the good will of Providence to provide necessarily for me" (August 2, 1805).

In June 1806, as his nineteenth birthday neared, he presented his brother with a "written address, asking advice & leave of going to Andover to school." His brother was willing to replace him for six months. Archelaus was aware of the instrumental uses of education: "I am not fond of leaving my native home where I have lived & enjoyed myself all my days. But I am of procuring learning of which I think a certain degree is absolutely necessary to a young man & is the best property to purchase with our money" (June 9, 1806). Suffering from homesickness, Archelaus nonetheless stayed at school in Andover for the second half of the seventeen-week term. His brother's business prevented his return for the fall term. Instead, he proposed tutoring at home. Almost twenty, again working for his brother, busy with an active social life and regional travels, Archelaus had still not progressed far along his path. His quandaries were neither resolved nor forgotten. In May 1807 he inquired about lessons in stenography in Salem, but found them too expensive. His birthday brought an outpouring:

> June 19. This day completes my 20th year. I have composed & penned the following lines on the occasion.
>
>> Alas! what is this life, & all its train.
>> But little pleasure & a deal of pain.
>> My childhood now has vanished away,
>> All seems a dream, a shadow, but a day.
>> All puerile thoughts & toys are laid aside,
>> Those playful days are swept as with the tide,
>> Maturer years unfold sublimer themes, While those that're
>>   past, like a vagary seems.
>> My active powers now tend toward middle age,
>> On what & where, these powers shall I engage.
>> Here I'm placed in life & preserved for why;
>> Where am I bound or where's my destiny;
>> I'm stumbled at the thought, then think again,
>> But yet my reason cannot make it plain, etc.

The mundane but painful lament underscores the depth and intensity of the conflicts that accompanied his efforts to find a career.

Archelaus persevered. In the fall he proposed to a former classmate, now in Salem, "to correspond by letter for the improvement of the mind" (September 19, 1807). In 1808 he took his improvement campaign to the community, seeking to establish a social library, a private school, and shared subscriptions to the Boston papers. In April, approaching his twenty-first birthday, he "conceived it my duty to consult with my brother Nathl. about my affairs" (April 21, 1808). The brothers disagreed over what Archelaus was owed for his work in the store. He consented to stay with his brother in return for $100, "a freedom suit," and a trunk, as well as the privilege of selling items that his brother did not sell and use of the horse and chaise. Although the bargain did not secure his independence, it brought independence closer.

In his diary Archelaus recognized his persisting financial dependency and his difficulties in taking action in his own interest. His account of his twenty-first birthday is colored by irony: "Twenty-one years of my existence on this territorial orb have passed irrecoverable. I was attacked and resistance was vain. Neighbors plundered my liberality of what their palate delighted in, and repaid for it, they supposed by their munificence in dealing out a huge mass of toasts & wishes which would affect me no otherwise than by making me sick" (June 20, 1808).

In 1809 he recorded a spell of youthful wanderlust: "I am almost resolved to abandon my present employment, considering the few hopes of success in it. An anxiety to see the world, get information and try my fortune are powerful inducements in favor of going to sea" (March 10, 1809). Archelaus desired to share in the "spirit of enterprize" in U.S. commercial activity following the partial lifting of the British embargo, as well as to pursue his independence.

May 1809 brought a new turn of events. His term with his brother expired, and he leased an apothecary shop in the nearby town of Lynn. At age twenty-two he found leaving home was not easy: "I am now on the verge of leaving Danvers New Mills, my birthplace & abode, where I was nursed and nourished & spent my life, where good will & understanding have been collateral with the intercourse I have had with the people, where reside my brothers, sisters, & near & familiar connexions. To be transplanted into an untried soil where it is doubtful if I shall take root & live, much more grow & flourish" (June 4, 1809). Young Putnam settled into Lynn commerce and society. But by November he was losing business, and by January 1810 he had disposed of his stock and furniture, paid his debts, and returned to work for his brother.

In May 1815 Archelaus began another business of his own, an apothecary, hardware, and crockery store, and moved out of his brother's house.

He took the remaining steps toward adult maturity in 1817 at age thirty, when he "hired a tenement, purchased the remaining articles wanted for housekeeping and received a visit from her whom I anticipate as my helpmeet in life" (May 24). On June 2 he reports: "Public notice was given yesterday in this and the town of Andover of an intention of marriage between myself and Sarah W. Noyes." Here the diary ends.

Somewhat more resolute and perhaps less idiosyncratic was the route that Ephraim Bateman took on his transitional path. Born in 1780 in Fairfield, Connecticut, one of seven children, Ephraim began a journal at age nineteen.[44] His father, a weaver who also tended a grist mill, died when the boy was thirteen. Young Ephraim had assisted him in both jobs. After his father's death Ephraim went to school between his fourteenth and sixteenth years and learned Latin. He records that "it is more than probable I should have remained at the Languages & prest on a liberal Education had not our tutor left us in order to study Divinity" (57).

Instead, Ephraim left home to learn a tailor's trade. Although the eighteen-year-old notes that he "had got my trade so as to work tolerably well" (58), when his master died he quit, and went to work in a store. In February 1799, living at home, Ephraim returned to school, on his friends' advice, to gain the credentials to succeed the local schoolmaster: "Their advice I reluctantly complied with I was however more easily persuaded to it by the consideration of my frail Constitution & bad state of health. In this project I succeeded . . . I was unanimously elected to the important post" (58). His poor health complicated his pursuit of career and independence: "Study I find is very unfavorable & as study seems to be the only way of subsistence I am at a loss to determine what Course to pursue. When I look around on my companions & see them strong active & Healthy I am apt to harbor hard thoughts . . . The cause of this indisposition I attribute to a days work wheeling wood on board of the sloop Morning Star . . . about September 98 when I . . . overstrained myself & setting at the taylors trade afterward I believe I brought on me the present disease" (82).

Ephraim alternated teaching with studying, troubling over his future, and occasional relapses of his "constitutional disease." He blamed himself for his condition and his inability to rise above it: "When I approach nearest to health then I am most easy 'drawn away by my own lust' fall an easy prey to irregularities & fall into a stupid indifference concerning my duty but few emotions of gratitude & these few exceeding weak & my affections placed on worldly pleasures & enjoyments" (87).

A career crisis erupted in April 1801, when Bateman was offered an opportunity to study medicine, toward which he was inclined. He feared "even if I should get a degree of Physic that I should not live long enough to pay the cost & trouble of acquiring it" (131). His friends urged him to make the attempt. With great uncertainty and pleas for providential aid, he did. Ephraim lived to complete his studies and practice medicine. In October 1802, aged twenty-two, he took sixteen-year-old Sally Bateman (perhaps a cousin) as his bride. His son and his son's son became physicians, establishing a new family tradition.

Precocity

Daniel Drake was a noted physician, scientist, and civic builder of Cincinnati. His published account of his life, written in the form of a series of letters to his adult children, provides evidence of the value placed on precocious self-making in an era of great change.[45]

Drake, a "pioneer boy," was born in a log cabin in 1785—in New Jersey. The family moved three years later to the wilderness, in 1788 clearing a farm in Mays Lick, Kentucky. Drake dated his lifelong interest in science to his curiosity about nature from age four or five. Country life was his pedagogue. Daniel also credited a local physician: "Already, when five years old, I had been promised to him as a student; and among the remembrances of that period is my being called Dr. Drake" (26). Whether this story is apocryphal or not, Daniel's path to the medical profession was inseparably intertwined with his path of growing up.

Daniel attended rough-hewn country schools from age five to age nine. In 1794 his father moved the family to a larger farm. For the next six years the hard labor, perils, and privations of farm work took up much of Daniel's time. He later claimed that his appreciation of the value of hard work and his interest in engineering derived from these labors. The children also did indoor chores. The family was unable to afford a hired girl and opposed to keeping slaves.

Reflecting values new to the late eighteenth century, Daniel reverently praised his mother's influence on his moral cultivation. He writes: "I was preserved from many temptations, and practically taught self-denial . . . I was taught to practice economy . . . I was taught the value of learning . . . I was taught the value of time" (110). Daniel's emphasis on maternal morality was typical of the mid-nineteenth century, when he wrote his memoirs. Yet even before 1800 the new ideology of moral motherhood was beginning its rise to cultural hegemony, with its doctrine of proper, middle-class, maternal-centered and mother-dominated character formation.[46] New currents of thought flowed through frontier Kentucky as through more developed areas in the early years of the Republic. Daniel continues: "I grew up with love and obedience to my mother, and received from her an early moral training, to which, in conjunction with that of my father, I owe, perhaps, more of my humble preparation of life to come, than to any other influence" (110).

Daniel describes his mother as "more illiterate" than his father. Her piety was based in her Bible, *Pilgrim's Progress*, and her hymnal. "Her natural understanding was tolerable only, but she comprehended the principles of domestic and Christian duty, and sought to inculcate them. This she never did by protracted lectures [nor force or punishment], but mixed them up with all our daily labors. Thus my monitor was always by my side, and ready with her reproof, or admonition, or rewarding smile, as occasion or opportunity arose" (111).

Although Daniel's outside schooling was interrupted by his family's move, he was able to progress at home, mastering penmanship with the aid of a local teenager. By the time he was eleven, a small log schoolhouse had been built, and he returned to his lessons. He went on to a better school in 1800, when he was fifteen, where he gained the "finishing touches" before his medical training. From his cousin Dr. John Drake, who had studied medicine in Philadelphia, Daniel learned his early medical lessons. By the time he was ready to leave home in pursuit of his career, young Daniel felt a great sense of accomplishment, especially in the formation of his character (171).

Feeling that he "had a natural and acquired preparation to become a useful physician" (173), Daniel moved to the nearest metropolis, Cincinnati, to begin his formal study of medicine. By age nineteen in May 1804 he had begun to practice. In 1805–6 Drake moved to Philadelphia for further medical studies at the University of Pennsylvania. Eventually securing his diploma, he returned to Cincinnati and took up his practice. In December 1807, after early establishing professional independence, he married a woman to whom he later credited his further professional and civic accomplishments. Drake was twenty-two years old. His path of growing up can be seen as a transitional one between the traditional and the modern way, the informal and flexible and the scheduled, the country and the city.

Connecticut-born Elihu Hubbard Smith's diaries convey some of the problems of precocity while also suggesting the variety of this route.[47] "I was born on the morning of the fourth of September 1771, a healthy and vigorous infant," his journal begins (17). His capacity for memorization, on which he prided himself, gave him an early start on schooling, between the ages of two and four. From four or five Elihu "in the short space of six months, learned to read, with fluency, in the Bible—then the highest school-book in the New England common schools. I also learnt many things by rote; & remember to have spoken in public, at a quarterly exhibition of our school, a little poem of Dr. Watts" (18). At the age of five he "began to have some relish for reading." By age seven he read well and had improved in writing and speaking. His progress was limited mainly by the irregular coming and going of teachers and schools, but by eight or nine he was learning Latin, and by ten Greek.

Elihu's father, a physician and "a man of more cultivated taste, than is generally found . . . in our little country towns" encouraged his son (4). Especially stimulating was his time at the academy in Litchfield, where he studied with a group of older boys preparing for Yale. Despite his father's intention that Elihu should study until age sixteen before seeking admission to college, the eleven-year-old boy entered Yale with his academy classmates. Accompanying them to New Haven for their entrance examinations, young Elihu was also examined. He did well and a tutor urged him to enroll. The average age of his enrolling class was seventeen; four were fourteen. Although his age apparently kept him from committing the excesses of his fellow students, Elihu was active in two literary societies and a social society. From these societies he gained access to library books the college lacked.

Graduation presented a quandary. As his diary's editor puts it: "To his father he was now a problem child, a Yale B.A. just turned fifteen, too young to study for the law or to begin medical training, with not enough Latin even to write a prescription, in no way equipped to be much of anything" (4). As a solution his father sent Elihu to a preparatory school, Timothy Dwight's academy at Green Hill in Fairfield, Connecticut, soon known as one of the new nation's finest. Under Dwight's progressive pedagogy Elihu blossomed. In particular he retained Dwight's conviction that the duty of an intelligent man is to strive for the betterment of humanity.

In 1787 he returned home to begin "a kind of apprenticeship" in the family apothecary shop and study with a local physician (9). In 1790, now nineteen, Elihu went to Philadelphia to study medicine with the renowned Dr. Benjamin Rush. From Rush he not only learned a progressive approach to medicine but also gained an interest in social reform. Barred from receiving a medical degree until he turned twenty-four, Elihu cut short his formal training.

Returning home to Litchfield in 1791, Elihu found "he could not be his own man: living at home meant either regular attendance at Sunday services or serious disagreements with his father" (9). After a few months he moved to Wethersfield and formed a close association with the Connecticut Wits, a literary circle. Elihu edited and published a seminal anthology of American poetry, *American Poems: Selected and Original*. He moved to New York City in 1793, where he was approved to practice medicine, although he never established a practice. Instead, he was active in literary undertakings, promoted the manumission of slaves, established a school for children of slaves, and served without compensation in the city dispensary. Elihu also fell in love, apparently unrequited. To his diary he confided his persisting sense of failure to achieve adult male independence, in part because of a lack of success with his literary projects and in part because of his lacking confirmed religious belief. In September 1795 he wrote: "I could scarcely hope ever to attain that independency which would place me above the fear of want, & necessity of labour; & which would allow me to devote all my time to the service of my fellow-men." Elihu also feared that knowledge of his irreligion would deeply hurt his parents (45).

Elihu persisted in trying to find his way. He confided to his diary: "The precariousness of my situation; & a restless uncertainty as to what plan I had best adopt; have perplexed me more than I ought to let them. Thousands are worse situated than I am; enter life with worse prospects; struggle with more opposition; & surmount greater difficulties. Considerations of this kind have made me half ashamed of relinquishing my Profession. What could I not accomplish therein, if I would exert the resolution of a man" (54). At twenty-seven, in 1798, he died in New York during an epidemic of yellow fever, without achievements to match his early promise.[48] In a time of transformation, precocity was sometimes an asset, at other times an obstacle. It was not always its own reward.

Precocity captured people's imaginations in later years. In the cultural myths assigned to men of humble beginnings, often frontier log cabin origins, who succeeded while young, reality and rhetoric intertwine inseparably. Cultural pressures in growing up henceforth carried this burden. Yet succeeding generations also came to fear precocity, and attempted to standardize the processes of growing up in the dual cause of protecting presumably vulnerable young persons and systematizing the age and institutional relations of coming of age. Both exceptionally early and exceptionally late development, more common as increasing numbers of young men from modest backgrounds attempted to make their way, were targets of reform.

Religiosity

The route through evangelical conversion was a journey of a decidedly different nature. Too easily and superficially cast as "traditional," this was instead a broad avenue whose population swelled at spiritual awakenings, "great" and otherwise. Studies of religious revivals in both the mid-eighteenth and early nineteenth centuries point to a relationship between conversion and massive social change, with special pressures falling on women and the young.

Devereux Jarratt, a leader of the so-called evangelical revolt in Virginia, was born in 1732. Jarratt's conversion and regeneration were somewhat tardy. Douglass Adair, an editor of Jarratt's autobiography, terms it "an eighteenth-century Alger-boy story."[49] He notes that Jarratt crossed the class divide of Virginia, climbed up the institutional ladder of the church, and achieved "intellectualism." The fact that his achievements followed his rebirth marks his avenue as transitional.

The son of a carpenter, Devereux Jarratt began his days among the plain folk of Virginia. As he describes it: "My parents neither sought nor expected any titles, honors, or great things, either for themselves or children. Their highest ambition was to teach their children to read, write, and understand the fundamental rules of arithmetic. I remember also, they taught us short prayers, and made us very perfect in repeating the *Church Catechism*. They wished us all to be brought up in some honest calling, that we might earn our bread, by the sweat of our brow, as they did" (361).

Devereux's father died suddenly when the boy was six; his eldest son inherited intestate. From an early age young Jarratt "discovered a pregnancy of genius" in his ability to learn and to memorize (362). He attended grammar school for four or five years, to about age twelve or thirteen, "though not without great interruptions," until his schooling ended with his mother's death (363).

In his brother's care Devereux was permitted "all the indulgences a depraved nature, and an evil heart could desire" (363), without correction of his morals, restraint of vices, or attendance at church. He assisted with racehorses, gamecocks, and plantation work. At seventeen he quit the plow for carpentry. In retrospect he saw that he was in spiritual danger—ignorant of God, careless of religion, copying the example of his brothers: "*Cards, racing, dancing, &c.* which are still the favourite sport and diversion of the wicked and ungodly, were then much in vogue" (363). Skilled in the "division of crops and the rule of three," he opened a school at nineteen (366–367). That pursuit did not last long.

Devereux next boarded as a servant to a wealthy gentleman. The pious matron of the house influenced his spiritual regeneration. Jarratt's religious worries commenced. Slowly he pursued the new education of his soul: "I was assaulted with very uncommon trials . . . sorrow, trouble, and perplexity, continued long and painful—perhaps for twelve months" (377). As he came to know religion and experienced conversion, Jarratt began to preach, for which he found he had a great talent, and also continued to teach school.

Reorienting his route toward adulthood, he went on to study divinity and prepare for ordination in the Church of England. This path took him to London in 1762, when he was approaching thirty. In 1763 he took up his first parish. A long and difficult transitional path—"the experience was traumatic and left scars"—led to regeneration and a new destination (347–348).

Peter Cartwright, born in 1785, in Amherst County on the James River in Virginia and known as "the backwoods preacher," followed another course of growing up through conversion.[50] Twists of time and migration shaped his way. His impoverished family migrated to Kentucky in search of opportunity. In their pioneer settlement there was no newspaper, mill, or "school worth the name" (24). Although Peter's mother was an active Episcopal Methodist, "Sunday was a day set apart for hunting, fishing, horse-racing, card-playing, balls, dances, and all kinds of jollity and mirth" (25). Peter recalls: "My father restrained me but little, though my mother often talked to me, wept over me, and prayed for me, and often drew tears from my eyes; and though I often wept under preaching, and resolved to do better and seek religion, yet I broke my vows" (27). Taught by a schoolmaster "not well-qualified to teach correctly," he made little progress. Meanwhile, Peter became "a very successful young gambler" (27).

In 1801, when Peter was sixteen, his religious moment came. Returning home from drinking and dancing at a wedding, he "began to reflect on the manner in which I had spent the day and evening. I felt guilty and condemned. I rose and walked the floor . . . all of a sudden, my blood rushed to my head, my heart palpitated, in a few minutes I turned blind; an awful impression rested on my mind that death had come and I was unprepared to die. I fell on my knees and began to ask God to have mercy on me" (34).

His mother rushed to his side, praying and exhorting him to look to Christ for mercy. Peter promised that if he were spared, he "would seek and serve him" (34). After this incident, young Cartwright gave up racing and cards. He fasted, read Scripture, and prayed for salvation. "I was so distressed and miserable, that I was incapable for any regular business" (35). Peter's father feared for his son's life.

At a Saturday night revival meeting, Peter's inner storm ended:

> In the midst of a solemn struggle for my soul, an impression was made on my mind, as though a voice said to me, "Thy sins are all forgiven thee." Divine light flashed all around me, unspeakable joy sprung up in my soul. I rose to my feet, opened my eyes, and it really seemed as if I was in heaven; the trees, the leaves on them, and everything seemed, and I really thought were, praising God. My mother raised the shout, my Christian friends crowded around me and joined me in praising God; and though I have been since then, in many instances, unfaithful, yet I have never, for one moment, doubted that the Lord, then and there, forgive my sins and give me religion. (37–38)

In 1801 he joined the Methodist Episcopal church. His path redirected, a new profession developed. The next year Peter was granted permission to "exercise his gifts as an exhorter." He was authorized to travel, hold meetings, organize classes, and form a circuit. He spent a term studying in an academy, and then at the age of eighteen, with his mother's urging and his father's hard-won assent, Peter went out on the western circuit. He converted an infidel his first night. He was ordained in 1806, was married in 1808, and was ordained an elder the same year. Just as Peter's initial path was shaped by the circumstances of migration, settlement, and social development, so too were his renewed journey and his transformed adolescence and youth. On the circuit his adult labors contributed to additional transitions.[51]

Female Paths

Although "modern" notions of gender were barely visible in the middle of the eighteenth century, the extent to which the experiences of the sexes differed—in growing up as in all else—is unmistakable, despite important commonalities. Differences increased over time. The historical meanings of dependence and independence, maturity and adulthood, all varied with gender.[52] Despite ample evidence of the complexity of women's routes to adulthood, historians have slighted female experience.[53] Problems of missing paths and distortions owing to contemporary categories and gender bias as well as preservation of sources plague this domain. In the first-person accounts, nevertheless, the traditional, transitional, and emergent paths can be seen to constitute the majority of female experience, underscoring the crucial interplay of similarity to and divergence from the lives of their brothers.

Traditional

The traditional path for women in the second half of the eighteenth century led from family home and filial responsibilities to courtship, marriage, and removal to a home and rearing a new family.[54] In her diary covering fifty-four years of life in Hadley, Massachusetts, Elizabeth Porter Phelps recorded just such a journey.[55] Born in 1747, Elizabeth was the only child of the wealthy Moses and Elizabeth Porter. Married to Charles Phelps in 1770, at the typical age of twenty-three, she lived her seventy years in one town, and "became one of the distinguished matrons of the area" (3).

At the age of eight, Elizabeth lost her father in the French and Indian War. Her mother never recovered from the loss; she lived as an invalid, dependent on opium, for her remaining forty-three years. Elizabeth's father's family assumed responsibility for the child's care and education "as was fitting for the daughter of the town's hero" (4). Elizabeth often stayed with her kin and accompanied them to Boston and Hartford. As with most of her peers, female and male, her growing up reflected the absence of impermeable lines between nuclear families and extended kin and community. Similarly, there was no demarcation between artificially defined categories of "childhood" and "adolescence" or "youth," although such stages were recognized.

In 1763 sixteen-year-old Elizabeth began in a handmade copybook her diary of the ensuing half century. Her active social world of well-to-do friends and family, church, local events, the weather, and illness, births, and deaths fill the diary's pages. She learned singing from a tutor, went out "a-strawberrying" or to pick whortleberries. She reports her many diversions, along with her occasional lapses in keeping "account of the texts and other things as I ought to have done." Female peers were especially close and important to her, although her society included both males and females.

Elizabeth records surprisingly little about her courtship with Charles Phelps, Jr., of Northampton, a lawyer. Having mentioned him only a few times in her diary, she writes on June 14, 1770: "A few minutes before 4 oclock I gave my hand to Charles Phelps—Polly Porter and Dorothy Phelps Bride maids—we had about 30 couples at weding." Her friends Polly and Pen are greater presences. After the marriage date entries concerning activities and associates suggest that not much had changed for Elizabeth, other than her name. Courtship, engagement, and marriage came to her at the expected age with the expected conventions of her station and her times.

A woman with a rather different personality, Elizabeth Cranch experienced a similar traditional journey.[56] Born in 1763 in Haverhill, Massachusetts, she was the daughter of Judge Richard and Mary Smith Cranch. Her mother was the sister of Abigail Adams. She later married the Reverend Jacob Norton of Weymouth. Her journal commences in October 1785, when she was twenty-two.

Many names of family, female friends, and male callers fill Elizabeth's journal. Her closest friend, Polly White, was a center of her attention. Elizabeth found men physically and intellectually attractive. She took piano lessons, danced, went on sleigh rides, read, sewed, made lace, and dressed for balls. She enjoyed reading *La nouvelle Heloise* by Jean-Jacques Rousseau. Uncle John Quincy Adams "is monstrously severe upon the follies of mankind—upon our sex particularly but tis only our follies—he condemns—I must *mortifyingly* confess *they are just*—but when we see our foibles exposed to ridicule they should be warnings to us to avoid & fly them" (28).

Elizabeth expresses serious concern about the proper way to achieve happiness. Reporting intimate conversations, she asks if contentment is all one should seek, if happiness and solitude are incompatible (10). Such dilemmas shaped her concerns about relations with men: "Must flattery be a part in the composition of every young man who makes it his aim to please? . . . The Fair was as susceptible of the poison as he could wish" (11). In contrast, her time with Polly provided relief and mutual pleasure: "Polly & I sat and chatted by ourselves & amused ourselves with forming imaginary schemes of future pleasure" (12).

Very much on the minds of Elizabeth and her circle (including at least one man, Polly's brother Leonard White) was its dispersal by the members' marriage and career plans. The strain and fear were likely more deeply felt among young women than the homesickness and wrench at leaving that young men report in comparable expressions. When women left home, they shifted from dependence on family to dependence on a husband. Their premarital bonds, more commonly with other women but sometimes with men, were deeply valued. Elizabeth's opinion about love, its risks and costs, formed a key part of this emotional parcel: "How doth love so extend & expand our affections but in proportion, we encrease our cares & pains every object of our Love sometimes causes our Grief—the avenues to pleasure are equally open to pain" (30). Elizabeth's journal makes no mention of her future spouse.[57]

Many women were widowed young and remarried. Ruth Henshaw Bascom, born in Leicester, Massachusetts, in 1772, was part of a large, active, and influential family.[58] She attended classes at the Leicester Academy, and reported in her diary an active world of social, domestic, and religious labors and recreations. In 1804 she married Asa Miles, a Dartmouth graduate and a physician. Miles died within the first year of marriage, and the twenty-three-year-old widow returned to her parents' home.

Ruth quickly remarried. In 1806 she became the wife of the Reverend Ezekiel Lysander Bascom. With no children of their own, the Bascoms raised the only child from the second of his previous marriages. For thirty-five years Ruth assisted her husband with his work. She also traveled a great deal and acquired some renown for her skill at drawing profiles.

In this era many young women, especially those without a large patrimony, began to gain more choice in marriage partners. This was one way in which traditional female paths of growing up were being transformed.[59]

Transitional

Among women growing up in the second half of the eighteenth century, transitional paths were richly varied and increasingly common. Among those recorded in personal testimony are paths characterized by religiosity, the influence of romanticism, and precocity.

As with young men, evangelical religious currents shaped the female experience of growing up. Spirituality sometimes worked to determine individual actions or redirect life's path. Esther Edwards Burr's route to marriage illustrates this influence.[60] Born in Northampton, Massachusetts, in 1732, the third of eleven children, Esther was the daughter of the Reverend Jonathan Edwards; she married Aaron Burr, minister and president of the College of New Jersey (now Princeton). Her journal, written in the form of letters to her long-time friend in Boston, Sally Prince, begins in 1754, when, at age twenty-two, she had been married for two years.

Esther grew up with the Great Awakening, in which her father played a leading role. Active evangelicalism in home and community permeated her world. She also learned the value and limits of women's proper role, serving—and obeying—men and God, in distinction to that of men, who need serve only God. As a child she witnessed the personal strains suffered by her mother, and their resolution in spiritual regeneration. Her journal reveals the pressure she felt when she chafed against her own and others' expectations, and it shows the value she placed on close female friends such as Sarah Prince.

At age twenty Esther married Burr, an evangelical minister sixteen years her senior, the pastor of Newark's Presbyterian church as well as a college president. Their courtship and "way of marrying" evoked comment from family and friends. Although they were barely acquainted and Burr had not seen her for six years, he journeyed to Massachusetts to ask Esther to be his bride. After five days they were married; her mother was the only family member at the ceremony. Two weeks later Esther moved to Newark. Her sudden decision may have stemmed from the family crisis precipitated by her father's ouster from the Northampton pastorate in a dispute over the conversion of new church members. His three eldest daughters married during this period, their paths clearly influenced by the family's circumstances.

Separated from family and friends, Esther felt isolated. Pregnancies and child care filled her time, and she records feelings of inadequacy under her burdens. Growing up in a minister's household had only partly prepared her for her responsibilities. Friendships came slowly; there were few married women her age nearby. She also had to manage the family removal with the college to Princeton. Although her relations with her husband were affectionate, even playful, convention dictated that she always refer to him as "Mr. Burr" in the journal. In 1757, after five years of marriage, he died during a malaria outbreak. Less than a year later, Esther died at the age of twenty-six, in the same year as her father.

The last decades of the eighteenth century began the era in which Lee Chambers-Schiller locates the emergence of spinsterhood, or "liberty," as a significant option for women. During the next century both average age at first marriage and the proportion of those never married rose among women as well as men. At the same time, new cultural currents that blended elements of the Enlightenment, romanticism, and religious spiritualism began to influence young persons in curious and complex ways.[61] The impact on growing up was mixed.

Martha (Patty) Rogers's exceptional diary provides a rare window on certain elements of this transitional path that looked to the future.[62] Born in New Hampshire in 1761, daughter of the controversial Harvard-trained "New Light" minister Daniel Rogers, Patty Rogers strikingly felt the new romantic cultural currents, although she struggled to counter their force. Her diary's rich record of the year 1785 reveals how personally costly the intersection of these currents with existing social patterns could be. It also shows the multiple bonds that constrained young women.

Patty recorded her activities as well as self-criticism and her intimate feelings about her romantic interests and her constraining responsibilities in caring for her infirm father. Her mother is never mentioned in the diary and was apparently deceased. Patty was active socially; she quilted, sewed, rode, sledded, danced (with her father's permission) at balls and assemblies, wrote letters and poetry, and attended teas, dinners, and other gatherings. She read romantic novels as well as the classics. Well educated, she was nonetheless critical of her accomplishments. At the age of twenty-three or twenty-four, she stood uncomfortably between being a dependent daughter living under the paternal roof and a young woman seeking self-fulfillment.

Patty found it hard to reconcile her feelings about marriage and love with cultural expectations. Teased by peers about her marital prospects, she took marriage seriously. She feared being made a fool by a man, had real doubts about being dependent on a husband, and did not wish to risk the loss of love through death. Patty had at least two suitors, a minister and a physician, to whom she gave classical code names in the diary. On March 7, 1785, she wrote: "Once I shall myself more than happy! when with him for a few *fleeting* moments and each bossom glow, I with friendship for each—other—But I dare not indulge myself in a moments pleasing reflection, lest my memory retentive of past scenes—should make me *wretched!* But what a *contrast* in my mind—*feelings* and *situations*—between this and the past year—but I'll be content, & hope for happiness *still*." Torn, she also dreamed of her own death in a shocking fit (March 11, 1785).

Romantic longings and bitter memories of unhappy past loves contended with her emotions over her father's illness and her responsibilities toward him. Although she was self-sacrificingly obedient, she still chafed at the ties that bound her. On March 12 of the same year she remarked that she "must deny myself everything for the present—my F—*very* Ill—O! how I wish to see some of my good friends." Those whom she most desired to see were the two suitors, "Portius" and "Philomen."

Beyond her romantic troubles, Patty struggled to achieve a sense of self-worth. On March 18 she wrote: "*Why have I friends—who am so worthless a creature.*" Suppressing her struggle with her father's evangelicalism, she hoped for happiness from God, not from a "vain world" not worth a thought. Her reflections swing from resolutions to be happy and to spend her time profitably; to regrets for her years of vanity, dissipation, and folly; to a search for spiritual peace; to longing for human, sexual love.

Still dreaming of Portius, Patty turned her hopes to Philomen. After seeing him, she wrote on July 1: "I enjoyed that happiness, which I seldom feel! O! could I dream away my Life in his arms, how *happy! exquisitely happy!*" Learning from friends that he was courting another, she struggled: "I only *feel* a friendship for him! I'll *steel* my heart to every *sentiment* of *love* . . . For who would consent a *second time to be a fool—not I!*" (July 13, 1785). Patty's struggle with her emotions stimulated her to reflect on relations between the sexes: "The controversies between man and wife are shocking—I think I could conform to a Husband's wishes in everything, and should certainly think it my duty, too, provided they were not inconsistent with propriety" (July 19, 1785).

On August 4 she recorded Philomen's attempt to take sexual liberties with her during their carriage rides. But whereas Philomen thought he was in love with her, she felt only "an ardent friendship." In response, he deemed her of "foolish heart." Patty strove to discipline her behavior around him. She turned criticism against herself: how good he was to "spend an evening with such a *dull unentertaining* girl as I am" (September 11, 1785). "I wish I could conduct with more prudence—I could bite my fingers off when I reflect on a little *manuver* in the preceding evening" (September 14, 1785). Patty also continued to long for Portius, now married. The diary ends with Patty, her love unrequited, hoping for the best for Philomen.

Patty's father died shortly thereafter, on December 9, 1785. Patty, who may have been the model for the character Dorcasina Sheldon in *Female Quixotism* (1801) by Samuel Tenney (her Philomen), never married.[63]

As with young men, precocity in young women reflected in part the flexibility inherent in growing up at this time. With fewer and very different avenues to the future open to them, precocity also cut differently for young women. For some, though certainly not all, it blended with, and sometimes built upon, spoiling by wealthy, indulgent parents, who thereby contributed to exceptional early experiences.

Since at least the late eighteenth century, Western and especially American culture has confronted the "precocious" child with deep ambivalence. Spoiling children is censured. Yet precocious children possess a certain attraction. In some cases childhood precocity contributed to significant adult achievement. In rejecting formal, institutionally based patterns of growing up, such individuals maintained some connection to the past, or at least to images of tradition; but in other ways, such as in the concern with children as individuals special in and of themselves, their paths looked to the future.

The popular Victorian novelist Catharine Maria Sedgwick, born in 1789 in Massachusetts, followed such a path. Sedgwick recounts her childhood in the form of a series of letters to a favorite niece written in the 1850s.[64] She began life in privileged circumstances. Her father was a prosperous lawyer who served in the U.S. Congress. He was married three times. Joined in what her daughter called "a perfect marriage," Catharine's mother, his second wife, found that responsibilities weighed heavily on her fragile health and delicate temperament. She died at age fifty-four, when Catharine was eighteen. Her husband remarried a woman Catharine deemed unsuited for domestic duties. Seven children filled the household.

Because of these domestic upheavals Catharine could write, "How faint and few are the recollections of a childhood that flowed smoothly on the current of love!" (39). The novelist continues unassumingly, "How trivial, too, are the recollections of childhood!" (40). More telling is Catharine's declaration that her childhood education was "fragmentary": "How different from the thoughtful, careful (whether judicious or injudicious) education of the present day" (43). She found her early environment nurturing: "No one dictated my studies or overlooked my progress. I remember feeling an intense ambition to be the head of my class, and generally being there. Our minds were not weakened by too much study" (44). Her precocity and ambition flowered from these roots.

Growing up in Stockbridge, Massachusetts, Catharine was "most happy." She "enjoyed unrestrained the pleasures of a rural childhood" with nature her "play-fellow." She had many companions. From her family she acquired a sense of nature's "picture language, so rich and universal." Scornfully she contrasted her joys with pedagogy's stress on learning "ologies" and summer holidays spent stitching "wretched samplers" (44). She writes: "Oh, how different was my miscellaneous childhood from the driving study and the elaborate accomplishments of children of my class of the present day!" (46). Sedgwick saw in country life—including its mix of social classes—an education that stimulated in her a sense of freedom.

Her nature was also a crucial factor. "I was a favorite with my schoolmates, partly, I fear, because I had what the phrenologists term an excessive love of approbation" (46).[65] For Catharine, nature joined with wealth and class. She was a favorite in part because she "had, more than the rest, the means of gratifying them" (46): credit at the store!

Reading "pleasant books" and "being petted by pleasant people" she preferred to "the task of learning lessons"—including those offered to her at age eleven by eminent dancing and French masters in New York City (55). Catharine's two years at a finishing school in Albany did not change her opinion of lessons. What school provided was female friendship. Catharine recalled "another gifted girl," Mary North: "She became a *lover* of mine, and was very jealous of every schoolgirl that I liked" (58). Frequent and significant, these bonds between girls likely reduced adolescent traumas and buffered gender conflicts. Sedgwick's experience puts "homosocial" relationships squarely within the emerging bourgeois paths of growing up.[66] Mary North was ideally suited to Catharine's imaginative and psychological needs: she was affectionate, true, handsome, and superior—and she died at seventeen. Years later Catharine fondly recalled "in my school-days—the elevating society and friendship of a superior woman, and cultivated companions and friends" (58). Boarding at Mr. Payne's school in Boston for six months at age fifteen, Catharine did not feel her time was well spent. "When I came home from Boston I felt the deepest mortification at my waste of time and money" (77). Her privileged circumstances did not prevent her from criticizing herself, and apparently correcting her faults.

Catharine's sense of self and self-confidence were among the consequences of her chosen path of growing up. She fashioned an independent single life and a career. But the cultural pressures facing professional women, single or married, were heavy.[67]

Emergent

Hardly rare, working prior to marriage constituted an increasingly common emergent female path of growing up.[68] Working for remuneration outside the domestic unit, followed by marriage, was not yet acceptable in terms of respectable gender norms, despite its frequency. Censured especially among the genteel, this route was a response to social and economic transformations that attracted, or in some cases propelled, young women into the labor market. For some, expanding opportunities in education paralleled those in work; for others, the realization that work and its rewards were even harder to come by than schooling was a difficult one. Nonetheless, in the second half of the eighteenth century the pattern of work before marriage was followed by a growing number of young women.[69]

Born in Pepperell, Massachusetts, in September 1773, Elizabeth Bancroft married for the first time in 1814. She was forty-one. Elizabeth's diary, kept from June 1793 to October 1795, reveals an active life.[70] Apparently living apart from her parents at the age of nineteen, she gives no hint of other supervision. She probably had some formal education to prepare her for her work as a schoolteacher. She kept a school of forty pupils. Most Sundays Elizabeth went to meeting; she also participated in quilting bees and visited friends and relatives regularly. She does not comment on her lack of a husband or fiancé. The matter-of-fact entries describe a satisfying life led by a competent and confident young woman.

On her birthday in 1793 Elizabeth sang: "O! it is my birthday to day. I can hardly believe it—is it possible that I have seen twenty years." The next day, a Sunday, after reporting on the preacher and the text at church, she adds: "As for me, I will behold thy face in righteousness; I shall be satisfied, when I awake, with thy likeness,—it begins to be almost bed time I'll drop my pen and read a chapter and then go to bed." Elizabeth also records her pleasure in dancing and singing in local "schools."

In June 1794 the name of John Hosley, her eventual husband, first appears: he came "to get me to keep school." The next mention is in February 1795, when she attended the funeral of "old Mr Hosley." In April she "went to Mr John Hosleys with Patty, spent the afternoon." Several weeks later she visited his mother. The Hosleys then disappear from the diary. Elizabeth continued her work and social life as a relatively independent, unmarried working woman. Nineteen years later she married John Hosley. She lived as his wife for seventeen years and then passed another thirty-six years as his widow.

Emergent Paths

Emergent routes for young men constitute this chapter's final set of paths. They look more toward the new century than to its past as they shift increasingly away from traditional and transitional patterns. Three routes in particular command our attention: the self-conscious, self-directed, Ben Franklin–style path; the path of higher education and advancement; and capitalist-commercial paths to adulthood.

Self-Directed

Benjamin Franklin's *Autobiography* strikingly describes an emergent path that some American men strove to follow from the late eighteenth century on. Silas Felton, son of a farming family in Marlborough, Massachusetts, claimed that reading the *Autobiography* had a profound effect on the course of his life.[71] Franklin's influence clearly permeates Silas's presentation of his own more ordinary existence.

Born in February 1776, Silas Felton belonged to an old New England family. He spent his childhood years in the usual routine of school alternating with farm work. His preference for the former became evident early: "Being more fond of School than of work I generally had more praises bestowed upon me at school than at home. When at home I was call'd rather lazy, but at School I almost always was at the head of the class of which I belonged" (126). Writing at the turn of the century, Silas took issue with the traditional child-rearing notions of his youth:

Experience has since taught me that people do not pay attention enough to the Inclinations of their children, but commonly put them to the same kind of business, which they themselves follow, and when they find them not attentive to those particular occupations accuse them of being idle . . . Being chastised for such things, it often damps their spirits, which renders them careless of what they do, and sometimes leads to looseness of manners; whereas if the leading inclinations of the children were sought after, and when found, permitted to follow them, [it] might prove highly advantageous to themselves, their parents and Society. (127)

For most of his teens Silas worked on the farm, read when he could, "roved" in the neighborhood with other boys. From fourteen to nineteen he "followed the schools only a part of the time they kept, but practised carrying my book home on the evenings, to study, because I was generally ambitious to excel in learning" (127). Silas also improved himself by frequent use of a subscription library established in 1792. When Franklin's "life and writings fell into my hands," he says, "I perused them attentively, and found many very valuable precepts, which I endeavoured to treasure up and follow. And I believe I may safely say they kept me from many Errors, for from that time I determined to *adhere strictly to Reason, Industry, and good Economy, to Always examine both sides, to keep my mind free from prejudice of any kind whatever, always to practice reason and truth,* believing it is better to follow the dictates of Reason and Conscience" (129).

In 1795 Silas began to teach school, despite his low estimation of his own learning: "Intending to take another School as soon as convenient, and knowing that my knowledge of Grammar was very small, I solicited my father, and at length gained his consent to attend an academy a few months" (132). His studies at Leicester Academy completed, he resumed teaching, again alternating with work on the family farm. All the while he agonized over his on-again, off-again courtship with Lucretia Fay. Now twenty-two years old, Silas counted his pennies, weighing carefully his future path: "I now began seriously to consider what I could do with a family, that if I did not intend to marry it was time our courtship was ended. My fortune was small and my prospects of gaining it, to any considerable amount, was also gloomy . . . often when going in the evening to visit her, did I form to myself a determination that this should be the last, but after spending the night agreeably and the morning appearing, I as often thought I would come once more" (136). Lucretia's attraction was strong. Reckoning together, they chose the path to the altar in January 1799.

Silas continued to teach successfully. With the aid of a partner and a loan from his father, he added storekeeping to schoolkeeping. The end of his path to adult independence was symbolized in March 1799, when, after marrying and opening his store, Silas was chosen assessor for the town of Marlborough. This civic work also contributed to his support. Thus, rational calculation and instrumental education proved their value for Silas Felton.[72]

Higher Education

College attendance as a route to a career was among the least common of the emerging paths; very few young men attempted it. Formal institutional training and credentials were not yet required for most professions, nor were ages of entering and graduating from college prescribed. Students came to colleges at many different ages and from many different origins. Not until the late nineteenth century did collegiate study play a significant part in an increasing number of professional careers.

Timothy Fuller, Jr., took one such path.[73] Born in Chilmark on Martha's Vineyard in July 1778, Timothy was the son of the Harvard-educated Reverend Timothy Fuller. He attended Harvard College from 1798 to 1801, taking his undergraduate degree. After briefly teaching at Leicester Academy and studying law in Worcester, he began to practice law in Boston in 1802.

Timothy's diary of his undergraduate years captures the emergent qualities of his route. Mixed with reports of many social activities is a serious and censorious note on students who did not "act on liberal principles uninfluenced by temporary applause or disapprobation" (35). His coffee club debated questions such as "whether the learned languages be too much studied at the University" (36).

The diary shows him to have been a diligent student. Timothy took pride in doing well and improving in his recitations and essays; he regularly visited Boston and attended intellectual as well as social and cultural events. He taught winter school during his freshman year. More social club activities marked his later terms, and we find restrained and judicious entries on the growing conflicts between students and college authorities. In October 1800 Fuller himself was fined by a tutor "for having a noise in our room an unseasonable hour last night" (49). More stridently, he notes on October 26: "Mr. Hedge read to our class some of the recent laws of the college, one of which prohibited leaning forward in class and enjoined us to 'sit in an erect position'! What admirable legislation! Such laws call for prompt opposition" (50). In December four fifths of the students signed a formal remonstrance against the laws and formed a committee to promote an orderly protest. Despite these distractions Fuller pursued his education to its conclusion. Professional training, consisting of traditional study in the office of a lawyer, immediately followed graduation. Marriage came only after he established an independent practice. Thus were middle-class paths being fashioned.

Capitalist-Commercial

The most noteworthy historical development propelling young men on emergent (and some transitional) paths was the spread of commercial capitalism. This economic change affected social relations in town and country; in offices, shops, and farms; in diverse families and regions; and across virtually all social divisions.

William Johnson, born in Newton, New Jersey, in 1779, was one of six sons and two daughters of Captain Henry Johnson, an officer in the War of Independence.[74] Johnson grew up in Newton and moved to New York City, where he became a successful merchant. His diary records significant steps along his path and their intersection with the uneven course of regional and national economic development.

William's diary opens with an account of his journey to New Orleans in 1800. With stops along the way for William and his brother Sammy to purchase agricultural produce and horses to trade, the trip took seven months. Once in New Orleans, the brothers dispatched their business, earning "a tolerable good speck" (56). Purchasing flour at a favorable price, Sammy sailed to the West Indies, while William returned to New York with a load of cotton to trade. Such commercial opportunities for young men were expanding; they propelled the transformations of growing up.

William's extensive commercial activities centered on New York. In June 1802 he rented a storehouse there and purchased dry goods to resell. But he still found time to travel to Newton to see family and friends. Eventually he decided to move his residence to the city. At twenty-six William Johnson still suffered from homesickness (153), although the city was where he built his social circle. In 1807 we find frequent notice of the comings and goings of "Miss B." or "my dear Rosaline," his poetic name for Susan Bray of New Jersey, whom he was to marry.

The interference of the British with shipping complicated his trading, but William continued to prosper. In 1810 he settled with his partners, noting on April 27: "This day opened store for the first in my life without a partner" (318). A month earlier he had penned: "In a couple of weeks I shall take a partner for life, and will be under the firm of 'Susan & William'" (318). His father's formal permission to marry having been granted, William and Susan were joined on May 10, 1810 (318).[75] William was thirty-one, a successful independent businessman who still retained ties to his family.[76]

John Griscom, Sr., is another young man whose growing up was affected by the transformation of society, the economy, and the culture. After traditional beginnings Griscom became a professor and a leading promoter of social reform in New York City. He recalls in his mid-nineteenth-century autobiography his early years of domestic tranquillity and comfort in his Quaker parents' small house in the village of Hancocks Bridge, New Jersey.[77]

At home, he writes, "I learned the alphabet without the aid of books. My father's [harness-making] work-shop was adjacent to our dwelling. He would often place me on his shop-board, or counter, while he pursued his work, giving me tools, etc., for my amusement. Many of the tools were stamped with the makers' names" (22). John early acquired a taste for reading. At about six he was placed at school twelve miles from home. In six months he learned to write, but an injury brought him home. Farm work, which he recalls doing well, occupied the next few years. John partially compensated for his curtailed education with his own reading.

Among his key early influences was his mother, "seconded" by his father. From her came "the excellent counsel, the watchful care, the sympathy, the mingled tenderness and firmness, of a pious and much beloved mother" (23). The family regularly trod the three miles to the nearest Friends' meetinghouse.

Because of the youth's reputation for love of learning and steady deportment, some neighbors appealed to the seventeen-year-old to open a school. Since his father had a claim on his services, John offered to share the profits. He soon discovered that a schoolmaster's labor was easier and more to his taste than farm work. His father relinquished his claim and allowed John to go in his own direction. Young Griscom assumed that teaching school would be "the probable business of my life" (26). In 1793 he went to the Friends' Academy in Philadelphia to improve his qualifications, especially in mathematics, but an outbreak of yellow fever cut short his stay in the city. He continued teaching in New Jersey, however, settling at the Burlington Academy.

With his career apparently in place, John turned to other steps on his path toward adult independence: "In the course of four or five years, I thought it would be right for me to become settled in domestic life" (43). He was boarding with a local family, one of whose four daughters was near his age. They married in 1800, when John was twenty-six. In the next five years three daughters arrived.

John began to feel the limits on his enterprise and earnings. His wife bore a heavy domestic burden of caring for family and boarders. Then a new opportunity beckoned. One of his memorialists writes: "His New York friends, some of whose sons had received their instruction chiefly from him, had several times intimated that he would find in that city, in all probability, a sphere in which he might reap a better reward for his labors" (51). In 1807, now thirty-two, John visited New York. He was well received, and was offered a school under his own control with a munificent initial salary of $2,250.

Despite the risks, he and his family made the move. Encouraged by his friends, John offered public lectures in chemistry. When the school lost its underwriters as a result of poor trade conditions, he reestablished it on his own. The Griscoms also reestablished private family life in a proper home removed from the bustle of the city. Their "rather quaint and rural tenement"—at 234 William Street (56)—was a forerunner of the middle-class family residential ideal in the nineteenth and twentieth centuries.

John became involved in an impressively wide range of reform and educational activities, emerging as one of New York City's leaders. After growing up in a traditional way, John Griscom began again on a new path with a new destination and form of independence, seizing emerging urban opportunities in a world marked by transformation.

Born in Lynnfield, Massachusetts, in 1788, Asa Goodell Sheldon also pursued an emergent path that reflected the spread of commerce and changes in social relations. He recorded his experience in a memoir published in 1870.[78] Born the fourth of eight children, Asa spent his early years in the comfort of his parents' rural home. He claims to have had early commercial interests. In his memoir, following pious praise of his mother's character, Asa reports: "Well do I remember, in the days of my childhood, the first copper ever earned with my own hands" (5). Saving (with a reference to Benjamin Franklin) followed, and with help he made his first purchases: a pewter porringer and a primer. Asa recounts his "first contract made for a day's work," six and a quarter cents for helping to fill a cart with stones when he was six, followed by many other odd jobs for pennies (8). His calling these informal arrangements "contracts" was one sign of the spreading market economy's impact on the culture and language of everyday life. Significant, too, is the cash basis of these transactions. The shift from traditional unpaid apprenticeship to paid work was under way.[79]

At eight Asa began his schooling, reading from the Old Testament and memorizing lessons. He suffered sleepless nights and mental distress owing to his inability to understand Christ's suffering and death until a sermon on salvation lightened his burden. Alternating school in winter (boarding one winter with his grandmother) with farm work in summer, Asa earned enough to buy schoolbooks and clothing. In December 1796 his father bought a lot of standing wood, employing his son to drive a team to drag away the timber, an unusually formal arrangement for a son's family labor.

"We now come to an important period in the history of a youth—I refer to leaving home," Asa intones. "What a privilege to parents it is, to be able to employ their children at home, and thus keep them around them under their careful scrutiny, and what a blessed privilege to children to live under the care and guidance of discreet parents" (13). That was neither Asa's experience nor his parents' option. Not yet nine years old, Asa was chosen by David Parker to live with and work for him. He joined a family of four; Mrs. Parker, who cared for him, told Asa to call her Mother. "I commenced my servitude here without time or remuneration being stated, which . . . is a circumstance liable to produce difficulty," he cautions his readers (13).

The bargain permitted Asa to continue his schooling in seasonal rotation with farm work. At the beginning of the third year, Parker urged that the eleven-year-old boy be formally bound to him, in return for $20 cash to his father now and $100 to Asa on his twenty-first birthday. The boy would also receive a few pennies and some opportunity to practice his petty entrepreneurship. His father agreed, although Asa's mother expressed anguish at making her son a "bond slave" (15). In his memoir Asa expresses satisfaction that "this inhuman practice has passed away": "O fathers, never be guilty of such a rash act. Never bind your children to service of any kind, and above all without the consent of [the child's mother]" (15).

Asa unhappily served Parker for almost eight years before he acted on his threats to leave. In his sixteenth year the lad returned to his own family. Parker asked him to remain for three years in return for $200 and one month of school each winter, but young Sheldon refused. Willing to serve only for pay and with a right to end the arrangement at any time, Asa negotiated a new signed and witnessed agreement. Parker proved unable to abide by it, and Asa finally left him after a few months.

After working for a neighboring farmer, Asa was hired as a "waiting man" in a Salem gentleman's family. Considering the wife "unsufferable," he gave notice and left. Returning to his "old neighborhood in North Reading," Asa continued school seasonally, sometimes driving loads to market on "vacant school days" (40). He also served the tavernkeeper at North Danvers for a year. Frequent shifts of residence accompanied greater regularity in work, punctuated by seasonal schooling. Together they defined Asa's teen years.

At about age twenty Asa purchased a sawmill with John Nelson. Much of his business was in lumbering, work that he felt suited him. Soon the sole owner, Asa added a winter grist mill. At age twenty-one, which he marked by treating his friends to liquor, Asa seemed to have the financial foundation for independence well in hand. His various businesses were doing well, and Asa expanded into hauling larger loads over longer distances. In June 1812 he began to carry hops and shoes to southern markets by way of New York City, learning to protect his monetary dealings. His business acumen expanded with experience. Asa did well during the War of 1812.

One major step remained on Asa's path to maturity: "We now come to that important period in the history of an individual, on which hangs so much of future weal or woe. My marriage with Clarissa Eames, was consummated Oct. 4, 1815. I was then 27 years old, and she 17" (73–74).

Asa Sheldon's business success continued. He expanded his transport and worked on New England's early rail lines. Although he continued to call himself a farmer, his ventures in commercial capitalism were many. In the conclusion of his memoir, with benefit of hindsight, he expresses his views on religion and child rearing and their accommodation to a new liberal social order: "I cannot believe that God has created a world full of children without one particle of goodness in any of them . . . We find great encouragement to live a good, moral life . . . Adopt the rule today, to do undo others as you would have them do unto you. Follow this rule, and you will soon love God, and he will be sure to love you. It may not make you rich, but take my word for it, it will make you happy" (181–182).[80] Is happiness its own reward? Sheldon does not offer that conclusion, nor does he claim that wealth obstructed happiness as values and ideologies contended with the many transformations effected by commercial capitalism.

These paths to adulthood in late colonial and early republican America mark only the beginnings of the epochal nineteenth-century remaking of growing up. In the eighteenth century young people seldom encountered sharp distinctions between "private" and "public" or fixed demarcations between the nuclear family and larger kin and community circles. Although the great import of early experience was recognized, childhood was rarely seen as a time of innocence and vulnerability. Childhood and adolescence were not prolonged, although youth certainly could be. There was relatively little of what has come to be called age synchronization, a standardized march through childhood, adolescence, and youth on the road to adulthood.

Yet the recognition of the importance of the early years of life was already contributing to a reevaluation of the needs of the young. One continuing debate concerned the proper role of young people in determining their path and destination. Youths began planning for their future, sometimes through formal institutions such as schools. The concept of the "moral mother" was emerging, along with more child-oriented families. The spread of commercial capitalism and market exchange created new opportunities and relationships, as well as new challenges. Among these were early waves of migration to urban areas and to the frontier. Class and gender, along with race, ethnicity, geographic location, and family circumstances, emerged to play major roles.

CHAPTER THREE

Hops, Skips, and Jumps
into the Nineteenth Century

"IN 1775, the character of American society was very similar to what it had been in 1700," write the historians James Henretta and Gregory Nobles. Freeholding farm families formed a majority of the New England and Middle Atlantic colony populations. Continuity also marked southern society. "Then," they note, "came a period of far-reaching social and economic evolution." Beginning slowly, the transformations became more rapid after 1790. "By 1820, the United States had become a highly developed preindustrial society with a diverse economy and a complex social structure."[1] Ever-larger commercially driven markets developed in inseparable connection with westward migration, transportation and other internal improvements, urban growth, early industrialization, and social stratification. A fundamentally new social order of classes and cultures was forming, striking different persons and places at different times and with differing effects.[2]

An era of revolutions, as its students proclaim, from that of the "common man" to those of market, commerce and finance, communications, institutions, and politics, this period saw sweeping transformations in realms rural and urban, agricultural and industrial, with dramatic impact on work, residential, family, gender, and age relations. For some, new opportunities arose, while others found themselves confronted by obstacles and crises, especially in the long-settled eastern rural areas. As Sean Wilentz writes:

Those who benefited most from the market revolution—merchants and manufacturers, lawyers and others professionals, and successful commercial farmers, along with their families—faced life situations very different from those known to earlier generations. The decline of the household as the locus of production led directly to a growing impersonality in the economic realm; household heads, instead of directing family enterprises or small shops, often had to find ways to recruit and discipline a wage-labor force; in all cases, they had to stay abreast of or even surpass their creditors . . . Less fortunate northeasterners faced a very different reality, dominated by the new dependencies created by the market revolution.[3]

While some persons strove for gain, others struggled to achieve social and economic independence, or just to make ends meet.

Many from the North and South went west; immigrants and other internal migrants shifted toward the cities. Each group, including the so-called new yeomanry, faced difficulties. Rural settlers contended with Native Americans, as well as speculators and creditors. Most managed to own their own farms. In time, the integration of farmers into commercial markets and the specialized production of cash crops brought prosperity to some but failure to others. Wilentz observes: "The rise of capitalist agriculture in the Northwest, as in the Northeast, produced new classes of independent and dependent Americans."[4] The changes that struck the South were characterized by the constant racial struggles between masters and slaves on the one hand and the class conflicts between the white yeomanry and the planter elite on the other.

Changes in means, modes, and relations of production were neither exceptional nor isolated. Especially profound changes remade the spheres of women and men into separate realms of private and public, most visibly in the emerging middle class but among others as well. Both the reality and the ideology of work, politics, residence, gender, and child rearing were all reconstructed according to new standards, rights, responsibilities, and social and cultural relationships. Wilentz concludes that from the point of view of recent scholarship, the main lines of antebellum history "begin to look very different . . . But in order to come to terms with these matters, historians have had to find out how Americans of different classes, races, and regions experienced the enormous structural changes that confronted them, and how they acted upon those new understandings."[5] Among those new understandings and experiences are those stimulating the continuing transformations of growing up.

As in the previous era, four principal paths of growing up dominate the record in this seminal epoch: *traditional, transitional, female,* and *emerging social class* patterns. The paths of African Americans and native peoples are not detailed here, for reasons I have discussed. Other absent or underrepresented subjects include female servants, unmarried women, the poor, the unskilled, and European immigrants, among other working-class men and women.[6] Compared to the previous period's paths, these nineteenth-century routes reflect both continuity and change. Both traditional and transitional paths were changing along with emerging social class lines. The female path, also in transformation, joined gender to class and race as constituting factors in the experience of growing up.

To a degree unappreciated in most earlier studies of this period, the extent of change in major patterns of growing up, much of it in transitions toward more modern paths, is remarkable. In addition to their early appearance, among the key aspects of these transformations are the appearance of a recognizable experience of adolescence, the pivotal place of age-related peer groups and peer culture, and movement, physical as well as symbolic. These transitions characterized paths toward adulthood much as they typified the era itself.

As in earlier eras, traditional paths comprised principally two subpaths: that of sons following fathers and that of rural migrants moving within or to the periphery of developed areas (in contrast to the movement of pioneers and other long-distance migrants). Traditional modes of growing up were declining, though not rapidly disappearing. Underlying important continuities while maintaining traditions—some of which were remade into powerful new cultural lore and mythologies—traditional paths reclaimed an increasing influence even as their numbers diminished.[7]

The transitional path of growing up in many ways characterized this period of social transformation. Its margins blurring with those of the traditional paths, on one side, and emerging class paths, on the other, this route reflects its central position in growing up as well as an overall indefinability of boundaries. Transitional patterns embraced and reflected the influence of geographic location and place of residence, definitions of dependence and autonomy, school and other institutions, family and community, peers, and work. These relationships defined the totality of growing up.

The artisan-apprentice route is the first of four transitional subpaths. In many respects traditional, this route was nonetheless changing. Artisanal work was shifting under the impact of commercial and early industrial capitalism and the resulting new modes and relations of production. In both craft and commercial-professional spheres, the practice of apprenticeship unevenly declined as formal institutions developed to take its place and as young people gained access to work in new ways. Transitional avenues were connected inextricably to the increasingly differentiated styles of working-class, middle-class and upper-class growing up.[8]

Constituting the second subpath, discontinuous routes to traditional middle-class destinations share some characteristics of the artisan-apprentice path. They included, but were not limited to, the older professions such as the ministry, medicine, and law, variously incorporating schooling, leaving home, college, and schoolteaching. Such transitional routes often overlapped with traditional modes of socialization and occupational preparation. They too were evolving, unevenly, in the direction of modern middle- and upper-class paths of growing up.[9] Young persons confronted a confusing proliferation of opportunities between the fixed boundaries of the traditional paths and emerging modern ways, with their stringent new order and discipline.

Rural and/or western migration, typically pioneering, forms the third transitional subpath. Affected by traditions of rural migration, its sagas contributing to new stereotypes and cultural mythologies of growing up—the advice to "go West, young man"—this avenue included youths migrating with their families or on their own, including young women migrating with their husbands. These lengthy and difficult journeys—part of the myth of "how the West was won"—had their impact on reshaping the process of growing up. Those who followed this path built on these beginnings to redefine American adulthood, as tradition and transformation were linked in the movement toward national expansion and continental settlement.[10]

The fourth subpath is that of youthful religious conversion. First rising, then declining in frequency throughout the nineteenth century, this route was shaped by the variable role of religion in growing up and by the peculiar relations of religiosity—in form, structure, meaning, and expression—to young persons. A consistent feature of transitional paths despite twists and turns, this subpath often blended with others along the way.[11]

Female paths constitute the third principal avenue of growing up in this period. This concept emphasizes the power of gender in shaping the life course as young women were propelled along routes that diverged from their brothers'. Such differences increased in this era with the fashioning of modern gender assumptions and roles and their broadening social and cultural expression. The powerful influence of class, race, and ethnicity brought sharp conflict and contradiction to norms and expectations, new and old. At the same time, class and race also underlay the basic commonalities with male peers that cut across gender distinctions, including assumptions about the nature of childhood and adolescence, schooling, residence, family, and the like.

The principal lines of growing up for women span and link, sometimes confusingly, traditional, transitional, and emergent class paths. For many young women of the period, three subpaths of growing up dominated their experience. (Largely missing from this account are female servants and unskilled and immigrant working-class women.) First, the traditional way, familiar from the preceding era, was tightly bound by family and marriage. In some ways traditional norms were redefined into emerging class paths. Traditional routes also took many women to newly settled areas.

The second subpath, the transitional, was the route of work and migration away from home and family. Schoolteaching, domestic service, and textile mill labor were the most common and, despite some conflict, culturally approved pursuits. Daughters of farmers joined those of middle- and working-class families, rural and urban, in following new routes and acquiring novel experiences, including more schooling and autonomy. Some young women moved to larger urban centers (skewing sex ratios), but that was neither their only nor their final destination. Some went west. Often marriage followed. This new avenue was in part a traditional teenage form of home-leaving.

The emerging bourgeois pattern constitutes the third and final female subpath. Often cited and surely most stereotyped, this was the sphere of middle-class formation. An intricate, highly contradictory process that remade home, family, childhood and adolescence, and womanhood itself, this development redefined bourgeois women and the ways in which they grew up. From new modes of child rearing to more advanced, formal preparation for conducting and exercising the responsibilities and powers of "women's sphere," this route was filled with conflicts and wrought massive transformations.

The fourth major path—the emerging path for working-, middle-, and upper-class males—conveyed unmistakable if incomplete signs of the transformation toward new modes of growing up. As the century progressed, the influence of social class, gender, race, and ethnicity became more noticeable. Many of the new forces that would contribute to modern social class relations, reshaping childhood, adolescence, and youth over more than a century, first appeared in this period. Although much was shared across class lines—including, in some part, new assumptions about the nature of childhood, formal schooling, extension of dependence, prolonged family residence, cults of home and mother, the influence of peer groups and culture, and the like—there were significant divergences. Even points of commonality—strategies and resources in family economies; traditions and values; activities of children, adolescents, and youth, especially relating to work and preparation for work; avenues to autonomy and home-leaving—yielded diverse results.

Although modern growing up is often viewed as a homogenizing experience across social lines, and although middle-class norms and values are often accorded a descriptive hegemony, the historical development of class-bound paths of growing up contradicts such easy notions. Growing up was a much more complex, uneven, and contradictory experience than it has appeared to observers. Emerging class paths gave rise to three predominant subpaths—the working-, middle-, and upper-class routes. Some variation existed within each subpath, as individuals and families blended old and new ways into strategies for preparing the young for a future of altered circumstances. Conflicts old and new shaped these developments, influencing, if sometimes indirectly, those in other classes.[12]

First-person testimonies of growing up show, in this era of epochal change, that tradition was becoming redefined. As the American social order was remade, so too were the ways in which young persons grew up.[13]

The notion of transition captures the overall flux of a world in which the young were struggling to find their places. It also clarifies the part that cultural thought and ideology, religion, social institutions, family, residential changes, peer groups, and the like played in refashioning childhood, adolescence, and youth. The ways in which these forces came together in the nineteenth century helped shape the modern concept and experiences of growing up. In strategies and socialization, family, institutions, and peers played seminal parts. Neither in this era nor in the next, however, was growing up completely remade into modern class-, gender-, and race-dominated paths. That struggle continued.

Amid this unstable blend of ingredients, the social and cultural meanings of age and life course were remade rhetorically and experientially. The period from the late eighteenth through the first half of the nineteenth century contributed to these ends, often earlier than previously presumed.[14] In this reinterpretation the familiar and the novel sometimes combine, sometimes clash. The many colors and shapes on our canvas include family strategies and adaptations to economic and cultural changes; new notions and expectations about childhood, adolescence, and youth; changing ideas about and experiences of gender; social class formation; changes in the modes and relations of production, patterns of residence, migration, and settlement; theory and practice of education; peer and voluntary groups; shifting meanings of public and private spheres; and state and institution building. Joining them were the forces of republicanism; evangelicalism; cultural currents such as Enlightenment rationality, human malleability and perfectibility, environmentalism, romanticism, and sentimentality; and concerns about order and disorder at a time of enormous and disconcerting change. In reading the tale through the personal stories of which it is made, we call the roll of major changes of the era as an aid to comprehending the transformed paths these lives illustrate.

Traditional Paths

Traditional paths show how continuity carried strongly into a transitional era. They remained a significant form of passage to adulthood, even as they were evolving through social change into transitional and emerging class patterns. Traditional paths are found mainly among those growing up in relatively settled, often rural areas. There is no doubt that this pattern was declining, but over a long term, slowly changing as new circumstances challenged and stimulated responses. At the same time, tradition itself was being redefined in the crucible of societal transformation.[15] The recreation of tradition is a basic human action. "New" traditions shaped perceptions and responses; "tradition" could connote either approbation or derision.[16]

Moses Porter, born in 1794, was one of four children of farming parents in Putnamville, Massachusetts. He followed his father into farming, long residing at the family homestead. In his diary Moses matter-of-factly recorded his activities for the two years before he married at age thirty-two.[17] He was comfortable with his circumstances. His regular rounds of farm work included marketing produce as capitalism reorganized rural life in Massachusetts. He attended meeting, enjoyed singing, spent time with his family and peers, including Fanny, whom he would marry and about whom he notes mundanely: "In the evening went over to see Fanny once more . . . Found her well and pleasant as usual, carried her 3 Tortoise shell combs for her to take on. Carried over the first Vol. of Henry K. White's remains for her to read" (45). Encapsulating in a word his traditional path, Moses refers to his father as "Sir."

Porter's path was hardly unique. His involvement in markets, locally and regionally, indicates some change in the pattern of growing up. The paths of those able and willing to follow their fathers were more alike than different. Almost fifty years later Charles Ross followed a path that was remarkably similar.[18] Born in rural Vermont in 1838, aged twenty-two when he began his diary, Charles worked at his father's farm in Lower Waterford. He threshed, drew and chopped wood, did chores for an uncle and other farmers, and performed road work. He attended singing school two evenings each week, lyceum one evening, and church services twice on Sunday, and he visited relatives, neighbors, and friends. He was strongly religious and maintained close ties to family and friends.

Under his father's authority Charles earned money for his labors, keeping daily cash accounts of purchases and expenditures. Charles's father invested his savings for him. He was fond of his son, glad to have him earn his living, and pleased to have him (one of two sons) at home. Charles got on well with his stepmother, who raised him, and his stepbrother.

Charles also taught school, living away from home. He was serious, if not enthusiastic, about schoolteaching, which he found hard work. His pupils did not know how to "mind." Discouraged, he nonetheless refused to give up, "for I will not be run over." His choices, he realized, were limited to farm labor and teaching (76).

At the end of term in January 1862, the trustees decided to disband the school. First, Charles returned to his father's farm. Then in August he enlisted in the U.S. Army with a cousin and neighbor: "Father was very much opposed & feels bad, but Mother is not so bad. I am sure it is my duty so I go forward" (120). As Charles's son later commented, "This year 1861 was the last year of CR's boyhood."

Elliott Story's journey reveals a less sanguine attitude toward following the traditional path.[19] Born in Virginia in 1821, the eldest of six children, Elliott combined family farm work with school until he stopped going at age sixteen. In January 1838, a month shy of eighteen, Elliott began to teach at a nearby free school. Living at home, he helped with farm work when not in the classroom. Nearing nineteen and clearing "hardly a hundred dollars," he was unhappy (146). Elliott wanted to leave home to teach in a larger, better school in another county. "The money was needed at home," however, so he agreed to stay. Several years of teaching exacerbated his frustration (146). Like Charles Ross, he had trouble in the classroom with attendance and discipline, and he was also dissatisfied with his unimproving earnings. In his early twenties he noted, "It [farming] is a business in which it is not probable I shall ever engage [full-time], unless I was able to have it cultivated without my own labour" (147).

In 1848, three years after his father's death, Elliot took over the farm. Still teaching, he had a vision of becoming a farmer, a calling whose natural and spiritual dignity he tried to justify. Facing drought in 1848, Story caught the western fever: "The rising west employs many of my moments of thought and I have often longed to go and seek my fortune there, but there are ties that bind me to Old Virginia" (147). In 1853, after fifteen years of teaching and farming, Story entered a mercantile partnership, borrowing his share. The venture was short-lived: his partner died, and Elliott sold out. With three decisions taken in 1856 at age 35, Elliott Story acquiesced in his traditional path: he married, purchased the family homestead from his mother, and built his house on the land. Unable to repay his debts and make a living just farming, he resumed teaching three years later. In his traditional path Elliott Story "never left home."[20] Traditions could bind tightly. Traumatic times such as the Civil War, stimulated their reemphasis and re-creation.[21]

In the nineteenth century, traditional paths of growing up contributed to the great migrations west and efforts to transplant customs and values from well-settled to newly developing areas. Deep-seated social changes were both cause and consequence of the ways in which the young were growing up. There is neither irony nor contradiction in grasping the many complex means whereby tradition and change played on and reshaped each other. Those interactions are visible in experiences ranging from "hardscrabble boyhood" in "poverty's vale" in western New York State to the life of pioneering settlements in the Old Northwest and beyond.[22]

In his 1891–92 memoir Henry Conklin (1832–1915) told a pioneer family's tale of growing up in frontier poverty in western New York. He and his siblings followed traditional paths in their struggle for subsistence and adult maturity. Typically among the first settlers in a wilderness, the family spun and wove its clothing and produced much of its food. Poverty is the main theme of Henry's memoirs. His path compellingly illustrates the connections that tied poverty to traditional modes of growing up in rural areas. Yet he grew up happy in a united family.[23]

His parents, especially his mother, stand out in his early memories: "My own dear mother, who had given me birth and nourished and cared for me until I knew her from the rest. Oh, that sweet childhood memory of my dearest one I ever knew on earth" (19).[24] Henry also recalled his pride in wearing his first pair of pants at age three to watch a circus caravan pass near home.

The woods were the grounds for play and informal learning with his siblings. As a young child Henry gathered wool for his mother and sister to card for spinning. Moving his family frequently but remaining poor, Henry's father worked farms on shares or for hire. He also drank. Only his mother's constant labor kept the family fed and clothed.

In his third home Henry had his first school experience. All summer his sister led him more than a mile through woods and clearings. Here Henry learned to read. His sister attended little; she spun at home, and went away to work in the fall. In other summers different siblings went with him, "but as soon as any of the children got old enough to work out, school was neglected" (32). The size and composition of the family constantly changed as children were sent out to work and then returned home. Similarly, they moved in and out of schools. Most of the children got "a very scanty education." Henry's older brothers and sisters found this a "discouraging" way to grow up (37). Reflecting back, Henry hesitated to cast blame.

Living at home, attending school when free from work, at age six Henry entered what he calls "the land of youth." "Childhood was fleeting. . . . Oh glorious awakening to youth and sweet childhood" (37). Precocious, romanticized youth lasted from about his sixth to his sixteenth years. In part this view reflects his expanding domestic role. As older siblings, especially sisters, left home, Henry took on more indoor chores. His sense of gender roles was flexible: "I was my mother's boy girl and I believed it for mother said so" (39). These were among the happiest of his memories of home. At seven years Henry added milking to his domestic tasks, a symbolic step: "I thought that if I could only milk I would soon be a man" (45).

Regular school attendance and his first case of "boy love" for a "best girl" marked Henry's ninth year. He and Ann sat in school and studied together. She was "the dearest, sweetest one I knew then and many a kiss did we snatch and take, and talked of the years to come" (58–59). Time with Ann and attendant childish notions provided some respite from labor. His sister Ruth married when Henry was ten, escaping "poverty's vale" by leaving home. The others spent their adolescence and early adult lives "toing and froing." The crush at home, at times exacerbated by his father's outbursts, led Henry to run away. Lured back by his mother's ill health, he was welcomed with a whipping by his father (the first and last, he notes). Frequent partings and returnings were emotionally wrenching, as when his brother Sammy came home from the farm to which he had been bound for four years bearing obvious signs of mistreatment.

After six years—up to Henry's "middle youth"—the family moved again. Parting from Ann and her brother, his best chum, was difficult. But with nostalgia and irony Henry reflects on his family of twelve children: "We were all well and healthy, thanks to plain food, plenty of outdoor exercise and a father and mother with iron constitutions and no hereditary disease lurking in their bodies. What a tough lot of children we were. Although poor and at times pinched with hunger we were comparatively happy going to our new home in the wilderness" (100–101).

But, Henry observes: "My youth was passing now like the fleeting wind and I was awakening to duty, sorrow, passion and pain" (118). He enjoyed the last summer of his irregular schooling: "My youthful school days ended and with what sad regrets, as many and many a time have I looked back over those ten years that were past. Ten years of youth and the reader will say is that not enough? No I was not satisfied. I wished for an eternal youth . . . I had passed through my boyhood love and manhood's budding morn was now beaming upon me and I was only sweet sixteen" (120).

That fall Henry left home to work, a major transition. "Well along" in his studies, his education "as good as the average teacher" (120), he needed only one more term to qualify to teach. But that was not possible. Henry, too, spent the next few years "toing and froing," according to his family's labor needs and opportunities for lumber work in the developing community.

At local revivals during this time Henry found religion. Rising in witness one night at age eighteen, he was baptized and given full membership in the church. Community substituted for family as his brothers and sisters increasingly scattered over a widening area.[25]

In about his twentieth year Henry began to court a young woman named Almira. Smitten with her, he would stay, kissing passionately late into the night. About the future they spoke in a "businesslike way not with any dilly dally foolishness as some lovers style it" (138–139). Before long they were engaged. Around the same time Henry began his own homestead, purchasing eighty-one acres for $100. Although his living came from working for others and he continued boarding, he and his brother worked the farm until 1861.

As marriage neared, Almira's feelings changed. The week before their nuptials she informed Henry that despite her love for him she could not marry, for she had no clothes to wear, and her folks were too poor to provide the household items she wanted. Responding to the poverty and plight of the women around her, she burst out "that whoever she did marry she would never have any family and that she never would wear her life out taking care of a mess of squalling brats as her poor mother has always done." With this declaration Henry's courtship and "imaginary happiness" ended: "All my air castles had crumbled at my feet" (156–157).

By boarding, working, and saving, Henry was able to pay for his farm. By 1854 Henry, now twenty-two had a new love, Elizabeth, another schoolmate. Although her "tyrant" of a father made courting difficult, they quietly sought out "trysting places" (159–161). Henry journeyed to his Uncle Henry Curtis's new farm in Wisconsin, where he worked as a carpenter and enjoyed himself with neighboring young people. Then, "tired of tramping and depending on strangers for work," he decided to "go home to York State" (181).

Henry returned warmly to Elizabeth, with whom he had kept in touch, his desire to wed heightened by her brother's marriage to Henry's sister. They resumed their courtship. Anticipating marriage, Henry "could spark and work also." This time he "had no fears of [Elizabeth] giving me the slip as Almira did . . . I knew she loved me." The couple did not share their secret with anyone. Finally, on October 12, 1856, they wed (198). To farm, cabin, and cow Henry added wife. Their family, which eventually reached nine children, grew steadily. Henry had achieved adulthood and independence. Interrupted temporarily by his Civil War service, Henry's traditional rural path of growing up, with its twists and turns, ended happily.

There were more similarities than differences between traditional paths such as Henry's and those of his contemporaries in the West. Branson Harris's experiences in frontier Indiana, and those of Elisa Keyes, who moved as a child from Vermont to Wisconsin, testify to powerful continuities as well as to the potential for change within traditional life-styles.[26] These paths were inextricably tied to national development, expansion through migration and settlement, and the formation of local communities. Born in Wayne County, Indiana, in 1817, Branson Harris was a first-generation Hoosier. His father had migrated with his family in 1807 at the age of sixteen. By the time Branson was born, his father was working his second farm. When the boy was nine, his father moved to his third and last homestead. With his father's early arrival in the county, Branson witnessed its settlement from the beginning; his growth paralleled the community's. With its house and barn raisings and corn shuckings, hard labor in a land lacking wagons and technological aids required communal cooperation and sociability across age, gender, and other lines. Nearby Indian villages added to Branson's awareness of growing up on the frontier.

His father's buying a new farm stood out in Branson's memory. To a boy of nine or ten, the move was exciting. Corn was a fast-growing crop, and markets were far away until the railroad came through. At twelve Branson saw his first town, Indianapolis, the state capital, "no great city at that time."

Much production centered on family subsistence. Working with flax took the labor of men and boys as well as women. "Many a day I had to stay at home from school when a boy to swingle flax to get it ready for mother to spin" (46), he recalls. "In the evenings the young men would come [to wool picking] too, and all would have what we called in those days a frolic" (47). As a small boy Branson helped his mother by putting the warp of the woolen thread on the beams of the loom.

Branson learned his ABCs in primitive schoolhouses. Teachers humiliated their charges. Some beat the pupils with ferrules. Oral recitation, copy work, and spelling dominated the curriculum. Spelling schools were common. So was the Christmas custom of turning out the master "to make him treat us to two bushels of apples" (15).[27]

Like others who recalled traditional paths of growing up, Branson Harris romanticized, and he had his ax to grind. His censure fell on the young of later years in a monotonous refrain:

> The young men of to-day, as soon as they get old enough to go out in company, must have a horse and buggy. To this I do not object. It is all right. When I was but a lad the boys and girls, when they went anywhere, usually went afoot . . . The young people often had parties. The married people would have wood choppings, flax pullings, and apple cuttings and quiltings and ask the young men and women to come in and help them. At night they could have their frolic. I was one of the boys who enjoyed going to those parties and taking an active part in our sport and amusement as well as any one. (56–57)

Other "frolics" mixing age groups as well as the sexes fell on election days (Branson first voted at twenty, not knowing he was not supposed to until age twenty-one, a sign of imprecise but incipient age consciousness) and at weddings, the young people's favorite gatherings. At twenty-two, Branson married Martha Young. After the ceremony and a dinner party with sweet wine, the newlyweds were escorted to Branson's parents' house, where Martha was welcomed into the family. The couple established housekeeping as Branson completed his traditional path of growing up in developing rural Indiana. He lived his more than ninety years in the same neighborhood in which he was born.

Elisa Keyes's no less traditional path was shaped by migration. When he was seven years old in 1837, his father moved the family of four children from Vermont to Lake Mills, Wisconsin. Growing up was more or less communal as settlers banded together, learning by trial and error. Elisa attended his first school at Aztalan in the summer of 1838. "I used to walk the distance most of the time on barefoot," he later recalled. "It was then thought quite a task" (22). Elisa's father decided that a school was needed closer to home. A district was formed. Local interest in churches also ran strong.

With settlers came sociability. "The utmost friendliness and good feeling prevailed," says Elisa (28). Social gatherings were frequent; women visited one another at home. The Fourth of July was a major annual celebration. For the young, social norms were rapidly set:

> The same kindly feeling was seen in the intercourse of the younger people of the families—the boys and girls—and as soon as civilization, so to speak, had advanced far enough, a regular ball was announced . . . Cards of invitation were issued. When rather young I was invited, and my mother insisted that I was big enough to go, and that I should invite a girl and take my place in line with those who were older. As I remember I was a timid lad, and it required a good deal of courage to (what seemed to me at that time a terrible ordeal) invite a girl to go to the ball with me, but with the help of my good mother it was made easy. (28)

Elisa's brother Abel, it turned out, had already asked Elisa's intended partner. When their mother learned this, she "knocked him out in the first round." Elisa proudly made it through the evening "without any discredit" (29).

Fulfilling a lengthening roster of domestic chores, Elisa proudly drove the ox cart in which his mother and her friends rode when visiting. In addition to farm work, with friends he "hunted and hallooed through the woods skirting yonder lake," fishing, swimming, engaging in sports, and going to school (43). Hunting, fishing, and digging potatoes were all children's activities that contributed to family sustenance. Elisa learned early to run the sawmill and gristmill built by his father. He too grew up along with the village. With his mother and Abel he ran the farm while his father built more mills. In the traditional passage of growing up, Elisa worked and boarded as a "farmer boy" at the home of a family named Phillips when he was seventeen.

Traditional paths did not always lead to traditional ends. Elisa's youthful aspirations were cut from the cloth of tradition: "It was then the ambition of my life to become a farmer . . . The sale of the farm destroyed all my hopes and aspirations for a farmer's life, and in '50 I turned my footsteps toward Madison, where I have resided ever since" (53).

Transitional Paths

Elisa Keyes ended his traditional path with a major transition. His story shows how suddenly and unexpectedly change could arise. Not all transitions were so explicit. Opportunities and constraints varied. Stories of how the young struggled with changes in their circumstances and confronted the conflicts accompanying those transformations constitute the heart of this chapter. The linchpins in the remaking of growing up were the transitional paths.

In this period the major transitional paths were those of the artisan-apprentice, the traditional but changing middle class, the western migrant or pioneer, and the preadult religious convert. Patterns of discontinuity in residence, dependence, and peer group provide one set of keys to understanding this route; new roles of families and their relationships with institutions offer another. Economic transformation had a critical impact on work and occupations. Let us see how individual youths and their families coped with these forces.

Artisan-Apprentice

John Albee's boyhood in rural and small-town Massachusetts offers one portrait of the transitional paths that reshaped growing up.[28] Born in 1833 in Bellingham, John grew up in parallel with the commercial and industrial remaking of New England. In his memoir he idealizes the early industrial society of his youth, despite his own struggles within it.[29]

Lacking the means to pay for his extended education, and "not feel[ing] able nor competent to manage me when I should be older" (151), John's widowed mother decided to have John apprenticed. He went to live with his bootmaker uncle in the next town at the young age of eight. John found the work and hours insufferable. He wept constantly for three weeks. He later wrote: "My nature was changed from that time; a kind of depression and melancholy, took the place of my natural gaiety. I can readily believe, such were my misery and agony, that one might die of homesickness" (151). The uncle returned the boy to his mother, who looked upon him for days with "sorrowful eyes."

Happier, John progressed in school and rejoiced in play. At ten he was apprenticed to a millwright. Schooling in summer and a new suit each year were the terms. He never received the latter, but living near his mother, seeing her daily, and having time to play kept him content until a severe illness two years later ended the apprenticeship. At this stage John "had no ambitions, no special talent nor practical faculty," nor any expectations for the future (167–168).

John moved with his mother and a sister to Hopkinton, where stitching boots was the town's predominant work. Bored by the bootmakers' politics, he "learned all the tricks and sleight-of-hand with which the bootmakers amused themselves and puzzled each other in the shops" (173). John completed his daily labors in time for afternoon ball playing. Too old to play with girls, he took up with mischievous boys; his education was neglected. That changed when one of his sisters, a teacher, took him to live with her and attend the private school where she taught in Norwich, Connecticut. Adjusting quickly to "a very different class of children," he learned to be comfortable among the "highbred." John's pleasant new life ended when his mother called him home; six months later, after teasing and coaxing, he returned to Norwich. With his sisters' and new peers' influence, he grew intellectually and socially.

Full-time schooling and recreation were "a temporary expedient." A new place in a dry goods store, earning board and clothing, was offered nearby. The shift was abrupt: "Without warning I fell completely out of the ranks of the elect and again returned to servitude as a shop boy, a runner of errands, a builder of fires and floor sweeper" (192). Despite the wrenching discontinuity, John felt "rather proud" standing behind the counter waiting on customers. Clothed and well fed, he lived with the store's "not unkind" proprietor. He took as role models the two clerks, one a poet, admiring their efforts at stylishness.

John also discovered a secret society of adolescent peers: boys of similar age, in similar professional and social situations, who had banded together to ease one another's transitions in growing up. He joined the group, indulging in its adolescent ways, after

> having been tested as to strength, reliability, and other qualifications. Our badge was a red morocco star, worn under the left lappet. The only purpose of the club that I could ever discover, was to lick every boy who did not belong to it! I was expected to celebrate my initiation by challenging three nonmembers, which I proceeded to do, licked two and met my match in the third. Then I was warned to attack only boys smaller than myself. The morals of the club were meant to be on a par with those of much older boys, but signally failed. We were as bad as we knew how to be; none of us had the courage or the enterprise to do the naughty things which so excited our emulation in our elders. However, we insulted and beat all the goody-good boys in our way, swore small oaths, smoked and swaggered until sick with nausea, and crowning achievement, learned what a Tom and Jerry tasted like, enticed merely by the name. (197)

Lacking money, the boys were the town's scavengers, sneaking into the shows that passed through and spending their small sums on raw oysters at their wharf rendezvous, where they imitated the sailors and local toughs.

They never mustered the courage to fulfill their ultimate ambition of getting drunk. Fear of being caught heightened the adventure. "Nothing saved us from the realization of our ideals but our extreme youth and native innocence, and perhaps some lurking sense that we were playing at vice, with fire that did not burn and water that would not drown" (199). Their juvenile activities, however, must not blind us to evidence of the early appearance and significance of peer groups and peer culture in the remaking of growing up.[30]

When the shop door closed behind him, his path was open-ended again: "What was to be my occupation did not give me one thought; I had as yet no choice, no preference. Wherever there were boys was my world and my trade" (204). Opportunity next came from his sister's patrons. A Worcester pistolmaker found John a place, continuing his transition between skilled labor and commercial status, another sign of the times. Doing finishing tasks, John was the only boy among skilled mechanics.

Now in his mid-teens, John "seemed in a fair way at last of acquiring a trade" (205). The accident of his place of boarding shifted his path again. John now had his first contact with scholars. While advancing in his sexual knowledge in backstairs encounters with an older, pretty waitress, John, lacking male peers, spent his leisure time with the student boarders. Appreciating their learning, John recognized his own ignorance: "The bitter seeds of unrest, and ambitions without opportunities, were at the same time planted in a fruitful soil" (213).

At first he tried to escape this inner conflict by returning to Bellingham to become a farmer. When that proved impossible, John suffered what later generations deemed an adolescent identity crisis: "There is no human experience more acutely painful than when one awakens to the fact that he is a person, an ego, unrelated to people or things, with no real claim to assert save that of habit or associations. The sense of isolation and loneliness is at first overpowering . . . The awakening may come in mature years, it may come in youth; but at what time it appears, the old earth crumbles and the soul faces its own destiny and recognizes that it must walk alone" (220).

The next summer John's path began to lead through books and learning. "Two awakenings, the intellectual and the spiritual," were under way (225). Whelpley's *Compend of History* and Emerson's *Representative Men* were the lanterns. "Overcome," John was "carried . . . this way and that" (225) by reading. Byron had a powerful impact, from moods to fashions in clothes and hair: "I began to turn down my Sunday linen collar which had stood up to my ears, and to wear my hair long and careless . . . I let it hang over my forehead and neck . . . Melancholy was the wear, and for this, in my present temper, not much effort was required . . . In turn one book after another held me like a captive lover, and I endeavored to conform my life to what I read, no sooner enthralled by one than I found another more enchanting" (225–226).

John took another step on his new path when he persuaded his sister to send him to Worcester Academy for a term. In youth "impressionable and plastic," he blossomed. Fittingly, the "one book which we all read with greatest diligence was Todd's Student's Manual . . . what may, without offense, be called the mechanical apparatus for the acquirement of education and character" (237). Only in its advice to keep a diary did John admit to failing.[31]

John managed a few terms at the academy, skimping on meals and supporting himself by a variety of odd jobs. He was accepted as a schoolmaster in the neighboring town of Grafton, returning to Worcester Academy "feeling older and more sobered" (249–250). Now learning Latin, he had "a dim idea of going to college, how and when, I did not dare to forecast" (250). A student at the nearby women's academy helped him to pass the time pleasantly. Finding no country schools open to male teachers in the summer and his funds dwindling, John hired out for farm work with an uncle.

Come fall, he returned to the academy resolved to devote himself to study. College—the idea of which he "still cherished"—remained distant. Public affairs and Free Soil party politics captured his interest. Emerson's *Representative Men* worked its magic, as Alcott, Thoreau, and Emerson guided him "into companionship" with poets and thinkers (262). The next step lay in moving on to Phillips Academy, Andover, with several of his classmates, to be readied for college by "the most eminent school and drill-master in New England," Dr. Samuel H. Taylor (263). The path led to Harvard, then "bitter" disappointment in dropping out with illness. Nevertheless, "in another year I began a new career which brought me happiness, new opportunities, new friends and dividends from Utopian investments . . . My destiny became my choice" (265). Albee became a writer.

John Albee's winding path is exceptional in encapsulating what so many contemporaries confronted in part: residential, educational, and occupational discontinuities; multiple transitions and blurred paths; family and institutional connections; peer groups and adolescent culture; a blend of traditional and novel experiences.

Many transitional paths led to cities, spanning the gaps between town or country and the potentially dangerous temptations of the metropolis.[32] Francis Bennett, Jr., son of a Gloucester, Massachusetts, seaman, records one experience in his teenage diary.[33] Born in 1837, Francis began his daily record in 1852, as he finished school and started work in a dry goods store in March. He celebrated his fifteenth birthday in August by going "berrying" (and giving his berries "all away to a young lady"). He lived at home.

From March 1852 until March 1854, Francis spent his mid-teen years working and socializing with the girls and "b'hoys" at parties, picnics, panoramas, rambles, beach walks, steamer exhibitions, fireworks, and circus caravans.[34] He had a "heighe time" playing "Ponds," "Roll the Cover," and "Drop the Pillow." Francis also had a serious side. He bought gifts for his mother, and he attended a Negro concert. His social life included both peer group and other activities where young people and adults mixed. He regularly attended lyceum lectures on a wide variety of topics, and he subscribed to a paper. He attended meeting on Sundays and went to auctions.[35] He and his friends celebrated Valentine's Day and April Fools' Day. Election days were the "most welcome" of all "holydays." Francis liked to buy himself sweets. In March 1853, his year at the store up, he extended his stay for $110; the shopkeeper Mr. Stevens presented him with "a very nice pair of pants."

Turning seventeen in August 1854, Francis Bennett agreed to a storekeeping position in Boston for "the liberal sum" of $250 the first year. He made arrangements, collecting his note from Stevens and depositing $311 in the savings bank. Francis "rusticated" for a week prior to his big move. The day of departure was difficult: "I left home I found it pretty hard to keep from crying on leaving the home of my childhood. But I have resolved to be as manly as possible about it."

Boston excited him. Placed at "the desk," he helped to open the splendid new store. Francis wrote dutifully to his mother, and was proposed for and admitted to the Young Men's Christian Association to ease his adaptation to the city. He exercised at gymnastics, attended concerts, the theater, and lyceum, Union, and Mercantile lectures, and read at the Union. He kept company with "other Gloucester boys" in the city, and proudly showed off the store to his visiting father. With numerous other young people Francis chased fires and fire engines. Proper young store clerk and YMCA member, he taught a class of poor children at the Pitts Street Chapel. He also made the rounds of city churches.

Francis's transition to the city proved smooth, and his prospects for middle-class life appeared good. Nonetheless, work demands sometimes obstructed pleasure, and home and family tugged. At the end of 1854 he reflected, "I left my beloved home and mother and little sister to seek my fortune in the great city." That was one price for young persons in transition on the changing paths of growing up.

Charles Howe (1822–1915) of South Brookfield, Massachusetts, took a similar path, traveling a greater distance in his transition from rural to urban life.[36] For him, kin were instrumental. Looking back in 1895, this farmer's son emphasized his traditional growing up: "In those days, farmer boys must work. It was their *business* to work, as may hardly be said of the boys of today" (13–14). Charles's rural idyll ended with his "New Life." At about age fourteen or fifteen he "was taken from farm work and placed in my father's store" (53). Interested in studying, he was encouraged to continue his education. He recited with a nearby minister, and until the age of eighteen he attended the academy at Monson "for several successive terms."

"But, ah me," he recalled, "quickly came the 'parting of the ways.' The decision must be made. Should I continue my studies, work for a college course with view to a literary life or abandoning, take a position in the store of one of my Uncles in the city of Boston" (56–57). Charles faced a problem of choice in paths of growing up very much of the historical moment. Few youths had the option of higher education, but negotiating life's uncertainties in choosing a career plagued many. His health unsteady and the city an attraction, Charles followed a merchant's path to Boston.

Charles commenced his business career at his relatives' firm J. C. Howe & Co., Importers. Beginning at the bottom, he was expected to work his way up by learning the entire business. He lived with a relation of his aunt's. His wealthy, socially prominent kin steered his affairs with propriety. Suffering from ambition, however, Charles was unsatisfied with his deliberate rate of advancement. He instead entered into his own business, which failed because he was too young and had insufficient capital.

In 1855 he left Boston for the West, following another developing path. He admitted leaving with "very little except experience" (62). Romantically nostalgic, he quipped that he had great wealth—his wife—and his wealth grew as they produced children. Youthful missteps aside, with supportive relatives and a successful marriage, Charles Howe survived his transitions with the advantages of his early experiences.

Some transitions were shorter in terms of both physical and psychological distance. Another white collar apprentice, James Whittier, was working in a Boston bank when he began his diary of 1830–31.[37] Born in Charlestown, Massachusetts, in 1816, first apprenticed at age nine, James now fourteen, was boarding in Boston. At times he worked hard; at other times he was not very busy. James kept in close touch with his family, going home for a sister's birthday and seeing his sisters in the city. Social, cultural, and intellectual activities filled his time outside work. He regularly saw friends, took walks around town, and went bathing in South Boston. He went to church (and wrote long accounts of sermons), the Young Men's Tract Society, Sunday school, public school visitations, mechanics' lyceums, educational reform meetings, and antislavery and anti-Masonry meetings.

James experienced youthful misbehavior at his Sunday school. A lack of teachers led to noise and disorder. The Reverend Mr. Hague attempted to impress upon the children their advantages in comparison to others. Not immediately grasping the point, the children in the gallery made so much noise that the minister had to stop speaking. Many of the sermons James reports addressed children and youth on the importance of developing piety and morality. Organized religion in the city typically reflected age-grading and age consciousness. Showing *his* age, James kept a scrap box of pictures he cut out. One friend with whom he spent his evenings put on a "brilliant *display*" of homemade fireworks, including a rocket (September 24, 1830).

His time at the bank passed quickly. On September 1, 1830, James had completed three years there: "The 3 years do not seem more than as many days." On November 15 he stated his intention of leaving the bank. He had earned $350. He moved to a new dry goods store, beginning with stocking and tagging goods. Shifting his place of apprenticeship apparently merited no comment. Business, he notes, was brisk.

James lost his new position because of illness. Still only fourteen, he was not especially concerned. Tending shop for Ma Grubb during the day, he writes: "I therefore am without a place now, though I have a prospect of soon getting one . . . It is Messrs. Thurston and Co's 'Stereotype Foundry'" (February 4, 1831). Thurston's asked him to call again in a fortnight. In the meantime, James filled in for sick clerks at the bank.

Spring brought a season of revival meetings, he reports, in Rochester and Utica, New York, as well as in Boston, along with a multitude of baptisms. At Sunday school prayers for the conversion of the scholars occupied the day. In the midst of this activity James's birthday arrived on April 6: "My Birth Day 15 years old to day. How short the time seems to look back. How long to look forward. Not much business at the Bank. Evening attended a prayer meeting."

In June the tumult of Election day brought a different rhythm of activities. In adolescent ambles with his friends, James walked the Common and visited places such as the Navy Yard (where they boarded a man-of-war) and the state prison (where they were unable to gain admission without paying twenty-five cents). Their rambles ended with the monthly concert of prayer at the Second Meeting House.

James's own conversion neared. On June 19 a speaker from the Reverend Mr. Malcolm's society proclaimed "that in that society there seemed to be a complete revolution, so many had been made to feel that they are sinners, or to hope that they have found mercy." On June 21 James addressed the Reverend Hague and the committee of the church for the examination of candidates: "Although I did not expect anything of the kind [a conversion], yet I related my experience to them, as did four others who were present." The next day Hague related the committee's pleasure with him and requested him to attend the next Friday meeting. "I feel it is a duty, as well as privilege to come out and declare to the world that I am not ashamed to be called a Christian, although I have very many doubts" (June 22, 1831).

Those words end James's journal. He had completed one part of his path in accord with current ideals. He leaves little doubt that he was well along a stable road through adolescence and youth, his spirit secure. His was the rising urban world of white collar workers in transition to a new middle-class path, involving voluntary associations and other urban institutions. With both age and occupational peers James adapted to new and changing environments, sometimes in age or social segregation, sometimes in more mixed company, in his search for success.

Others' artisan-apprentice paths took them outside or beyond the metropolis. Throughout the century most people grew up in small towns or rural areas, yet their paths of growing up were no less challenged or reshaped by social transformations. For some the search for adulthood was intensified.

Edward Jenner Carpenter, an apprentice carpenter in Greenfield, Massachusetts, was born in Bernardston, just north of Greenfield, the first of eight children.[38] Edward (1825–1900) was the son of a physician. The family's modest resources were strained. With no land or patrimony to offer their many children, the Carpenters had to develop other strategies. Family resources allowed Edward to attend an academy, but college was out of the question. On his father's death in 1855 he inherited five dollars. For him and for three of his brothers the path to adulthood lay in apprenticeship or clerkship. After a short spell in a factory village, Edward was apprenticed at sixteen (bound until nineteen) to the Greenfield cabinetmaking firm of Miles & Lyon. In his nineteenth year, 1844–45, Edward Carpenter kept a daily journal.

His familiar path began close to home. Boarding away from but geographically close to his family, Edward in his late teens combined work with social, cultural, and intellectual events. In general, his transitional path was shaped by a variety of associations and activities. Visiting home, he felt "homesick before night for there is not so much going on here as in Greenfield."

While learning his craft, he was sometimes frustrated by the cheaply made products he was assigned to work on as an apprentice. He wanted more varied tasks and a different regimen than that of ceaselessly turning out secretaries, bureaus, and coffins. His work reflected changes in production and the market for handmade goods, specifically a shift toward standardized products. His working conditions were flexible, his time much his own to complete jobs. This, too, was sometimes a source of friction with his bosses.

Activities outside of work took up much of his time. With other apprentices constituting a relatively uniformly age-graded peer group, Edward enjoyed ball games, swimming, fishing, walks, skating, berrying, watching the militia, and generally "loafing around" with friends. He attended picnics and parties. A regular at literary society debates and lyceum lectures, he avidly read newspapers and books. He played cards—only "for amusement"—with friends of his own age and fellow workers. Sharing status and steps toward growing up bound his group as age-mates and also as "mechanics." They exhibited their class consciousness and sense of superiority over white collar workers in literary society debates and comments criticizing the "big bugs" of the town aristocracy. Edward found friends to share his bed when his fellow apprentice was away. He kept in touch with a large number of young people. Addicted to chewing tobacco, most likely a common habit in his circle, Edward struggled to give it up. His interest in the fit and style of clothing grew as he matured. Dancing was practically another addiction. With his peers he flocked to a new dancing school, which, at four dollars per couple, stimulated informal social intercourse between young women and men. From awkward beginnings, greater social ease followed, culminating in a supper ball for forty couples.

Edward's intellectual interests were broad. His interest in reading ranged from uplifting nonfiction and fiction ("Easy Nat or Boston Bar and Boston Boys"—on the evils of drink) to romance novels, which he all but devoured, and which come to predominate over the course of his journal. He took several newspapers, including the *Rural Repository,* the *Dispatch,* and the *Washingtonian.* He followed the antislavery and temperance movements, although he drank small beer, and, to a degree, politics. At the lyceum Edward attended lecture series on physiology and phrenology, a topic popular with young people in search of routes to success.

Edward's progress toward adulthood reflects the status of a young man on a transitional path at a transitional time. Hovering between dependence and independence; new class culture and trade traditions; family, peer, and work circles; reform interests and novel reading, drinking, card playing, and tobacco chewing; not yet courting but delighting in dancing and parties, Edward looked toward his twenty-first birthday and becoming his "own man." He was aware of the hard times facing his trade. At twenty-four, just before marrying a local woman, Edward Carpenter moved a few miles north to Brattleboro, Vermont. After following a crafts path to early adulthood, he eventually fashioned a successful career selling the printed works he so avidly consumed.

Some transitional paths traversed greater distances. Trans-Atlantic immigration and other long-distance migrations characterized the experiences of some. Charles Camden's journey spanned the Atlantic Ocean, from Worcestershire, England, to Long Island, New York, and beyond.[39] Camden's autobiography underscores the relationship between youth and movement, age and major transitions.

Born in 1817 to a "well-to-do farmer" in Worcestershire, Charles was one of thirteen children. Early on he set his sights on migration, an element of long standing in the cultural mythology of growing up. "In my earliest remembrance," he writes, "I had a strong desire to leave home, 'to see the world.' Restraint I could not bear, hence I would not go to school, but would rather work on the farm; the result was I left home at seventeen years of age almost without any education" (1–2). At seventeen, "a dunce of a boy . . . full of ambition," he determined to go to "AMERICA" (2). The third son to leave home, Charles found it hard to leave his mother. Promising to return a rich man, he arrived in New York with the twelve shillings, sixpence, his father had given him.

Agricultural and commercial opportunities awaited him: "Naturally I went to live and work with brother Thomas who was engaged farming and gardening on Long Island" (2). At four dollars and board each month, he found no quick riches. In May 1835 he hired out for harvest and boat work for eleven dollars, then fifteen dollars. Accumulating money, he longed to become his own boss. Hearing that opportunities were better down South, Charles sailed for New Orleans in October 1835. There he made plows, returning to New York to run a milk route. Visiting his brother Richard, who farmed in Pennsylvania, Charles profited from trading cows. He returned to making plows in Louisiana, joined by a newly arriving brother, Henry. The brothers signed a number of lumbering contracts. After a trip to Texas, they worked their way up the Mississippi River. Charles was now twenty-one.

The pair were in "a quandary what to do next; we had accumulated quite a little sum of money and several things occurred to us as being full of promise" (18–19). Agreeing to work the winter in Louisiana, Charles returned to Long Island and Henry to England, seeking to marry. In February, again working milk routes for his brother Thomas, Charles "began to look around for our future business and saw satisfactory opportunities of procuring just what we wanted" (20). He returned to New Orleans. Sensing profits, he bought three drays and teams. In time this venture proved seasonally profitable. In the United States Charles's close kin formed a kind of network of opportunity within which he moved, alternating between Louisiana and his brothers' homes. Tying commerce to agriculture, these youthful movements were seasonally determined as Charles's path shifted cyclically.

Selling his business in 1841, Charles accepted an offer to run a store in Jackson, Louisiana. "Bad breaks" on loans he made took most of his savings. For two years he ran the store, turning down offers to manage plantations, for the idea of being a "slave driver" was repugnant to him. But while considering the possibility of learning Spanish and going to South America, he accepted the management of a plantation for a year in a continuing search for wealth: "The salary offered was large for one so young" (32). Enjoying "everything belonging to the cultivation of the soil" and feeling that with fair treatment and respect he had ameliorated the slaves' burden, Charles completed the year (37). Returning to Jackson, "which seemed like my home," he studied Spanish at a nearby female academy. There "arose a little difficulty about my being admitted," Charles writes, but he was deemed "not 'very dangerous'" (39). For four months he boarded and studied. At the end of March 1845 Charles, now twenty-seven, left New Orleans for New York, seeking passage to Valparaiso.

On his way north he visited his brothers. A delay in his journey was "provoking," yet "these idle days afforded time to renew . . . the pleasurable occupation of my first, earnest courtship." He left the young woman reluctantly, for "our acquaintance had gone through the regular course and become an engagement, and was to be consummated in full when I returned from South America—rich, of course" (44). Charles's intended tired of waiting, however, and married another man. In any case, he found female company on the voyage. Eventually he settled in California, where he was married.

The long-distance travels of Charles Camden were more dramatic than the regional moves of many young men from small towns and rural areas, regardless of national origin. David Clapp (1806–1893), an apprentice printer, was more typical.[40] One striking feature of transitional paths of growing up in this period is the shift between traditional and emerging norms of behavior—not "normlessness" but a blurring of expected routines, rules, relationships, and assumptions with respect to place of residence and work, family and peer relations, schooling and job training, degrees of autonomy, styles of life, destinations, and so on. That blurring encompassed similarities between transitional ways of preparing for skilled manual and white collar work, as well as overlap in social class location. For both kinds of work some form of apprenticeship was required, but the concept itself was changing.

Clapp's journal (1820–1824) charted his passage to the city and his trade. In May 1820 fourteen-year-old David was living in his hometown of Dorchester, Massachusetts, with his master, a Mr. White. Apprenticeship was shifting toward a cash relationship; he was paid a wage of five dollars per month. He stayed with White for five months. Returning home in

December 1820, David went to school then left the following April and went back to White. Parties and berrying filled some of his spare time. In November David left White again, "having staid 6 months"; he received Cummings' *Geography and Atlas*, a quire of paper, and a bunch of quills. His shifting routine continued: from December to April David attended school, studying arithmetic and bookkeeping. In April he worked on the family farm.

David's major move came in May 1822, when he was apprenticed to a printer. His sister took the sixteen-year-old to Boston, where he boarded not with his master but with a private family, another change in the pattern of apprenticeship. This relocation was wrenching: "It being the first night I ever slept in Boston, and the whole family entire strangers to me, I was rather inclined to wakefulness through the night, though less disturbed than I anticipated." He feared being ridiculed for his country ways and ignorance.

Anxious about his apprenticeship, David had a keen sense of the importance of this stage of his life. The printing office became "the scene of my labours—of my industry or laziness for years to come; where I shall form new connections, new habits and desires, and where perhaps the die will be cast for my future character in life; so that in a great measure my prospects depend upon my good or bad behavior in this office, as youth is the time we are most susceptible of impressions, and impressions formed in youth generally have an influence over our conduct through life" (May 13, 1822).

The situation turned worse than David had feared. His master's failure to pay for his board became a major embarrassment for David. Finally he had to move to his master's home. He shared a bed with a thirteen-year-old son with whom he did not get along, and was assigned many domestic chores. In the shop of an absentee master, the foreman was a drunkard, and peer rivalries and jealousies proliferated. As the youngest hand David was exploited by the others, while his zeal to learn went unappreciated. The master amassed heavy debts and was jailed, forcing his father to take over the business.

Fortunately for David his new employer took a special interest in him and arranged for him to complete his apprenticeship. David went on to work for him after his apprenticeship and helped him start his own printing business. Such accidents of fortune were among the paving stones of transitional paths. Many were not as fortunate as David Clapp.[41]

Traditional Middle-Class

The second major subpath—the traditional middle-class and professional route—reveals especially clearly the pivotal role that transitional paths played in the transformation of growing up. Here I refer primarily to the professions of law, medicine, the ministry, and college teaching, and to a lesser extent schoolteaching and commerce. The routes that young men took toward these destinations illustrate variations in individual life courses, family strategies, educational and professional institutions, professional standards and requirements, and the impact of social, cultural, and economic transformations.

Transition permeates this historical moment. And this subpath, more than others, highlights the way relatively well placed young persons and their families responded to the changes occurring around them. Such changes were not exclusively urban, nor were they closely related to industrialization. Material change and its social and cultural concomitants were the catalysts. As flexibility persisted, shifting circumstances encouraged new connections between social change and the process of growing up. Lucien Boynton's path toward his destination as a lawyer was anything but direct.[42] His discontinuous twists and turns in search of career, personal satisfaction, and independence underscore both the possibilities and the problems that faced an ambitious young man who attempted three different professions.[43]

Born in 1811 in Weathersfield, Vermont, Lucien graduated from Middlebury College in 1834. He briefly taught school, then in 1835, the year he commenced his lengthy journal, he entered Andover Theological Seminary. Beginning the term late, he managed to catch up quickly. Lucien credited his "systematic course of exercise" and the "very plain fare in Commons" with maintaining his health; in his studies he overcame several bad habits. With his progress in piety he was less satisfied. He hinted at what plagued his development more generally: "Near the beginning of the term, I had some seasons of very high religious enjoyment . . . some due sense of my sinfulness and a strong desire for the promotion of Christ. At other times . . . I seemed to have no religious enjoyment . . . I feel the fault was mine. Have had many struggles with ambition, and selfishness, and wrong feelings towards others. Find it difficult to keep these in subjection to the great and holy principle of living to God, and of loving others as myself" (331–332). These qualities haunted him. Toward the end of his course he expressed doubts about his qualification to preach: "I know not whither I shall go or what I shall do . . . perhaps I ought not to have undertaken [the theology course] . . . I think, I might have done well in the Law, and should have liked the profession" (337).

Graduating in 1838, Lucien failed to find a church. He taught school in Delaware, where he had cousins, for more than a year, and for five years in Virginia. His struggle over "high notions of myself" continued (338). Falling in love, he penned a roster of desirable traits in women to justify his doubts about this woman. Lucien remained troubled by his inconsistent piety and lack of spiritual progress. Meanwhile, he broke off his relationship with one woman and courted another whose manner with other men troubled him. No more able to find satisfaction in another than in himself, Lucien was harder on others, especially women, in whom he condemned insufficient education, artfulness, and coquetry. His problem was ambition. He could no more tolerate it in others than he could resolve his own. The fault lay in his character.

Despite achieving status and compensation as president of a Virginia academy, Lucien began to study law in 1842. Making this decision only "after much thought and deliberation," he declared, "I am aware that I have not all the requisites of a first-rate lawyer. But I believe I can acquire and sustain a respectable standing in the profession" (351–352). In his journal he rationalized his failure to become a minister, citing a characteristic but potentially debilitating blend of traditional and more modern notions: "Neither my talents, my taste, nor my inclination fit me for that office . . . The ministerial character does not become me. When I put it on, or when others put it on me, I feel awkward and uncomfortable in it, like a boy in his father's, or uncle's coat" (352). Lucien also admitted his lack of faith and spiritual ardor.

For teaching he was perhaps as well qualified as for any pursuit. Despite many attributes, which he lists, he admits "that weakness, (if it may so be called,) which I possess in common with many of my fellow beings, of taking pleasure in wielding 'a little brief authority'" (352). A professorship or a college presidency might have suited his ambition, but he had not begun his higher education early enough nor had he achieved a reputation for scholarship. Although he thought he could likely gain a position in "some Western college" in the institution's "infancy," his post would be insecure. "All-wise Providence" had not shaped his path in that direction. The choice, Lucien reasoned, came to teaching or the law. It was the latter he now chose, attracted by its respectability and "higher standing in Society" (353).

Lucien returned north to continue reading law. In 1846, aged thirty-five, trained or experienced in three different professions, he was admitted to the Vermont bar in Woodstock, and in 1847 the Massachusetts bar in Worcester. His career quandary resolved, he now fretted about the best location for his legal office. Settling down in Worcester, he married a widow, Sarah Judson Cole, in 1852. The bride's charms, the diary's editor hints, may have been pecuniary; at least that consideration seems to have quelled his criticism of women. Lucien and Sarah took their wedding journey to Niagara Falls.

Caught between traditional and evolving paths of growing up, Lucien

Boynton was engaged in a lengthy, complicated, and difficult passage to maturity. If his many discontinuous moves sometimes seem unproductive, his reflections were typical of his time, and his use of institutions and their requirements, as well as his scrutiny of character and his concern about his age, were indicative of new paths.

In his journey toward the medical profession, Samuel Busey also moved between traditional and newer paths.[44] His course of study, timing of transitions, physical location, and starting circumstances differ from Boynton's. Samuel was born in 1828 on a farm in Montgomery County, Maryland. His father died when Samuel was four, his mother when he was almost sixteen.

His mother "was careful to inculcate the highest qualities of good morals, probity, and frugality, but was, perhaps, more especially concerned in regard to our education" (23). She believed in "hardening boys for the struggles of manhood life," something her son never appreciated (53). She impressed on her sons "the importance of diligence in the acquisition of learning" in light of their small inheritance (23). Traditional means were put to new uses as Samuel's path took him from the life of a gentleman farmer to one of urban professionalism. He left home first to attend Rockville Academy from 1841 to 1845, and then permanently at seventeen to study medicine in the office of a Georgetown physician in Washington, D.C.

Samuel's mother refused to allow him to accept an appointment to West Point, "persistently" designating the profession of medicine regardless of his wishes. Nor would she leave him any farmland. Even with his share of a great-uncle's estate, Samuel's inheritance could not provide for his support and education. The help of a close family friend allowed him to take his medical degree.

For sixteen years, Samuel recalls, "boyhood ran its course of joyous but heedless pleasure and happiness" (30). Only one sentence later he restricts that experience to his first nine years, after which he attended a country school five miles from home, where he boarded for five years. Sentimental and romantic recollections of his early life on the farm he dates from those first nine years, time and memory blurring the images of an important transition (33).

"Closer associations" with the girls at school worked "a very happy influence in restraining the excesses and minor vices to which boys are so prone" (61). Samuel recalls the "rivalry between a pretty winsome red-haired girl and myself for head-place in certain classes, which . . . made the competitive struggle one of general comment and suggestive innuendo." He met his future bride at a private "selected" school, closer to home (61).

In 1841, while he was a student at Rockville Academy, Samuel's childhood "joys, deviltries, and pastimes" (72) ceased as he experienced another transition. He began "the struggle with the problems of a higher curriculum, where gratification came only through the higher marks of success and proficiency" (72). At the academy from ages thirteen to sixteen Samuel boarded with various families. Separated from peers in boarding-houses, he read or studied or took an "occasional ramble." He went home each weekend, and often visited his girlfriend until she was sent to boarding school. Samuel lived "to win her love" (77). His teenage insecurities made him a target of her sisters' gossip about his rivals.

In Georgetown, where his girlfriend finished her seminary studies and he commenced his medical training, Samuel was "at liberty to make my visits at my pleasure and her convenience" (77). The "smoothness" in their courtship was broken when Samuel departed for Philadelphia to "enter the private office of Prof. George B. Wood" (78) and study at the University of Pennsylvania, where he took his degree in 1848 at age twenty. Engagement followed his establishing a practice in Washington. The wedding took place a year later; Samuel was twenty-one. From traditional genteel early socialization and family influence, to a blend of old and newer forms of education and a forward-looking passage to medical education, professional practice, and marriage, Samuel's experience embodies the changing paths of growing up. Despite his conflict with his mother over his education and his choice of career, as well as the relative constraints of his inheritance, Samuel's transitions, especially in comparison to Lucien Boynton's, were smooth.[45]

Formal institutions, especially schools of all kinds, increasingly occupied a pivotal place. Riley Adams's path was marked by his teenage experiences as a cadet at a novel kind of age-specific institution, a private military academy—the "celebrated" American Literary, Scientific, and Military Academy of Norwich, Vermont.[46]

Riley (1808–1894) was born in Bristol, Vermont. After common schooling in his native town and study at Middlebury, "agreable [sic] to the arrangements of my parents," he was sent at sixteen to the military academy. Homesickness struck immediately: "After looking about some time I began to be uneasy . . . I began to be sorry I come but still did not like to own it to my father" (12). He "wished himself home . . . and remained lonesome during the day" (12). Immersed in Latin and "Arithmetick," writing and drilling twice each afternoon, Riley "began to be much consolated again" (12–13). He also studied agriculture, mineralogy, topography, and music. After about two weeks young Riley felt better.

Study, drill, and excursions kept the cadets busy. Collegiate tradition and more than a bit of adolescent high spirits combined in outbreaks of disorder. The cadets who stayed behind on one occasion "had not managed themselves with propriety during the Capt's absence, but on the contrary had managed very badly by trying to blow up the building"! Two cadets were dismissed (60).

Riley's lonesomeness persisted, along with doubts about his path: "My thoughts were carried home a greater part of the day thinking on the busy scenes of a farmer . . . My old classmate Edward Willis had entered college. This news troubled me a good deal. I was sorry I had not entered college with my class" (75). He dreamed about being at home (86).

Riley constantly reports mischief. One cadet was put in the guardhouse for throwing hot coals down his roommate's neck—"a bare trick" (76). Firecrackers exploded at night, breaking windows. Money was stolen. The captain investigated. Rumors abounded of a justice coming to "swear all the cadets" (76). All this misbehavior disturbed priggish Riley, who refrained from such misdeeds.

Peer groups and conflicts at the school formed along regional lines. Riley was troubled by southern students, one of whom played "a shameful trick . . . scandalous and vile," with a platter of meat at the boardinghouse table. After drill that afternoon one of the southerners insulted Riley, accusing him of being the culprit. "I was greatly enraged. I expressed to him that if he told me another falsehood I would knock him down, that I would rather be found stealing than be caught in such a trick and thus after supper I returned to my home enjoying myself with the realization of a clear conscience" (107).

Riley also remembers a conversation with a southerner early in the term to whom he said in jest that southerners were cowards. Word circulated. When the southerners confronted him en masse, a group of northern students appeared on the scene. The southerners did not accept Riley's version of the story, and only the captain's arrival prevented a brawl. His inquiries proved Riley right. The northerners prepared for a "bloody fight." Aware of the captain's threat of dismissal for breaking into anyone's room, sixteen-year-old Riley and his adolescent peers stayed on guard: "We armed ourselves with bayonets and clubs, being determined to run the first one through that entered the room. Not only to do what was required of us, but to defend our rights" (156).

At roll call the next morning the southern students appeared vindictive and surly. On the way to breakfast one insulted Riley, who made no response. A northerner at Riley's side, however, threatened to make a "corps" of the southerner. As soon as Riley was alone, the student struck him. Unwilling to take on a gang, Riley delayed until night. Then he retaliated.

After police duty the next day Riley was confronted again and "asked if I chose to fight [the student] or let him pound me" (157). Riley agreed to fight. Supportive northern students bolstered his courage, "but he was to [sic] stout for me and took me down which was the cause of my getting the disadvantage. I struggled some time and was obliged to give up, but was not blamed by the Northerners as I did the best I could, but was rather commended" (157). Individual conflicts continued, and rumors of a major outbreak remained rife. Riley awaited further assaults. His military school journal ends December 11, 1824. "In the afternoon I was examined in the studies for the last week. No war waged today. Yet it was hinted to us by the same South. that we should have a battle at Christmas Day" (158–159). Such was adolescent peer society at a private military school in the 1820s. Growing up was sometimes a physical struggle as peers reinterpreted adult roles while shaping their paths and experiences.

As they came increasingly to set boundaries for growing up, formal institutions differed among themselves. Those distinctions could make an enormous difference. William Northey's 1843 Quaker boarding school experience was far calmer, and likely more common, than Riley Adams's.[47] It was more attuned to changing ideas about growing up. The son of a Salem family of prosperous Quaker merchants and shippers, at age fourteen he attended the summer term at the Friends Boarding School in Providence.

William's letters to his mother show a serious young man, intent on keeping her abreast of his activities. Fellow students, boys and girls, ranged in age from twelve to twenty. William was permitted to stay up until nine o'clock. He confronted the harmless pranks of the other boys who "plague[d]" him and whom he did not like. He studied arithmetic, geography, grammar, spelling and "defineing," and history, and wrote compositions. William complained about boys who tried to steal his food treats and whined about mornings on which he'd rather not study. Ill with a cold, he wrote that he'd rather be at home, keeping his mother company. He thanked her for suggesting a subject for a composition: the benefits of industry and perseverance. He dreaded his upcoming exams. On July 4 he complained that there was no play, only hard study. For exercise he sawed wood. He also collected minerals.

His deportment and studies were commendable. William stayed at least until the end of the year. Study with a tutor in Salem followed to help him qualify for admission to English High School. Rather than going on to college, he entered the family business in Salem, a traditional path. The transitional aspect of his experience lay in his time away from home in early adolescence. Sheltered and dependent, preparing with a minimum of pressures and prolonging his juvenile status, despite his complaints William found in the Quaker school a surrogate family.[48]

The early years of precocious Cyrus Bradley demonstrate the flexibility inherent in institutions at the time.[49] Born in 1818 in the country town of Canterbury, New Hampshire, Cyrus, with no brothers or male peers, found company in animals, inanimate objects, and manual labor. Early affected by a love of books, he also found time to play ball with other children.

His father's rural political activities led to an appointment in 1829 as state librarian, and the family moved to Concord. Not only did Cyrus find books there, but he also gained patrons willing to contribute to the classical education his family could not afford. Admitted as a "charity scholar" to Exeter Academy in 1830, he left home at age twelve. After completing his preparatory course in one year, he continued on to Dartmouth. Advisers at the time railed against this kind of rapid advancement, considering it potentially dangerous. This attitude was one result of the new movement toward age-graded educational institutions, and of contemporary child-rearing strictures. The breakdown of Cyrus's health after two years of college appears to indicate the critics.[50] Illness and a lack of funds led to his dropping out of school for a year. Cyrus taught and did literary work to secure the means to return to Dartmouth.

His health and spirits improved, Cyrus stood high in his class in all subjects but mathematics. He wrote editorials for the *Herald of Freedom* and *Newport Argus,* sent historical and antiquarian pieces to literary journals, and completed a "Biography of Hon. Isaac Hill," a prominent New Hampshire politician. Cyrus also participated in canoe races and football games, observed surgical operations, and hunted for botanical and geological specimens. His lengthy senior public address was deemed masterly. He was considered a genius, the equal or superior of Daniel Webster, Rufus Choate, and Salmon P. Chase. The institutions within his reach as well as influential supporters were willing to accept his precocity, despite doubts about the value of early development. This precocity marked Cyrus Bradley's path as transitional. Unfortunately, although mortality levels were falling, early death still plagued the paths of the young. This promising youth died at nineteen.[51]

Less precocious and gifted himself, Richard Fuller nonetheless experienced the transitional path typical of a young person from an exceptional family. Son of Timothy Fuller and brother of Margaret, Richard (1824–1869) was born in Cambridge, Massachusetts.[52] When his father died of cholera in 1835, the burden of caring for a large family fell on Margaret, the eldest child. Both the loss of his father and the guidance of his sister shaped Richard's path, as his 1840 diary reveals. For him, educational institutions combined with family connections to make the difference in his life.

With his father's death Timothy felt that he must give up his plans to attend Harvard and instead go into business to aid the family. In comparison with his sister, Richard thought himself unambitious and slow to understand, despite her efforts to stimulate him. While his mother stayed in lodgings with the younger children and Margaret taught in Providence, Richard boarded with a neighbor while he attended school and cared for the family cattle in Groton. The farm was sold, and the family moved to a house in Boston that Margaret rented. Relying in part on his sister's earnings from "lady pupils," fifteen-year-old Richard made rapid progress in school. "I was fitted for college, and my teacher strenuously advocated my graduating. But Margaret and Mother thought I had better engage in mercantile life" (218).

Richard secured a position with a dry goods jobber through his uncle Henry Fuller, a Boston lawyer. That proved unsatisfying. He wrote that a store "which had given me any enlarged views of commerce might perhaps have engaged my interest. But here I was boy to sweep and dust and carry heavy bundles over the city, in short to 'grunt and sweat under a weary life,' with no initiation into business methods" (218). Afraid to blemish his reputation by appearing "unsteady," though clearly chafing in conflict with his goals, he struggled on. Finding his responsibilities far less interesting than they had been on the farm, and suffering the lack of rural scenery, he "resolved to go to college, and to enter, if possible, far enough in advance to make up for the year I had lost." He was determined to do this "at a very small cost" (218).

With a letter from Margaret, Richard set off for Concord to seek Ralph Waldo Emerson's wisdom. Expecting little, for Emerson was a "great man and myself a little one," Richard met no condescension. He received encouragement to pursue learning and to begin by studying in Concord. For five months he lived cheaply in a rented room and "by rigid economy and by hard study" achieved his goal of entering Harvard as a sophomore. Thoreau's school and his companionship, along with the Reverend Frost's and Elizabeth Hoar's aid, and Mrs. Emerson's pies, nourished him. Individual effort, family connections, influence, and institutional support joined to propel Richard on his transitional path and allow him to compensate for his deficiencies. Entering in his mid-sophomore year, Richard graduated in 1844 at age twenty. He found the debating clubs valuable. But "a greater aid," another paving stone on his distinctive path, was "the society of my beloved family." During his last two years at Harvard, Margaret rented a house in Cambridge.

In its relation to family and to institutions, Richard Fuller's path highlights our sense of the dynamic interplay among the varieties of transitional middle-class paths of growing up. College populations in antebellum America were also dynamic: in numbers of students and institutions, and in the wide range of student origins, discontinuous studies, and behavior. Institutional change and its influence on growing up was not limited to formal institutions at the precollegiate level, although changes there touched far more lives. For increasing numbers of middle-class youths on transitional paths, college began to take on a new prominence as a step along the way. As these lives show, the transition to modern, rigidly age-graded growing up in a series of institutions was a lengthy and variable process for the individuals whose lives it touched.[53]

Living most of his life in or near Port Penn, Delaware, Joseph Cleaver (1833–1909) attended Delaware College, graduating with the class of 1856.[54] His diary for the year 1853–54 presents the collegiate experience of an unremarkable but serious midcentury student moving toward adulthood. However significantly his college years shaped his growing up, they did not influence his destination. He inherited and managed his father's store and farm.

In his account of his twenty-first year, apparently his first in college, Joseph's late adolescent passage from timidity and uncertainty to the greater confidence of a maturing person is striking. At first, he reflects, "I am glad to live with an old boy because I will learn my way faster" (August 31, 1853). Joseph did not feel a part of college life; the diary was part of his effort to become so. Meeting people, beginning his studies, learning the routine took up his early weeks.

Central to his initiation were student societies, especially the Athenean Society: "Sept. 3. I have had three invitations to join Athenean Society and some of the boys have had invitations to apply for both societies." Joseph was elected and initiated. He liked the Greek symbols and pictures on the walls of the meeting hall. He began declaiming a week later. Wanting to do well, he worked hard and "did better than I feared." A week later he debated the question of abolishing capital punishment. Society meetings complemented a student life otherwise consisting of classes and preparation, sermons, and rather dull parties.

He reports that student disorder was often a result of drinking. Compared to behavior common early in the century or the unrest at Riley Adams's military academy, this was tame. It was also increasingly sophomoric, and more "modern," perhaps, for that. Relations respecting women also seem more juvenile that those represented in earlier records: "Nov. 25. I gave a little girl a kiss who was crying in the street but she cried louder and put her arms around my neck and I had a chore drying her tears and finding her way home. Now I am the but [*sic*] of a lot of wit bearing on young ladies." On Valentine's Day he notes: "We made a Valentine for Ashmead as if it was from a young lady and he blushed and stammered and opened himself to a great deal of wit." The "fair sex,"

Joseph reports, was "a great subject of conversation among us and no doubt [a female visit] has happened but is oftener told of than it happens" (October 29, 1854). Occasionally a student was socially persecuted for inappropriate behavior or attitudes. Popcorn, ice cream, and oysters were favorite student treats and excesses.

Joseph mundanely outlines an emerging agenda: "March 22. Examinations began . . . There was a Phrenologist at the Ball Room and about sixty people but some left when they saw it was educational and scientific instead of entertainment. He told us about our natural abilities and what we ought to do and avoid. I am musical and emotional and I must watch that I finish the things that I start. I must try to keep the friendships I begin. I must keep the things I own in better order." Joseph struggled to grow up appropriately. On May 5, he records, "I dreamed I bagged school and went nutting and gathered coat buttons." In June he notes that a bull was let into a college building but was unable to descend the stairs after he had been lured up. In the fall of 1854 Joseph rose to become president of the Athenean.

College may not have prepared Joseph to manage his inheritance or transmitted specific skills. Its contribution lay more in developing his character and sense of himself, and in providing a transition from home and dependence in the form of an intermediate space and time in which to grow. That was no small contribution.[55]

A member of the Amherst College class of 1849, William Gardiner Hammond of Newport, Rhode Island, offers an instructive contrast within a context of broad similarities.[56] William's intellectual aspirations, or perhaps pretensions, were stronger than Joseph Cleaver's. He labored for his literary society, the Academian, and had his juvenile escapades, such as nailing college doors shut. Despite the frivolity, he studied hard. William lived in a boardinghouse, unlike Joseph, who seems to have resided in a dormitory. The most interesting difference concerns their relations with young women. William was more active socially. The editor of a portion of his diary notes: "His susceptibility to the allurements of one young lady after another lends zest to the narrative" (2). William apparently visited Mount Holyoke College regularly. Leaving campus and friends after graduation, he wrote that he was going out into "the cold, cold world," a new notion of leaving home and other supporting institutions. Hammond's path led him to study law, practice in New York, and then migrate west.[57]

Within the middle-class and professional subpath transitional journeys like Hammond's traversed geographic distance as well as other chasms. Like the subpath of rural migrants and pioneers, this route sometimes wended toward the wide open West and back again, creating new challenges and opportunities.[58]

Born in Beaver County, Pennsylvania, Joseph Baldwin (1827–1899) took a route to career and success in Texas which combined professional and migrant subpaths.[59] A student who began his diary at eighteen, Joseph was devoutly religious. "Saved" during a serious illness at fourteen, he continued to struggle with his "direful condition" in a search for salvation. He visited the sick and dying and attended the dead. Conversion and baptism renewed him (April 23, 1845), and he dedicated himself to serving Christ (May 1). Secular reading was one of his distractions. He lamented: "I have spent a considerable portion of my time in reading History and Biography and thus have neglected the most important of books to wit the Bible. May in future make this my study and may I use it as my sword" (September 14). First becoming a teacher, then a school founder and an educational reformer, Joseph set himself a difficult path to follow. Completing his eighteenth year, he rededicated himself to his saving mission. He focused on "Youth" (such as himself), deserving of eternal punishment but saved, to whom "Duty, Justice, Reason, Honour, Happiness, and Conscience" all called.

In the new year, 1846, Joseph reports that he had been studying since November with good teachers in a select school in New Castle, Pennsylvania. The previous March through November he had worked for his father. In 1847, his twentieth year, he attended school a full forty weeks and worked about a month and a half. He was proud of his progress. Joseph's labor paid for his board, clothing, and tuition. Practicing what he preached, when he was invited to a party, he chose to spend his time studying rather "than in hurtful folly" (February 6). Passing a room where "many youths were engaged in mirthful danceing [*sic*]," he writes, "I was struck with the reflection that all these thoughtless youths must soon appear before the judge of all" (March 10). As for his ambitions: "I long to become an orator; that I may do good to my fellow men."

In 1848 Joseph took another step by entering Bethany College. There he studied, recited, debated, and helped to form an "economical society" whose members pledged to assist one another in case of sickness; he became its president. Joseph performed well, ranking first or second in his classes. His censure of other youths, including his fellow students, continued: "Alas follish [*sic*] young men! You do not feal [*sic*] the values of life" (April 5, 1849).

In summer he taught Sunday school, spoke at meeting, and worked on the farm. At twenty-two his attentions began to fall on young women, another step on his path. In August 1849 he went to the county meeting in the company of Emaline McC., "whom I think would make a suitable companion for me for life . . . If it is the will of God to spare my life &

hers, and if he so permit, we may be united by the bans of matrimony; after I have completed my College course." Joseph knew the proper sequence of life's events.

Back in school in September, Joseph spent his days writing to Miss Emaline, studying hard, and finding "Pope Homers Illiad" truly admirable, if filled with much of which he disapproved. Reading Cicero, writing compositions and orations, Joseph did his best. Partly contradicting his dedication to a higher spirit is his self-puffery: "Declaimed in society a piece called 'The Whiskers.' Succeeded better than ever before. One remarked publicly that it was the best he had ever heard. But O! how far short of what I desire, what vast heights still remain to be assended [*sic*]."

After graduation Joseph Baldwin went west to pursue the newly emerging professional career of a college professor. In 1853 he taught at the Platte City Male and Female Academy in Missouri, and by 1855 he was co-principal of a collegiate institution in Savannah, Missouri. It was then that he married.

Joseph became a career-long school builder and promoter. His conflicts remained mainly within himself. He had followed a transitional path that took him across the country, spreading the pan-protestant ideology of public education. Founding institutions and contributing to the foundation of a new middle-class professional career path for men and women, he established his own place in a period of transition.[60]

Jeremiah Curtin's Wisconsin boyhood and subsequent turns east to seek a profession form a reverse twist on Joseph Baldwin's route.[61] Moving counter to the more familiar westward rush, and underscoring the sometimes surprising flexibility of transitional paths in this period, Curtin's route to success took him geographically and socially far from his farm boy roots. His story reminds us of the many paths that went into forming the middle class.

Jeremiah, who was born in 1835, began his memoir at his family's Greenfield, Wisconsin, farm. He grew up with at least four sisters. By the time he entered school, his mother had taught him the alphabet and he could read a little. Learning with ease, Jeremiah pleased his teacher. At age twelve he progressed to a winter school at "the crossroads." He first triumphed over many older scholars there at a spelling school.

Jeremiah read the Bible, Bunyan's "Siege of Mansoul," and "all the books I could buy or borrow and was thinking of what I was going to do in life. My idea was that I must learn, learn everything, and young as I was I thought much about how I could learn most in the shortest time" (37). But his help was needed at home. Jeremiah's schooling stopped the summer after he turned thirteen. Greatly disappointed, he found that he was too tired to study in the evenings. Outdoor labor he did not mind, but he missed his books. From thirteen to eighteen he alternated summer farm work with winter schooling.

Despite his need for his son's labor, Jeremiah's father had decided early that the boy should have a college education. But without another son old enough to work, he could not yet let Jeremiah go. In 1856 the father died of pneumonia, and the son despaired over his loss. Farm responsibilities remained his primary burden. "Evenings and nights were spent over books. I was depressed, struggling, trying to decide what I was to do in life" (42). Aged about twenty-one, Jeremiah struggled "between which I must choose were on the one hand a useful and pleasant, but circumscribed life, a life mainly personal, devoted to things local; and on the other hand a life in which I might work for great results" (43). He struggled for months: "Shall I go to college, or shall I stay on the farm?" Finally he made his choice: "Now began the struggle to go to Harvard college" (43). At last a strong, honest man turned up looking for work managing a farm. Jeremiah rushed off to Carroll College, late for the term. He prepared himself, especially in Greek and Latin, for Harvard. Embarking in October 1859, he "feared [an] insurmountable obstacle to meet: I must win the consent of the Harvard faculty to admit me out of the regular course and, if they consented, must face a private examination in each required study. My only chance was that the faculty would take into consideration that I lived in the Far West, that the death of my father had delayed my preparation for college and thrown many cares upon my shoulders" (47). Petitioning the president and gaining Professor Louis Agassiz's support, Jeremiah "went through the ordeal very well, and was admitted" (51). Thus, educational institutions provided the ground for his transition; they too were in transition to their later, more orderly, structured forms.

College had another, less formal benefit: providing useful contacts, which served Jeremiah well. Making friends who would later be of assistance, he delighted in the intellectual life of Cambridge and Boston. European languages and literature became a favorite subject. He considered his class of 1863 "wonderfully fortunate" in its instructors. On the eve of graduation Jeremiah reflected: "Each man was thinking of the future, asking himself: 'Will my life be a success or a failure?' Each student had a number of intimate friends whom he would like to keep near him always, and he dreaded the parting of ways" (67).

Jeremiah Curtin's path took him to New York City to study law. With letters from James Russell Lowell, he connected with the literary lights. Seeking work to meet his expenses, he gained appointment through his contacts to the Sanitary Commission at $50 a month; he also served as a private tutor in languages. Language study, now Russian, competed with his legal work. Influenced by Russians he met, Jeremiah decided to seek a diplomatic appointment. He used the influence of prestigious Harvard and New York men to support his application. In 1864, far from the farm and the Wisconsin frontier, Curtin became secretary of the U.S. legation in St. Petersburg.[62]

William H. McIntosh's novel path of growing up fittingly concludes this exploration of middle-class and professional transitions in the first half of the nineteenth century. In general direction as well as in many of its specific aspects, McIntosh's life captures the meaning of these seminal transitions. Various threads woven together point toward new middle-class modes of growing up, while others recall tradition.

William titled his autobiography "The Story of a Life," beginning with a sound statement of age consciousness: "There must be five epochs to a life, viz:—Infancy, Childhood, Youth, Manhood, and Old Age."[63] Distinguishing youth from childhood and manhood, he thus recognized adolescence in its new construction.[64] Born in 1837, he was one of three children whom his out-of-work father moved from Albany to Wisconsin in 1843 in search of security. His father worked as a railroad superintendent while his mother reared the "little family and sought to give them education and train them in the tenets of religion" (1–2). Through nostalgia and sentimentality, William retained a vivid childhood vision:

> A child in red, black-dotted flannel playing by a brook bank in a valley by a rude small house delighted to watch the quick movements of the speckled trout. At school, teased by roguish girls and punished by the mistress for futile attempts at retaliation. With sled, playing on the streets of Albany and hiding behind doors to elude pursuing policeman; at least select school, ferruled for every failure in spelling, and at church receiving colored vine-inscribed cards and forming a unit of the hundred gathered with banners for celebration. (2)

Moving first to the village of Racine, where his father bought a house and struggled to support the family, William and his older brother were "crudely taught" in the boys' school. They "soon struck up acquaintance with the village boys and learned the boundaries of the place" (5). School and church effectively defined his childhood. "Mother was very desirous that we should be educated, and induced father to send us to the Academy, of which Prof. Stowe was one of the best teachers."

Joined by another brother in 1845, the boys learned more at home, especially the limits of acceptable behavior. William's gullibility elicited correction from his mother, still "decidedly Scottish in language and ideas." His father was often away, improving his farm and struggling to manage it, while the family lived in town. When expenses forced them to move to the farm, William found the conditions new and strange. Their novelty quickly wore off. Free from farm chores, he enjoyed leisure in the fields and fruit from the vines much more than the local school. William also learned, in part from his father's failings, a stern sense of economy.

Showing his age consciousness, William offers a concise notion of what was becoming recognized as adolescence: "A Man is as his youth has been passed and youth begins at about twelve years of age, with many much earlier. He is influenced by heredity, parentage, associates, and surroundings. I had . . . a strong desire for company but my parents saw fit to restrain their children from attending placements of amusement and taking part in the gatherings that enlivened the monotony of long winter nights" (23). Parental correction made him unfit for company. He saw himself as better than other boys, but in seeking seclusion, he missed society.

The year 1853 was a critical one. Term after term the boys had gone to winter school, making no progress. Disappointed, their mother visited Racine and arranged for one son to attend the city school. James, the eldest, was asked first; he declined, giving William his chance, and he "willingly" accepted. When fall work was finished, the sixteen-year-old left home to board with a family in Racine and attend the new high school. The transition was not easy: "I was a raw country boy and felt the contrast with the city boys who for a while gave me rough usage, but I made no complaint and then though small was tough and managed to hold my own" (29). William suffered from loneliness. His studies, too, were difficult. But he became accustomed to them and to his new routines, which included Sunday church services. He settled into a regimen of farm work in summer and school during the other seasons. School life was "wearisome," but there was activity on the streets and lectures and political speeches as well as sermons to occupy the teenager. As he progressed at school, William helped to organize a debating club. He ranked high, but found his instruction faulty in its mindless repetition, and the results were discouraging.

In addition to his other interests there were girls: "Society of the girls had attraction that was fast driving thought of education into the background. There were parties on two or three evenings each week which I attended with great pleasure and much profit, as this social intercourse steadily wore off the rusticity engendered by my solitary farm life. The young ladies were handsome, bright and delightful company and these evenings were better passed than in study" (33). William was soon tempted away from his proper path. The schoolmaster noticed his growing indifference to study and spoke to him. Undeterred, the boy continued "near the road to ruin," his pleasures outweighing any higher instincts. His acts of juvenile degeneracy extended as far as drinking until he made himself sick, smoking a cigar, and participating in a wedding shivaree with Racine College students. Here a centuries-old peer group practice in which the young exercised their limited powers still formed part of the adolescent repertoire in a mid-nineteenth-century town.[65]

The family with whom he boarded influenced William to mend his ways. A year shy of graduation, he left the city school and in 1856 entered the preparatory department of Beloit College, moving into a dormitory. He made excellent progress in Greek, Latin, English grammar, algebra, and bookkeeping. When other students left to teach winter school, nineteen-year-old William stayed at his studies and kept up his health by playing cricket and football, "sometimes very earnest and very violent." As a junior student William suffered the practical jokes of the seniors, from burning outhouses to invading his room and filling it with tobacco smoke. William "gave [his studies] all my time and mind" (41).

William's roommate exemplifies yet another symptom of the rescripting of adolescence and youth: "My room mate of the fall term, Jerome Davis, had during the closing weeks grown very morbid and melancholy. He had thoughts of suicide and it became evident that his mind was giving way, and he was withdrawn from college where his career had sorrowfully ended" (42). The influence of young Werther, and the "pressure cooker" educational and career strains under which young persons struggled at the time and later, struck here.[66] William addresses another theme of the time which presumably reduced such impacts: "The outside world was 'terra incognita' to us in our seclusion. I lived within the college bounds, rarely going to town save for letters" (43). Not quite the family home as a "haven against the cold, cruel world," college for William nonetheless provided a surrogate.

Beloit College like many others at the time, had been founded to prepare ministers, specifically Congregational ministers. It required church attendance and prayers at chapel. "In the course of events," William recalls, "a revival sprang up, class exercises were temporarily made secondary to religious meetings" (44). He was one of the few students who were unable to convert. He showed no lasting anxiety and never claimed more than a belief in the creed and practice of religion. Debating drew his greater passion; president of the debate society, he found educational value in cultivating oral expression. He excelled in spelling, but worked hard to improve in public reading and speaking.

Finishing third in the preparatory class, William matriculated as a freshman. At home for the summer, free from enforced attendance at church and chapel and, he admitted, from books, he worked on the farm. Proud of his son, his father bought him a hat for $3.50, "in the slimness of his means, practically voicing his regard for my interest in the farm and his pride in my appearance" (52). William celebrated his twentieth birthday with a dinner of pigeons he had shot, "served up admirably" by his mother (54).

As summer ended, William's enthusiasm for college cooled: "I had somehow lost my zeal in study and the prospective duties of a student, so different from the farmer's life, looked difficult and wearisome, but none the less did I resolve on going, not a hint did I let fall of being tired of it" (57). Delayed by harvest, he arrived at Beloit one week late but caught up. Hard study was the rule, the necessity, and the object of the "whole expensive system of a collegiate course." He suffered constantly from financial fears. December's recitations proved to be his last. He worked at home during the next term and earned his own way thereafter.

A sense of endings and beginnings marked William's ruminations on his twenty-first birthday: "I was only conscious of the one fact that I had reached an age when manhood is wont to be asserted and when the young man in natural course must rely on himself." Manhood "is the preserved vitality of youth, its impulses, its outgrowth, its powers of action and its self control." William grasped that he had learned to think and look out for himself. The pressure of debt led him to seek employment "whereby to return some of his outlay and help my father to regain his independence, for he was practically a slave to his creditors" (62). The desire to achieve his independence intertwined with the needs of his family.

He claims to have enjoyed this interim period of work, of sitting many hours by the window, looking out or reading Shakespeare and Thomas Dick. With winter approaching, an invitation to teach in a district school opened up a path leading away from the farm. Although he anticipated problems, he took on the task with pledges of good conduct. After a "farcical examination" by the town superintendent, William was engaged at $21 for twenty-two days each month, boarding round. Despite the usual problems, he succeeded.

In 1859 or 1860 William journeyed through Missouri to "see slavery as it was and learn something of the country." During this brief period of wanderlust, he taught in Kansas and Missouri. He also did some writing, won prizes at county fairs, and attended a teacher's institute from which he received a first-class license. In Missouri William was harassed as a northerner. With the outbreak of the Civil War, he expected to enlist in the Union forces. Then his brother James was reported killed at Bull Run: "The blow to my parents was very heavy and I could not persuade myself that my duty to them was less than to my country and so resolved to defer enlistment for the time" (92).[67]

Working on the farm and serving as principal of the local schools, William "could not be spared to go, tried to reason myself into the belief that I would better serve my country by teaching" (93). His salary paid off the mortgage on the family farm: "So at last, their pains to give me an education had borne rich fruit, as to my improvement in intellect had come the ransom of the old farm," no small benefit (96). Then, to the family's joy, word came that James was alive in a Richmond hospital. Now freed from his conflict between obligation to family and to country, William enlisted as a volunteer in the Twenty-second Wisconsin Infantry for three years: "It was with a lighter heart that I now began to consider the home leave taking" (98).

William saw little combat. Taken prisoner and then paroled, he did garrison service and was dispatched in December 1863 to teach in a "colored school" in Tennessee. He had the assistance of young women teachers, one of whom, Anna Cosper, from DeKalb County, Illinois, was William's special favorite. "It had come to be understood," he writes, that they would marry before William returned to battle. Within the year he reports, "The momentous step had been taken" (207–208). He was twenty-seven years old.

William returned from the war unharmed and resumed teaching in Wisconsin. Independent, his path confirmed, William combined educational work, local officeholding, journalism, and apple selling. This roster encapsulates his transitional professional path, which evolving school structures played a special role in forming.

Migrant and Pioneer

William McIntosh and his family in Wisconsin took part in fashioning a new transitional path to growing up that spanned country and town, family and outside world, farm work and careers in nascent bureaucracies such as school systems. William himself showed a new awareness of age and stages of growing up.

A great many of his contemporaries were closely tied to another transitional feature of the time—the western movement. Many were shaped by a life on the land, often in pioneering circumstances: transcontinental migration followed by the choice whether to farm, ranch, mine, or seek their fortunes in the new western cities. The young took their place among the waves of settlers moving across the young republic and contributed to territorial development. Mixing tradition with change, their experiences constitute the third subpath along the transitional route.

Rhode Island–born Harvey Alexander Adams (1812–1895) provides one typical example.[68] His path took him in stages from Rhode Island to Ohio and to Texas via New Orleans. His diary testifies to basic conflicts, personal defeats combined with victories. Harvey spent his childhood in Providence, where he went to school. His father, "a Sterne man," chastised his children for their errors, though his son deemed him fair: "I do not believe he corrected his child through passion as many parents do." He was especially concerned about their physical safety (9).[69]

In financial straits, Harvey's father journeyed west, first seeking opportunity near Columbus, Ohio. He moved the family before Harvey was twelve, limiting the children's schooling. His daughters received better schooling than his sons, for he recognized that his girls needed a different preparation for adult life, and that additional education would open up teaching as a means of making their way, but no such perception shaped his approach to his sons. By age twelve Harvey and his brother were working. Living at home, the boys sometimes took advantage of the situation. On at least one occasion they drank so much that they couldn't do their work, and Harvey just missed being severely injured. They were firmly disciplined.

In his later teens Harvey left the small family farm. For several months he worked on the national road, breaking stone. Returning to the farm, he looked for better employment. He exchanged a horse and gun for a bit of property but soon considered himself badly swindled. Moving to Columbus, he was plagued by legal problems over the note on his property.

Harvey also attempted to renew his acquaintance with a young women to whom he had earlier taken a fancy. "Miss S.B. [Susan Burke] had been the idol of my affections for many years. . . . Her image was engraved on my heart, I thought of no one else, and I loved none else. I contemplated that as soon as I became of age I would offer my addresses to her, but my prospects, my hopes, my affection, were not realized by her. Time had erased the early affection of her heart, as she never expected to see me again" (19). Calling at a quilting, he stated his intentions in a note. "But I was disappointed for it contained the history of my defeat" (20). Engaged to marry another man in three weeks, she sent Harvey away. Had he arrived three months earlier, he would have succeeded, she said. Disappointed and "deprived of his honor," Harvey left, reflecting that "an affection formed and inculcated at so early an age, where it continues for any length of time it is generally lasting . . . The journey of Life may in some respects resemble a road through a mountainous country through which we travel on for some time amid a continuation of the same kind of scenery, till suddenly a new winding of the path brings us upon a landscape entirely dissimilar from that we have just left behind us" (20). For Harvey, this proved to be more than a metaphor.

In Columbus he worked "to considerable advantage" in carpentry and construction, hoping to save enough to travel. He bought a lot and built a house. But falling into debt, he had to give his creditors his tools, house frame, and books, sacrificing a large amount of property for the small amount owed. Deeply disappointed, Harvey returned home and worked on improving the family farm.

Eventually Harvey's search for independence took him farther west. In February 1836, aged twenty-four, he started out for New Orleans. His family had tried to talk him out of his plan: "My sisters almost went into fits to think that I was going so far from home that they never would see me again, my Mother in particular grieved me very much . . . Oh, said she, Harvey, I never shall see you again if you go so far from home" (26). She made him promise to return in a year's time. Unlike many of his peers, Harvey showed no comparable pangs at parting. From New Orleans he proceeded to Texas and began to build his homestead in Fayette County, a pioneer in a pioneer territory.

Others initiated their paths to success in the West from different beginnings. Many were attracted by the discovery of gold near San Francisco in the 1840s. But there was more than one West to win. Edward Bosqui, born in Montreal in 1832, took a typical route in migrating to California.[70] Despite the lure of mineral wealth, his destination lay in the city and in commerce.

Edward was the eldest son in a family of seven children born to a French-Canadian cabinetmaker and a Scottish-Canadian mother. "With few exceptions," he writes, "my earliest memories were clouded by the anxiety I felt for my parents, who were struggling to make a living" (9–10). From the age of nine or ten, he recalls in his autobiography, Edward hoped to find a position from which he could help his parents. At eleven he took a job in a bookstore, apparently boarding with the owner's family. His pay of two dollars a month came in the form of coppers, one hundred to the dollar: "How well I remember my feeling of pride when this heap of coin was placed in my mother's hands each month!" (10). Business was poor at the store, so he proposed peddling books and stationery door to door. Edward's occasional success did not prevent the store from closing.

He spent the next two years with his aunt in the village of Laprarie, near Montreal. He next worked with another bookseller in Montreal, earning ten dollars a month. His duties were "light and pleasant," he had time to read. In addition to helping his parents, he writes, "my great ambition was to become a painter . . . I soon realized that I possessed no marked ability" (16).

Meeting the head of the Geological Survey of Canada stirred Edward's interest in travel, exploration, and nature. That influenced his response to news of the discovery of gold in California in 1848: "Like almost every one, I caught the gold fever and determined to go to that far-away country" (21). Requesting a loan of $125 from an uncle in Georgia, the sixteen-year-old got advice instead. But "the idea of going constantly occupied my thoughts and manifested its seductive power in my dreams," and his determination increased (22). Sharing his excitement with another young man, Edward read the travel account of Richard Henry Dana and John C. Fremont. The two planned to go to California together.

To placate his mother's "great distress" and meet the nay sayers, Edward temporarily borrowed a roll of 150 one-dollar bills to show he had resources. "The deception worked like a charm, and she gave me her consent to go" (24). Bidding his family farewell, Edward, now eighteen, and his friend left for New York in March 1850. They booked passage to Mexico. After exploring Chihuahua and Arizona, on his eighteenth birthday in July, they arrived in San Francisco.

Edward sought work. After several unsuccessful efforts he was encouraged by a Mr. Cook of the bank of Palmer, Cook & Company, where he had presented his letters of introduction. He was hired to work at $80 per month: "My heart was full of gratitude and delight at being duly installed as bank messenger, porter, clerk and general factotum. My feeling of relief at this sudden change from a wandering adventurer to a bank attache may be imagined but not described" (48). Relief also came from purchasing clean new clothing with his first wages.

By December 1850 dissatisfaction with the menial, routine work given him by the firm's junior partner had led Edward to think seriously about leaving for the mines. The discovery of a rich pocket in the Josephine Mine at Mariposa stirred him. Cook sagely told him: "Very well, you will never be contented until you have gone to the mines and seen the elephant." Giving him a letter to his brother, who was in charge of a Fremont mine, Cook told him, "Should you not succeed, return at any time to San Francisco and you will have a place with us" (59).

Edward's encounter with the mine was a comedy of errors: "It was soon ascertained that my sphere of usefulness in the mines was quite limited . . . The fact was soon apparent that I had 'seen the elephant'" (59). He returned to San Francisco, the bank, and Mr. Cook. As the bank prospered, Edward rose to department head, in effect ending his path from artisanal origins in Montreal. Homesick, he visited Canada. At twenty-five Edward met the woman he would marry two years later.

As we see from Edward Bosqui's story, paths west led to the city as well as the land and the mines. Some paths proved the stuff of legends, of country-conquering models of American achievement; others were no less salient for personal and national development.[71]

With incredibly high rates of movement across the American landscape, many personal transitions were tied closely to migratory paths within the developing countryside. Two particular stories advance our understanding of this common route.[72] Despite major differences, each reflects with exceptional clarity the possibilities and conflicts offered by rural, western, and migratory patterns. Each captures aspects of the transition that were shared widely during the era; each reflects a young man making his way across a terrain in seismic social and economic upheaval. Both show the reciprocal relations between social development and individual life prospects.

Benjamin F. Gue was born in 1828 in Greene City, New York, the second child and eldest son of a Quaker family.[73] In his early years the family moved to Ontario County. Then, when Benjamin was ten, his father died, leaving his wife to raise six children. The eldest son assumed responsibility, as he was able, until the farm was sold and the family dispersed in 1851. Thus, from a very early age Benjamin occupied the place of "man of the family," a role that propelled but also complicated his growing up. He considered many routes, from mercantile work in New York City and legal studies to joining the California gold rush. He followed one path to teacher training, then another to the West. His course reflected the rural, migrant, and western transitions as well as emerging middle-class paths and the choices leading to them.

Benjamin began his diary at age nineteen in 1847 while studying and boarding at Canandaigua Academy. Despite his (perhaps stylized) fears about December's examinations, he scored 100. Delighted, he went "down street" and spent nearly all his money in celebration. On Saturday, December 25, he celebrated his nineteenth birthday. He hints at his interest in "a certain scholar," a young woman.

Despite his family responsibilities Benjamin was a typical teenager of his time and place. In addition to attending school, he actively followed politics and reform activities, going to many meetings and to church, dancing school, singing school, and parties and attending court trials. His sober, almost intolerant side surfaced in response to the juvenile misbehavior of fellow students, who ripped up beds, disturbed worship, and made rude noises in class when the master was absent. He belonged to a society to guard against the "plots" of mischievous peers, including one plot to lock students in their rooms (March 14, 1848). After an informal social visit, he comments: "We enjoyed ourselves much better than we often do to a large fashionable party where there is nothing going on but dancing, marching, talking, nonsense and kissing, it is strange that any one can enjoy such parties. But 'it takes all kinds of people to make a world'" (March 13, 1848).

At home after five months in school, Benjamin resumed farm routines and responsibility for his younger siblings, and he went to many meetings. In August he attended to legal matters involving the family estate which had long plagued him. His sister Sarah Ann married and left for New York City, prompting an outpouring of nascent family sentimentality.

With fall came harvest and meetings on suffrage, religion, slavery, and temperance. In 1849 Benjamin continued to work the farm. In April he writes, "Had my head examined by a Prof. of Phonology [*sic*]." He did not report what guidance he gained from analysis of his character and prospects.

In December Benjamin received an appointment to the Normal School at East Bloomfield. On arriving he "had to be stared at as *a new scholar*" (December 5, 1849). In a reflection on his pursuit of professional training, or perhaps on his age, he refers to his fellow students as "Gents" and "Ladies." Contradicting his earlier position on student behavior, Benjamin and his cronies engaged in a sort of shivaree involving violins, tin pans, a bell, and banging desktops, after locking the doors and stairs on Christmas Eve. The "serenade" lasted until 10:30 and ended with a closing "salute." His twenty-first birthday on Christmas, the next day, was quiet.

In the new year exciting events overtook the school. Learning that one of their fellows had been expelled and another was likely to follow, the students went into "council" to fashion their response. Another student "got his *walking* papers" without being told the cause. The male students accompanied the two to the stagecoach and sent them off with three long cheers. Tensions—"the Prof. . . . looked daggers"—continued until the next night when "the Prof.," a Professor Clark, asked to see "the gentlemen" and commanded that all sign a pledge of good behavior. Clark pulled out his pen and laid down the paper. "Now came the trial of *grit*," writes Benjamin. As Clark called their names, virtually all the students were cowed into submitting; one who refused was told to leave immediately. At his turn Benjamin responded: "If it is necessary I will sign the paper so far as relates to my conduct, but I will not sign the last part of it which pledges to be informers." An argument ensued. Others followed Gue's course. The professor then said he would wait until the next day to require the pledge. Nothing further was said, although Clark, without luck, tried to persuade Benjamin, who writes: "This was the last we every heared [*sic*] about it, when he found he must back out or expell 7 of his largest schollars he seemed to think it was most prudent to back out. And he was wise in doing it for it would have nearly broken up the school" (January 2–May 10, 1850).

Benjamin was greatly excited about California. With several others he set about raising money and planning to leave. After bidding farewell to their friends at the academy and arriving in New York City, they found they could not book passage until June. Although Benjamin saw the sights of the metropolis, the plan came to naught.

At around this time, Benjamin and his family were stunned by news of his sister Sarah Ann's unexpected death. Working on the farm, observing the rituals of different religious sects, visiting friends, and attending political and fraternal meetings constituted much of Benjamin's time in 1850 and 1851. He felt deeply for a female friend who was forced into marriage by a father who did not believe her happiness carried any importance, especially when money was involved (September 10, 1850).

By September of the following year Benjamin had sold the family farm for $40 an acre and was anxiously awaiting news concerning the next steps on his path. He was expecting to hear from his brother in New York: "This suspense is provoking—very—when I know what is coming or what I am going to do—I can make up my mind to it however bad—but waiting between hope and fear is horrible. The content of that letter will decide my course for life in all probability for I am out of business just having sold the farm and I am now waiting to hear if James finds any business for me in New York." He was also preparing to part for a time from his girlfriend, Delia: "How I love that girl—she is everything I could ask—and no wonder I can hardly stay away three days—wonder if it will always last" (September 11, 1851). (It did not.)[74] Benjamin waited at home, reading Byron. He also responded to newspaper ads. But without any business contacts, his brother's efforts in New York turned up nothing.

By late October Benjamin was struggling with choices about his future: "Tried to make up my mind what to do. Whether to buy our old farm—teach school—go in a store or study law or go west" (October 20). Offered a place for winter school, he asked for fifteen dollars a month but was offered twelve: "I would see them in the warm place first" (October 22). Yet, teaching school is what he eventually did. On Christmas Day 1851, his twenty-third birthday, Benjamin plaintively penned: "Today I am twenty-three years old—how time does pass along, to look back it only seems a few days since I was 18 . . . Wonder where I shall be next Christmas, in all probability I shall be hundreds of miles from here away out west somewhere in Iowa or Illinois . . . But years bring changes and changes have just begun with me."

Benjamin began 1852 with a sense of the changes to come. Since his New York hopes had come to naught, he resolved to take other steps toward independence. By February he had packed to go west, first to Cleveland and then on to Iowa in March, where he and his brother bought land and began pioneering. By the mid-1850s they had achieved enough security to marry and regather their families. His path found and taken, Benjamin prospered. Although, in his early twenties, growing up often seemed to Benjamin a road without markers or end, it was neither. His route spanned tradition and transitions toward new ways of development, both individual and collective.

Benjamin's contemporary John H. Rhea (1827–1896) confronted a wilder West in the "Arkansaw" of the 1830s, 1840s, and 1850s.[75] In 1829 John and his brother moved with their parents from Tennessee to Arkansas—the untamed West, with all its privations, challenges, and rewards, as he recollected in his memoir. Children were brought up amid the "feet washing and close communion," "spitting and foaming" preaching, and the uncontrollable excitement of their parents' Hard Shell Baptism.

John began school at age seven. Encouraged by an uncle to be "saucy," John accused his teacher of lying when he insisted that the second letter of the alphabet was called B. Offended, the teacher gave him "a severe drubbing. This gave me a decided disrelish for books and schoolmasters. Hence, my education did not advance rapidly, not being able to master my alphabet in three months, the time of Mr. Sexton's school" (5).

As John grew up, "a better civilization sprang up" with the settlement of the area. At nineteen, in 1846, he left home seeking an education: "Had no money—no clothes—no books—no anything that a boy ought to have to be at a boarding school." Traveling forty-five miles to Mount Comfort seminary, he found the boardinghouse keeper willing to wait for his rent ($1.25 per week) until John earned it. From his limited foundation school was a struggle: "I could barely read and write a very little. I can never forget the embarrassment of the situation. I could not even be graded in a class with the smallest boys admitted. After a few weeks, by hard study, I climbed up to some of the lower classes. Having no money to spend and nothing to do but study, I soon had the satisfaction of entering the first classes" (11).

That achievement confirmed the migratory and teaching path that John would take toward and through adulthood. With Arkansas's early educational and cultural institutions developing, John was "connected with" Arkansas College in Fayetteville in 1853–54. He then taught at Berryville Academy, a school of "high grade in Carroll County," from 1854 to 1859. He became a Southern Methodist preacher, converting in 1851. Moving next to Springfield, Missouri, he took charge of a church and a female institute.

Then the Civil War came. "Although a Southern man . . . we loved the union more than the south and slavery" (12). Running for his life, John closed the school just days before Confederate troops were battling nearby. He took his family north to the free states of Illinois and Iowa.

Despite the melodramatic style in which John Rhea tells of the adventures on his path to growing up, he was securely placed within the realm of midcentury sentimental domesticity rather than romantic adventurism: "In all the tragic history of my life I have not yielded to the enchantment of the wild and romantic spirit of the times in which I lived . . . I only regret that the 30 years of my life spent in Arkansaw had not been when there were more advantages for gaining knowledge and fitting for usefulness . . . The sweet recollections of home in the cabin, and mother and father, brothers and sisters, as we sat before the great fire in the rude home of my childhood, bring the tear to my eye and the sigh from my bosom" (12). The tale was there for the telling, and John told it well. In this way the West was won, and young people fashioned their paths and their stories of transition.

Religious Conversion

John Rhea's Hard Shell Baptist upbringing suggests the fourth course within the transitional path: preadult conversion and paths to adulthood that reflect that influence.[76] Given the common expectations for conversion among many evangelical Protestant sects—with conversions at an early age increasing during the Second Great Awakening—in isolating this pathway one may risk distorting the overall picture. Nonetheless, the experience of conversion evidently predominated among females, though it crossed all lines of social division.

The increasing frequency of early conversion is clearly related to the complex social changes that contributed to the remaking of growing up.[77] The modern idea of adolescence emerged in connection with teenage conversion, a link perceived in the last century.[78] It became a major source of conflict among ministers and their flocks. Some applauded the practice, while others decried it. On the link between the adolescent years and conversion, Hillel Schwartz argues: "Whether or not revival descriptions were accurate, whether or not youth made up the majority of revival converts, adults expected revival conversions to betray an adolescent style . . . Revival accounts in ante-bellum Boston may be . . . a reflection of the common adult belief that adolescents by their very nature responded to religious revivals."[79] In that connection, the emerging view of adolescence and adolescents becomes something of an ambiguous legacy.

William McKnight was born in Rootstown, Portage County, Ohio, in 1815, the only son of an Irish father and a Pennsylvania Dutch mother.[80] During his childhood, he recalls in his memoir, the family lived "in rather low circumstances, and so far as I know, they were not professors of religion" (5). When William was two, his father was killed by a falling tree limb. Widowed with three small children, his mother remarried. William worked on the family farm.

At twelve he left and "sought a home among strangers in a strange land" (5). With no prospects or clear path before him, he reports, "I was a wicked boy until I was about 13 years old but at that time I would have some serious thought on the subject of religion. I have no recollection of hearing but one sermon [by a Methodist preacher] before I experienced religion." He attended two or three Sabbath schools and received a lesson on the Psalms of David. William was ripe for the call of conversion: "When I was between 12 and 14 years old, in the winter . . . I attended a prayer meeting one evening . . . A strange feeling came over me and I did not know what was the matter, but I was afraid of dying, and I called on the name of the Lord for mercy and the brethren prayed for me and before the meeting closed that evening, the Lord spoke peace to my soul and I shouted 'Glory to God in the Highest, Peace on Earth and Goodwill to Men.' I remember distinctly how happy I felt. I went home singing and shouting and praising the Lord" (5). This experience led William to join the Methodist Episcopal Church; he was baptized by a traveling preacher.

After a period of probation he was received into the church "in full connection." For three years he tried to live a Christian life. Supporting the views of contemporaries who mistrusted the sincerity and depth of early religious experiences, William lost his active spirituality. When a "difficulty" divided the local church, his stepfather "compelled" William and his sister to leave it, refusing to allow them to associate with so many "hypocrits." For the boy, the consequences were dire: "I lost all relish for going and lost my enjoyment and gave up prayer, or nearly so, and therefore I back slid from God. And I lived, as near as I can remember, in this state about two years but would pray at times when I felt bad. If I was irritated, I would swear sometimes. Then I felt ashamed afterwards and thus I enjoyed no peace of mind while I lived in this state" (6).

Like other converts, William came to a crisis point from which he might renew his faith through a serious illness from which he was not expected to recover in the winter before his seventeenth birthday. Although he was often delirious, he writes,

> during my illness, my Methodist brethren would talk to me about dying. I there promised to God that if He could spare my life and restore me to health and strength, I would serve Him all the days of my life. After I was restored to health, I did not forget my vow, as many do, but went to work praying to God to give me peace . . . It was impressed on my mind that I must go to the prayer meeting and take up the cross in public and then I would receive the blesing . . . God, for Christ's sake, wrought the pardon on my heart. I shouted "Glory to God who has given me victory." (6)

His regeneration was permanent.

Until the age of twenty-six William worked at carpentry and farming. In 1836, aged twenty-one, he married and began a family, residing in the "east part" of his father-in-law's house. William built a log cabin on some land he had inherited from his father and grandfather, establishing an independent residence. In 1841 he received his preacher's license, which allowed him to spread the Word in pioneer territories in the quest to build the kingdom of the Lord on earth and combat the agents of the devil. With many riders he took his message on the road. Merging his mission and his life's work, he shifted his path. William's is the kind of story that was told to children in the hope of harvesting their souls.[81]

William's experience pales in comparison with the journey of poor, abused, orphaned Hosea Smith.[82] Undoubtedly exaggerated, the story of Smith's life highlights the social relations governing the paths of growing up and their intersections with conversion. In the early mill town of Slatersville in Smithfield, Rhode Island, fate dealt Hosea a cruel hand. Kept hungry and cold by his master and mistress, Hosea confronted cruelty early. Punishment constantly befell him.

At four he entered the cotton mill to work. "The overseer would pull my ears till the blood would run down my neck, and pull my hair till my head ached, and when I went home I was often sent back to the factory as hungry as I came" (4). Only the kindness and affection of a few neighbors and some men in the factory kept him going. Weakened by mistreatment, he was punished for being ill. At six he glimpsed the Lord's hand in creating the world; he felt that he would have to try to meet that Lord. At seven, virtually abandoned by the family who had kept him, Hosea was passed to another family who treated him even worse. Physically, spiritually, and psychologically he sank lower and lower: "I looked upon the brute creatures; I thought they were better off than I was. I envied every thing I saw their happiness . . . I reflected upon my situation and did weep and lament" (8).

When he was twelve a revival meeting came to his neighborhood. Hosea's clothing was so poor that he "was deprived the privilege of going to meeting" (9). Seeing the hopeful, happy converts confused him: "When I saw them so happy I was convinced that there was an eternal reality in religion. I then saw myself a sinner and without religion I must be eternally miserable. I thought that if I would have religion I must pray. The enemy then began to reason with me, and told me that there was no need of praying, for I had not done any thing very bad. I then began to inquire what I had done that was worth repenting for. The good spirit of the Lord then asked me if I never told a lie. I said yes" (10). That recognition led to others and to prayer for forgiveness.

At nineteen Hosea could no longer bear the family. Alternating periods of work in a number of nearby factories with periods of illness, from time to time he found his mind "awakened" to his spiritual condition, the specter of death, and the need to get religion. Attracted to the Shakers, he journeyed to Enfield, Connecticut. But their way of absolving sins disappointed him, so Hosea resumed work in the Rhode Island mills.

After befriending a "truly pious man" at his boardinghouse, Hosea began attending meeting, sincerely seeking religion. One minister led him to a grove and prayed with him. The next day he returned. They "prayed that the Lord would convert my soul that night. I fell on my face and prayed to the Lord, saying, O Lord, have mercy on me or I perish: my strength fails me, and I am sinking down to hell! I then raised my face from the ground. Every thing seemed light, and darkness had turned into light. I had lost my burden, and my mourning was turned into rejoicing . . . I prayed for an evidence . . . I thought I heard the most beautiful singing that I ever heard in my life—it seemed to come from heaven" (27).

Praying when not at work, Hosea searched for conviction. One day it came to him: eight lines of religious verse leaped into his mind: "I felt evidence that I was born of God. I felt to rejoice in his love. I experienced that joy and peace in my soul that I cannot describe with pen and ink" (31). At age twenty, having found religion, Hosea began to pray to help others, and this pointed him toward a new path to adulthood.

Moving from mill town to mill town for work and boarding, Hosea knew his physical and spiritual paths were not yet one: "I wished I was a beast of the field or a tree of the forest, or a rock in yonder ledge, or any thing that had not an immortal soul. But the worst of it . . . I thought I had rather die than undertake to preach" (40). Hosea soon heard the Lord's voice. The message was: "Go preach my gospel to a dying world— warn your fellow-men to flee from the wrath to come and lay hold on eternal life" (41).

Continuing to work in the mills, Hosea struggled with this burden. In time he accepted it, promising that if he were spared, he would do his duty. Telling his brethren he had been called to the ministry, Hosea received their approval to preach. Preach he did, gaining peace of mind. His youthful wanderings ended in the path of an itinerant evangelical preacher, confirming Hosea Smith in his adult calling. Studying doctrine in a church school, Smith received a license to preach in the Church of Christ. Other young men like him carried out the work of the Second Great Awakening and brought to countless young persons salvation during their crises of growing up.

If truth is sometimes stranger than fiction, we find evidence of that truism in the life of James J. Strang.[83] Strang grew up in New York State's "Burned Over District." His conversion-influenced path of growing up was an extreme form of transition, but one that in its uniqueness influenced U.S. history, for he was among the founders of the Mormon church. The son of a farming family, Strang was born in 1813 in Scipio, New York. His path was in many ways typical of the rural-born but professionally destined. As the introspective diary he kept from ages eighteen to twenty-three powerfully demonstrates, his path evolved in ways that were anything but typical.

James's diary opens with omens of conflicts to come. On July 31, 1831, he notes "Our debating school was given up as soon as it went into operation to prevent contention with the [p]rejudiced bigots." On October 16, the eighteen-year-old wrote: "Last night we had a sharp debate on the question is man more inclined to good than evil? I was never before so wearied with speaking. I have imbibed a habit of speaking very loud, last night was heard distinctly twenty rods in a house." He delighted in "training"—tongue-lashing—his opponents. He also felt slights easily.

More mundanely, James taught school, aiming at "regulating them and learning them what to do, without punishing a single schollar" (December 31, 1831). Given his bleak view of humanity and its prospects, that was no simple goal. Undeterred, he sensed a place for himself and a path to follow in this morass: "I ask no more than what this life may give—if it will but I tremble when I look forward to future prospects. I am resolved to [devote] my life to the service of mankind" (January 15, 1832). How to achieve that mission was not yet clear. Religion, relations with others, and sense of self emerge as central sources of conflict. As for religion, "it is all a mere mock of sounds with me for I can no longer believe in nice speculative contradictions of our divine theologians of our age. Indeed it is a long time since I have really believed these dogmas" (January 15, 1832).

Strang occupied himself writing poetry and "preparing for my great designs (of revolutionizeing government and countrie[s])." His delusions and grandiosity constitute a caricature of twentieth-century psychologies which are themselves caricatures of adolescence: "I have everything to surmount, but if I can completely surmount my disposition to indolen[ce] I shall consider the race half run; but I have another discouragement from the fact that I have never done one great thing" (February 19, 1832).

On his nineteenth birthday James repeated his ambitions and limitations, admitting that he was at a loss about what path to pursue: working for a fur company, studying the law, speculating in this or a foreign country. In May he tried to contrive a plan to marry the heir to the English throne. In June he wrote: "This is a flying time for me. Indeed I know not what to do. Sometimes I have almost a mind to become a priest but that i[s] to[o] small business for me. Cursed is every man and every beast he has subjected." On July 27 he declared himself a "perfect atheist, but do not profess it less I bring my father grey hair with sorrow to the grave."

Twenty years old, Strang took up the law in December 1832, claiming he would practice only if he were unafraid of encountering any person of equal experience in the state. Flights of fancy soar and plunge from page to page of his diary. On March 21, 1833, his twentieth birthday, Strang's hopes rose, then fell: "Bright prospects are before me, but all depends on the most untiring exertion. Twenty years of my life are allready-passed, and what have I done? Ah, what have I done? Nothing! Nothing! Nothing but commenced doing."

With the new year, 1834, Strang continued teaching, studying law, and debating. On February 22 "night finds me the most down that I have been these three years. Indeed I am about worn out for the present. School teaching does not agree with my health generally, but this winter my labours have been intolerable." Election to constable on the "people's ticket" rewarded him with $300 a year and "good exercise while studying" (March 3 and 9, 1834).

At the end of a busy year James remained uncertain about his course. On December 13 he wrote: "There is something radically wrong in my course of study or I am totally unfit for it. Besides this I am earning nothing. Perhaps I was born for poverty and disappointment but I do not believe it. I have as yet succeeded as well as could possibly be expected. True I have done nothing in all my life and am a fool yet but that is not so poorly as most have done who like me have had no oppo[r]tunities." As he ended his twenty-second year, James was still at sea, decisions unmade, path uncertain: "Perhaps it is erroneous to indulge such hopes as mine . . . If my present aspirations are too high, I may as well abandon my future hopes; mark out a different course" (March 18, 1835). Even in the "sparking line" he did "a dull business" (May 7, 1835).

For all his adolescent then youthful uncertainty, angst, and evident pathology, when James's path finally came into focus, he stayed with it for seven years before it took some startling turns. He returned to serious legal study and renewed his engagement to Mary Perce, gaining admission to the New York bar. He married Mary and settled down, finding independence and stability. James prospered from legal work, lecturing, politics, and publishing, and he served as postmaster. For seven years he lived in "conventional mediocrity" to please Mary and her orthodox mentors.

Then at age thirty, in 1843, unsatisfied and no longer willing to subdue his freethinking or his dreams of empire and immortal fame, James moved to Wisconsin and joined the pioneer Mormons, who included some of his wife's family. His imagination soared anew, and his abilities were recognized. He became one of the leaders of the Beaver Island Mormons. Strang later struggled with Brigham Young for the leadership of the church. He did not win that battle. He was murdered in 1856 at the age of forty-three.

Not all transitional paths were clear, consistent, or comprehensible in social-psychological terms. But neither did most experiences of adolescence and youth border on the clinically pathological. Always complicated and varied, growing up was changing. It was often difficult. Transitional paths remade the possibilities for growing up amid the many transformations that marked American society in the first half of the nineteenth century.

Female Paths

Female paths form the third of the main lines of growing up, comprising three subpaths, two of which cross emerging class lines. The major avenues are the traditional, work and migration, and the emerging bourgeois. Missing, as we have seen, are the experiences of servants and working-class and immigrant working women, as well as women who remained unmarried.[84] These female paths took shape during the historical moment in which modern gender roles crystallized. The heterogeneity of experience among young women growing up is nonetheless unmistakable. Both traditional and more novel paths demand emphasis; both pushed and pulled, sometimes contradictorily, sometimes simultaneously, at women growing to adulthood.

The three female subpaths parallel the traditional, transitional, and emergent class paths of their brothers. Women shared in major aspects of the transformation of growing up: they remained longer at home, experienced new modes of socialization, attended school more regularly and for longer periods, and prepared for one or another form of "women's work" at home or, sometimes, elsewhere. In other ways, girls' experiences differed from boys: in the point and timing of transition, the nature and length of dependence, the meaning of leaving home. No simple balance sheet of comparisons and contrasts is possible or useful. The dynamic, sometimes contradictory intersections of gender with tradition, emerging social class, race, ethnicity, religion, family circumstances, geographic location, and the like not only set the bounds for actions and expectations but also shaped central conflicts.

Despite its neglect by historians, the story of how girls grew up constitutes a significant chapter in our history. The fundamental reconstruction of women's place both followed from and stimulated changes in growing up.[85] And these changes in turn influenced the course of social and cultural change. In that dialectical relationship key conflicts and contradictions—between gender and class in particular—arose.

Traditional

We begin by examining the powerful presence of traditional yet evolving paths of growing up female in an era of transformation. More striking than in comparable accounts by men, the invention of sentimental, romanticized imagery—amounting to the creation of new traditions—formed a cornerstone of American culture in this era. This process of cultural construction both complements and complicates our efforts.[86] Tradition and change intermixed, sometimes subtly, sometimes not. Education, religion, family circumstances, demography, western migration, and chance all influenced traditional experiences. In a period of evangelical fervor, religious influences worked to support both conservative and more progressive outcomes.

Fanny Newell's memoir centers on her struggle from an early age to achieve salvation.[87] Born in 1793 in Kennebec, Maine, she died in 1824, her life marked as that of a martyr. The narrative opens in 1818: "At a very early period of my life, I was drawn to seek the living God. But alas! I rejected the many calls of this most merciful God" (5). At age five she first confronted death when one of her "little companions" died; as a result she feared to go anywhere alone or be left in the dark. One day, she writes, "it came into my mind with great weight and power, You must pray or be DAMNED." With little notion of the meaning of prayer but without hesitation, she knelt down, prayed, and wept. The respite she gained was only temporary. Her relish for "childlike play" returned, and she "grew up in pride and vanity, for which I now mourn and lament" (5).

A desire for repentance overtook Fanny. She feared her mother's death as well as her own and resolved to be more obedient to her parents and more loving to her brothers and sisters. Again, however, her conviction left her. She found herself "more than ever filled with lightness, vanity, and sins of many descriptions" (7). With her father's influence and instruction, Fanny at fifteen commenced her prolonged journey to regeneration: "At length the thunders from Mount Sinai struck my heart, rent my garment, and I was left naked before God" (12). After taking Methodist instruction, she was baptized. She continued to confront trials and temptations: "The enemy of righteousness tried hard to ensnare my soul." With her father's help, she conquered that enemy and found salvation. At age eighteen, ending her path early, Fanny married a Methodist minister. She died in April 1824 at thirty. Her life of regeneration and martyrdom for the Lord's cause constituted Fanny Newell's legacy to her sisters and daughters, an exemplary path of spirit versus the flesh, a tradition suited to a turbulent time.

Growing up with the privileges of a wealthy family was another key determinant in following a traditional path. In rural areas such origins readily lent themselves to creative and influential uses. In their excesses, however, they shaped by negative example new middle-class paths and contributed damning stereotypes of the useless young woman of leisure.[88]

Two New England women exemplify this particular traditional pattern. In her reminiscences composed in the late nineteenth century, Caroline Clapp Briggs records her childhood, evoking idyllic gatherings of three generations of family members, recalling memories of sitting on her grandfather's lap and listening to stories of the Grumpuses, "famous old bears that never did children any harm."[89]

Caroline was born in 1822 to a family that was close and loving. Her father, a tailor and public official, was "too indulgent; he never attempted to govern us" (10–11). On religion, morality, and politics, her Unitarian father was uncompromising. Devoted to his home, he instilled his love of nature in his children. And he was a famous storyteller. Caroline's mother, his second wife, was "a most devoted slave. We were watched over and guarded day and night, indulged in everything which she could possibly procure for us,—wept over, prayed over, but never controlled" (19). Growing up "wild as a deer," Caroline gave her mother much trouble (19). She was rewarded with toys.

Caroline's family lived in a "rambling old house" in Northampton, Massachusetts, with a household staff of three. She recovered quickly from childhood ailments when "wise Dr. Flint" prescribed—radically for the times, she recalled—fresh air and outdoor activity. "I was as a child a strange mixture of bravery and timidity, too impulsive to withhold speech when my feelings were injured or when I saw injustice done to others, but much too proud to let my inner thoughts be seen," she wrote (48). Caroline's emotions fluctuated up and down; she was frequently but briefly angry and jealous. Only at age fifteen, after reading Miss Martineau's "Deerbrook," did she understand herself and "for the first time in my life was ready to make full and free confession to those I loved best for every word I had spoken from my childhood up" (49). She was also full of "imaginary terrors," among which death stood out. Less severe but still frightful were strange sounds, house noises, rats.

The small group of Unitarians in Northampton kept a private school which their children attended. Pupils helped tend the schoolroom. "The teaching was almost uniformly good,—of rather a desultory sort, but generally made interesting to the children" by their female instructor (24). One year Caroline attended the "seminary" at Springfield. Living with an aunt, she was "deadly" homesick. When the Unitarian school disbanded and the family could not afford to send her away, more informal tutelage sufficed. Her mother wanted her to teach, but she never trained. A teacher told her, "'Talents wasted, time misspent.' I richly deserved the rebuke" (26).

Sundays were her "bête-noir": "At sunset Saturday night the straight-jacket was put on . . . The wildest dissipation was the repeating of hymns, which I abhorred . . . All the time I was struggling for my freedom, now and then stealing a story book from some hidden place" (52). Parties were frequent on other days. Wednesday and Saturday afternoons were spent with friends. Caroline had special girlfriends whom she "reverenced as a Catholic does his saint" (30). Good like a saint, Caroline's Susan was her partner in what Carroll Smith-Rosenberg has termed "the female world of love and ritual."

Only at age nineteen did Caroline journey from home, to western New York to visit a friend. When she was twenty-two, her father lost his businesses, and the family moved. Caroline and her sister "took up the laboring oar for the support of the family" by sewing, copying, taking in boarders, anything they could do (77). Caroline later married. Her comfortable, traditional path of growing up did not preclude a sudden reversal that turned the daughters into the family's breadwinners.

In partial contrast, with its own mix of tradition and novelty, was Caroline Wells Healey Dall's privileged Boston youth.[90] Her precocity and her place in Boston society stand out in her memoir. Caroline (1822–1912) grew up among the elite. She recalls her large house, her nurse, and her early schooling at age three at a nearby dame school. She idolized her father, the central figure in her memoir. At eighteen months she knew her letters; her father taught her from the large type of the front page of the *Christian Register.* She later taught her children in the same way from *Mother Goose.*

At age eight Caroline was sent to a school to begin her domestic instruction. Two maiden ladies taught the girls how to make a linen shirt, a skill Caroline later used. She attended small private schools in the city. But the learning about which she expresses greatest enthusiasm came less formally, from her father's bookshelves. She claims to have mastered by age twelve the English classics and others in translation. Other Boston private libraries were open to her. From a writing master she learned penmanship. Between the ages of thirteen and fifteen she learned Latin and modern languages, reading the classics and works in Spanish and Italian with the aid of Joseph Hale Abbott and tutors. Abbott's school served "a superior class of young women whom I have loved from that time to this" (40). Caroline's precocious learning was not an unmixed blessing: "One unfortunate result followed: I began to write for the press while I was still a child" (70).

Caroline also played and rambled throughout the city's environs with two favorite companions. Despite the lack of swimming schools for girls as there were for boys, Caroline swam in local waters. There were parties, too. She enjoyed visiting the central wharf with her father, an Indies merchant. Riding with her parents in the chaise, Caroline took drives in the suburbs. When her mother's health failed when Caroline was thirteen, housekeeping for her father added a burden. Still, balls, tea parties, and social visits alternated with study and domestic chores. In her mid-teens Caroline attended exhibitions and commencements in Cambridge, and "had such intimate relations with many students that I felt as if I too were a pupil at Harvard" (42). Long before her marriage, she saw her future husband at such events. Caroline also attended public lectures with her father.

According to custom, young ladies were introduced into society at coming out parties at age sixteen. At her own party Caroline's colors were white and green; five hundred camellias mixed with myrtle (at a dollar apiece) adorned the table and the house. Declining to open the dancing at her own ball, she was praised for her self-restraint. The real reason went undetected: she had no respect for the young man with whom she was supposed to dance.

Caroline taught Sunday school until her marriage. Her major early religious influences were Dr. Charles Lowell and Dr. Joseph Tuckerman. She attended educational reform groups and met activist women. Yet Caroline did not speak or lecture in public until after she was married. In her memoir she complains about women's lack of knowledge and access to money within the family and their consequent dependence on their husbands (who distrusted them) even for their charitable contributions. Growing up rich, precocious, and active prepared her for more. Her path shows the flexibility—within limits—permitted in traditional female experience. The balance was sometimes tricky to strike for the advantaged and for other women as well.

What growing up rich prepared women to do in adulthood depended on circumstances. One's own expectations, as well as those of adults and peers, shaped girls' experiences in ways that contrasted with those of their brothers. The simplistic view that all contrasts denigrate women fails to capture the complexities inherent in these privileged lives.[91] Orleana Ellery Walden-Pell's *Recollections of a Long Life* (1810–1895) demonstrate this complexity.[92] Orleana was the daughter of second-generation wealth. Her father, a well-connected New York lawyer born in Newport, Rhode Island, married the daughter of Baron von Weissenfels, a Revolutionary War volunteer. Moving to New Orleans, he soon joined the state Supreme Court.

New Orleans provided a rich environment for Orleana's childhood. Privilege marked her course; her recollections were of "infinite delight" (11). A country home exposed her to animals, tame and wild, and the fruits of the sea. She studied piano and attended a day school for girls, where she was punished for her mischief by being "placed outside the door crowned with a fool's cap, so that passers-by might jeer. But I enjoyed it immensely" (10). No wonder her father observed, "That child will turn out remarkable, either for good or bad.'" Pressures to conform to the norms of behavior for privileged females did not overly constrain her.

Reflecting both her status and her location, at seven Orleana joined her sister at a convent school. At age eight she began to receive "pin-money once a week," an early example of a child's allowance. To her mother's surprise, she sometimes saved her pence to buy treats for poor old people. Her mother then added her own contribution to this precocious noblesse oblige. From her mother she also learned elegance and grace, in part from watching her tutor her father in his courtroom gestures.

Orleana was not quite nine when her father died during a yellow fever epidemic. Unlike so many others who lost parents, she lost neither status nor comforts. The family returned to Newport. Orleana was glad to leave New Orleans and the cruelty of slavery. In Newport her schooling continued. She first attended a "boy's and girls' school mixed, [where] some of the lessons were given separately" (23). A board partition from floor to ceiling divided the sexes, but Orleana and one boy managed to communicate through a hole he cut in it. Her social life widened to include Assembly dances, "a great treat," and she attended a French dancing master's classes.

"Like other attractive girls, I was very young when I received my first offer of marriage," she recalls (26). When a German man proposed to her, she refused on grounds that she did not and could not love him. He responded with the "stereotyped remark in such cases, 'Love will follow.'" Orleana publicly embarrassed him. Her action looked to the future of gender relations as the young increasingly gained control over their marital choices. Often considered a mark of the emerging middle class, these changes affected the upper class as well.

Appropriately for her class and her future, Orleana and her sisters "finished" their education in New York. They excelled in piano, harp, and guitar. They met and sometimes became intimate with accomplished foreigners and highly placed Americans, including President Jackson. The rich also enjoyed a form of entertainment which added color to Orleana's last stages of growing up and marked her distinctive path. With other young women she took "part in some *Tableaux Vivants*. I went as Psyche and was much applauded" (31). Invoking other traditions, Orleana was three times a bridesmaid before she married. She was well prepared to continue on her own path, on both sides of the Atlantic, exhibiting the eccentricity that her class comforts facilitated. She had gained the rare capacity to laugh at herself, an ability that was typical neither of the rising middle class nor of its predecessors.

With the exception of her New Orleans childhood, Orleana Walden-Pell's path centered on the eastern seaboard and, later, on Europe. Traditions of society and wealth joined in determining that course. For many young men and for women, too, including those whose paths of growing up were traditional, the road headed westward to national settlement and development.

Elizabeth Caldwell Smith (Mrs. Joseph Duncan) experienced the intersection of a privileged eastern upbringing with westward movement on her marriage.[93] Born in 1808, Elizabeth was the daughter of a successful New York shipping merchant. She began her diary when she was a sixteen-year-old boarding school student. She continued irregularly throughout her life in Jacksonville, Illinois, after marriage at age twenty to thirty-four-year-old General Joseph Duncan, U.S. Representative for Illinois, soon to be governor. It shows her to have been a serious and religious teenager. Her father died when she was ten, her mother when she was seventeen.

Elizabeth was very social, constantly visiting or being visited. Every New Year's Day she received "Male Friends." She met her future husband in Washington; they married after a brief courtship. Elizabeth's adult life demanded more than her growing up had directly prepared her for. An "intrepid" traveler, she adapted her experience to the West, accepting personal loss (Duncan died in 1844 after financial reverses and political problems) and using her training in hospitality and sociability. She was active in social reform causes, from female education to temperance, abolition and colonization, and circulating libraries. Deeply concerned about her own daughters, she expressed pride in their growing up.

Sixteen-year-old Elizabeth delighted in the "romantick scenery and falls around" her boarding school (November 15, 1824). She sought to do well at the Ark Institute. On reading a composition to the class she notes, they "were such great criticks that I made several mistakes but on accounting of never having read before I escaped bad marks." When a headache ended plans to work on a composition, she played the piano to amuse herself and the company, reducing her pain. With adolescent romantic spirit she writes: "I found that Musick is a good relief to the mind, when it becomes fatigued and languid by close application to study. O yes tis Musick that inspires the soul and leads us captive with its power." Elizabeth also expresses romantic dreams of nature (December 3, 1824). In addition to attending church services on Sundays, she sometimes participated in Sunday school. On Mondays she went to the "Priccilla [*sic*] society in the afternoon, and read for the young ladies" (December 20, 1824). On other days Sunday school teachers' meetings and Bible classes filled her time after school.

Social life permeated the school term. On February 5, 1825, Elizabeth accepted an invitation from a Mr. Van Doren to ride to Paterson, New Jersey, with seven persons, five women and three men. They dined before returning. Much of her time was taken up with studies, Sunday and Bible schools, and debate society. Her teen years prepared her for her later involvement in various societies in Illinois. That spirit, faith, and perseverance proved necessary in later years. Her academy education was a basic training of the mind and character that contributed more broadly.[94] In her confrontation with the frontier and her struggles against adversity, her romanticism likely played a part.

Other women moved west under very different circumstances and at different points in their lives. Tradition came in many hues. As an infant, Eleanora Garner Colton moved with her family from Ohio to the newly founded town of Columbus City, Iowa, where her father started a mercantile business.[95] She grew up along with the town. Life was hard but full: "Each child could do something useful about the home" (15). A sense of tradition shapes her memoirs: "The life of the people in those early days, and especially of the young folk, was more serious than in the present day. Amusements were just as enjoyable as those now, but so different. They enjoyed dancing, but it was more dignified than the dances of today" (7). Singing schools and clubs, spelling and geography schools, and the skating pond were prime gathering places. As a teacher, Eleanor later passed on her views.[96]

Lucy Gillmore Cowles's (1833–1914) *Memories* (1833–1914) of her youth in Ohio and Iowa ring a familiar bell.[97] The challenges and uncertainties of a new life in the West confronted her family in its efforts to establish for her a traditional female path. Her memoirs begin in Athens, Ohio, where her father "located that his sons might have the benefit of the educational advantages there" (9). After her mother died in Lucy's fourth year, the family made its home with an aunt. Her father then married the principal of the local female seminary, a Mount Holyoke graduate, for whom Lucy's "admiration was extreme" (10).

Giving up what Lucy thought was a lucrative business, her father bought a farm along the National Road in Granville, Ohio. Having lost one brother, and finding Granville uninteresting, Lucy and her sister, Helen, "were surely dependent on each other, and were often very lonely and unhappy" (11). This common experience in growing up in new territories, especially among women, is sometimes lost amid nostalgia. Women's strong kin and sibling bonds eased their transitions.

Life on the farm, Fairmount, was interesting. A steady stream of visitors, including traveling clergymen, stopped by for entertainment. The house was also a station on the Underground Railroad and a site of abolitionist councils. Exciting encounters with fugitives and the men pursuing them influenced Lucy's growing up. Lucy and Helen were supervised by governesses and their elderly grandmother. In the evening their father would read from the Bible as the family sang hymns around the fire. He also read from newspapers, often the *New York Tribune*. They played music and sometimes danced. The girls' Boston-reared grandmother criticized their social awkwardness.

After selling the farm and sending Lucy to an aunt in Circleville, Ohio, to go to school, while Helen was in Athens, Ohio, the father moved west to Keokuk, Iowa, in 1850. Although Lucy was already sixteen, she later associated her "early girlhood," meaning adolescence, with Keokuk. She spent time with nearby nuns and passed one summer at a Quincy, Illinois, school organized by Catherine Beecher.

A center of navigation on the Mississippi, Keokuk experienced a "great boom." "There were more young men than girls, so all were belles," Lucy recalled (21). Excursions to St. Louis were major social events. Lucy was an undoubted belle on the boats. Her father's business losses led her "to make the most of what I could get . . . I think I usually compared favorably with the other girls, and was ever among those invited first, and always by some of the foremost young men" (22). Her early romances took place here. An engagement to a Quincy attorney much older than she did not last. Spending much of her time at the home of a cousin who had two daughters near her own age, Lucy "was spoken of as much too wild," to her mind a charge without merit (23).

By the outbreak of Civil War, Lucy was married with two small children. After the war, which temporarily delayed her path to marital stability, her new family headed west, often operating hotels on main railroad lines, a fitting metaphor for migrants' paths.

In contrast to Lucy Cowles's peripatetic rural path was Mary Ann Hubbard's migration from Massachusetts to Chicago, where she spent her teen and young adult years.[98] Her father was a merchant who had previously relocated from Newark to Vermont, and then to Middleboro, Massachusetts, where Mary Ann (1820–1909) spent her first sixteen years. When his business suffered during the 1812 embargo, her mother's brothers, who had long provided assistance, bought a farm where Mary Ann's family lived. With Sabbath and secular schooling, and instruction in knitting and sewing, her upbringing was traditional.

In 1836, when Mary Ann was sixteen, the family followed her brother to Chicago, where he had gone into business. Settling into the fledging town, Mary Ann experienced a major conflict with her parents. She wanted to continue her schooling, but they wished her to enter society. An unsatisfactory but proper solution lay in sending her to Iowa to care for her sister. Mary Ann thus took a traditional path as family housekeeper.

At twenty-three Mary Ann freed herself from her family bonds by marrying Gurdon Hubbard. Repeating the tradition of extended family by taking in young female kin, Mary Ann presided over a home that included two nieces and a servant. Family-centered before and after marriage, Mary Ann concluded that her life had been "long and beautiful." For her, urban migration had been neither liberating nor improperly tempting. For some of her peers the country proved more exciting than the city was for her; for others it was the city that made the difference.[99]

For other young women growing up along the broad and pliable traditional path, migration and family wove different connections and different routes. Nancy A. Hunt's trail to California was long but comparatively simple.[100] It came at the end of her youth. Family and migration are inseparable in her narrative, and movement was part of her heritage. Nancy's parents were born and raised on Ohio's farming frontier. Once married, they wasted no time in following family migration habits. Their wedding trip consisted of moving to Indiana, where they built a home and farm. Her mother developed rheumatism, and both parents suffered from chills and fever; this led them to join a paternal uncle's family in Illinois. At the time Nancy was three years old, her sister Sarah six weeks: "Pretty young to be an emigrant to a new country, to be one of the pioneers!" (319).

"Here my school days began," she writes. "Scholars being scarce, the teacher got my parents to let me go, although a baby not four years old yet" (319). Primitive conditions did not restrain gender differentiation: "The girls never studied arithmetic in the school there, but did study grammar: the boys studied arithmetic, but no grammar" (320). Nancy's mother suffering as an invalid, the children were put to work early in and outside the house, the girls doing most of the housework. Religion was central to family life. Nancy's immersion took place too early for her to remember the age "when I began the Christian warfare." She recalls being "a bashful, timid Christian when I was young" (320).

Her single life ended early: "At seventeen and a half years I was married: no one seemed to think I was too young, nor my husband, Alexander Cotton, who was just past nineteen" (320). Taking no wedding trip, they shared a wedding night custom: "The company came thronging at the door to catch a glimpse of us in bed. Then they left us" (320–321).

Settling nearby, the new couple worked an eighty-acre farm that Nancy's father gave them. With their own labor and her father's assistance, they did well: "I fully believe there never was a happier couple" (321). Proximity to family and former homes made early adulthood satisfying, but Nancy's happiness was short-lived. Her husband's health deteriorated; he developed "the dread disease, consumption. Then our troubles began" (321). The youngest of their three small children "inherited" her father's weakness and died. In 1854 doctors said "that the only chance for my husband to live was to come to California that year" (321). With her father already suffering California fever, Nancy's family joined in the move. The trip, from March to August 1854, was long and difficult. Alexander died just as they entered California.

At first Nancy and her young sons remained with her parents. But women were scarce, and "so many came to ask me to work for them, I concluded to hire out to work, although I had never worked away from home" (326). Offered $50 to $75 a month, she left the children with her

mother. Nancy's first new acquaintance was R. D. Hunt, "an old bachelor," four years in California. He drove her to the large country hotel
where she was to work. Return to the marital state followed a short span
of partial independence.

Nancy Hunt's relatively straightforward path of growing up, with many
moves and challenges against a background of tradition, took her across
the continent, tying growing up and family formation to western migration
and settlement, and to tradition and change. For other women, as for men,
migration across the Atlantic Ocean was a key part of growing up. Such
long-distance paths could be relatively simple or quite complicated.

The memoirs of German-born Ottilie Fuchs Goeth (1836–1926) tell one
such tale.[101] At the age of ten, she migrated with her family in 1845 from
a town in Mecklenburg. They came as part of an organized migration
scheme, the Adelsverein or Society for the Protection of German Immigrants in Texas. Ottilie's father was a pastor and a musician. He chafed at
church policy and lacked sufficient income for his growing family. His
children were unaware of the family financial situation. Ottilie recalls:
"Our childhood was carefree and gay, the environment of our home
providing the best possible opportunity for our development . . . Mother
looked after us with unfailing care and kindness, while Father taught us as
best he could and time allowed" (14). Her parents "never mentioned [emi-
gration] around the children. In any case, we had all studied English" (20).

Ottilie's memories blend tradition and change, creating the former anew.
Her father had two motives in emigrating. First, he no longer wished to
earn his living by preaching, but in Germany he lacked opportunities to
use his musical and literary talents to support his family. Second, "he
wished to provide greater opportunities for his children, rather than allowing them to be stifled, body and soul, through the miserable conditions
prevailing in Germany" (21). The family sailed from Bremen in 1846. In
Galveston reports on the Adelsverein were so discouraging that Ottilie's
father decided to settle on his own. Concluding that children are adapt-
able, Ottilie recalls that she "soon felt at home in Texas. It became my
second fatherland" (39).

Admitting his failure at farming, her father decided to teach music, first
as a private tutor, then at an "institute for young ladies." The gift of a
large tract of land on the Colorado River became the family's permanent
settlement in Texas, a place the sons could inherit, achieving their father's
goal. Settled, comfortable family life took root. The Fuchses purchased a
piano, which her father taught Ottilie to play.

Among their many visitors was Carl Goeth, whom Ottilie first met in
1855: "I was nineteen years old and did not at first entertain such thoughts
[of marriage]. The early death of my sister Lulu made a deep impression

on me as a child, and I felt disinclined to marry very young. Additionally, I had been deeply occupied with the reading of Schiller" (60). Classically educated and trained as a printer, Goeth could find no work in his trade, so he worked as a saddler in New Braunfels. Compared to other young men, he "was certainly not too obvious in his advances" (60). Occupied with domestic labors, Ottilie lost sight of him. The pressures she felt to conform to tradition were affected by her sisters' experiences: "I did not marry quite as young as was the general custom of the day. Because it upset Mother when my two older sisters became engaged so very young, I had determined not to do likewise. I had decided not to become engaged until I could be sure that my parents would be pleased and in favor of the idea. In those days there was ample opportunity for a young lady to marry. There were hordes of cultured and attractive young men in Texas, constantly on the lookout for a wife. Young women, on the other hand, were scarce" (66–68).

On her twenty-third birthday Ottilie wondered "if the one I cared for might be thinking of me—my Posa and Carlos fantasies probably having subsided somewhat" (68). Then a letter—"doubtlessly a much more straightforward love letter than any Carlos might have composed"—came from Carl (68). Marriage in September 1859 followed a chance meeting at Christmas 1858. With marriage came removal to New Ulm, where Carl worked and had a house. Leaving home after twenty-four years of close-knit, happy family life was hard for Ottilie, who "shed many tears" as she left her parents' home: "At most I had been away from home for a few days at a time and had come to believe that my beloved little mother could not get along without me" (73).

As these experiences show, migration shaped paths of growing up for many individuals and families. These movements both challenged and reinforced traditions. The impacts were multiple and long-lasting, and they rippled out like waves, affecting later developments. The memories of Sabrina Ann Loomis Hills provide an excellent example of a life influenced at virtually every major point by movement within one region.[102] Born in 1811 in Madrid, St. Lawrence County, New York, she was one of three children of a Vermont-born father and a Connecticut-born mother.

Physical relocation punctuated Sabrina's earliest years. The War of 1812 led the family to Poultney, Vermont, before Sabrina was three. A year later they moved to Albany, New York, an exciting town to a child. Significant family disruptions resulted when her parents contracted typhus when she was eight. The family rejoined Sabrina's grandparents in Vermont to give her parents an opportunity to restore their health. Disposing of their household goods provoked battles between mother and children over what "prizes" to keep. Parting with friends was also difficult, but the novelty of the journey captured the children's attention. On the farm in Charlotte, they encountered "a bewildering number of names of uncles and aunts and cousins," all wishing to see them and "take us out on exhibition" (11). Three months later Sabrina's parents established their own home nearby, and she began to attend the district school.

By the spring of 1820, when Sabrina was almost ten, her parents rented a house in the town of Vergennes, Vermont, twelve miles away. "This caused general regret" was Sabrina's later understatement (13). The country "had more real attraction for us children than the confines of a city life." Sabrina missed winter evenings of paring bees, spelling schools, and sleigh rides, as well as family gatherings, harvests, and domestic activities.

For Sabrina the "delightful" ride to her new home was sufficient transition. Liking their new environs, the children went to school, first to Mr. Edmund, then to Mrs. Cook, and then to Miss Smith. Town life was active. A military academy opened nearby, and traveling entertainments were performed. A missionary enterprise to a "separate village" of French-Canadian workers began, with a number of girls "deputized to induce the children," to attend Sunday school (14). Sabrina called on members of the church and storekeepers to donate clothing. The benevolent "were rewarded by seeing them coming into Sunday school bright and happy" (14). She also recalled the high level of cultivation among Vergennes's citizens.

After four years the family moved to Whitehall, New York. Leaving was hard: "The parting with my young friends was so affecting that I was obliged to keep my berth most of the day. My father and mother often being moved to tears" (17). Their new home was a thriving town of three thousand on the route to Lake Champlain and Montreal.

Changes threatened all mobile families. Sabrina recalls: "In the fall a new trial awaited us." Her eighteen-year-old brother wanted to go to New York City and get a clerkship. "In this he was opposed, but after awhile my parents yielded to his wishes." At his parting everyone tried to be cheerful, "but O, those treacherous tears, that have so often betrayed my feelings" (18). Prior moves had made the family closer and new departures more difficult. For Sabrina frequent migration combined the pleasure of new places with the pain of constant separation.

An aunt in New York now urged fifteen-year-old Sabrina to visit. Her brother added his voice, and her parents consented. "My time was almost wholly taken up in sight-seeing, visiting museums and places of arts" (20). Sabrina returned with her aunt, who also visited Charlotte and Vergennes. The value of such connections, especially for the mobile, was great. Sabrina's family next faced the question of their teenage daughter's path: "Now came a trial; aunt could not think of returning without me. My parents were equally loth to part with me, but on thinking it over came to the conclusion that it was best, as my brother was desirous for me to come also" (21). She spent a happy year in New York.

Returning for the last year of her unmarried life, Sabrina found several of her peers "on the married list, and others contemplating the same step" (22). Although marriage was expected and unquestioningly planned, it nonetheless posed another trial of family separation. At nineteen, Sabrina recalls: "I had also been solicited to give my heart and hand to Nathan Cushman Hills . . . I found cousins and friends in the same dilemma. This afforded us means of speculation and conjecture, rather enviable, nevertheless, and was a new tie to our affections" (22–23). The pain of separation from extended family, a hint of underlying doubt, and powerful female bonds all percolate through those words.

Her marriage consummated, her path of growing up completed, one transition awaited. Sabrina expresses it without irony: "The next summer it was evident that my husband had caught the Western fever, and there was no alternative but to make up our minds to be pioneers to the, then, far West. This decision caused my parents and myself many a wakeful night" (23). Like her father before her, Sabrina at twenty parted from home and family traditions.

Sabrina Hills's relocation after marriage highlights the role of marriage in both traditional and newer paths, for departure from the family home was a major juncture at the end of growing up. In a time when migration was common and very much a part of childhood and youth, the links between marriage and migration took on special meaning, and sometimes a real poignance.

The story of Harriet Hutchinson and Lucius Salisbury in the mid-1840s captures this aspect of growing up.[103] Harriet waited in Vermont for four years while her intended went to Missouri in search of economic independence prior to marriage. He had planned to return to Vermont to marry after one year. After a number of false starts in farming and store clerking, much suffering on Harriet's part, and strains between the two, Lucius returned and they married. Harriet, as her letters make clear, feared leaving Vermont, but she also feared losing her fiancé. She wondered if he would ever return for her. When he went west, Lucius was nineteen and Harriet eighteen.

Just after Lucius left, Harriet wrote him on October 16, 1843: "It must have been hard parting with your friends the morning you left . . . I believe all the young people are going to the West" (275). In July 1844 she warned him that if he planned to farm, she would be of little help, for she had had an indulgent mother. Harriet feared that Lucius's sister had been writing falsely about her: "I am sure Lucius if you were here I should not be any more strict than what I am now. Your friends are watching me every chance they can get I suppose, but I do not blame them for that" (277). In February 1845, obviously unhappy, Harriet wrote: "I should like to be the one to comfort and console you in your lonely moments. I suppose you have someone as well as myself . . . I should like to know how you have spent these long winter days and evenings? You did not tell who you have to keep house for you" (278). Urging him to come home, she penned: "You should not feel that you are obliged to be married as soon as you come for you are not. We have better wait until you can engage in some business that would suit you but we might enjoy ourselves so much better if you were here so we could see each other often" (278).

For his part, Lucius made it clear that he had no prospects in New England, that they could live "cheaper, better and easier" in the West. He urged Harriet to come west with his brother and sister-in-law (279). Harriet recognized that had she known that separation and delay in marriage would be so lengthy, she would never have believed he would return to her. She was reluctant to leave her mother. She feared for Lucius's health and worried that he might enlist to fight in the Mexican War.

At the end of 1846, Lucius and Harriet decided that he would come home in the spring, and that Harriet would return west with him. On April 13, 1847, Lucius and Harriet were married. They moved to Keytesville, Missouri, where Lucius ran a general merchandise partnership. In 1858 they moved to a farm, and in 1860 they laid out the town of Salisbury and built a store and post office; Harriet delivered the mail. In 1892 they moved to another farm in Kenton, Ohio. With marriage Harriet set out on a path of constant movement, mixing tradition and change.

Usually but sometimes misleadingly dissociated from histories of migration are the experiences of southern women, especially in planter families. They constitute one segment of the traditional female pattern, with contradictions and conflicts that on occasion challenged the lines of tradition. As with others along this route, southern traditions were sometimes of rather recent vintage, and the lines between change and tradition were blurred. Despite myths to the contrary, for example, serious schooling even for the daughters of privilege was new to the early republic, and in plantation society that learning was limited. For many girls their academy years, often spent away from home among other young women, were their one period of intellectual development and semi-independence. Among the many contradictions of plantation life for southern white women was a protected, sheltered childhood and adolescence in the care of the slaves they were expected to command. Mothers played the major role in domestic socialization and training.[104] Furthermore, as Steven Stowe observes, "the distinctness of woman's realm, and the intensity of the homosocial bonds it fostered, coexisted with the strong social claims of marriage and the family. Ideally, woman's sphere was to intersect with the world of men in a harmonious bond. Yet this coexistence between intense female friendships and the claims of marriage generated tension that many antebellum women had to confront as they matured."[105]

Emily Virginia Semple's *Reminiscences of My Early Life and Relatives* shows the elemental conflicts and contradictions in growing up a part of the southern planter class.[106] Caught between idyll and isolation, her memories are telling. Born in 1829 in Lowndes County, Alabama, on the land on which her grandfather had settled his children as they married, Emily passed what she remembered as a happy childhood. She kept in contact with kin throughout the South, traveling with her grandparents or her mother to see them.

Her mother, Emily reports, disliked living on the plantation six miles from her grandfather's house. Plantation life was isolated and lonely for women and children. Emily's closest childhood relationship was with her grandmother: "I loved my grandmother better than my own parents—always cried and begged to be left with her which was usually done. I have never forgotten the loss she was to me when she died. Never wanted anything that was denied me without thinking 'If grandma was only living she would give it to me.'" A famous beauty, grandmother "reigned supreme in her sphere, husband and children bowing to her dictum as family law" (5). Her other grandmother, a hundred miles away in Mobile, stood out for her force of character and strength of will: "No familiarity even with her own children. Hers was to command and theirs to obey. Her duties were stern and fulfilled to the letter" (11). Emily at age sixteen spent a winter with her. Other than her relatives she had few consistent female role models.

In 1840, when Emily was about eleven, her father sold his property and moved to Clarke County, Alabama, "to the distress of my mother and all the children" (13). This move greatly disturbed domestic life. Emily was left in Montgomery with her aunt to attend school until a new plantation was built and a school started. Her father bought her first piano in Mobile and advertised for a music teacher. He also hired a "regular 'Irish school teacher,'" to whom he paid a salary and who brought along his other students. Into the boys he "whaled" the "Rule," along with Latin, Greek, and mathematics. "The girls were spared on the idea then prevailing, I supposed, that it was not as necessary for girls to be taught as it was for the boys" (15). Emily's brother was sent away to college, but her tutoring stopped when she was sixteen. Every Friday a dancing master taught either at Emily's or at her uncle's house. Lessons were followed by "a grand Virginia Reel in which all the older people joined . . . Those were happy days," Emily recalled. On Sundays the family would go to her grandmother's church and "sit as mute as mice and listen to the sermon, relieved as I then thought by singing the beautiful old hymns" (17).

Emily spent the "greater part of my time as a young lady"—her adolescence—with her aunt in Montgomery, "a gay place" in antebellum years, where she finished her social training. "The strictest propriety reigned in the intercourse of young people, but no lack of fun and frolic. We were strictly prohibited from attending public balls where the company was indiscriminate. There were private parties enough given for the young people to meet and do all the courting necessary to bring about the marriages of myself, all my cousins and friends" (19). Emily was married in November 1848, at the age of nineteen, in a Catholic ceremony, "Mr. Semple" having been received into the church a year earlier. Hardly alone in her era, she wove her own fabric of traditions old and new.[107]

Work and Migration

Tradition and change also combined to affect work and migration, the second female subpath. As with others who followed more traditional female paths, these young women's responses, strategies, and resources took different forms. Often rooted in traditional assumptions about the family economy to which all members contributed, the paths that developed took women away from home, physically and psychologically. Changes in productive relations impinged on individual and family dynamics.

Those whose growing up followed this route confronted questions of authority, relationship, and dependence, on the one hand, and autonomy, individual development, and choice of paths, on the other. Conflict with parents and employers marked such journeys, and struggles within oneself were sometimes severe. The shifting connections between gender and social change were pronounced, especially as both work before marriage and manual labor became acceptable, at least temporarily, for rural and poor girls. Questions about the legitimacy of women's work outside the home persisted, however, as new middle-class gender notions developed partly in opposition to the idea of women in the work force. Movement by many young women across middle- and working-class lines—schoolteachers and textile millhands, for example—marked this era and its contradictions. This path thus contributes to the story of class formation and gender definition.

Contradictory at their core were the blurred borders between traditional family connections and dependence, as opportunities increased for movement and for greater degree of personal freedom and sense of agency. That complex cultural symbol the mill girl captures these contradictions, as the tales of Lucy Larcom and Harriet Hanson Robinson, and their subsequent cultural appropriation, show.[108]

Work and migration became acceptable if ambivalent routes away from declining rural areas with few economic or marital prospects. This acceptance also spurred increasingly normative strictures against outside work for middle- and upper-class women and about which kinds of work were suitable. As a factory proletariat developed by the fifth decade of the century, gender and class formed new interconnections, and the sphere of legitimacy contracted.[109] Socioeconomic changes, cultural development, and transformations of growing up were related in intimate and complex ways. First-person sources make us privy to the experiences and meanings that resulted from such choices, whether the authors pursued novel paths or strove to combine change with tradition, and whether schoolroom, mill, workshop, or domestic labor was the destination.

Confronting their circumstances growing up in Cowbell Corner, later Derry, New Hampshire, in the 1830s, Hannah and Mary Adams chose the path of the needle trades: millinery and tailoring.[110] First- and third-born children, the two eldest daughters among eight children in a fifth-generation New England farming family, they grew to late adolescence in a long-settled, integrated rural community—a setting they missed when they left home for a busy commercial town.

The sisters left primarily because of economic pressures. Although their father owned two farms, livestock, and a sawmill, his income did not support the large family. In the 1830s each of the four eldest children, on reaching their late teens or early twenties, sought an independent economic course. Hannah left home in 1831 at age twenty-one to teach in the adjoining town of Sandown. Educated in the Salem district schools and at Atkinson Academy, she had good qualifications. Illness forced her to return home, where she spent most of the next two years recuperating, living with an aunt and uncle.

Like most girls who shared her family circumstances, Hannah's sister Mary had been taught to sew. She took an apprenticeship with a Nashua, New Hampshire, tailor in October 1833, when she was twenty-one. With Mary's help, Hannah obtained a millinery apprenticeship in Nashua the next spring. A third daughter, Eliza, left home to work in the weaving room of the Nashua Corporation but stayed there less than six months. The eldest son, John, went to Maine seeking lumber work. By 1834 only four children remained at home. One girl made straw hats and helped her mother, two sons assisted their father in the sawmill, and the youngest son learned his letters.[111]

Moving to Nashua in late adolescence, Hannah and Mary confronted a new world, as their letters reveal. They had to learn a skill from a person outside family or community which would provide them with an income. Learning a trade was no simple task, given the transformations of commercial and early industrial capitalism. There were far more young persons seeking apprenticeships (a declining practice) and other learning situations than there were employers to provide them. The Adams brothers encountered the same problems. Hannah's letters home suggest no trouble with Miss Brown, her employer; Mary, however, struggled long to get Mr. Hickey to fulfill his promise to train her in cutting out patterns. Wanting to acquire the full range of skills, she had carefully and tenaciously bargained the terms of her apprenticeship in advance, and she sought to combat his efforts to exploit her labor. The sisters sent home patterns, information on styles, and detailed instructions on hatmaking for the family to use in domestic production.

In addition to conflicts with employers, these young women also faced a new world of regulated time controlled by others.[112] The sisters complained of long hours, of being "hurried," and of unaccustomed supervision. With breaks for meals, Hannah worked eleven or twelve hours a day and Mary fourteen. That left little time for leisure. They felt socially isolated and missed the female company they had had in working at home. In particular they chafed at the close supervision and changing moods of their employers.

The sisters' adjustment to their new lives in Nashua accommodated changes in their family relationships. Mary continued to refer to herself as "one of the family circle" and sent advice to her siblings, but she had lost her authority over them and her place as her mother's chief assistant. Both sisters admitted feeling a loosening of family ties. Within a year of leaving home their relationship to the family economy also changed. Despite earning wages, they still requested—sometimes without success—that food be sent to them from the farm. Hannah wondered about the appropriateness of their request: "You will think we are pretty good beggars but as it is from a fathers house I supposed we shall be excusable" (29). With time and relocation, norms and expectations changed. Separation reduced dependence, but not always as designed or expected.

Although conflicts were many, new working and living conditions difficult, and separation from family painful, the Adams sisters found their environment interesting and enjoyable. Meeting people, attending local events and holiday celebrations, going to church, and the like provided pleasures. They heard about other work opportunities. They traveled a bit. Whatever they needed or wanted had to be purchased: "Everything costs money," Mary wrote (30). Gaining new skills and aspirations, Mary and Hannah preserved certain traditional ways as they pursued their paths. Hannah assured her mother, for example, "We had an excellent discourse . . . upon dress . . . and unnecessary caution to me for I have not the wherewith to be gaudy" (30).

In 1838 the sisters moved to Manchester, New Hampshire, where they opened their own tailoring shop in an act of sisterly independence. Business prospered until they retired in 1880. Concerned with maintaining family connections, Mary preserved their letters. The sisters, we discover, negotiated their paths well.[113]

A generation earlier Lucy Fletcher Kellogg's diary reflected well the mixing of new and old and the blurring of class and family lines as she traveled her path to adulthood in a time of fundamental change.[114] Lucy (1793–1891) was the third child of a Sutton, Massachusetts, farming family. A small farm inherited from Lucy's grandfather was insufficient to support the family. As Lucy put it, "In accordance with the instincts of New England people, they must sell their farm and move to New Hampshire or some other new place." The family moved to Croydon, New Hampshire, for five years, where the father "merchandized." They next bought a farm in Worcester, Massachusetts, in 1800, where the family of five children remained for eighteen years.

"Worcester is the town where I spent my youth," writes Lucy. "We had good common school advantages. My father lived in a large house and kept a tavern. When I was twelve years old, I attended a dancing school, with my brothers and two sisters, which I enjoyed much." At sixteen she attended a boarding school in Sutton, "where I learned some things not taught in the common schools in those days, such as geography with the use of maps, needlework, drawing and painting in watercolors." Despite these comforts, Lucy had other occupation:

> Before my boarding school experience, when I was thirteen, my sister Fanny and myself went into a town adjoining Worcester, to learn the art of braiding straw. After that we earned our own clothes . . . My father owned a small farm, but had not a sufficient income to supply his daughters with all their wants. But the war of 1812 coming on, the straw business failed, and we changed our business. We got a couple of looms and set them up in our east room, and we took cotton yarn from the factories, which were beginning to spread in Massachusetts, and wove fine shirtings, gingham, and bed tickings for the factories, and for ourselves, as English goods were not to be had . . . We continued our business of weaving four or five years.

Thus, Lucy's family developed a flexible economic strategy that allowed their early adolescent daughters to gain practical income-producing skills prior to completing school. Straw braiding was useful at the least to offset the cost of the daughters' "wants." It also provided a basis for a shift to weaving as an economic venture to capitalize on wartime privations and generate needed income. Lucy's experience shows how such productive and remunerative skills could add to the family economy while the girls remained at home, leaving only to learn the skill (and for boarding school). The course was similar for their brothers'. Living at home, one went into his father's brickmaking business; the other was apprenticed to the printer Isaiah Thomas. All the children acquired craft skills, although there is no doubt that both old and new expectations about their use differed, at least in part, according to gender.

Fanny married and in 1817 moved to Chautauqua County, New York. With their mother's consent, Lucy accompanied the newlyweds to help her delicate sister. "This was a romantic journey for me," she writes. Lucy had been told that the justice of the peace was single. The sisters "enjoyed the new country well." Lucy applied to teach at a small local school, a new line of work offering potentially greater autonomy in living apart from her family. After teaching for several years, she met Titus Kellogg, who boarded at the same place. She married him the next winter at the age of twenty-five. Lucy's adolescent training and experience surely paid off in helping her meet her new family's needs.

A common presence in the lore about young migrating and working women is the fabled New England mill girls. The literary abilities (and excesses) displayed in Lucy Larcom's *New England Girlhood,* Harriet Hansen Robinson's *Loom and Spindle,* and the pages of the *Lowell Offering* ensure their place in history.[115] Historical research qualifies impressions based on the literary self-representations of exceptional individuals. What remains striking about the original presentations is the sensitive portrayal of the girls' ambivalence at leaving home, migrating to work in new mills that were exciting but also frightening places in their mechanized order and pace. The youth of these girls, in many cases from declining farming areas—though most were older than eleven-year-old Lucy, they were commonly in their mid- to late teens and early twenties—is striking. Mill girls from migrating families, often female-headed ones like Harriet Robinson's and Lucy Larcom's, continued to reside at home and were somewhat younger than rural migrants. With links not only of work but also of place of origin and kinship, a community formed in the boarding-houses which eased adaptation and the pain of separation. It also encouraged collective actions, from literary production to strikes.[116]

As cause and consequence of their narrative production, the girls created a collective literary identity. Though important to their shared consciousness, it complicates the study of mill migration and work as a path of growing up.[117] Nancy Cott has identified the contradictions in expression such as Lucy Larcom's. One is the clash between a traditional emphasis on the usefulness of work as compared, on the one hand, to work as the end of childhood innocence and, on the other hand, to industrial labor as temporary and not self-defining. These attitudes allowed Lucy and her scribbling sisters to treat their industrial experience as a form of education, a stage of growing up that mediated between ideal rural childhood and the relative independence of adulthood. As Cott notes, the representation of "woman's sphere" is also contradictory. For example, Lucy criticizes domesticity as "narrowing" and celebrates collectivity, education, and paid work. But she concludes her memoir: "I have always regarded it as a better ambition to be a true woman than to become a successful writer . . . I never had a career."[118]

Born in 1824, Lucy Larcom entered the mills of Lowell, Massachusetts, in 1835. If precocious, her path was otherwise typical. Born and raised in Beverly, where her father had a store, she later romanticized her early years of communal, familial rural bliss and her schooling and religious foundation. The "fall" came after her father died, leaving her widowed mother with eight children. With few choices, her mother moved to Lowell to operate a corporation boardinghouse. After a brief period at grammar school, to which she later returned, Lucy joined the labor force.

To Lucy, poetry and mill work were inextricably combined. She relates the importance of communal connections among the girls and the place of the literary magazines within the collective culture that formed around the workplace. With boardinghouses, churches, and voluntary associations in close proximity, the girls collectively refashioned their paths of growing up. For many migrants such associations made mill work acceptable. Sisterly relations among the girls allowed them to share their experiences, deal with demands, and make sacrifices together.[119] Nor were the wages, higher than teachers' salaries before the 1840s, an insignificant factor in the prominence of mill work along the paths of many young girls.

Lucy lived in Lowell from 1835 to 1845, working much of the time but also studying, writing, and producing a literary magazine. When she left, she joined another great migration of young persons to the West. She was lured through her church, by the chance to teach or engage in missionary work, a calling in which some of her Lowell acquaintances preceded her. The combination in late adolescence and early adulthood of work as a mill girl and schoolteaching was then neither jarring nor unusual. Each was a common experience for women in this era, and both were routes away from declining opportunities elsewhere. One sign of class lines in flux was that daughters from middle-class families could work as either or both.[120]

In 1846 Lucy and a roommate who was preparing to be a teacher went west to Illinois along with Lucy's sister and ailing brother-in-law. Attending Monticello Seminary, Lucy prepared, then taught, returning to Massachusetts in 1852 to write. To Lucy's tale, with small alterations, may be compared the equally fabled representations of Harriet Robinson, a sister in letters as well as in textile work. The two shared ambitions for education and literary expression. Leaving the mills and marrying, Harriet went on to a literary career.

Other young women who followed similar paths to, and from, the mills placed a different emphasis in their accounts, as we find in the diaries of Susan E. Parsons Brown Forbes (1824–1910).[121] Mill work took her from a farm in Epsom, New Hampshire, to the Middlesex Woolen Mills in Lowell in 1843 at age nineteen. Her journey continued with schoolteaching from 1845 to 1859, when she married.

Susan began her diary in 1841 when she was a seventeen-year-old academy student boarding in Pittsfield, Massachusetts. Her adolescent activities included classes, singing school, church meetings, sewing circle, calls by a peddler, and visits from her parents. This typical life continued until January 1843, when Susan left for Lowell to board at Mrs. Stuckney's and to work in the mills. She was joined by her sister within a week. Her experience, however, was not like Lucy Larcom's.

Susan enjoyed a full social and cultural life in Lowell. She has virtually nothing to say about the mills or her work other than reporting wages received and times not spent working. On May 11, 1843, she wrote: "In the Mill as usual. Wish I was at Epsom or Pitts.[field] or Pembroke." A week later, more vehemently, she wrote that she was still within the "brick walls of a hate Factory" (May 20). In July Susan noted that it was six months since she had come to Lowell. She now reported month by month: "Eight months since I first entered the Middlesex—Since I saw home! Alone among strangers! Oh, when shall I return?" (August 18). Lowell and its mills were places she strongly desired to escape.

By January 1845 (there is no diary for 1844) Susan, now twenty-one, was back in Pittsfield. Apparently not working, she shared a bed with other young women. In May she was engaged to teach school. She also traveled with female friends. In August she took up a private school position that barely lasted the month. September brought another teaching post. Often her father would drive her to the school; sometimes she walked. Susan also visited friends and relatives and attended concerts and singing school. Sometimes she lived at home; at other times she boarded out. Usually though not always teaching, she remained close to kin and friends, male and female. Sewing and quilting circles occupied her, as did church meetings, including some for "we young folks." Susan attended to her wardrobe and maintained an especially close relationship with a young woman she signifies as "JDR." In 1847 she was teaching in Deerfield, New Hampshire. Her many visitors included several young men. Summer found her teaching and boarding in New Rye.

With her major relocation to the Lowell mills, then a lengthy period of teaching and moving back and forth between home and boardinghouses,

Susan found continuity in her relationships and associations both formal and informal. Her path, at least from age seventeen at the academy in Pittsfield to age thirty-five, when she married in 1859, was one of almost continuous movement over relatively small distances to work in factory or school. A traditional form of youth for a young man perhaps a generation or more earlier, this was a new pattern for a young woman. This prolonged period of single and migrant working took Susan to schools in Georgetown, Massachusetts, in 1847; Pittsfield, Massachusetts, and Deerfield, New Hampshire, in 1848–1851; Mardentown, New Hampshire, in 1852; Marlboro, New Hampshire, in 1854; and the Jewish School in Boston in 1856–1859. In 1856 Susan also worked in Remick's Department Store in Boston.

At about that time she met Alexander Barclay Forbes, a Scottish immigrant and later founder of Forbes and Wallace Department Stores in Springfield, Massachusetts. They married in 1859; she continued teaching for a while. Later activities in voluntary and charitable organizations, and successful assumption of Alexander's financial affairs after his 1895 retirement owing to ill health, likely were anchored in her lengthy work experience and her pattern of growing up.

The widely published author Emily Chubbock Judson suffered much more severely from her time in the mills than did Susan. That was one cost of a path shaped by migration and work within the context of a family's struggle with poverty. In her *Life and Letters* Emily shows that she had learned from her early experiences the necessity of independence for women.[122]

Emily was born near Hamilton, New York, where her poor but respectable family had moved from New Hampshire in search of improved circumstances. Her father lacked shrewdness and energy, and he was often ill. Emily was a delicate child; her mother feared that she would have her daughter but a short time. Emily writes, "I remember being much petted and indulged during my first years" (15).

In 1828, when Emily was eleven, the family moved to Pratt's Hollow, a small village with a woolen factory. "We . . . did not know on one day what we should eat the next," Emily recalls, "otherwise, I should not have been placed at such hard work." Early work permanently weakened her. "My principal recollections during this summer are of noise and filth, bleeding hands and aching feet, and a very sad heart" (16). When ice stopped the factory's waterwheel, Emily had the respite and satisfaction of two months in the district school, adding to what her sister had taught her after work.

In March 1829 the factory reopened. In June Emily's long-ailing sister Lavinia died, and Emily's health failed soon after. A physician recommended the fresh air and freedom of a farm, but this was not possible. Emily gained some relief, in her imagination at least, from novels borrowed from other factory girls. This reading sparked her idea of becoming one of the fictional characters or "a brilliant poetess (my verse were greatly admired by my brother and sisters), and my name would be famous while the world stood. But nothing satisfied me. Whatever I became, I should die and lose it all" (19). The romantic notion of missionary work in a foreign land also caught Emily's sometimes morbid fancy.

In November 1829 the family moved to a farm. Her brother entered a printing office; her sister returned from a half year with cousins. They suffered from cold but had enough plain food to keep from being hungry. Their father distributed newspapers, further harming his health. With her mother and sister Emily dug up fallen wood from the snowy fields to fuel the fire. She and a sister attended district school whenever possible. The new year brought a season of revivals, including her sister Harriet's conversion and baptism while Emily watched "almost broken-hearted . . . I recollect feeling myself very heart-heavy, because the revival had passed without my being converted. I grew mopish and absent-minded" (21). She and her sister joined twice-weekly Bible classes. This pleased their father.

With spring her father and a son who had returned from five years of farm employment built fences and did other seasonal work. Their large house drew frequent company—pious persons and Hamilton College students. Among these acquaintances were two women who tutored thirteen-year-old Emily in English composition, rhetoric, natural philosophy, eighteenth-century English and French authors, and poetry, especially Byron, who had a lasting impact. Life on the farm improved Emily's health.

By November 1830 her father's attempt at farming had failed. The family moved, huddling in a two-room house. Two sons returned to places elsewhere; one sister took in sewing; two younger children went to school. Emily twisted thread for a weaver. She was among the first to attend an academy that opened in the village. Each night she labored to meet that day's expenses. When the first term ended in August, she resumed work for the threadmaker. One brother purchased a share in a town library and gave Emily the privilege of taking out one book a week. She read Paine's *Age of Reason*, alarming her father.

As winter approached, the family moved into the village, having to meet costs by taking in academy students. Harriet soon died from pneumonia; with a houseful of boarders, the family could not even mourn quietly. Their income did allow them to hire a maid, and Emily returned to school. To make ends meet she rose at two o'clock on Monday mornings to do the washing before nine; on Thursday she did the ironing; on Saturday, with only a half day of school, she baked. She also took in sewing "and so contributed to make good the time consumed in school. My class-mates had spent all their lives in school, and they now had plenty of leisure for study. They were also, all but one, older than myself, and I therefore found it a difficult task to keep up with them without robbing my sleeping hours. I seldom got any rest till one or two o'clock, and then I read French and solved mathematical problems in my sleep" (26).

Emily's health failed again. On the doctor's advice she left school. Her mother hinted that she might find in millinery a good business. Emily disagreed. "'But what do you intend to do?' asked my mother; 'here you are almost fifteen, and you can not go to school always.' That was true enough, and I went away to *think*. At length I proposed attending school one year more, and preparing to be a teacher. But our boarders had proved less profitable than we anticipated; father had been underbid, and so lost one mail route; and then another year in might kill me. I must think of something else" (26–27). Her mother spoke to a milliner, Miss B., about taking Emily into her shop. Good terms were offered, but Emily cried all night.

Hesitantly, the girl approached her teacher and asked if he deemed her capable of teaching school. "'Yes,' said he, 'but you are not half big enough.'" Pretending to visit a farm to improve her health, Emily sought a post. With anxiety, and friends' help, she obtained a teaching job for seventy-five cents and boarding per week. The family was satisfied with the arrangement; her mother "was highly pleased, particularly with the ability I had shown to help myself" (29). In her first boardinghouse, Emily fell homesick, but a weekend at home salved her blues. She taught until August 1832, then returned home happily.

That fall Emily, now fifteen years old, attended the academy, again sewing to pay her way. She writes: "I began to think more of my personal appearance, and of intercourse with my fellow-students; hence I advanced less rapidly in my studies than formerly, though I still made very respectable proficiency" (30–31). Perceiving certain feminine failings, Emily wanted to add dancing school to her activities against her parents' strong strictures about present waste and future danger. She wanted to share the activities of the other girls in the village, to be like them: "I believed what I had often heard and read about the usefulness of this accomplishment, and I knew that a pleasing personal presence, and elegance of manner were invaluable to a woman" (31).

Seeking greater autonomy, Emily told her mother than she would board in the village, "for, as I had my own fortune to look after, I ought to be allowed to follow my own plans" (31). Emily grasped explicitly what many young women and men understood more implicitly: balances of authority and leverage were shifting within families as more young people were earning an income and fewer families were promising inheritances or other inducements for accepting their sway. Distressed, her mother admitted that she'd rather allow dancing than have her daughter move out. After her father admitted failing his children financially and warned that "the village girls whom I wished to imitate were by no means the ladylike models that I supposed," Emily resolved never to dance (31–32). As she grew up, her struggle for self continued.

Through and beyond her teen years Emily taught, boarding in nearby villages, moving from school to school, season to season. Her abilities acknowledged, she was in demand. She studied in the evenings, advancing to Greek. Health and financial problems placed a heavy burden on her. She struggled with her religion, feeling antagonism and unable to experience conversion. Her missionary impulses gained new strength.

In 1839, when Emily was twenty-two, family troubles reached a crisis. Her own health was poor, and her mother was near death. Like many young women Emily turned to a female friend of long standing, Maria Dawson, for comfort. In moving letters to Maria, she expressed her emotions and fears. Emily worried deeply about her femininity as well as her teaching and her family; she feared for her present and future in this world and beyond. She wrote about ill health, ungovernable classrooms, and hopeless schoolkeeping efforts. She wrote, too, about her loneliness and fears over her ability to give and receive love. Maria's recent marriage no doubt stimulated some of Emily's outpourings.

Emily also wrote about contentment, for example, "I have taken my pen to tell you how much happier I am to-day than I was yesterday—happier because, I *will* be" (51). Another friend found her, at twenty-three, a free place at Utica Female Seminary for a term. Her health improved and her learning increased. In 1841, aged twenty-five, Emily was appointed assistant instructor in English. She continued writing, sending poetry and other pieces to local papers. By fall she was heading the composition department at a salary of $150, and was beginning to publish novels such as *Charles Linn* (1841) and *The Great Secret, or How to be Happy* (1842). Early stories, published under the name Fanny Forrester, told of young girls who left farm families for millinery, mills, or service. Some failed; some succeeded.

Added to her family burdens, this workload led to a physical breakdown in 1845. In 1846, however, now almost thirty, Emily finally ended her quest for a romantic end to her long and tortuous path of growing up. With some ambivalence toward the prospect of matrimony, she married a widowed fifty-seven-year-old missionary, the Reverend Dr. Judson. Judson had sought Emily's acquaintance in an effort to secure a literary memorial to his dead wife; he gained her hand.

Once married, Emily joined in Judson's missionary work. Unlike her heroines who found in missionary life their reward, Emily lost her husband in 1850 to disease in the Orient. She died shortly after returning to western New York State in 1851 on the very day on which she was said to have hoped to die, the anniversary of her sister's death and her own marriage.

In its details and emphases Emily's path was more exaggerated than exceptional. She did not live to reap the same rewards as Lucy Larcom, Susan Parsons and their peers. If her experience was extreme, in early death she was not alone.

Less sentimental but no less telling is the story of another woman who taught before marriage, Caroline Barrett White. Recorded in an extraordinary diary she kept for sixty-five years, her experiences testify to her movement, her career in teaching, her transition to marriage, and her self-criticism.[123] Born in Ashburnham, Massachusetts, Caroline (1828–1915) and her family moved in 1830 to Fitchburg, Massachusetts, and later to Newport, New Hampshire. By the time she began her diary—to improve herself, control and observe her emotions and conduct, make impartial judgments, and exercise her penmanship—in 1849 at age twenty-one, she was already teaching school. After acquiring her certification, she taught for two long years before her marriage in 1851, a very common step among women's paths in growing up.

Teaching was hard, exhausting work. It made her weary and prompted her to ask questions about her future. Diary entries mix notes on her family, social life, and voluntary association activities with typical metaphysical and romantic musings over nature and God, self-criticism about dwelling on worldly matters rather than spiritual happiness, and wrenching concerns about her own path and her abilities. On January 18, 1850, Caroline, no feminist, attended a lecture on slavery by Lucy Stone. She found this a "moving sight, to see a woman rise up before such an audience—with all the *undaunted courage* which we are accustomed to think belongs exclusively to the sterner position of mankind. I believe that she is *out of woman's proper sphere*—though I presume she is sincere in thinking her duty calls her into the field."

Caroline worried about her own preoccupation with human selfishness and practicality. More immediately, she noted her weight, at 112 pounds "greater than ever before!" and was anxious about finding a post for the coming season. She gave music lessons, and with numerous peers read Byron's poetry.

Foremost in her jottings was Frank White, her intended, a partner in a Boston tannery. She frequently related her marital fears and hopes to her wavering sense of self and lack of confidence in her character and capabilities. Caroline regularly worried about Frank's health, comfort, and future with her. She did not trust her emotions or responses. When he was ill during the summer of 1850, she attended him. "Would I could do more. No one can [word illegible] sympathy when in suffering more than myself . . . I have some misgivings as to the future—I distrust myself—I know my own weakness so well—but by the aid of my heavenly Father I hope to perform the duties of life acceptably to Him, and to my fellow man."

In the spirit of contemporary domesticity, Caroline was nurtured to internalize guilt and moral responsibility, to treat them as individual and personal issues. Her equally common romanticism interlaced with her internalized morality. Given her doubts about her abilities, Caroline was at risk of painful self-censure, one outcome of the new style of child rearing: "In viewing the day that has passed—I do not feel satisfied with my own improvement of its precious hours" (September 7, 1850). She sometimes traced her sense of failure to her qualifications for teaching: "I am sensible of my disqualification for the office of teacher—but I am in hopes so to exercise the little talent I possess" (September 18, 1850). Caroline expressed a particularly but not uniquely female assimilation of new introspective psychological and characterological emphases. These were signs of the times, and mixed benefits to those striving to reach adulthood. Caroline seemed certain that blame lay within oneself: "I have been examining myself, and my course for the last few years and find that I have been waiting for a lucky turn in the current of affairs—whereby I might be enabled to earn a respectable livelihood—but I cannot see that I have ever made any decided effort" (September 22, 1850). She vowed to persevere.

Caroline's concerns went well beyond her teaching posts. The stage of life she called youth was ending for Caroline and her peers. On a childhood friend's marriage, reminiscing and hoping, but also admitting the loss of womanly youth and companionship, she wrote ambivalently on October 28, 1850:

Feel in the best of spirits tonight. They are ready to overflow—and had I a boon companion with me, who was in the same hilarious mood I should enjoy a frolic right well . . . I wish I could be with her tonight, as then. Have those days passed forever away—and will none other arise like unto them? I trust there are more in store for me, though perhaps they comport not with the dignity of womanhood—and surely E. & I have arrived at that dignified period of existence. Our girlhood has gone! Oh! sad sad thought. And now life with all its active duties, its stern realities and solemn responsibilities is upon us! But the merry shout of girlhood—the ringing laugh of youth is sounding in my ears, and I am young again.

Caroline struggled to balance the uncertain emotions that accompanied the major transitions of adulthood and marriage. The confusion was hardly hers alone. Growing up brought losses as well as gains. Each had its attractions.

Her responses to teaching are typical of her concerns, swinging from nadir to zenith and back again. On September 2, 1850, essaying a balance, she wrote: "I have been in school to-day—& no more encouragement than I received last week. I will not despair however, but 'wait a little longer' . . . I will endeavor to do what I can." Yet on September 5: "Have enjoyed myself in school to-day very much—believe I have tried to discharge my duties faithfully." On other days she deemed herself unqualified. Peaceful government was her goal. Caroline vowed to correct her behavior and keep trying. Authority in the classroom, a general concern of the time and a special concern for women teachers, plagued her and limited her confidence.[124]

Caroline also chafed at the small pecuniary returns from her anxious labors. The task, especially of regularly opening schools for new and different pupils, was trying: "This is the first day of school—task is begun and when I first went in and looked about on the rude countenances before me I almost despaired of finding anything like intelligence among them but as I became accustomed to the different countenances they assumed a more human face" (November 12 and 15, 1850).

Boarding while teaching, Caroline fell prey to loneliness. Receiving two letters on October 23, 1850, one from Frank, the other from her mother, she penned her thanks: "The tears will flow in spite of the pleasure derived from their perusal. I have been separated so long from my mother." Short visits from Frank elicited mixed responses. After a visit one night Caroline noted: "Am glad he came . . . he should have waited longer though by so doing he might have been able to have protracted his stay" (October 26). But on January 20, 1851: "Came home and was sitting by the fire writing, when I heard a rap on the door—opening it I was delighted to see Frank standing before me *large as life*. So after all my disappointment was only for a little season. How pleasant this meeting of friends—yet in the middle of our joy the sad thought that we must soon part, casts a shadow."

As marriage drew near, Caroline made peace with herself. She admitted her fears but with a greater sense of control, expectation, and maturity: "The prospect of my being his 'for better or for worse'—seemed approaching. With many hopes—with many fears do I look upon the consummation of that event which will link my destiny irrecoverably with his." On March 21 at the end of the term: "Received a letter from F. which filled my heart with inward joy though I may not express it." Finally, on June 25, 1851, the eve of her wedding, she balanced her emotional and social accounts:

"This is the last night of my girl's life! The thought makes me sober but not unhappy at all. A new life is to begin tomorrow—a life less free—more anxious—more responsible it may be—but nevertheless I trust—it will not be less happy than the past has been. For my own case there are fewer ties to be broken than is the case with many. I have no home to leave—about which all the sweet associations of childhood and youth cluster . . . Now I go gladly, and I would invoke the blessing of God upon the union about to be formed." Caroline and Frank moved to his "mansion" in Boston, which she found beautiful. According to Caroline their marriage was happy, unlike her teaching career and courtship.

Different in location and circumstances but similar in the role of movement and teaching is the case of Ellen Augusta Parker in Wisconsin.[125] Lacking Caroline's introspection, Ellen had a special sensitivity to moving and the attendant losses and pain it caused young people. When she was three, Ellen's family migrated to Wisconsin. She began her journal in 1852 at age nineteen, living at the time in Muskego with her family. As her account opens, Ellen is busy with domestic work, visits in the neighborhood, and journeys to Milwaukee to shop.

In March of that year Ellen and her friend Louisa attended a Teacher's Institute at Genesee, Wisconsin. They met other young women for tea in a tavern before the evening lecture. Classes alternated with social functions. After one party Ellen unabashedly noted: "Had quite a pleasant time. Danced till two or three o'clock. It was dark and very muddy, and going home we ran against a stump and broke our wagon . . . We did not get to our boarding house till daylight" (March 24, 1852). Arising late, Ellen was dull and sleepy in school.

Returning from the ten-day institute, Ellen resumed her domestic work, churchgoing, and visiting. Nathan Cobb, whom she later married, was among her callers. Her father traveled to his native New Hampshire in June in the hope of improving his poor health. He returned in September "somewhat better," but unable to work much (September 30, 1852).

In the new year, 1853, Ellen reports that she was teaching school and residing at "a very good boarding place" for four weeks in Mr. Peck's district (January 8, 1853). Holiday balls kept her enjoyably occupied, but school presented the usual problems: "Oh dear! Everything has gone wrong today; the young ones have not half got their lessons, and such a *racket* as there has been all day cannot be equaled. And what a lonely, dismal day we have had" (February 11).

With friends regularly coming and going, and herself moving in and out of the family home, Ellen, like so many of her peers, sentimentally but realistically mused: "The same company will never all meet again together. One of them is now gone, another is going ere long, perhaps never to return. Oh, why must friends so soon leave each other's society, where they have enjoyed many happy moments, and wander among strangers who look upon them coldly, and seem to care not what may be their fate? Yet such is the lot of man." This was the problem of a mobile society, and a particular problem of growing up.

Change and mobility are explicit themes in Ellen's frontier diary, typical in certain ways of the experiences of many young people. On her twentieth birthday she comments: "How differently am I situated from what I was one year ago today. Michael Post started for the gold region. Where shall I be one year from this day? None but the great Ruler of all can tell" (March 16, 1853). Ellen also expected to feel loneliness after leaving her pupils at the end of term. Her transitions from home to school and boarding merited no comment; she took them in her stride. Being at home also implied some loneliness: "Another long day has passed into eternity. How slowly time passed to me. I am here all alone with our folks, and not a soul has been here all week . . . I should like to be placed in California for a few minutes this evening, and have a chat with our friend Michael Post" (April 15). Receiving "another letter from Mr. C. [Nathan Cobb] today. I did not expect it. I should be happy to see him this evening, and Persis [her sister], too. She has not been at home in a long time" (April 20).

For more than half a year Ellen neglected her journal. Returning to it in February 1854, she penned: "Under very different circumstances do I now write. My father has gone to his last resting-place. He died the 17th of June last. My brother and sister were married the 9th of November. I have lived with Persis the most of the time this winter" (February 12, 1854). She also had rejected one man's courtship.

In March, washing, ironing, sewing at home, and busy socially, Ellen was almost obsessed with the passage of time and people. She talked about "old times" with several friends, including men who were leaving; she found it hard to grasp that almost a year had passed since she taught at the district school. With a friend Ellen vowed to write in one year's time, wherever they were.

Ellen married Nathan Cobb in October 1854. He died less than two years later. Her sense of loss and loneliness lasted for years. Earlier experiences did not prepare her for the pain of the final departure. The domesticity and sentimentality of Ellen's era and class likely intensified her hardship.

The countless native-born and immigrant daughters who served in the homes of others while growing up, typically between leaving home in their teen or later years and trying to establish their independence, represent one more lane of this subpath. Domestic service was at once an exceptionally broad path often linking growing up and geographic mobility, and an exceedingly contradictory one.[126] Not surprisingly, there are few first-person accounts.

Lizzie A. Wilson Goodenough provides us with one testament.[127] Born in 1844, Lizzie was orphaned in 1860. Residing in Brattleboro, Vermont, to support herself, she worked as a domestic servant prior to her 1869 marriage to Henry F. Goodenough. She worked for several families and sometimes for a merchant tailor firm. From their beginning in 1865, her diary entries testify to the onerous lives of self-supporting young women who had few available alternatives. Faced with financial difficulties, she lamented her lot: "Oh how I wish the time would come when the time would seem pleasant to me. Something to think about besides working away from home and friends past for money. Long years have past since I had a Father home to go to" (March 19, 1865).

Lizzie records endless work: washing, ironing, dressmaking, knitting, baking, cooking, mopping, cleaning up after children. The work was dull. She was often lonely. Time dragged. She worked like a slave, on some days never leaving the house. Sometimes she imagined life without this drudgery; she wished for someone or something to remove her from service. In 1869 Lizzie looked forward to Henry Goodenough's evening visits. On July 4 they walked to a hilltop to pick strawberries, a pleasure contrasting with the demands of her domestic labor. In November the end of service was in sight. She finished making her wedding dress and a shirt for Henry, and they married and moved to their own home. Though still doing domestic labor, Lizzie now worked in her own household. That was one critical step in her passage.

Countless poor working women grew up in circumstances far worse in material or personal terms than those we read about in these experiences of work and migration. Whether native-born or immigrant, they left few accounts. Recent studies sketch the contours, chances, and dangers of growing up on the streets or in the fields. Paths diverged for both sons and daughters from the patterns discussed here. Growing up seemingly undisciplined, without parental authority, protection, and moral socialization, was condemned as a failing, and as preparation for a brief, unhappy life of crime and sin. In literary lore and in the work of reformers such as Charles Loring Brace, the poor were sometimes romanticized and mythologized. Seen through the distorting lens of a middle class in the midst of its own anxious self-formation, the poor constituted a powerful negative image against which bourgeois family life could be constructed.

It is necessary to look through a different lens to grasp the significance of family economies to which all contributed, in workshops and on the streets; of the adaptation of traditional ways of workers, immigrants, and the poor to the new scale of life; of the extraordinary sacrifices made, especially by poor mothers for the sake of their children; of the resourceful and "streetwise" learning of children and youths; and of conflicts, dangers, costs, and human losses. The young were not always bound agreeably to family economies when the environment appeared to offer other opportunities. Conflict permeated relations across generations, genders, and classes, as the poor and the alien faced new standards of conduct and civility increasingly embedded in social institutions, policy and law, and normative expectations. In grasping these issues, we also see the ways in which these lives overlapped with those of other contemporaries, including some I have discussed here.

Emergent

The struggles of young women and their families in a changing world led to new expectations and norms for growing up properly female. This historical moment was seen as an especially dangerous and demanding time for "true women," but also was perceived as requiring the contribution of women, at home and increasingly in legitimated roles outside the family. As with their brothers', women's class-defined paths do not encompass the totality of experience. They did speak to the future. Emerging middle-class ideals and behavior influenced policy, institutions, and normative expectations for one's own kind and others. Those are only a few of the complex legacies of the first half of the nineteenth century.

Mary Anna Longstreth's memoir introduces us to middle-class experience as it was forming.[128] Born to Philadelphia Quaker parents, Mary Anna (1811–1884) was "an infant greatly desired and joyfully welcomed" (12). Hers were "modern" parents, and the infant responded to their love. In perfect health, she "was never heard to cry" (12). Concern about precocity being as yet uncommon, Mary Anna began school at the age of two and a half when her sister was born.

At first she went to a dame school. "Actual study" began at age five. Mary Anna attended a school run by the Misses Cox for five years. Although fond of reading and grammar, she had difficulty learning to write. When she was seven, her father died, and her mother's sister joined the family to assist in socializing and educating her nieces and nephews. Since no school in Philadelphia taught Latin or Greek to girls, a private master was employed. A minister awaiting missionary assignment in Burma, he sparked Mary Anna's lifelong interest in and support of missionaries. Greek and French masters followed him.

In 1824 John Brewer opened a girls' school that taught Latin and Greek. Thirteen-year-old Mary Anna was one of the first scholars and one of the best. She also taught Latin to her younger sister. Before she was twelve, Mary Anna had read all of Virgil. Brewer engaged her as an assistant while she continued her own studies over the next three years. The first payment for her services was a great delight: a "little diary" that "bears witness to the deepening earnestness with which she looked upon her vocation as a teacher" (16–17).

In the diary Mary Anna thanked family and God for their aid and blessings, and vowed to repay them with her life by always improving, always doing good. She was grateful for the peace and tranquillity she felt in her soul. On her eighteenth birthday, confessing a deep sense of responsibility, Mary Anna rededicated her purpose, surrendering herself to her God to do "my 'most reasonable service'" (20). In the spring of 1829 the sisters began to teach "on their own account." Mary Anna, eighteen, and Susan, sixteen, opened a school for girls "under the protection of their mother's roof." After a week, it "succeeds delightfully" with eight students, and after two weeks with fourteen. On her nineteenth birthday, the school "prospering," Mary Anna repeated her covenant. She made education her career, a proper path for a middle-class woman: working for the young, aiding them along their way.

Always improving themselves, the sisters took lessons in drawing and perspective, attended lectures on chemistry and natural philosophy, read constantly. Mary Anna also "loved an innocent jest as much as any one, and her habitual brightness, even gayety of manner, her quick smile and genial laughter, and above all, the rare sweetness of face, the very 'lineaments of gospel books,' left no room for the reproach that her religion was an austere one" (29). Little disturbed her. Combining in her patience and spirituality the qualities of "true women," fashioning in growing up a life of virtue and a contribution to her class and gender, Mary Anna Longstreth served spiritually and maternally three generations of Philadelphia children.[129]

Mary Anna allows one glimpse into the emerging middle-class path of growing up. Piety and spiritually on the one hand and education on the other were its banners. In their implications for self-definition and expanding schooling for women, they began to redefine growing up. Quakerism provided Mary Anna's emphasis. Other influences derived from romanticism and sentimentality, enormously popular cultural currents.

An Autobiography by R.L.B, or Harriet G. Doutney (Storer) (1822–1907), shows this form of influence and complementary experience with almost painful clarity.[130] Full of excesses, the account pronounces on its first page: "Byron by force of inspiration, wrote his 'Bride of Abydos,' in one night. I, by force of poverty, write my book in one week. He wrote for fame! I write to pay my board. His motive was the more elevated! Mine, the more urgent" (7–8). The author continues in the Byronic vein: "Behold the reason why I write a book! That it will be sensational, is not my fault; my life has been one long sensation" (9).

First child of a romantic young mother and a wild but generous-hearted father, baby Harriet was "welcomed with smiles and prayers," though deprived of her mother's breast owing to complications of her birth. "Still, I throve" (17). Fear stimulated her first step, as she found her feet, but "being of the 'female persuasion,' I did not have to hunt for my tongue" (19). As she grew, Harriet romantically "combined the elements of two distinct lives. The one, bright and joyous; mischief and prank filling the house with sunshine. The other, dreamy and sad; influenced by emotions difficult to explain, but *with* which my playmates had no sympathy" (21).

Girlhood followed babyhood and childhood; she precisely subdivides the stages of the early life course. The deaths of her sister and grandfather changed the family's circumstances: "My grandfather dead, my parents moved to a large manufacturing place; and my mother's eldest sister, having no daughters of her own, claimed me for an unlimited time" (26). The girl's "very worst characteristic," pride, was fostered, but her religion proved firm. With sleigh rides in winter and circus rides in summer, "life [was] now gala!"

When her father died, the family needed money, so Harriet "eloped": left home to teach school. That did not take. "Hiding my light, as it were, under a bushel; unknown to my friends, I entered a leading store as saleswoman. *My* world was immediately turned upside down!" (40). Her talent for business shocked and shamed her family for it transgressed the limits of legitimate middle-class women's work. After she met the gifted son of a Methodist preacher, her life took a new direction: "My whole being recognized, and went out to its new master—LOVE" (42). Their engagement caused a stir; Methodists were beneath the station deemed proper for her class to marry. Pressures to break the match only increased the couple's resolve. Eloping, they took the train to Providence, Rhode Island, "in those days the 'Gretna Green' of persecuted lovers!" (44). Now married, Harriet began to contemplate the meaning of "obey": "In fluttering happiness, *I* exchanged my maiden freedom for the soft restraint of a blushing bride!" (45). From that point followed the ups and downs and subsequent debts that inspired her to write her breezy, romantic life story.

Caroline Cowles Richards describes the developing middle-class female path of growing up more realistically and more credibly in the rich account of her 1852–1872 diary.[131] From the time of her mother's death, Caroline (1842–1913) and her sister lived with their grandparents in the town of Canandaigua, New York. Her father lived in Litchfield, Connecticut, where he kept a school in the old Beecher house; her brothers boarded at an academy. Living away from parents, although not unusual for the time, given mortality, morbidity, and mobility levels, was the major way in which Caroline's early life diverged from an emerging middle-class ideal. Despite some traditional fussiness, her grandparents were exemplary surrogate parents. If not a metropolis, their place of residence did not prevent the girls from encountering new currents of thought.

Caroline begins her two-decade diary on her birthday in 1852: "I am ten years old to-day . . . I have lived with my Grandfather and Grandmother Beals ever since I was seven years old, and Anna, too, since she was four" (November 21, 1852). The sisters attended a district school.

Whimsy was one of this lively young girl's attractive qualities. Love, kindness, a bit of indulgence, and consistent concern with shaping character and inculcating proper morality governed Caroline's and her sister's rearing. She often saw her father and brothers. When their father visited, he bought the girls candy. They felt his absence. He wrote, reminding them to read the Bible, say their prayers, brush their teeth, and be good little girls. This moral inculcation seems to have succeeded.

Caroline reports that her grandfather's usual response to a challenge was to say, "The girls were not old enough." Their grandmother employed many effective disciplinary devices. The girls had regular domestic chores; her grandmother chastised Caroline about the example she set for her younger sister. She offered eleven-year-old Caroline ten cents to learn her verses from the New England primer. She had Caroline read three Bible chapters each morning before school and five on Sunday; thus she was able to complete the book in a year. For Sunday school, Caroline learned seven verses each week and recited catechism and hymns in the evenings. Their father sent the girls *Gulliver's Travels*. Disapproving of the pictures of the giant, their grandmother pasted a piece of pink calico over him from the waist down. At thirteen Caroline read the *Harper's* serialization of Dickens's *Little Dorritt* and found it very interesting.

Their grandmother's kindly moral tutelage mixed well with the Reverend Mr. Tousley's preaching to the children about the steps along the road to being bad: from lying at first, to disobeying parents, Sabbath breaking, swearing, stealing, and drunkenness. "I don't remember just the order they came. It was very interesting," wrote Caroline, "for he told lots of stories and we sang a great many songs." When Caroline and Anna disobeyed, they were chastised; when sorry, they were forgiven.

Their grandmother had a ready moral for all occasions. When Caroline asked for a verse, she was told, "To be happy and live long the three grand essentials are: Be busy, love somebody and have high aims." Caroline deemed this a satisfactory motto but had doubts about her own or her sister's ability to practice it. Her Grandfather said simply: be like Grandmother! Their grandmother also taught them the social graces. She taught them to sew, stitch, and knit. When they received five dollars from an uncle, she allowed the girls to purchase whatever they wished.

Classroom and recess activities kept Caroline busy at school. She recalls playing snap the whip: "I was on the end and was snapped off against the fence. It hurt me so, that Anna cried. It is not a very good game for girls, especially for the one at the end." By age eleven Caroline had a special favorite among her female classmates. Her friend Abbie taught her to play "mumble te peg," which she found "fun, but rather dangerous." Composition writing was sometimes trying, and spelling gave her problems. Music lessons and "spelldowns" lightened the classroom grind.

Beginning in 1855 Anna and Caroline attended a seminary. In February 1858 they and other boarders put on a tableau, a charade with music. Anna was fond of acting. But "Grandmother told Anna she must choose between going on the stage and living with her Grandmother, so Anna gave it up and some one else took her part." Spiritualism was the current rage; the girls attempted a séance. Caroline thought they had made a table move, but others denied it. "There is nothing very spirituelle about any of us," she concluded. In December 1855 Susan B. Anthony spoke in the town, requesting that the seminary girls attend along with other women and girls. Caroline "could not make Grandmother agree with [Anthony] at all and she said we might better all of us stayed at home."

As Caroline entered her teen years, she thought increasingly about fashion, shopping, and style. Once she stayed home from school to have a new dress fitted. Her grandfather gave her a malachite comb for her hair, but when Caroline asked for a gold chain like the one worn by another girl, her grandmother recited a verse about the relative merits of outward adornments and inward graces. When Shaker bonnets, costing one dollar, became the thing to wear to school, Caroline vowed to wear hers until it wore out. Grandmother readily declared that those who seek to please everyone please no one.

As they grew up, the girls tried to dress in ways they deemed more mature. Preparing for a party in May 1856, Caroline wrote: "The girls all told us at school that they were going to wear low neck and short sleeves. We have caps on the sleeves of our best dresses and we tried to get the sleeves out, so we could go bare arms, but we couldn't get them out. We had a very nice time, though, at the party. Some of these Academy boys were there and they asked us to dance but of course we couldn't do that. We promenaded around the rooms and went out to supper with them."

In 1859, aged seventeen, Caroline had her ears pierced. The current fashion was for the girls to cut and curl their hair: "It wouldn't be comfortable for us to sleep with curl papers all over our heads, but we must do it now." Their grandmother did not accept or allow all new styles. Caroline comments: "It is nice, though to dress in style and look like other people. I have a Garibaldi waist and a Zouave jacket and a Balmoral skirt." With their peers, the sisters dressed up in "new fangled costumes." They wore them to school, with some dresses almost to the knee and others trailing on the ground, their hair twisted into knots or hanging down the back.

Mystic books—bound books with blank pages—were also the rage. The girls and boys wrote in them, then turned the page twice over and sealed it with wafers or wax, writing on it the day it might be opened, say, a year hence. "That," Caroline remarked, "is a long time to wait . . . We have autograph albums too and Horace Finley gave us lots of small photographs. We paste them in the books and then ask the people to write their names . . . We are going to keep them always." Adolescent culture clearly flowered in Canandaigua in the mid-1850s.

The teen years brought parties, and the issue of dancing. Although Caroline's grandparents had met at a ball, her grandmother had not danced since she had become a "professing Christian" more than fifty years earlier, and she did not want the girls to dance. Whenever boys came to their house, once the clock struck nine, their grandfather scraped up the ashes in the fire, a signal to bid goodnight. "'We won't go home till morning' is a song that will never be sung in this house," Caroline quipped. A variety of shows, from General Tom Thumb to Barnum's circus, came to town. Their grandmother forbade the girls to go to the circus, which featured half-dressed women riding and jumping.

In January 1859 Caroline and Anna joined other boys and girls in a singing school in their chapel. Their master told them if they practiced they might have a concert: "What a treat that will be!" As they girls grew up, their treats blended the pleasures of childishness and adolescence. Games with other girls included "Simon says" or chanting "Rich man, poor man, beggar man, thief" to discover whom they might marry.

Given the girls' social inclinations, their teacher doubted their intellectual commitment. Caroline notes in December 1859:

> I think some one must have shown some verses that we girls wrote, to Mrs. Grundy and made her think that our minds were more upon the young men than they were upon our studies, but if people knew how much time we spent on Paley's 'Evidence of Christianity' and Butler's Analogy and Kames' Elements of Criticism and Tyler's Ancient History and Olmstead's Mathematical Astronomy and our French and Latin and arithmetic and algebra and geometry and trigonometry and bookkeeping, they would know we had very little time to think of the masculine gender.

Recognizing her march to maturity, her grandfather gave fifteen-year-old Caroline his sets of the Waverly novels and Shakespeare's plays. "He is so good. Anna says perhaps he thinks I am going to be married and go to housekeeping some day. Well, perhaps he does. Stranger things have happened."

Between her studies and her grandmother's moral inculcation, on the one hand, and fads, fun, peer culture, and Anna's tricks and puns, on the other hand, lay the realities of Caroline's middle-class youth. Nearing eighteen years of age, on New Year's Day 1860 she wrote, "We felt quite grownup today." Asked her approval to teach in the "colored" Sunday school, Caroline's grandmother remarked that the girl had shown no interest in "the colored race" and likely just wanted an excuse for a walk: "Grandmother said that when she saw [Noah Clarke's brother] opening the gate for me, she understood my zeal in missionary work." Changing tone, she writes: "'The dear little lady,' as we often call her, has always been noted for her keen discernment and wonderful sagacity and loses none of it as she advanced in years."

With the outbreak of the Civil War in 1861, Caroline reports that many young men were going off bravely and patriotically to fight. Groups of girls would go to the train station, taking flowers to the soldiers. Ladies sewed garments, and young ladies wrote notes to cheer the soldiers. In this atmosphere Caroline graduated from the seminary in May at age nineteen. As her teens ended, she looked to the future. When one of her friends said, "'How nice it would be if our lives could run along as smoothly as this stream.' I said I thought it would be too monotonous. Laura Chapin said she supposed I would rather have an 'eddy' in mine."

Anna decided to write a poem for Caroline's twentieth birthday in 1862. After working all night, she presented her sister with what she called "An Effort": "One hundred years from now, Carrie, dear, In all probability you'll not be here; But we'll all be in the same boat, too, And there'll be no one left To say boo hoo!" Grandfather gave her books, one of which had been presented to their mother as a prize. His death in April 1863 was the "saddest day" of Caroline's life. Anna graduated in June, valedictorian of her class despite her mischief-making. Caroline was teaching Sunday school.

With 1866 and the end of the war came parties, fairs, and fetes. Among them was Caroline's wedding day. Her grandmother could take pride in the exemplary children she had nurtured along a new middle-class path.

With frontier settlement the spread of new middle-class female paths of growing up was impressive in its speed and extent. As the very different accounts of settlers tell us, "proper" middle-class morality encompassed a wide range of behaviors. That could present a problem in judging others, including potential suitors. A new focus on educating young women, a development that elevated women's school attendance and literacy, provides a revealing view of variations along emerging paths.[132] A number of types—matronly and moral, seriously studious, sincerely social, or saccharinely silly—hint at more complicated realities.

Rebecca Ann Lamar, daughter of Mirabeau Lamar, a founding father of Texas, spent part of her teen years there, moving after the Mexican War from her native Georgia. She kept a diary from July 1838 to April 1839.[133] In frontier Texas district signs were appearing of emerging class paths and the problems they created for a daughter seeking to please her father. Journeying to New Orleans, Rebecca wondered if a certain "gentleman" loved her, or "was it because my Father stood very high in Texas?" (July 22, 1838). This was a persistent, often difficult question for female children of successful families whose concern about authenticity and artifice in social relations was often justified. Rebecca's position brought her many introductions and gifts. Without self-consciousness or coyness, she deemed herself "lucky."

Rebecca was aware of her frivolity. Sometimes it disturbed her, and sometimes she vowed to mend her ways: "Although my time has not been as profitably employed as My Dear Father would wish, I have not read much but hope what little I have read has been an improvement to me. My Dear Aunt has often requested to me to read or write. And I know she always wishes me to be benefited by her advice. I must acknowledge I have not been industrious. And have resolved to improve the time I have to remain in Texas" (September 25, 1838). Confirming her observations if not her resolve, two days later she added, "This morning I have been engaged in reading Queen Elizabeth's reign . . . She was not very pretty herself."

During the fall of 1838 Rebecca traveled to Galveston and Houston with her aunts and grandmother. She missed a ball because her aunt, a Methodist, "did not attend such places, and I was not willing to go without her." In November she began Christian lessons under an aunt's instruction. Rebecca admitted that she had neglected her journal and been idle and was very sorry for it, "for I want to improve every day I grow older" (November 19, 1838).

Rebecca also attended school, though her diary indicates that she was at least as concerned with society as with her studies. Despite persistent self-denigration—of the diary she writes it "is a very poor one for the length of time I have been at it"—she showed no sign of reform: "I have let a long time pass without writing in my journal I have been going to school and I had no time but to please my dear papa I have began to write" (January 28, 1839).

In February Rebecca was too tired to write after school. She was beginning to succeed in her classes. Journal writing was hard "because it takes a great deal of study and thinking to compose a journal or anything else. I was head of three classes this week Grammar Reading and Dictionary." Her aunt and father wanted her to write in order to improve; she wanted his praise (February 1839). This was one force in the formation of middle-class paths of growing up: the desire of girls to please their fathers and other men. They also hoped to improve themselves. Patricia Mercer's 1840–41 Galveston schoolgirl diary reflects the same tensions, especially about applying oneself to studies perceived as little more than a grind.[134]

In sharp contrast is the studious Anna May, a senior at the New Hampton Institution in New Hampshire, who kept a diary during the 1857 academic year.[135] The school offered English and classical courses similar to those in female collegiate institutes. A child of her times, Anna May opens her diary with a typically romantic lyrical passage: "Treasure of my thoughts! Dear companion of solitary hours! . . . Herein I inscribe the workings of my secret soul."

More seriously, Anna registers her sadness at leaving home to return to school and her struggle for emotional control: "I must not yield to my inclinations but must go. Farewell, Mother, Father, Home, and Friends! May I soon return to find them in health . . . I have spent rather a lonely day. My studies as yet are not settled . . . Am I homesick? I hope not, the first day! Oh no, it must not be, I must control my feelings and not yield to them thus" (February 4). Still lonely the next day, Anna wept. Recovering rapidly, she settled into her studies. Among the costs of being close to her mother was that she missed her deeply. But with studies, teachers, fellow students, and Sabbath services to occupy her, Anna found herself "becoming more weaned from home. . . . I become engrossed in my studies and thus do not so often think of them . . . Oh dear! The pleasures and sorrows of a school girl!" (February 11).

Anna experienced "regular blue days," a normal aspect of her age and school situation. These feelings also derived from her search for religious faith. And she was self-critical as a result of her early socialization. She writes, for example: "Would that I were calm and cool and never did things in haste to repent of afterwards. But I am hasty and impetuous. I must try to think more before I speak. This is the first and I mean it to be the last time I do in this manner" (February 21).

Letters from home and a friend cheered her. But Anna lacked a close school friend to share and counteract her blues: "If I only had some congenial spirit to commune with me, my sorrow would quickly be dispelled like dew before the sun. Oh, if that one, my beau ideal of human excellence, were only here, how pleased I should be! . . . What nonsense am I writing? What if you, oh my journal, should meet some other eye than my own?" (February 24). Anna later repeated her longing: "It is just such a night as those in which dear ones hold sweet communion with each other, but alas, I have no dear one here with whom to hold communion. Would that I had! I think a moonlight evening the sweetest of all ties" (April 7).

In addition to her studies and religious activities, Anna was an active member of the Germanae Dilectae Scientiae and the Young Ladies Literary Society. She enjoyed the meetings but admitted, "I do not think that they tend to increase our interest in our studies at all." Anna revealed: "Excitement is my life, but a bad one for me to follow, I am so nervous and excitable" (March 12). Symptoms of the multiple strains of middle-class womanhood, these feelings were common.

Anna May kept up her studies: "I have recited much as usual today. I was obliged to study pretty hard in order to learn my lessons" (March 12). She studied so much that she was "weary." When not doing well, Anna severely berated herself: "I study nearly all of the time, but I do not do well at all. I fear my rank will be very, very bad this term. If it is in my power I will have good lessons tomorrow, if I study all night to do it . . . I think that this is the anniversary of the death of my darling only brother" (May 11). The next day she reports doing much better.

Peer pressure and desire to be with the other girls conflicted with studies and good sense. On March 19 Anna wrote: "Tonight, silly girl that I was, I went away with most all of the girls to a long walk . . . I fear that I may take cold, and I do not think that the enjoyment will pay for it." What she struggled to achieve was a proper balance in her feelings and responses. As she wrote on April 10: "I stopped all evening and had a fine jovial time . . . I think that it is not well to try to be too dignified, if, indeed, I am ever dignified. I fear that I am never dignified enough."

Anna also struggled with pressures and conflicts over religion. In March she reports talking and praying with Elder Stewart. Combined with her other anxieties, this resulted in severe stress: "I am so nervous that I want to take hold of everything and slat it to pieces. What shall I do? Oh dearie me!" (March 23).

Amid these conflicts Anna lost her sense of humor. On April 1 what she thought to be a letter from a friend turned out to be an "April Fool": "I was a little amused. I think one may spend their time in a better manner than in playing such jokes upon another, but I do not care for it at all."

More plaintively, under multiple strains, Anna struggled with adolescent anxieties and mood swings:

I do fear that I am losing all of my ambition in my studies. I feel it a task to learn every lesson that I undertake. I wish I did not . . . I am really getting impatient to go home . . . but no, I do not really want to go, only for I am weary . . . I am a strange being tonight, I am so wild and gay. I have received some praise tonight from our Principal for my Latin class. The teacher says that I am doing finely, and there were quite a number of compliments for me on that account. I am so glad he thinks so. Is it true? Am I vain to write it? My mood is very changeful. I am now sad, now gay. Why is it thus? (April 6)

Saturdays provided some respite, freeing her from the tensions, anxieties, and weariness of the week.

At home in April for the change of terms, Anna at first was ecstatic, then lonely for schoolmates (April 18). This shifting of sentiments is another sign of emerging adolescence for young women of the middle class. Returning to school, she relived her earlier trauma, limiting her progress on her senior essay to be read at graduation. In addition, "I feel sad to think that is my last term here at New Hampton. I should like ever so much to go to College if I only could, but my health will not allow" (May 15, 18, and 19). Then restoring discipline: "I must lay aside my dear companion [the diary] and turn my thoughts to my Botany lesson. It is now 9:15 P.M. and I have permission to sit up till 10:30. I must improve my time" (May 20). The diary does not tell us if Anna's health literally prevented her from attending college or if assumptions about the detrimental impact of advanced study on women's health were to blame.[136] To benefit her health, Anna walked a mile most days.

Among the senior girls, marriage was in the air: "I have been talking with some of the girls . . . and one of them laughingly remarked that in two or three years I should be married. I, of course, denied it, and do not believe one word of it, no, indeed, not that! Of course I shall not. What a ludicrous idea, and not even any signs of a beau as yet, without which I could not very well be married" (May 17).

The end of her last term in school brought the blues. On June 10 Anna wrote: "I am very weary indeed tonight. I have studied hard all day long . . . I am really glad that school is done, or, at least, that my school days are nearly ended. I am also sad when I think of them as being so. Oh, I am, I believe, a little tinged with the blues tonight." Parting was painful. She feared loneliness (June 16).

Confronting the end of this stage of her life, Anna wallowed in sentimentality: "Sad will be the parting hour. Oh dear, how mournful it will be to me to think that I am never coming back to New Hampton again" (June 20). Her nerves became harder to control (June 22). She longed for "some near and dear friend with whom to hold communion" (June 28). The pressures and weariness mounted with the prospect of final recitations: "I fear very much that I shall fail in my recitation next week . . . I dread the thought of it. I am almost crazy tonight. I cannot write or think anything connectedly" (July 2).

Despite her state, Anna accepted an invitation from "a certain gentle-man" to accompany him on a July 4 ride: "This to me is a day ever to be remembered. How happy I have been, all day long!" Eight couples rode partway up a mountain in Bridgewater, then walked to the summit. After refreshments, "we indulged in social converse sweet." Self-criticism limited her enjoyment: "I think that never did I enjoy a day more than I have this. I have done some things that I regret, perhaps. I was somewhat too wild. I am apt to forget myself when in company." Anna was properly wary of losing self-control, a major failing in her socialization and a threat to her proper path.

With her classmates Anna cried over their separation: "Oh, it seems as if my heart would break when I think of the parting" (July 5). With final lessons and recitations over, graduation exercises took place. She "commenced about seven to dress for the grand exercises. I was very, very nervous. Our class were all dressed in pure white muslin, with lace waists, white kids, ribbon, etc. My hair was dressed plain, with geranium leaves, fuchsias, and rose buds." The procession began at 8:00. Miniatures were taken before the exercises in the church. The fifth graduate to read, Anna was less frightened than she had expected. Diplomas were distributed, and "very affecting" remarks were made. She almost wept, but she managed to control her feelings. Her gentleman friend accompanied her home. Anna penned: "Oh dear, what conflicting emotions have agitated my breast this day!" (July 9). Here Anna May completed the adolescent portion of her path of growing up.

The matter-of-fact journal of Hannah (Anna) Gale of Northborough, Massachusetts, is a relief from Anna May's anxieties. Anna Gale kept her record while a nineteen-year-old student of Margaret's Fuller's at the re-nowned Greene Street School in Providence.[137] Preparing to teach, Anna spent a term at Hiram Fuller's school before her father's financial reverses ended her attendance. The school's cardinal qualities were its stress on order in all things and, especially for Margaret Fuller's students, an em-phasis on self-analysis and independent thought, in part through keeping journals. Despite opening-day jitters, Anna found the environment pleas-ing and comforting. She imbibed the heady romanticism underlying the pedagogy.

Anna found journal keeping a trial. She had to conquer a tendency toward procrastination. By dictum and experience she learned to be prompt and to control her emotions. Proper middle-class socialization and charac-ter training were indistinguishable from the lessons she learned at school. Although she often complained, and sometimes doubted her ability to master her studies, at the end of the term Anna was sad to have her stay cut short. She felt she had lost her chance to improve herself, "to retrieve my character as a scholar. I am very far from being in the least satisfied with what I have done. I do not think I have even done justice to myself" (February 28, 1838).

By mid-century more (mainly but not exclusively) middle-class daughters were seeking and gaining a college education. Advanced female seminaries added for some another step on their path of growing up between completing seminary or academy and leaving home for marriage, work, or other responsibilities. The campaign for women's higher education was long and hard-fought, and colleges occupied places of material and symbolic importance in the transformations of growing up. These experiences were neither simply liberating nor conservative. What David Allmendinger sees as "meeting the need for life planning" at Mount Holyoke College combined premarital training with training for a career, teaching in particular. The "diffusion of feminist values" which Ann Firor Scott finds at Troy Female Seminary formed another component.[138]

The experience of one Mount Holyoke student, Mary Olivia Nutting, reveals the impact of higher education on growing up.[139] In 1850 Mary, the youngest child of Squire Nutting of Randolph Center, Vermont, left home at nineteen to attend the college. She and her father thought one year sufficient to complete her education. The trip to South Hadley, Massachusetts, was her first time "abroad" and her first travel "in the cars." A review of her previous education showed that more than a year would be needed for her studies. The college's curricular requirements were firm. Mary passed out of Latin and was placed in the "Middle Class." She wrote to her father: "I value the advantages of learning to be systematic, punctual, industrious, &c. in anything, in short the advantages which are common to all who are *here* . . . Instead of fretting because I cannot do all I hoped to, I am glad, more and more, every day, that I am here at all. I should not think the expense of my being here by any means thrown away, if I should do no more than finish the Middle studies, nor would you, dear father, if you knew all the privileges we have here" (183–184).

Mary was impressed with life at Mount Holyoke. Founder Mary Lyon's moderate standard for expenses, $60 for forty weeks, was achieved with a domestic system in which each student, as a member of the "family," gave time to housework in groups called "circles." Mary was one of 280 women living in one large four-story brick building and sharing beds, three to a room, one of whom was usually an "old" scholar. Previously acquainted, the other two in Mary's room shared the bed; she slept "out" in the public sleeping room.

Mary grasped the need to be systematic, punctual, and industrious to achieve her goals. Her schedule kept her occupied from early morning until night with chores, studies and recitations, devotions, physical exercise, and meals. She wrote her father: "I generally retire very soon after this, because I get sleepy, and I am not going to learn myself any different habits from what you brought me up in, especially when I rise so early" (189).

As a junior, Mary studied history, algebra, Greene's analysis, physiology, Euclid, chemistry, and natural philosophy. The next term she expected to study rhetoric, astronomy, botany, and natural philosophy. Gaining her father's permission to attend a second year, Mary graduated in 1852. She then taught school for some years, as Mount Holyoke students were prepared and expected to do. In 1870 she returned to the college to become its first librarian.

Mary Olivia Nutting evidently never married. Her path to adulthood concluded with college graduation and advancement to a career. For most young women the next major and, in theory, "final" step—sometimes after a period of working—lay in marriage. Marriage was the socially approved, culturally legitimated realm in which young women of the middle class could practice their carefully cultivated moral domesticity. The meaning of the transition to marriage in this period is a subject of debate between historians such as Ellen Rothman, who argue for relatively "modern," close and affectionate courtship and marriage in this period, and those such as Carroll Smith-Rosenberg, who see rigidifying gender role distinctions and close same-sex bonds, both of which could make marriage difficult. The first-person sources show a range of actions and reactions. Together they emphasize that many young persons, for varying reasons, took their steps into marriage with great concern and care.[140]

Lizzie Scott Neblett's midcentury Texas diary is an exceptional testament on the final step in a female's growing up.[141] Lizzie, at the age of nineteen, began her diary a few months before she married William H. Neblett in Anderson, Texas, in May 1852. Born in 1833 in Raymond, Mississippi, Lizzie moved as a child with her family to Fanthorp Springs near the small town of Anderson. She lived at home. Her family was well-to-do, and her fiancé's family was wealthy. As the diary opens, Lizzie all but sings: "My heart is now young full of hope, life, animation." Before long, her tune began to change. Will, her fiancé, "appeared more indifferent and careless than I had ever noticed before," she writes (March 17, 1852). His detachment alarmed her. A few days later, with all the allusions at her command, she poured out:

> I am feeling so sad, so despairing. When I think how full of hope, how happy I was only two weeks ago, I can hardly recognize, that, it is one and the same spirit that inhabits, my bosom. Now I feel joyless, alone, unappreciated, and bitter feelings are continually rising . . . My feelings are deeply, painfully,

acute, and here even among those who I know love me better than any one else does I am often pained and wounded, beyond the power of expression, and for my own happiness, I strive to persuade myself that, the wound was not intentional I cannot cheat my heart with such reasoning: too well, too feelingly, is the knowledge taught, that, I am *bound to be unloved,* or with Mad. de Staael [*sic*] I can feelingly say, and with the conviction deeply rooted "Never never, will I be loved as I love." (March 20)

As her overwrought romantic sentiments indicate, Lizzie felt that her situation was dire. The meaning of marriage and the need for hopeful expectations were so important that her emotional stability could topple quickly. Much was at stake; her suffering was great.

Lizzie filled the pages of her diary with anguish. She accused herself of selfishness, of wishing for too much, virtually blaming herself for her injured feelings. She expressed doubts about her choice of Will over a former beau. In contrast to her state was Will's: "He will instead of showing me any error, if there be one, mock, at my wishes, or else say nothing" (March 20, 1852). Lizzie was not ready to reject him or change her path. There was a history with Will. But her father had reservations about the match, and this was not the first time the two had moved toward the altar. "I am sorry that these pages should have opened with complaints against Will. I do love him, inspite of all, and in May I am to become his wife. Pa has yielded a rather reluctant consent, and Will has not yet said anything to Mother about it. I feel confident that we will be married this time after being twice engaged to him before" (March 20, 1852).

Their relationship was six years old; it was almost five years since he had first declared his love for her, and more than three years since their first engagement. Lizzie admitted her conflict: "I have grown cold some-what in my affection three times, but every time have returned to my old love true as the magnet to the pole . . . It seems I can never be rid of him as a lover until I convert him into a husband. I wonder how we will get along. I know I will be loved well enough. I feel many fears about Will" (April 19).

Lizzie's hesitations stemmed from general concerns as well as specific slights. The question of financial support was one issue for her. She refused to be dependent on their parents: "Will is poor, so am I. I have nothing, to give him but myself and my whole heart, and, I know ours will be a life of toil, yet a life I hope where love will abound. Pa and Mother seem to have a great many fears, that, we will come to them, to be supported, by them. But me, I could suffer in penury and want, all my life before I would implore their aid. Will can support me, I know, or, he would never have sought, to wed me" (April 2).

More than pride figured here. The humiliation of dependence on one's parents after marriage was a great fear for many for whom marriage and independence, despite their gender imbalances, were inseparable. "I am determined while there is strength in my arm," she declares, "and a little sense in my head I will not be dependent on my parents. never! never!" (April 14). That was one meaning of female autonomy.

Another aspect of Lizzie's problem was her sense of isolation and loneliness. All her friends had deserted her. Two women in particular had not written in four or five months; nor was this correspondence likely to be renewed, for Lizzie "would not answer a letter from either of them now." Female friends were unavailable to support, counsel, or calm her in her hour of need: "I have been deceived in those girls they I do not believe were ever my friends and were ever making remarks about me" (April 3).

By April 10 Lizzie's spirits had improved, in part because a reassuring letter from Will pleased her. In a more metaphorical mood she struggled to be philosophical and self-critical. This effort stemmed in part from her middle-class upbringing: "My future has many bright colors, tho' I know there must be shades. I have every confidence in Will, and distrust myself more than I do him. I have so many faults and fears, I have not been proven sufficient to overcome them. Will must practice forebearance. He too must have faults tho' now I may see as 'through a glass darkly' yet I know Human nature is a mass of imperfections. As long as love lasts I shall feel no fears but alas! when love *dies*. 'There's the rub'" (April 10). Self-doubt, romanticism, and the press of expectations were a bitter brew.

Not hearing from Will for several weeks revived Lizzie's doubts: "I wish I was as good as Will thinks I am. He tells me I will get to Heaven anyhow. My virtues are few, and my foibles, their name is legion. Will for your sake I would and do wish I was better and more worthy. I dreamed of Will last night but thought it was Ben [another suitor] and I called him Will" (April 21). Her misgivings mounted. So did those of her parents. Lizzie feared living in tiny Marlin, Texas, where they planned to reside. She wanted to teach school to occupy herself and earn income. Fearing Will's opposition, Lizzie planned to "try every means to persuade him" (May 9). Her independence was at issue. And there was also the question of adapting to life in so small a town.

On May 10 her parents' attempted intervention stimulated a crisis that exposed deep-rooted family conflict. Lizzie's father asked her if she "intended having that affair over with." She told him, yes. He then asked if she were not ashamed of herself:

> He knew that I did not love that man, and I saw what a hell it was, if love was absent. meaning himself and mother. I told him he did not know what I thought or anything about me, in answer to his saying that I did not love

Will, and he says the hell & devil I don't. mother said I could not love a man more than a week and would be so in all of my life, and if I did marry *'that man'* I would not live long with him, and I was marrying him to rule him that I thought I was smarter, and that I would make him do all that I wished. a *good* deal more was said. he cursed me and told mother he had great mind to *cow hide* me. Such expressions for a *father,* and it was because Mother was and is too busy to make him some pantaloons, and I will not do it. let me get the taylor to make. I am so proud that my days are nearly at end here, and I am done being cursed and threatened to be *cow hided.* I'll warrant I'll never trouble with my company when I am married I want nothing from him, even if wished to give me anything. no I'll work my finger nails off before I'll be dependent on him and if Will and I do sepperate, I'll never come back to him. I'll support myself. Tomorrow is the day Will is to come and make some definite arrangement.

In her rage Lizzie grasped "even if I did not love Will, I should be tempted to marry him, if I had the chance to get away from here. Mother does not see a moment of happiness" (May 10). Surely Lizzie was not the only daughter to perceive this, nor hers the only family lacking in love.

Lizzie Scott and Will Neblett married on May 25, a fortnight after the family fracas. Two weeks later, residing for the moment with Will's family, Lizzie expressed her happiness. She later wrote about continuing problems in the marriage but also of reconciliation with her parents, whose aid had become important. Lizzie's mother attended her births; her father bought the couple their first house and also trained Will to practice law. This rings of new middle-class efforts to establish one's children securely, but also of family traditions.[142] The conflicts and contradictions of growing up, including those stemming from new middle-class socialization and changing marital expectations, shaped and reshaped courting and the transitional passage to marriage, among the roads taken by women.

Compared with the preceding period, female paths of growing up now seem to narrow in number. Appearances, however, are misleading. In the critical transitional period from the late eighteenth through the mid-nineteenth centuries, complexity, variety, and flux serve better as signifiers. They are attested to by paths in which tradition and change overlapped, blurring the margins, and by conflicts and contradictions that speak to the struggles confronted by young women and their families and the strategies they developed. New stages and destinations sometimes complemented, sometimes complicated, old and new restrictions based on gender, family, culture, social origins, and the like. At the same time, opportunities for education, work, relocation, autonomy, and maturity advanced, often rubbing against restraints.

Traditional female paths, while a major presence, were also changing in telling ways. Routes characterized by premarital work and migration mediated between older and newer paths of growing up. The unevenness, ambiguity, and ambivalence of life course transformations and the impact of gender come clearly into view. Class-determined paths—those of the emerging middle class in particular—simultaneously stand as summaries of change, routes to the future, and cradles of conflict: the stuff of change itself.

Emergent Class Paths

Among the most crucial transformations of growing up in this era is the emergence of new paths determined by social class. In an age of class formation, which saw the rise of modern divisions into working, middle, and upper classes, the dynamic relationships that tied class formation to the forging of new family strategies and modes of individual socialization are seminal if complicated and sometimes contradictory. Class-related paths of growing up originated in part in earlier eras, and in part in transitional paths. As they took shape in early national and antebellum eras, these paths looked to the future of growing up.

It is essential to recognize the cumulative impact of changes such as reduction in family size and marital fertility; new modes of socialization within the home, with new responsibilities for mothers and new notions of human development; novel relations between home and outside world; new relations with social institutions, especially schools; prolonged residence with families of origin; new notions of parents' contributions to their children's future; and shifts in timing in the transition from home to school, work, separate residence, and marriage. Our sense of how people respond to change must be flexible and sophisticated. So must our understanding of the uneven pace of change itself. Individual testimony about growing up takes us beyond abstract generalizations as we mediate between aggregate actions and expressions of personal experience.

For the sake of clarity in this book I focus on three principal classes: working, middle, and upper. I also note distinctions within each class as well as characteristics shared across their sometimes blurred lines. I find especially notable the ways in which the actions of one class influenced those of another, and the manner in which developing middle-class norms and expectations came to stand in judgment of the behavior of others. Middle-class family practices were used as standards for evaluating the extent of deviance ("failure") among working-class and sometimes upper-class families. They were also used as metaphors and models to fashion institutional responses ("reform") aimed at homes and parents presumed deviant and to "correct" the potentially dangerous ways of their young.

They contributed, for example, to the development of private schools for the upper classes and correctional institutions for the lower.

My interpretive approach identifies social class, its emergence, and its concomitants as motivating forces in modern historical development. This requires no crude caricature of human beings as one-dimensional, as bourgeoisie or proletariat. Not only do important differences exist within each class, as against notions of homogenization or standardization, but also I recognize gender, race, and to some extent ethnicity as at least partly independent forces that cut across class lines. Although modern growing up is usually viewed as a homogenizing and standardizing experience across social divisions, and although middle-class norms and values are accorded a descriptive (if often deceptive) hegemony, the historical development of class paths revises such notions. In this account I cut into an ongoing process of transformation.

As elsewhere in this account, the experiences of the poor and other groups are missing. Upper-class paths are also less frequently documented than middle-class routes. On both sides the principal contrast is with the emerging middle class for the simple reason that the middle class is the emergent class par excellence of the era.

Middle Class
The middle-class path of growing up was formed in the crucible of great transformations by the example of that class's and others' actions and reactions. It shared some qualities with transitional paths; that was part of the historical process. The incomplete and emergent qualities of class paths in formation is another part.

First-person sources locate family and school as central in their role as shapers of character and career. Eight-year-old William Hoppin's diary, begun on the new year, 1821, at the request of his Providence, Rhode Island, auctioneer father, shows his early experiences in the light of new class-defined paths.[143] His father's request stemmed from both traditional and newer impulses. As his diary-keeping habit formed, William found that every day it became easier to "collect subjects to write down."

William's experiences combined play with school tasks and the moral character formation of family socialization. Living at home, he skated before school. In the evenings, "after tea [I] set down by a good fire and read and do anything that comes into my head sometime get an astronomy lesson or recall or talk with papa or with anybody else" (January, 1821). In February he started flute lessons. Like many of his peers, he chased after firefighters. In school, William, notes, he began Virgil and "got 30 lines in." He started to read a history of America. He also read Cicero and was learning Greek ("although the letters look so unintelligible yet when you get an insight into it is easier than Latin").

Permeating these activities was the moral mode of child rearing, which the boy dutifully recapitulated. The lessons for this winter of 1821 ranged from appreciating his place in society ("There are many poor children who have no home nor no fire to go to, and had not we who have so many comforts, thank God for this and the many other comforts we enjoy"), to knowing the worth of efficiency ("I am afraid we boys think little of the value of time"), self-improvement ("The examination took place in our school today and papa said we done very well but not so well as might have done and I think so to [sic]"), trying harder ("Accord to my resolution yesterday I went to school and got 65 lines in Virgill when as other days I did not get but 50 and thought that I could not get any more in 3 hours and I supposed if I was to try harder I could get still more"), industry ("the importance of cultivating industry when we are young, and it will grow with us"), and achievement ("The schollars seem to be very ambitious but if I mind the instructions of my father I think I would be the first schollar in it and I think if the boys would give more time to study and less to play we would not have to say as most men do that they wished they had studied more"). Warmer weather, he remarked, "will be a great relief to the poor." The specter of time wasted playing ball haunted his conscience: "Did not stay long for to [sic] much sauce spoils the pudding I dont think I wasted the day as such . . . I felt better pleased with myself." So did his father, one suspects. Little William Hoppin early consumed the sauce on the pudding of proper middle-class growing up.

The same spirit of youthful molding emerges in the 1817 diary of a Kingston, Massachusetts, minister's son, Samuel Bartlett Parris (1806– 1827).[144] Eleven-year-old Samuel's journal commences: "I intend to record everything material that happened . . . and also my faults that by looking on this I may remember them and do so no more." Reflecting various relationships in a transitional time, Samuel lived at the academy where his father was master, combining home and boarding. His brief journal reveals a blend of youthful play, diligent study, and vigilant work at molding the future man. Samuel kept a separate journal to list his studies: "This week I studied Horace for some time . . . I played some ball today" (March 26, 1817). "I have lately wrote a history and a dialogue" (March 29). Samuel regularly records that he "got" his lines from Horace, counting up his daily achievements. He also expresses concern about his mother and domestic demands: "I hope We shall take no boarders. Mama is Yet unwell. I am afraid the Academy will stop. For We can [word illegible] nobody to keep it" (March 27). Wishes for a private family home and his mother's health conflicted with the economic needs of the school, which depended on boarders. The problem challenged his understanding as it pulled at his elders. Even the sons of academy-keeping ministers sometimes slipped from the straight path: "I did not come into the school to-day because

David Turner from Duxbury came here last night & I staid out with him to-day. I have been put out I am ashamed of it," Samuel wrote on May 2. That sense of shame shows his internalization of "proper" character traits.

Like Samuel's, Merrill Ober's life was cut short in its twenty-first year. Merrill was an extraordinarily precocious sixteen-year-old growing up in the village of Monkton, Vermont. In his 1848 diary he reminds us that new class-determined paths did not directly depend on or follow from urbanization or industrialization.[145] The child of a storekeeper, not regularly in school, he does not appear to have been working, either, evidence of the lengthening period of dependence along the middle-class path. Beginning his record, the adolescent translated traditional motivations for diary keeping into a modern emphasis:

> Sept. 2, 1848. This day I commence a private journal. I think it will be a pleasure to me to look back when I shall have grown to manhood on my past life to see how I have spent my time & besides being a mere pleasure it will be instructive. It will accustom me to picture my thoughts on paper. I shall see my thoughts and they will in a manner be continually before me & seeing them may have an effect to reform them. This day I am sixteen years old . . . Yes, 16 years ago today I first saw light or rather light first saw me. I have spent my life mostly in mental occupation. I have been to school a great deal (i.e. to a select school taught in this place every fall & sometimes in the winter & spring).

His "mental occupations" made a long list. Out of school the previous summer, he had read Rollins's history and "many other useful books besides some that were not so useful." Learning Greek and progressing with Latin, he read Shakespeare, Milton, Byron, and Sue's *El Gitanos*. He wrote compositions for school. On some days, playing, copying, or recording music occupied him. After finishing "a book called Jane Eyre," Merrill played the violin and "spent the rest of the day at the store hearing politics talked," especially "a great 'free soil' movement." Politics was his abiding interest, perhaps the best amusement in town. He refers to studying "phonography," Pitman's system of shorthand. This suggests that in addition to his wide studies, he was also preparing for a commercial career. Merrill sought more cultural and intellectual fare than Monkton offered. After a lecture, George Perkins Marsh offered him the use of his 1,500-book library in Burlington.

The spirit of Merrill's youthfulness, what a later generation would term adolescence, pokes through the serious record: "I played checkers with Clarkson to day & licked him" (September 16). He listened to poetry, eagerly read periodicals, and played ball. A juvenile enthusiasm underlies his impressive studies: "Sept. 29. I finished Cicero's first oration against

Cateline [*sic*]. It is great." Merrill's moralism and internalized socialization also permeate the record. The coming of fall sparks comment on the impermanence of mortal life and the immortal soul (September 22). His moral maxims reflect character training and a correct orientation to life.

Merrill also reflected on his future. Despite his ambitions and precocity, he was in no hurry to set his career course. For him and for increasing numbers of his peers, migration was likely. This period of reflection and a moratorium on early decision making, sometimes combined with extended schooling, was a characteristic of new paths of growing up, and one that led to prolonged residence at home. In Merrill Ober's 1848 diary we find the new phase developing, though not yet the codified norm enshrined at the end of the century by G. Stanley Hall.[146] Merrill wrote: "I am now 16 & have not decided what business I will follow through life. But I shall probably teach for a spell anyway. I must keep on studying & learn all I can. A man can not learn too much. If what he learns is of no temporal use it certainly will be of mental use" (September 8). Still pursuing his path, Merrill unfortunately died at the age of twenty-one.[147]

Other interesting examples of middle-class growing up appear in the experience of children in exceptional circumstances. Ralph Waldo Emerson's son Edward (born in 1844) reminisced about his early years in Concord.[148] With associates such as Bronson Alcott and Thoreau, the elder Emerson pioneered and publicized intellectual currents that permeated new approaches to child rearing and education. Reflecting the new domesticity and the potential it offered for loving familial relations for fathers as well as mothers, his son recalled: "He had love and tenderness for very small children, and his skill in taking and handling a baby was in remarkable contrast to his awkwardness with animals or tools" (425). If unusual, Emerson's paternal care left a deep impression on his children.[149]

Unlike increasing numbers of his peers, Ralph Waldo Emerson worked at home. In his family there was no daily separation between domesticity on the one hand and a father making his way in the outside world on the other. Edward remembered: "A very small child always had the entrance and run of his study, where it was first carried around the room and shown the Flaxman statuette of Psyche with the butterfly wings, with little bronze Goethe, the copy of Michael Angelo's Fates . . . The pictures in the old 'Penny Magazine' were the next treat, and then, if the child wanted to stay, pencil and letter-back were furnished for him to draw with. After a time, if the visitor became too exacting, he was kindly dismissed" (425). This exceptional paternal role incorporated aspects of the new maternal domesticity, including amusing while simultaneously manipulating and training the conscience and character of children.

Emerson made clear his desire for his children's success in school, especially at learning Latin and Greek, in part by reading with them. He sympathized with their dislike of mathematics. His son writes: "He was uneasy at seeing the multitude of books for young people that had begun to appear which prevented our reading the standard authors as children, as he and his brother had done."[150] He required Edward to read two pages of Plutarch's *Lives* every schoolday and ten pages on Saturdays and vacations.

Emerson's approach to questions about his children's future departed from tradition and leaned toward the emerging class paths. Edward writes: "He had the grace to leave to his children, after they began to grow up, the responsibility of deciding in more important questions concerning themselves, for which they cannot be too grateful to him; he did not command or forbid, but laid the principles and the facts before us and left the case in our hands" (428). Emerson invested in his children with lengthened schooling and prolonged residence at home. Similarly, he adopted new views of the nature of the child and ideal childhood experiences: "Affectionate and with a marked respect for their personality, as if perhaps their inspiration or ideal might be better than his own, yet dignified and elevating by his expectations. He was at ease with them and questioned them kindly, but as if expecting from them something better than had yet appeared, so that he always inspired affection and awe, but never fear" (428–429).

Emerson seldom romped with his children or tolerated silliness, gossip, or meanness. He barely permitted indoor games and juvenile playacting. Only an interest in nature and books drew his unqualified praise. When the children were in bed, he would come to them "and sitting by us in the twilight, chant, to our great delight, a goodnight song . . . to the trees, the birds, the flowers, the members of the family, even the cow and the cat" (429).

An idyllic way to grow up, this program included explicit and implicit intolerances, manipulations, and unstated assumptions about human nature and psychology. Emerson's child rearing theories and practices, as recollected by his children, reflect implicit conflicts and contradictions. Standing in awe of one's father was preferable to standing in fear. The contradictions of the new philosophy of human development appeared in the manipulation of affection, the difficult relation between emotions and family bonds, and preparation for independence and autonomy in extended dependence.

A delightful contrast to the seriousness of the Emerson household is the youthful experience of Edmund Quincy Sewall (1828–1908).[151] At twelve he spent one term as a boarding student in Henry and John Thoreau's private school in Concord. His boarding place housed three other students. These advantaged young men were only partly divided by age and class status, segregated in school and at peer play but less so in residence and extracurricular activities. That segregation was a transition in progress.

Thoreau placed a "natural" emphasis on education. Edmund's diary reflects such a program: mornings devoted to solid geometry, geography, and grammar; afternoons to reading, spelling and definitions, Latin, and algebra. He was to write each morning; Saturdays were for compositions. Writing his first composition about birds, Edmund's purposes crossed Thoreau's: "Mr. Thoreau said that he should give me something to write about of which I did not know much about so I wrote on the Ostrich the Eagle and Falcon which every body knows something about. I suppose he thought I should write about Bobolinks and Chickadees of which I am wholly ignorant. I cunningly took half a sheet of paper to write on whole I managed to fill out my pages. In the afternoon went to the jail with the boys" (April 2, 1840).

For all the discipline of his schedule, Edmund's diary tells a more nuanced tale. March 28, 1840, was "a day of misfortunes." Edmund and a fellow boarder "fired" on a party of boys going by. A "skirmish" followed. "Inferior in force" to the others, they were chased by the "marauders" back to their residence. In racing to spy on their pursuers from a window, they knocked over a pudding. This misadventure culminated at dinner, consisting only of salt fish, "which I hate." Edmund compensated by eating berries, purchasing apples and figs, and receiving another fig from "Mr. John." He writes: "I did very well till supper time." Later that day the boys broke a chair and upset an ink bottle on the tablecloth. With no irony, Edmund closes the day's entry: "P.S. I'm sorry the pudding was lost for it was a baked rice one such as I should have liked."

The students also went to the lyceum, mixing with persons of varied age and status. Once the phrenologist who was due to lecture never arrived. After a display of skulls, the audience heard instead a lecture on Roger Williams of Rhode Island. Edmund's diary also mentions eating clams. On April 1 he responded emotionally to a note from home; homesickness spread in the wake of domestic reminders.

About his daily studies the diary reports less and less. The final entry is much like early ones: "Saturday. I wrote composition. Mr. John at first told me to write about 'Yankee ingenuity and enterprise' but I did not see how I could possibly make anything of it so he gave me 'the biography of my uncle Ben' to write" (April 16).

Although these reports show that young Edmund Sewall was not always practicing proper middle-class habits, he was nonetheless preparing for his later path from home and school out into the world. On the eve of adolescence, Edmund was ripe for the emerging course of development and transition.

If Edmund is refreshing, some of his more virtuous peers are close to insufferable. John Bannan Douglas (1832–1889) of Orwigsburg, Pennsylvania, was a member of the Yale College class of 1852. A studious but not gifted young man, he kept a diary for 1849–1853, from age seventeen to twenty-one.[152] With all the banality of his age, his era, and his middle-class, John's diary evinces moralism and moralizing, a stress on self-discipline and character formation, and the notion of self-making central to the emerging middle class. No doubt strong early socialization by his mother with internalization of self-control lay behind the sentiments recorded in this late adolescent's diary.

John's mundane memoranda display a superficial morality and piety. He mentions the "brotherhood" of his Greek letter society, which provided a surrogate home at college. He often comments on his own and others' habits. On December 7, 1849, he notes the classroom games of "typical students . . . manifesting the usual agony of a student straining his memory." Rather tough on himself, he airs his faults and errors, seeking to improve them: "Arose this morning between five and six oclock. washed my face. Now, there is no time to lie at ease but is a time for vigorous exertion in attainment the greatest improvement mentally and spiritually . . . We cannot occupy a middle position between God and the Devil. There is no use of mincing matters (as they say) about giving oneself to doing right or wrong" (December 13, 1849).

John reports Christmas "riots" between students and faculty and tutors and ritualized interaction between members of different classes. More revealing is his habit of writing moralistic clichés at the top of each diary page, along with doodles. The diary entries have their own ritual form, beginning with his hour of rising and ending with his time of going to bed, giving a sense of his schoolwork for the day, and incorporating a moralistic maxim related to his conduct and lapses. The latter include, for example, "Vice is a clog on human progress" (November 1850). John often notes his need to develop the power of memory. He seems almost obsessively concerned about his efficiency, propriety, and success, and the impressions he made on others, all essential traits of character. He wanted to be respected and to progress.

John displayed proper middle-class character inconsistently, sometimes behaving immaturely. Regretting that he did not introduce his friends to a Miss Ludwig, he writes, "I am quite bashful" (May 7, 1850).[153] His superficiality surfaces in the petty tests he set himself for self-improvement, such as finishing and mailing a letter to a cousin. Despite his rhetoric, we note that John regularly slept past the time for prayers in the college chapel.

John Douglas's final diary entry speaks loudly about the gaps between the theory and practice of character. Now employed as a public school teacher in Pottsville, Pennsylvania, he writes:

> I did not arrive at the School in good time in the morning. It is absolutely necessary that a School Master should set an example of punctuality to his pupils. I must lay out for myself a course of instruction and discipline which I must follow firmly and mildly. In order to do this I must obtain an accurate knowledge of the disposition of each pupil, this obtained and only when this is obtained will I be able to lay down a course which will be best suited for their advancement in knowledge and sobriety. In the first place I must excite their desire for knowledge, their desire to become acquainted with the Great truths that govern themselves and Society. (February 26, 1853)

Knowing which virtues count and striving to make them his own, he reminds us (and himself) that proper middle-class behavior was not always easily or quickly mastered. It was hard work, and could lead to thinly disguised superficiality.[154]

The emerging male middle-class path had ramifications for the final rungs on the ladder of growing up: choosing a career, leaving home, marrying, and establishing a new domestic unit to reproduce middle-class standing.[155] First-person testimonies by women are more forthcoming about these events, but accounts by both men and women show that leaving home was emotionally difficult. With home sentimentalized, romanticized, and starkly juxtaposed to a "cold, cruel world," leaving it to make one's own way could only be seen as hard.[156] Sources of advice ranging from phrenology to numerous voluntary associations and institutions aimed at aiding and protecting migrants and other young persons who were experiencing major life transitions.

Steps toward marriage and an independent household were being taken increasingly prudentially. Ages at first marriage for both men and women increased, and the proportion of people remaining unmarried also rose during the nineteenth century. With difficulty, new rules and rituals for courtship were established. Shifting notions and norms of the individual, gender, and family led to tensions and contradictions along the developing middle-class route. Tantalizing hints about these issues come from correspondence between couples. The courting letters between the thirty-one-year-old New Hampshire physician Elijah Colburn (a graduate of Phillips Exeter Academy and Harvard Medical College) and his future wife, twenty-year-old Sally Belnap, in 1826, provide one view.[157] Although their courtship moved rapidly from February meeting to June wedding and their expressions are bold, the letters tell a tale of caution and concern about intentions, meanings, and actions. Fear of misunderstanding and being misunderstood score the pages. Blending his role as suitor with that of instructor, in response to Sarah's query Elijah speaks volumes about gender difference and proper male concerns: "You cannot at this time so well realise the importance of the most strict attention to my practical concerns as at some future day, when I hope it will be more convenient to enter into particulars than at the present time . . . You may think my mind is to [*sic*] much engaged in my practice, that I appear rather cold and indifferent towards yourself, think however you do not judge this. Please excuse me. I indeed frequently think of you and as frequently lament the unfortunate distance you are situated from me" (March 2, 1826).

In striving for balance on the tightrope of middle-class love and marriage, Elijah and Sarah were hardly alone. Albion Tourgee conflicted directly with his intended about proper female behavior when he argued against her further education. Conflict because of common gender-based imbalances in norms, expectations, and authority marked their lengthy married life. For couples whose differences were better controlled, tension and caution nonetheless remained commonplace. By comparison, what stands out about Elijah Colburn and Sarah Belnap is their apparently successful containment of conflicts. In general, marital tensions remained among the central dilemmas in the new middle-class "pursuit of happiness."

Upper Class

The American upper class was also forming in this era, though constituting the experience of a far smaller population. Two broad patterns of growing up coexisted. The first, more traditional, is described by Joseph Kett and Bernard Farber: relatively limited formal education to perhaps the early teen years, followed by preparation for future work and leadership in the family enterprise.[158] Examples range from the sons of a merchant clerking from age thirteen or fifteen to sons of a merchant-shipper serving on crews for extended voyages or working in offices in London, Edinburgh, or the Caribbean. College or formal professional training was less common. The wealthy had long been ambivalent about higher education, variously considering it a luxury, a confirmation of status, or a utilitarian tool. That attitude was changing, along with values favoring closer family relations.

Like the emerging middle class and some members of the higher levels of the working class, upper-class families began to develop new structures, strategies, and paths of growing up. In part this involved establishing and endowing an array of institutions. Some were meant to maintain, protect, and expand their wealth, from corporations to testamentary, charitable, and philanthropic trusts. Others were entrusted with preparing heirs for their position; typically these were new or re-formed private day or boarding schools and colleges such as Harvard. Upper-class families turned increasingly to these new organizations, although regional (principally northern versus southern) differences and other idiosyncratic variations are striking. William and Jane Pease's comparative study of elites in antebellum Boston and Charleston shows the variable roles of mothers and fathers, education and institutions, and career training.[159] As it formed, and as new paths of growing up became part of that process, the upper class was far less obsessed with uniformity of response and action and a narrow code of character than was the emerging middle class. That difference was itself a class characteristic to which growing up contributed.

Despite the persistence of earlier traditions, two sets of experiences suggest the terms of growing up in the emerging upper class. Stephen Salisbury III, heir to a Worcester, Massachusetts, family fortune, exemplifies a youth born to wealth, whose adult responsibility was to maintain, expand, and use it well in the interests of family, class, and social obligation. His path of growing up prepared him for that role.[160]

An only son, Stephen (1835–1905) attended several public and private schools. For him, as for many of his peers, attendance at an elite boarding school was becoming a new norm. In time this was one of the ways in which a national upper class formed. Preparing for his expected role as heir to a family fortune and cultural leader of local and other institutions, Stephen took his undergraduate degree at Harvard College with the class of 1856. The Boston aristocracy was then completing its remolding of Harvard for its greater utility in the reproduction of class status.[161] With the leisure allowed by family wealth and intellectual interests of his own, Stephen departed on a grand tour focused on study. Returning home in 1858, he completed his preparation at Harvard Law School, class of 1861. That accomplishment foreshadowed his position at the top of the class structure. In 1862 he celebrated by making the first of two expeditions to Central America to pursue his interest in Mayan ruins.

Taking his expected place, Stephen Salisbury III served as trustee of State Mutual Life Assurance, director and president of the Worcester National Bank and Worcester County Institution for Savings, and many railroads and industrial enterprises. His activities and obligations included directorships of and contributions to civic and charitable organizations. Young Salisbury successfully and directly negotiated his upper-class path.

A slightly different route was taken by another upper-class son who also moved within the bounds of class status. Born in Salem in 1832, Joseph Hodges Choate differed from Salisbury by residing and practicing law in the national financial and mercantile capital, New York City.[162] His father was a prosperous physician, and Choate added to the family fortune and position through his achievements in the law. His path also led through the gates of Harvard Yard. And, like Stephen Salisbury, he took his class responsibilities seriously, devoting much of his last eighteen years to "remarkable public services that distinguished [his] life."

As we will further see in the next chapter, upper-class paths of growing up show how youthful experiences and social transformations formed and reformed one another. Conflicts between fathers and sons reflected the anomalous position of privilege within the emerging bourgeois cultural and social order. The Peases conclude that the upper class "was hard-nosed about training its young and assessing their capacity. For the benefits it bestowed, it demanded conformity and ostracized those who rejected its values. While it gave those who strayed a second chance, it did not compromise with them."[163] Intergenerational conflicts were common.

On another level, the upper class's divergence from certain new notions about human development and child rearing created a different sort of contradiction in comparison to emerging middle-class norms. This difference was central to the development and popularization of single-sex, boarding, but family-oriented upper-class institutions for adolescent character training. So, too, was the upper-class family a different environment for child rearing in terms of the persisting distinction between practical, experiential education as against institutional preparation for career and duties. The full import and impact of upper-class paths of growing up emerges from the larger contexts of class, culture, and their contradictions.

Class, culture, contradictions: along with gender and transition, these few words powerfully evoke the accelerating transformations of growing up in the seminal era that embraced the late eighteenth through the mid-nineteenth centuries. In studying this dynamically developing process, we find neither a simple summary nor a casual conclusion possible. This age of transformation saw no culmination. Its significance looms large whether one views its contribution looking backward from a later date or forward from an earlier time.

The principal paths of growing up are best seen as transitional themselves, from those characterized by tradition or transition to those scored by gender or class. Each major path embraced variations and differences among its own divisions. Traditional paths were often in transition themselves. They remained common well into the nineteenth century, even if their resemblance to their counterparts in the preceding period was partial.

Most significant for this era, however, are the paths identified by their transitional qualities, for both young men and young women. Giving the era a historical distinctiveness in their mediation between the often overlapping boundaries between tradition and change, transitional paths were most salient for young people seeking their way amid the confusion of epochal social transformations. Increasingly complex relations with families, institutions, jobs and professions, migration and residential shifts, forms and extent of autonomy are especially telling in marking out the many connections that tie growing up to social change and development. In these linkages, causes and consequences rebound back and forth upon one another with all factors and facets in motion and few simple causes and effects. Individuals and families seeking secure paths to adulthood were simultaneously contributors to and receptors of shifts in the world around them.

Critical elements of modern growing up formed in connection with modern social structures, including gender, race, and ethnicity, which were undergoing redefinition. A world of the young that would be recognizable to the late twentieth century was under construction. By the mid-nineteenth century it was only partially in place, incomplete in its articulation and diffusion, and contradictory to its core. In the next era the refashioning of growing up began to coalesce. Its historical course is no less complicated for that.

CHAPTER FOUR

Paving the Paths in the Nineteenth Century

LOOKING back on an era in American history commonly, almost stereo-typically, associated with unprecedented change, Richard L. McCormick writes in "Public Life in Industrial America, 1877–1917": "Virtually every man, woman, and child in America had to face the unsettling consequences of industrialization." Exaggerating for emphasis, he elaborates: "Railroad and telegraph (and later, telephone) lines penetrated the countryside, factories multiplied in size and number, millions of migrants from the farms of America and Europe found their way to our cities . . . Scarcely a person remained unaffected; scarcely anyone's daily life was untouched. Many people made their peace with these developments—or failed to make it—in individual, private ways . . . But others supplemented their private decisions with public efforts." Among those "ways"—sometimes embracing change, sometimes resisting its impacts, often attempting an uncomfortable balancing act—was the continuing transformation of growing up. "Many organized efforts to cope with the consequences of industrialism produced unexpected results," McCormick notes. "Virtually every feature of American life was being transformed, and no one could have anticipated where the changes would lead."[1]

The voices of young persons growing up between the middle decades of the nineteenth and the early years of the twentieth centuries, heard in this chapter, proclaim unequivocally that more private, individual, and familial efforts shared in that quality of change. From either dimension, responses to change often included efforts at conservation and turns back toward tradition which intertwined in complex ways with broader transformations. Some failed where others succeeded. Shifting norms and expectations and their spreading stratification by social class, gender, race, and ethnicity simultaneously simplified and complicated the attribution of failure or success as well as the very paths by which the young came of age.

The extent of change can be and often is exaggerated by students of childhood, adolescence, and youth, as it is by social, economic, cultural, and political historians. Lost in that emphasis is the presence and power of traditions that were themselves changing within the crucible of societal reformation. Among the continuities with earlier eras, for example, were the ongoing processes of class formation, gender reconstruction, cultural redefinition, institutional mediation of change, and the struggle for the terms and powers of social order. The extent of shifts and the magnitude of effects, the scale of life, the size and complexity of the continental nation, the numbers of people, and the degrees of apparent difference were nevertheless unprecedented.

Focusing on organized public actions, McCormick argues:

> Most people confronted variations on a common problem: the defense of their families and communities against outside forces emanating from industrial growth and the increasing heterogeneity of the population. Americans faced that problem, moreover, within a common environment: a rapidly expanding economy that was causing massive dislocations, frequent depressions, and widespread unemployment. Yet whatever the commonalities, these conditions were experienced by diverse, often antagonistic groups with unequal capacities for shaping public choices.[2]

The same stimuli and the same range of possibilities and restraints faced individuals and families who sought to refashion their strategies for growing up to accord with their perception of the social disorder around them. Public and private life overlapped, blurring their margins, regardless of ideologies that promoted rigid separation. For those whose growing up was buffeted by these transitions and transformations, concepts of both public and of private took their toll.

An epoch marked by political crises that led to the ruptures of Civil War and the incomplete reunification of Reconstruction; major depressions that marked each decade except the war-buoyed 1860s; violent clashes of capital, state, and labor; rural reorganization and protest; and growing antinomies of class, gender, race, and ethnicity could not escape collateral charges of crises in growing up made by contemporaries and later students. McCormick writes: "Within a single decade [the 1890s], immigration from southern and eastern Europe emerged as one of the greatest forces . . . A new culture of leisure and consumption . . . made its first tentative appearance. The movement toward consolidation in business and industry took long strides toward permanently transforming the nation's economy." Political parties dramatically realigned, and the United States "burst onto the world stage." Thus, "most people experienced those years as a time of crisis, of economic depression, and perhaps even of severe personal disorientation."[3] Responses ranged widely, from the privatization of middle-class families and their careful socialization shared by home and school to the rise of interest groups aimed at transforming the habits of the alien at home, in private and public institutions, and under public laws and policies. Innovations stood more or less uncomfortably alongside reconstructions of supposedly tried and true traditions now imposed on young persons and cultural groups presumed to be ignorant of them. Crises perceived and proclaimed are not always crises experienced. Tradition, transition, transformation, in new and shifting balances, marked the manner in which the young struggled to make their way toward the maturity and independence of adulthood.

For this era a limited set of images of young persons dominates most viewpoints and shapes our understanding: child laborers in factories or tenement workshops, "newsies" on street corners, city urchins swept off to farm or reformatory, scrubbed and pampered suburban youngsters, high school and college students forming new peer cultures, farm lads and lasses steeling their moral fiber against the sinful cities to which many would migrate. As with so many clichés and stereotypes, these representations are not so much wrong as biased and incomplete. The context that informs our comprehension of them is shaped by the growing up experiences of the preceding century. Those transformation of paths of growing up did not await the increased pace of industrialization, urbanization, and immigration of the second half of the nineteenth century. In many ways, basic changes preceded this period, laying the foundations for the future.

As we consider the principal paths in this perspective, continuities gain a new emphasis: these are continuities with respect to the further development of transitional paths and, increasingly, class-determined paths of growing up. No path was static; their development advanced in this period. Less novel by the second half of the nineteenth century, transitional paths were no less significant or powerful. More pervasive directly and indirectly, they were also more influential. One of the most seminal developments, whose beginning we glimpsed earlier, was the way in which emerging middle-class paths affected growing up across the nation and the social order. The boundaries between class and transitional paths blurred at their margins.

For this era three principal paths predominate in the configurations of growing up. They are the transitional and class-determined paths for young men and the female paths. Missing paths include those of the rural and urban working class and the poor, servants, many immigrants, and persons of color. Institutionalized young persons and prison inmates constitute another noteworthy absence. In comparison with preceding periods, the smaller number of principal paths is striking. But as the first-person testimonies make abundantly clear, the array of paths is no less complicated, if somewhat less varied. We find no linear convergence toward homogeneity. The reduction of paths represents a more complex, contradictory process related to social, economic, and cultural development, regional and national. Growing up was closely, dialectically, but seldom neatly connected to changes in all these areas.

With wide-ranging implications for the young and their families, paths previously designated as traditional diminished. Some were reconstructed to an extent within transitional, class, and gender paths, as we shall see. A lengthy process, this shift incorporated changes in norms and expectations of growing up and the evolving correlates of age and early life course stages. In part it pivoted on the process whereby traditional craft apprenticeship and professional preparation gradually eroded and in time were replaced by new institutional forms of education and certification. This in turn was closely tied to the ongoing work of class formation. In part it also pivoted on the capitalist transformation of the countryside as regional and national markets remade social and intergenerational relationships. In part it stemmed from immigration, the construction of ethnicity, and internal migration. And in large part it was tied to gender development, as many women's paths tended to reflect a cultural re-formation, an invention of "traditional" ways that diverged from men's experiences and from past practices. Men's paths had their parallels for women. With the passing of tradition came its reassertion in cultural mythology, nostalgia for "old days" good and not so good. The testimonies reveal this complex cultural process and allow us to witness its invention, diffusion, and enduring impact. These elements stand out sharply among the contradictions that mark this era in the history of growing up.

Standing between the assumed extremes of tradition and change, transitional paths of growing up took on new and different qualities. Some of their characteristics were defined or at least perceived as "traditional," irrespective of the extent or experience of change, for example, among those taking small-town, southern, and/or rurally rooted paths. Despite their relative novelty in comparison to paths more accurately termed traditional, western and major migratory paths were subjected to similar cultural appropriation. In these cultural manipulations lay powerful and sometimes dangerous legacies for the future, especially when such redefined "traditions" confronted new class, ethnic, racial, and gender formations, typically but not always deemed inferior to the "old" ways.[4] A striking new hegemony of class-determined paths, sometimes in association with paths linked to ethnicity, also marked this period. Its power can be understood only in the complicated conjuncture of changes, continuities, and shifting cultural currents that developed amid the material and social relations underlying and accelerating class formation.

The first of the principal paths we shall consider is the transitional. It incorporated three major subpaths for men. One is the rural, small town, southern route, blending and blurring older, traditional forms of growing up with various degrees of social and economic change. A second, equally a part of the historical stuff of national development, is the route informed and shaped by western migration. The third, another blend of tradition and change, is the discontinuous passage often but not exclusively to middle-class and professional destinations. None of these was new to the second half of the nineteenth century. Each took a different shape and meaning as circumstances and balances of opportunities and limitations shifted. The very salience of transition as a metaphor for experience and expression was recast as conditions and expectations changed and growing up was itself transformed.

The second principal path is the female path of growing up. Seemingly more diverse and complicated than male paths, it reflects the impact of gender differentiation and the influence of social class on the one hand and, on the other, the multiple, conflicting demands on and roles for women. Female growing up consisted of two major subpaths. The transitional one incorporated the three distinct but overlapping avenues of rural, southern; older, more settled rural; and major migration, especially to the West. This variation contradicts notions of female growing up as a homogeneous experience and evinces both the domain that was shared and the domain that was differentiated among brothers and sisters. Social class increasingly influenced these transitional avenues. The second major subpath is the class-linked pattern, comprising the three lanes of upper-, middle-, and working-class (including urban and immigrant) life.

The third principal path is the class-linked path for men. Its major routes, each of which developed in encounters with the others as well as with paths of tradition and transition, are the upper-, middle-, and working-class avenues. Although their evolution remained uneven and incomplete, and there is a notable degree of overlap, the lines are nonetheless distinct, for example, in terms of family relations, institutions such as schools, modes of socialization and career preparation, social relations, expectations, and changing norms. If not unprecedented, these social class paths achieved new heights in number and influence, by example and through familial, institutional, and normative transformations. Along with gender paths, they framed much of the future of growing up.

Transitional Paths

In the second half of the nineteenth century, as traditional paths of growing up diminished, countless individuals and families struggled to cope with the actual and perceived threats of social change. Transitional paths occupied much of the shifting terrain between efforts aimed at maintaining continuity and the embracing of change. The lines between traditional and transitional paths blurred, sometimes through attempts to redefine or reconstruct new traditions as older ways were eclipsed. A rhetoric of supposed "tradition" permeated many responses to change and difference. Such "traditions" of growing up took on great value; for example, individual striving and sacrifice were compared favorably with institutionally aided advances, class advantages, or new strategies of prolonged dependence and preparation for adult challenges.

Experiences of growing up reflected in poignant and sometimes powerful personal testimony can be distorting or misunderstood. Nevertheless, expressions of traditions newly reconstructed, or sometimes newly lost, are central to the overall transformations of growing up. They are telling both in themselves and in their complex relation to change. New cultural mythologies were created and diffused as legacies to present and future. Especially significant, singly and collectively, are those emanating from small-town, rural, and southern origins; western migration; and paths to middle-class or professional destinations marked by discontinuities.

Transitional paths covered a wide range of routes. They confused the lines between old ways and new, continuity and change. They differentiated between traditional ways and modern class, gender, and racial paths, even as they advanced the latter. They represented social processes with long-term cultural impacts central to regional and national, class, and ethnic development, whether great human migrations or discontinuous journeys to professional or middle-class status. Issues of particular significance are the uses, impacts, and interactions of social institutions, the market, relations between fathers and sons, peer interactions, and social as well as geographic mobility. It is no exaggeration to claim that these transitional paths constitute a keystone of the transformation of growing up.

Rural

Columbus B. Campbell, born on December 20, 1856, near Calhoun in Gordon County, Georgia, aptly introduces the theme of rural, southern, small-town growing up as experienced and recollected.[5] His memoir begins: "At the time of my birth my parents were in very meager circumstances . . . neither side of my grandparents owned any Negroes" (1). His maternal grandparents were strict Presbyterians, in good farming circumstances. Their children were trained early in the Bible. Columbus deemed his upbringing "a great help": "A lot of people were not as strict as my mother's parents . . . Many times the 'rod' was used. We were taught to obey our parents . . . I fear we spare the rod too much at this day and time" (2).

The Civil War changed his family's course.[6] With his father serving in the "Rebel" army and his mother left to care for four sons under eight, times were hard. Living on their maternal grandparents' farm until the Confederate army surrendered, Columbus and his brothers learned important lessons "by working hard and saving" (4).

After being transported to Indiana with captured forces, his father found work there once the war ended and sent for his family. In the fall of 1865 family life recommenced in a rented log house five miles from New Providence, Indiana. An uncle, also a freed prisoner of war, added to the family's labor force and the children's entertainment. The boys worked in the fields, while Pa and Uncle Andy cut cross-ties for the railroad. In spring the boys helped by cutting timber. When their landlord relocated, they moved into his larger and more comfortable home, joined by another uncle and a male cousin.

Despite the example of their grandparents, the family only occasionally attended the nearby Christian Campbellite church. The boys had no religious education. "But," Columbus reports, "when I spent all day Sunday romping round with other boys, when night came I felt mean and conscious that I hadn't kept the Sabbath as I was taught to when I was at Grand Pa's." He blamed the lapse on his "environment" (13). Schooling, too, was irregular, limited to three months of free school in the winter term. "Here I will have to brag on myself a little," he writes. "I learned my A,B,C's in one day and the multiplication tables in a short time." But in general, he writes, "our schooling was very limited the five years we lived in Indiana." The boys picked chestnuts in the fall, which they sold in town for ten cents a quart. "That was our spending money" (13).

Moving from one rented farm to another, the family gradually improved their circumstances. They did well planting tobacco, and Pa continued cutting logs. By the time they were ten or older, the boys were expected to work at home. They helped their mother with washing and tending the younger children, and they assisted with farm and lumber work. With no daughters old enough to work, gender role conflicts were absent. The boys enjoyed their work. But there were "losses," as Columbus termed them. Childhood playmates came from neighboring farms, and included the sons of a fellow Georgian who had served in the army with Pa. "This made an inseparable tie," writes Columbus (15). Sundays were spent with a nearby Methodist family: "They would have us come to their home of Sundays and have Sunday School by reading and telling Bible stories. We liked them and felt much better when Sunday night came" (15).

After five years in Indiana, the family followed Ma's father to Arkansas. "Glowing news of the prospects" for cotton growing combined with the desire to see their kin. Columbus was about fourteen. His family now consisted of six sons and one daughter. A great family reunion took place.

Columbus recalls: "The five years we were in Indiana I had acquired quite an education and was proud to tell Aunt Lizzie and Uncle Joe about it. They in turn would brag on me . . . I was pretty well advanced for the short time I had spent in school and I was pardonably proud of it" (18).

Columbus's family rented a farm on a large creek and planned to raise corn and cotton. Several of the boys, including Columbus, were big enough for regular farm work, including plowing, planting, and harvesting. The brothers attended school in the summer when it was too hot for farm work. In time Pa purchased land. They built a house, and began to clear and fence land for planting corn. Columbus "was old enough to work out and make enough money to buy groceries" (23). Grand Pa bought a neighboring farm, and other relatives settled nearby, recreating a world of kin. Frequent visiting knitted the youngsters into a reconstructed traditional web of family.

More active religious participation had an influence on teenaged Columbus: "We had a good Brush Arbor meeting and I felt my first conviction that I was a sinner and needed salvation. I went up as mourner . . . I think it was a Baptist meeting. I was not converted" (23–24).

The land eventually proved too dry to farm. Visiting a brother in Missouri, Pa found he liked that country and rented a farm in Barry County, to which he moved his family—now seven boys and two girls—in 1876. Satisfied with the new farm, the children found playmates nearby. Three miles away was a little village with store, blacksmith, gristmill, and schoolhouse. The main trading town, Pierce City on the railroad line, was farther away.

The Campbells were soon joined by two uncles and their families. Kinship nets widened and contracted and then widened again. Helping an uncle move, Columbus gained another lesson: his aunt and uncle's quarreling he writes, "just disgusted me. I thought if I ever married and had to live that kind of life, I would rather not marry. Consequently I was very careful about choosing a mate . . . put off marrying until I was almost thirty years old . . . If there is any thing in this life I cherish it is PEACE AND HARMONY in my family life. So I hesitated a long time, never telling anyone my reason" (27).

His social life expanded in Missouri: "Young people always want to get together and have a lively time. Most of the families were religious so we had singings one or two nights a week" (28). They also had play parties at people's homes. This was not his cup of tea, Columbus reminisced. In an age before movies, "we had to get up something of our own to entertain ourselves. Young people just will have some place to go. I was never a right good hand at the play parties. I would go to be with the crowd and take part, but I didn't feel at home like I did at the singings" (29).

In his early twenties Columbus still remained at home, working the family farm. In no rush to move or marry, he purchased forty acres and improved it, growing corn and sharing work. His siblings began to wed. Many settled nearby, constructing apparently traditional family arrangements that were made possible in part by new market, railroad, and agricultural technology. Columbus's own hesitation and tardy marriage was as much a modern as a traditional choice. He was in no hurry to declare his independence. That was one lesson he learned growing up at home: "I remember the day I was 21. Pa told me I was a free man . . . to look out for myself. I had to take a little cry. I was always tender hearted. I had always worked under order; had nothing but my horse, bridle and saddle; had never hired out and so I was at a loss to know how I was going to start in" (34).

Twenty-one years of age represented no milestone on the road to autonomy for Columbus. His transition was a gradual one. In part it involved planting his own corn. He began to produce sorghum, first with Uncle Lee and later with his brother Rome. Columbus developed his forty acres, adding to it and building a house.

Approaching thirty, enjoying some economic security, and feeling more confident about himself and his place in his world, Columbus

> had begun to think about getting me a help meet . . . There were several nice girls I had been going with. Somehow there was one I couldn't get off my mind. She was a good religious girl and I thought I could get her. Something seemed to tell me she would make me a good wife. I decided to see if I could have any luck. I hadn't made up my mind how I was going to kill myself if she refused, but I dreaded the ordeal. One Sunday after Church, we had taken a buggy ride and then sat in the shade of a tree and talked it all over. Everything was all right.
>
> I never had asked a girl to marry me or even approached the subject. It wasn't near as dangerous as I thought it would be. We got along fine and finally decided the great day would be November 19, 1885.

Following a "simple wedding at home" for Ona Lucinda and Columbus, he wrote, "From now on it will be we" (37). Setting up housekeeping with his wife in their new home, Columbus considered himself fortunate. "I was always thankful for the chance Pap and Ma gave me in giving me a home until I could provide a home to take my wife to. I was always good and kind to my father and mother" (38).

Blurring simple distinctions, traditional and more modern influences combined to shape Columbus Campbell's transitional path. In its timing and pace of transition, the path he trod resembled traditional forms of growing up in an earlier America. But a fuller perspective incorporates the

Civil War and its disruption; numerous family moves for the sake of a better life; the ebb and flow of kinship; and opportunities made possible by the market, technology, railroad, and the like. Basic elements of his domestic arrangements and his slow approach to autonomy were new if not unprecedented. Columbus's path was transitional in its mix of tradition and change. The gloss of tradition is increased in hindsight by nostalgia and rhetoric, but among all the apparent continuities, change asserts its presence.

Despite differences in origin and destination, the path that Samuel E. Tillman (1847–1942) followed from his plantation boyhood took a similarly transitional shape.[7] His growing up was reshaped by the Civil War and national institutions. Sammy's route took him far from Tennessee and planter traditions. Born the fourth son among eleven children of Lewis and Mary Catherine Tillman of Bedford County, Tennessee (his father was a Seminole War veteran, county officeholder, newspaper editor, and plantation owner), Sammy grew up with the plantation as his playground. Both slave and white children were his playmates.

With his brothers, Sammy received a more or less classical academy education, interrupted by the Civil War. Schooling began when he was seven and a half and continued for seven years. While attending the Duck River Male Academy, taught mainly by his uncle, Sammy lived with his grandparents thirteen miles from home. Most of the boys lived within five miles of the school; a few, from as far as Nashville and New Orleans, boarded. Only during vacations did Sammy return to his parents' home, where he played, fished, bathed, and observed farm operations.

His progress at school left more lasting memories than the plantation did: "What was accomplished by that one teacher at the Duck River Male Acad. [was] quite astounding . . . we all seemed to progress about equally. When I began school in 1854, I knew the alphabet but had not learned to spell; and so [I] was near the beginning of my school education" (150). Students were divided by size rather than by class. Ballgames, bathing, swinging, and chasing rabbits occupied the boys outside the classroom. On occasion the teacher permitted them to bring their hounds to school and allowed an hour in the afternoon for "drag racing." With the outbreak of war, the school closed in 1861.

One older Tillman son joined the Confederate army, although their father was opposed to secession. The three schoolboys stayed at home for the duration of the conflict. He wanted them to be occupied productively: "Father concluded that idleness *could not* be permitted, and that he would depart from the prevailing custom and informed us, who were old enough and capable of regular work, that we must become regular day workers, taking part with the colored people in such classes of work as we could do" (153). Under the unofficial supervision of "old Uncle Jim," a trusted slave and plantation foreman in all but name, the boys kept busy for four years: "To assist in the plantation labors added our element of difference between ourselves and the boys of our well-to-do neighbors." Sammy's "natural inclination" for outdoor life (as well as an "intense interest" in the war) eased this novel transition to home and to work (153). Sammy also wrote "passes" for male slaves to visit their families and friends on neighboring plantations free from punishment by "patrollers."

On the recommendation of Andrew Johnson, military governor of Union-occupied Tennessee and a family friend, in 1865 young Sammy Tillman was appointed by President Lincoln to the United States Military Academy at West Point. This diverted his path far from the South and plantation life. After prepping for a few months at Miami (Ohio) University, Plebe Tillman joined the class of 1869. He graduated near the top as Lieutenant Tillman. His first assignment took him to frontier service in Kansas. After a few months he was called back to West Point as an instructor in chemistry, geology, and mineralogy. Three years later Sammy left to serve with the army engineers surveying and mapping in the West. A service career culminated in his appointment as superintendent of West Point during the First World War.

The shift from traditional plantation boyhood to new professional career was certainly a significant moment in Sammy Tillman's path of growing up. His education, his father's atypical attitude toward his sons, the war, patronage, national institutions such as the military academy and the armed forces, and new career options all contributed to shaping his transitional route from Tennessee to the wider world.

From rural Tennessee to Binghamton, New York, from rural South to small-town North, transitional paths abounded. Elements of tradition and change blended to create opportunities, constraints, and outcomes that were as distinctive to the era and the transformation of growing up as they were contradictory. Born December 14, 1847, Morris Treadwell began at age twelve a diary he would keep for the next decade.[8] Reflecting a proliferating age consciousness, Morris listed not only his birth date and age but also the ages of his parents and siblings, and on each birthday he reported his age as well as his height and weight.[9]

Morris's life was familiar and ordinary. His farmer father sometimes taught school. Morris helped with farm work, attended school and lectures and often went to meeting in town with his sisters. At home he read his Bible on Sundays and received the *Sunday School Advocate* and *Good News*. At twelve he took the temperance pledge. With his siblings he enjoyed watching the firemen perform on the Fourth of July. He enjoyed school, studying geography, arithmetic, and grammar, and attending school exhibitions. He liked to read, and read often—history, for example. Morris reports these varied activities in his journal without distinguishing among them. They constituted a boy's standard routine and regimen.

Morris's social life with peers expanded as he entered his teens. At fifteen he reports: "Surprise party at our house of young folks in the evening. We had a very pleasant visit, and an excellent good time" (February 19, 1863). His circle showed other signs of adolescent culture. He reports on May 3, 1863: "Sunday. I went up to the school house meeting in the evening to hear Hiram Gale. The young folks laughed & joked through meeting, much to his discomfiture." In May a small circus and menagerie came to town; in the fall a singing school formed. A magic lantern exhibition also passed through. In July the wartime draft began: "Pay $300 or go." In December Morris read *Uncle Tom's Cabin*. When he was sixteen hunting and trapping captured his interest. We get a sense of juvenile adventure and masculine bravado mixed in an adolescent brew: "Getting to like Hunting and Trapping very much. I like to hunt, or trap, better than to go to parties, ride down hill, go to town, Fourth of July or other amusements which young people generally like better. I had rather shoot a squirrel or other animal or trap a skunk or weasel than to go to a Circus any day . . . I think I should like to be a hunter & trapper when I am a man if I lived, and go where game is plenty" (December 31, 1863).[10]

Though an avid student and reader, the sixteen-year-old ran into teenage trouble in January 1864. At spelling school "a cud of tobacco was threw at the teacher which partly broke it up. It was laid to me, but the wrong one." Ten days later, on February 6, "the teacher called at noon & had an altercation about a little matter at school from which I think I shall not go to school any more."[11] Busy with farm work and other activities, Morris never admitted missing the classroom after his abrupt withdrawal. He continued reading. With his sisters and another girl he toured the institutions of the local metropolis, from the Binghamton courthouse and jail to the poorhouse, which held a perverse attraction. Male peer activities and peer culture were distinct. With his friends Morris "went down to river in the evening . . . & went in swimming. I cannot swim any yet. We wrestled, tried out strength in different ways & had a bully old time" (June 18, 1864). They pitched quoits. Morris also tried his hand at painting pictures; friends found them "very nice."

An incipiently modern teenager, Morris had bouts of feeling low. On October 16, 1864, he noted, "I have been very low spirited this week, thinking over old times and other matters." He was sixteen. A year later he disappeared for several days without notice, to visit a friend eighty miles away. His parents were not pleased. Social activities were a partial antidote to low spirits. Three days after reporting his blues, Morris took part in a husking bee and he "had a first rate time of it. Husked off about 100 bushels. Laughed an awful sight." The next day, in mixed-age company, he and two sisters "went over to Uncle Augustus's to a party & dance in the evening. Had playing, fiddling & dancing & we had a first rate good time of it. About 75 persons there. Young folks & old folks & all went off very nice" (October 20, 1864). Age-segregation in the activities of the young, a phenomenon of increasing consequence, did not yet dominate society; social life embraced both inclusive and exclusive age and gender groupings.

Among young people conflicts sparked. Morris had spats with boys and with girls. On December 8, 1865: "I went home with Lizzie last night & today I heard that Frank Barlow was angry because I had stepped in his way. I lost all interest in the meeting. I had a talk with both of them after meeting. With Frank it was all right. But Lizzie felt very cold towards me." Morris reveals his frustration and anger with Lizzie: "Lizzie would not speak till I did first. I will never speak to her again until she does first. She may go to the old harry!" (December 9). The next day, he reports, she "came round all right."

His eighteenth birthday raised new questions for Morris and his family. He talked with his father about leaving home to try to fashion a life from hunting and trapping or other work (December 29, 1865). Notions of adventure in the Wild West lured him. On January 18, 1866, Morris had a successful conversion: "I experience religion today & last night. I feel safe. I spoke down to meeting at night. It made many hearts rejoice." He took communion and "the right hand of fellowship," and further pondered his future. At the end of the year he wrote simply, "I should like to go west & I shall some day" (December 31, 1866). Stimulated by the marriage of friends in the new year, Morris showed more frequent concern about his future. By late winter and spring 1868, the twenty-year-old still "hope[d] in a short time to be out west or somewhere among thousands of game where I think I can live contented. My greatest ambition now is to be a Good Hunter & Trapper" (June 8, 1866).

On turning twenty-one (which he celebrated by hunting fox), Morris prepared to leave home. On December 15 he went to the city to buy a new coat and an account book: "I expect to start for myself in life now. Earn my own living, fight my own way, and do the best I can." Morris had imbibed a litany of new middle-class values, which he blended with the romance of masculine adventure in the West. His lengthy delay in growing up and his caution also reflect a new consensus about the difficulty and dangers of starting out alone in life and leaving the protection of the family home. Morris's quest for western adventure likely had the contradictory effect of making it more difficult for him to depart from home. It had its juvenile elements, too.

Finally, in March 1869, with his father's assistance, Morris actively prepared to leave: "We packed my trunk for my journey. I rather hate to leave the old hills and valleys of my native home where I have perhaps enjoyed the happiest hours that I will in my life." Morris spent almost two years with cousins in the Midwest. On his next birthday he confided: "Another year is here. I am now 22 years of age. In 22 more, much of my life will be spent. I am realizing more and more the value of time and life for various things. I am here in Illinois enjoying myself with my friends. I expect to be home in a year if all goes well." Without career quandaries or definite plans, he returned in late fall 1870. Morris took up beekeeping and honey making. Clearing his own piece of land, he remained there, filling up his journal. For all his "bully" ambitions, Morris Treadwell's path turned home. Traditional and new aspects of growing up intertwined in that conclusion to his path.[12]

The new nostalgia that developed along small-town and rural transitional paths soon took the form of a potent cultural mythology. Contradictory at their core, such myths were used to laud, applaud, and sometimes attempt to preserve so-called traditional opportunities for growing up, in contrast with major migrations and urban ways. Sometimes, however, they were used to damn the sorry sight that rural and small-town America presented to some by the end of the century. They were also used to justify efforts to "save" poor or "deviant" city children by removing them from their families to supposedly more nurturing rural environments. Seldom were these views accurate.[13] The myths nevertheless provided sticks for beating the cities and their residents, generation after generation. Among the cultural consequences of the transformation of growing up, cultural mythologies and transitional paths went hand and hand.

Western Migration

Among formative experiences and their cultural legacy, the impact of western migration and/or pioneer life on transitional paths of growing up was equally powerful.[14] Some of the stories provide a highly dramatic impact. Unusually diverse in comparison to those of other periods and paths, they reach new heights of representational resonance in their stirring portrayals of paths taken and their personal meaning. "Tradition" was discovered and proclaimed in what were often in fact novel experiences. More significant and subtle mixes of change and tradition can be lost in the ensuing confusion.[15]

Beyond a recurring bravado, many of these testimonies present revealing views of a new style of growing up. They illustrate significant paths for the second half of the nineteenth century. Richard Henry Alexander, for one, recorded his experiences in diary and narrative form.[16] Born on March 26, 1844, in Edinburgh, Richard emigrated with his parents to Canada when he was eleven. They settled in Toronto, where he attended an elite academy, Upper Canada College, and the Model Grammar School. Matriculating at age seventeen at the University of Toronto, Richard planned to study medicine after he took his bachelor's degree. He seemed firmly established on a middle-class path to the professions.

His mother's death, however, and his father's intention to return to Scotland upset his plans. Richard chose to stay in Canada and support himself, a radically different course. He filled several minor business positions until spring 1862, when news of the discovery of gold in Caribou, British Columbia, reached Ontario. When several former schoolmates decided to travel overland to the gold fields, Richard joined them. Arriving in New Westminster in November, he got a job chopping firewood. He later worked for John Robson, editor of the *British Columbian*. In spring 1863 Richard reached the gold fields. He did not find quick success. Eventually he settled in Vancouver, where he lived until his death in 1915.

Leaving the middle-class path temporarily to follow the trail of mass movement, adventure, and risk-taking that marked the gold rush was a typical transitional course to the West, part of the process of peopling the cities and towns of the Great Plains and the Pacific coast. Less dramatic, and different in origin as well as destination, but no less prominent among the transitional paths of growing up was James Granville Rouse's experience, which was inseparable from his geographic movements. In his nineties he recollected his life in the 1860s to 1880s.[17] Born August 14, 1855, at Garnettsville in Meade County, Kentucky, James was the fifth child of his twenty-six-year-old mother and twenty-eight-year-old father. His mother died when he was six. His memory of his strict and stern father was etched more deeply. His father's firm sense of right and wrong permanently impressed the son.

James grew up around his father's blacksmith shop. When not singing or swearing, his father would tell the boy stories of his Old Virginia childhood. James looked up to him and to his older brother Will. The arrival of the stagecoach, and its occasional stay while a horseshoe was replaced, was the boy's sole exposure to the larger world. James recalled his early life as pleasant and comfortable despite his mother's death. His father remarried his wife's sister, a widow with a daughter, "almost before we realized our motherless state" (8). Ill with consumption, she died giving birth. "Children of a century ago had to accept death stoically," James remarks. "Parents then fully expected at least half of their offspring to die before maturity" (8).

After the Civil War, James's father sold his property and moved the family by steamboat to Owensboro, seventy-five miles away. For James a formative succession of migrations began. Always "searching for additional ways to add to his worldly good," his father leased a coal mine, planted a tobacco field, and leased strips of woodland that Will and hired men worked for lumber. Against the wishes of his fourteen-year-old daughter, James's father married the sister of his two previous wives. "My new stepmother was twenty and father forty," James writes, "but she fitted into our circle, for she had a faculty of making friends and was more like an older sister to the girls than a stepmother" (12).

James began his formal schooling in a private house, where he learned spelling, reading, and numbers. The schoolday lasted from early morning to almost sunset with "pretty strict" discipline from a teacher whose ability to keep order was valued more than "book larnin'." In retrospect, James found the monotonous memorization and chanting of the multiplication tables valuable in work and commercial dealings. Sunday mornings were a special delight, not only because the family indulged in biscuits with honey, but also because "my parents didn't go in for religion enough to spoil Sunday for us" (16). Instead it was a day for recreation. When they did go to church, they tried different ones, as young men did when courting; they went on foot, "uncomfortable and aching in unaccustomed shoes" (16). For many, church was a form of entertainment. Under his father's influence, James remained skeptical of religion.

After one brother left home and several sisters married, the five remaining children moved with their parents to Illinois in 1871. Their father rented a farm with a blacksmith shop in Clifton County, near his sister and Springfield. The move was exciting for fourteen-year-old James. The young people went to parties and dances in their new community. Unlike Kentucky, Illinois had free schools. James and his school-age siblings immediately enrolled. Though no scholar, James later concluded that a good memory was worth as much as schooling "because my mind isn't cluttered with learning that I have little use for" (20).

In another year the family moved again, renting a farm and blacksmith shop from an uncle near Taylorville. Another child was born. In addition to working on the farm, James drove a wagon for trading and shopping in Springfield. Helping raise corn and hogs, James usually did not start school each year until January, and he attended only until March, when he resumed his farm labors. He liked school, but there was no chance for him to attend the university like his rich uncle's children.

Then came another change: "After long years work in Kentucky and Illinois my father had but $400 capital, which was not getting ahead very fast so he decided to go to Kansas and homestead" (22). After several false starts and further diminution of cash, in January 1877 the family moved to Bristow, where another blacksmith shop awaited. Within a year, James's father had his own shop.

In 1880, now aged twenty-five, James left home for the first time. Taking advantage of congressional extension of the Homestead Act, he returned to Illinois to work. The next fall he went back to Kansas. With "$75 in my pockets, I thought I hadn't done bad, since I had sent some money home" (25). "Sometime later," with his brother-in-law, James joined a crew of laborers working on the Kansas-Pacific Railroad. In his mid-twentys, he alternately left and returned home as jobs and opportunities punctuated the discontinuous rhythms that combined traditional and novel paths. The state, the railroad, and the market, as well as family connections, sounded an uneven beat, to which his movements responded. Railroad work continued to drive James's migrations, eventually taking him to Colorado.

After that experience, he writes, "it was good to be going home, even if we hadn't much money. People asked along the way, 'Got your tax money and going home, hey?' They knew we had been working to pay taxes on our land back home when we had proved up on our claims. The tax was only $10 or $15 but it was harder to raise than several hundred would be now" (25). That his parents continued to pull up stakes and "try another locality in the manner of real pioneers" did not make it easier (25–26). Even in Bristow, "the place they had been searching for all the years," money was scarce, and his father had to trade blacksmithing for food, feed, and household goods (26). The nearest market was thirty-five miles away; a round-trip took three days.

Working for his family and others, James also advanced along his own path, "proving up" a land claim by working it six months each year for five years, and putting a certain number of acres under cultivation. He began to build a house. With another local man he set out to earn extra money by breaking prairie land for three dollars an acre. In 1879 they hired out to do grading for the B&M Railroad. Pioneer life was hard and dangerous. James was impressed that many stuck with it rather than giving up and returning east. Friendship, community, and necessary interdependence flourished in this environment. "Having always played the fiddle," James recalls, "I was in demand constantly to play for dances" (30).

In 1884, one year shy of his thirtieth birthday, James Rouse married Jessie Benton McClellan. She had arrived at age twenty to teach in the Briston, Kansas, district school, having taught and boarded around since she was fifteen. For the newlyweds need stood above any notion of genteel domesticity: "School teachers made as much as $25 a month and after our marriage Jessie taught several terms, one year before our son, Tom, was born and two afterward. I think my wife was the most ambitious woman I ever knew" (31). Ending his peripatetic and prolonged adolescence and youth, James established an independent household and family. With crop failure from 1884 to 1888, Jessie's teaching ensured their subsistence; the baby was cared for by relatives—one kind of dependency in a family economy. James Rouse's extended transitional path of growing up was forged by family circumstances and historical forces, including the construction of the railroads, government land policy, and educational institutions.[18]

Thomas Arthur Whitaker's family took a different path from the city to the West.[19] Thomas, born in 1857, lived in Waltham, Massachusetts. He worked oiling looms at a nearby textile mill when he began his diary at age seventeen. His journal, which spans five years, was begun in 1874 in a daybook Thomas's father gave him, along with copies of several poems and a list of the letters he received in 1873. Thomas daily recorded his familiar teenage activities. Living at home, in addition to working, he attended various churches, studied his Sunday school lessons, went to prayer meetings, and read the Bible. With friends he picnicked, took walks, participated in socials, talked, played, and read. He visited relatives and took music lessons, practicing on the church organ.

Although much of Thomas's reading was religious, he also read advice for young men. Sometimes he attended lectures, on temperance and the physiological damage of drink, for example. He enjoyed the usual entertainments. On some evenings, with his brother or a friend, he would pay visits to girls. He inquired about positions for organists. He appreciated a good sermon, like one at the Universalist church on "young men—Subject—aiming at high things in life—It was an excellent sermon—I was much taken up with it" (November 29, 1874). Although he was frequently engaged in family activities, Thomas's social affairs were influenced by age grouping. He spent much time with his male peers, and often visited or escorted young women. Sometimes girls called on him. Many socials were specifically for the young, as were some of his church activities, from Sunday school to young people's meeting and lectures aimed at youth.

With little forewarning, in early August 1875 Thomas and his family packed up and paid their farewells. They traveled from Boston on the Grand Trunk Railroad, crossing through Canada, to Iowa. In Plainfield they stopped to see Thomas's sister and her family. Settling into a new home, Thomas worked for his family and for others. In September his organ arrived, and he joined the Plainfield church. With local boys he went shooting. In the fall he picked beans and plowed. Social life was a pale reflection of what he had known in Waltham. He shopped, went to Sunday school, participated in socials, helped form a mutual improvement society.

He read his daily chapter in the Bible. Thomas wrote a piece for the *Evening Times* on self-improvement. Letters and visitors were common. Then in November his sister and her family left for England. Parting was difficult. On November 26, 1875, after a Thanksgiving Day on which he was too busy to take a holiday, Thomas celebrated his eighteenth birthday. "The Lord has been good in sparing my life to the present day: Oh may I spend my future days far better: and more profitable is my true desire. To day we husked corn. Read my chap."

Farm work was now Thomas's central occupation. It took more space in his diary, and likely more time and effort, than his mill work. Planting hay and corn, threshing, seeding, cultivating, cutting, harvesting, logging, hauling, repairing, going to town all kept him busy. Still, he had time for "the literary," where he "had a real good time," as well as a family Christmas. In the new year he added spelling school and debating to his activities. Thomas took the negative on the subject: "Resolved that country life is preferable to city life." The affirmative won. He started a weekly singing school, which he conducted. At the end of the year he observed: "I feel that I have made some progress in the divine life during the year" (December 31, 1876).

In February 1877 Thomas attended a teachers' institute and began to go to school. By March, however, farm work precluded further education. He went to the schoolhouse only for social events. In the summer he visited other towns with family and neighbors. Then in November he suffered a serious injury while plowing. Between his own troubles and the death of several young friends, Thomas's tone was low. He commented on the year on his twentieth birthday: "This is my Birthday. Age 20 years. Thus my life has been spared to see my 20th Birthday. Oh how little I have done for the Master yet. I feel I have left many things undone that ought to have been done. During the year that is Past. Yet I feel resolved to do better in the future and to labor more for the Master. May God help me and mark out my Path is my prayer" (November 26, 1877).

The new year began on a cheerier note. Thomas busily attended meetings at school, at Eddy's Cheese Factory, and at the Young Folks society. After February he neglected his diary until November. By then it had become a difficult year. The singing school had failed. Times were hard, and it was impossible to raise money. As was his way, Thomas tried stoically to balance the bad with the good: "This year has been somewhat discouraging. But then we have things to be thankful for health and food fully supplied ... We have been preserved from all harm." Although many of his plans had come to naught, "I still make new plans asking God to lead me in the right path and to show me what is my mission" (November 20, 1878). Questions about his path of growing up lurk between the lines. Thomas notes that many of his friends had married.

Thomas Whitaker's diary stops at the end of 1878. On his twenty-first birthday he recited thanks to God and his parents for his life as a man, for a good home, and for good religious influences around him. Fittingly for the symbolically charged coming of age that this birthday marked, Thomas penned hopefully: "All that I have to regret in my past life is: that I can see so little I have accomplished. But I feel determined to try and commence and make my life more useful to live nearer my Heavenly Father and to endeavor to be of good to my fellow men. I find many temptations. But God is my helper in Him will I trust" (November 26, 1878). This rite of passage brought no other transitions on his path toward adulthood. Thomas's final entry on December 31 reports on the poverty, hard times, disgrace, shortage of clothing, and other trials he faced. Still on his transitional path, he claimed to believe firmly that all was working for the best: "I think I can see good from it." Growing up was hard, and transitional paths in particular were seldom easy. Thomas faced his unquestioningly. This route to adulthood often required some kind of faith. In this he was neither especially modern nor traditional.

Discontinuous

A third avenue within the transitional path strikes a familiar chord. Discontinuous paths mainly toward middle-class or professional destinations blended traditional elements with new influences and circumstances. Exceptional testimony comes from the memoir of a westerner, a child of Scandinavian immigrants, Victor Lincoln Albjerg.[20] As was common among his peers, Victor Albjerg's and his family's path incorporated major cultural tendencies, "traditional" and new.

Victor (1892–1973) was the son of Danish immigrants who left behind declining prospects and crossed the Atlantic, his father in 1883 and his mother a year later. As Victor declared in his memoir, they came "for release from economic thralldom; and to establish a new Scandinavian Jerusalem, for to them Minnesota was an economic rainbow" (1).[21] By coincidence, they both settled in Fergus Falls, Minnesota. Victor's father purchased eighty acres ten miles from town. In church and town Victor's parents renewed their prior acquaintance. Three months later they married. They worked hard. His mother gave birth to nine children, of whom Victor was the third. Like his pioneer neighbors, Victor's father endorsed schooling for his children within "thrifty limits." Family farm work came first.

To the seriousness of schooling and the powerful mythology of success, Victor testified: "An atmosphere of earnestness prevailed . . . We pursued our 'subjects' as if mastery of them constituted an open sesame to distinction. Even as youngsters the more conscientious had one characteristic in common with Sinclair Lewis, they wanted 'to be somebody.' Public acclaim was ours if we could pass the state board examination" (6–7). Not everyone shared this belief: "Some were resistant to praise or blame. They viewed studying with an aversion similar to table-waiting in Hades. They envisaged numerous pursuits beyond schools far more interesting than the acquisition of information. They were the chief troublemakers" (7). A birch rod for discipline accompanied a narrow curriculum.

Neither Victor nor his family contemplated advanced education. To them, schoolteaching seemed a possible and promising path and a well-trod traditional path. Victor's father took him to town, where the school super-intendent admitted him for the additional secondary courses he needed to prepare for the teaching certificate examination. He sought employment to defray costs. Hired by the college on the town's outskirts, he milked four cows morning and night in exchange for room and board.

Victor applied himself to his studies: "I cheerfully pursued my courses for 'I wanted to be somebody'—a rural school teacher." Given his late start and the example of his parents' accents, English proved his most difficult subject. Nonetheless, after one year at the college he passed the teacher's examination in all eight fields, and in 1909 he gained an appointment for three months at $40 per month. For $10 a Norwegian family provided room, board, and laundry. At seventeen, Victor now had to learn how to teach.

The next summer he returned to Fergus Falls. He took summer courses in algebra and agriculture to meet requirements for a first-grade teacher's license. He also took a teaching position in another one-room school with excellent students, but with the equivalent of thirty-two classes a day. When the 1911 school year ended, Victor enrolled for the third time in summer school at Morehead Teachers' College, this time to study geometry and physics with a number of other rural teachers seeking advancement. Receiving his first-grade certificate, he applied for a position paying $50 per month at a school six miles from Fergus Falls.

Now in his early twenties, Victor desired to extend his path, but his ambitions outran his current status and his prospects: "I saw only a small future in it, when, after four years of teaching, I was receiving only fifty-six dollars a month. During my teaching career I had, through frugality, accumulated $1300, enough to make a down payment on a farm, but farming at that time was a career for those who could function in no other enterprise" (19).

Victor discovered that he could complete high school in a year by taking almost a double course load, thereby qualifying for the university. Devoting all his time to his seven courses, he ignored extracurricular activities and had only one date. At the end of the year he stood highest among the male graduates. He won a tuition scholarship good at any of the state's small colleges. His choice driven by economics and recommendations, Victor enrolled at Hamline University in September 1914 as a twenty-two-year-old freshman: "My career there left much to be desired. Poverty compelled me to work for my board and room. During my freshman year I served as janitor of the gymnasium. During my sophomore year I was promoted to kitchen scullion in the ladies dormitory, and as a junior I was elevated to the rank of table waiter. This reduced the time I could devote to scholarship" (20). He also participated in track, the literary society, and the debating team, and was elected president of the college religious society. His grades were mostly good. "I rationalized the low grades," he writes, "with my need for agreeable social relationship with young men and women. As a farm boy I had had very little social experience. I realized my inadequacy, and I strove to compensate for it" (20).

Learning to value scholarship over "bogus popularity," Victor extended his path to the University of Minnesota: "There I got what I was looking for, scholarship in the field of history" (21). He also took courses in education to qualify for high school teaching. He had barely completed his undergraduate studies when he was called up for the U.S. naval forces in the First World War. As combat drew to a close, illness led to an early discharge. Victor returned to the university to do graduate work in educational administration. In 1920 he became superintendent of schools in Gary, South Dakota, a peripatetic twenty-eight-year-old educator at last on an adult professional path. After two years Victor found there were too many distractions and demands in the post. He also wanted to complete his master's degree. A visit to Wisconsin to consult advice led him to a doctoral program at the University of Wisconsin. In 1923, at the age of thirty-one and with resources of only $500, he struggled to continue his studies under difficult economic conditions.

Victor felt that his life was incomplete: "My effort to secure an advanced degree had compelled me to throttle any inclination toward romance . . . I had stifled every inclination that might have ended in matrimony. It was a life of silent, repeated self-denials" (28). He began to fear that he might never marry: "I resolved to emancipate myself from self-imposed inhibitions and respond to my inborn proclivity" (28). Nearing the end of his studies, he began to see Marguerite Hall, holder of the President Adams Fellowship in American History, "the only woman until then to merit that distinction." After a year's "agreeable association," they became engaged. She took her Ph.D. in 1925 and for two years headed the history department at the Alabama State College for Women. Victor completed his degree in 1926, and accepted a teaching post at Purdue. In 1927 they married.

Victor was thirty-five before his lengthy path to independence, marriage, and a professional position could be completed. His transition drew on the growth of educational institutions and their hierarchies, the modern university, and the professionalization of the academic disciplines. At this stage it also allowed flexibility in the course he followed. Marguerite's path did not offer the transitional career choices her husband's made possible. She took a part-time teaching post at Purdue, which she held until after the Second World War. Husband and wife published two books together.

Female Paths

Female paths of growing up during the second half of the nineteenth century also blended tradition and change, transitional and class-determined characteristics, commonality and difference. The mix of elements, more complicated than in previous eras, contributed to a sometimes confusing landscape of genders and generations. That confusion, at this time and later, is itself a part of the great transformation of growing up. Evolving discourses of gender as they intertwined with traditions old and new, on the one hand, and shifting experiences, on the other, complicate our understanding just as they provide clues for comprehension. In cultural and social transformations gender linked experiences of young women from different class, ethnic, racial, geographic, and family circumstances, and yet the same characteristics also divided them. Intersecting with traditions and powerful forces of change, the paths of female growing up and their historical expression were transformed in seminal, subtle, sometimes misleading, but nonetheless telling ways.

Women's courses of transformation toward modern ways shared with men's principal patterns, influences, actions, and reactions. They also differed as a result of crystallizing gender notions and norms, including some that reinterpreted new ways as "traditional." Of great significance, for example, are the use and impact of social institutions such as schools and families, and the meanings, expectations, and experiences of major life course transitions such as entering or leaving school, home, work, or marriage. Relationships with peers within and across boundaries of gender and age also contributed strikingly to the remaking of childhood and especially adolescence and youth. Dependency was perceived more than ever before at the core of growing up, a perception that also varied with the historical context as well as with gender, class, ethnicity, race, and geography.

Not all young women were affected similarly by the constellations of change and continuity that marked this era. Their impact was mediated by the familiar list of social factors. Neither homogeneity nor linearity contributed to or resulted from the remaking of growing up. The conflicts and contradictions surrounding gender were nonetheless of epochal significance. The lasting effect of changes whose origins I discussed earlier add perspective to this canvas. The experiences of poor, immigrant, minority, and working women continue to be underrepresented.

Like their brothers', women's paths were defined, on the one hand, by transitional routes and, on the other hand, by social class. Among the former, three major lanes dominate: the rural, southern mix of tradition and change; the western, migratory pattern punctuated by middle-class elements; and the settled, rural, nonsouthern blend of change and tradition. In these paths, as in those shaped by social class, we find persuasive evidence of the variety, flexibility, and complexity typical of female adolescence, despite historians' cavalier dismissal and neglect of women's experiences. Female growing up merits interpretation on its own terms as well as in terms of what it shared with that of men.

Upper-, middle-, and working-class urban immigrant routes are the subdivisions of the social class path. Gender may have mitigated the new power of the social class. Each forcefully influenced the other. The impact of traditions as they intermeshed with transition in turn contributed to contradictory consequences for many young women. These "traditions" were in large part newly invented, involving gender and class and their cultural mythologies, a factor that complicated the paths taken by females. We are heirs to this legacy.

Transitional

RURAL SOUTHERN

The rural southern female path is one of the most telling of the transitional ways of growing up at this time. Concentrating on tradition not only obscures the novelty of many of those seemingly timeless choices but also detracts attention from the dynamic elements of the path. In the recognitions and responses of young women and their families to the challenges, opportunities, obstacles, and contradictions around them, we discover forces of change as well as continuity. For many the effects of the Civil War added to other factors variously remaking growing up.[22]

Eleanor Agnes Lee (1841–1873), fifth child of Robert E. Lee, spent her early years at the family's Arlington House plantation in Virginia.[23] From 1852 to 1855 she lived at West Point while her father was superintendent of the U.S. Military Academy. He was often away, her mother often ill. From 1852 to 1858 Agnes kept a diary, initially at the insistence of her governess. Her personal record reveals a teenager at odds with dominant images and stereotypes. Complex and interesting, her account is a telling one in its testimony about a distinctive transitional female path.

Agnes began her journal during the busy Christmas and New Year's season of 1852–53. In the midst of family ritual she looked forward to resuming her studies: "When I am at school it is a different matter then I am obliged to perform my duties" (January 5, 1853). At home, family and neighborhood sociability provided a focal point of her attention. In May she expressed anguish at the death of her Grandmamma, "the first person I loved that had ever been taken from me" (May 4, 1853). Agnes struggled to "write more connectedly" about the death. With this loss her "delightful anticipations" of West Point gave way to persistent bitterness: "I am almost tempted to murmur against God" (May 25). Her identification of Arlington House as "always *my home*" deepened (June 1). Her sense of loss, her sentimentality, and her expectations combine in her reaction to a sermon two months later: "I solemnly determined to dedicate myself to God & I have tried, but Oh! I don't think I have improved in the least there is so much to try me. I do wish I was a christian! but it is so hard to be one" (July 20). The urge to improve influenced her schoolwork as well as her approach to social responsibilities.

At West Point, Agnes was homesick. Almost thirteen, in transition to adolescence, she and her sister Annie adjusted with difficulty to their new northern home. The cadets frightened Agnes: "I am so dreadfully diffident I believe . . . Annie & I generally sitting on the steps & having a good cry than remaining in the parlour to enjoy their society" (November 8, 1853). In late December, still confused about her feelings at this difficult time, Agnes wrote: "To be surrounded by several cadets at once is no very pleasant feeling, but I am overcoming my bashfulness a little. I don't know it is any great advantage in one so young. I fear I am getting corrupted by the world" (December 29). Incipient maturity interfered with her regular diary keeping: "What a different creature I am this year. In one year I have learnt & experienced a great deal. I feel differently too; young as I am I must sit up & talk & walk as a young lady and be constantly greeted with ladies do this & that & think so all as if I was twenty but enough of this" (January 22, 1854).

Agnes's socialization to mores of gender and station advanced rapidly. By February 2 she was reporting "Flirtation." She now enjoyed the social rounds at "W.P.," finding some cadets charming. By June she could write: "Generally I prefer the society of boys—perhaps because I am *used* to them, I don't know so much about playing with girls—then you need only be with boys when you feel in the humour for it" (June 20). Happy to be spending the summer at Arlington, she admitted: "I really have a kind of home feeling for the place & can look back to the winter we passed there as a very happy period of my long life for I have reached the respectable age of thirteen. How well I remember the first few months. I am naturally so reserved and retired I used to suffer 'agonies'" (July 16).

That summer, as before, Agnes continued the family tradition of teaching slave children. She vowed to write twice a week in her journal to improve her style and her handwriting. Taking pride in her intellectual as well as her social accomplishments, she notes: "I think we learned a great deal. I conquered a good deal of my diffidence & learned to conduct myself in society with tolerable self-possession" (July 18). Yet by the end of the year Agnes feared that "far the greater portion" of her time had been "mispent or wasted" (December 31).

By March 1855 Agnes had bloomed into adolescence. Lamenting that she and Annie received fewer Valentine cards than their siblings, she felt neglected: "I had only one. But the quality of this one! I was compared to sugar—clarified at that, molasses, honey & all things sweet" (March 11). At her mother's Valentine's Day party for cadets, Agnes drew the name of "about the greatest lady's man in the room. I showed my appreciation by behaving just as badly as such a retiring young damsel could behave." After meeting the new class of plebes, she wrote: "They were very nice boys it hardly becomes *me* to call them boys, but, though young in years, my residence at W.P. has given me the experience of an ancient & enables me to look down upon young people generally from a great height" (March 13). Still she suffered from social anxieties.

The family left West Point and resettled in Arlington in time for Agnes's fourteenth summer. She admitted, surprising herself, missing "W.P.," but here at "*home*" she was very happy, reading, writing, gardening, teaching slave children, visiting and being visited, receiving letters from her "Valentine," celebrating the Fourth of July.

In September 1855 Agnes and Annie entered the Virginia Female Institute in Staunton, a relatively new institution under the auspices of the Episcopal church of Virginia. Agnes referred to it as "Staunton Jail" (March 16, 1856).[24] Its many activities kept her sufficiently occupied that she made few diary entries. She evaluated the faculty in terms of their handsomeness and age, as well as their teaching skill. She dreaded being examined, a new experience. Drawing classes and playing with other girls were much more fun. She also suffered "blue Mondays" (March 11, 1856).

In the middle of adolescence, boarding away from home, Agnes struggled with her emotions. In part her crisis involved religion. On Easter Sunday she wrote expansively about her complicated adolescent feelings:

> The girls have all gone to church so alone, home sick & in pain I must pour out my sad thoughts to my journal . . . But why I am so miserable I can't find out. I am not in love certainly . . . I only know I want to go home O so much! & I want to go to West Point . . . How happy we were . . . How silly I was then! & how silly now, I almost believe I am losing my senses to write in this way. But I have such longings sometimes, such *yearnings* for something I know not what. Is it to be loved, to be worshiped by something or some

one—No—that is *sinful*, silly & impossible . . . I am one of those who are never to be good—one of the doomed. I am generally I am thought—I feel—bright & gay as other girls are, but I confess there are times when I feel scarcely sensible, when my poor weak, miserable nature makes me despise myself with a force which no language of mine can describe, then every slight, every sarcasm, every neglect seems to go my very heart almost to breaking. (March 23)

Agnes decided to "scratch some of my foolishness." Fancy dress balls took some of her attention. At one dress ball she lost her heart to another girl. Reading fiction also gave relief. Agnes read her Bible at length but "then poured [*sic*] over Madeline to forget my pain . . . I wish Madeline was a real character I am sure I should have loved her. I have never read a book which has taken such hold of my heart & imagination before. Perhaps it is I love to read so much & this has like such a *refreshment* among all my Philosophies & Ologies generally" (March 27).

At school the girls presented their learning in soirees. At one the first French class spoke, some played music, and Agnes and another girl read compositions. Frightened initially, she performed satisfactorily but found fault with the social wiles of other girls (March 27). Mathematics plagued her. Her adolescent feelings swung wildly: "I feel tired discontented & *mad* so little disposed for writing but here sitting on the bed my book on my knee I will try" (April 11). Social functions, spring clothes, and bonnets provided distraction, and knowing that "each rolling week brings us nearer *home*" helped a great deal. She struggled in part because she was no longer the center of attention as she had been at West Point: "But I was a young lady then though one of thirteen & now—I am only an *insignificant* schoolgirl!" (April 20).

At school the next fall Agnes's adolescent ups and downs continued. "I am alone," she wrote on October 20. "I am sick I am at Staunton what more do I want to make me unhappy . . . My schoolmates have been very kind I like them better this year. I feel so much more confident in myself so much more independent!" She was growing up. Returning to Arlington in the summer of 1857 after her graduation, nearing her passage to young womanhood, she wrote: "This is Sunday night and Oh!—I am weary of being wicked!" (September 14). Happily she informed the diary of her confirmation in the Episcopal church and her trust in the Lord's mercy and love.

That test passed, Agnes's next trial came with her grandfather's death. Her deeply felt response was more measured and brief than that for her grandmother. The teenager revealed her own awareness of her progress toward maturity. "I look back: first upon those happy school days, those cold months, when careless girls to-gether we gave our whole time to our studies, enjoying the pleasure of gaining knowledge, while our *hard* lessons, our momentary annoyances were the subject of many a laugh & threat of vengeance" (December 13, 1857). Thus Agnes Lee concluded her journal, and that portion of her journey toward adulthood.

Superficially contrasting with the growing up of the socially prominent Agnes Lee, the experiences of Letitia Pendleton were nonetheless quite similar. Her journal, written while she was a student at Mary Sharpe College in Tennessee (1854–1856), reflects the influence of broad currents of change for women in the mid-nineteenth century.[25] These forces crossed lines of class, family, and region, and intertwined tradition with change.

Letitia began her journal on August 1, 1854, voicing the familiar pangs over leaving home for school. It "was a sad day to me," she wrote, "for it was in the morning of that day, that I left my dear 'Home' and so dear to me." She immediately caught herself and shifted emphasis: "But when I thought that I was leaving home to get an *Education* I soon forgot all my bad feelings for I knew that if it had not been for *that* my dear parents would never have suffered me to be absent from them so long."

Letitia's journal documents regular study, classes, music lessons, letter writing, and assiduous performance at schoolwork. A proper child of her time, she writes: "When I think over the past year it makes me feel sad to think how little I have accomplished and how little good I have done, which, as a christian, I should have done" (January 8, 1856). Her many statements of personal and scholarly progress provide a counterpoise to this ritualistic refrain, which served as a charge to herself and a reminder of her goals and her human frailties. It was also a cultural reflex against undue pride and immodesty. She writes: "I believe I feel the importance of an education more and more the older I grow and I therefore resolve to be more studious . . . And I intend to quit talking as foolishly . . . And as I am getting older my actions must accord with my age. I will no longer be looked upon as a mere child, but soon I will take my place in society, and my influence for good will depend very much on how I improve my present opportunities" (January 8). Aware that she was growing up, Letitia grasped the burdens and opportunities of maturity. Now a blossoming adolescent, she remarks on sending a valentine anonymously to a gentleman friend, who thought it was from someone else.

A similar passage between tradition and change was taken by Ann Browder of Barbour City, Alabama.[26] Fifteen years old when she began her diary in 1858, the plantation-born Ann was a serious student at the local academy. Her wealthy family encouraged her. But the Civil War would place obstacles in her transitional path.

Writing on September 27, 1858, Ann remarks: "START TO SCHOOL IN AM, with the determination to improve myself so much it would be noticed by every one of my former companions." She "found all the girls smiling and speaking of how they spent the vacation. We had a very good beginning though not a great many scholars." Ann's studies included algebra, geometry, natural philosophy, chemistry, astronomy, logic, Latin, botany, rhetoric, and composition, as well as French and music. Her schooling ranged from scholarly to surface finishing. A boarding student, she often was visited by her parents or traveled home. She reports doing well in her classes and studying regularly. She also comments on other girls and on fashions. When an eighteen-year-old eloped, Ann piously penned: "I think when such children think of marrying it is just because they do not know any better but before I proceed any further I will correct the grand mistake I made on the opposite page. I said children . . . for Lucy Patterson is eighteen . . . She had better take my advice, which is to come to school and gain knowledge before she thinks of marrying" (November 23).

Ann priggishly suffered writing a composition on the theme "What Makes Me Happy" because so many of the other girls had written on it (December 10). She would have preferred the teacher to assign each pupil her own subject: "I find so many faults in those I select myself" (March 18). Ann learned embroidery and singing, and expresses a wish for guitar instruction. She remarks of *"Gody's"* [*sic*] *Lady's Book:* "I think it improves every year. I will take Home Magazine and Peterson's too." Her father sometimes brought her *Harper's Magazine* (December 15).

In the New Year she summed up her progress: "Happy New Year Journal, as I hope I'll have. A great many changes have taken place since I said so before. I am still a school girl, a Junior. Last year I was a Sophomore. I've improved a good deal in music, am a great deal taller and a whole year older. I think I've gained some knowledge from my school book, and other important ones" (January 3, 1859).

Regardless of her desire to achieve and her success in her studies, Ann's attitudes and expressions are typically adolescent. On February 9 she wrote: "Journal, I know you would laugh it you could see me. I am sitting in a very large rocking chair, with my feet on a stool—a flannel rag around my neck, my mouth about half open, a double shawl on, and my hair tucked up in a single knot behind—and surrounded by old news-papers, school books, letters and magazines." Told her writing was too stiff, she commented, "I'll try to make it appear more like a girls of UNION COLLEGE" (February 21). Two days later, noting that she planned to go to school for two more years but that her classmates had asked to graduate early if the trustees would allow, "I would laugh if they would blast their hopes." As if in response, ceiling plaster fell on her head, giving her a bump and a headache (February 23).

Perhaps unintentionally, Ann captures the flavor of her female academy education: "Mr McIntosh is going to give us lectures next week in Philosophy and Chemistry. I will like that so much. Mrs McIntosh read us a chapter today about things we shouldn't do or say. We shouldn't cross our feet or tip our chairs back. Negatives in a sentence is inelegant, and 'no more'; toat [tote] is vulgar, and a great many other things." She wished she could go to the plantation the next week: "I always go rambling on the creek . . . I don't believe I was born to live in town" (March 3).

Ann's attitudes toward society and its rules were no less conflicted. Separating herself from her peers, she wrote censoriously: "The schoolgirls received invitation to the party yesterday. I don't see any use in sending them invitations when it is against the rules of the school." On learning that the trustees had given the girls permission to go, she added, "I don't see any use of having that for a rule if they are going to let the girls go to every party that is given" (March 11). A bit later she recounts: "I went to the lecture Saturday night. The subject was 'Love and Matrimony.' Professor Mott seems to be in favor of both. It was really amusing" (March 14). On April 1, noting that "the girls were all April fooling each other," she remarks, "It is sweet to love and to be loved." She "took a 'big' cry" when she was unable to attend a picnic (May 2). Consistency and a mature confidence were not yet hers at this relatively early point on her transitional path.

Ann's summer consisted of travels, socials, dances, games, and the like, typical amusements for a girl of her class and place. Summer also provided time for more expansive judgments of her peers. Likes and dislikes cluster in the adolescent manner of her class and gender, revealing much about their author's discernment and biases:

> Alice Wyche is surely the most undignified girl I ever saw. She talks all the time—she is at the table in the rudest of manner, just to attract attention. Everybody hates her. Her brother is dying to marry, and his wife just died this late winter. I'm sure I hate him more than anybody I ever saw. He makes himself perfectly ridiculous trying to wait on the girls. He isn't intelligent by any means and he is ugly anyway. Miss Sallie Russell is just the opposite of Alice—so dignified, gentle, quiet and unassuming in her manners. She is very refined, though not pretty by any means (August 31).

Of another female peer she writes: "Puss Watkins is so sweet—I dearly love—she is modest yet she loves to laugh when gets fully acquainted with any one, and one of the best friends, and Laura so friendly and sociable, and so funny one couldn't help loving her. She is Puss' best friend" (August 31). A few days later she notes: "I got acquainted with Mr. Flanders from Macon—he is a fast young man—he looks so foppish, but is of course a great beau—he wears a charming moustache, and I think is quite proud of it. He has been here all the summer, but is going away next week" (September 2). Without hesitation she declares: "The 'Fancy Balls' are now all over with, and I'm glad of it . . . I don't see why they CALLED those balls 'Fancy' any way, for they didn't have any fancy costumes" (September 2).

Three weeks later Ann bade farewell to the journal, closing her record of adolescence in progress. She also kept a diary for 1866–67, when she was about twenty-four. After the Civil War, in January 1866, Ann was less sure of herself and her world than she had been at fifteen. Admitting doubts about her own abilities, she deemed the Christmas just past "much dreaded," though it went off without the anticipated murders and with the "Negroes behav[ing] remarkably well, better than usual—obedient, polite, so many Negroes in town that ladies couldnt go" (January 8, 1866). She "began to realize poverty now." She found herself restless, in waiting, morose, low-spirited, and with a strange sadness when alone. On January 19, 1866, she wrote: "Yesterday was my birthday. I am so old—almost an old maid, but I don't care."

Ann now feared that she was wasting the life God had given her. Common concerns of adolescence and early adulthood intensified in these troubled times. Her self-image and ego were fragile, and she was often confused. With a wrench of pain unlike the probing of her teenage years, she begged:

> What was I made for?—just to breathe and move and nothing else?—shall no one be made better by my example?—shall no one point to me as a benefactor?—shall die 'unloved, unhonored, unwept and unsung'? God forbid, but make me a true hearted, noble, and useful woman, one who will be blessed by all by whom I am surrounded. I am so wicked . . . yet there are some who seem to love me. What it is they love I do not know, but make me worth all the love that falls to my lot whatever may be the incentive—make me kind, polite and affectionate to them at all times and make true to them forever. (January 19, 1866)

Ann's travails in part resulted from her marital status. This was not a good time or place to be a single woman. Writing on her next birthday after months of silence, still feeling sorry for herself but less self-indicting, Ann observed with more composure:

> I can hardly realize it—almost an old maid, still I feel younger, and am in better health and look better than ever before—one year ago I was an old woman—and a deep, deep trouble made me old. I thought I could "nevermore" find pleasure in society—had absented myself from it for more than a year and was still O-so unhappy. I remembered my duty to my parents and to myself, and have been in society nearly all the time . . . In my heart there

is a "void this world can never fill"—a longing for "something to love me—something to bless," yet never finding my ideal. The unforgotten past still clings to me. (January 18, 1867).

For months she struggled to gain a more accurate sense of herself and her situation. Perspective and maturity returned. She desired a husband, one major step on her path that war had complicated greatly. A May revival gave her some relief. On July 3, however, she admitted: "I have done a very absurd thing today. I have written to this Madam Thornton who professes to produce a life-like picture of the one you are to marry—together with date of marriage, position in life—leading traits of character, etc. . . . I shall look anxiously now for her answer."

Living at home, Ann found herself lonely and lazy. She was unable to sew for more than ten minutes at a time, and attempting to read put her to sleep. Her sense of herself expanded: "I wish the ladies would visit more. I am decidedly a social being. I cannot live within myself, I am going out visiting soon, and going to see everybody" (July 5). Later that month she notes: "I received, to my surprise, this morning, my fortune from Madame Thornton, and a photograph of my destiny. I am to be married the 4th of January, 1869 . . . The photograph is right handsome . . . He has a good deal of depth of expression—looks very calculating. I'm about half in love with him now" (July 23).

By fall Ann had men actively involved in her life. She was pursued by a Major Pruett, who proposed, but she didn't want to marry him; she claims that he made her sick. By October 20, however, Ann was engaged to him. On November 10 she wrote: "I do not know how I feel about it—it is so strange—I feel all the time I am dreaming." The wedding was set for December 3.

By November 24 Ann had begun to feel more secure in her plans: "Everyone talks about my marriage—it is so strange how everyone found it out . . . I do not yet realize it, but I shall marry confident of happiness afterwards. He is a sober, industrious man—kind hearted and everything— but all this will be nothing unless he loves—my happiness even now depends on it." After the ceremony was postponed for a week, Ann's strange feelings continued. She feared leaving her family. She wanted a beautiful wedding. She was finally married on December 10. Ann reports on Christmas Eve that all was well: "I have been married two weeks today—and am so happy." The long year ended on a note of love, as she looked happily toward the future. Ann completed her war-torn and de-layed course of growing up, demonstrating a new maturity and confidence in her transitions.

Ann Browder left no record about the war itself, testifying less directly to its continuing impact than Lucy Breckinridge of Grove Hill, Virginia, who left an exceptional journal for the years 1862–1864.[27] Daughter of a well-established planter family, Lucy was raised a southern lady—more so than her peers in these pages—with all the ambiguity and contradiction that term carries. The traumas of war exacerbated those contradictions despite her comfortable material conditions. Along with voicing her wartime worries about men she knew, she makes acerbic and equivocal comments about the place of women, an attitude that marks her growing up as transitional.

Lucy Gilmer Breckinridge was eighteen when war erupted. The diary covers her twenty-second to twenty-fourth years. Born in 1843, she was the sixth of nine children. Lucy began her journal to assuage her boredom, for she had no visitors, no materials on which to work, and little incentive for other activity. Her observations speak to the special circumstances of her age and stage of development, as well as more general issues of gender, society, and war.

Lucy shows both a critical, questioning tone and her loneliness in her first entry, dated August 11, 1862, when she asked:

> What sort of friend shall I choose? . . . A discreet female of advanced age? A respectable maiden aunt? A young and intimate school mate? Or an old and attached governess or tutor? It is a hard question to decide. Upon reflection, I think I shall select a female, rather older than myself and a great deal smarter, but whose sweet and gentle disposition shall call forth all my confidence, an expression of all my feelings and doubts, etc., and whose deep and loving interest in my family shall induce me to write anything which concerns them. I never had such a friend and I shall love her so much.

Drawing on her education and imagination, Lucy created in her journal the close female friend she lacked and whom she needed so deeply.

The journal addresses Lucy's stage of growing up in the midst of the dangers of war. The pivotal issue for her was love and marriage. Her brother Gilmer advised Lucy and her sisters not to marry for love, for few find happiness after marriage. No romantic, she replied: "From observation, my theory is that wives generally love their husbands more . . . The wife's love grows . . . while the husband's almost invariably cools down into a sort of patronizing friendship." She found her brother "very inconsistent," for he had married for love, and he "does and always will love his wife as much as she does him" (August 12).

At the same time, Lucy listened "neutrally" to an argument about which sex is superior: "I rather incline to the opinion that women are purer and better than men, but, then, they are so guarded from evil and temptation, while men are exposed to every temptation to wickedness, and have so many disadvantages to struggle with; and (I think) they have not the moral courage that women have." Lucy had no doubt that women had more trouble and suffering, between demands of children and husband, "unless there was an immense amount of love" (August 12). A year later, about to reject one suitor, she exclaimed: "I cannot love that fellow! I can never learn to love any man. Oh, what would I not give for a *wife!* Some pure, lovely girl who would be mine and never learn to love any male, but the poor weak things will do that. Women are so lovely, so angelic, what a pity they have to unite their fates with such coarse, brutal creatures as men, but some of them are *right* good" (August 15, 1863).

Lucy's affections centered on a Captain Houston, of whom her parents disapproved. Visiting officers, handsome young men, sometimes also caught her or her sisters' fancy. Brother George warned her, however, "'Do not get married until after the war is over. There are many reasons why you should not; for instance, you might be a widow in a short time.' Then, after thinking a few minutes, it seemed to strike him that it would not be such a bad thing to be a pretty young widow" (August 24, 1862). One brother had been killed in the war. Death weighed on the living.

At this strained time, Lucy and her mother were in conflict: "There never was such a sweet, loving Mamma as ours. I wish I could be more industrious and useful for her sake. She can't help thinking that I am a good-for-nothing, lazy girl, and my good qualities, if I have any, are so hidden by the bad ones" (August 27, 1862). The next day she wrote: "Ma said something to me about my affairs which distressed me very much. She never had seemed to be satisfied with me since last March. She does not seem to love me as she used to, and her love to me is more precious than anyone else's. When we came home I went into the parlor and took a good cry, and gallantly determined to break off that engagement [to Captain Houston], because I know Papa and Mamma would never like it . . . I do feel terribly perplexed and distressed" (August 28). The following day Lucy and her mother talked. Though her mother was sorry, kind, and gentle, Lucy deemed the situation "miserable": "[Houston] ought to love me a great deal. I do not think, myself, that we shall be very happy after we are married, and I am not at all anxious to hurry that event. I do tremble at the idea of ever being married, but I do not expect to be more sensible and stronger than other women. And I love him enough to risk my happiness for his sake" (August 29). Afraid of marrying, she was not convinced by her own arguments. The engagement was on again, off again, before it was finally broken off (October 3, 1862).

With no men to occupy her, Lucy wryly admitted: "I feel so alone. I can't people the room with sweet fancies and imaginations now . . . When I was in love, some four or five months ago, I always had something interesting to think of, but now that I have cast aside all such follies and settled down to discreet, matter-of-fact old-maidism, I have nothing to think of but darning socks and working for poor soldiers. I'll be a sweet old maid" (December 19, 1862). Faced with contrary advice, Lucy reminded herself that she did not "want any grumblesome husband to be sewing and cooking for all the time, nor any disagreeable, colicky little babies, always getting their little noses and mouths soiled and keeping me awake all night." Spinsterhood was preferable, or so she tried to persuade herself, without complete success (December 22).

Other suitors pressed their claims after Houston. Toward the end of 1863, Lieutenant Thomas Bassett appeared on the scene. He "made himself very interesting, and tried to make me promise to be Mrs. B., but I did not quite do it, though, I do not recognize him as my *fate*" (November 17, 1863). Nonetheless accepting his proposal four days later, she declared that she did "love him very much—not the same way I loved Mr. Houston" (November 21). With her doubts about ever marrying, she resolved to be firm about *this* engagement: "After the others retired, I sat some time in the sitting room with Lieut. Bassett and had a wretched time. I'll tell him some of these days how terribly he has worried me, sometimes, so much that I have almost sworn to cut his acquaintance, but *that man* wiles me. If he looks at all unhappy I can't stand it, and must ever pardon and love him. Heigho! How I have changed, but I am afraid when his influence is withdrawn that some miserable reminiscences will make me dislike him" (January 9, 1864). Her fears that her engagement would not lead to marriage and that marriage would not lead to love or happiness were exacerbated by war. She suffered "sad forebodings." With heightened emotions Lucy celebrated her twenty-first birthday on February 1, 1864: "I am 21 today! Of age! Independent! I feel right old now."

A daughter of her social order, Lucy struggled over her religion: "I am so sinful, so weak to resist temptation. I am always doing wrong, and yet my heart thrills with love for Christ" (October 5, 1862). Her doubts about herself as well as others led her to pray for God's goodness. Fiction, especially novels such as Miss Pardoe's *Confessions of a Pretty Woman*— "too much like French novels"—gave no relief. More satisfying were tomes such as *The Lays of the Scottish Cavaliers,* the *Spectator,* and Tennyson's poetry. When lonely, Lucy found companionship in reading.

Despite the risks of war and her forebodings, Lucy Breckinridge married Tommy Bassett on January 28, 1865, at Grove Hill. On June 16, after only five months of marriage in war-torn conditions, Lucy died of typhoid fever and was buried beside her brother John. She was twenty-three. The final stages of her growing up were transformed by war and the mores of southern society, marked by her criticism of gender distinctions in her culture, and marred by ambivalence and worry.[28] Lucy barely experienced her adulthood. That was a real loss.

RURAL NONSOUTHERN

As in the plantation South, in "traditional" or established rural places in the North, female growing up was also in transition. This route constitutes the second transitional subpath. Here, too, both traditions and paths of growing up were in transition, altering images and experiences.[29]

At age thirteen in January 1873, in Oswego County, New York, Ada Harris began to keep a diary.[30] Consisting of brief entries of activities, weather, and family affairs, her jottings, according to their editor, Robert Clark, "read in sequence, are repetitious, routine, a little dull, but sorted out and fitted together like pieces of a jigsaw puzzle, they tell the story of a lively and delightful teenager" (29). A farmer's daughter, Ada lived in Amboy, three and a half miles from the village of Williamstown, the local market. Her Methodist parents both grew up there. By 1873 her father had enlarged his farm, valued at $3,000, to 150 acres, producing for the market and family consumption. Ada's two younger brothers, a grand-mother, and an orphaned nineteen-year-old female cousin lived with the family.

Ada attended winter term at the schoolhouse a quarter mile from home. An indifferent student, she went infrequently: "I do not go to school now, I am helping Ma get the sewing done," she noted on January 16 (31). She went to school only twice that month. Weather permitting, her attendance was more regular in February. She never names the subjects she studied, but she does report learning to "play penny," and having "some fun" with Allie Laing, exchanging valentines (31).

Ada was more interested in her domestic work, a reflection of normative gender roles and expectations. She baked, sometimes spending the whole day in the "citchen" making jellies, preserves, pickles, maple sugar, and the like. On Mondays she helped her mother with the wash; on Saturdays they cleaned. A list of her household labors is lengthy. Rising early each morning, Ada also worked in the family garden and sometimes in the fields with her father.

As Clark describes her, "she was not always serious, by no means a slave to her work. Only thirteen, she was sometimes a child in her delight in simple things, or a giggling adolescent, or a young woman heartbroken in her fantasies of love" (33). Ada was an adolescent growing up in new but increasingly typical ways. She delighted in her aunt's gift of a pipe to blow bubbles and her mother's purchase of fabric and ribbon for a new dress. She collected locks of hair from school friends, relatives, cousins, a teacher, and boys she liked, mounting them in a scrapbook. She corresponded with friends and relatives near and far. Church was a dominant factor in her life. Clark notes: "Stone Hill was a congenial setting for the activities of the young, a tightly knit community of fifteen or twenty families, their houses close together, their relationships interdependent and supportive" (35). Visiting, especially among relatives, was constant. Ada visited her best friend, Nellie Wilson, frequently. They walked to school or into the country, had long talks, and sometimes stayed up late at night.

On occasion, with other young folks, the two girls held evening socials at one or another's home. Sometimes they stayed out until midnight. Christmas and birthdays called for major celebrations. Unable to join the group on one occasion, Ada was regretful: "All the young folks but me went to Cornelia's exabition [*sic*] tonight" (37). She didn't go out with boys, and when Nellie suggested that they do so, Ada replied negatively. Admirers three or four years her senior would walk her home from school or meeting, call on her, or see her at parties.

Adolescent Ada had a romantic streak typical of the age and time. A new moon or a rainbow would captivate her. When moody or lonesome she liked to walk in the woods. Marriages she recorded in capital letters across the top of two pages. As with so many of her peers, thoughts of love and death captured her imagination. In her diary she attempted to express these sentiments poetically.[31] Death was a common presence in the community. Children and adolescents were not yet "protected" from it.

Growing up comfortably in a commercialized rural area, Ada Harris experienced a typical early adolescence. Her path combined traditional with newer emphases in thought and action, with no recognition of discontinuity. Increasing evidence of a more protected growing up—bounded by school, peer culture, and family—evidently stimulated little conflict, at least at this point. In December 1877 Ada married Warren Clark, putting an early end to childhood. After two more years in New York State, they rented a farm in Iowa for five years, then homesteaded in Nebraska. She thus continued her transitional journey in parallel with the reshaping of the country.

How different was sixteen-year-old Victoria Lodge's experience.[32] Daughter of a farmer in Morrisana, Westchester County, New York, she trained to be a seamstress and spent much of her time making clothes for a tailor. Victoria experienced regular conflicts in her relationship with her mother, which she recorded in her journal of 1874–75. The demands made on the teenager at this stage of growing up may have been more than she could accommodate. Victoria states her problems at the beginning of her brief record. As experience and expression, they ring true as those of a developing adolescent of the late nineteenth-century, though she seems unaware that her problems were not unusual:

I am going to try to write a journal. I do not know whether I shall succeed.
I don't know as I shall have much to write about. I often try to run away
from my thoughts by reading light reading. I know it is not right for me to
do so, but how can I help it? I want to be good and do good but I almost
always end there. I read Stepping Heavenward to day and in it I read that
just so far as we obey God just so far we love him. I wish I was a Christian
I wish I loved to pray, but I dont. I wonder if I ever will? I got up this morning
and helped to get breakfast. Mother washed up the dishes I am not very
bright to day do not like to study my Sunday school lesson. I am also given
to saying uncharitable things about different people. I wish I could stop
speaking sharply to mother. It is disrespectful and wrong. Must stop now and
study my lesson. (August 2, 1874)

Learning her lesson brought praise from her mother and a vow to be good
that week.

Victoria next clashed with her mother over cleaning as opposed to going
out. The family's forgetting her mother's birthday on August 4 did not help
matters. Two days later Victoria reported that her father was "mad about
something." When her mother asked her to get a pail of water, the contrary
teen "said I would not but I did. Why cant I do things pleasantly and
with-out words?" she asked (August 8). A week later, after Victoria had
spent Tuesday doing a large wash and Wednesday ironing, she was informed by her mother that she could not make a skirt that had been
ordered: "I got mad and Scolded Mother. Poor Mother. I wonder if we are
all made quick tempered, and what for?" (August 16).

Victoria spent most of her time learning to make pants. She thought that
she might "like this business," and she liked Mrs. Provost, who was
teaching her to sew. They made eighteen pair of pants in a week. With her
earnings, Victoria bought ribbon for a bow and a lace ruffle, as well as ice
cream and candy; for her mother she bought beef for soup (August 24).
The next day she went on a Sunday school picnic.

Victoria's hopes for self-improvement were not fulfilled. She sadly and
contritely writes: "I am afraid I shall be very sure to break all my promises
if I make any. So the safest way will be to stop making any. I wish I could
behave myself. Tom Eggert was over to Mrs Provosts today and we carried
on like time I won't do so again if I can help it. I promised mother I would
fill and clean the lamp this noon but I did not do it. I must stop and go
to bed now. I hope I did not do anything wrong to day. I did not mean to.
I pray God to forgive me all the wrongs I have this day done and to lead
me not into temptation" (August 26). Victoria knew what was expected
in terms of proper behavior and relations with her mother. Though she
worked hard on her sewing and did a good deal of household work, this
adolescent, like others, was unable to practice what was preached.

When Victoria makes her final entry on January 30, after a five-month silence, she does not mention the usual conflict with her mother or unpersuasive hopes about her behavior or beliefs. In a hopeful tone she reports acquiring her own sewing machine (for $15 down on a total cost of $65). She had a good Christmas: "God has been *very very* good to me indeed and I hope I feel grateful for all my blessings." Conversion at this age, a common event fifty or more years before, was now less frequently a solution to the strains of growing up. The kinks in Victoria's mid-adolescent path—living at home, balancing demands of home and work, religion, parental authority, and a maturing self—may have begun to smooth out.

A third "traditional" rural example emphasizes the mix of diversity and common experience in growing up female in this era. Elmira Sexton Newcomb was born in 1848 and died in 1867 at age nineteen.[33] She grew up on an estate outside Hyde Park, New York. In 1859 her father sold the mansion and lands and moved the family into Hyde Park. When Elmira took ill, apparently with tuberculosis, she was sent to New York City in 1866 to live with her aunts. She returned to Hyde Park, where she died November 26, 1867.

Despite her serious illness, Elmira's stay in New York City was demanding. This eighteen-year-old was no patient confined to a sickroom. Her diary of her nine months there records her membership in a Presbyterian church, religious meetings and church fairs, drives in Central Park, visiting, occasional schoolwork, Sunday school teaching, and French and riding lessons. She details dress purchases, bonnet trimmings, and reactions to people she met. Most of all, with no apparent contradiction, she records her constant struggle for religious awakening and her doubts about her Christianity. Elmira's aunts encouraged her religious devotion, but like many teenagers in different circumstances, the young woman often felt unwilling or unworthy. She fought against facing death. More traditional resolutions didn't satisfy her. Elmira was also confused in her feelings toward Dr. Paxton, the parish minister, and Mrs. Roberts, her religious meeting leader, who took an active interest in her spiritual state.

In February 1867 Elmira confided that she felt obliged to say little and hide her feelings at home. She found the thought of going to meeting at once dreadful and hopeful. She felt pressure to attend from her aunts as well as Dr. Paxton. On March 16 she writes: "Tomorrow is Communion and I am still wavering between irresolution and decision. I feel that there is sort of a delicate desire to go although when I pray and ask God to help me to decide rightly, the thought comes up to my mind, that I do not love Jesus." That morning, out of sorts and depressed, when her Aunt Emm "said something about turning all my failures over to Jesus and trusting within entirely I nearly broke down, so she sat down and took me on her lap; there we sat, I sometimes crying and sometimes talking." When Aunt Emm asked if they should pray, Elmira could only answer indifferently. She could not bear pressure over religion so close to home (March 17).

As with Victoria, teenage conversion was neither as usual nor as easy a solution to the problems of growing up as it had been earlier in the century. For Elmira it simply was not possible. Some months before her death she confessed: "I resolved this morning to go and ask Dr. Paxton about giving up dancing, but . . . I feel as if every *serious thought or feeling* had gone. I am just as undecided as ever about going with Mrs. Roberts . . . Oh! I wish there was some way, by which I could be sure I was right" (April 30). Elmira Newcomb's path of growing up stopped short at age nineteen.

THE WEST AND MIGRATION

Transitional female paths of growing up are particularly common among the experiences distinguished by major migrations, especially to the expanding western frontier.[34] Recent research illustrates the variety of new opportunities as well as the challenges to "proper" growing up that moved many adult contemporaries to fear for the future of their young. The perception that traditions were being threatened and lost propelled efforts to create them anew. Experiences of growing up amid westward movement give richer evidence of transformation—of individual lives, geographic regions, growing up itself—than even the most durable myths and stereotypes suggest.

Young people and their families reacted to the very different environments around them with a mixture of hope and fear, decisiveness and constraint, change and tradition. Personal stories relate the pressure and interplay of new influences on female growing up. In areas settled relatively recently, "tradition" intermixed with new middle-class and other transitional paths, though migration and settlement contributed to some significant differences from urban middle-class ideals. The resulting patterns of growing up owed much to traditions and expectations, including those concerning proper womanhood, which were even then being revised. Our journey into this set of transitional female experiences begins with lives influenced by westward migration and continues with the stories of women whose youth was spent entirely in the West.[35]

In the spring of 1857 Mollie Dorsey moved from Indianapolis to the Nebraska Territory with her parents and seven siblings.[36] She was eighteen years old. Her father's search for economic opportunity for himself and his sons led him to uproot the family and move to where land was available at a good price. Fears of such a major relocation prodded Mollie to keep a diary, "to have a confidante or bosom friend, now that I am to leave so many near and dear. I go among strangers, into a strange land,

and it may be a long time before I find one to whom I can confide my joys and sorrows" (March 23, 1857). In this exceptional diary Mollie recorded her late adolescence and early adulthood experiences, transformed by migration, a tale of challenges, conflicts, and new opportunities. With regret she left behind her Sunday school students, classmates, close female friends, church, and "dear old home." But Mollie was also "glad to go from here 'heart whole and fancy free,'" especially after a disastrous love affair two years earlier. All in all, she was excited about the move.

The family headed west at the end of March. The journey to Nebraska City by train, boat, and wagon took two weeks. The arrival of Mollie and her sisters visibly changed the sex ratio. Men on the streets as well as their landlady announced their pleasure at the presence of young women. The girls found that walking down the street was enough to cause "a sensation." Offered six dollars a week to work in a hotel, one sister took offense. Mollie reflected, "I was more amused than insulted, and said 'I thought six dollars a week pretty good wages, and if the worst came to the worst *I* might go.'" She was aware of her father's financial burden: "Perhaps all of this may be for our good . . . that we might help by our efforts" (April 16).

Settling in town was exciting at first. Mollie matured with the experience. She was learning to deal with the company of single men more informally if rather egotistically. Bored at times, she tired of waiting while her father looked at land. Visiting the wives of local merchants provided some sociability and routine to the sisters' lives. On one call Mollie "told Mrs. B. that as there was but *one* good young man in town, the prospects looked gloomy enough for young company. She advised me to 'set my cap': for a Mr. By Sanford, a friend of theirs, who arrived here yesterday from Indiana . . . A good-looking enough fellow. *I'll see about it*" (May 5).

Mollie's late adolescent thoughts about love and marriage were filled with the usual doubts and questions: "I do not know whether I will *ever* love any man well enough to marry him or not. If by the time I am twenty-one, I find a sensible fellow that won't talk silly flattery, I may transfer my maiden heart to his keeping. I don't know *what* the matter is. I so soon tire of the gentlemen, that is, if they get *too* sentimental. And I am sentimental too myself" (May 5). Waiting in town deepened Mollie's ambivalence about her new life in the West. Unwarranted male attentions only heightened her wish to move on. But, she knew, "then I'll have no place to go nor no one to take me. O! dear, the gloomy prospect ahead!" (May 18). Mollie felt "caged" in town, but she was also confused about men and marriage, unsure of her desires (May 22).

In June the family moved to their new log cabin home more than fourteen miles from town. Family members differed in their reactions.

"Mother hardly enters into extacies [*sic*]," wrote Mollie. "She no doubt realizes what it is to bring a young rising family away from the advantages of the world. To *me,* it seems a glorious holiday, a freedom from restraint, and I believe it will be a blessing to we girls. We were getting too fond of style, too unhappy not to have the necessary things to carry it out . . . Home! Sweet Home! There's no place so dear, no charm so sacred." That outburst spurred another outpouring of more personal criticism: "I want to be *good.* I *try* to be, but some way, I fall into many grievous errors. Perhaps my light frivolous nature was given me to help those differently constituted. I'll try to keep from going into any foolish excesses" (June 5). Tradition and novelty blended in Mollie's struggle for self.

Working at home provided distraction. Yet she felt "a little homesick," thinking of her "many dear friends of the past. My life is not what I pictured it a year ago. My airy castles have tumbled, and I feel *so* far away" (June 23). Mollie had no doubts, however, that relocation was the best thing for the family. But the eighteen-year-old also recognized her mother's ambivalence: "I can see and feel that it chafes Mother's spirit. It worries her to think that we are in such straitened circumstances . . . If the country would only fill up, if there were only schools or churches, or even some society. We do not see a woman at all. All men, single, or bachelors, and one gets tired of them" (June 27). Growing up meant learning to sacrifice, especially for women. Her mother's and Mollie's sacrifices differed from each other's, from their earlier ones in Indianapolis, and from the men's. They had to teach the younger children at home. Mollie's mother feared that her daughter would lose her dignity on the frontier.

Mollie's interest intensified with exposure to the wagon driver By Sanford. "I don't know *why* I should call Mr. Sanford 'mine,'" she writes, "unless because the folks have assigned him to me, and because I like him. He is the cutest fellow I ever met" (July 2). A few days later she confessed: "I like him *very* much . . . He measures people by their worth more than looks, and dear me! I'm afraid I haven't either" (July 6). In August he began to farm only three miles away: "I am teased about him until I wonder if I do not care a little for him? for an allusion to him even makes my cheeks burn and my heart beat quicker" (August 10).

Mollie's late adolescent experience involved more than courtship, conflicting emotions, and confusion about love. She did "not know what this wild life is going to develop in me anyway. Guess I am going to be a 'mejium' or spiritualist whether I want to be or not." Her family, who she guessed "won't be surprised at *anything* I do these days," already called her "prophet" and "witch." Mollie and the girls went on a "long tramp" with the "store boys" to pick plums: peer group activity in a newly settled place (September 15). Other excitement came with her seventeen-year-old sister Dora's courtship. Mollie predicted: "She will be married perhaps before myself, and I, to use a homely phrase, will be left 'dancing in the hog trough.' Boo! hoo! Boo! hoo!" (September 17). Doubt and irony underlie her humor.

Domestic life improved with an addition to the cabin of a room to serve as a parlor and with the arrival of the grandparents. By fall, self-critical Mollie was registering an improvement in her own demeanor, too: "I do not run into the woods any more . . . I have subsided into a very quiet young lady, with all my native dignity when occasion calls for it, as it did when Mr. Andrew Jackson Cook came to pay his distresses to me the other day. Said he was on the hunt for a wife, and hearing there was a 'hull lot of girls' here, he thought he would 'come around.' I tried to freeze him but don't think I did, as he announced he would call again" (October 26).

On December 17, 1857, Mollie celebrated her first birthday in Nebraska. Major questions of present and future weighed on her: "My 19th birthday, and O! dear, I feel 25 years if a day. I have grown years, it seems to me, in the last 6 months. I ought to be doing something or making something of myself. There is not much that is flattering in the prospect . . . Now I am ready for something else. Father's burdens are increasing. He needs help, and I shall not mope down here always. By spring I hope something will 'turn up' to give me an opportunity to satisfy my ambition." Further doubts clouded on the marital front: "I sometimes try to picture out my future . . . Will I be a happy beloved wife, with good husband, happy home, and small family, or an abused, deserted one, with 8 or 9 small children crying for their daily bread? Or won't I marry at all? If I live to be an *old maid,* I will be one of the odd kind that is a friend to everybody and that everyone loves. If I *do* marry it will be someone I *love, very, very, very* much, better than anyone yet, except—except. Well, if he does love me a *little* he may not think of marriage. I'll wait until he asks me." Mollie alluded to By Sanford. In her mix of fear, ambivalence, and criticism of woman's place, Mollie in Nebraska shared elemental concerns about self and significant others with Lucy Breckinridge in Virginia and many other young women. They were indeed part of growing up.

Some of Mollie's doubts began to disappear. On March 1, 1858, she confided: "I have a secret, Journal dear . . . I have had a letter, a *sweet* letter . . . By loves me tenderly, truly, and has asked my heart in return, and I know now that I can place my hand in his . . . We did not fall madly in love as I had always expected to, but have gradually 'grown into love.'" More confident of herself and her prospects, Mollie evinces a greater maturity as she approaches the end of her path of growing up, facing the future with courage and hope.

Acting on the resolve of her birthday, in May 1858 Mollie moved to town. Boarding with Mrs. Burnham and "enjoying my feeling of independence," she became "Mollie E. Dorsey, dressmaker and seamstress." Mollie and By got better acquainted: "There's no danger of disenchantment there. By is so witty and full of dry fun that he amuses and interests me." Despite being engaged, they had made no definite plans. "But as I have said before," writes Mollie, "I will not marry until I am twenty-one, and by that time, we will be already with a home of our own. We will both work for that consummation" (June 1).

Homesick in July, Mollie returned to the farm to find Dora grieving, having heard nothing from her fiancé for some time. With "piety of the severe type, where it is almost a sin to laugh," Grandpa lectured her constantly. Mollie worried about her own character: "O! why am I not always good? I am afraid I am too frivolous, that is, to do other people much good" (August 10). She struggled with her sentimentality. When By sent a valentine, she felt ambivalent: "Sometimes I wish By was a little bit more demonstrative, a trifle more sentimental. He is very matter-of-fact, and yet I presume if he were, I would soon tire of him. I *know* that he loves me, and that is enough for a sensible girl" (February 15, 1859).

Returning to town in March, Mollie took a teaching position. Teaching was hard work, but it went well. At the end of June she returned home ill and tired. When By left to visit his dying stepfather, Mollie confessed to turning sentimental and mawkish, fearing that "if he goes I shall never see him again. No lack of faith in him, but a fatality that would follow" (August 5). By late August she was prepared to resume working, preferring sewing to teaching "unless I could be a first-class teacher" (August 20).

Business was good, and Mollie enjoyed life in town. She tried to be discreet and cautious in her conversations with men. By returned only to leave for Iowa, "superintending the making of a canal or ditch." Mollie spent her twenty-first birthday (December 17, 1859) in town, missing her home and her mother. On February 1, 1860, Mollie noted that she had told two or three friends that she would marry that month: "There has been so many comments on the affair, as there always are about long engagements." She repeated her trust in By: "I have no doubts or misgivings in regard to him. I trust him fully and truly. I trust we may enter this new life in the right spirit. Just as thou art, my darling, I take thee. Just as I am thou takest me. We promise to love in prosperity or adversity." On February 19, a Sunday, By married Mollie, "a happy bride," completing at age twenty-one, as she had vowed, her path of growing up. Mollie matured in her years in the West, as marriage extended her path to Colorado.

In Martha Farnsworth, known as Mattie, Mollie had a fellow traveler.[37] Despite sharing migration and other experiences, Mattie was unlike Mollie in many ways, too. Sometimes she pushed hard against family, age, and gender boundaries.

Born in Iowa in 1867, Mattie Farnsworth moved at age five to a village near Winfield, Kansas. She kept a record from age fourteen. Although we follow her path only to marriage, her journey continued. After a terrible first marriage, she remarried. In addition to being a housewife, bereaved mother, and widow, Mattie was a reader, teacher, waitress, suffragist, social worker, and political cartoonist.[38] Her teen years were full and complicated. Motherless and often living away from home, Mattie experienced many conflicts. She was socially and sexually precocious, full of juvenile bravado, constantly struggling for autonomy. But such an adolescence, including her problems at home, is surprisingly typical of the time and place, contradicting our distorted images of historical experiences. In her degree of autonomy, lack of maternal influence, and disconnection from the family home, Mattie's experience diverged from the emerging norm. But she was not in all ways exceptional.

At first Mattie kept her journal sparingly, in 1882 reporting little more than school attendance, occasional community events, and the weather. The following year Mattie bloomed into adolescence, showing an interest in boys and affairs of the heart. Her social world expanded. She had her "jolliest, best times at Literary [society]," with her father, her sisters, and Bert, who walked her home. At school she had "such good times," including baseball games at noontime, when the girls played, and beat, the boys' team. Bert had competition; two other boys also wanted to walk with Mattie, but she stuck with Bert. Both were fifteen and "heavy for our ages, and everyone says, we are *'an awful cute little couple.'*" His interest pleased Mattie but not her stepmother: "[She says] if I don't quit letting the boys walk home with me, she will put us all to bed, for we are only children: *she can't put me to bed, anyhow,*" Mattie more than hints at their difficult relationship (January 23, 1883).

Mattie considered herself ill treated and spent much of her time away from home. She writes: "At Mr. Thompson's, they want to *adopt* me; 'the very idea'; I would not be anyone's girl but Pa's and I wish my stepmother was good to me, so I could stay home more" (June 4). Adolescent bravado was not only a male trait.[39] After riding a wild colt Mattie asserts: "I *Dearly love daring.*" Only fifteen, she stayed out at a party until 3:30 A.M. She had a *"jolly good* time . . . but I'm *not stuck*" on the boy who kept her out so late (September 12).

Mattie further reveals the tenor of her adolescence when she reports that she and her female peers "made life miserable" for a new, bashful young teacher (November 1 and 4). In December Jozie Calvin walked her home. In an early form of "rating and dating" Mattie reports: "Bert is *'not in it'* so much this winter . . . I've 'got my eye' on a 'new fellow' . . . I'm the envy of all the girls, but they can have Jozie, for I'm going to catch this 'new fellow'" (December 7). She goes on: "My step-mother says I'm too young to go with the Boys. I'm 16 and not very small, either, cause I'm *awful fat.* my legs, measure 14 inches around the 'calf' and I'm big all over. *I'm* big enough to go, whether *I'm* old enough or not. I weigh 129" (December 31).

In the new year, 1884, Mattie added dancing to her whirl of social activities. She danced with "the new fellow, *'Mr. Carman,'*" until 4:00 A.M., at a party on January 31. "Everyone says I'm such a pretty dancer . . . Every young man wants me to dance with him." When Jamie Carman stunned her by asking "rather abruptly, *'Will you marry me'?* Well, it was so sudden and unexpected that I answered, simply, *'Yes'* without hardly knowing what I was saying." Mattie wondered

> if that is the way everyone *"gets engaged."* I always thought people "made love" first . . . He says we will get married when ever I get ready to quit school. This is my first *"proposal"*: just think! I'm the first one, of all this crowd of school-girls and boys to be engaged, and I'm *young, too young:* just *"sweet 16"* and Jamie is 20 . . . but I must go to school a long time first. I'll have to give up my other "sweet hearts" when we get married, so I'm going to wait a long time: Jamie asked me to "kiss" him goodnight and I had to do it: but I don't think he is near so nice for doing it. I never kissed him before. I don't like to *kiss boys.* (March 7)

A few days later Mattie returned to Winfield, where she boarded while attending the grammar department at the central school. She helped pay for her board by assisting a former teacher "because my stepmother didn't want me to come and this will settle the 'expense' question" (March 11). A week later, her bravado failing, she admitted homesickness for "all the young folks," and vowed to be at the next Friday literary society meeting (March 19). By April Mattie was enjoying school and making new friends: "I see I've made two new 'conquests' in Gene Mc & Will Finch: wonder who will come out 'best.' Gene is ahead now. Poor Jamie Carman is being forgotten I'm afraid. Well I *don't love* him anyway and never did, and people ought to *love* when they marry" (April 14). Mattie also joined a small circle of girls her age. They attended church, played games such as "Author," and took long walks. They teased Will Finch and made him walk with girls other than Mattie. Knowing that her father "won't like it very well," she had her ears pierced (May 3). At the end of the term Mattie won promotion to the high school.

Once she had broken her engagement, Mattie's relations with Will intensified: "This little love affair is mutual, and in dead earnest; not like it was with Jamie: With Will & I it was 'love at first sight' tho' both of us were engaged to someone else; but I've broken mine and it waits to be seen whether Will can his or not. I hope he can" (June 3). Two weeks later the seventeen-year-old reported, "No wonder Will & I are 'falling so much in love,' we see each other, day and night and all the time" (June 20). Alas, Will broke Mattie's heart when he left to take a position in a mill in Elk Falls, Kansas: "I've been 'blue' all evening, I couldn't eat any supper and I've nearly cried my eyes out. I didn't know I did care so much for him, until now he is gone: how can I ever stand it" (July 15). But a week later Mattie had a new man pursuing her. Her former teacher Clem Bradshaw "*proposed* to me and I told him I would not marry until I was an 'old maid' and that would be 13 years from now." He replied that he would wait; Mattie considered his chances "slim," given her feelings for Will (July 23).

Jamie next threatened suicide. Feeling sorry for him, Mattie "made up" with him (August 23). Undiscouraged, Clem sought her love. Her parents were opposed to her "going with Will," whom she met secretly and who repeatedly broke her heart. In confusion and frustration she declared: "I wish Will had stayed here, then Jamie could not have had a chance to 'coax' me back. Oh! Well I may get over it; a girl of 17 is not expected to know *what* or *who* she wants and is excusable for most anything she does. I'll try to be good to Jamie" (August 26). Taking her admonition seriously and claiming loneliness, Mattie added Harvey McClellan to her list of suitors.

Her estrangement from her family increased. One diary entry hints that Mattie may have been beaten at home. Secret meetings with Will continued: "*All is fair, in love and war*" (November 3). Meanwhile, Mattie continued her schooling. But in December she began to skip school when Will was in town; three late nights of dancing she deemed "*disappating*" (December 19).

In January 1885 Will told her that he had at last broken his engagement. He asked her to marry him: "I was so happy, I cried. I don't think there is two happier people any where, than Will & I" (January 12). Planning to marry in the fall, eighteen-year-old Mattie sought to "get work of some kind to do . . . and I will have to get my clothes, for it will be against my folks' wishes I know" (February 23). She helped temporarily at the Central Hotel. Then "Pa came for me to go out home . . . Pa says they need me at home" (February 27). This meant leaving school. It also meant loss of autonomy. At first she was lonesome, but she soon had a full round of activities, including church and rambling with other young men and women. She sometimes stayed with girlfriends. Her ability to assimilate an abrupt shift of circumstances is typical of the transitional path of growing up.

In April Mattie began to teach. "I don't know whether I can change myself from a 'romping tom-boy' to a sober little school ma'am, or not, but I can try" (April 6, 1885). After a week in the classroom, she reported that she liked teaching "real well: find some of my pupils quite mischievous" (April 10). In accord with gender divisions, she went to parties with boys and attended prayer meetings with female friends. At the end of the month she prepared a major celebration for her eighteenth birthday, sending out more than one hundred invitations. "We had just the *jolliest, best* time," she reports. "Every one said they had a most splendid time. I was dressed in White and received compliments from every side. Also many handsome presents" (April 27). In early May, Will visited.

Conditions at home worsened. In June Mattie feared that her sister had "run off," as she had threatened. "Our Stepmother is so cross we can hardly live together . . . No one knows how unkind our stepmother is to us" (June 12 and 14). Summer also brought normal school, socials, and outdoor dancing. Girls walked home with boys after the dances "on the *sly*" (August 10). At the end of August Mattie ominously wrote, "Sent Will a letter today that I'm sure will *'break us up*" (August 29). He replied by asking her to release him from their engagement. Melodramatically she penned: "I'd rather have died, than live to see this day. Will, that woman does not and never will live, who will love you as I do, and you *will* live to regret this day, most bitterly . . . I suffer now, *you* will suffer later" (September 5). Broken-hearted, she released him.

Still vowing her love for Will, Mattie went out with other boys. She thought "so much of *Will* and yet am having such a good time, guess my heart won't break" (November 4). Seeing him again and talking into the late hours led only to tears: "Will has promised to come to me in one year" (December 19). They would then marry "'if all is well,' tho' 'twas not said in so many words." Their ambiguous relationship was extended (December 21).

Mattie stayed home only when she had nowhere else to go. In January 1886 she recognized that she might have to leave because of her stepmother: "We have such jolly times at home, but our step-mother makes it hard for us, threatening to 'mash our mouths' or do something dreadful for the least little thing. She doesn't want Belle and I at home at all, and says if we don't leave she will. Pa doesn't know 100th part of how she treats us and some times seems to take her part" (January 27).

In 1886 Mattie added to her roster of suitors. One fellow was "playing sweet" with her and a second girl at the same time. "That won't go with me," she contradictorily declared. "He can go with me when *I'm* doing that, if he wishes, but won't go with him when *he* is doing it. *Independence*" (January 3). On the sly she met men her parents opposed, letting them walk her to church, singing school, or a dance, the institutions that constituted teen and youth society. Mattie continued dancing and staying out until the wee hours of the morning without chaperones. Her bravado turned to shame at rejecting from one man "a pure, honest love, that I ought to respect, even if I cannot return it . . . A less heartless girl than I, would surely, have asked forgiveness and promised at once to marry him. I only laughed at him" (April 17). Turning down another suitor, she had no scruples in hinting at the imbalances of gender relations: "He is too badly *'stuck on me'*. Why can't a girl go with a fellow a *few times* any way, without his getting so stuck on her, that she must marry him, or quit going with him. *Foolish boys*" (June 29).

At the end of April, Mattie regretfully moved back to Winfield, boarding with Judge Torrance, shifting location and status again. "I wish my step-mother was willing for me to stay home," she writes. "I can't bear to be away from dear sister Belle" (April 27). With her new "independence," however, she soon was contented and busy socially.

In July she moved to Medicine Lodge to work at the Grand Central Hotel. As before, she took the job to earn money because "my stepmother gets angry everytime Pa spends a 'penny' on we girls. None of my folks know I came here and Pa will be awfully angry if I stay here to work, but I can't see any harm in it" (July 21). With great emotion she learned in late August that her beloved sister Belle had died from typhoid fever. Mattie was hurt that her family had sent no word in advance of the telegram of the death. "I feel the folks have wronged us both," she wrote sadly, her estrangement worsening (August 30). In Medicine Lodge she found a new "home. I ought to be happy here, with so many friends who are *continually* paying me some *pretty* compliment. A girl friend told me today that everyone were saying they, 'never knew a *jollier* girl than Mattie Van.' How little they know, how my heart is *bleeding* for dear Belle" (October 6).

While slowly recovering from a long illness at home at the end of the year, Mattie records that her "old sweet-heart, Will Finch, gave me a great surprise this morning, by coming to spend the day with me. I didn't know he was within 200 miles of me . . . I was real glad to see him and enjoyed his visit, but he wanted me to promise to marry him, as soon as I was strong enough, which I could not do. The old love is gone: *killed* by his own *heartlessness*. He knew I loved him and felt *so sure* of me, that he thought to let me suffer on, to his own good time" (December 29). Despite her vanity and her ego, Mattie was slowly maturing and gaining some perspective on her affairs: "I think I treated Will *too cool* yesterday, for he is *so good*: but my heart would not respond to his 'overtures' of love'; instead it resented, and felt repulsive to every loving word and look: he let my heart suffer and *break* unjustly, and lost the *purest, best* love a woman ever gave to a man, by doing so" (December 30).

By February Mattie's stepmother was insisting "I *'have to go'* as soon as I am strong enough tho; and I want to stay home *so much*" (February 2, 1887). "God *pity* a girl, that can call *no place home*" (February 14). Still weak, she left for a boardinghouse. Her father stopped to say goodbye on his way to Colorado. "I love *Frontier life* and wanted to go too, but he wouldn't let me, for I'm not strong enough yet," writes Mattie (March 4).

Recovering, she turned her attention to the new telegraph operator, Oren Kettlewell. "I didn't get an introduction, tho' I think I'll 'mash' him, to see what he's made of" (March 23). By June the two were carrying on a "nice *flirtation* . . . I believe he is an awful *Flirt*" (June 12). His admission that he was "only flirting" because he was engaged to someone else led her to take a new tack in the battle of the sexes: "He said when he came to this little Village, he thought it such a little *country* place, he'd have a great time *mashing* all the girls and I pleased him most and he wanted to go with me." Mattie vowed to "*show* him, that *Flirting* is a game *two can play*, and *I vow, I will make him love me and he will ask me to be his wife before three months from now; now see if I don't. See if I don't prove to be the best flirt of the two. I feel sorry for the other girl, but I shall leave nothing undone, to win him*" (June 15).

Exerting her efforts in this direction, Mattie consciously risked breaking her own heart in order to break Oren's, a perverse plan. By mid-September she had him. Mattie's late adolescent flights of fancy knew few bounds. To salve his feelings temporarily and to escape, she agreed to an engagement, thinking "it will be easy enough to get out of it again" (September 24). He seemed happier, but by November she felt that there would be trouble between them.

In the new year, 1888, Mattie reported that she and Oren were quarreling "so much, we are about to *'quit.'*" Her eye caught a "little Mail carrier," John Shaw, "just a little dandy. Pretty brown eyes, and awfully cute . . . He told Sadie today, in my presence, that I was *'sweet enough to be kissed.'* I don't like such remarks at all" (January 28). Mattie was waiting, she claimed, for a "good, honest man" who wanted a wife: "I've got a *whole heart* to give him" (January 31). Mattie discovered that she was in a *"peck of trouble"*: Oren would not agree to break their engagement, and Will Finch was at home, remembering an old promise. Mattie was almost snared in her own traps. "So what I am to do. A girl likes to keep on the *good side* of all these nice Boys. God Bless them, what would we do without them. *The very thought of marrying now, is so distasteful* to me, that I can't do it" (February 24). The next day she returned to Topeka and her mail carrier. Mattie observed her twenty-first birthday on April 26, 1888. Expressing concern about her future, she enrolled in an evening "Short-hand School." As she learned stenography, John Shaw persisted in his suit despite their frequent spats.

By summer Mattie had begun to accept him: "I begin to like the Boy, he is so good to me" (July 11). "Mr. Shaw seems very devoted and some say he would *love* me if I'd let him; some say he is *very much in love* with me and *all* say it is *shameful* way I treat him" (August 1). By the end of October she could report: "He is winning me over, thro' his goodness and kindness. I've always had a *presentiment* that I would marry that man and I don't want to, at all, yet I seem to be drawn on and on, towards him, against my own will" (October 27). Another "presentiment" came on Election Day, when Shaw responded with angry jealousy to seeing her— innocently—with another man. She reports being *"very much hurt"* (November 14). Shaw apologized; they continued to see each other. At year's end Mattie hoped that 1889 would bring her more happiness than 1888, "tho' 1888 has been very happy since I got O. Kettlewell off my Hands" (December 31).

Shaw talked of matrimony. On February 2, 1889, he proposed. Mattie's reactions were complicated: "I am Oh! so happy; he is so good and honest I know he will always be true and good to me, yet I don't think I ever shed so many tears, for some way, I don't feel just satisfied; I feel half afraid and yet I love him so much, yet there is an uneasiness I cannot explain; but I am happy." She identifies the source of her fears about "Johnny": his "little *fits* of *temper* that I'm afraid of: makes me feel that trouble may come of it, in the future, after marriage" (March 2). Time proved her correct.

Summer brought wedding plans. Mattie hoped that her dress "will please my Boy. I never got such a thing for any other man and never will again: it is my *first* and *last wedding dress.* I never was so lonesome as I am away from Johnny" (August 12). They set the wedding date for September 4. "And while I think I'm very happy," she writes, "there is a constant kind of dread or presentiment, that, 'all will not be well' and I shall be unhappy; but I drive such fears away" (August 1). Mattie's anticipation of happiness was compromised. Isolation increased her vulnerability. Her youthful independence had its costs as well as benefits; a long estrangement from family and early autonomy could be mixed blessings in confronting a transition such as marriage.

Mattie's wedding day began happily, but with the arrival of rain her spirits fell. She was determined not to cry: "I love Johnny and I know he does me, yet it seems as tho' he has thought more of how things shall look, at the wedding, than of me; he has hurried me all day and not given me one little pleasant word concerning what is to be. My heart feels hungry and not satisfied" (September 4). With evening came the ceremony, followed by a light supper with beer. Happy the next day, Mattie found being Mrs. J. W. Shaw "is more like keeping 'Play house.' It seems so funny to be married" (September 5).

In the middle of their first month of marriage, Johnny's temper flared, foretelling the unhappiness of Mattie's years with him. To the problem of temper he added drunkenness. Domestic tragedies punctuated long periods of boredom. Mattie's lengthy, intensely self-centered path of growing up had ill prepared her for the shock and pain of Johnny's anger and jealousy and his drinking. She suffered several miscarriages, as well as a forced trip to Colorado during one of her pregnancies. Johnny's death from consumption brought relief. Mattie married again. With her second husband, Fred Farnsworth, she had a long and satisfying relationship. For Mattie, adolescence was at once a vital preparation for future independence and a training ground for a false sense of self and a failed first marriage.

Contrasting but complementing the lives of Mattie Farnsworth and Mollie Dorsey is Mary R. Luster's experience of growing up, also shaped by western migration and residence.[40] For her, a family's quest for fortune made the difference, as did the effects of the Civil War. Drawing on transitional experiences shared by many of her male and female contemporaries, Mary's memories, set down late in life, also reflect nostalgia, a mythologizing of her family's experiences. Ninth child "in the family that must have been a great care and burden to an over worked mother," Mary was born July 5, 1853, in Spring Creek, McDonough County, on the Illinois prairie (12). Her parents had moved from Kentucky and Indiana about twelve years earlier. Near them resided her mother's father and two sisters. Family visiting was frequent. During Mary's early years her grandfather Searles lived with the family. He would tell stories and sing songs of his War of 1812 adventures, petting and spoiling Mary.

Mary retained a clear picture of a path in which tradition and change, old ways and new influences, intermingled. She recalls, without any sense of conflict or contradiction: "So eager were we for any thing that brought change into the monotony of our lives, and yet we did not know we were either lonely or heart hungry for companionship outside of our own home. We were, I think, contented and happy . . . kept busy and responded with perfect obedience to the commands of our parents . . . Mother would endure any sort of sacrifice to see that not an hour even of the precious school time was lost" (14). One older sister left home to teach at seventeen; she married at eighteen.

The common urge to "make one big venture and obtain this needed wealth" to care for a growing family threatened the precarious stability of farm life (19). Mary's father mortgaged the farm in order to increase his herd of livestock. A bad market—"It was the old story"—ended the dream (19). When Mary was three, her family moved to a small village nearby. Her father took charge of a mill, her grandfather made barrels for the flour—Mary "reveled in the long curling shavings" (20)—and her mother took in boarders. This venture failed within a year, and the family moved to Missouri.

Joined by a married daughter and her family, their eldest son clerking in a store nearby, the family first rented a farm. After a year Mary's father found "an ideal place . . . where we lived [for five years] until the tragedies of the Civil War drove us roaming again" (28). Inheriting her mother's skill with children, Mary "was very early made custodian and interpreter for my baby brother George," a slow learner (31).

Church and school were strong early influences. With few toys, the children made their own diversions. In the evenings "we would tell the same story over and over again vying with each other as to which could tell it best," Mary recalls (35). At six Mary started winter school, but when schools in the area closed at the outbreak of Civil War, the mothers brought their children together and taught them in circumstances that dramatically affected Mary's family. "I did not know what it was all about, but I imbibed enough of the spirit of the times to be very enthusiastic in my patriotism for the 'Southern Confederacy,'" she writes (37). The war hit home: one of Mary's brothers was in combat, and soldiers raided their farm, taking timber and a horse. "Nearly all" of the older and more prosperous residents of the community were "rebels," and eventually three of Mary's brothers fought for the Confederacy. But her father—"Perhaps father was not discreet"—was arrested and imprisoned for several weeks in Alton, Illinois (41). His spirit broken, he took an oath of loyalty to the Union then returned home. He was run off by his neighbors, and the family home was threatened with arson.

In the spring of 1863 Mary's mother and the younger children followed her father to Illinois, where they had relatives. They stayed until the next spring, when they trekked "across the Plains." The fears that ten-year-old Mary suffered were erased by time, although she later remembered the shock and grief at her older brother's death in combat. "But we children could not understand. We had never seen death" (51).

New plans to move were stimulated in part by one son's and a son-in-law's draft eligibility, which might literally set brother against brother. The family joined the "great tide of emigration that went West . . . It seemed like going to another country to leave the States," Mary writes. They settled near Boise and built a new home. Mary's early adolescence in Idaho featured more sociability beyond the family circle than her childhood had. "Big brothers were always ready to take me to the few entertainments that came our way." Her first party—Mary was thirteen—seized the family's attention: "Every one was telling me something to do or not to do in the advent into society when Eva, the little four-year-old, piped out, 'Be sure and keep your stocking tied up'" (75–76).

Schooling was limited despite the children's eagerness. Mary writes: "Had my first beau during this school experience. There were only two large girls who attended, in fact only two in the valley . . . We were very popular. We could dance and felt quite grown up and young Frank Murray continued to pay me considerable attention for the next year and a half . . . Once or twice each week during our school term the teacher and Mr. Murray gave us dancing lessons, both boys and girls" (77–78). Both community and peer cultures formed, within limits, with the support of this kind of teaching.

After five years the family returned to Missouri in 1868. For fifteen-year-old Mary this was a major transition to a place where there were peers of her own age and regular private schooling. (There were no public schools.) She writes: "I was permitted to take my place among girls and boys of my own age. My study at home had been sufficient . . . I was most happy to find I was equal to the requirements in every branch of study" (92). Society for teenagers included magic lantern shows and dances. The school prohibited dancing, so "children's parties played 'Post Office,' 'Clap in and Clap out,' and such. They were rather tame to both of us [Mary and her brother] for we had been dancing with the 'grown up' for the past two years, but we were happy in our school work and formed many warm friendships" (93). Mary rivaled a teacher's son for class honors.

Because of her success in school, says Mary: "I realized I had learned much . . . and thought I could teach." Through her teacher's recommendation and the help of a neighbor, Mary secured a school position. Unable to pass the county examination, however, she "had to forgo [her] ambition for that time." Mary appreciated the foundation she had gained in country schools, "so I was able to lead my classes when I had the next opportunity to attend a city school" (96). During school sessions, spelling matches and singing parties provided amusement, especially for the young.

Family life changed again in 1871, "the year our paths diverged" (101). The younger children now began to grow up and leave home. Mary moved to Brunswick to live with her sister and attend high school. Graduating in the class of 1872 at age eighteen, she had the highest grades and took valedictory honors. In Brunswick she met Charles Luster, editor of the local paper and a frequent visitor to the house. Mary and Charles were not "very congenial, perhaps each was a little jealous of the other's standing in [her sister's] family." Mary was "aware of his good looks and . . . admired his literary promise, but he was sarcastic and very indifferent and I never for a moment in that first year of our acquaintance thought of him as a possible sweetheart" (103).

As their acquaintance lengthened, they found they "had become interested in each other." Before spring they were engaged: "It was not a case of 'falling in love,' it was one of growing in love. I do not believe that two young people, male and female, can be so intimately associated as we were without a very definite interest in each other developing." Mary wasn't alone in this experience. Charles was the first "really educated" young man she had ever known. She enjoyed talking to him, hearing him recite poetry "by the yard," along with "some pat quotation ready on every occasion." Eager for learning, Mary faced an increasingly common conundrum: "It was very appealing. I had no thought of marriage, however, when I said yes. I had decided on teaching as a career and our marriage was to be a long way in the future" (105).

In the summer of 1872 Mary worked in the newspaper office, learning to set type. She considered becoming a printer: "It was before any vocation but teaching and housework was open to women and the curious gaze of the men who came to the office annoyed me greatly but I kept valiantly at the task until I could earn $1.50 a day, which was better wages than teaching was at that time" (105–106). Unable to match Luster's faster typesetting, however, she quit. The following spring, aged twenty, Mary secured the post of teacher at the neighborhood school near home. She received $105 for the three-month term, happily spending the summer with her mother.

Attracting the attention of the local physician, she nonetheless remained "too loyal" to Luster: "I was very soon left to my own resources" (109). Later in 1873 Mary married Charles Luster. After progressing toward adult maturity and independence by living away from home and gaining competence in teaching and printing, she took the next step on her path. They moved to St. Louis, where Charles became an editor and Mary taught school for $35 a week and $40 a month, respectively.[41]

These young women's lives stand out as mixtures of newer and older ways of growing up, of accommodations to tradition and change influenced more or less directly by westward migration. Individually and collectively the women defy easy summary or stereotype as migrants or westerners. That is important to keep in mind as we consider the similarities in their stories. Their lives are distinguished, too, by the relatively early transitions they made, if not to full autonomy at least in the direction of decreased dependence on family. We also note key intersections of age, institutions, peers, work, and family relations. The process of making those connections captures in part what Mattie Farnsworth meant by seeking female "independence" in her relationships.

The early life course experiences of women who grew up in the West, in comparison with those also shaped by internal movement, testify to a breadth of patterns within this wide transitional female subpath. What is especially clear in these lives is the striking presence of new middle-class elements of growing up in places where we might not expect to find them. These include the critical place and associations of families, institutions, peers and their culture, notions and expectations about childhood and adolescence, and connections with both ideas and experiences of gender, dependency, and autonomy. That is only part of the story.

As we follow the path of growing up across the West, we encounter Blanche Beal Lowe, who spent her first four years on the prairie at Conway Springs, Kansas.[42] A farmer until he invented a barbed wire tightener in 1894, her father gained business know-how and capital in partnership with a cousin in Wichita. In 1896 Blanche's mama and papa (both thirty) and their five children moved to the city. Blanche's pattern of growing up altered with the move, but her memoir tells us that city and country, significantly, shared a great deal.

Blanche's parents axiomatically valued the linked institutions of home, church, and school. Home life was central. The children had assigned responsibilities whose importance grew with their father's increased business travels. Whenever he left, "he'd say to Ralph, 'Son, you're man of the house while I'm away. Take good care of Mama.' To Mama he'd say, 'Wife, think these young'uns have enough chores to keep them out of mischief?' And Mama would say, 'If not, I'm real good at thinking up others.' And they'd both laugh." Blanche remarks: "Town people had chores to do much like country people. For behind every house in our neighborhood there was a barn and a chicken house, fruit trees, and a big garden. Some people also used vacant lots to grow bigger gardens or alfalfa for livestock" (40). Producing wood fuel and coal was also labor-intensive. The lines between growing up in city and country blurred. Many domestic tasks marked the family economy of both. A clear gender division of labor ruled these chores; for instance, the girls washed the dishes and ironed when they became old enough. The children teased one another and argued about who was shirking his or her fair share.

The constant extensive labor required by turn-of-the-century domesticity mocks contemporary and later notions of idle middle-class youngsters in contrast with hardworking country kids. Town life called for different tasks. "The magic for her," Blanche writes of her mother, "was living where they were so many lamps to light . . . a town where everybody, even a farm woman like Mama, already past thirty years old, had a chance to learn and do and be things they'd hardly dreamed of" (45). Urban residence also meant that "the whole family was in the middle of things, being part of a real church with a regular preacher, a good graded Sunday school, young people's groups, and women's societies" (49). Growing up in a town or city also imposed the cultural divisions of age and gender that population concentration made possible. That segregation in turn transformed the experience of growing up. Middle-class practices gained support and advanced.

Of her education in town Blanche writes: "We were in the middle of things in schools too, and proud (except maybe Carl) when Mama came to visit each of our grades. And prouder still when one of our teachers came to our house for dinner" (50). Homework was part of the serious business of growing up. In this family, as in many others, supervising the children's schooling fell within the mother's preserve. When he was home, however, Blanche's father signed the report cards. "Papa and Mama had so little chance to go to school," she remarks, "they weren't going to let us waste our chance" (50). The piano was another focal point of family activity.

On a business trip Blanche's papa fell in love with California. In 1902 he decided to risk indebtedness to purchase a run-down sheep and cattle ranch north of San Francisco. The older children's tears over leaving high school did not deter him. Six years after settling in Wichita the family moved again, from rural life to urban and back to the frontier; Blanche was ten, her parents were thirty-six.

In California, Blanche recalls, "we children learned new skills and to some degree developed qualities that pioneer life taught our parents: qualities like adaptability, self-reliance, responsibility" (53). Formal schooling consisted only of a one-room schoolhouse. After the first year the children took turns going to a high school fifty miles away and helping on the ranch. The eldest daughter married, and the eldest son, Ralph, graduated from high school and taught while saving for college. Blanche's father eventually sold the ranch and bought into a business in Palo Alto. Three children entered high school there, while Ralph entered Stanford. Voicing the rhetoric of transitional growing up, Blanche attributes a design to parental action which may or may not have existed originally: "I never heard Papa speak of opportunities for us children, only of 'advantages' to help us 'get ahead in the world.' By settling in Palo Alto, a college town, Mama and Papa had done what they set out to do: put college education within reach of their sons. For daughters, higher learning was hardly worthwhile; 'they'd just get married anyway'" (53). Such gender differences went unquestioned; the girls married college graduates, and the boys graduated from college and then married. Thus traditions, in new or updated forms, emerged amid major transformations in this as in other families; in turn they reciprocally shaped and were reshaped by changes along the paths of growing up.

The lines that blur in the movements of a family such as Blanche's gain clarity from other experiences of growing up in the developing society of the American West in the second half of the nineteenth century. Five personal testimonies of young women growing up in Texas, contemporaneous records from diaries, provide an exceptional focus on life patterns and processes. The records cluster around major transitions such as schooling, leaving home, and marriage. They contribute a comparative perspective, a sharpness and immediacy that Blanche Lowe's and Mary Luster's nostalgic accounts tend to lack. They tell a crucial tale of the spread of new middle-class patterns, as well as their limits.

Mary P. Burke's diary of February–November 1861, an account of her year at the Live Oak Female Seminary in Houston, is an exemplary tale of a teenager uprooted from home to a private boarding academy in a fledgling metropolis.[43] Mary reminds us that in areas still in the frontier stage of social development, families and individuals were faced with certain limits on their choices. An important consideration for increasing numbers of families and young persons—for improving their chances in life, meeting norms, conferring status, and protecting children at vulnerable ages, among other reasons—was that secondary schooling was not available without leaving home. Therefore, in a curious contradiction, families who wished to prolong their children's dependence in accord with their sense of their children's best interests, but who lived in remote places without secondary schools, had to send the children away. In terms of emerging middle-class patterns, this meant violating one cardinal stricture—prolonged residence at home—in order to secure another, prolonged schooling and institutional dependence.

That contradiction was part of Mary Burke's lived experience. She begins her diary: "Sun. morning Feb. 10, 1861. arrived yesterday. Frank Noble left here this morning. oh I did hate to see him go away so bad. I am so homesick I am nearly dead. home sweet home. oh Allie you nearly broke my heart when you told me good bye. how long will it be before we meet again. oh *how long how long*. it may be that we *never will meet* again. if I thought so my heart would break. yes indeed it would." Mary carries on in this manner for several entries before heeding advice to complete the year. She testifies to the wrench she felt in leaving home and friends of both sexes. Her tone probably represents her effort to express herself in imitation of popular, overly romanticized genres. Is it ironic or simply sentimental that by July, anticipating vacation, she writes: "Still it is very sad, for who can tell how many of us meet in this schoolroom again as teachers and taught?" (July 24, 1861). Mary's problem was not only separation from home and family but also separation from the young man she loved (July 28). Another element of Mary's adolescent development emerges in the gendered peer culture of the school: "Tonight is Sunday and we have had so much fun. Fannie and Georgia dressed up in boys clothes. Fannie now was Jack??? Georgia's name was Thomas Conklin" (August 19).

Mary remained lonesome and homesick during her entire time at school. On September 11 she wrote: "Six months since I left home oh I do want to go home." Five days later an entry reads: "I do feel so bad to day. I do not believe I am going to live long. I would give worlds if I was at home with my own dear mother and I want to see pa so bad bless his dear good soul if there ever was a man on earth as oh me I cant stay up here three months it is impossible I do believe it will kill me" (September 16). Mary dreamed about home, her mother, her boyfriend Chris—"he is a strange boy. to think he has not written to me in a whole month but I am going to break my heart after him certain" (October 6). She hoped for a visit from her mother: "If she dont I dont know what I will do. oh I do want to see all of the loved ones at home so bad" (October 6). In six weeks she would be "at my own dear home and wont I be happy yes indeed happy happy happy happy . . . We will have so much fun going home that night after the concert" (October 16).

At home on vacation, with no sense of contradiction, she writes: "Thoughts at the close of School. The term has again closed and we are compelled to speak that sweet old word *Good Bye*. It is spoken with a tearful eye and heavy heart to think it may be the last time we may ever meet again as teacher and scholar" (October 29). Sentimentality overmisted leaving school for this adolescent much as it colored her leaving home for school and going home again. New traditions were spreading in social relations and their cultural applications.

Mary Burke was not exceptional in her teenage sentiments and experience. Her path of growing up, middle-class influenced but western-based, was a broad one, typical of its time. Ella Cole, another schoolgirl who grew up in Austin, College Station, and Waco, Texas, was different from Mary in that she lived at home while in school. Her father was a professor at Texas A & M in College Station. Her diary spanned October 1883 to April 1884.[44]

Following convention, Ella sophomorically addresses her entries to "Dear Journal." Her record begins with school, which consisted of a small number of pupils studying with a teacher hired by parents to teach in their homes: "At last succeeded in getting at our books, a teacher from Waco this time . . . Papa and Mrs. Allen look over old rusty books and decided what we should study. I will name some of the books I study. US History, Clark's Grammar, Mental Arithmetic, Writing, Written Arithmetic, Latin and Speller" (October 22, 1883). Ella found Latin difficult; music and Friday evening spelling matches were more enjoyable. Since she lived at home, her education included regular household chores as well as schoolwork. Both were meant to prepare her for her anticipated course.

In mid-November the arrival of a circus disrupted the usual routines:

"How we enjoyed ourselves, our trip is indescribable." Reflecting a spreading age consciousness, Ella mentions her father's forty-fourth birthday: "None of us had a birthday present for him" (November 17). What with circus and birthdays, it is not surprising that Ella notes: "I have not known hardly any of my lessons to day, I had to stay in for missing two words in my spelling. We had calisthenics to day instead of singing" (November 19). Here we find evidence of a trend toward increased emphasis on physical education for the young, including girls, to ensure their healthy development.[45] The next day Ella proudly regained her standing, achieving impressively while chafing over discipline and attesting to her adolescent feelings: "I have known all of my lesson to day . . . I will tell my grades. History 94. Grammar 94. Mental Arithmetic 100. Written arithmetic 99. Latin Grammar 86. Spelling 99. Writing 96. Music 83. We had singing to day. Miss Imogen gave me a demerit to day for not getting to the piano in three minutes. She makes us stand around and has so many different rules that we are afraid to turn around. I have got the blues to night. Dear old Journal. Good evening—Ella Cole" (November 20).

Ella studied dancing in the evenings, learning to waltz, as well as skating and music. Miss Imogen also trained her pupils' character and deportment: "Oh me! we have some more new rules. If we do not hold ourselves up straight we get demerits and to stay in too" (December 19). A change of teachers in January made no difference to Ella. In February 1884 the school prepared a concert: "We all looked cute and *very* nice," she notes. Although Ella was nervous, the music, boys' and girls' calisthenics, wand exercises, and speeches went well (February 8). Testifying to the interests of her age, Ella closed the diary by remarking that she was going to watch the cadets play ball.

Mabel Montgomery Minter of Abilene kept a diary in 1893–94 while she was a student at the Stuart Seminary in Austin, Texas.[46] She begins typically: "Dear Diary: . . . I hope, as this resolution to write to you, My Diary, differs from others in these material points, that it will be remarkable of all remarkable things—an unbroken resolution" (August 2, 1893). Mabel expresses a hope that "when my school-days are over, I may read [the diary] not from instruction, but that I may live again with pleasure the days that now seem so long and wearisome" (August 2). Mabel pursued a collegiate course. She was uncertain what degree to take, a reflection on female education and higher education at this time.

Schoolwork was not Mabel's major preoccupation. Boys and romances among her friends take up more diary space. "Dere Diary" was far more attractive than Mental Philosophy. Mabel's active social life included male admirers. At a dance at the beginning of the fall term, she had a "lovely time" (September 5, 1893). Yet proper relations with men required careful negotiation over intentions, actions, and significant others. On Valentine's Day, she writes, "much to my astonishment I actually received a valentine" sent anonymously. When the sender was revealed on "Birthington's Washday," it was "not so pleasing as I anticipated. Rather more disturbing than otherwise . . . Well!! I haven't any comment to make. A man of his age, and the second time I have met him!! I can truely [*sic*] say 'That makes me tired'" (February 23, 1894). Relations among the girls at the school could also be stressful.

Adolescent peer culture was a shaping influence on the female students. "Cutting up" during study hour—throwing sticks of kindling across the room—was one form of entertainment. So was "swapping" beds or changing rooms, and "jumping ditches, this evening playing in the sand," part of exercise class. One Friday night the girls romped and played blindfolded. Mabel admonished herself when she "played handkerchief" in front of two men, surprised or pretending surprise that as a "senior" she could "so condescend" (February 22, 1894).

Elocution class "was quite killing yesterday. We shouted Othello etc; once we were all reciting in concert, but soon 'on alas, I found that I was singing there alone.' They laughed a little, I am told, but I had done my best" (February 17). The "rations" in the dining hall were "pretty good." Receiving letters defined a good week. And Mabel reports falling in love with other girls. The girls avoided one peer who ate onions. They worried about gaining weight. All these preoccupations were part of adolescent growing up in the halls of the seminary. In Mabel's estimation, "Things at Stuart's are *quite tame*" (February 22).

"The greatest thing of the season. *Senior's Reception*" brought excitement. Given but a day's notice, "Oh how we tore around (The juniors tore around but for a different reason)," making "programs or lists or what ever you call them." Lacking an evening dress, Mabel borrowed a white cashmere. She "represented 'Measure for Measure' with two medicine glasses pouring meal from one to the other." At the party she met two young men—"both very nice. Mr. C. especially handsome. Mr. L. said something *awfully* nice about me. Hope I'll see them both again" (February 27). On other evenings the girls played "Blind Man's Bluff" in the moonlight or "Weavely Wheat," or "extinguished ourselves in spelling" (March 7).

In March Mabel experienced "the first trouble of my life worth mentioning"—apparently her failure to graduate. Mable deemed herself "*cowardly* to take it this way . . . This is one of the *saddest* nights of my life . . . I will have to write to mama Monday and tell her about it, and what she says will change the course of my life for years. Oh why can't I tell somebody? How will I bear it by myself. Is it right that one should be happy and gay with never a thought of trouble and the next have her dearest hope and ambition crushed by one blow that seems as if all the foundation aim and joy of her life is broken and cast away as if by a careless wind?" (March 10). The next day Mabel explains the problem: she wasn't able to complete the degree. "The *Idea* that I had to give up my A.B. course was too much for me," she writes. "I don't know how I can stand it in June if I decide not to take my diploma but return next year and receive the A.B. degree" (March 11). Unless she intended to marry, the school wanted her to return.

Past the initial shock and much relieved, Mabel regained her interest in men and tennis. Still awaiting word from her mother, she writes: "We had a splendid old see-saw last evening and then played Blind Man and 'Charlie'. Don't you want to know how old all are? Well we have to be children sometimes, and Mr. Purcell makes it so lively its lots of fun" (March 18). A letter arrived from home advising her to return the next year as contemplated. The question of a fall roommate occupied her (March 18).

The trauma behind her, Mabel's concern shifted to other failings. Observing strong relationships between some of the girls, she wrote: "Unfortunately I'm one of *these* here people that ought to have someone to love them and show it and I have not that necessary article here. I love M. dearly, dear old girl. I may someday have to say with Marietta 'I loved her dearly but my love wasn't reciprocated.' I think Mamie likes me right well. I wish I could make her love me better than anyone else but am afraid it's a vain wish." Ira, another girl, didn't like her; they had once loved the same girl. When Ira said that she was vain and conceited, Mabel admitted, "It hurts me, awfully at first, but I have no business being so sensitive." One friend counseled that she hadn't been at boarding school long enough. Some solace came when she was told "I was the *prettiest girl in school*" (March 27). Mabel struggled with her teenage emotions.

Turning seventeen in April and awaiting a new dress from her mother, Mabel remarks: "I wonder what will come to me during the year I have begun only a few hours ago! Will it be tiresome, humdrum and unmomentous, or a busy time with no spare minutes to hope or wish and bother about better, or full of strange happenings and adventures" (April 10). She hoped for the latter: "My studies will be few and far between and I expect to hear a few classes, a sort of apprenticeship as it were for my 'future brilliant career as a teacher.' Ah!!" She celebrated her birthday with banana cream pie. Mabel now counted fifty-one days until she would return home.

Mabel went on outings to an ice factory and a lunatic asylum, and clashed with a schoolmate. An essay won her praise, but, she writes, "I'm certain I wont read at the concert though, because even if mine was judged the best it would look very strange indeed to omit one of the bona fide graduates and have *me* to read" (April 21). In spring she took a number of "splendid rides." More seriously, the faculty belatedly discovered "how terribly the girls have been carrying on with these workmen. (Had to be told at that. I wont express my opinion of the one that took upon herself the privilege of telling)." The punishment of exercise in the hot sun, of "we innocent ones for the foolishness of five; that all the school is subjected to such treatment" was unfair. "The greatest injustice" was the suspicion that fell on her friend Mattie: "It is right that the guilty should suffer but I would do almost anything to clear her. She doesn't know how bad the company she has been keeping lately makes things look . . . Just think how awful it would be if she wasn't allowed to graduate just for this mere fancy" (April 28).

The situation worsened. An "idict of quarentine" was imposed. The girls were not allowed to visit one another's rooms for the remainder of the term. For Mabel, thinking about going home made these circumstances bearable. She nevertheless worried, contradictorily: "Will they like me at home. I know that really *at home* there's no danger of their love for me ever changing, but I mean will the dear old boys and girls I've know *always* and love so long till they seem an essential part of my life, will they decide that 'Mabel is not like she used to be' and with careless indifference return to their pleasure among themselves treating me as an outsider? If so I know I will be glad when the time comes to return to dreary old Stuarts" (May 4). Caught between her Scylla and Charybdis, Mabel quipped: "Anyone reading the last part of this would think I had become a monomaniac on the subject of going home" (May 17).

Examinations and dresses took center stage at the end of term. Mabel hoped to get out of examinations (she placed out of all but one) and "be a lady of leisure," looking forward to a final recital and refreshments. Her new dress from home, lemon "crepon" with white lace and ribbon, fit perfectly. Young men and male instructors reminded her of cute boys at home. Baccalaureate day was quite a spectacle. Saying goodbye to the girls was hard.

Mabel's travail-filled year at boarding school ended with her return home in mid-June. Happy and secure in returning to familiar places and people, she saw her friends and went dancing. She concludes her journal, writing: "I will put you away but over and over will I turn these pages in the future" (June 15). Mabel had taken basic steps on her path of growing up in contending with school, peers of both sexes, and other transitional demands typical of her life course stage. Other steps awaited.

Tennessee Keys Embree, who attended "the old Female College at Waco" in her teens, had already taken some but not all of those steps.[47] At age sixteen in 1856 she had studied at the female boarding academy, living away from home. Her 1862 diary finds her at home in Bosqueville, Texas, twenty-two years old, unmarried, and unhappy, suffering old and new problems of the age. Hers was the familiar problem of having a stepmother and stepsister. She was also limited by her circumstances at this stage of growing up.

Tennessee was lonely, in part because many young men were away in wartime service. She occupied herself with "one thing and another"—sewing, ironing, a "little exercise"—as she prepared for a domestic future: "I wish to learn how to do all such work before it is necessary for to have to know" (August 4). This course was not satisfying in itself. She wrote on August 9: "I have not felt happy today but oh, I dare not tell why, it seems to me that a revelation of such feelings would display a weak mind. I hope to learn contentment so perfect that I cease to record sadness." Calling herself a "coward," she refused to go visiting by herself. Isolation and insecurity played on each other; self-criticism was not always constructive.

Nor did sermons provide ease: "My mind seemed to [*sic*] much occupied with other things to be good and do good" (August 24). Reading helped somewhat more. A long, lonesome day, she writes, could be refreshing to her feelings. She read to pass the time: "Spent the day mostly in reading a work titled 'Amy Lee.' I do not know that I have been very much benefited by reading the book for I think it is a fictious [*sic*] work, but I do think such books will do to read once and a while to respond the imagination and teach us human nature" (July 31). Reading allowed her to escape temporarily the dreadful reality of war. Tennessee read history as well as fiction, likely an academy influence.

In the stores in Waco she found little to buy. She returned home with the resolve to make herself useful at the spinning wheel. She made some progress: "At work hard most of the day I think and I also believe I am learning to be very domestic and I am very fond of industry" (September 16). Assimilating lessons stressing industry but lacking suitable occupations she found exacerbated rather than resolved her conflicts. Teaching Sunday school offered Tennessee a worthy outlet for her energies. Church attendance and church work seemed to make her feel better, but also caused her to indict herself self-critically: "Thank God for religion, but oh, for a heart that can love him more and serve him better." Phrenology offered little help (December 3).

Living at home in the small Texas town at age twenty-two during the Civil War, without close companions of either sex or much activity, Tennessee could not see ahead to the remaining steps on her path. Environment and location, as always, made the difference. It could have been worse. The experience that Margaret Armstrong Bowie recorded in her diary of 1872–1877 leads us to that conclusion.[48] Born in 1857 on a frontier farm in Jack County, Texas, she was one of two daughters of a father who had migrated from Tennessee. Her diary relates the strains and conflicts of growing up under isolated frontier conditions. The early end of her path was a happy one, however.

Margaret sets the tone at age fifteen in December 1872: "This is a lonely life we don't see a person once in six months, if we did not have lot of house work to do we could be at a loss how to kill time. Even the little shuttle sewing machine turned by hand does not take all my spare time." Farm work did not break the tedium and isolation. There was no school or church within six miles. On turning sixteen she lamented: "It seems that birthdays are the only thing we have for certain in this lonely country, and not even a party to go with it. I'm 16 today, and was just old enough to begin having company and a good time when Pa had to leave town for this quiet humdrum place farm" (October 12, 1873). Discontent seethes between the lines.

Her mother's example showed the adolescent the impact of this kind of life on women. To her diary Margaret confided: "Ma has been married low [sic] these many years . . . She says she would not go to school longer as her parents wished her to, but silly like she perfered [sic] to get married and settle down to a life of seclusion as all the country seems to be. But there is a future to it all and some day it may work out for the best" (October 20, 1873). Her sense of time passing, time wasting, was only accentuated when on February 14, 1874, she remembered that she had received two valentines the year before they had moved.

Country life was not completely empty. With her sister Annie, Margaret visited Jane and Charity Wood: "They are real nice girls but rather plain and old fashioned country folks, and sing the good old camp meeting songs very well" (June 6, 1874). She occupied herself making shirts and drawers for a bachelor cousin, Jasper. Margaret struggled to maintain a balance: "It is now two years since we moved back to the farm, and it looks quite changed for the better, as we have plenty of house room, and can go out oftener. If only we had a school house and church in our own neighborhood it would seem more like home" (August 26).

On her seventeenth birthday Margaret avoided her usual laments: "I feel most like a young lady, and weigh 137 lbs. so guess I am large enough already" (October 12, 1874). On November 1 her mother—with a new baby, a family of seven girls and one boy—was thirty-seven years old. When Margaret received a letter from a young preacher, she chose not to answer, for "ma does not approve of girls writing to any man" (November 15). At Christmas, at last, she reports a party: "All the boys and girls came and we had a real jolly time of it, playing games singing till midnight" (December 25).

In 1875 the family began to attend church in Black Springs and socialize with others. On February 10, Margaret records meeting George Bowie at a dinner after services through a "Miss Sophia," who "remarked there would be a wedding soon as most couples she introduced got married sooner or later. No telling her profesy [*sic*] may come true." Bowie, who had replaced the local teacher, was to board at Margaret's home. They became engaged. With this Margaret's tone and concerns shift. New problems and complications accompany expectations of happiness. She worries about Bowie's health and the social restrictions on their being together (September 3). On her eighteenth birthday George gave her a pair of kid gloves: "He is so kind and thoughtful, and is looking as well now as usual. We spend many an evening playing checkers. He reading to me or we try singing for a change" (October 12). This courting couple lacked both the peer and mixed society that Mollie Dorsey and Mattie Farnsworth drew upon. The wedding was set for November 18. Bowie selected Margaret's white satin dress (October 20). He moved from her house while wedding preparations were under way.

On Thursday, November 18, 1875, Margaret's spirits soared: "Well this is the great day of my life and it is a beautiful one bright and clear, and hope it is emblematic of all through our love." The couple planned to live with Margaret's family until the school term ended, then move to the village of Springs (November 19). A month later Margaret observed: "And I am just as busy as before I married for I do the house work just the same; while we live here and let Annie go to school. Though there is not much change otherwise as there is no place to go" (December 20).

She wanted change. "I would rather be to our selves," she writes (February 6, 1876). In March the newlyweds moved six miles away, boarding at first while waiting for their house to be ready (April 7). She reports "many nice walks after school of an evening" (April 28). By May Margaret had finished six quilts, and they had moved, buying her cousin Jasper's home and twenty-acre farm a mile from her parents. Margaret valued this proximity: "I went down and spent the evening with ma. I get real lonesome some days but I keep busy most of the time" (July 19).

Margaret's transition at age eighteen from dependent daughter to wife consisted of a subtle, undramatic shift in location, yet it carried real significance. On January 23, 1877, her first son arrived, likely making more changes for the nineteen-year-old. Margaret Bowie complained no more to her diary. Her last entry reads: "This is my 20th birthday and here I am married and have a most lovable husband and one of the finest blue eyed baby boys in the land" (October 12, 1877). Her path had ended well.

Growing up in frontier Oregon gave Elizabeth Reed Brent a very different sense of her early life course.[49] Frontier farm loneliness, marriage to the schoolteacher, adolescent schoolgirl silliness, conflicts with stepmothers, the prized status of young women in frontier areas with unbalanced sex ratios, Mattie Farnsworth's "independence" and misalliance: these constituted the stuff of diffuse, sometimes contradictory cultural myths of growing up in the West. Elizabeth's reminiscences, set down in old age, express the powerful mythologies of growing up on the frontier that were bequeathed to the future. "I am inordinately grateful for my pioneer childhood," she writes. "It was a wonderful life for children who were in an atmosphere of loving protection and security. Also, we were required by our very isolation to use imagination and invent many of our own pastimes and games. We became familiar with many of the old children's games, handed down from antiquity. There was plenty to keep us busy and occupied. My own parents were unusually protective. We were never allowed to attend the public dances, but we had our own folkdances and rollicking around games" (128). In creating her memoir, Elizabeth was aware of the nostalgia and romanticism working upon her memory. Not confronting these influences critically, neither did she admit the implicit contrast with modern urban images. In old age she felt sympathy for "that child I was so long ago" (117). Her memories are vivid. Her account drips with sentimental touches. Those of her peers provide balance.

In search of a brighter financial future and "the benefit of high altitude to his health," in 1891 her Iowa-born father, with his wife, two sons and two daughters, and "some misgivings I'm sure," journeyed by train and wagon to Keno, Oregon, where he bought an interest in a general merchandise store (118–119). Elizabeth was born on March 25, 1895. Two years later the family moved to homestead land in Picard, California, "a typical western cowtown" with a branch of the general store. A remote forty miles from the nearest railroad terminal, Picard was surrounded by ranches. Elizabeth was soon joined by two more babies. Despite tales of accident, hazard, and isolation, Elizabeth recalls mostly the happiness of her early life. All was a "joy." Her nostalgia is visibly at work.[50]

Elizabeth's initial transition to school was difficult, in part as a result of normal conflicts of growing up: "Life for any child of six is difficult. He has always felt so inferior, almost at the mercy of adults who are so much bigger and who know so much more. But now he had begun to reason for himself" (146). She also romanticizes her mother's rigid scheduling.

Changes shook her path of growing up: "For some time my parents had been feeling unsettled" (151). Her mother wanted to move to the Butte Valley to secure schooling for her daughters equal to that of their brothers. Another important factor was the reduction of open range land as settlement increased, and with it the reduced profitability of the cattle business. Her father sold his holdings and settled on Chico, California, "as the most promising town in the valley, beautiful and with excellent educational opportunities" (151). At age nine, Elizabeth moved with her family to the fledgling town.

Elizabeth Reed Brent's blend of nostalgia and myth ends our journey through the transitional routes, the first of two principal subpaths of female growing up in the second half of the nineteenth century. We turn now to paths determined by social class. Their impact on the early life course for young women was at least as dramatic as for their brothers. Especially notable is the way details of these principal patterns of growing up overlap: in the mix of tradition and change, old and new, and the intricate ways in which these currents came together in individual and family responses to specific situations. Both the continuity and the increasing penetration of social class bound these lives and the paths they followed to one another and to the future.[51]

Social Class Paths

Paths constituted by social class are the second major course of female growing up in this era.[52] For both young women and young men classdefined paths (upper-, middle-, and working-class) represent more than a culmination of a century's shifts in the ways in which young persons grew up, responded to the changing world around them, and sought a way toward adulthood and maturity. The central reciprocal intersections of class and gender are at once unmistakable and epochal. A critical step in understanding these seminal modern transformations in their historical situation involves grasping the complex relations of class and gender differences and similarities: young women and men fashioned and followed new paths in ways that simultaneously diverged from and resembled one another. These lengthy and uneven but accelerating processes blended new and old, change and tradition. As we see throughout this book, ethnicity, race, age, geographic location, time, and other key factors cut across and influence the impact of gender and class, precluding outcomes that many observers have claimed to discover.

Major signs of the transition to paths with emergent middle-class ideals at their center include smaller families; longer periods of supposedly protected residence at home; closer and more intense socialization by mothers, aided by other personal and institutional influences; greater use of and dependence on formal institutions; extended dependence on family; new concerns and expectations about the cultural, psychological, and physiological characteristics of age—childhood, adolescence, and early adulthood and the fears attendant on each stage—and the presence of peer culture among diversely located young persons. Despite some sharing, women and men differed fundamentally with respect, for example, to specific expectations and locations, preparations for adulthood, relationships to families and institutions, value of work, meaning of dependence and autonomy, and destinations.

On both sides the transformation of growing up involved remaking norms, expectations, and cultural mythologies, including traditions of domesticity, femininity, and respectable and disreputable behavior—notions both newly created and inherited. Sociocultural interactions that tied gender to social class or that followed from their intersections gave the female class-related paths their distinctiveness. They endowed the experience of growing up female with a complex range of evolving norms, expectations, and behavioral codes strikingly different from those affecting men. Scholarly neglect of women's experiences of growing up obstructs our appreciation of this key variation. Overall social transformation reduced the number of paths available to women in this period and into the next century while leaving the paths that did remain more contradictory than before. The legacy bequeathed by these signal developments, still felt today, touched law, policy, institutions, norms, expectations, behavior, and conflicts.

In this and the next section we listen to young persons who occupied various places in the class hierarchy as they express as best they were able their experiences and their efforts to make sense of the great transformations of their time. To us they reveal the simultaneous integration and differentiation that lay at the heart of class and gender relations.

UPPER-CLASS PATHS

Blending aspects of traditional, transitional, and class-related paths, if not always consistently or comfortably, upper-class patterns of growing up emerged and advanced with the increasing accumulation and consolidation of wealth. One extraordinarily consequential element of nineteenth-century capitalist class formation was the adaptation of both new and existing social, cultural, and institutional forms for distinctively unequal, status-confirming use and display.[53] From family estates to private social and cultural institutions, whether educational institutions for the children of the rich, private clubs, or art museums and symphonies, among others, this was an epoch of active formation of the culture of the wealthy. The upper-class experience of growing up was intimately linked with the refashioning of a diverse, less formalized social class path. The impacts for women included a reputation for superficiality and idleness that was not always a fair representation of their lives. The upper-class path in fact accommodated a wide variety of routes through childhood, adolescence, and youth.

Born in Chicago in 1853, Julia Newberry was one of two daughters of the successful Chicago merchant Walter L. Newberry and his wife.[54] Julia kept a diary that focused on her social world, activities, schooling, and illness (she died in 1876 at age twenty-three) from 1869 to 1871, from the ages of fifteen to seventeen. That testimony reveals the hopes and fears of a rich adolescent, spoiled and indulged, who nonetheless tried to achieve self-control and improve herself.

Julia's diary opens with her return to Chicago in June 1869 after travel in Europe. She was happy to be back: "I am home . . . in the old house, where I was born, & where I wish I could always live; it is the dearest place on earth to me, & worth all London Paris & New York put together." Returning home was in another respect "very sad, & strange, but *that* is a subject I can not talk, nor write about either." Here she refers to her father's death at sea six months earlier en route to France to join his family (June 6, 1869). Coming home meant a return to familiar routines, to seeing friends and relatives. Julia exclaims at how much her girlfriends had grown. One "look[ed] like a young lady . . . We inspected each other mutually, & with curious eyes" (June 6). So did the boys.

The rules of society, enforced by upper-class mothers, influenced sociability. Julia's mother and godmother ceased writing over their differences about a young man's suitability as companion for sixteen-year-old Julia (June 13). Although they might disagree, both mothers and daughters were quick to rate young men and others by physical features, wealth, character, or social demeanor. Julia also chafed under her older sister's efforts to guide her in society: "Sister acts as if I were eighteen she is so afraid of my seeing any one. That she will never marry I am morally convinced, fifteen have already sued in vain, & fifteen more would sue with equal success. She is an old granny, & rules this establishment with a rod of iron." Julia looked toward her eighteenth birthday, when greater independence would come with control of her allowance (June 18).

Julia was influenced by middle-class notions of virtue, character, and occupation as well as expectations of wealth and luxury. She piously and jejunely observes: "There is nothing like constant occupation to keep people from feeling blase, the minute I cease doing something I feel disgusted with everything . . . I wonder if the knowledge that we acquire here, will be useful to us in our future state? Certainly reading, writing, drawing, painting & playing on the piano wont do us any good" (July 4). Her occupations were not those of her less advantaged sisters. At the end of July, for example, her family went to Richfield Springs, New York, for the mineral waters and society. The Newberry girls played croquet with the Pierrepont boys. With potential suitors present, Julia's mother was at times "rather nervous." Evidently some young women intrigued to manipulate one another and the men. Julia wrote on September 5, "I'm tired to death of having company"; she found a number of the men "absurd."

Several of her girlfriends planned to attend Vassar College, reflecting a new phase in growing up for their class and gender. Another would go to Farmington. "There will be very few left at home of the girls next Winter," noted Julia on July 3. Before the season ended, she recorded her educational destination: "My going to Miss Haines [a school in New York City] is fully decided" (September 5).[55] She found Miss Haines "*supremely* gracious, & called me 'my dear' all the time.—She sat on the sofa & her eyes twinkled; she must have been very pretty; I made several original remarks that seemed to amuse her immensely . . . I expect I shall like it, & I hope to goodness I wont be sickish" (September 20).

Ready to begin her residence at school, Julia anxiously prepared herself: "*Now* all the girls whom I shall know so well in a month are perfect strangers. There will be nice, pretty, clever girls, & horrid, disagreeable, nasty ones. I never went to a large school before, & I feel the tug of war is coming. I intend to *behave, to like school, & not* to be *home-sick.*" Assessing her scholarly strengths and weaknesses, Julia ascribed some of the latter to "being abroad so much, & traveling all the time. I hav'n't announced the fact, but *privately* I intend to study hard this Winter, & do *something;* that is if I can only have my health. I've made one grand resolution & that is to *hold my tongue!!!!!!* It certainly is a 'little member, & kindleth a great fire.' 'Be somebody, July,' Papa always used to say, & 'be somebody,' I WILL.—I've always been told I had plenty of brains, & every natural advantage; so why shouldn't I be Somebody??? *Laziness* is the bane of my existence" (September 24).

The term's good start socially and academically was short-lived. Julia took ill and had to leave school: "I'm green, & pale, weak as a cat, I have chills, no appetite, & my head heavy as lead. To day I'm up, tomorrow I'll be down, one day better, the next worse." The doctor said that an immediate return to school was impossible: "It is so horrid for I like it so much" (October 20). After three months the doctor advised that Julia be taken to Florida. She thought herself improving slowly, and indeed she was well enough to be seen socially and to engage in correspondence. She kept up her reading with the *Iliad,* Shelley, Keats, Coleridge, Chatterton, *Héloise et Abelard,* "travels in Spain." When strong enough, she painted. But her health did not improve. On the eve of her sixteenth birthday, December 27, 1869, Julia lamented: "This is the last night I shall ever be fifteen; tomorrow I shall be sixteen & when once a person is sixteen, though they are still very young, they can never be called, 'child.'—*Oh Papa, were* YOU but here! I am still sick & miserable, & shall have but a dreary birthday, I'm not even well enough to invite a friend to dinner. I have been sick so long, I almost wonder if I shall ever be well . . . I have grown old the last year. I feel it, though the idea may be exaggerated by my feeling so blue tonight."

The new year found Julia still in Florida but feeling better. She and her sister

appeared in several tableaux, and Julia had a new suitor—the twenty-
three-year-old blueblood Jack Foster. With mixed feelings she left Florida
in late March for New York City and the spring season. From late April
she was in Chicago, where she resumed her active social life insofar as her
health allowed. Julia indulged in her love of music and painting and
reading. The family planned to travel to Europe again. Her life, she wrote,
"would be very pleasant . . . if I only felt well." Enforced leisure, "with
plenty of fainting & hysterics in between," did not please her. She didn't
look forward to being sent east for her health, for her girlfriends were due
in town by the end of the month (June 2). Julia was in demand among the
young men, a number of whom she refused to see.

Spending another birthday in Nice stimulated typically effusive upper-
class adolescent stock-taking:

> I slept until eleven this morning, & when I awoke I could not believe I was
> really seventeen years old. Seventeen rather eventful years take them alto-
> gether. I have been twice to Florida, & three times to Europe. I have been to
> two boarding-schools, & have gained a great many friends in different ways.
> Have been runaway with twice, & had my portrait painted. I have learned
> how to faint, & have inheireted [sic] a fortune. Have been through a long
> illness & had a terrible sorrow! And I might have been married if I had
> choosen.
>
> On the other hand I have never had on a long dress, or been into society as
> a young-lady; Nor in the conventual form, have I been to my first ball.—I
> have never given my photograph to a young man, or any other souvenir
> either, nor have I made my hair uneven by distributing locks, among my
> friends. I have never waved my hankerchief, to a male biped on the other side
> of the street, or appointed a rendezvous on my way to school.—I have never
> sworn eternal friendship to any one, nor written poetry since I was eleven
> years old.
>
> I have never fancied myself in love, even in extreme youth, with either a little
> boy in knickerbockers, or a *man* with side-whiskers.
>
> Nor can I say I have been much in want of attention from the opposite sex.
> I can not remember when I *first* ran away from them, & their gallantries. I
> have a great many nice *friends,* & what I am chiefly proud of, *"old gentle-
> men" friends,* whom I can look up to with respect.
>
> Besides there are number who are particularly fond of me, & whom I par-
> ticularly hate. (December 28, 1870).

Preparing to return home, in October 1870 Julia learned of the great
Chicago fire. She was "perfectly bewildered": "It is too awful to believe,
to [sic] dreadful to think about" (October 13, 1870).

Julia Newberry's ill health continued to plague her. Neither wealth nor connections could prevent her death, in April 1876 in Rome, of "sudden inflammation of the throat."

Adeline Atwater, born around 1887, also from Chicago, was a generation younger than Julia.[56] Her path of growing up was also typical of the upper class. She shared the leisure and luxuries of surplus wealth, material comfort, and a tolerant family. Not burdened by the loss of her father or by chronic and debilitating poor health, Adeline had a very different personality and familial milieu. She describes her life with great flourish and exaggeration in her manuscript memoir, "The Autobiography of an Extravert." Adeline's path was marked more by dramatic behavior and outlandish ideas allowed and indulged if not approved. (During part of her childhood, Adeline's mother took a "rest cure" in a sanatorium.)

Adeline's irreverent self-portrait mocks other autobiographers. Her sensibility is modern: "To me, life means being and becoming, and it's fun to write a book, especially in the first person. Everyone loves to talk about himself, and I am no exception . . . I shall try to be truthful . . . yet I wonder how much . . . I have confused fact for fiction . . . Strange that memory and imagination can become so blended" (8).

In her own recollections Adeline's character was marked by "insatiable curiosity," boldness, and lying from an early age. A terror, she would push other small children into the pond and stuff mushy biscuits into all her baby sister's orifices. Wonderful summers in a rented house, called Ledgemere, in Highland Park, twenty-five miles from Chicago, gave space for play. In terms of cultural motifs, Adeline's influences were more modern psychological notions of personality and post-Victorian female development than romantic nostalgia or Victorian ideals: "No malicious emotions urged me to my acts of cruelty" (12). Her penchant for undressing other children distinguished her "sadistic period" at age four. She was a spoiled child, she admits: "I've always been unafraid of the consequences of my actions . . . I had a dare-devil-spirit—or was I just a brat?" (15). Adeline also enjoyed the challenge of punishment.

In her next stage of development, which she humorously titles "In Which I Grow a Conscience," Adeline specialized in lying, "despite all efforts of progressive educational methods." Her mother, "always ahead of her time," followed Elisabeth Harrison and later John Dewey. "Though my actions were often inexcusable, I was never a misunderstood child with tyrannical parents," she writes (20). "My sociable tendencies which conformed to no standards of society annoyed mother. When she would have welcomed a day of rest I would invite large numbers of children to the house" (24).

Adeline's ingeniousness and energies were sometimes directed more productively. With her brother and their friends, she ran lemonade stands and put on a show to benefit a relief fund for soldiers in the Spanish-American War, "making the vast sum of seven dollars—to us a fortune—oh, the sweet simplicity of childhood." This "ingenious" show included "coon songs" performed in blackface. She danced and sang while her brother accompanied her on the banjo.

Adeline's education began at the Loring School, "a private place of learning for the sweet and refined daughters of the so-called fortunate." In her mother's judgment the discipline was insufficient, so she transferred her daughter to the public school, "where in a large and imposing edifice of red brick, I was one among hundreds. It was here that I became a real insurgent." She chafed under the rule-bound ordering of the mass of students. "I had to wiggle or I would have exploded," she recalls. "The hour after school would find me 'kept in' usually with a lot of boys of also excessive vitality. And the crime might be nothing worse than throwing 'spit balls.'" Outgrowing her impulses to steal or lie, she turned "smug and self-righteous" instead (30). "I hated this whole business of learning. When spring came and the seats didn't get any softer I writhed with the agony of a growing child and gazed out of the window . . . I wanted freedom!" (31). One day Adeline kissed her mother goodbye, but instead of going to school she visited a very old woman who thought the child was on vacation and was flattered by her interest. When her mother learned of this, Adeline was escorted to the school door each day. The child "soon became reconciled, for in my class there was an East Indian boy. He was beautiful." His life seemed to epitomize "all that was romantic." She saw him as a "self-made boy," selling newspapers (32). Even at this early age an "urge to do something" marked Adeline as an upper-class woman discontented with a life of leisure but lacking direction.[57]

At about age eight Adeline advanced to the next stage of childhood, or as she titles it, "My Sense of Values Develops": "When my sense of right or justice was outraged, I would go to extremes—my wrath became the terror of the neighborhood." She found "many causes of one kind or another" to espouse, thus venting her outrage. Among them was facing down her schoolmates who were jeering a girl whose father had been imprisoned (35). She delighted in having her hair cut short and wearing her brother's outgrown suits, in which she could play more easily: "Though I like the freedom of men's clothes, I've never regretted that I was born a woman . . . People would say, 'what an energetic little boy you have, madam!' And mother never contradicted them. Little girls in those days were supposed to sit at home, look pretty and sew" (34). A wider curiosity also marked this age. Adeline began to realize that her brother had more privileges than she did owing to his being older, and that she was "just a pest" to him and his friends. She also learned "how babies were born" (37).[58]

Extensive reading was another part of Adeline's childhood: "By the time I was twelve I had read all of the books children don't read today—Sir Walter Scott's books, Byron, Thackeray and Dickens." She "devoured" Sherlock Holmes, who made her imagination "work over time." Long before today's cavils about the "loss of childhood," Adeline wondered, "Are [these books] too long, or is life speeded up to such an extent that youngsters prefer their literature in more compact form, like a pill. No time today for dreaming and spending days in quiet reflection. Someone's automobile is too ready to take you anywhere."

And then there were boys. Much of Adeline's attention in late childhood and adolescence was reserved for Hunt (Huntington), her brother's friend: "We were love's young dream, and though people called it 'puppy love' it was sweet" (46). She recalls: "Although I was a tom-boy . . . the boys seemed to like me. I evidently had the dear old s.a.! (Sex Appeal)" (47). Kissing "was a serious business then!" After her first kiss—"I mean the one that took effect"—at sixteen from Hunt, he told her that he loved her; they "knew some day" they would marry. "And in our reasoning, it was the kiss and not the companionship of which it was the symbol, that caused us to think ourselves forever plighted." Adeline reflects: "We were old then, older than I feel today, and we had a high purpose. Yet we think OUR children are mere babies at that age" (49).

Next came what she titles the stage of growing up "In Which I Adolesce." She dated it from the moment at age twelve when she first went to a matinee alone with a boy. This was a precocious start. "Still old fashioned in her viewpoint," her mother refused to allow her to go out unchaperoned with a boy for several more years. This part of her path was also marked, she notes without irony, by Sunday school at All Soul's Church: "With all the passionate fervor of youth hero-worship, I loved Jenkin Lloyd Jones," her Sunday school teacher. With Hunt and her brother Charlie, Adeline "sat in a Browning class at his feet"; she also attended his class on the great religions of the world. Jones gave his pupils "the joy of an open mind, responsive and ready for new impressions, new ideas . . . Each Sunday, inspired by his teaching, I ardently longed to accomplish great things. How important is the adolescent period in which to plant the seeds that we hope will later bear fruit. That striving after ideals" (57). At sixteen atheistic Adeline joined the church: "I felt there was noble work to be done" (58).

As she "adolesced," Adeline was, in her words, "Making Character." As she recovered from a heart ailment, lengthy rest had its influence: "The muscle of character is developed. When you're at the age of youthful activity, when dancing, athletics of all sorts, are your joy, and you are obliged to give them up, it does something to your morals—it strengthened mine. That patience and forebearance which had been left out of my original make-up, was that year forced into me" (61). The illness had a more direct effect. Mount Vernon Seminary, in Washington, D.C., with its warmer climate, became, instead of Bryn Mawr College, the next stop on her path away from home. At the end of her teens Adeline spent two years in Washington: "It was a school where one is taught to be a lady. You see the parents were still hopeful! It was one of the those finishing institutions of learning . . . For a boarding school we had a good deal of freedom— nevertheless I felt caged . . . In my studies I was always on the Honor Roll, and my behavior was so perfect that Mrs. Somers selected me to be one of a handful of girls on whom she bestowed, 'The Order of the Lily'" (62). She also was a member of a secret social society at the school for those who felt superior to the others. The humiliating initiation made her miserable (68–69).

Adeline enjoyed the city more than the school. She met President Theodore Roosevelt. She delighted in shopping without chaperones and going to the theater. Yet, she writes, "I was in love—always depressing to others and I wanted to go home. Hunt wrote me a letter a day, sometimes two or three, and they were sweet. Mostly said the same thing, if I remember correctly, but I was never bored" (63). Hunt attended the University of Chicago. Adeline went to proms at Brown and Yale, where Charlie was a student, and senior week at Harvard. Calling this "her college career," she attended—as a "college widow"—eight proms. "Those were the days! Not a worry. Of course, we tried to manufacture them . . . I looked forward toward my future with all the confidence of ignorance" (72).

At age seventeen in 1904, Adeline took a grand tour in Europe after her first year of finishing school. She graduated a year later. "Now," she writes, "my life began in earnest. I was nineteen" (94). Returning to Chicago, she learned French at Berlitz and studied music; she also ran a girls' club at Lincoln Center, a settlement house. Not unusual for recently graduated young women of some wealth, such volunteer service left its impression on them and on social welfare.[59] Also, "after years of faithful devotion, Hunt and I became officially engaged . . . everything looked rosy, no breakers ahead" (96). The end of her path of growing up seemed firmly in sight.

Then, to his parent's dismay, Hunt left the University of Chicago without a degree and took a job as a glove salesman. Marriage was put off until he was established in business. Adeline later wrote: "Perhaps that was where we made our first mistake!" (97). She went with her parents on a journey around the world, a trip that reshaped her path. On the voyage

Adeline met Burton Holmes, who was photographing throughout the East. In two weeks, she writes, he changed "the whole tenor of my life. There seems to be no way of safety in happiness or love . . . I was shocked out of my sureness and the structure of my twenty-one years of building collapsed" (108). A divorced Englishman, Herbert James Ibbotson, next swept her off her feet and stirred a major emotional conflict. Crying across Russia, Adeline wrote to Hunt, ending their engagement.

Before long she met Henry Atwater, who "had everything in his favor"—good looks, family, occupation. They married. But they were opposites in most respects, and the marriage was doomed. Adeline continued her quest. She had the resources. For the upper class, growing up could be different, but also not so different.

MIDDLE-CLASS PATHS

Although the forces stimulating life course change and patterns of action and reaction were felt similarly among women in the upper class and among many who followed transitional paths, it was the daughters of the middle class who most clearly exemplified the normative new class-linked path of growing up. In this they stand at once as symbols of theory—in the form of norms, expectations, and anticipations—and of practice, in the form of behavior in accordance with those strictures and ideals. The experiences of reshaped paths of growing up, as we have seen, are the culmination of the previous century's transformations and the foundation for future paths. The middle-class route spanned a wide range socially as well as geographically.

Born September 12, 1846, near Springfield, Vermont, Etta R. Harlow was the daughter of an inventor and paper manufacturer.[60] She began a diary on her fourteenth birthday in 1860, observing: "As to day is my birthday I thought it would be good time to commence journal. Attended School. Hattie staid with me this noon." Her life was bounded by home and school. Etta had a close female friend. A tone of propriety and ordinariness marks her diary and her life.

By day Etta attended school. In the evening she went to singing school. Her father was often away on business, but mother and daughter stayed safely in this small family's private domestic domain. One Saturday she wrote: "It seems quite natural to be at home all day. I had been at home [on school vacation] so long that I had quite forgotten how to act when school kept. Father is home to night" (September 15, 1860). Etta's work at home tired her. She reports having shopped and bought herself a pair of kid gloves for eighty cents.

The spheres in which Etta moved were divided by age. Beyond the bounds of home and school, she participated in the age-graded voluntary temperance association, the Band of Hope. She attended the "Children's meeting" at her church, as well as mixed-age "Home Educational" meetings, which she found "very dull indeed . . . I got so tired [from the lengthy speeches] that I wished I had staid at home" (October 8). She also took part in a sewing circle.

Attending school, she grasped, had an import apart from its intellectual contribution: "School has been rather small to day. I myself did not feel as though I had ambition to learn much but thought that I [had better] not be absent" (September 24). When a new teacher reopened the school in mid-December, "it seem[ed] quite natural to go to school again. I like the appearance of the new teacher very well" (December 16). Such was Etta Harlow's properly ordinary middle-class life in Vermont in the early 1860s. Appearances were indeed important.

Almost two thousand miles away in Mount Pleasant, Texas, Mariana Thompson was also growing up along a middle-class path.[61] Born in 1845, Etta's contemporary kept a diary of her mid- to late teen years, from July 1861 to September 1864. Mariana announces her middle-class sensibility, age consciousness, and path of growing up in her initial entry: "I am sixteen years old to-day and I have always thought that when I got that old I should be a young lady, and I would keep a journal take care of my own clothes but how different I feel from what I have always expected I do not feel much nearer a young lady than I did three years ago. And as for keeping a journal I think I shall try that" (July 30, 1861). Becoming a proper young woman took time and effort. Mariana resolved to use the journal in her effort to be a better and nobler girl, though she feared she might fill it with careless thoughts. The journal was not filled with much at all. Mariana made rather ordinary entries every month or two. She went to school and church. Religion was important, for she was concerned with behaving sufficiently seriously. She had a number of friends. The Civil War appears in references to camps of soldiers. There was a college in the town, where she attended exhibitions and met young men.

In April 1864 Mariana, now nineteen, attempted to assess her teenage development. She sought in vain to discover progress in herself, that quintessential middle-class marker: "I do not feel much change in myself and feel some times rather discouraged that I do not make more progress have not been at school for a year and done but little studying" (April 3). Idleness was a sin in the middle-class moral canon. In her next entry Mariana laments at length:

> Oh! how long since I have penned any in this book . . . But it is perhaps as well for I do not know that I shall ever want to see or hear of many foolish fancies which frequently crowd my brain but to night I was trying to write

to Bernard and thought seemed to come slowly and with but little to them when I happened to think of my long neglected journal . . . I feel that I have greatly changed since I first recorded in this book but I do not know from that it is much for better Ideas come in a different [word illegible] and I some-times look around me or give utterance to my sentiments for fear that they will suddenly prove false and leave me in the dark but some solid facts are to be placed here. (August 28, 1864)

Mariana was in a muddle. During the summer between these entries she considered going to college. In preparation she began to study Greek, "but it was too much for my health and had to be dropped" (August 28). To benefit her health, she traveled instead.

Mariana confided the names of her friends and men she met to her diary. She evidently desired more male society. Prior to leaving to spend the winter in Pennsylvania, she took part in her Soldiers' Sisters' Aid Society's tableaux and festival. Arranging to depart, Mariana resigned her voluntary society offices. Ending on a very ambiguous note, she wrote: "I will close this for the present great changes over me ere I write in or see this journal again" (September 23). Perhaps Mariana foresaw "progress" or a suitor as her path approached its next destination.[62]

Attending college, as Mariana contemplated, was a goal, and increasingly a reality, for many young women of the late nineteenth century. It often conflicted with "traditional" notions of society, especially those held by fathers, medical men, and some educators. Arguments ranged from the physical and reproductive damage that precociously studious young women would do to themselves and their "race" (thus lowering fertility rates), to the waste that advanced study would prove to be. Regardless, more and more women, primarily middle class, went to college, where they enjoyed novel and formative experiences. By 1900, 85,000 women were enrolled in institutions of higher education (compared to 11,000 in 1870), making up 37 percent of all students enrolled (compared to 21 percent in 1870). College students represented almost 3 percent of all women eighteen to twenty-one (compared with 0.7 percent in 1870).[63]

Among them was Mary Roselle Davis, who attended Vassar College in Poughkeepsie, New York, a new college endowed for the advancement of higher learning for women.[64] Rosie, as she called herself, began her diary, a gift from her mother, with the new year 1876 and kept a journal for the entire year. Rosie's mother lived nearby, and the two saw each other regularly. The student lived and took her meals at the college, and socialized with her friends among the students.

In accord with contemporary thinking, students' time was finely divided and highly disciplined. Rosie "got along very well in my classes," always knew "my lessons tolerably." She went to class, studied, cleaned her room, prayed and attended Bible class, practiced music, did gymnastics—exercise was deemed essential to protect the feminine constitution from physical injury or impairment from excessive study—and visited, leaving her card.[65] In the midst of her routine, reflecting her concern, on January 11 she penned without explanation, "I hope I may be happier." By the next week she seemed to be, attending a concert with other girls: "Oh, it was elegant" (January 17, 1876).

Still, something was troubling Rosie. She appears to have been struggling to gain self-confidence and sense of her own ability and achievement. In this quest she is reminiscent of other young women and more broadly evocative of cultural concerns about female intelligence, accomplishment, and confidence. On January 31 she wrote: "Oh! I will never be a clever girl. My good resolutions are of little effect I'm afraid." On February 4: "Did not get along very well with my lessons. No letters. Went over and staid all the afternoon with Mama. We had a very nice time talking together about some [word illegible]. But oh, I felt so wicked I did not love to talk much." Rosie's concern is repeated irregularly: "This is another unhappy day" (March 15). She assisted a fellow student in writing an essay and read her daily Bible chapter.

Rosie sometimes escaped her doldrums and doubts and managed to apply herself. April found her enjoying croquet. She reports in her diary: "I finished reading 'Great Expectations' this day. I was very much excited over it and was as nervous as could be, the girls laughed at me for being so easily freighted and excited over a fictitious story. I liked the book very much but it did not end exactly as I wanted it to" (April 12). Exoteric, a student society, was "very good indeed tonight," she also reports. But "I have done nothing today. I expected to do a great deal. Oh! Why am I still so unhappy" (April 29). Expectations weighed heavily, resulting in critical self-judgments.

Rosie's problems also stemmed from her relations with at least one young man and concerns about her future. On May 5 she confided that she "had a gay old dream last night about *some one*. I wish it could be realized. I often want to know what will be my future destiny but I fear I will be none the happier for knowing. What was I made and put in this world for any way? I hope I may know sometime." In search of answers to such questions, many turned to phrenology, advisers of one kind or another, or advice literature. Struggling with such difficult issues was part of middle-class adolescence and youth. Rosie was no exception.

In the summer of 1876 Rosie attended the great centennial in Philadelphia. She began to read *Sex in Education* by Dr. Clarke. She occupied herself with cleaning, sewing, and visiting and being visited. Beginning in May and continuing through September, Rosie received letters or wrote to a young man, Clem, who "is improving in more ways than one" and "is wonderfully smart" (May 17). Although she seems pleased whenever she mentions him, she never describes their relationship. In September she wished to see him but had no idea when she might. Fall brought few entries. On the page for November 9, 1876, Rosie writes, inexplicably, "Tues. Aug. 21, 1877 The event that is to decide my future happiness transpired on the 21st of Aug. 1877." Usually if not always, middle-class paths took predictable steps.

Alongside the clichés and stereotypes with which the modern middle-class path of growing up became laden, an experience that strained at its boundaries provides a rich sense of the limits but also the possibilities contained within this path. Margaret Deland's autobiographical account, *Golden Yesterdays,* represents as a literary effort both her own and her future husband's stories of growing up.[66] She was born Margaretta Campbell, near Pittsburgh in 1857, and was raised a Calvinist. Her future husband, born in Boston in 1855, was a New England Yankee and a Unitarian liberal.

Margaret's mother died at her birth; she was raised by her aunt and uncle in a large, generous household. Calling her aunt and uncle Mama and Papa, and her cousin Sister, Margaret felt no lack of family: "It was a family life of such happiness and discipline that when I was sixteen, and Fate began to arrange matters to turn me into a Yankee, I was still incredibly a child" (10). In childish innocence, at sixteen Margaret was thrilled by the "sentimentality" of an older man's interest. Influenced by the novels she read, she was tempted. Her aunt informed her that her father's consent was required. That was that. "It never occurred to me to rebel," she remarks (16). "So endeth childhood" (21).

Margaret's adoptive parents decided to send her to an environment designed and suited for those of her age and class, a private boarding school away from home. She went to Pelham Priory near New Rochelle, New York, "kept by very early Victorian English ladies." Opened in the 1830s, the school catered to "young females of good family connections" (23). The Priory was more finishing school than academic institution. This appealed to Margaret. The school emphasized religion and deportment. It was influential in her impressionable mid-teen years, though not always as intended. One "important memory" focused on "the apparently trivial matter of a school friendship . . . a 'crush' I think it was called, the sort of thing that is a holdover from childhood, a play, yet a sort of religious experience." "Ecstatic" together, Margaret and her beloved Lizzie promised "everlasting devotion to each other" (30).

At seventeen, wanting to see Lizzie in the summer, Margaret grasped the need for money of her own and the independence it might bring. "But, if

I supported myself, wouldn't I have the right to spend my money as I wanted to? The difficulty was to think of any way in which I could support myself" (33–34). Her family refused her permission even to run to Lizzie's sickbed. Youth and age struggled against freedom and authority. Only when her young Aunt Sadie offered to chaperone was Margaret able to go. In the aftermath of this conflict Mama allowed Margaret to accompany her brother Harry to New York, where she could see Lizzie and, though she told no one, Cooper Union. "I had read somewhere that girls studying industrial drawing there, were fitted to earn their living by designing wallpapers, or calicoes, or whatnot" (48). Her family wished her "to 'settle down,' and behave like any other young lady." However the trip to New York "encouraged that new and (as the connection felt) unlovely idea of 'independence.'" Unhappy back at home, she told herself that her relatives "didn't like me any more," and recognized that she did not like "that 'me' very much" either (48).

With the consent and encouragement of a Quaker aunt, Margaret began teaching school. She also visited Lizzie in New York, this time without family opposition. The next summer, having "tasted freedom—and liked it," Margaret joined Lizzie and her sisters in a Vermont boardinghouse (50–51). While her family "waited patiently for me to 'come to my senses'— and indeed, I was gradually growing more sensible," Margaret entered her name at Cooper Union (52). How she would support herself remained a discouraging subject. "But before this point of necessity was reached," she learned of "a competitive examination before the Board of Education, of applicants for the position of assistant teacher of drawing" at the Girls' Normal College (52). Margaret won the post at $800 per annum. She stayed with Lizzie's family in New York City.

The next summer Margaret returned to Vermont with Lizzie and friends. While recovering from the shock of her cousin's death, she met Emily Deland of Boston, sister of her future husband. Having heard incessantly about Margaret, brother Leland (Lorin), who sought an acting career against his family's wish that he attend Harvard, traveled to Grafton, Vermont, the next summer to "see this Miss Campbell for himself" (65). That he did in 1878, when he was twenty-three and Margaret twenty-one. They met at five o'clock on a Saturday in August, and by half-past nine they had fallen in love. Margaret writes: "We knew we were in love, but we didn't say anything about being engaged; we called it 'an understanding.' I think this was because we were conscious that both sets of relations . . . really believed . . . that an engagement as well as a marriage, should be entered into 'soberly, discreetly, and in the fear of God.' Obviously, an engagement based on an acquaintance of two weeks, was neither sober nor discreet" (79). Margaret continued teaching art in New York;

Lorin, working in his father's office, saved. "Like old people" they drew up budgets and lists of items to purchase for housekeeping. Despite Lorin's father's sudden death, the marriage went ahead: "It was a strange, unreal time, those three or four days before the wedding—a time to me, as to most girls, I fancy, of misgivings. I was in love—oh, yes, certainly. But getting married? That was different—it was as final as dying, I thought," Margaret observes (96).

Margaret ended her path of growing up well within middle-class margins. Her experiences had strained the boundaries of norms and expectations for legitimate behavior—in the loss of her parents, early marriage offers, boarding school, her search for independence and income, her romances—but it never broke those bounds. Her slightly risqué actions and her irreverence align with the cultural mythology of the independent "new" woman. Evidencing the course of change, her path confirmed the limits and possibilities of middle-class growing up.

From Margaret Campbell Deland's strains and romps to Ethel Spencer's turn-of-the-century suburban Pittsburgh family memoir seems a great leap.[67] But the distance separating Ethel's and her six siblings' youth from Margaret's was not so great. Both fit within the definition of middle-class paths. If Margaret risked "deviance," the Spencers exhibited typical, almost quintessential qualities of the new upper-middle-class "traditions" as they took root. Ethel's nostalgia-leavened look backward testifies to the achievements of the middle class and its ways of growing up.

With seven children, all surviving, the Spencer family was large. That all were born within a twelve-year span indicates some exercise of family planning, marking their social status and correlative behavior. That they lived within a stone's throw of other close kin, as mandated by the family patriarch, Ethel's maternal grandfather, Judge Acheson, also distinguishes them. Their residing as a nuclear family in a large private house in the upper-middle-class suburb of Shadyside also indicates their typical social status. From commercial origins, Mrs. Spencer's family early left the central city, first for fashionable Allegheny City across the Allegheny River, and when that area began to decline, for Shadyside. The judge settled there in 1877 and created a family cluster by building houses for several of his children. Mr. Spencer's family followed a more direct route to Shadyside.

For those able to afford it, residence separated family life from business life, private life from public life, and growing up—childhood and adolescence—from contaminating influences. Prior to the development of mass transit, native-born Anglo-Saxon professional or high-ranking business families belonging to Shadyside's Presbyterian church constituted the majority of the suburb's population. Ethel's father was an agent for the wealthy, powerful Pittsburgher Henry Clay Frick.

Thoroughly middle class, the family took special care in educating its children and overseeing their growing up. Both private and public schools contributed to social class reproduction. The number of children in the Spencer family prompted a strategy that made use of public institutions. The children started school earlier and remained longer than had been traditional, with secondary schooling a certainty and higher education increasingly common. Their adolescence was characterized by school rather than work, by dependency, social training, and peer group activities.

Preserving family connections was important. Aside from the father's work, most activities of the family pivoted around home, from play to hobbies—Mr. Spencer specialized in family photography—voluntary activities, vacations, holidays, and celebrations. The family always came first. As befit their status, the Spencers' child-rearing emphases combined a normative stress on achievement and right conduct—the children internalized proper notions of conscience and responsibility—with a general level of permissiveness. Neither discipline nor privacy was rigidly enforced. The children shared bedrooms and play spaces. The house provided an environment in which the mother was the central presence and domestic power. She had servants to assist her.[68]

The Spencer children grew up in a society that was, in part, age-segregated. Amberson Avenue "has always been a neighborhood of children," Ethel recalls. "Though relatives were an integral part of life during our childhood, they were not, since they were mostly grown-ups, on quite the same level of importance as the friends of our own age with whom we played every day" (58). Age and gender cut across lines of playmates; peer groups formed and reformed, especially with the numerous McClintock children next door. With their mother giving the children "the freedom of the house" by day, the Spencer household formed the gathering point of the neighborhood. Elsewhere children were confined to the nursery. Their many games divided indoors and outdoors into "casual play and formal games."[69]

"Sometimes," Ethel writes, "the orderly routine of our days was interrupted by illness." All except one brother were "reasonably healthy children . . . We had all the normal diseases of childhood. And because there were seven of us, a disease, once started, often swept through the family knocking us all down like ten pins one after another" (70). Given the ubiquity of disease and the limits of medicine, Ethel considered it lucky that all seven siblings survived childhood without needing surgery. Convalescence could be fun, especially their mother's reading.

She continues: "Play, unfortunately we thought, was too often interrupted by far less important activities. Of these school, of course, was the most time-consuming. The education of their seven children posed a problem for our parents, but unaware of the speed with which their family would grow, they started off their two eldest in aristocratic fashion" (74). Before settling on an affordable strategy, the Spencers joined with neighbors to employ a German governess to teach the oldest girls at home. After two years the girls entered the nearby Alinda School, a prestigious private school.

When they developed discipline problems, the children were shifted to the neighborhood public school, "small and in a sufficiently residential section of the city to supply us with suitable companions," Ethel recalls. "On the whole it was a good school" (76). There the children were taught the fundamentals, and their ambitions were nurtured: "We never received rewards, however, for doing well in school; no bright silver dollars came to us for good reports, as they came to some of our friends. Our parents expected us to reach the top of our classes, and sometimes we did" (77). This was the middle-class faith in achieving to the best of one's ability, not always the reality. Other middle-class children felt greater pressures.

When they reached the end of the public school's eight grades, the children went on to private school.[70] Only one attended a public high school. This was a complicated issue: "We lived in a neighborhood where children went to private, not public, schools. Our parents, I think, felt that free education for seven children was worth a little social sacrifice and that it would not hurt us to be separated from our friends during the early years. When we reached adolescence and social life was beginning, more snobbish motives prevailed and our public schooling came to an end" (79). Age and gender as well as class distinguished the children in adolescent years. The girls attended their private secondary school, going on to their later educational destinations. Of the five sisters, two completed college— Ethel at Radcliffe, Mary at Smith. A third attended Bryn Mawr for two years, and the other two took secretarial courses. Both sons went to college.

Mr. Spencer's efforts to provide for his family by curtailing extravagance worked against further schooling for the girls.[71] "It never occurred to him," writes Ethel, "that it would have been better to educate his daughters so that they could make a living for themselves. Actually in the world he knew there was nothing women could do but take in boarders or teach" (83). Mrs. Spencer, however, "believed wholeheartedly in college education for girls." She had attended college and loved it, and wanted that experience for her daughters (83). Living frugally, borrowing money, and doing the laundry the children sent home helped pay the school bills but harmed their mother's health.

Ethel considered her mother "far ahead of her times." She was emphatically a middle-class mother who sacrificed for all her children. She also

appreciated that not all girls would "finish school, 'come out[
and live happily ever after" (84). Ethel reports that it "took se[
years of doing nothing more interesting than making clothes [
a Sunday School class to make me realize that I wanted a colle[
after all" (84). The youngest daughter made the same dec[
rapidly. Nevertheless, whereas the sons became a minister and a[
ant, the daughters worked as secretaries, teachers, a medical t[
one became an antique dealer after marriage. Their mother c[
change the world (although middle-class mothers have been ac[
attempting to do just that for their children).

The Spencer children went to dancing school, dressing the pa[
meeting their peers of the opposite sex. The girls were given music l[
with varying degrees of success. The boys had less training of this[
Only one child, a daughter, exhibited any artistic ability.

Marking hers as a typical middle-class family, Ethel recognized that[
moved at an even pace in our youth; the weeks, the months, the years v[
an orderly routine, as I suppose they still are in well regulated famil[
School and play that filled six days of the week gave way every seventh d[
to the special routine of Sunday" (92). Here respectability was promote[
Here, too, tradition—sometimes old, sometimes recently invented—wa[
supported. On Sundays the Spencer children were not allowed to play or[
"do anything that was primarily fun" (93). Preparing for and professing[
faith for "joining the church" at about age eleven or twelve carried neither[
meaning nor excitement. That had to do with more than faith alone. It
was one among many mandates that first transformed and then signified
the transformation of paths of growing up along middle-class lines.

WORKING-CLASS PATHS

As with earlier periods, we lack sufficient examples of personal testimonial
sources for the growing numbers of native-born and immigrant working-
class women, poor rural women, African American and other minority
women. They were less likely to create such records in the first place; and,
if created, their records are even less likely to have been preserved. Working-class paths of growing up are thus both less well documented and more
susceptible to stereotyping and distortion than upper- or middle-class experiences. Nonetheless, among women records of lower-class life are slightly
more available than among men. The use of oral history among the elderly
population now brings a much greater range of lives, especially immigrant
lives, into focus. Among the benefits are a clearer understanding of the
influences of ethnicity as well as historical time and location, especially as
they intersected with class and gender. Some of these studies deal with
youth and childhood.[72] Though they usefully supplement our incomplete

-class paths of growing up in the nineteenth century,
the problems.
kno⟩n a limited number of experiences is incomplete at
the⟨ult even to discern the outlines of working-class
⟨ith other class-linked and transitional paths. Also,
⟨which the middle-class path achieved public domi-
focus. The ways in which the various class-related
own or others' (mis)perceptions, which were then
r cultural stereotypes and/or mythologies, are also
ss formation and the transformation of growing up
:enth-century foundations, assessing changes and con-
ed baseline becomes risky.
mited evidence and powerful assumptions, commen-
⟩rical and sometimes socially biased arguments about
⟨ing up and notions of family life "trickling down"
orking-class "imitation" of middle-class mores; about
"selfish," or "ignorant" class failing to plan or sac-
.ers (a characterization especially applied to women);
.ing "mass culture" advancing like a steamroller, caus-
⟩n" of social control or cultural hegemony. None of these
ides a satisfactory explanation, though some carry more
.hers.[73] Pursuit of these issues demands a more flexible and
⟨oach to cultural and structural variation within the working
.fferential actions and responses across the class among young
.d their families. I make only a limited beginning here.
ng-class paths of growing up were transformed during the era,
⟨h the process required much of the next half century and more for
naking. A source of many misconceptions, this transformation some-
.s resembled, sometimes overlapped, middle- and upper-class patterns.
.e transformation stemmed in part from ethnic, economic, and geo-
⟨raphic variables, including lengthier exposure to schooling and longer
periods of residence at home; more frequent interaction and confrontation
with social institutions and legal authority; and increasing potential for
conflict with new norms and expectations governing youthful conduct.
The appearance of informality, indulgence, or absence of intergenerational
sacrifice spurred denigrating comparisons between upper and lower classes.
Fluidity, especially on the margins between classes, was another source of
confusion or strain.

Gender, race, and ethnicity all cut across class and contributed to the
resulting conflicts. For many growing up in the working class, their place
within the family economy and the need to contribute to its upkeep made
for radical differences from the mores of other classes.[74] The age and

class-cultural formations that evolved among the young va
from class to class but also within classes, sometimes acco
nomic resources, but also following ethnic, generational, and
ditions. The contradictions of growing up stand out strikingly
confusing relationships. Gender, as we might expect, proved an
ally powerful force for conflict.

Lizzie Cora Goodenough, like her mother, Lizzie A. Wilson (se
3), also kept a diary.[75] In 1901 she was twenty-seven years old bu
leading an independent adult life. For Lizzie gender, class, depende
family needs intertwined painfully. She worked in her brother's an
in-law's Brattleboro, Vermont, home as a servant in fact if not in
an arrangement that made her very unhappy (April 22, 1901). Wh
expressing deep dissatisfaction with her circumstances, Lizzie rec
unceasing work: washing, ironing, gardening, farm chores, child
Housework was her main occupation, and one she seems to have
formed for several different households. The labor was endless, her co
plaints almost as frequent. She writes of being "cross" and feeling ill w
"sick headaches"—likely job-related symptoms. Work and her respons
to it varied a bit. On August 14 she reports: "Have got along nicely with th
children today." But the next day: "Children have acted like Satan all day.

Lizzie's only respite seemed to be "going to the street," to the centra
shopping area. Sometimes she went along with or met other women.
Sometimes she purchased items for herself or her niece Freda. Lizzie drew
no satisfaction from her routines. Her refrains—"Words wont express my
thought," "Im more than disgusted," "I am cross"—ring loudly and poignantly, telling of a path without end. None of the comforts of growing up
in the middle or upper class were hers; her dependence, exacerbated by her
gender, was of an extreme order.

The metropolises of the late nineteenth century burgeoned with migrants
of all kinds, among them countless young working-class and immigrant
women. In her reminiscences Catharine Brody captures the spirit and
rhythms of growing up along the margins of the relatively stable immigrant working and lower-middle classes in New York City around the turn
of the century.[76] Brody's retrospective view reflects the inextricable play of
gender, class, and ethnicity. Her sensitive vision also shows the risks of
romanticizing and mythologizing one's past:

> One's early years must have been spent in close communion with the metro-
> politan sidewalks . . . And it was among the lower middle class [and working
> class] of the unfashionable West Side, that the sidewalks permeated most fully
> the lives of the children. The streets were the true homes of the small guineas,
> micks and sheenies, the small Italians, Irish and Jews . . . Sweets tasted better
> in the streets; a new dress waited for the verdict of the streets; a beating or a

:he beatings and scoldings audible and visible
's on the streets.

terms" in public on the streets, differences
1 (57).

2 romance of the streets (as do scholars such
iodman), Brody asserts that the experiences
is those of country children: "We could not
or the first violets, but on the day that the
chalked boxes and numbers of 'potsies,' on
; had come" (58).

each day, a second round of play began.
to the street with pennies to spend. Matrons
or gathered on the cluttered pavement. Gender,
egation and integration roughly coexisted. Amid
ses, and a blend of languages, little girls met their
d to the store, sometimes chanting ditties. Older
voices thinly, half song, half wail, in a folksong . . .
pes and their ambitions, their customs and their man-
2ir pronunciations of English" (59). Girls clustered to-
fear of "boys in the aggregate, all boys who were not
oys would chase them just for the fun of chasing them and
2m; the boys stopped them on their way to school, stole their
, dumped their books into wet cellars" (60). Girls looked out
/ for one another.

country children with regular chores, Brody thought (implicitly
questions about the accuracy of her observations), city boys were
free, and almost the only duty that devolved upon the girls was
ing the current baby. Perhaps among the very poor the to-do about
ie Mothers may have been justified, but I do not remember that baby-
iding was a laborious task for us" (60).[77] She thought mothers passed
.long their chores reluctantly, owing to their perfectionism on the one
hand and on the other "a subconscious determination to save their children from the clutches of that drudgery into which they had themselves
fallen" (61). Each new domestic task represented another step in growing
up, a "symbol of maturity, a recognition of growing sense and responsibility" (61).

And there was school: "Most of our time was taken up by school, but
schooldays, despite the songs, are the least fruitful in memories" (62).
Brody claims to have forgotten everything except simple arithmetic, reading, and writing. But she recalls "the glamour of the lady teachers . . . all
fused and molded into one symbolic figure" (62).[78] For girls in particular,

the teachers were important role models. She recalls, too, that "there were all sorts of clans and boundaries in school, not only of religion and nationality, but also based on pull, on the work one's father did, on the presents one could afford to give the teacher for Christmas." Those unable to give nice gifts suffered a "suffocating sense of inferiority" (62). Here class cut across other divisions.

What counted in schools for immigrant children, "beyond all marks and studies, was to be clean and to have a clean head. It was a praiseworthy idea, but engineered with such lack of tact as to bring torture and tears to children penalized for the ignorance of their parents" (63). Brody accepts this necessity, but not the bewildering and fatiguing music and drawing lessons that disconnected their subjects from music and art. Weekend and holiday trips to Coney Island were the capstone of these children's experience of growing up in the city.[79] Unlike peers whose class status and material comforts exceeded theirs, they lived in, learned from, and grew up in the city's streets. This was a special space, one that presented great opportunities and great dangers.[80] Paths and futures were in flux. The various immigrant, ethnic, and working-class paths differed from others, although they shared some characteristics. They also differed among themselves in the many intricate interactions of class, gender, ethnicity, and place.

A final, fuller view of this path gives pride of place to another immigrant daughter, Mary Antin, born in Russia in 1881, migrant to Boston in 1894, and interpreter of American civilization for countless readers.[81] *The Promised Land,* Antin's classic memoir of growing up in the Old World and the New, is a fitting symbol and source of cultural mythology. Antin's moving effort to essay the meaning of America not only for herself and her family but also for countless other immigrants, casts her transit explicitly in terms of her path through childhood, adolescence, and youth.[82]

Mary Antin begins *The Promised Land:* "I was born, I have lived, and I have been made over" (xix). At about age thirty she looked back, recognizing: "My life has been unusual, but by no means unique. And this is the very core of the matter. It is because I understand my history, in its larger outlines, to be typical of many, that I consider it worth recording . . . My age alone, my true age, would be reason enough for my writing. I began life in the Middle Ages . . . and here am I still, your contemporary in the twentieth century" (xxi).

Mary was born and spent her first thirteen years in the Russian Pale in the town of Polotzk. Life in "medieval" Russia and the Jewish ghetto shackled her, the latter in gender restrictions on learning and wealth, the former in other social and economic restrictions as well as spiritual and physical threats on account of her religion. She grew up with fear and a sense of injustice among the legacies of her ethnic origins: "I remember little children in Polotzk with old, old faces and eyes glazed with secrets. I knew how to dodge and cringe and dissemble before I knew the names of the seasons. And I had plenty of time to ponder on these things, because I was so idle. If they had let me go to school, now—But of course they didn't" (26). In local schools places for Jewish boys were limited; for girls there were no free schools at all. Even when parents could afford private tuition, educational opportunities for females remained severely restricted. Women were also excluded from studying the Torah. This was another restraint against which young Mary chafed. The dream on which she was nurtured at her mother's breast was that of God's covenant with his people. Following her own dream, her mother had sought higher education and had become an excellent businesswoman, more adept than her husband.

Mary was born the second of four children. Since her mother worked, a nurse cared for the youngest children. Mary recalls that her younger sister's nurse terrorized them with superstitious tales of the evil eye and other horrors. Their grandmothers spoiled them. Mary's father was "the real disciplinarian," for "it was fear of his displeasure that kept us on the straight and narrow path" (70). Her mother's presence was limited but no less valued by her children.

Until business reverses impoverished them, the children "had everything we needed, and almost everything we wanted" (75). They had a "comfortable sense of being well-off" (75). And they had a mixed group of female playmates. "We were human little girls," writes Mary, "so our amusements mimicked the life about us. We played house, we played soldiers, we played Gentiles, we celebrated weddings and funerals" (105). There were few toys. They danced, sometimes for entire afternoons, making their own music. Mary's best times were spent alone: "Idle child though I was, the day was not long enough sometimes for my idleness" (109).

As the children grew up, their parents gave them an education, the legacy of their ethnicity and class: "For the ideal of a modern education was the priceless ware that my father brought back with him from his travels in distant parts" (75). He hoped that his children might live free and that their education would contribute to that end. As long as possible the two older daughters studied with a rebbe (rabbi) and a secular teacher. Proudly and eagerly Mary learned in Hebrew and in Russian. Change mixed with tradition. Setbacks in business, illness, and other troubles conspired to limit this special opportunity. Her father's hopes "of leading his children beyond the intellectual limits of Polotzk were trampled down by the monster poverty who showed his evil visage just as my sister and I were fairly started on a broader path" (120–121). The family's problems planted the seeds of their emigration to the United States, "the promised land." Because of their parents' illness, their father's search for work, and the family's impoverishment, the children were sent away to stay with relatives over the next few years. Mary's elder sister Fetchke at age twelve took on the burden of child care and housework while their mother tramped the streets peddling with her basket.

With aid from a charitable society, their father journeyed to America in 1891. He wrote about the great prospects there and encouraged the children to prepare themselves for emigration: "Education would be ours for the asking, and economic independence also, as soon as we were prepared. He wanted Fetchke and me to be taught some trade; so my sister was apprenticed to a dressmaker and I to a milliner" (149). Fetchke succeeded at her trade; Mary did not.

With few pangs at leaving, Mary and her family joined their father, who sought without luck to earn the riches he had foreseen as a peddler and street seller in Boston. On their arrival the world of America had seemed so wide and bright: "Our initiation into American ways began with the first step on the new soil. My father found occasion to instruct or correct us even on the way from the Pier" (184–185). Every experience and sight was a lesson. There was a profusion of good things: lights in the streets, music to enjoy. And education was free.

In their first summer in Boston the children became immediately Americanized in clothing, language, even names. From Maryashe, or Mashke for short, the author became Mary. Fetchke became Frieda. The fact that her father was "Mr." Antin helped allay his own sense of loss. Many good people helped. For Mary the world grew larger. The "apex of my civic pride and personal contentment," she writes, came in September, when she entered school. Never would she forget that day whose significance was "a hundred times magnified, on account of the years I had waited, the road I had come, and the conscious ambitions I entertained" (198). Their father took the children to school the first day, seeking for them what he had not achieved for himself.

With the guidance of several fine women teachers, Mary progressed, learning the language and its usage, learning to love it, skipping grades. A teacher arranged publication in a pedagogical journal of one of Mary's first compositions, foreshadowing her career and fueling the flame of her burning ambition: "Nothing so wonderful had ever happened to me before. My whole consciousness was suddenly transformed. I suppose that was the moment when I became a writer" (212–213). Promoted to grammar school, she felt she was "a *student* now, in earnest, not merely a school-girl learning to spell and cipher. I was learning out-of-the-way things, things that had nothing to do with ordinary life—things to *know*" (216). As she was learning, Mary was also growing up, maturing in her sense of herself as well as the world. "So I was forced to revise my own estimate of myself. But the twin of my new-born humility, paradoxical as it may seem, was a sense of dignity I had never known before" (224). Mary gained a country, "my country" of which she was "a citizen."

Her success in school and writing continued. She became a celebrity, a "show pupil." Although she struggled not to be seen as "stuck-up" by her schoolmates, she enjoyed her special status. She also clashed over her lack of religious beliefs with some peers who adhered to stricter ethnic and religious traditions. In part this was an inevitable result of the passage from the first to the second immigrant generation. For teenaged Mary, what was most important was that "I considered myself absolutely, eternally, delightfully emancipated from the yoke of indefensible superstition . . . I was very much in love with my enlightenment, and eager for opportunities to give proof of it" (249). This, too, was part of growing up, regardless (or perhaps because) of the conflicts it brought. Her sister Frieda, by contrast, worked in the hope of acquiring "good things"; she lacked "self-analysis." After two years in the United States she was engaged to be married. For other young people the demands of ethnicity cut more deeply; different paths developed.

Among Mary's discoveries was the public library. It became her home away from home. She read "pretty nearly everything that came to my hand . . . Something must have directed me, for I read a great many of the books that are written for children" as well as "every kind of printed rubbish that came into the house" (257). She still had the time and will to play. With boys as her favorite playmates, she played at theater and hide-and-seek. Mary also had her best girlfriends: "There was one occasion in the week when I was ever willing to put away my book, no matter how entrancing were its pages. That was Saturday night, when Bessie Finklestein called for me; and Bessie and I, with arms entwined, called for Sadie Rabinowitch; and Bessie and Sadie and I, still further entwined, called for Annie Reilly; and Bessie, etc., etc., inextricably wound up, marched up Broadway, and took possession of all we saw, heard, guessed, or desired, from end to end of that main thoroughfare of Chelsea" (260–261).

This freedom of movement, unconstrained, was another sharp contrast with the past: "In Polotzk we had been trained and watched, our days had been regulated, our conduct prescribed. In America, suddenly, we were let loose on the streets" (270). To Mary this freedom stemmed from her father's renunciation of his faith and her mother's uncertainty about her own: "Chaos took the place of system; uncertainty, inconsistency undermined discipline. My parents knew only that they desired us to be like American children; and seeing how their neighbors gave their children boundless liberty, they turned us also loose, never doubting but that the

American way was the best way," and lacking new standards of their own (271). For many this stimulated conflict, but not for Mary's family.

Not all their contemporaries shared their views. Children did not all run freely in the streets. In the immigrant neighborhoods where Mary's family lived, there were numerous clubs and lots of playmates. Mary withdrew from these activities, slipping home to write melancholy poetry. She wondered, "What had come over me? Why was I, the confident, the ambitious, suddenly grown so shy and meek? . . . I did not know why. I only knew that I was lonely and troubled and sore; and I went home to write sad poetry" (274). She gave up her male playmates and the dancing club, and wrote long letters to her former teacher, Miss Dillingham. The teacher comforted her, telling her to bear her sorrows, to soothe her irritations, to live each day. This advice comforted her better than promises that all would be better. As Miss Dillingham recognized, Mary had entered adolescence. This unhappiness, "or something like this, had to be repeated many times, as anybody will know who was present at the slow birth of his manhood. From now on, for some years, of course, I must weep and laugh out of season, stand on tiptoe to pluck the stars in heaven, love and hate immoderately, propound theories of the destiny of man, and not know what is going on in my own heart" (275).

Despite her family's economic problems, Mary's education did not end at her grammar school graduation or the legal working age: "As I understood it, my business was to go to school, to learn everything there was to know, to write poetry, become famous and make the family rich" (291–292). In his ambitions for her, her father was "as bad as" she was. With encouragement and support at home, "it is no wonder if I got along rapidly" (292). Thus, Mary entered the Girls' Latin School alongside her social superiors. There she gained the help of schoolmates who judged her democratically by her scholarship. They invited her home, but except for one close "chum," she "had no time for visiting; schoolwork and reading and family affairs occupied all the daytime, and much of the night time. I did not 'go with' any of the girls, in the school-girl sense of the phrase" (295).

Mary recognized her difference from the other girls: "It seemed to me that I had been pursuing a single adventure since the beginning of the world . . . What that purpose was . . . was an absorbing mystery to me" (297). She was happy, learning Latin, mathematics, history, "the things that suffice a studious girl in the middle teens" (297). There were moments, she admitted, when her home in the slums depressed her. She spent hours walking the streets blindly. The tenants' fear of the landlady also affected her. Here too adolescence reared its head, along with the effects of ethnicity and class.

Mary found various outlets for her intellectual energy. There was the library. Fond of reading boys' books, she writes, "I could put myself in the place of any one of those heroes, and delight in their delights" (322). And there was Hale House Natural History Club, to which she was steered when a girls' club did not interest her. Overall,

> the busy years flew by, when from morning till night I was preoccupied with the process of becoming an American; and no question arose in my mind that my books or my teachers could not fully answer. Then came a time when the ordinary business of my girl's life discharged itself automatically, and I had leisure once more to look over and around things. This period coinciding with my moody adolescence, I rapidly entangled myself in a net of doubts and questions, after the well-known manner of a growing girl. I asked once more, How did I come to be?—and I found that I was no whit wiser than poor Reb' Lebe, whom I had despised for his ignorance. For all my years of America and schooling, I could give no better answer to my clamoring questions than the teacher of my childhood. (332)

Mary neither found satisfaction nor allayed her doubts. Still she quested: "Thinking in aeons and in races, instead of in years and individuals, somehow lightened the burden of intelligence, and filled me anew with a sense of youth and well-being, that I had almost lost in the pit of my stomach" (333). Although it gave no answer, the study of science and natural history showed "something of life that is not revealed to poetizing girls" (333). This learning did not make her "a finished philosopher" (335). It made her more girlish. As she grew and matured, Mary realized how much she had learned outside formal channels: from Frieda's fat baby, a drunken neighbor, the girls on the corner.

Mary Antin's academic and literary success and the connections she developed gained her a scholarship to Radcliffe College, though she did not attend. Mary had met and fallen in love with Amadeus William Grabau, ten years older than her, the son and grandson of Lutheran pastors, at the Hale House natural science club. Educated at MIT and Harvard, he taught at Tufts and Rensselaer Polytechnic Institute. They were married in Boston in 1901. Instead of going to Radcliffe, she settled with him in New York, where he taught at Columbia, and they had a child. She studied at Barnard and Teachers' College. The marriage ended, but her career as a writer and lecturer had been launched. Mary later wrote, acknowledging the grocer whose credit helped make her path possible: "The world belongs to those who can use it to the best advantage . . . From my little room on Dover Street I reached out for the world, and the world came to me" (335). In some ways similar to, in some ways different from other young persons during this epoch, Mary followed her path. Her route was that of the "emancipated immigrant." Hers was a success story. Others' were not. For both winners and losers, the costs could be high.

Social Class Paths for Males

For young men, as for young women, among the critical features of growing up during the second half of the nineteenth century were, on the one hand, the increasing resemblance of transitional paths to new class-defined paths and, on the other hand, the character, meaning, and uses of those class-linked paths. Paths defined by social class represented the culmination of more than a century of changes in the way young persons grew up, responded to opportunities and constraints, and moved toward adulthood. Gender, as we have seen, interacted critically with class, and other key influences such as ethnicity, race, geographic location, age, and time cut across them both. Turning to the narratives of men in this final section, we explore the similarities and differences, according to gender and to social class, in the transformations wrought in large measure by class formation and its consequences.

As with their sisters, for boys growing up the principal signs of the transition to class-related paths ordered by middle-class ideals included longer residence at home, safe from the "dangers" of the outside world; decreasing family size; extended dependence on the family; intense maternal socialization aimed at inculcating "character"; increased use of formal institutions; growth of age-related peer culture; and a shift in expectations about the stages of childhood, adolescence, and youth, including a sense of private versus public "spheres" and of growing up as a period of respite from life's burdens.

The class-defined paths of this era—upper-class, middle-class, and working-class—emerged in part in contrast to transitional routes, and were both consequences and causes of the ongoing remaking of society. They derived from the actions of families and individuals, voluntary and collective, as well as of private and public persons, associations, and institutions all struggling with the epochal transformation of their world. Quantitatively and qualitatively, the increasing but incomplete hegemony of distinctive social class paths truly marked the period, and in turn they were marked by it. Together their legacies are powerful.

Upper-Class Paths

In an era of active formation of the class culture of the wealthy, a distinctive class structure was taking shape.[83] What they were growing toward may have been clearer to upper-class youths, if not how they were to get there. Class and gender intertwined in ways both distinctive and common.

In diaries from age seven through twenty-two, Granville Howland Norcross of Boston detailed his upper-class youth.[84] Born into a wealthy lawyer's family, young Norcross (1854–1937) lived an exemplary life of advantage. He prepared for an elite private education and an elite professional career with the resources his family commanded. His growing up prepared him not only for adult independence but also to follow his father into the law. Granville dutifully reproduced his family's position in the social order. Compared to other paths, the path of the upper class retained certain inconsistencies in its apparent flexibility and indulgence.

Granville's diary opens on February 2, 1861, as his all-male private day school celebrated his seventh birthday with the relatively novel ritual of a birthday party. Cultural consciousness of age and the practice of marking birthdays were spreading.[85] He also celebrated in private with his doting family, who gave him books and a toy pistol. His father in particular encouraged reading by giving him books from the Rollo series to fairy tales and a pictorial geography of the world. His mother helped by listening to him spell. The boy's father also encouraged his interest in collecting natural "curiosities."

Class and material wealth characterized Granville's childhood world, marked by frequent visiting and celebrations and the incessant giving of gifts. They also encouraged a somewhat cavalier approach to school and church attendance. Granville, age seven, records: "Went to school and lost my shoe coming home. Too bad!" (April 5). Among his school peers childish pranks such as writing on one another's backs with chalk were common. Like many youngsters, he was susceptible to illness. When he was well, it was his responsibility to keep his room neat. Granville played juvenile card games, such as Old Maid, and backgammon with his mother. While summering on the shore in Cohassett, Granville played and read. He grew up in a close and caring family environment which included aunts and a grandmother as well as parents and siblings. This was no stereotypically aristocratic household of too busy mother and distant father. The Norcrosses' family life approximated the new middle-class ideal.

As Granville advanced through childhood, home and school were his primary domains. He read widely, from history and natural history to *Bruin the Grand Bear*. The new genre of juvenile literature aimed at a specific age or gender, now pouring off the presses, was well represented on his shelves, from *Turtle Catcher* and *Peon Prince* to *Tom Bright's Boyhood*. In school he did well. He continued to collect natural specimens, his interests deepening with visits to Boston museums. He played ball, chess, dominoes, and rings with his friends. He formed a company of "Garibaldi Guards" among the boys. His class advantages are striking when he notes gold prices and lists Christmas gifts in his diary. In time, he would add accounts of his cash.

When he was ten his social world expanded to include dancing lessons, an early preparation for the mixed-sex peer society to follow. Gender expectations and socialization marked many of his activities and environments. An organizer, Granville formed the "Suffolk Club" among his peers, with himself as president; the club did not last a month. More serious was his new habit of copying out extracts from the Boston press in his diary. Like countless other youngsters, he showed a great interest in fires.

Granville's education now included the new practice of writing letters to his father. He records classroom fracases, imitating the teacher, and having "fun" with a Negro boy, as the school struggled to maintain discipline and order. Schoolwork competed with his many activities. Public speaking and composition held his interest more than his other courses. Reflecting age consciousness and new social rituals, Granville began to record his parents' birthdays and ages and to give them little gifts. Performances aimed at the young sparked an interest in theater; among those he attended he lists "the play of the forty thieves," "Jack and the Beanstock," and "The Enchanted Forest."

Granville graduated from the Phillips School in the fifteen-member class of 1867 and entered the all-male Boston Latin High School, living at home rather than going away to a private boarding school. He did well, especially in speaking and on his examinations. At thirteen he received a cat from an uncle. He continued to collect, to attend dancing school, and to go on theater outings. Although he indulged in scant reflection about himself as a child and an early adolescent, the activities Granville notes were typical of his age as well as his class.

Occupied with *The Last of the Mohicans,* borrowed from the public library, and events such as a visit by Kit Carson and Ute chiefs to his school, with the scholars singing in praise of Indians, Granville found his class standing slipping—to second place: "Received my monthly report for March as it had for a remark, 'He seems to have become second in rank from choice,' father gave me quite a scolding and wrote in answer 'I must regret Granville should give you occasion to make such a remark and trust it will not occur again'" (April 3). The boy continued to focus his attention elsewhere: "Went to the Cretan Fair at the Music Hall. Paid ten cents to see the 'Railroad to the Moon' and it was the greatest cheat I ever came across. Went to the fourth meeting of the Lowell Society in the Vestry. After the refreshments 'the younger members of the society with the festiveness peculiar to youth' played shouting proverbs, stagecoach, characters, animals, and scandal" (April 14).

Granville's standing improved to first among seven in his class. Paths of growing up were not rigid. Of one peer who left school Granville writes, "As he does not intend to go to college, he thinks it would be better for him to go to Comer's Commercial College" (October 1). Only two members of the original class remained. Granville organized a baseball club, with himself as secretary-treasurer. He lists the books he read each month. In 1870 Granville was promoted to the school's first division and given a medal. Despite his first-place rank in the lower division, Granville's new teacher, Mr. Gay, called him "unwilling to do his best. Needs to do it now" (February 1869). This was not news to Granville, who made no comment, reporting instead on wide-ranging activities in and out of school. By July he ranked seventh of eighteen, fourteenth in conduct. Pressure from his teachers did not motivate him. Despite his father's reprimands, the boy's unconcern, perhaps an effect of his social class, persisted.

The next fall Granville still showed no signs of being disturbed by his mediocre rank or his failing grades in ancient and modern languages. He continued to perform well in speaking and composition but failed in arithmetic and had to stay late at school to make up his work. Hinting at his method, and his ability, he writes: "I read 20 lines advance in Virgil, which I had not looked before recitation, with only 3 mistakes!" (December 3). In 1869 he showed more initiative in privately reading sixty-six books than in his schoolwork. His December report card read: "'Fair: ought to do better with his abilities.' my father was very much provoked at the remark but I do not think that a teacher ought to make such a remark on a boy's report," he writes. Father–son conflict was evidently low-key.

At sixteen Granville finished third among the four in his class who planned to attend college. Examinations twice a week prepared them for senior year and admission to Harvard. In September 1870 he returned for his final year of high school. Time for college preparation was running out. His class now numbered twenty-six boys. Granville's report for September read: "'Earnest and steady work is necessary if he wishes to enter college in July.'" Marking his gender, age, and incipient transition from high school to college, Granville received a gold watch from his father for Christmas.

When he was seventeen, Granville's social life blossomed: "Had my hair cut and immense crop of whiskers removed at the Tremont House. In evening went to Miss Helen Sandiford's party at Mrs. Wheelwright's, No. 127 Beacon St. with Florie and Nellie Stevens . . . As I do not waltz I did not enjoy myself very much in dancing. I gave a bouquet to Miss Lothrop and received a rose from Miss Deanne" (February 21, 1871). His activities now regularly included young women.

In June Granville graduated from the Latin School fourth in his class. He wrote ritualistically: "We were all sorry to leave the school; most of the class had been there for six years; Charles Lord and I are the only boys left of the original 'Out of Course 4th' that entered in Sept., 1867" (June 23). The next week, in a three-day period, he took his Harvard entrance examinations in Latin composition, Greek grammar, geography, arithmetic, history, geometry, algebra, Xenophon, Virgil, and Cicero and was admitted for the fall.

Granville's college days began with required 6:45 A.M. prayers. Whatever demands his studies made, he found time for socializing, gymnasium, visiting home, euchre, bowling, other games, and young women. He went to the theater with Nellie Stevens; Hattie Andrews he took to the fair. He does report studying, recitation, and cramming. He scored in the sixties and seventies on his end-of-year examinations, and reports having found them "very hard indeed." They did not affect his social life; indeed, his college path was not cramped by academic demands. Yet despite his relative inattention to his studies, Granville did not fare poorly. His grades improved to seventies and eighties.

In November 1873, his march toward maturity and his progress on his path deemed satisfactory, Granville arranged with his father for an allowance of $450 per year. His upper-class elite institution left room for play and other presumed necessities of his age, including "bread fights" among students. In January 1874 he was initiated into a student society. Blindfolded and dressed as a black pelican, he took his oath of secrecy, enjoying the farce that was performed afterward.

In October 1874 Granville began his senior year at Harvard. Although classes remained of secondary importance to other activities, he had improved his grades to achieve a three-year average between 80 and 85 percent and stood eighteenth in his class. Granville petitioned the faculty to be excused from writing his part in the graduation proceedings. Reaching his majority at twenty-one years in February 1875, he participated in organizing a Phi Alpha Society for the class of 1875, with himself as secretary-treasurer. Such activities, virtually normative preparation for adult life, were expected for a youth of Granville's background. In April he was elected to Phi Beta Kappa. Nearing the end of his undergraduate years and a major transition in his path of growing up, Granville donated $100 each to the Class Fund and the Class Subscription Fund. Only a young man with wealth of his own at his disposal could have contemplated these actions. For his last set of examinations he studied seriously.

On Class Day in June, Granville held a reception in his rooms. He issued about four hundred invitations for "my spread, inviting some 550 persons of whom over 250 present . . . Everything connected with my spread passed off successfully." At five o'clock the class reassembled in old clothes and shabby hats. They marched through Harvard Yard, to the Class Day tree, cheering the buildings. The customary exercises took place, with the singing of the class song. This was followed by dancing and promenading in the Yard.

At commencement Granville received his A.B. degree cum laude. He stood twenty-seventh in his class. After the usual summer vacation he took the next unsurprising step on his path of growing up: in September, he notes, "signed my name as a member" of Harvard Law School. Equally unsurprisingly, his socializing continued. In October he adds, "I am to read in the office of Healy & Norcross, 9 Pemberton Square when not in Cambridge." Fittingly, that concludes Granville Norcross's account of growing up upper class.

Middle-Class Paths

Along with the advantages of wealth and privilege, Granville Norcross's upbringing illustrates the new modes of growing up that influenced the paths of children and adolescents from a variety of social origins and locations. Especially in contrast with earlier patterns, these changes typically are associated with the formation of the modern middle class. Despite the clichés and caricatures that designation carries, it still contains a core of historical truth. In its own development in response to the transforming world around it, and to an important degree regardless of geographic location, the middle class led in the restructuring and refashioning of growing up along the lines we now uncritically term modern.

In the preceding chapters, and in aspects of transitional and upper-class paths in this period, the articulation and extension of new social class paths becomes increasingly visible. In first-person accounts we are able to examine experiences of middle-class growing up directly. In particular, attention centers on key relationships such as location; ties with family, school, and other institutions; work and preparation for it; voluntary associations; leaving home and other transitions; forms and duration of dependency; and peer connections and culture. By following these themes of middle-class life, we gain new understanding of process, timing, diffusion, conflicts, and their meanings for individuals and families, and all of society, then and later.

In his diary at least Amos Armsby found his life and activities "pleasant."[86] The saccharine language of this academy student, living near Worcester, Massachusetts, highlights the superficiality, the thinness—as Mary Ryan terms it, the puerile quality—of much developing adolescent culture.[87] Exemplifying trends in growing up within the middle class, Amos "resolved to keep a list of all books I read this year." The issue before his debating society, fittingly, "was on the abilities of the sexes. I spoke the ground that woman was inferior to man. It was decided against me. Majority" (January 31, 1853).

His time was taken up with school, debates, reading, sermons, Methodist meetings, lectures, woodwork, and socializing. Amos was clearly a busy boy. He was ambivalent about continuing in school. Religion claimed him more directly. "The [sermon] was very solemn, seemed to have a more realizing sense of my significance," he writes (April 3). Amos's reaction was likely a response to the pressures he faced in his teen years. Looming over him were questions of schooling, leaving home, where to live, what occupation to pursue. Amos confronted these concerns: "Father says I can't stay at home long" (March 5). The diary stops before the next steps on his path to adulthood become clear.

James Ferdinand Fiske, Amos's contemporary in Holliston, Massachusetts, was more forthcoming.[88] James (1841–1901) was a sixteen-year-old student employed at several part-time jobs when he began four years of diary keeping in 1857. He later became town postmaster, a new middleclass occupation. Romantic passions permeate his otherwise typical teens. In January 1857 the youth was in school. He did well on his examinations, sleighed—sometimes taking girls to school—and attended singing school. James attended a variety of lectures, temperance meetings, churches, and concerts. He saw his relatives frequently, and did chores on his father's farm. In summer he assisted the town librarian, a "business" he liked "very well indeed" (July 12). Returning to school in the fall, he planned to study philosophy, history, and rhetoric. James's adolescence seems quite normal in its regular rounds of school, recreation, limited work, and family orientation. His society included both peer and more inclusive groups.

In 1858 James added to his voluntary associations. He joined the debating club, becoming its secretary a year later. With his family he participated in the new Benevolent Society. James contributed to subscriptions for the Congregational and American Missionary Society, whose lectures he attended. With peers he joined the young men's prayer meeting. He frequently went to parties. His singing school gave a successful concert, raising $60. He began to play the piano. James's chores now included farm work for his grandfather as well as his father, and for the sewing circle, meetinghouse, and library. As he entered his late teens, James's activities reflected an increasing maturity. In August 1858 he wrote a new constitution and bylaws for the debating club. In September the seventeen-year-old, still in school, began bookkeeping lessons, preparing for future work.

One of James's distinctive adolescent characteristics was his frankly admitted interest in young women. His diary records his loves and travails. His distinction lies especially in his writing down his feelings (December 2 and 14, 1858; January 1, 1859).[89] In the summer of 1859 James's passions heated. On August 5 he confided to his diary: "I saw Elmira Maser and if she does not suit my idea of good girl in every sensible respect I will give up. Oh, that I were truly intimately acquainted with her." Elmira disappeared. In September he wrote regularly to several other girls, and in mid-October he took afternoon rides and had cider "with the girls." His active social life was so full that the moments without activity stand out, as when he wrote, "It was rather dull after dinner not any thing in particular going on" on November 25, 1859.

By January 1860 James's amorous urges were directed at Sarah Craige. She did not share his feelings (January 21 and 30; February 1). Undeterred in his pursuit of love, James turned to a girl called Stella. On February 15 he declared: "Stella told me to night that she loved me and I told her the same. May we always do so and I think that I shall have some splendid times in the enjoyment of each other's society. Oh! how I love Stella." Two days later: "Carried Stella and other girls to the sing and back. I love Stella more and more and I hope that she does me at least I do not know but that she does. May she never prove false hearted. They [Sarah and Stella] are both good girls and I like them much." For Sarah, James vowed: "I shall do my utmost to see that [she] does go with some one (if any one) who is good and respectable." From suitor to big brother in barely three weeks. Modern adolescence was emerging.

James left little to chance, spending as much time with Stella as he could. He had good times with her at singing school and socials, and taking her home. After a town meeting on March 5, James "had a short and delightful private interview with her in the parler [*sic*] and I think that she truly loves me. I certainly do her."

Their romance quickly heated up to the point at which James grew concerned: "Staid alone with Stella too long or rather [word illegible]. Must not again. We love each other so too hard to separate and the time passes away so insensibly when we are alone that before we can [word illegible] it is very late. Must in future start earlier for home. Wonder what Stellas mother thought of us. She must and I think will excuse for this once erring" (March 12). Mindful of proprieties and his own susceptibilities, if not his projections, James admitted the next day: "Much apologies to Stellas mother for sitting up so late last night. What an influence Stella does exert over me and it for good. It was but a mere accident that formed our so far pleasant acquaintance yet I hope it may prove the era of my life. Oh that I could always have lived in the enjoyment of the companionship of some amiable and loving creature like Stella. It would have saved one many a painful and [word illegible] hour and have smoothed my now extremely rough exterior of heart and manner." The line between description and an adolescent's romantic hyperbole blurred.

All was not well with Stella. On March 20 James was worried: "Stella made some remarks to night which were rather ambiguous. Shall have to find out what she meant." James did not easily tolerate ambiguity in his romantic passions. The next day, in his familiar desires and ideals, he revealed more about contemporary gender relations and their likely conflicts: "There is nothing I like better than to see a young girl independent of style and [word illegible] so much as to not be afraid to wait on company without awaiting 1/2 hour to dress. I admire Stell for a great many qualities within an exterior perhaps not so fair as some others which I have seen but she is good looking enough for any body. What is in a name the exterior the actions the heart &c. are the criterions by which to go on choosing associates."

Shortly thereafter Stella's ambiguity was resolved, but not in James's favor. She evidently wished to withdraw her involvement and diminish the intensity of their passion. Public discretion was one strong motive, a mark of class and gender. Together they

> decided that it was not but for us to be so much together as it has been and will create talk. It has been I think all for the better that we have been together so much as we have as no very serious consequences have arise therefrom and it has been a good opportunity for us to look into each others dispositions characters &c. and given us a chance to become more intimately acquainted. And now as that result has been so partially well acquainted we shall I hope in future [be] the more discreet in our actions and conversation so as to give to the slightest possible opportunity from the censure or remarks of an ever critical community. (March 23)

Given his earlier statements, James's somewhat reflective tone belies deeper feelings. Easily hurt, the insecure adolescent was not satisfied with this resolution. On March 30 he stopped at a party. Struggling with his ensuing emotions, he relates:

> Did not stop long. It was an invited party and there were other gentlemen there. Wonder why I did not have an invitation. Shall and do not feel offended in consequence. Came home and retired to my room and shed many bitter tears over imaginary or anticipated events for which I really have as yet no proof. How foolish to do this. I think it has done me good; I feel better about the matter now. Wonder if Stell is going to prove false in her confessions to me. She seemed rather distant I thought to night. Hope she will not. If she ever does I shall think as much of her as ever and try not to show by any of [my] actions that I am offended; its no use and will bring unhappiness. I shall take the liberty as heretofore to consider always myself as a friend of the family.

A bundle of fears and hopes, James struggled to behave respectably and correctly but in his ardor perhaps frightened young women away. He worried repeatedly about Stella's proving false. The more he worried, the more deeply he unsettled himself. James desired more from late adolescent relationships than he was able to solicit, not unlike some of the young women we met earlier. Doubting both himself and his female friend, seeing himself in a "cold world," he continued to struggle for self-persuasion and balance: "Perhaps all my unhappiness is owing to my imagination. I really hope it is. Will Stell tell me a falsehood. I know she will not and she assured me again of her affection for me. But is something wanting some pledge unspoken. This is a cold world and it hath [been] said that man is false but if they could know my heart they would not say so" (April 6).

James's doubts were well founded. His emotions masked by an unconvincing declaration of happiness, he rationalized: "Just what I expect would did happen to night and I am so glad of that I don't know what to say. Went home with Stell as usual and she told me or rather asked if [I] thought we had not better separate so far as being [word illegible] and being obliged to go with each other was concerned . . . We agreed to do so and now I feel so much happier than I did before for if we can both go with any one and do things without any fear of offending each other" (April 6). Returning home after eleven, poor James met the further injury of a lecture.

Revealingly and sensitively, James admits that he had problems with young women. The trouble lay within himself, he confessed in a adolescent mix of self-knowledge, confusion, angst, and need: "I don't care for myself. what troubles me more than anything else is that I should be the cause of any such feelings as I suppose to exist. What a world in which to live [word illegible] and learn. O that I would have some friend to whom I could go in true confidence and who would sympathize with me in all my trials &c. It seems to me that there are very few persons of such a nature" (April 25).[90]

The diary suggests that the nineteen-year-old attempted to bury his feelings, perhaps sublimating them, in work at church and at home. The Sons of Temperance, church services, a magic show, circus, and menagerie, singing, and a visit to Boston kept him busy all summer. In the fall he engaged in various jobs. He makes scant mention of young women.

James Fiske's adolescence was apparently ending as he neared the close of his twentieth year. The diary stops in October 1860, when he was placed on the Literary Committee. James later became town librarian and evidently married Sarah Craige. Adolescence for this middle-class young man was a sometimes difficult, conflict-ridden path.

Almost a generation younger than Fiske, Benjamin Sands followed a more privileged and leisurely middle-class path to the professions.[91] His path reflects differences in location and origin as well as historical time. His path was built on family tradition. The grandson and son of doctors trained at Columbia University College of Physicians and Surgeons, Benjamin, born in 1869, followed in their footsteps after attending Harvard. His path began in suburban Port Chester, New York. He kept a diary for 1882. It begins on March 27: "Today is my birthday and I am thirteen years old. I received three five dollar gold pieces, one from Papa, one from Mama, and one from Pa Sands . . . There has been two dancing bears in the street today."

When not in school, Bennie assisted his father, for example in measuring land, or visited nearby relatives. With family relations living close by his suburban residence, he had many contacts; deaths among kin he took in stride. He took private music lessons, befitting his family's position and their expectations of his reproducing it.

Schooling was important to Bennie and his family, and the boy took his studies seriously. On examination day in physics and arithmetic he confessed to exhaustion. Studying physics at age thirteen was precocious. Yet at his age play was also central. His family encouraged his pleasures as part of middle-class child rearing. They rode the train to New York City to see Barnum's circus one Saturday. Bennie delighted in the enormous elephant Jumbo and other animals new to him (April 15). The next day he went to Sunday school and church. After school he cultivated a little vegetable garden at his grandparents' home. With due respect to gender roles, Bennie went riding with his father and tended hens with his mother in his suburban domain.

During summer vacation Bennie records tending hens and ducks and a garden, taking music lessons, riding, going to parties and concerts. He was briefly ill. He also notes a two-week journey to Block Island, where the family took a room in a house called Rose Cottage. After drinking at a spring, he writes, "we went down to Ocean View Hotel a little way from our house tonight and sat on the veranda and look[ed] in the large windows, to see the people dance. Little girls can dance splendidly. They dance every night" (July 22).

Back home, with his sisters and cousin enacting a typically pampered middle-class childhood, practicing for the future, he "decided to give a kind of concert a little while ago and the audience was to be no one but Papa, Mama, Pa Green, Ma Green, and Jeanie. We further decided to have it tonight. In the day we had a grand rehearsal of all the songs, recitations, and tableaux. To-night we began a little after nine because Papa could not come sooner. We had twenty-six things on the program . . . We collected one dollar and thirteen cents" (August 8).

A final summer excursion took the children to Coney Island. These were the pleasures of middle-class life in a family devoted to the progress and entertainment of children nurtured in innocence, with carefully chosen activities and environments, a good education, and prolonged dependency.

Two of the three Sands children, including one daughter, followed their father and grandfather into medical practice. The other daughter graduated from Vassar. To the extent that they followed family traditions, their path of growing up was solidly middle class. Continuities and changes subtly blended as new ways themselves became traditions.

As normative ideas and expectations evolved in the direction of modern, especially middle-class, paths of growing up, and institutions and social policies shifted accordingly, the range of acceptable, even tolerable behavior was redefined. Between the presumptions surrounding the pampered, supposedly innocent, prolonged dependence of the young (which Bennie Sands enjoyed) and the enlarging sphere of youth peer culture (in which James Fiske functioned), the effects were contradictory and often gave rise to inconsistencies. In part this meant the scope of sanctioned expectations for the young was reduced while the range of future choices supposedly widened. This was a highly contradictory development. The range of behavior considered proper also narrowed. As Viviana Zelizer has noted, these developments resulted in the increase in the "value" of children, and their simultaneous removal from productive life.[92]

That contradiction parallels what Kirstin Drotner has termed the "structural paradox" of childhood: "The young are brought up to adulthood at a remove from the social experiences and activities of their elders. [This creates] a discontinuity between the juveniles' present situation and their future station, a separation of personal learning and social use, of the process and result of socialization."[93] Norton Grubb and Marvin Lazerson's *Broken Promises* suggests many of the policy, institutional, and social consequences of the development Drotner notes. Class, gender, race, ethnicity, age, cultural traditions, institutions, and policies constituted new and different relations in the remaking of growing up along paths determined by social class.

Stephen F. Littlefield's diaries reflect this experience of change.[94] Born in 1868 in Worcester, Massachusetts, as an infant Stephen moved with his family to Rutland, Massachusetts. They returned to Worcester in 1876. Starting his diaries in the late 1880s, Stephen looked back. What he wrote about his teen years is striking. He recollected his encounter with the relatively novel phenomenon of the school truant officer, one element of the new movement to enforce schooling for a specific range of ages, and the consequent redefinition of childhood and adolescence. The same norms and expectations caused his parents to worry, he recalls, when he explored the town one afternoon instead of coming home directly from school. Those memories counter Stephen's "recollections of school days very pleasant to me in recalling the scenes and incidents which I passed through in preparing for the higher studies in the High School." His selective recollections make school a source of fond memories. Theses "fond recollections" include one from 1878, when he was ten or eleven: "Of course we were always up to tricks with new teachers, and I received many 'whippings,' with the rattan."

Contradictions and inconsistencies pervade Stephen's recollections. One event he recalls is his departure from high school, premature by newly forming middle-class standards:

> I did not enter the High School with the intention of remaining any length of time, and even if I did have any intention of completing the course, I would have been prevented from doing so, for before one year was finished, I had trouble with Mr. Roe, who was then principal, and before I would do so as he requested me,—an apology for some nonsensical act—I took my books and left the High School, Easter Monday morning, 1884. My studies were all completed in a very satisfactory manner . . . But I seemed to be a Jonah in actions, for I was always invariably caught.

Stephen left school at sixteen not for reasons of academic failure or family need but for failing to behave in accordance with normative expectations (or, in his view, for being unlucky enough to be caught). Middle-class mores were becoming embodied in institutions and policies that were themselves inseparable from class-linked paths of growing up. Any failure to meet these standards, even relatively minor deviance, if detected and punished could lead to drastic consequences, including more deviance and delinquency. This new order increasingly impinged on the young of other classes, especially on working-class, immigrant, and other minority youth.

At this time the consequences of failing to complete high school were slight. Writing a few years later, Stephen was not troubled by them. He continued to read literature and history. At age twenty in 1888, involved in local politics, he found a career path in newspaper work, a spiritual path in temperance and Catholicism, and a social path in literary, political, and religious associations. He found friends and female companions. In his newspaper career, much of it spent with the Catholic press, he combined these respectable pursuits.

Stephen Littlefield's middle-class path, if incomplete in some ways, reflects the limits on norms and actions, still themselves limited for the moment. The new definitions of deviance had a powerful effect in practice and in cultural symbolism. Helping to define deviance were new stereotypes of adolescents as prone to misbehaving in a variety of ways.[95]

From the self-consciously aesthetic pose of young men such as Henry Blake Fuller,[96] clichés and stereotypes flowed. Some of them contributed to dangerously false notions and expectations, codified into psychological theories by G. Stanley Hall and his successors. Cultural elements from romantic notions typified for many, including Fuller, by German authors such as Schilling and Goethe, as well as the French and English aesthetes, blended with views about growing up that featured notions of crisis, rebellion, alienation, *Sturm und Drang*. Some led to more positive ideals. We in the late twentieth century are heirs to these developments and must appreciate the power, for good and ill, of efforts to define adolescence and growing up more generally in this way. Over the last several decades the young have tried to teach us (as have some psychologists) about the terribly high personal and social costs of these stereotypical expectations.[97]

Henry Blake Fuller (1857–1929), son of a New York–born bank cashier, was born in Chicago. He attended Chicago city schools. His diary of 1876–1879 captures the spirit of a young man who was crafting, at least in part consciously, an aesthetic and homosocial identity for himself. The diary reveals a pompous, precocious youth, but it also raises crucial questions for historians of men and gender, and comparisons with homosocial friendships among women.

Henry records in detail his summer at the seashore, singing in the parlor, and evenings of charades in Platonic or romantic styles. He read Goethe and Schiller in translation. He lists many women among his acquaintances. Henry writes in stylized tones of his quest for a male confidant: "I am meditating an advertisement for a bosom friend, though, so solemnly assured by Goldsmith that friendship is but a name. Please step back Oliver!; I must have my way." He continues: "It may seem incredible that I have paddled so far out into the sea of life without hailing a bosom friend. Such is the melancholy fact. I have never yet found a thoroughly congenial person whom I could make friend and confidante . . . perhaps I am too fastidious."

Henry's qualifications for such a friend begin with the physical. First, the youth must be handsome: "I would pass by twenty beautiful women to look up a handsome man. A man with a fine form, a beautiful head, and a handsome face is a feast for my eyes. Why could I not have lived with Sophocles? Why could I not have caught a glimpse of Byron's glorious head?" He must have similar aesthetic interests: "Again my youth must be of aesthetic tastes. He shall love literature, art & music. Oh, to find a few in this rough and tumble squabble for dollars and cents; who can find in books something better than bullion, and in culture something higher than cash." He must be virtuous: "Third my youth must be moral; I don't ask for religion, but for morality. He will be honest, conscientious. In our days, when the Almighty dollar is the highest goal of man's ambitions, it is a grand, proud thing to be a man of truth and honor." In sum: "Here in general outline are the essentials—physical, mental, moral. The advertisement will appear in the Sunday Tribune; answers to Orestes, box so and so."

Whether the advertisement actually ran in the newspaper we may doubt. Henry soon had a new obsession, architecture, which precluded for some time almost anything else. We see how easily he folded cultural interests into his romantic quest, and into his own identity. His middle-class origins and education, and his evident leisure in traversing the passages and rites of late adolescence and youth, contributed to the shaping of his path. We see, too, how easily he reshaped his images and stereotypes of youth, transforming them into powerful operational mythologies to bring to bear on others, whether for the sake of denouncing them as immoral (that is, by his own standards of morality) or applauding their purity and transcendence of materialism. That Fuller became a novelist rather than an architect is not surprising.

Henry Seidel Canby's classic account of his hometown, *The Age of Confidence: Life in the Nineties,* presents a culmination of the development, diffusion, and elaboration of the middle-class path of growing up by the end of the century.[98] Canby's point of origin and point of view were those of bourgeois society in turn-of-the century Wilmington, Delaware, although his concerns and conclusions transcend any one place. Trusting memory rather than documents—and acknowledging that his method would be frowned on by historians—Canby created a memorable portrait. He recognized the spirit of middle-class child rearing. At the same time, he neglected, as children were supposed to, the manipulations and interventions aimed at moral character formation in early socialization. Underlying the spirit he identified was the "confidence" that parents of the 1890s had in "their civilization." Here was the flowering of the middle-class order, for adults and their offspring. The struggles of the nineteenth century had culminated in this sense of security. The children's confidence was "set in a lower key . . . We lived then in a laissez-faire world of childhood, where authority was always upstairs but did not have to show itself often" (35). There was always something to do, and a place to do it, ranging from play to solitude, but little time for introspection.

"Of study the parents took care," he notes. "It was part of the chores, but there were not many other chores, since servants were cheap and abundant" (36). Nonetheless, life "was no Utopia."

> Every little boy had a big boy who bullied him . . . Every boy, too, had a crush on some girl, the phrase then, of course, was "stuck on her." Usually he just made eyes and never got as far as a kiss, indeed I remember a two-year courtship conducted by glances which ended in the hideous embarrassment of meeting with nothing to say on either side. Some girls were "onery" . . . It was a term not used before parents, and referred, I see now, to the high-spirited and over-sexed, and was applied by us with a derogatory smirk to someone with whom you could take liberties, twitch a garter, and probably go further. (37)

Such girls, Canby adds, almost always ended as model housewives and mothers. In their pre-Freudian innocence, children were not yet inhibited.

And with so much else to do, sex did not become a preoccupation: "We never questioned the moral code of society . . . Nobody rebelled that I can remember, for homes were no longer stern and there was nothing to rebel against except an easy life" (38). In their teens and early twenties the sexes freely associated. They fell in and out of love. Sex was a hard adjustment for young adults; it did not accommodate well to confidence or security.

In school and in Sunday school morality was lightly taught. Everyone knew what was right and wrong, Canby notes. Discipline, especially physical force, was used only infrequently. An easy sense of "Us" and "Them," he says, ruled the children's social relations. Overt conflict between groups erupted in boys' scuffles on the way to and from school, largely "the micks," or Catholics, against "Us." He and his peers missed much, physically, intellectually, and aesthetically, Canby admits. Only in terms of discipline did the school ever attempt to raise the standards of the community. Art and music were foreign; girls played the piano but stopped as soon as they married. As a result, Canby writes: "We emerged . . . narrowly educated, imperfectly developed physically, and intensely local. We had been, I think, very happy as children because we had been let alone in a good environment. As youth, when the life of the community, seen nearer, began to lose complexity and glamour, we had rushed after the nearest new experience" (48). Such were the culminations, and the contradictions, of the dialectical forces which had forged the middle-class path of growing up, a path in full flower by the "confident 1890s." Authority was maintained in a "secret bond of deference," with "a tacit agreement that parental opinion had the right of way." In family life there was more unity but less honesty. There was also less companionship but more affection. "Democracy had after all touched the home only superficially" (68–69).

The breach between the generations was wide and, in a rapidly changing world, widening. In part, that accounted for the respect accorded to tradition: "Tradition dictated an immense respect for the women of our own class. A girl at a ball was still a woman on show, a custodian of honor and the home" (91). At school it was no different: "There were no frills and little nonsense in our school, or any school that I knew, in those days. We heard much of integrity and hard work, very little of school spirit and the 'ideals' of youth,' nothing of self-expression. We went to school to work, our play was done elsewhere" (104). School was for learning facts. The children received little education but got "valuable experience in taking educational punishment" (105). Canby writes: "The school as I knew it, and the university also, was growing intolerable to active youth. With no emotional outlets, our intellects were being cramped into a routine which we were asked to take on faith" (206). Reading was wide but seldom profound or guided: "Our deep reading was in Scott and the other romancers," who provided an escape from commonplace life (193). Only in new courses in science and literature did a sense of humanity intrude. With stifling boredom dominating the classroom, the social life of school and college was easily romanticized into glamour. School reflected community—and its contradictions: "Ethics breathed through every brick of it [the school] except the boys' (and perhaps the girls') latrines . . . Even physics and chemistry were made to demonstrate the perfectibility of the world" (115). In short: "Contradictions lay all about us in a town that drank, cheated, fornicated, tyrannized, and was mean" (118). From such bases the young as they matured either "sunk into the mass" or changed in order to escape the environment. Canby himself escaped into a world without stability and certainty, often confused, without confidence. As he concluded in 1934: "We are paying grudgingly now for whatever harm was done us by this lost American age, but we have taken our profits without gratitude" (260).[99]

Canby's experience represents one broad synthesis of middle-class growing up at century's end. It was limited by its urban setting and a well-developed sociocultural order, as well as by the author's emphases. For balance, and to underscore the diversity within the middle-class path, we turn to the frontier. Edwin B. Hancock's diary of 1872–73 details growing up middle class in the very different social order of Austin, Texas, the state capital but still very much a frontier town.[100] Edwin's diary reveals how widely the principal elements of middle-class paths spread, as well as the limits on that distribution. This was even clearer with respect to girls' growing up.

Edwin Hancock was a sixteen-year old Austin schoolboy when he began his diary in November 1872. His parents' departure for Washington, D.C., and their return in April 1873 defined the period it covers. Edwin was born into a well-established family. His Alabama-born lawyer father migrated to Texas in 1847 to join a brother who was a merchant. Successful at the law, he held a number of offices; from 1871 to 1877 he served in the U.S. House of Representatives. Edwin was an only child who followed his father's path to a career as a scholarly, well-informed lawyer, engaged in social and civic activities. In his one major deviation from the middle-class path of growing up, while his parents were in Washington, Edwin stayed in Austin, living with the family of his closest friend, James Raymond. The boys attended the S. G. Sneed Private School, one of six in the town. (Public education developed slowly in Texas.) The Raymond family was a close substitute for his own, and in other ways—his pastimes, his associations, his frame of mind—Edwin moved along a typical middle-class teenage route.

In the absence of his parents, Edwin's school provided familiarity and security. "After a years [*sic*] absence from my old school," he writes, "everything seems as home like as when I left. The studies are conducted in the same manner; and I think they are conducted in the best way a school can be." He set out to do well, reporting after his first day without his parents: "I tried hard today, to perfect myself in my tasks but failed to learn them all as I reached school so late in the day. Nevertheless I had the satisfaction of feeling that I had done my best" (November 25, 1872). Edwin and his fellow students were pleased when Mr. Sneed announced in December that the philosophy and rhetoric classes were "on"; that news contributed to a noticeable improvement among the students (December 4). Despite his intentions, Edwin admits that it was hard for him to find time to read. He also notes throughout the winter months low levels of school attendance: "Winter bring [*sic*] with him sorrow, as well as pleasure, and to correspond, he has his gloomy, as well as, his bright days" (January 7, 1873).

Debate was a part of the curriculum that Edwin particularly enjoyed, whether listening to others or participating himself. Excitedly he reports his school's challenge to a spelling match with the young ladies of Miss Alice Bacon's school. "I am very much afraid that the '*Austin Normal*' [his school] will be conquored [*sic*], that is, if there are many such spellers as myself among 'The Chosen Sixteen'" (December 4, 1872). He wrote a month later: "I feel as confident that the young ladies of this school will vanquish us as if the battle had been fought and lost" (January 7, 1873).

Boys and girls came together on other common ground. They met socially in school peer groups. In April the boys were invited by Miss Bacon to share in a candy pull at her school. Mr. Sneed dismissed them early to "get ready for the occasion" (April 12). Edwin writes: "We needed no formal introduction to all the girls; but were soon engaged in a game of which I never heard before, called 'Stealing Partners.' All were very much amused by this game. After playing this game awhile, the candy pulling was in order. In this many were anxious to engage; but as the candy was very hot all became very inpatient [*sic*], and began to grab into the hot dishes without care for the heat" (April 15). A dance followed the candy pull. Two weeks later the boys and girls met again at a picnic: "The grounds were thronged with a merry host of young people. I was introduced by Miss Gertrude Bacon to four or five young ladies and soon joined them in a game of Croquette." The event tired the sixteen-year-old enough "to enjoy a good night's rest" (April 25).

The boys had petitioned Mr. Sneed for an outing to Barton's Creek to explore the caves. Edwin thought "the trip would be as improving as it would be interesting." He was not sure that there were caves at that site, "but if there are none it is a beautiful walk to the creek and would afford relaxation to the minds of the pupils. I do not think there are many in our school who are injuring their constitutions studying" (January 21).

Typically, attempts at discipline and control sparked conflicts. On January 30 Edwin reports that Mr. Sneed "has become very strict lately." The adolescent chafed when his sense of justice and desire for consistency were offended: "Today he told me to *remain in* for an offense which I think he has seen me commit numerous times, and yesterday, he told me to stay in simply because I smiled. I do not *know*; but I *think* boys can smile and not laugh boisterously. When Mr. Sneed is lenient atall [*sic*] he is very lenient and when he makes a *resolution* to be strict and to establish a rigid code of laws, he does it to perfection." Not surprisingly, the boys' efforts to persuade Mr. Sneed to take them to Galveston for Mardi Gras failed: "I do not think it would be much valuable time lost either to teacher or pupils; but perhaps the teacher's opinions clash with the opinions of the pupil. If so good by to Mardi Gras and all its pleasures" (February 15) The lesson wasn't hard to learn.

When not in school, Edwin and his friend James hunted, often with little success. That was one reason why he complains about being "sick and tired of hunting" and notes that he passed up some opportunities. They also "took" physical exercise on their outings. Edwin also attended concerts. Like many other young persons, he had a great interest in fires. Notorious trials attracted his interest; Edwin and James received permission to miss school to be present for the arguments of one Supreme Court case. A double hanging of two convicted murderers claimed his attention. Reflecting the times, Edwin also had a sharp interest in locomotives and the building of railroad bridges. Regular train service had just come to Austin. The boy also actively watched the changeable Texas weather. With his cousin Willie and friend James, Edwin played poker. Tiring of that game, they turned to "Twenty One, (I have forgotten the French name for it) which is by far the most interesting of the two)" (January 18). They also played chess. For the boys and the community the opening of the state legislature in January 1873 was a major event. Hotels overflowed; amusements vied for attention.

A tale Edwin tells on himself reflects the nature of his adolescent conflicts: "Yesterday evening, played myself such a trick as has never happened to me before. I left home with a calico shirt on; and when I reached town the first thing I did was to change my shirt. I put on a clean one and when I began to feel for the buttons I remembered that I had left them at home" (10 March). On the eve of his parents' return, with James's help, Edwin cleaned the yard of their house in anticipation of their arrival. He writes: "I am looking forward with great pleasure to the time when Mother and Father will come into Austin. I have spent a pleasant winter out of their company and hope to spend a pleasanter summer with them" (March 8). That was the way it was supposed to be for teenage children on middle-class paths of growing up.

Changes in the direction of new class-linked paths were neither simple nor linear, as the experience of Charles Doak, son of a Philadelphia textile mill owner, shows.[101] Growing up with the material comforts of his class and the expectation of succeeding his father as proprietor of the family firm, Charles graduated from Manual Training High School in 1898. The school was chosen for its relevance to his anticipated adult destination. His path combined new aspects with traditional elements of apprenticeship. For a boy of his family and class position, this was no anachronism.

After high school Charles began a "manufacturing apprenticeship" to prepare for his partnership and his expected directorship. Succession in leadership was a real issue, for Charles's father was sixty-one when his son graduated from high school. In 1899, after a year in the "Wool room" assisting the sorters, he was dispatched to Drexel Institute for a three-year course in mechanics. After graduating in 1902, he returned to the mill; during the next two years he worked in each division. In 1904–5 he acted as mill superintendent. Charles then served as a "roving quality-control engineer" until he assumed the firm's presidency on his father's death in 1916.

An apprenticeship and a long period of partial dependence mark this as a middle-class path. The combination of professional education with shop floor experience, as his father deemed necessary and proper, did not simplify or shorten Charles Doak's route to growing up, although they may have eased if not speeded his transition. Philip Scranton notes: "The earlier format of direct apprenticeship and rudimentary schooling have been superseded here by a more complex preparation for entrepreneurship appropriate to the level of manufacturing development achieved by the turn of the century. Whereas James Doak, Jr., son of a failed handweaver, matured as a factory worker before finding a commercial backer for his entry to the proprietor's world, his own son was carefully prepared for the role of 'practical manufacturer.'"[102] This path also gave fathers the opportunity to observe and evaluate their sons' potential and ability. That was no small benefit, whether we deem it traditional or modern.

Working-Class Paths
The working-class path of growing up was also transformed during this era, although by way of an uneven process that required the next half century and more for its completion. A source of many misconceptions, these transformations overlapped in part but also clashed with those affecting the middle and upper classes. This process included the trend

toward increased exposure to schooling and longer periods of residence at home; more frequent interaction and confrontation with social institutions, policy, and the law; and increasing potential for conflict with new norms and expectations governing youthful conduct and cross-generational interaction. Fluidity, especially along the margins between classes, was another source of strain. Gender, race, and ethnicity contributed to the resulting differentials and conflicts. For many growing up in the working class, the need to contribute to the family economy was the primary difference separating them from the ways of other classes. Young persons' own age and class-cultural formations, as well as their responses to others, varied not only from class to class but also within classes, sometimes according to economic resources but for other reasons as well, including ethnic, generational, peer, and cultural traditions. The contradictions of growing up stand out strikingly among these various relationships.

As with working-class women, for men too there is a lack of sufficient useful examples of first-person sources.[103] In addition, questions of class are not easily disentangled from those of ethnicity. There is also the obdurate issue of the relations between normative middle-class developments and their institutional and policy articulations and contemporary transformations among the working class. The merging of the boundaries of the working class with those of the lower-middle or "underclass" complicates precise location and sound comparisons, since the lack of a distinct baseline interferes with assessing the extent of change and continuity.[104] In addition, there are the further problems of perception and misperception, types and stereotypes, particularly in middle-class and institutional or professional observations and collections of testimonies, telling in their own right, which contaminate many texts. I elect reluctantly to leave for now another missing path. Chapter 5, tracing the tale of transformation into the first decades of the twentieth century, serves appropriately as the conclusion to this lengthy exploration.

CHAPTER FIVE

The Beat of Different Drummers into the Early Twentieth Century

THE PERIOD from the end of the nineteenth century through the first decades of the twentieth embraces the historical culmination of the previous centuries' transformation of growing up.[1] In referring to this as a historical culmination, I claim neither that a long and complicated process was complete nor that all lives had been similarly and simultaneously reshaped. Rather I mean to underscore the appearance and substantial impact of large-scale changes in paths of growing up toward a pattern we associate with modernity. To deem those paths transformed, to call the complicated process transformative, is only to begin to suggest the power, depth, and breadth of the seismic reshaping of the early life course.

To locate this achievement by the first part of the twentieth century clashes with commonly held views that place the blooming of "modern" growing up in the mid-twentieth century—not until the 1950s and 1960s.[2] Reformulating the chronology is central to reconceptualizing the historical development of growing up. My earlier location of the "big change" in growing up and the lengthy process of its arrival contributes to a fuller historical conceptualization of childhood, adolescence, and youth. Thus, G. Stanley Hall's seminal codification of adolescence in 1904 stands out as a crystallization of the remaking of growing up, but not as an announcement of unprecedented or novel occurrences in the history of human development. The years spanned by this chapter played a different if still highly consequential role in the remaking of growing up from the one often assigned to them. The struggles to establish the juvenile court and mothers' pensions, and the resulting compromises and contradictions, are telling signs.[3] They are best located within the continuing sweep of historical time, the clash of conflicting paths, the intertwining of tradition and transformation.

As every schoolgirl and schoolboy knows, this period was marked by resounding developments in immigration; class, ethnic, and racial populations and their relations; the growth of cities; business, industry, and work; economic and social institutions and organizations; norms, expectations, and social theory, with corresponding shifts in law and policy, especially with respect to the young and to women, in particular mothers; and gender roles and families and their relation to state and formal institutions, among numerous others. They have helped to give this period its many labels, from the progressive era to the age of capitalism.

To place growing up within the pantheon of social change risks condemning those whose paths were reshaped to a passive functionalism. One then loses sight of the active responses of the young and their families to shifts in circumstances, opportunities, and constraints, and the *longue durée* of the transformation itself. These seminal developments carried a great deal of meaning for the young, but certainly not the unbounded and unprecedented salience often accorded them. The testimony of personal experiences portrays these consequences and their complications clearly, often poignantly.

Without exaggerating either the novelty or the extent of their impact, we must consider how certain crucial developments affected the paths of growing up. They include the dramatic new levels of attention accorded the young, in part as a result of "new" psychologies and concerns about social order and progress for a nation confronting unprecedented levels of immigration and other forms of growth and transformation. Children and juveniles, at once the hope of tomorrow and the fear of today, symbolize the resurgence of reform. Movements to educate and assist mothers and families, to compel and extend schooling, to promote proper play and peer groups, to restrict work and enhance health all portrayed the young as victims to be "saved." Ambiguities, ambivalences, and contradictions marred goals that at first glance seemed faultless, as the intrusion of the state into family life, the extension of professional influence, the articulation of welfare bureaucracies, and the socialization of reproduction developed and spread. Major debates, still unresolved today, revolved around questions of the responsibilities of private versus public spheres, families versus institutions as proper environments for dependent youngsters, the appropriate roles and powers of government, the removal of children from their families—the rights of parents and of the young themselves.

As children were increasingly defined as worthless economically but priceless in emotional and sentimental terms, regardless of individual families' needs and values, their enforced dependency increased, along with institutional age segregation. Similarities among differently situated children, adolescents, and youth in the length of schooling and residence at home as well as in peer group associations, cultural trappings, and behavior, though often superficial, led to misleading presumptions of homogeneity, and in turn stimulated further anxieties about families and young people. A narrowing of normative expectations closely accompanied the anticipation of "crises" for adolescents among a lengthening roster of problems now deemed inherent to growing up. Adding to the blurring of lines between difference and deviance, not surprisingly, were issues of social class, race, and gender and their sociocultural correlates.

The paths whose gradual rise to hegemony after the second half of the eighteenth century has been recounted here dominate the pattern of growing up in the first decades of the twentieth century. Paths of class and gender, as well as those of race, increasingly incorporated the additional contributions of ethnicity, family relations, geography, age, and time.[4] Having observed the emergence and shaping of these paths over several centuries and numerous lives, we no longer need to search for novelty. We must seek instead concrete historical relationships within specific contexts. The stories told in this chapter embrace the old and the new, the traditional and the novel, the expected and the surprising.

For boys and young men growing up, the facts of social class cut across the powerful forces of ethnicity, family, geography, gender, and age. The interactions among these key factors had an inestimable significance, promoting diversity within common consequences, commonality within differences. Social class also achieved an overriding if not fully independent significance. Ethnicity, as familial or geographic circumstances facilitated or restricted its expression, played a strong part in child rearing and adolescence, sometimes alleviating conflicts, sometimes aggravating them. It intertwined all but inseparably with class. Gender, the second major path, also cut across and took its shape from its relationships with other social factors. So did race, especially for black, Hispanic, and Asian youth. As we shall see in Chapter 6, race contributed more powerfully as an independent element than did class, gender, or ethnicity, despite their considerable influence.

What might ironically be deemed "the triumph" of class, gender, and race in modern America, mixed with expressions of profound ambivalence toward the young—especially toward "other people's children"—marked the period, leaving behind a legacy of deep divisions.[5] Hallmarks of the era include the development of institutions for both "normal" and "deviant" or "dependent" young persons, from high schools to juvenile courts and "homes" of all kinds; new psychologies and social theories; narrower notions of normality and wider constructions of delinquency, including so-called status offenses against age-linked expectations; shifting norms relating to age and to family; the concomitant reconstruction of childhood and adolescence in primarily middle-class terms; the further spread of youth peer culture, conveying a superficial sense of homogeneity and uniformity; seemingly endless efforts to reform the young and the environments presumed to shape them; and changes for individuals and families in the wake of economic transformations and massive migrations.

With increasing dependence came rising levels of segregation by age. In fact, dependency in various forms came increasingly to mark the experience of growing up. Changes in family structure are one example of both the causes and the consequences of a lengthened period of dependency. Schools, along with other institutions aimed specifically at "deviants," took on a new and larger role. These were joined by other organizations embodying their own contradictions and conflicts, from scouts to street gangs. Struggles between generations and other conflicts over authority marked the era, especially for immigrant families. In turn, they set the foundations and defined the complications for our own times. Shifting and conflicting economic and political contests formed one arena in which this complex history was acted out; private and, increasingly, public social services, state legislation, and policy served as another. The perceived, imputed, and sometimes very real crises of youth and family formed a third.

Despite the undoubted "triumph" of modern class, gender, and racial paths of growing up, this culminating age is aptly viewed as transitional. Underscoring the developments, still in process, that continue to mix transformation and tradition, experience and expectation, difference and homogeneity, "drift" and "mastery" (to use David Matza's evocative terms) in the late twentieth century, an approach that emphasizes transition guards against overly abstract reifications of class or gender or race.[6] The testimonies of growing up flatly contradict such simplifications of historical process and experience.

Unlike Chapters 2, 3, and 4, this chapter explores patterns of experience across a smaller canvas.[7] It spans a briefer time frame—approximately one third of a century, from the 1890s into the 1920s—and a narrower range of paths, reflecting the ongoing transformations of growing up and the circumstances that shaped them. Fittingly, I think, the chapter is itself transitional: it takes us from the in-depth exploration of numerous primary sources in Chapters 2, 3, and 4 to the rapid survey of the mid- to late twentieth century in the chapter that concludes this account. As in earlier chapters, however, the problem of "missing paths" persists.[8]

Social Class Paths

Growing up in rural Michigan, near Tecumseh, seventeen-year-old Ray Binns went to school and assisted on the family farm.[9] With fellow teenagers he participated in contemporary youth culture. A conscientious youngster and a good student, he grew up in a rural world now permeated with products, forms, and influences of a fundamentally commercial, urbanized culture. In many ways Ray's "year in the life" evokes images of traditional country living. At the same time, his activities, sensibilities, norms, and expectations were shaped by the transformation in paths of growing up along modern social class lines. We read in his diary for 1910 about a path that was middle class in its typical small-town way.

Ray's peer group of boys and girls in large measure organized his social activity, some of which was organized by gender as well. With three male friends he sledded on an ice-covered pond. His sister Ina went to hear the mission band and attended parties. On January 25 he writes: "I went up to see Wilfred Mills, one of my schoolmates, this evening. We had a very nice time. We studied, played checkers and ate pop-corn." The next morning Ray took his examinations in English and algebra. The study session paid off: he scored 97 in English and 88 in algebra. On January 30 he celebrated his seventeenth birthday, noting that a young woman, Olive Bloomer, "was down this forenoon." Age-grading influenced Ray's religious as well as his school life. He was a regular at Sunday school, where he served as secretary and treasurer. He attended weekly Bible classes and wrote two Bible stories for "The Young People's Weekly."

Ray's rural world was far from rigidly segregated by age or gender. Both his immediate and his extended family shared many activities. Reflecting his era's increasingly intense nuclear family relations, Ray displayed a special happiness whenever he was at home: "I guess I am so glad to get home [from nearby Tecumseh] that I cannot remember what I ought to do" (January 22). This feeling did not detract from his pleasure in being with other kin. Marking his affection for his mother and her place in family life, he sent her cards even when he was only a short distance away, and he celebrated her birthday. Prefiguring later developments, Ray's father often drove him, in buggy or sleigh, to his destinations, including school six miles away.

His adolescent humor and high jinks were typically sophomoric. "'Liv[ing] to[o] high'" at dinner, Ray ate egg "sandwitchs," "hickery-nut" cake, cream and "pre-plant" pie. This led to his fainting and falling out of his chair in school. Like many other boys, Ray had a keen interest in fires. More serious was an exemplary new hobby: "May 5. I have started to collect the birthdays of noted persons. One person for each day of the year." By the next night he had seventy-eight names: "That is pretty good for two nights." By his own plan he began to write "diary letters" to his friends: "You write a little each day as many days as you wish to, there being no special length of time stated" (June 9). Reading a life of Robert Burns inspired him: "It makes one feel like being better; not that Burns was a good man, but I think he tried to do right" (May 10). Reading his *Youth's Companion* brought pleasure, as did learning short poems from a library copy of *Poems Every Child Should Know* (June 14). Ray apparently thought this was something, like a normative convention, he should do.

By mid-spring Ray was counting down the number of days remaining in the term: "Only thirty-nine more days of school. I am anxious for vacation" (April 13). Scoring 99 on an English test, he admitted that "I like English best of all my studies." Verse, however, was not his strength. On April 29 he recorded his ode to an "April day, that broke so gray / You're setting rather gay." At the end of May the class studied argumentation and debated the question that capital punishment should be abolished: "I was leader of the negative, the side that did not win. I had to fight against myself as well as my opponents because I do not believe in capital punishment" (May 26).

During the school year Ray apparently did no regular farm work. In the spring he sowed flower and vegetable seeds in the garden: "That they may grow and do some good and I also grow and do some good in the world is my wish," he piously penned (April 26). Once the school year was out, Ray and Ina helped with house cleaning. Ina took music lessons, to which Ray often drove her. Together they began a "potato business." In addition to family outings and ice cream socials, Ina went to the Maccabee Memorial Exercises, and Ray read "Munsey Magazines." They played croquet with friends. He worked regularly in the fields and garden. The family had "a sane Fourth at home." Fittingly for a middle-class teenager in his eighteenth year, Ray Binns returned to school in September 1910: "I study English, German, Vergil, and Physics. I like English best" (September 11).

After a ten-month hiatus the diary resumes with a new tone. Ray's sensibility now reflects teenage pride, priggishness, even vituperativeness (July 14, 1911), while it evidences an almost stereotypically adolescent unfulfilled romantic bent:

> It's been a melancholy day. This morning the burning northern forests first greeted my awakened senses. The smoky horizon and the cool north-eastern breeze seemed more like a September day than one in July. The smoky white sky, pouring glaringly down, made me think of Van Der Velde's painting "Landscape," which I can never look at without having a home-sick feeling. To-day "I am aweary, aweary" and "the melancholy days have come" have repeated themselves in my ear. To-night as I sat on the porch I saw the low-lying western sky all saffron, the gloomy blue above, a few solemn stars and I heard the northwestern breeze rustle the leaves, sadly, and the cry of some [word illegible]. And I thought of one who was gone and one who remained, one whom I think loved me and one whom I love and I desired friendship and love. (July 12, 1911)

At least his prose style had improved. Ray's diary ends with thoughts of a friend who had died. In the experiences of Ray Binns we find on a family farm in rural Michigan in 1911 the twentieth-century synthesis of class-oriented growing up.

Ray Binns's diary reflects transitional as well as more modern middle-class patterns in part but not solely as a result of his rural location. It was more a balance of key characteristics, rather than any single factor such as location, that determined the path a young person's life would take. These characteristics included family economic base, labor needs, traditions, the proximity of opportunities (for education as well as employment), and personal goals. The varied paths of Everett Ludley in Iowa,[10] Charles McKenzie in small-town Alberta,[11] and Loren Reid in small-town Missouri and Iowa[12] underscore the contribution of class in its interplay with other factors.

Everett Ludley's youth in Iowa embraced country and town. His family had moved to a new farm, he notes in his memoirs, "the year before I was to enter the first grade" (139) and then to the town of Manchester "in time for me to enter the second semester of the sixth grade" (140), remarks that reflect both age-grading and the significance of schooling. We see how industrial and commercial capitalism and the trappings of middle-class status had penetrated the countryside when he writes: "Father had bought Mother a Woodrow washer and a roller-wringer . . . powered by a Stover gasoline engine" (139–140). With the move to town came electricity and a phonograph to replace that middle-class symbol the piano, which only his mother could play.

Everett's memories of events in the 1910s, recalled from the perspective of the late 1980s, cast a veil of idyllic nostalgia over his family and childhood: "Dad and Mother both loved the land, but farming continued to be a challenge," especially given his father's physical handicap and asthma. In 1916 the family decided to rent out the farm, sell their machinery, and move to Manchester. Like countless other youngsters, Everett now faced great changes and the conflicts they entailed. He writes: "It was a frightening experience to transfer from a one-room country school to a graded city system . . . I was miserable that first day at recess time. It was cold and I hovered near the building, afraid to venture out to join in the games. I heard someone refer to me as a 'country kid' . . . Finally a couple of boys came over, asked my name, and invited me to join their group" (140). School, particularly music class, was the scene of humiliating experiences, including the snickering and laughter of one red-haired girl: "I wanted to hate her, but I couldn't because I had a crush on her" (141).

Town life brought new demands on Everett's parents, as well as a pronounced teenage culture: "Trading in the piano was the only way my folks felt that they could afford to yield to the pleadings of their teen-age children: 'Let's get a phonograph. Everyone else has one!' It was a beautiful oak console. Dad did manage to get the dealer to throw in a couple of extra records. Mother selected 'Beautiful Ohio' and 'Wonderful Words of Life.' The teenagers chose dance music by the Ted Lewis Jazz Band. Dad didn't get a choice; he just paid the bills" (141). The ability to pay those bills depended on "progress." As the horseless carriage replaced the horse-drawn and the town grew, his father's draying business shifted to trucking, primarily for residential relocations.

When Everett was fifteen, his parents decided to return to the farm. Turning to tradition in a time of transition, the boy remained in town, boarding with another family. Now a senior in high school, he also worked as a clerk in a grocery store. He had sold religious pictures and bluing papers to neighbors and *Liberty Magazine* to traveling salesmen at the railway station, delivered telegrams, weeded gardens and mowed lawns, tended the public library's furnace, and operated a button-covering ma-chine at the dry goods store, typical juvenile labors. He writes: "My job at Lafferty's [grocery] gave me opportunity to observe the adult world, which I would soon enter, as I followed the routine of opening and closing the store" (145). Retrospectively at least, he genuflected toward a tradi-tional but long-standing goal of growing up, one that was emphatically but not exclusively middle class, which seems to have lost its place outside of rhetorical repetition: "I considered all the changes I had experienced in those early years—growing up on a farm, moving into town, working at an array of jobs. I was grateful now that I had learned to work hard when I was young. Since then it has seemed to come natural" (145).

Despite differences in location, Charles McKenzie's story of growing up is similar. Born in 1897, he moved with his family, following kin west, from Watford, Ontario, to Okotoks, Alberta, at age eight; his brother was six. His father took extra training from the Deering Company to sell and service farm machinery in southern Alberta. Seizing an opportunity offered by corporate amalgamation, he worked for the new International Har-vester Company.

Traveling west by train, the children found "there was so much to see and do that we were never bored . . . At every stop, even the briefest, we jumped out and ran up and down the long line of cars" (14). From Calgary they moved twenty-five miles south to Okotoks, where their mother was more comfortable. "Life in a small town was much more interesting for two small boys than life in the city," Charles writes. "We had many playmates and we roamed all over. One of our favourite places was the mill pond, where we sailed boats and skipped stones and tried to walk logs" (15). Taught on a "competitive basis" by a "crusading old maid and a fine teacher," school was "an interesting experience . . . Usually, I was able to keep at or near the head of the line." Not all the boys could meet the teacher's high standards for her Anti-Cigarette League. Stories Charles read left a deeper impression than school lessons (16).

"The best part of living in the West was Uncle Dick's ranch," he recalls (16). Spending each summer there, Charles was happiest riding horses and exploring, catching gophers (for which he was paid by his uncle), picnicking, and dancing. After the death of his aunt, Charles's family lived on the ranch from the fall of 1910 to the spring of 1912, "a wonderful, although sometimes difficult, experience" (18). When Charles was in grade eight, their "little country school was already using the grade system in 1910" (19). The boys rode the two miles to school on horseback except in the coldest weather, when their father would drive them in a sleigh. They seldom missed a day, though later, in his teens, Charles took time off for plowing and sowing. In addition to seasonal field work, the boys rose early for their ranch and household chores. Their father nourished their intellectual and cultural development by organizing the Tongue Creek Literary Society, which met in members' homes twice each month, a wide range of ages participated.

In 1912 the family moved into a new house in High River. The father now sold automobiles. Fifteen-year-old Charles attended grade ten in the new high school, where he played on the school lacrosse team. Schools in the surrounding towns offered baseball, so Charles switched the next year and became team captain. But "there was more to grade 11 than baseball. It was a critical year for me academically," he writes. Excellent teachers taught "students how to love learning and how to enjoy working hard." Dr. Tory, president of the University of Alberta, gave a talk in town. He "was an excellent speaker and put forth many arguments in favour of a university education, but one argument really struck me. He proved to my satisfaction that every day I went to school would be worth $10 to me in my future life. I'm not sure why this reasoning appealed to me so much. Possibly because we had always been poor, or, maybe, it was only my Scot blood, but that day I resolved that I would go to the university" (21–23). The push and pull of various motives paved his path.

Passing grade eleven with the highest exam scores in the province, Charles received a four-year college scholarship. His parents would not allow the sixteen-year-old to leave home yet, although his mother, who had stopped teaching in order to be at home, clearly wished him to become a schoolteacher. With no grade twelve in High River, after "much discussion" Charles's parents sent the boy to high school in Calgary to prepare for the Normal School. Financial considerations weighed against university study. Boarding near the Central Collegiate Institute, Charles graduated with the highest marks in the class. He recalls: "I'm afraid I was pretty wise . . . Nobody could tell me anything . . . On top of all this smartness, I got religion." Looking back, he realized that he was "very immature" at seventeen (23).

Although he was supposedly too young to attend, the Normal School permitted Charles to enroll, removing that obstacle to his precocious middle-class, education-centered path. For the first time he stumbled in school, finding educational psychology difficult to grasp and "reassembling" what he learned in order to teach it. After a "miserable" four months, he earned a first class teacher's certificate and a job near home for $60 a month. Teaching in "a typical country school," he instructed and prepared work for grades one through nine; his pupils' ages ranged even more widely. The teenaged teacher struggled, quitting one job during what he deemed "the worst year of my life" (19). After two years teaching at several schools, in May 1918 Charles joined the Royal Flying Corps. When the First World War ended before his training was complete, he "actually felt more disappointment than relief" (21). He returned to High River in December 1918 and accepted a nearby school post.

He writes: "Sometime during my wonderful eighteen months teaching in Longview in 1918–19, I decided to go to university and take the medical course. It wasn't a sudden decision. I was alone much of the time and was able to think and consider what I had seen and learned. I also read many books and thought about them. I was still very religious and . . . had thought I might be a missionary" (25). Charles had "been intrigued" by the military doctors: "Prestige impressed me. I think I have always accepted positions which tickled my vanity and which I thought added to my prestige" (25). Enrolling in the six-year course at the University of Alberta medical school in 1920 and living with kin in the city, he set out on the next steps of his middle-class path of growing up. Despite another interruption when poor weather killed the farm crops, leaving no funds for medical school and necessitating his teaching for another year, Charles persevered. With financial assistance from home and summer jobs, he was graduated in 1927. Interning that year, despite his being "so shy" and she "so popular," he courted his future wife (32). Charles stepped more surely along his path, one suspects, than his retrospective testimony admits. His transition, however, led first through tradition: teaching.

Loren Reid, born in 1905, grew up in Gilman City, Missouri, where his parents ran a weekly newspaper and post office, and then in Osceola, Iowa, where they put out a larger newspaper. Small-town origins and family migration also shaped his path, as Loren relates in an account of his first twenty-eight years in a two-volume autobiography published in 1978 and 1981.

The Reids' ties to relatives crossed rural-urban lines, despite the middle-class town orientation of their life and livelihood. Print was more than a vocation at which all family members worked. "Ours was a reading family," Loren notes. "We had a better library at home than was available at school . . . I always read with such intense concentration that I became transported to the scene of the action" (145–146). Growing up in a printing office prepared Loren for rapid advancement in the public schools, despite beginning a year late at age seven.

Despite high dropout rates and hard lessons, he progressed through elementary, grammar, and high school. Teaching was "sharply geared to the textbook . . . Our instruction had a rugged thoroughness about it" (167).[13] If Loren can be believed, teenaged girls presented him with more obstacles than his lessons: "For the most part, girls gave me a bad time. The princesses I worshipped, and fell in love with, and would have served forever and ever, lent their smiles and charms to the bigger boys. The girls would not have been flattered, however, if they knew that what I really enjoyed was to go roller-skating in the evenings" (206). Parties, card games, and sports events dominated social life for the young and the not-so-young.

By the time he went to high school in 1919, Loren was living in Osceola. He stood out from the other students, especially in his speech. Children at the time, he recalls, sometimes "reach[ed] an age of readiness before their parents realize[d] it" (35). Loren learned to drive a car, something his father could not do. His hopes for college fell prey to family finances. Retrospectively he remarks: "I often wonder why Father and Mother did not send me either to Grinnell or to the University of Iowa immediately after graduation." Despite the fact that he had received scholarships to both, "Father skirted the college issue because he was swamped with mortgage payments and needed my help around the office" (57). So Loren trained in the family business as a linotype operator.

Paths of growing up at the time were narrowing but still remained flexible, accommodating a brief delay before college. When his brother replaced him on the paper a year later, Loren went to Grinnell in 1924, where he worked for the local paper. At Grinnell he also met his life's love. With breaks for summer newspaper work in Chicago, he completed college. Remaining in journalism, he subsequently attended graduate school and became a university professor of speech communications. Loren's middle-class path wound forward in its interplay of patterns old and new.

The lives of contemporary young persons growing up in larger cities express revealing similarities and differences. Replete with myths and fables, their stories sometimes mix, and mix up, themes of hope and opportunity, despair, temptation, and threats to the young. Both fears and hopes were based in key characteristics of the urban scene. Nonetheless, countless youngsters grew up with scant regard for clichés and cultural myths. Others struggled, sometimes later in life, to comprehend the meaning of their earlier years in the overall design of their lives. In their accounts, imputations of significance to ethnicity, class, and place typically accompany the tale of growing up.

Wilbur Cohen was born in Milwaukee in 1913 into a family of Polish Jews who had migrated first to England in 1870 and then to Milwaukee in 1892.[14] Wilbur grew up the son of storekeeper parents who had come to Milwaukee as young children. His middle-class, urban, ethnic path led to the Experimental College at the University of Wisconsin, Madison, and then to Washington, D.C., where he served in the federal government for almost four decades.

Looking back in 1984, Cohen admitted that his lens might be distorted: "I am one of those who believe that ancestry, early environment, family and teachers play an extremely important role in the personality, development and attitude of an individual" (82). Cohen internalized mythologies of ethnic success: "In appraising my genetic heritage, I have always assumed that I was indeed fortunate to have selected four grandparents who had the initiative and independence to leave their communities, their families and friends, and be willing to try to forge a new life on their own in the New World" (83).

This family of shopkeepers sacrificed for business success and prosperity. They did not strictly separate home from work:

> Even at that time for us, home and business were physically and economically interrelated, an advantage which my children and my grandchildren did not have. I worked in my parents' stores after school, on weekends and in the summer and accepted hard work, long hours, and a participatory role for mothers and children in the family business as a natural course of events. I learned from my father the importance of understanding the consumer's point of view . . . not merely in economics, but also on such important problems as health and education. (84)

Wilbur's grandmother and mother worked long hours in the stores the family owned. They created the environment in which Wilbur grew up, the roots of his life's work, mixing old and new, class and family, urban and ethnic to yield the benefits of tradition. From his father Wilbur gained his interest in politics and his desire for influence, though he had no wish to run for office.

Living in the center of the city near his father's shops was a key factor in Wilbur's growing up. He knew the streets and alleys "very well" and understood "how hard it was for storekeepers in the 1920s to make a living." But, he writes, "the most important aspect of my life . . . was the

very different ethnic groups who lived in the area in which I went to school
. . . We were proud of being a melting pot with over thirty different ethnic
groups . . . I treasure this as the most important experience I learned as a
boy growing up in Milwaukee" (86).

Constituting an irreplaceable education in itself, this early experience
combined with family support to give Wilbur a head start. He speaks of
the cultural processes of growing up and how they are subsequently remade in memory, ideology, and mythology:

> In growing up . . . I never felt our family was poor, but I never felt that our
> family was affluent. I did not feel that we were middle class or elitist, or that
> we were above or below any other group or individual. In other words, I grew
> up without any kind of class distinction in my mind whatsoever. While
> perhaps part of that derived from the attitude of my own parents, I attribute
> a significant part of this non-discriminatory attitude of the Milwaukee public
> schools which I attended and the melting pot ethos of the many ethnic groups
> that were represented, at least at that time. (86)

Growing up in Milwaukee, Wilbur claimed, significantly shaped him
and his path. His emphasis on formal institutions and organizations,
including those aimed specifically at the young, are typical of the time and
place, and the class, in which he grew up. At the Lapham Park Social
Center he learned to speak extemporaneously and to discuss public issues.
At the public library and museum he learned "to treasure libraries and
museums all over the nation and the world" (89). Like his father before
him, he went to the Milwaukee Boys' Club. Wilbur Cohen's childhood in
the city was shaped selectively by the parts of it he came to know and love,
and by the guidance and supervision of his mother. This was not a poor
child on the city's streets, or the success symbol of the "newsy" or other
working-class entrepreneur.[15] Neither should he be confused with other
boys whose middle-class paths began in the suburbs, distinguished by the
separation of home from the outside world, a portrait of sheltered and
innocent growing up in the mother's domain.[16] Urban ethnic lines contributed to the larger web of social class paths. Despite their differences, those
growing up shared more and more.

In contrast with Wilbur Cohen in Milwaukee, Harry Roskolenko was
born in 1907 "into a self-contained Yiddish ghetto" on the Lower East
Side of Manhattan.[17] He grew up largely following a working-class ethnic
path in a world of immigrants caught between tradition and change,
struggling to rise from poverty, create new traditions, and grapple with the
resulting contradictions. Similarities and differences at once pushed together and pulled apart urban ethnic working-class and middle-class routes
of growing up.

Roskolenko writes: "It was another time and another place, then, on Cherry Street. It was the lowest part of the East Side amid crowded-together, five-story, wash-hung tenements. Everything was immigrant laden, a bazaar of colors and bizarre languages" (11). This child of eastern European Jewish immigrant parents remembered his working-class upbringing sixty years later. Mythology, romanticism, nostalgia, and reality blend almost inseparably in the telling.[18] So did poverty, and the struggles to survive it and rise above it.

Harry stresses the active role of his family and ethnic and religious groups in shaping the environment in which he grew up: "Whether you lived in the front house or the rear house [in a tenement building], it was a home if your parents made it a home. We had a Russian-Jewish home . . . We wore what my father could buy for us. It meant old clothes, bought secondhand, for school and for play, and new clothes, firsthand for Sabbath" (12). A constant shifting between tradition and change, ethnicity and class, characterized the transformation of immigrant paths of growing up.

Harry's father labored as a cloak presser and slaughterhouse worker. "And he was never to know anything good no matter where he worked in New York," his son writes. "For it was the wrong time for a man of half skills who preferred God to the making of money to be in the United States of America. My mother, who was not financially illiterate, was soon calling America, 'America *Gonef*' (America the thief)" (12–13). Legend, and parental fears, had it that it was the children of immigrants who were stolen. Harry's parents' traditions interacted with those of the new land for their six children (of fourteen) who survived infancy. They were American children, "tougher, burlier, hardier, and better fed . . . We had more possibilities, if less of God," than their Russian-born parents (14). The city provided more for the children than the parents had known. Adapting to it was a long and difficult process, one that stimulated conflicts and contradictions. The challenges were different from those that confronted Wilbur Cohen. First, there were intergenerational conflicts: "As children, we were American-grained from the start. But to our parents we were always Jews, never American, though we lived within a perplexing set of physical and spiritual nuances" (18). Factories and living conditions made his Orthodox father a socialist, anarchist, and unionist. His mother, however, believed in "more God, more faith, more charity. These were enough to give her immortality and to make a family grow up on Cherry Street" (2).

Children lived amid death, pain, and ill health. Boys and young men suffered in the turf wars of ethnic gangs. These were as much the badges of social class as of immigrant districts. Poverty was a leveler. Spiritual conflicts caused pain of a different sort: ritualized and sometimes even physical struggle between "the rebbe" and young people growing up in a new environment full of American ways and rituals, from patriotic holidays and election campaigns to local boys' clubs and public schools. Like the strictures of socialism, Judaism, and concerned parents, the boys' clubs "kept the errant among us somewhat straight," Harry recalls. Cherry Street lacked a settlement house, so the children went to Madison House and the Henry Street settlement "for games of play that kept us from mass mayhem on the streets" (31).[19] The Neighborhood Playhouse on Grand Street, another institution, introduced Harry to the theater:

> But it was the Educational Alliance, a massive building on East Broadway, four blocks from my home, that was to have the major portion of our youthful allegiance . . . The Educational Alliance gave us what we could not learn at school, in a setting created for energetic scholarship . . . It was the intellectual heart of the Jewish ghetto. And there I could write my early poetry, have it read, then laughed at by my friends all the way home . . . For the Educational Alliance was an intellectual and moral testing ground for those not about to become antisocial gangsters and killers . . . For the Educational Alliance taught a sullen or a happy boy to be less violently errant, more decently dutiful, and almost properly American—with our East Side local combinations. (31–32, 211)

Working after school for five cents an hour was another path of transformation, perhaps leading to a trade, a way "to make real money." Harry writes: "My mother had a passion about success, American style. It was in the streets, easy to find. All that a boy or a man had to do was to seize the opportunity. It was not garbage, if you worked it over. It was for the sons of immigrants who were willing to apply themselves to stuff the American dream with the dollars of success." In this enterprise his mother was "a suddenly inspired banker," saving $1,500 from her sons' earnings, giving them an allowance—and new values—and later starting a successful business. Harry had the wrong interests (he read the English classics) and the wrong sort of friends to work in an ice cream parlor. For him, poetry rather than dollars became the goal, to his mother's chagrin. He and his comrades were condemned in Yiddish as fools. They went on to become professors, a scientist, an editor (and Soviet spy), a poet, a socialist organizer. Amid such romanticism, as he termed it—a love for poetry and literature in English and Russian, Marxism and Trotskyism—Harry grew up, gradually replacing that spirit with others of the city (33, 34).

Harry recalls the schools—day, night, Sunday, and other schools—"just off the greening buttocks of the Statue of Liberty." He writes: "Schooling in my time, at P.S. 31, was very stern. The teacher, though not a cop, was nevertheless a ruler-wielding teacher . . . I was never right at any time— said my parents, who were immediately told of each incident by a note from the teachers or the principal" (210). Some, like Harry, "learned quickly. There was no easy route to high school and college" (27–28). Some did not learn quickly; some did not learn at all. "If you learned nothing, you had to manage with ancient skills. Garbage collecting went to the classical Italians; becoming a cop or a fireman to the clanning Irish; pants pressing, tailoring, the garment trades, went to the ancient Jews" (210).

As a poet and socialist organizer, Harry found that his path led neither to new norms of mobility nor to dependence on ancient skills. Looking back, he found his youth romantic, an escape from *"growth,"* which of course it was not. It was an important path to maturity: "What I got besides nails, saws, hammers, lessons in dead reckoning, civics, the Torah, Yiddish poets, playwrights, lectures on *Eretz Yisroel*—was myself" (218). That is a great deal. In their difficult balancing act on the tightrope of growing up, Harry and his early twentieth-century peers forged their way along social class and ethnic paths, an increasingly common experience among immigrants and migrants in cities and towns.

The historian Henry May, born in 1915, the son of a lawyer in Berkeley, California, records experiences sometimes similar to, sometimes subtly different, and sometimes massively divergent from those of his middle-class and working-class contemporaries.[20] From age four Henry, the youngest of three children, lived in a single-family home in the developing, naturally beautiful Claremont district. While his father commuted to his San Francisco office, Henry grew up in suburban comfort, residing at home until 1937, when at age twenty-three he traveled east to begin graduate studies at Harvard. Despite his father's financial and emotional problems, the future intellectual historian's path exemplified the modern middle-class model: from maternal-centered family life to schooling, peer culture and socialization anchored in the high school, and personality development.[21]

Manners and culture, the latter "far more than a badge of class" (13), stood atop the hierarchy of family socialization, especially given his parents' and their peers' complaints about "America's vulgarity and lack of culture" (12). Even with his parents' financial worries, which May considers exceptional, they insisted on a middle-class life-style of commuting father, household overseen by the mother, and a brood of protected, increasingly dependent youngsters whose residence at home was prolonged in part by schooling, in part by economic considerations, and in part by up-to-date thinking about proper child development.

Peer society, from classmates to best friend—"better than school and more helpful than home"—gave the growing boy a "third world" (176). More than ever before that world's ties held children closer to school and its ancillary institutions. Deeming himself "odd," Henry relates his maladjustment to school and its social ways, from sports to relations with the opposite sex. From junior high school "what comes back most clearly is certainly not the classrooms, probably not even the schoolyard, but the locker room of the boys' gym . . . I remember acutely the smell . . . the steam . . . wet towels, snapped skillfully at bare behinds . . . boys singing obscene parodies of the latest hits. It is the gym that symbolizes for me the grubby jungle of junior high, the democracy in which I had to learn to survive" (178). By tenth grade "we were all emerging into the more interesting world of late adolescence . . . Our major new interest was girls" (178). For those choosing the college preparatory course, "intellectual skills became important. To be a star student was not as good as to be a star halfback or student body president, but it was something" (179). Despite continuing family problems, he writes, "my four years as an undergraduate at the University of California were a time of happiness and partial liberation. After my nineteenth-century upbringing, I was suddenly introduced to the culture of the twentieth century at a particularly stirring time" (185). In that Henry May was more normatively middle class than he realized: he stood in the vanguard of change, but neither alone nor unprecedented.[22]

Female Paths

Born in 1903, Sarah Flynn Penfield grew up and lived her life on a farm in southeastern Ohio. She joined five generations of her own and her future husband's families.[23] Conditions were sometimes primitive, but social, economic, and cultural changes were transforming women's lives and their paths of growing up. Sarah's horizons were shaped by the values of the rural lower-middle class, a path increasingly influenced by social class and by gender.[24] The ways in which these elements intersected with each other in her early life course reflect the transformations that affected growing up in this culminating modern era.

In seventy-nine years, aside from brief periods of schooling Sarah lived in only two dwellings three miles apart: her father's and her husband's farmhouses. That is unusual. But in other key respects her path of growing up followed emerging patterns. A mythology of rural self-sufficiency and unusually primitive arrangements accompanied family stories well into the twentieth century. Yet Sarah's father took on nonfarm work; he also earned money from royalties for gas wells dug on his land. "Farm and family required constant work, by parents and by children, too, as they came along," she later recalled. "Everybody at our house worked . . . Everybody had to . . . We had no conveniences . . . Years ago if a child went out and made a little money on the side, the parents usually took it" (84). With three girls and only one boy old enough to work—the other sons were still too young to help—no simple gender division of labor would serve. The girls worked both indoors and in the fields, although the boys did not do housework. As Sarah and her sister remembered it, even in their area it was unusual for girls to work outdoors. They also thought "that not only did girls work harder than boys but that, significantly, this carried through into later life, with women working harder than men in most families" (86). During the First World War the girls did the work of absent men.

Despite a grueling regime, Sarah's mother always attended to the family's needs, shaping her daughters directly and indirectly: "My mother was especially education-minded . . . Oh yes, she was interested in education. Of course she was raised in town," Sarah commented. Her mother loved to read, often staying up late to "keep up with things" (87). School was conveniently situated across the road from the house. In a strict gender distinction, none of the six boys attended beyond the one-room schoolhouse, whereas all five daughters went on to high school. Two became teachers, one a salesclerk (and later cook-manager of a bank dining room), and two became nurses. The boys had the opportunity to stay in school, but they "wouldn't take it . . . No, not to amount to anything" (85). Gender, and the opportunities of lower-middle-class status, etched their sometimes contradictory and conflicting patterns.[25]

Sarah's mother was what we consider traditional in wishing her children, especially the girls, to stay near home. Fear of illegitimate pregnancy was one factor in allowing less freedom to daughters than to sons. Sarah thought "that mother watched over us closer than she did the boys . . . because she didn't have the control over the boys she did over the girls . . . They had the silly idea that the boy could do the same thing, be guilty of the same thing as the girl, but it didn't hurt him like it did the girl" (88). So paralleling middle-class practice, her mother kept her children, especially the girls, thought to be in need of protection, at home. She would have had "a perfect family" if she could have kept all her children with her.

Especially for girls, home shaped growing up: "Social life consisted, then, of simple pleasures, all close to home" (90). Growing older, the girls increasingly took part in neighborhood activities. They danced, sometimes all night, at parties that crossed age and generational lines. School and church were social centers where peer groups took on ever-greater roles. Country schools, especially township schools, provided a common focus for social life from ballgames to socials, luncheons, spelling bees, and debates. At some events adults predominated; at others the younger people were most prominent. The church stood next in organizing social life. Revivals and Chautauquas were major events, along with meeting. Communal work crossed age boundaries but also brought the young together while bringing them into the community through labor and festivities. Rural isolation had its pleasures. Like her mother a "booklover," Sarah "retreated" into a world of literature, from English and American classics to Zane Grey and other western novels. School contributed to her taste for reading.

The First World War marked a transition from family and home. After his discharge, the eldest son left to work for the gas company. Then the eldest daughter left to teach nearby, and the next eldest to marry. Fourth in line, Sarah attended high school away from home, living first with a maternal aunt eight miles from home and later with her schoolteacher sister three miles away. Sarah followed her eldest sister's path to college in Athens, Ohio, to train for teaching. Attending three summers and one winter, she received a primary teaching certificate from Ohio University. Returning home to live, she taught for three years in the one-room school. She also bought a small parcel of land, which she sold for "a tidy profit" in a few years. Growing up was changing, but not in any simple, linear fashion.

While teaching, Sarah met a neighbor, Robert Penfield, who had also lived almost all his life on his parents' farm. They married in 1927. One sister married the high school teacher. As the sisters recollected, "plays and programs at the school and Friday night spelling bees were courting fare in the early twentieth century, with only an occasional movie" (109). Their parents went to the movies and went visiting with them, too: "We spent a lot of time going to church; we walked in groups . . . Often we'd maybe meet up with somebody and walk with a certain one or something and to tell the truth, I don't think that we brought too much company home," Sarah recalled (109). Their mother allowed them to attend parties, but the girls didn't want to have them at home. Domesticity could be limiting.

For these young women, time away from mother and home, even walking, was essential not only for meeting men but also for forming their own mature identities. In part this depended on their peer groups; in part it served the purpose of courtship. Marriage was expected; it was the time for leaving home to reside with a husband. Having experience of extended schooling or work prior to marriage did not necessarily have an impact. The girls mainly married local fellows, often schoolmates. With marriage came responsibilities; these marked adulthood. For Sarah, marriage meant continuity as much as change. In her household she became the focal maternal presence her own mother had been. For that, and a half century of hard work, her path of growing up prepared her.

Raised the child of Jewish immigrants in New York City, Kate Simon exemplifies the bonds and the boundaries of gender, social class, and ethnicity. Her memoir displays similarities to and differences from Harry

Roskolenko's, on the one hand, and Sarah Penfield's, on the other.[26] With her mother and baby brother, Kate followed her father from Poland at the age of three and a half. From age six she lived in a tenement in the Bronx and went to P.S. 58, in a neighborhood socially and economically distant from the ghetto of the Lower East Side. With her father accustomed from childhood to luxuries and her mother a shrewd businesswoman and family focal point—often her parents clashed—Kate's was a lower-middle-class path to "modern" childhood, adolescence, school-based peer culture, college, and adulthood. Despite what is exceptional about her memoirs—family idiosyncrasies and her own literary ability—her portraits of childhood and adolescence reflect typical twentieth-century notions and mythologies of growing up.

Lafontaine Street, where she lived, "offered several schools . . . School-school, P.S. 59, was sometimes nice," but not so nice on "cringing days," usually Fridays, with arithmetic drills. The library "made me my own absolutely special and private person with a card that belonged to no one but me, offered hundreds of books, all mine, and no tests on them, a brighter, more generous school than P.S. 59" (*BP,* 44). And the movies, the "brightest, most informative school," offering numerous lessons on living, loving, behaving, "Being Married," often in sharp contrast to the immediate world of experience, including her mother's:

> My mother didn't accept her fate as a forever thing. She began to work during our school hours after her English classes had taught her as much as they could, and while I was still young, certainly no more than ten, I began to get her lecture on being a woman. It ended with extraordinary statements, shocking in view of the street mores. "Study. Learn. Go to college. Be a school teacher," then a respected, privileged breed, "and don't get married until you have a profession. With a profession you can have men friends and even children, if you want. You're free . . ." My mother was already tagged "the Princess" because she never went into the street unless fully, carefully dressed. (*BP,* 48)

"Proud of her difference," Kate understood that her parents occupied separate worlds. Often centering on the children's conduct and their mother's permissiveness, the parents' fighting at times "threatened" Kate. They fought about money. They fought about her mother's relaxed judgments and relations with others, and about her father's relationships with other women.

What is striking is not only the lessons Kate imbibed. Other girls growing up learned them, but largely either by themselves or from peers or older role models, not so unambiguously from their own mothers.[27] This distinguished her path of growing up, perhaps no less than her fears that "we would all be swept away, my brother and I to a jungle where wild animals would eat us . . . School now offered the comforts of a church, the street its comforting familiarities, unchanging, predictable. We stayed out as long as we could . . . we read a lot, we went to bed early, anything to remove us from our private-faced parents, who made us feel unbearably shy" (*BP*, 53).

Outdoors, her block and, as she grew, the park over which Kate imagined herself queen provided another kind of school, especially in the summertime. Watching over her "kingdom" gave Kate her first sight of sexual intercourse, among dogs as well as humans. After the birth of her sister, two weeks at Coney Island extended her territory. Orchard Beach provided a summer respite closer to home. Tenement stoops were sites where young girls embroidered fall fashions and engaged in other peer activities.

When she was ten and a half, boys intruded on Kate's growing up. That spring she "was in love in Arthur, mostly because his name wasn't Sammy or Benny or Petey" (*BP*, 108). Kate was also in love with Mrs. Bender, "the teacher who stroked her large smooth breasts as she read 'Hiawatha.'" She was in love with poetry, music, the consumption that wasted and inspired Chopin, the neighbor's new poodle, her mother, her brother, "and I was in love with me, grown suddenly taller and thinner . . . Above all, I was in love with Helen Roth," bigger and older, and "Big Mouth," who had the "courage" to be left back in school (*BP*, 111). Kate was becoming an adolescent. Helen's Italian neighbor, a cellist, showed the children pictures that introduced them to new information about genitals, breasts, pubic hair, and varieties of human copulation. Startled, Kate feared the growth of body hair and breasts. She channeled her anxieties into her piano playing and her father's misplaced dream of a concert career. Falling behind her brother in feats of strength and sexual knowledge, she learned from peers such as "big, bosomy Italian Rosa [whose] specialty was the most important one . . . how it's done" (*BP*, 140–141). In her explicit awareness and especially her questioning expression of emerging sexuality and its conflicts, Kate's modernity distinguishes her from her predecessors and many of her peers.

Adolescence led to new conflicts with her parents and her maturing self: "I fought more with my disgusting mother and braved louder disobedience to my disgusting father, and while I fought, I tried to shape the breasts under her housedress and pierce the front buttons of his pants . . . [Everywhere] I looked for the shape of breasts—titties, Rosa had called them— and 'things,' not yet ready for 'prick.' I began to examine myself carefully, to search my armpits for hairs and my breasts for signs of swelling" (*BP*, 145). She tore out underarm hairs and bound her chest with ribbons and cloths, but still she "swelled."

Looking back, Kate recognized that "there were other matters involved, dimly reasoned, strongly felt. The ribbons were another test of strength, of stoicism, and a denial of sexuality, of being filthily conceived, the need for privacy an evolutionary step in the gathering of myself as me, solely me, a separation from the strangling claustrophobia of four people continuing too long to be one" (*BP*, 146). Struggling with bodily changes, she contended with the question of beauty. Her father, in particular, made her life difficult in ordering her to stay home, unlike "street girls." He shamed her by dragging her home in public.

School continued to provide a needed if incomplete distraction. Sixth grade was a decisive moment in her educational path. It was the point when the "smart ones" were separated from the others, sent on "rapid advance" to a junior high school to complete three years' work in two. Arithmetic "did her in," leaving Kate to face her father's "monumental" reaction: "Although he was eager to pull me out of school, this was a searing wound to his vanity" (*BP*, 157). Other problems of female growing up followed Kate to P.S. 57, from being "felt up" by the barber who cut her hair and the neighbor who took her to the movies, to a boy for whom she only felt sorry, who wanted her to be his girlfriend. Ignorant of and disgusted by sexuality, Kate desired the freedom denied to her by norms of age, gender, class, ethnicity, and parental authority. She searched for it in typically adolescent ways, wrestling with a boy until she was caught and reprimanded, following an older Italian high school athlete but only feeling more an outcast, "in dark cases of self-pity and gnawing jealousy," than she already did (*BP*, 169).

At thirteen, Kate declared her adolescent (semi)independence. Rejecting her father's dream for her of a concert career, she vowed to stay in school throughout high school, claiming it as her right. On graduating from elementary school, she symbolically exchanged her child's library card for an adult's. In the adult rooms perhaps she could find truth. Her menstruation began while she was reading Chekhov in the library. From her mother came the surprise of a new summer dress-up dress, shaped and fitted. Kate began to accept herself, body and all. Graduating from eighth grade "was a rite of passage that would call for light rejoicing, especially in the houses of immigrants" (*WW*, 6). Struggling with her father over her future—school or work—she confronted the contradictions of gender, class, and ethnicity. As Kate stood by in trepidation, her father read a letter from her teachers and principal stating that she was in the wrong school and that she should be in the general high school preparing for college. Faced with such authority, her father could only agree to her transfer to James Monroe High School, a new institution with an "unusually permissive curriculum" (*WW*, 8).

"James Monroe," she recalls, "was the first stage on which I created of myself a distinctive, conspicuous character." Dressed in earrings, odd hats and clothing, black stockings, she "could not be mistaken for anyone else in the world" (WW, 9). Kate concentrated on drama, poetry, literature, languages, and music. Encouraged by her teachers but with no plans for college, she was unworried by grades or her parents. She was rarely at home, now a workers' cooperative in which her father had invested his savings. For a while she enjoyed the "coops," especially their cultural activities and entertaining politics. But the center of her life had shifted to the school, to literature, to walks and talks with her new, small groups of peers after school when she was not at work. "Inhabit[ing] an exaggerated Mannerist world of overlarge, shocking values, alternating with deep niches," they spoke of literature, art, politics; they also talked of, but feared and were naive about, sex. Early efforts to overcome that fear did not succeed. Kate later saw that, in the terminology of modern psychology, they were "trying on a succession of identities" (WW, 19–21).

"In spite of the thickheaded school authorities, the melancholy fogs that touched me, life gradually became multistranded and rich," she writes (WW, 25). Kate received a raise at her laundry job. And she had two suitors, men in their late twenties, with whom she went to concerts, learned sad Russian songs, found cheap immigrant restaurants, and delved more deeply into New York's cultural life. At home Kate continued to fight: about men, her smoking, erratic eating, "crazy, schleppy" coat, and Isadora Duncan's morality. After a "monumental" fight over Duncan, the teenager "marched out and went to sleep with my friend Minnie, complaining into the night about the vulgar conventionalism, the narrow-minded insensitivity, of my bourgeois mother" (WW, 33).

From her mother she received no encouragement about domestic life. She was told: "'Any girl who isn't an idiot can learn everything there is to keeping a house clean and neat in a half hour. All it requires is that you must want to do it . . . I'd rather go to school or work' . . . She was right" (WW, 64).

Kate moved toward maturity, her path of growing up combining elements of working-class, middle-class, ethnic, urban bohemian, and feminist cultures. No longer willing to stay in her father's house, Kate received money from her mother, who silently acquiesced. She stayed with friends or worked as a live-in child- or elder-minder while continuing high school and part-time work. A woman English teacher took the teenager under her wing and served as a role model. She oversaw Kate's encounters with theater, music, cinema, art, and acquaintances, including a near-promise of a college scholarship from one of her associates, for which Kate's "deflowering" was to be the price. Although she tried to prepare herself,

Kate fell asleep while her intended lover talked on about nature and sex. Still a fearful teenager, Kate was not yet ready for sexual relations.

Despite her truancy, at seventeen Kate was determined to graduate from high school with the English medal, conquer math, and attend Hunter College, largely a place of and for women, "the only college I could afford." Hunter's "tacit ideal was to make cultivated women of us, and to good degree the Hunter of my years succeeded" (*WW,* 112). Nourished by a cluster of female English professors, she had a circle of friends who remained while others came and went, including her long-time close male friend, Davy. Her college friends were the girls of the Exchange room in the school cellar: the only "shelter for girls who smoked, our most forceful symbol, other than pregnancy, of freedom from parental prohibitions" (*WW,* 122). They talked, plotted, arranged to meet City College boys for political protests or outings to speakeasies. Seduced by books, the English majors dreamed. More independent than her peers, Kate took pleasure in her reputation, "this elevation to minor goddess, this ascension to utterly uninhibited sexpot and total free spirit. I neither confirmed nor denied the story" (*WW,* 128–129).

Renewing her family ties, she found the "irregularity" of her situation "beyond [her father's] capacity to understand and difficult to endure." He saw her "living 'free love' like wild anarchists," but wasn't able to protest much (*WW,* 137). With her mother and younger sister Kate had no such conflicts. Her Greenwich Village apartment attracted her sixteen-year old brother, who was popular among her female friends. Here she lived with Davy. "It was easier to avoid sex than to admit that the best we could do was stroke each other, penetration avoided," she writes. Fear of pregnancy inhibited them. Not trusting "rubbers," they had no money to consult doctors and no adults from whom to seek advice. Kate did not know how to bring up the subject with her mother, "nor could I easily confess failure of any kind to her." If nights were "embarrassed, frozen," days were "garlands of pleasure" (*WW,* 145).[28]

Whatever contradictions riddled her path and her life-style, they did not overly trouble Kate: "My independence had moved me into an ultimate mastery of life: a real, full apartment in Manhattan, a short walk from Greenwich Village, the haven of free love," she writes, overstating the case (*WW,* 148). Kate kept very busy; she had jobs, a house to clean, a full-time boyfriend (except when his mother ordered him to stay at home). School and work "engulfed" her. Sex hung over her peer group: "Most of our sexual encounters were truncated, gasping ventures . . . Virgins were rarely deflowered under these circumstances" (*WW,* 176). Finally, Kate was "un-virgined" and joined those who worried about periods, pregnancies, abortionists, and money. She had two abortions.

For Kate Simon, growing up was "a long, erratic labor, alternatively pulling away from and pushing toward a vague new condition, a faint goal reached with difficulty." Richly, metaphorically, her discourse retrospectively casts this as her time of "rebirth . . . In its wayward progress, there appear long, contemplative pauses for unaccustomed thoughts and new, firm decisions, clean of hesitancies and vacillations" (*WW*, 183–184). More mundanely but still metaphorically modern, her growing up meant "I had acquired the wisdom, during my rebirth passage, to know that job interviews for fulltime work after college would go badly if I was judged too odd, too affected . . . Telling transitions sometimes came when the rebirth struggle left me skinless and unprotected, not quite ready for the new human world" (*WW*, 184). In this recognition she joined many of her predecessors, even as she distanced herself from them in her self-awareness and self-expression. Kate finally "was no longer immune, no longer the mythical, separate, and privileged entity I had tried to design. I was earthbound and vulnerable, like anyone and everyone else" (*WW*, 184–185). Poetically put, this was the modern struggle of growing up shaped by gender, class, and ethnicity, with all their conflicts and contradictions.

A similar but in its particulars very different story—retold repeatedly *as* a story—was that of another Jewish immigrant girl in New York, Anzia Yezierska, whose early path was that of the immigrant working class.[29] In stories such as "Mostly about Myself," "America and I," and *Bread Givers,* Anzia tells her own tale, which is also that of her migrant generations. While celebrating the freedom of America, she also speaks of the struggles of poverty, generational clashes, the pain of assimilation and loss: "All the starved, unlived years crowd into my throat and choke me. I don't know whether it is joy or sorrow that hurts me so," she writes (9).

The experience of growing up in Poland (born in 1885, she emigrated in the 1890s) and New York City in numbing poverty made her the writer she became. When she began to write, she knew only about hunger "In the days of poverty I used to think there was no experience that tears through the bottom of the earth like the hunger for bread. But now I know, more terrible than the hunger for bread is the hunger for people" (18). Class, ethnicity, immigration, assimilation, the demands of growing up and the restrictions of gender came together violently. In her metaphor growing up meant transcending those different kinds of hunger: "In my early childhood, my people hammered me into defeat, defeat, because that was the way they accepted the crushing weight of life. Life had crushed my mother, so without knowing it she fed defeat with the milk of her bosom into the blood and bone of her children. But this thing that stunted the courage, the initiative, of the other children aroused the fighting devils in me" (20). Growing up meant conquering that defeat, rebelling, working her way beyond her mother's failure. Freedom meant not only free schools and colleges but the sweatshop, where the means to seek freedom and its fruits first had to be attained. Rent, bread, clothing, shoes, their prices always rising, preceded education, making it unattainable for the poor. Anzia was unwilling to accept "the America that gives the landlord the right to keep on raising my rent and to drive me to the streets when I do not earn enough to meet his rapacious demands" (27).

That refusal entailed in growing up meant tearing herself painfully from her family and their troubles and finding herself and her own America. It meant working as a servant and in a factory, learning English, joining Women's Association social clubs, losing her illusions and conquering drudgery, always learning, learning, learning, only in part at school and from books. It meant learning to make one's way in institutions and other formal settings, often with the support and help of friends to conquer loneliness. For Anzia it meant specifically gaining enough bread to continue her schooling, to become a teacher, then a writer, all the while fighting the loneliness of an immigrant in an alien land, caught between the Old World and the New. As Rachel in the story "Children of Loneliness" asks: "But am I really alone in my seeking? I'm one of the millions of immigrant children, children of loneliness, wandering between worlds that are at once too old and too new to live in" (123).

So was Anzia Yezierska, and so were countless others. Most did not possess the strained self-awareness that she as a writer had. Most did not follow the immigrant working-class path to material success. Growing up in these ways and creating a metaphorical, sometimes lyrical literary monument, women and men such as Anzia Yezierska redefined culturally, symbolically, and ideologically how we think about growing up and what we expect from it. A complex, contradictory legacy overflowing with its own conflicts, this was another contribution to modern social class and gender paths, as well as to the myths of growing up.

CHAPTER SIX

The Disappearance of Childhood
in Our Own Time?

"TROUBLED times force teens to grow up fast," blares the front page of the Sunday *Dallas Morning News,* March 8, 1992. "You don't have to be a parent to be alarmed by the headlines," reads the story. "Talk to enough of today's teens, and a picture begins to emerge: Children barely old enough to drive flirt with pregnancy and the possibility of AIDS. Students accosted at knifepoint give up their jewelry and $100 running shoes. Kids swagger through high school corridors, guns stashed in their belts." For better or for worse, this is no longer news. What is striking now is the very mundaneness of these powerful images of the young as tempted, threatened, or gone astray. No more ironic is the writer's concession in retreat that this view of teenagers "is exaggerated [although] studies suggest that most of them will at least witness violence."[1]

As the nineteenth century turned into the twentieth, the progressive "century of the child" was proclaimed. By midcentury an "age of adolescence" was upon us. To be sure, not everyone found that cause for celebration. Serious questions remain about the accuracy of the claims. Nonetheless, well before the century's end, commentators were informing fearful audiences of the coming "end of adolescence," the "disappearance" or "erosion" of childhood, "children without childhood," "endangered children," "adultlike children" (and "childlike adults"). The proclaimed "rise and fall" of the young supposedly includes a "postponed generation" that won't grow up and a "generation in search of adulthood." Worse, today's young, we—and they—are told perversely, are the first "modern" generation that won't fare as well materially as their parents. The political state is held responsible at once for insufficient action and for interfering with families' proper domains. Shifting expectations may generate new and dangerous myths.

Beyond the platitudinous proclamations of the doomsayers appear less vague and to many less threatening but no less stark realities. Constituting in part what Norton Grubb and Marvin Lazerson evocatively dub "broken promises: how Americans have failed their children," these facts include:

- One in every four to five American children lives in poverty. The United States ranks no higher than ninth in child poverty rates among industrialized nations. About 45 percent of African American and 39 percent of Hispanic children live in poverty. Forty percent of all poor people in the United States are children under age eighteen. In 1973, 83.6 per 100 poor children received Aid to Families with Dependent Children (AFDC); in 1987, despite rising population numbers, 59.8 per 100 received AFDC. The federal share of AFDC is less than 1 percent of the annual budget.

- One in every four homeless people in the cities is a child. Each night an estimated 100,000 children go to sleep homeless. One of every eight children goes hungry each day.

- The U.S. infant mortality rate is the worst among nineteen developed nations. With 7 percent of its infants born at low birth weights, the United States ranks twenty-ninth worldwide. Nonwhite infants are more than twice as likely to die as white ones; an African American child born in inner-city Boston has less chance to survive its first year of life than a child born in Panama, North or South Korea, or Uruguay.

- Homicide is the leading cause of injury-related deaths among children under one year old. In 1987 African American males aged fifteen to nineteen were ten times more likely to be shot and five times more likely to be killed by other violent means than white males.

- Between 9 and 12 million children under eighteen have no health insurance. Only 50 to 60 percent of two-year-olds in low-income urban areas have been properly immunized.

- Almost two thirds of all mothers in the work force raise their children alone or have husbands who earn less than $15,000 per year.

- Every day 501 girls under eighteen become parents; about 1 million teenagers became pregnant in 1989, most of them unmarried.[2]

These dramatic but partial data address only some of the concerns of the doomsayers. The poignant pictures dominated by young persons, often poor and of color, are seldom central to the canvases that portray America's own young "disappeared."[3] As in the past, poor and minority youth are "other people's children"; the other endangered children are closer—

symbolically or geographically (or racially or ethnically)—to one's own. This distinction is seldom made explicitly or clearly. That there are multiple paths to the contemporary "crises" of the young is obscured in most analyses. That both sets of young persons—and their images—are contradictory historical outcomes, not recent aberrations, attracts little attention. Powerful emotional and rhetorical outcries lack a sense of direction. In the final pages of *Conflicting Paths* I seek to direct that focus, to consider recent and contemporary continuities and connections as well as breaks from the past. Toward that end I briefly survey the twentieth century, purportedly the "century of children," the "era of adolescence." In contrast with preceding chapters, in this chapter an interpretation of selected patterns replaces personal testimony. Although the story spun so far cries out for "an ending," it finds no closure here. The press of the past on the present and future, inescapable in my understanding, demands recognition as a prelude to renewed action. The stakes, for the young and the world in which they struggle to make their way, are great. Creating a new past is one path to new presents and futures.

Few problems are so poorly understood as those relating to children, adolescents, and youth. In large part, as we have seen, this stems from the combined impact of dominant images, myths, theories, expectations, fears, and aspirations.[4] Typically lacking are larger, more complex interpretive contexts that include a necessary place for the history of growing up. This is as true with respect to David Hamburg's *Today's Children* and Donald Hernandez's *America's Children* as it is for shrill, less responsible statements. Among the key components of that "missing" force, on the one hand, is the persistent pressure of the powerful shaping factors of social class, gender, and race, and earlier in the century ethnicity and place. On the other hand are the myths about growing up, legacies of the past that powerfully shape expectations, presumptions, programs, and policies.

Contradictions and conflicts are central on both sides, perhaps seen more frequently and forcefully today than in the past. They deeply mark experiences of growing up as well as theories and norms about it. In their influential syntheses G. Stanley Hall and Sigmund Freud created major representations and anticipations with conflict at their center. Erik Erikson, whose ideas proved so powerful after midcentury, added to their legacy. Many followed them. More so now than ever before, we expect conflict in growing up, indeed we define it in part by reference to those conflicts, but we remain deeply conflicted ourselves about its definition. A certain "difference" or even "deviance" in growing up is deemed normal and is tolerated; other forms or sites of "deviance" are not. They are considered "delinquent." Anticipatory socialization, self-fulfilling and self-perpetuating for various forms of teen "rebellion" or "generational warfare," is indeed powerful. As John Modell, Frank Furstenberg, Theodore Hershberg, and Marlis Buchmann conclude from empirical investigations, twentieth-century patterns of early life course transitions, widely and sometimes wildly misunderstood, have *not* simplified or eased the struggles of coming of age. They may well have exacerbated them.

Among those easily oversimplified and misunderstood contradictions is what Viviana Zelizer identifies as the sentimental worth of children that increased as their productive value declined, crystallized in her evocative phrase "the priceless child." Class, gender, racial, ethnic, and geographic differences complicate her thesis of "sacralization." Never have all children been equally "priceless"; presumptions and expectations that stem from shifting cultural valuation touch most young lives unevenly.[5]

Closely associated is the deeply rooted, insidious ambivalence toward the young in American society, another historical legacy. Whereas the "classless" American dream has long been expressed in terms of improving our children's chances, reality never closely resembled the dream. Grubb and Lazerson assert the tragic failure of public responsibility: "Other people's children, those who are different from one's own, are to be mistrusted. They may be shiftless or dangerous influences . . . potential competitors . . . social costs . . . Class and racial biases harden the negative perception of other people's children." Gender also contributes. Ambivalence touches even our attitude toward our own children, and "is thus deeply embedded in modern conceptions of childhood and parent-child relationships," collective responses, and policies and institutions.[6] The inescapable historicity of the position of the young today—the present as outcome and our central notions as products of historical development—demands new paths to understanding and action.

Among epochal changes from the past is the extent and orientation of government activity at all levels, but especially that of federal programs, that mark the twentieth century. Simultaneously condemned for actions that are too large and omnipresent and too small and inconsistent, "state intervention into the lives of children has become a fact of life for all children, not those just those defined as problematic," observes Alan Wolfe. That intervention is not equal in its uses or its consequences. While un-doubted benefits have come to countless young persons, from public health and Head Start to enriched and advanced education in middle-class sub-urban schools, and while some common levels of institutionalization and standardization in paths of growing up have resulted, government policies also suffer from "broken promises," unequal allocation of resources, and lack of equity or equal opportunities. Private goals dominate public needs and goods; professional and interest groups triumph over the goals of benevolence and rehabilitation. Ambivalence, distrust of "other people's" children, and meanness defeat the potential of the state's power. Wolfe rightly identifies the contradictory nature of relations between children and the state and the resulting politicization that "places a tremendous burden on children, because it makes them the battleground upon which different conceptions of public policy are fought out."[7]

Viewed from this perspective, twentieth-century growing up is revealed as an unstable mix of the shaping and differentiating power of class, gender, and race, and to a slightly lesser extent ethnicity and geography; historical continuities as foundations for further shifts; and older and newer conflicts and contradictions, from demography and indicators of well-being to peer and consumer cultures, institutions such as the era-defining high school, deviance and delinquency, constructions of life course stages, and expectations for the attitudes and behaviors of the young. Clashes about cost, value, and pricelessness; needs for protection of vulnerable young innocents; lengthy dependency as a route to autonomy; segregation by age and other categories as preludes to presumed social integration; expected developmental "problems"; confusion of myth with actual experience; conflicting trends in indicators of well-being: these and other contradictions cloud the contemporary glass at a time when new and persisting social inequalities ravage the less advantaged. Differently placed youngsters continue to take their own paths toward growing up, regardless of myths to the contrary. Left unsaid at great loss is the truism that growing up is always hard to do. Lately it has not become any easier.[8]

Demography, like other important factors, reflects the clash of common opinion—codified in normative theory, policy, and expectations—and divided, complicated realities. In his overview of one hundred years, Peter Uhlenberg, for example, detects "a significant trend toward increasing uniformity for cohort members."[9] Emphasizing the convergence toward homogeneity and uniformity, demographic analyses reinforce misleading, superficial readings of trends. The problems lie in aggregate data and uncritical interpretation that together obscure irregular change and prominent factors such as social class, gender, and race. Uhlenberg reports that "changes in mortality, fertility, nuptiality, and migration since 1870 have led to successive birth cohorts living out their life courses under markedly different demographic conditions."[10] Demographic change is indeed one powerful engine plowing paths of growing up. Modern notions of innocent, secure childhood and dependent, prolonged adolescence developed in accord with falling fertility and lengthening longevity, though never in a linear, causal connection. And, contrary to presumptions such as Uhlenberg's, neither aggregate demographic trends nor urbanization, education, or assimilation leveled differences of class, ethnicity, race, gender, or geography, even when they partially reshaped and restructured their distinctions. Neither equal access nor equal participation follows from "a substantial decrease in cohort diversity."[11] Demography is not destiny, nor is it another name for egalitarian democracy. Persisting differences of race, class, gender, and region take a heavy toll today.

Uhlenberg's view fits well with common thinking about homogeneity, influenced by notions about schools and peer groups on the one hand and mass consumer culture on the other.[12] It provides often missing data to compare with, in the words of Modell, Furstenberg, and Hershberg, "our historical image [that] is the product of no research in particular, but is instead based on nostalgia and the need for a contrasting image to our concept of youth today."[13] Contradicting Uhlenberg, they paint a more complex portrait of a century of change. In some respects they find increasing uniformity in life course transitions; in others, such as marriage and household headship, they find little change. Data from 1970 indicate that young people needed less time than in 1880 to move from their parents' home, marry, and set up their own households, but that they were taking longer to complete their schooling. They were entering the work force earlier and in a more concentrated way. Overall, the patterns are varied and complex. On the one hand, "young people today are likely to be similar to one another in the age at which leave home, enter marriages, and set up their own households." In completing these transitions more rapidly, including leaving home, modern youths belie pervasive images of protracted growing up. On the other hand, also contradicting common images, today's transitions are more complicated in part because of overlapping statuses implied by school, work, marriage, and the like.[14]

Ironically, Modell and his associates find, some late nineteenth-century patterns still fit today's expectations: "Life-course organization in the nineteenth century was substantially the product of age-congruity. Most members of a cohort left one status before any entered another. Individuals today are forced to make more complex career decisions in a briefer period of time."[15] Transitions to adulthood were concentrated into a briefer period in 1970 (a trend that may have begun to reverse since that time). Among the consequences is an absence of uniformity across a cohort or age grade, and a lack of a lengthy period of postponement or moratorium in youth or adolescence, regardless of theories and expectations to the contrary, which nonetheless retain their force.

Although these data do not permit study of class or racial differences, other studies speak to their persistence, with a gradual decline through the middle decades of the century (sharper for distinctions of class and ethnicity than for race), then a recent increase. Gender difference makes a clear case. Over the course of the twentieth century, transitions became more integrated for women than for men. Since schooling for women conflicts with marriage, according to Modell it "must be tightly meshed into the schedule of family transitions." Although the two transitions are integrated, "the greater instrumental worth of continued education to men means that more is to be gained by staying in school even when married." Also unlike men, in both 1880 and 1970, women who remained home were more likely to work than those who left.[16] In recent years, with vacillations in rates of marriage, childlessness, and timing of first child— with mounting class and racial distinctions—contradictions shatter any previously clear notions of uniformity among women.

As aggregate demographic data as well as personal testimony suggest, great changes took place in the early life course and associated structures during the past two centuries. Some common images, such as the prevalence of the usual transitions, gain support. Others—such as those concerning the relative timing of status and transitions—do not. "Young people today face more complex sequencing decisions, rendered stressful," write Modell, Furstenberg, and Hershberg:

> Transitions are today more contingent, more integrated, because they are constrained by a set of formal institutions . . . [that] call for and reward precise behavior . . . The integrated mode does not in our way of thinking imply the reduction of strain. Growing up, as a process, has become briefer, more normful, bounded and consequential—and thereby more demanding on the individual participants . . . Scholars who see today's period of youth as extended, normless, lacking bounds, and without consequential decisions are responding—we believe—not to its essential characteristics, but to the expressions of those experiencing the phase of life. They reflect rather than analyze turmoil.[17]

Recent research, such as Thomas Held's for Europe and Marlis Buchmann's for the United States, reports a new shift away from, or at least some reduction in the extent of, the institutionalization, standardization, and individualization of the early life course that Modell and others identified. Buchmann argues that these changes do not indicate any easing of life course transitions to adulthood. On the contrary, increasing tensions have developed in the relationships between standardization and destandardization and bureaucratic allocation of status. Conflicts emerge in the "dialectics between action autonomy and action constraint."[18] "Historical time" and "growing up time" continue their awkward dance as the beat changes.

Today, as in the past, no one path serves all those growing up. Neither are there simple "rises" or "falls." Changes differently affect those who follow divergent paths. Complicated, uneven shifts in family economies, dependency among the young, and family structures (including the conse-quences of divorce) impinge on the environments in which the young grow up.[19] Many youngsters are now dependent in ways that were relatively uncommon a century or more ago. Some are not, though legally their sphere has narrowed greatly.[20] The active if selective role of state family interven-tion unequally redefines the playing field and the locus of authority.[21]

Divorce now touches the young to the same extent that death of a parent did in the past century. Their impacts are not easily comparable. Careful demographic estimates from 1800 to 1980 indicate a net gain in the amount of time children spend with any parent.[22] At the same time, data from the Panel Study of Income Dynamics show that by age seventeen, 19 percent of white children born between 1950 and 1954 lived with only one parent; by age seventeen, 70 percent of white children born in 1980 "are projected to have spent at least some time with only one parent." For African American children the percentages are 48 and 94, respectively. These estimates exaggerate the situation. Among whites, such children spend between 8 and 31 percent of their lives with only one parent, compared to 22 to 59 percent for blacks. Type of family at birth also shapes one's later experience.[23] Recent students such as Andrew Cherlin and Frank Furstenberg argue convincingly that relative advantages or disadvantages of class, gender, and race are more significant indicators than merely whether parents are coresident. Studies of the poor, both "new" and old, support their view.[24] For children born to unmarried adolescent mothers, especially among women of color, the facts of class, race, gender, and geography combine with the grip of an iron fist.

Data for 1990 indicate that 56 percent of African American families with children under eighteen living at home are headed by women, com-pared to 17 percent of white families. Mounting numbers of mothers are unmarried, and increasingly young when they first give birth. The rate of increase in these categories is higher for white than for nonwhite women. For both, these changes are relatively recent and reflect complicated socio-economic transformations, and are subject to much derogatory mythmak-ing. Regardless of debates about family structure, what is at base, as Cherlin asserts, "is not the lack of male presence but the lack of a male income."[25] Class and race intertwine in complex ways, connecting with long-standing and newer images. The hand of the past grasps that of the present. As Andrew Hacker summarizes:

> Such evidence as we have suggests that the forces propelling early parenthood cut across racial lines. One difference lies in the settings. Births among white teenagers tend to take place in depressed towns and rural areas, usually on the dreary side of the tracks where journalists seldom visit. Black out-of-wed-

lock births get much more attention, because more of them are clustered in central cities. Moreover, in low-income black areas, having babies out of marriage is seldom seen as an act of rebellion, let alone defiance directed at parents or the larger society . . . For the young fathers, being able to point to a child they have sired is seen as tangible evidence of manhood, an important laurel for men unable to achieve recognition in other areas.[26]

Ironically, there is less promiscuity among black teens than most reports suggest. Teenage girls know that their children will be their own responsibility, but still they desire a baby to love. As they have historically, many make enormous sacrifices for their young. Complications follow from immaturity and poverty, together with location, racism, and lack of institutional supports, as today's alarming poverty and mortality statistics indicate.

Among the many consequences are racially shaped paths of growing up. Whereas the paths of many children of middle-class and working-class African American families overlap with those of many white children (though clearly not all, given persisting differentials in opportunities and outcomes), those of poor, particularly inner-city blacks do not. For them, life course links with schooling, work, premarital sex and pregnancy, fertility, and marriage diverge sharply from the patterns and social norms of others. Some of this difference is not novel. Modell reports some variations among blacks and for blacks in comparison to other races earlier in the twentieth century, as in more severe effects resulting from the Great Depression in regard to schooling, premarital behavior, and marriage. By the 1960s, he notes, "whites and nonwhites basically shared the same temporal patterns, although the two had different age schedules of marriage, with nonwhites' timing throughout the era less uniform than whites'." Although he is less sensitive to intraracial differences, Modell concludes that "blacks differed so markedly in the way they typically constructed their life courses, that it at least suggests a subculturally distinctive (but no less dynamically changing, and in some of the same ways as for whites) normative structure . . . The flexibility of the black family has been often remarked, with differing evaluation. Their life courses, too, were flexible."[27]

For young women, gender continued to shape paths of growing up, influencing the course of twentieth-century transformations. Sensitive recent research such as that of Miriam Cohen and Kathy Peiss demonstrates the intricately shifting ties that bound gender to class, ethnicity, race, and geographic place. In the twentieth century, countless indicators reflect that females growing up forged new paths and experiences in education, work, and personal expression and stimulated new attention. These interconnected developments ranged from the feminization (numerically at least) of high schools, the consumer culture, lower-white-collar labor markets, and college campuses to the rise of a female-run dating and courtship system and shrill perceptions of the threat perceived in female deviance and delinquency.[28]

While women forged major new paths in life-styles and personal expression, education, and work, many of their routes ran up against notions and norms governing respectability, heterosexuality, home, marriage, and children which limited their range of opportunities. Concerns about gendered standards of propriety, laden with class-cultural connotations, restricted change and brought volumes of criticism and advice to millions of young women, their mothers, and teachers. Best reflected in the kinds of "status offenses" against age and gender expectations that labeled many female adolescents as deviant and at least potentially delinquent, the ongoing struggle for control of youthful sexuality was seldom far from the surface. Contradictions racked ideas about innocence and vulnerability and their often confusing, sometimes bizarre images.

Notions of difference, embedded in institutionalized (sometimes medicalized or psychologized) norms of proper conduct and closely connected to class, ethnicity, and race, connected contradictions in historical passages with contradictions in new paths. They also underlay the tremendous expansion of the institutionalization of growing up itself in environments such as the emblematic high school, with its many substructures, such as scouting and other peer groups, deeply conflicting and contradictory phenomena themselves.[29] From Middletown to Crestwood Heights, from River City to the West End of Boston, contests for authority and autonomy also took place within institutions and around peer groups that ranged from the adult-dominated to the semiautonomous.

Young women in high schools and colleges, viewed ambivalently, formed one flash point of danger and opportunity. Working women living away from their families of origin in urban areas constituted another. Change, little of it linear or simple, began to reshape female paths of growing up to include working outside the home; extending one's schooling to gain skills or certification newly demanded by labor markets; going to college away from home; or participating with same-sex or opposite-sex peers in a new consumer culture of amusements and markets.

Contradictions punctuated these developments. Young women differently placed by class, ethnicity, race, or geography participated and were influenced differentially, too. Women struggled to make their way, repaving or refashioning or detouring their paths as they could. Peiss, for example, notes that by the early twentieth century in New York City "working-class youth spent much of their leisure apart from their families and enjoyed greater social freedom . . . They fled the tenements for the streets, dance halls, and theaters . . . Adolescents formed social clubs, organized enter-tainments, shaping in effect a working-class youth culture expressed through leisure activity."[30] Their brothers had long had outlets for sociability, from militias and fire companies to gangs, clubs, pool halls, theaters, and dance halls. Both sexes stimulated reforms aimed at controlling them; both formed incomplete, awkward compromises with adult familial and external authori-ties. Neither radically reduced other inequalities of class, race, or gender.

Young women searching and striving for autonomy and independence along paths both new and old met responses that perceived them as threatening, disruptive, and dangerous to cultural and social order. The cure was "justice," juvenile or other, for the "precocious," "wayward," or misguided (or unguided). Women came to dominate the profession of "social" work, which offered diagnoses and treatments that dealt more strictly and severely with female than with male deviance and deviants. This in turn helped to create more professional and lower-level jobs in the process of building the organizational state and service economy. It also paralleled curricular and vocational "streaming" by gender (and class, a move that affected boys, too) in schools and colleges. By the 1960s and 1970s one result lay in the destructive myth of "liberated women" who could "have it all" but who risked losing their "distinctly feminine" attrib-utes while gaining "two full-time jobs": paid work and housework. Con-tradictorily, these developments contributed to an increase in both volun-tary and professional positions for women in social service, much as shifts in capitalist modes of production, bureaucratic expansion, and family economies swelled the numbers of jobs for women. For many families the achievement of the one-"breadwinner" family wage was short-lived.

To the extent that inequalities by gender as well as by race and class declined from the 1940s to the 1970s, their course was not irreversible. But since the 1980s at least, social gaps are widening again. Whether in Middletown in the 1920s or 1930s, Elmtown in the 1940s, River City in the 1940–1950s, Crestwood Heights in the 1950s, Boston's West End in the 1950s, Buffalo in the 1940s–1960s, or Francis Ianni's ten communities in the 1970s–1980s, education expanded, rates of participation and grades of school completed rose, institutionalization of growing up spread, peers came together, young people grew up. Deeply rooted differences and in-equalities among them, especially by class, gender, and race, persisted even as the educational floor was elevated and social configurations were re-shaped. Peer and extracurricular activities reflected and reinforced rather than seriously challenged those aspects of the social order. The ongoing order was largely reproduced in the processes and paths of growing up.

David Matza's classic 1961 and 1964 essays on traditions and the position and behavior of youth capture the interrelated facts of scholarly ignorance about and social difference among those coming of age.[31] No more had mass educational participation or mass cultural consumerism leveled the social hierarchy than the "century of the child" and "age of adolescence" homogenized the paths and destinations of young persons growing up. Despite their currency, such views are no more accurate than the equally common belief that "reports from schools and other sources indicate clearly that restlessness, turbulence, and emotional instability are increasing among adolescents everywhere. There is evidence also of increasing hostility toward adult authority," quoted by Modell, whose source dates not from the 1960s or the present but from the 1940s.[32] It was as true then as it is now that the young have never been so much studied or so little understood.

Even as our distance from the 1960s increases, the meanings and impacts of the decade's social and cultural movements remain confusing. Students of these events struggle uncomfortably with legacies that are still being debated, sometimes hotly.[33] Mary Ryan and Richard Busacca air one appealing version that places youth movements in historical context:

> The sons and daughters of the domestic ideal and the suburban home marked their transition out of the family with even greater panache [than working married women]. This bulging cohort of young men and women marched out of the family . . . to create or join the civil rights movement, the student movement, the antiwar movement, the counterculture movement, and the women's liberation movement . . . For this generation the experience of daily life was, to use the phrases of the day, a matter of growing up absurd in the lonely crowd created by organization men.

The sixties generation carried "more than the banner of a generation gap." They shouted out their origins and their dissatisfaction with "repressive, expressive" families by challenging society with "the family's cherished values of love, sharing, and caring."[34]

Undoubtedly accurate for *some* growing up in the 1950s and 1960s, this sketch depicts only one cohort of that "generation." Neither Dr. Spock nor suburban moms who (s)mothered or neglected their young bear the full weight of responsibility. As Elizabeth Douvan and Joseph Adelson first demonstrated in the mid-1960s—confirmed many times since, but not yet assimilated into most images of youth—relatively few young persons experience major adolescent crises in growing up.[35] A romantic (and increasingly nostalgic) mystique that weaves together the Beats, rebels with and without a cause, cultures counter and alternative, free love, political struggles for rights and for peace only rarely culminated in what Kenneth Keniston calls "postmodern" or "postconventional" youth. Most young people are "normal," in Douvan and Adelson's lexicon, a category that embraces a diverse range of individuals who are neither visionaries nor victims. Often the so-called normal, whether fairly or not, must carry the label of "conformist" rather than "activist."

Opposing one stereotype of grouping to another is not the point here, despite the lure of simplistic dichotomies and the psychologizing notions on which they often rest. Notwithstanding strong expectations and theories that stress powerful processes of convergence, uniformity, and homogenization, as a result of factors such as demographic transitions, economic growth, educational expansion, and a peer-based culture of consumption, young persons from the 1950s to the present have not all followed the same paths in growing up. Class, gender, and race stand out among a number of shaping factors.

Adelson, among others, argues that "dominant imaginings" are "inventions," useful for creating ambiguity as well as myth. Only partly does he overstate: "We invent because we must, for the young are in fact so diverse, complex, and obscure . . . Hence we invent what we wish to perceive. We invent the young so that they may, like figures in a morality play, take their places in that larger tableau of social action that our sins have devised."[36] Other "inventions" include "deviants" who are grudgingly tolerated (especially if they are "our own" rather than "other people's" children), "delinquents," "status offenders" and "real" criminals, "conformists," and "nonconformists."

Just as there is no one path in growing up, neither is there one youth culture. For better and for worse, claims that young persons can be fairly characterized by common orientation, alienation from adult roles and values, detachment, lack of commitment, and the like seldom hold up under scrutiny. Although Kenneth Keniston and others praise the potential consequences of the same traits some damn them to the point of diagnosing them as psychopathologies, study after study shows their minority, transitory character. Most young persons are in most respects conservative, neither deeply alienated nor activist, neither social problems nor progenitors of a different kind of future.[37]

Much more helpful is the sociologist Mike Brake's identification of "a complex kaleidoscope of several adolescent and youthful subcultures appealing to different age groups from different classes, involving different life styles." He concludes from comparative studies of the United States, Canada, and Great Britain that "these subcultures appeal to different self-images, values and behaviour and they bear a close relationship to their parent class culture."[38] Each student of the young has her or his own roster of subcultures. Typically they range more or less from "normal" or "respectable" to "delinquent," "cultural rebel" (Beat, bohemian, hippie) "politically militant" or "radical," and so on. In these subcultures Brake and others locate key elements that both define and differentiate paths of growing up. From the recognition that adolescence and youth are times for exploring relationships and shaping values and ideas, Brake argues that cultures or subcultures are important among the young because:

> They offer a solution, albeit at a "magical" level, to certain structural problems created by the internal contradictions of a socioeconomic structure, which are collectively experienced. The problems are often class problems experienced generationally.
>
> They offer a culture, from which can be selected certain cultural elements such as style, values, ideologies and life style. These can be used to develop an achieved identity outside the ascribed identity offered by work, home or school.
>
> As such, an alternative form of social reality is experienced, rooted in a class culture, but mediated by neighbourhood, or else a symbolic community transmitted through the mass media . . .
>
> Subcultures offer to the individual solutions to certain existential dilemmas.[39]

Brake notes that the last is often the preserve of young males, especially among the working class. Gender is a critical element that is still neglected. Divisions among the young are neither all of their own making nor wholly negative or positive.

For my own "Baby Boomer" generation (I was born in 1949), recent students distinguish the simultaneous presence and absence of common experiences, lack of single paths in growing up and singular consequences for the life course. They differentiate between those born early in the postwar period and those born after the mid-1950s, and increasingly by class, race, and gender as well. Paul Light cites common elements that define what he deems "the first standardized generation": history, television, economic expectations, hopes, fears, disillusionment, self-perception. How these attributes and experiences serve as defining and uniting principles is made clear; good studies such as Light's necessarily also emphasize diversity and division. Like other recent writers, Light stresses two population "waves" or "booms," defined by date of birth, whose members faced different sets of opportunities, or fortunes, in Richard Easterlin's term. Differences in paths of growing up resulting from class, gender, and race also continue to influence how differently placed young persons respond to expectations, increasing or diminishing. Among the Baby Boomers gaps of age, gender, and race as well as class claim more and more attention.[40]

Generational changes stemming from recent transformations in growing up are often exaggerated. Powerful images reflect judgments that sometimes have little to do with the young themselves. While hesitant to claim either "liberation" or great loss, I do not wish to argue against important changes that remain today controversial and incomplete. Major shifts in attitudes and behavior regarding sexuality and reproduction, marriage and divorce, among other elements of family life, relations between spheres considered public and private, public roles and work for women, and gender relations stand out among many asserted "revolutions" in morality, culture, and society. Others relate to shifts in attitudes toward authority and social change. As with changes in work and economic structures, education, and class and racial relations, their impact and course are uncertain. Despite claims to the contrary, I urge that we continue to hedge our bets on both the positive and negative, short-term and long-term consequences for growing up from epochal transformations whose ends are barely in sight. Neither cries of crisis nor paralyzing despair offers solace or guidance.

If a glut of print or electronic commentary could prove the presence of a "crisis in growing up," no doubts would exist about the plights of the present. From Vance Packard's *Our Endangered Children* to Marie Winn's *Children without Childhood*, Neil Postman's *Disappearance of Childhood*, Valerie Suransky's *Erosion of Childhood*, Sheryl Merser's *"Grown-Ups:" A Generation in Search of Adulthood*, Susan Littwin's *Postponed Generation*, or Donna Gaines' *Teenage Wasteland*, to media commentaries and documentaries, made-for-TV movies, the periodical and daily press, and much else, the message of "doom and gloom" is omnipresent, constant, and shrill, spreading alarm. I fear far more harm than good follows from the unabated flood of words and strong images. Surely those who care about the young—although about whose young varies greatly and tellingly—can do better than Marie Winn's assertion, "Something has happened." All the complications involved in studying the young carefully and sympathetically, many of them products of history, conspire to obstruct useful understanding and promote indiscriminate condemnation.[41]

The recent past and present constitute no golden age for the young. Much, indeed, has happened. A richly complex view of growing up in the late twentieth century may provide a more accurate and useful if less dramatic picture. Transformations in growing up need to be grasped in their connections with the massive remaking of national and international orders; modes of production; economic relations; political spheres and public policies; family structures and relations; interpersonal and gender relations; and deepening divisions over values, beliefs, and ideologies. Important continuities also mark growing up today. Both continuity and change stem from historical precedents and processes. Growing up and the place of children, adolescents, and youth have changed, and not always for the better—nor for the worse. Have there been serious, large-scale problems and declines? Yes. Have there been crises for poor young persons, especially those of color? Yes. Have *all* young persons been in crisis? No. Diversities and inequalities make balance a false ideal. Expectations for understanding fare better if we recognize deep divisions, differences, and the conflicts that underlie them.

Responding to those who take data on the well-being of the young out of meaningful contexts in order to assert a decline attributable to parents and families, Cherlin asks two important questions: Has children's well-being in fact declined? If so, can the decline be linked to changes in the family such as the spread of single-parent families or mothers' employment? He concludes: "Unfortunately, the evidence on these issues is far from definitive, and reasonable people might make differing interpretations. Nevertheless, the following conclusions seem warranted: In some important respects, children are less well off [in 1988] than two decades ago. But a portion of the decline in the well-being of children can be attributed to increasing marital instability or out-of-wedlock childbearing, and little or none of the decline can be clearly linked to the increasing number of mothers working outside the home."[42]

More specifically, in terms of family income, children's lot improved on average 46 percent between 1962 and 1983, owing to a rise in real incomes to 1973 and falling birthrates thereafter. But during the same period the gap between the family incomes of poor and better-off children widened. The proportion of all children living in poverty increased by 20 percent. Increasing marital disruption and out-of-wedlock births contributed to the declining economic position of children as the number and proportion of single-parent families grew. The increase in the numbers of working mothers, however, improved children's overall economic standing by raising the number of two-earner families.[43]

Divorce harms children economically. Fathers earn more than mothers, but after about 90 percent of divorces the children remain with their mothers. Middle-class families suffer the sharpest drop in income; few better-off children experience poverty as a consequence of divorce, "yet for children in families that are just getting by, a parental divorce often means a fall into poverty."[44] For some children this poverty persists, especially when fathers contribute little or no support.

Marital changes can also contribute to children's emotional problems. After the initial trauma, however, most children recover, resuming normal cognitive and emotional development. A minority seems to experience long-term negative consequences. "The studies suggest that the effects, if any, depend on a host of factors, such as social class, race, the mother's desire to work or not to work, and the age and sex of the child," Cherlin summarizes. Contrary to common opinion, the effects of various day care arrangements are not known. Studies point to both beneficial and harmful impacts; so far they fail to show pervasive harm. There is little reason, Cherlin avers, "for lumping the employment of mothers with other family behavior such as divorce, teenage childbearing, and family violence that nearly always produces short-term, if not long-term stress for children."[45]

Indicators of children's well-being reflect mixed trends. Children's health has improved, though at a slower rate in recent years. Overall death rates for infants and children have declined, but not for the poor and racial minorities. By international standards U.S. levels of infant mortality, rooted in social inequalities, are scandalously high. A general increase in parents' levels of education seems to have had a beneficial effect. Yet rates of juvenile arrest, suicide, marijuana use, and premarital sex increased from the early 1960s to the mid to late 1970s. Often ignored, however, is that most of these trends leveled off or declined from the mid to the late 1970s. Reports that cite trends from decade to decade miss this fact.

The decline in children's well-being has concentrated among disadvantaged groups. Their numbers and proportions are increasing, at least since the 1970s, as racial (particularly inner-city), gender (particularly single female heads of families), and class (rural and urban poor) differences also increase. Most telling are the joint consequences of these powerful forces. "Children growing up in mother-only households often face multiple burdens," Nicholas Zill and Carolyn Rogers have found. "Their mothers may have little education, low income, and high unemployment; in addition, many of these children lack contact with or support from their absent fathers, depend on government assistance, and face ethnic discrimination." In this, children of mothers who never married are more disadvantaged than children of divorced mothers.[46] In 1985 the median income of two-parent families was three times that of mother-only families with children, and the median income of white families with children was one and a half times that of Hispanics and almost twice that of African Americans.

Aggregate statistics regularly report that children are more likely to live in poverty than any other age group. In 1986, 20 percent of persons under eighteen were poor, compared to 14 percent of all people and less than 13 percent of those sixty-five or older. The proportion of poor children decreased sharply in the 1960s (to about 14 percent in 1969) but rose in the 1970s and 1980s, paralleling national economic declines. Data for 1986 show astonishingly high poverty rates for African American and Hispanic children: 43 and 37 percent and rising, respectively. For children living in mother-only families, the poverty rate has ranged between 51 and 56 percent since 1970. Government and private responses remain woefully inadequate to combat these alarming levels or to promote change. Health problems concentrate among the poor: pregnancy without medical attention; low birth weight in infants, with high mortality risk; lack of access to medical care, information, and insurance; and so on. As the news media tell us almost daily, accidental deaths and fatal violence seem ubiquitous among these populations, often the result of abuse and homicide. More an issue among middle-class adolescents, if often exaggerated, the teenage suicide rate has been falling for several years.

Regardless of the trustworthiness of data or interpretation, apparent trends in the social behavior and attitudes of the young constitute endless grist for the rhetorical mill. As Zill and Rogers write: "In the past three decades, the social behavior and attitudes of young people in the United States have changed profoundly. Some of the changes in teen behavior have been a source of great concern to older generations of Americans. Theft and violence, use of illicit drugs, and early sexual activity outside marriage are all more common than they were among the teens of 20 to 30 years ago."[47]

Careful research on sexual activity, including that of Phillips Cutright and John Modell, qualifies the sense of dramatic change and shows that shifts have stemmed from trends well under way before recent charges of apocalyptic epidemics. Lack of sex education stands out among the many causes of teenage pregnancy, abortion, childbirth, and sexually transmitted diseases. The early stages in ongoing cycles of poverty and "social problems," exacerbated and distributed unequally by class, gender, and race, become set in place. From 1970 to 1985 the proportion of births to unmarried teenagers doubled, from 30 to 59 percent. In 1985 unmarried mothers accounted for 45 percent of births to white teenagers and 90 percent to African American teens.

Over the past decade or so, write Zill and Rogers, "most indicators of undesirable behavior among teenagers and young adults have reached a plateau or declined somewhat."[48] Juvenile arrests have been declining since about 1975. Rates of victimization of teenagers by violence and theft, although declining, are almost double those of adults. Homicide trends parallel those of arrests; like adult levels, they may be rising along with gang activity. Owing to tougher policies aimed at longer incarceration of offenders, there has been a slight increase in the numbers of juveniles in custody. Males dominate among offenders, although the numbers of women in jail have increased faster than the numbers of men, with African Americans dominating the prison population. Young blacks are more likely than whites to be both victims and perpetrators of violent crime. Minority youths make up a disproportionate number of the juveniles arrested or held in correctional facilities.

Marijuana use has followed general trends. Among young people aged twelve to seventeen, it rose between 1972 and 1977, from 7 to 17 percent; in 1979 more than one half of high school seniors reported use of marijuana during the previous year, more than one third within the month. By 1982 nearly two thirds of young people aged eighteen to twenty-five surveyed had tried it. By 1985 surveys were reporting only the 1974 level of use for marijuana, the most popular drug. No drug rivaled alcohol, the most common adolescent intoxicant. In 1985 two thirds of high school seniors reported current use, whereas only one fourth admitted using marijuana. "Because youthful drinking is so widespread, it is likely that the negative personal and social effects of teenage alcohol abuse far exceed the effects attributable to teenage drug use," conclude Zill and Rogers.[49]

Students of youth find "positive implications for the well-being of current and future generations of children" in trends toward later marriage, smaller families, more widely spaced births, and declining black fertility. Surveys of high school students list marriage, children, and a happy family life, along with material success, high among their goals. These trends and others form the basis for new, but not unprecedented, paths of growing up, including the now common experiences of spending at least part of one's childhood with one parent, experiencing some early time in child care, staying home longer, and returning home after leaving.[50] Some patterns, including the promotion of (part-time) work for teenagers; the debate about relative roles of families, schools, and peer groups in socialization; contradictory worries about too much or too little independence; and questions about the efficacy of education or authority echo or repeat historical ones.[51] Others do not.

Loss of a parent is one among many parallels. Recognizing the difficulty of comparing the experience of losing a parent to death as opposed to loss by divorce only begins to hint at the obstacles that preclude quick judgments or predictions about the future effects of such loss. That is just one of many points at which class, race, and gender rear their heads as we ponder the plight of "other people's children."

Those who write sincerely and seriously today of "a generation in crisis," "lives on the edge," "declining fortunes," "fateful choices" relate much of import. The Carnegie Corporation's David Hamburg does not exaggerate when he declares that "a variety of indices indicate that we are suffering heavy casualties during the years of growth and development, and these casualties not only are tragic for the individuals but also bear heavy costs for American society." He continues, amid a rising chorus of voices in the early to mid-1990s: "Distressing as this bad news is, there is much more. Reports of domestic violence and child abuse are on the rise. Over the past several decades, the largely unrecognized tragedy of moderately severe child neglect has been added to the more visible, flagrant child neglect."[52] The roster of crises, costs, and consequences lengthens. The present is another moment of great fear and concern, another transition era for society and for growing up.

In pointing first and foremost to the "decline" of the intact nuclear family, on the one hand, while failing to specify clearly among the different paths to different destinations that the young continue to take in growing up, on the other, Hamburg's and many others' rhetorical and policy work loses focus and force, dissipating its energies and diminishing its impact. Myths of growing up, comparisons with an implicit or presumed past to the detriment of the present, universal notions of what "child" and "adolescent" mean abound in current diagnoses and prescriptions. History can teach us otherwise. That is the lesson that rings out from this overview of growing up in the past. The plight of the poor, whether inner-city or rural youngsters, and the crises of middle-class suburban youth may share elements, but they are not at all the same thing. Crisis mongering seldom leads to long-term problem solving. I fear for those young persons who have grown up under the dark clouds not only of the obscene possibility of nuclear holocaust and environmental poisoning but also of the perversely negative expectation that they will not fare better than their parents. The toll on them is heavy.

Growing up has always been hard to do. Especially for those who suffer disadvantages that remain widespread and powerful at the end of the twentieth century, "advanced modern" society makes it no easier. For some, perhaps for many, it has become even harder. Age itself as it is constructed and reconstructed is one of many disadvantages. It never stands alone, separate from class, race, gender, ethnicity, and geographic location, among many critical factors. For that legacy the past and present together share responsibility. Tomorrow who will speak for the children, whether "our children" or "other people's children"? Who will listen? Who will hear? Who will take action?

Notes on Sources

Information and commentary in this appendix complement and amplify but do not repeat that presented in the text.

Research Design and Strategy

Working first from published bibliographies and guides to first-person primary, testimonial, or narrative writings and ancillary sources, and then from scrutiny of notes and bibliographies of related secondary sources, I chose to focus my research on reading and evaluating *all* relevant items in these research centers, accompanied by extensive use of interlibrary loans, primary source anthologies, and collective biographies and family histories.

Major repositories:

American Antiquarian Society, Worcester, Mass.
The Newberry Library, Chicago
Barker Texas History Research Center, University of Texas at Austin
Texas State Archives and Library, Austin

I chose these institutions in part because of my prior knowledge of the value of their collections for this kind of project, in part because of their geographic distribution and varied collection strengths, and in part because of the availability of funding and reasonable access. In beginning to search out first-person accounts, one quickly discovers their tremendous number. A decades-long, all but limitless process of collecting and studying them gapes as one pitfall for the uninitiated researcher. I limited my gathering by the number of repositories I visited, the duration of time allotted for the primary research phase of the project, and the arbitrary

Average ages for key events

Age	All	Pre-1750			1750–1800			1800–1850			1850–1900			1900–1920+		
		M	F	All	M	F	All	M	F	All	M	F	All	M	F	All
Leaving home	16	7	—	7	15	20	17	16	17	16	16	18	17	15	—	15
Migration	17	—	—	—	17	20	18	18	15	17	15	14	14	19	4	16
First work	16	22	—	22	17	15	17	16	16	16	17	18	17	12	13	13
Marriage	26	22	—	22	27	25	26	27	23	25	31	26	27	30	22	25
Intercourse	17	—	—	—	—	—	—	—	—	—	—	—	—	—	—	—
Courtship	22	—	—	—	—	—	—	—	—	—	—	—	—	—	—	—

Note: Ns too small to calculate for intercourse and courtship by period.

decision that a database of approximately five hundred life accounts was sufficient for my goals. My method clearly remains open to criticism for lack of additional accounts and other aspects of the collection. More years spent garnering materials would in no way forestall such criticisms. The database is marked by the problems of "missing paths" and missing variables discussed throughout this volume. I am satisfied that this book is based on the largest collection of such sources of which I am aware. *Caveat lector.*

The Primary Source Database

All cases, on the basis of individuals not sources, were summarized and indexed in a dBaseIII+ file. This greatly aided my organization and categorization of the materials in developing the grid of paths of growing up that is central to this history. The actual writing depended not on the dBaseIII+ files but on copies and notes of the primary materials themselves. The summary information on the collection was generated by dBaseIII+.

The following lists categorize the first-person testimonial sources by time period, type, and sex of author:

Period		Source		Sex	
Pre-1750:	8	Autobiography:	83	Male:	256
1750–1800:	67	Diary:	126	Female:	219
1800–1850:	200	Memoir:	98		
1850–1900:	168	Letters:	31		
1900–1920+:	35	Other (collective biographies, etc.):	31		

In all, I examined first-person testimonial or narrative sources for approximately 520 individuals. These included separate items for about 480 individuals and collective materials on about another 40. Totals may be misleading owing to missing information on key topics. All numbers presented in this appendix should be taken as approximations. This is equally the case with the summary averages overall and by period in the table on the facing page. The average values that appear, excepting those in two periods, pre-1705 and 1900–1920+, where the number of cases is quite small, fall well within expected ranges. The revisions in the growing up history with respect to ages of leaving home and extent of (formal) child labor, discussed in the introduction, find support in the lack of great variation over time. The variations by age and gender are expected ones.

Notes

Preface

1. "Little Men and Women," *The Child's Friend,* 7 (February 1847): 202–203. Appearances to the contrary, I have made no effort to provide exhaustive citations to relevant secondary literature. This is a long book, and my efforts in drafts to list full guides to the many materials that shaped its contexts, comparisons, and conclusions made it much longer. Similarly, I have not attempted to cite every first-person source uncovered by my research; nor have I included any of the British sources that my comparatively framed research located.

2. Among a large and growing literature, see Marie Winn, *Children without Childhood: Growing Up Too Fast in the World of Drugs and Sex* (New York: Penguin, 1983); Valerie Polakow Suransky, *The Erosion of Childhood* (Chicago: University of Chicago Press, 1982); Vance Packard, *Our Endangered Children: Growing Up in a Changing World* (Boston: Little, Brown, 1984); Neil Postman, *The Disappearance of Childhood* (New York: Delacorte, 1982); Joshua Meyrowitz, "The Adultlike Child and the Childlike Adult: Socialization in an Electronic Age," *Daedalus,* 113 (1984): 19–48; Ruth Sidel, *Women and Children Last: The Plight of Poor Women in Affluent America* (New York: Viking, 1986); Donald Hernandez, *America's Children* (New York: Russell Sage Foundation, 1993).

3. Originally published as *L'enfant et la vie familiale sous l'ancien régime* (Paris: Librairie Plon, 1960). In subsequent editions, Ariès responded to some of his critics. For the English edition, see Philippe Ariès, *Centuries of Childhood: A Social History of Family Life,* trans. Robert Baldick (New York: Random House, 1962). Excellent introductions to the criticism appear in Adrian Wilson, "The Infancy of the History of Childhood: An Appraisal of Philippe Ariès," *History and Theory,* 19 (1980): 132–153; Richard T. Vann, "The Youth of *Centuries of Childhood,*" *History and Theory,* 21 (1982): 279–297;

Linda Pollock, *Forgotten Children: Parent-Child Relations from 1500 to 1900* (Cambridge: Cambridge University Press, 1983); Antony Burton, "Looking Forward from Ariès? Pictorial and Material Evidence for the History of Childhood and Family Life," *Continuity and Change,* 4 (1989): 203–229; *Journal of Family History,* 12.4 (1987), among a number of symposia.

4. See, among a large literature, Keith Thomas, "Children in Early Modern England," in *Children and Their Books: A Celebration of the Work of Iona and Peter Opie,* ed. Gillian Avery and Julia Briggs (Oxford: Oxford University Press, 1989), pp. 45–77; Ludmilla Jordanova, "Conceptualizing Childhood in the Eighteenth Century: The Problem of Child Labour," *British Journal for Eighteenth-Century Studies,* 10 (1987): 189–199, and "Children in History: Concepts of Nature and Society," in *Children, Parents, and Politics,* ed. Geoffrey Scarre (Cambridge: Cambridge University Press, 1989), pp. 3–24; Jan Kociumbas, "Childhood History as Ideology," *Labour History,* 47 (1984): 1–17; Hugh Cunningham, *The Children of the Poor: Representations of Childhood since the Seventeenth Century* (Oxford: Blackwell, 1991); Carolyn Steedman, Cathy Urwin, and Valerie Walkerdine, eds., *Language, Gender, and Childhood* (London: Routledge, 1985). See also Arlene Skolnick, "The Limits of Childhood: Conceptions of Child Development and Social Context," *Law and Contemporary Problems,* 39 (1975): 38–77. On discourse and its consequences, consider the contemporary, painful, and difficult example of child abuse. See Joel Best, *Threatened Children: Rhetoric and Concern about Child-Victims* (Chicago: University of Chicago Press, 1990); Ian Hacking, "The Making and Molding of Child Abuse," *Critical Inquiry,* 17 (1991): 253–288; D. Kelly Weisberg, "The 'Discovery' of Child Abuse," *University of California at Davis Law Review,* 18 (1984): 1–57; Jenny Kitzinger, "Defending Innocence: Ideologies of Childhood," *Feminist Review,* no. 28 (1988): 77–87.

5. See Lloyd DeMause, ed., *The History of Childhood* (New York: Psychohistory Press, 1974); C. John Sommerville, *The Rise and Fall of Childhood,* rev. ed. (New York: Vintage, 1991); John Demos, *Past, Present, and Personal* (New York: Oxford University Press, 1986); Joseph Kett, *Rites of Passage: Adolescence in America, 1790 to the Present* (New York: Basic Books, 1977); John Gillis, *Youth in History: Tradition and Change in European Age Relations, 1770–Present,* rev. ed. (New York: Academic Press, 1981); Michael Mitterauer and Reinhard Sieder, *The European Family: Patriarchy to Partnership from the Middle Ages to the Present,* trans. Karla Oosterveen and Manfred Hörzinger (Oxford: Blackwell, 1982); Michael Mitterauer, *A History of Youth,* trans. Graeme Dunphey (Oxford: Blackwell, 1992); Ariès, *Centuries;* and *American Childhood: A Research Guide and Historical Handbook* (Westport, Conn.: Greenwood, 1985) and *Children in Historical and Comparative Perspective: An International Handbook and Research Guide* (Westport, Conn.: Greenwood, 1991), both ed. Joseph M. Hawes and N. Ray Hiner.

6. Important examples include several essays by Bruce Bellingham: "The His-

tory of Childhood since the 'Invention of Childhood': Some Issues in the Eighties," *Journal of Family History,* 13 (1988): 347–358; "The 'Unspeakable Blessing': Street Children, Reform Rhetoric, and Misery in Early Industrial Capitalism," *Politics and Society,* 12 (1983): 303–330; "Institution and Family: An Alternative View of Nineteenth-Century Child Saving," *Social Problems,* 33 (1986): S33–57; "Waifs and Strays: Child Abandonment, Foster Care, and Families in Mid-Nineteenth-Century New York," in *The Uses of Charity,* ed. Peter Mandler (Philadelphia: University of Pennsylvania Press, 1990), pp. 123–160; and "'Little Wanderers': A Socio-Historical Study of the Nineteenth-Century Origins of Child Fostering and Adoption Reform, Based on Early Records of the New York Children's Aid Society" (Ph.D. diss., University of Pennsylvania, 1984). See also Kirsten Drotner, *English Children and Their Magazines, 1751–1945* (New Haven: Yale University Press, 1988); Viviana Zelizer, *Pricing the Priceless Child: The Changing Social Value of Children* (New York: Basic Books, 1985); Jordanova, "Children"; Cunningham, *Children;* Pat Thane, "Childhood in History," in *Childhood, Welfare, and Justice,* ed. Michael King (London: Batsford, 1981), pp. 6–25; W. Norton Grubb and Marvin Lazerson, *Broken Promises: How Americans Fail Their Children* (New York: Basic Books, 1982); Joseph Adelson, *Inventing Adolescence: The Political Psychology of Everyday Schooling* (New Brunswick, N.J.: Transaction, 1986).

7. See, for example, interpretations ranging from DeMause, *History,* to Edward Shorter, *The Making of the Modern Family* (New York: Basic Books, 1975), and Lawrence Stone, *The Family, Sex, and Marriage in England* (New York: Harper and Row, 1977).

8. See, for example, John Demos, "The Rise and Fall of Adolescence," in *Past,* and Sommerville, *Rise and Fall,* among numerous works on the "erosion" or "disappearance" of childhood.

9. Evidence spans the eras. See, for example, Ariès, *Centuries;* Sommerville, *Rise and Fall;* Demos, "Rise and Fall." Telling critiques include previously cited works by Bruce Bellingham, Ludmilla Jordanova, and Jan Kociumbas, as well as John Boswell, *The Kindness of Strangers: The Abandonment of Children in Western Europe from Late Antiquity to the Renaissance* (New York: Pantheon, 1988).

10. *Harper's* credits as its source *Animal Agenda,* a monthly magazine published by the Animal Rights Network.

11. Most of these cartoons were given to me by students, unfortunately without publication dates noted.

12. I presumed without question that it was the children to whom the father referred. Female students to whom I showed the cartoon sagely observed that he might well be including the wife!

13. Among the literature already cited, see especially essays by Bruce Bellingham and Ludmilla Jordanova, and Grubb and Lazerson, *Broken Promises,* among a vast literature.

14. In addition to critiques cited previously, see David Herlihy, "Medieval Chil-

dren," in *Essays in Medieval History,* ed. B. K. Lackner and K. R. Philp (Austin: University of Texas Press, 1978), pp. 109–142, among Herlihy's writings; Natalie Zemon Davis, "The Reasons of Misrule: Youth Groups and Charivaris in Sixteenth-Century France," *Past and Present,* 50 (1971): 41–75; Ross W. Beales, Jr., "In Search of the Historical Child: Miniature Adulthood and Youth in Colonial New England," *American Quarterly,* 27 (1975): 379–398; Charles Tilly, "Population and Pedagogy in France," *History of Education Quarterly,* 13 (1973): 113–128.

15. See also my essays "The History of Childhood and Youth: Beyond Infancy?," *History of Education Quarterly,* 26 (1986): 95–109; "Early Adolescence in Antebellum America: The Remaking of Growing Up," *Journal of Early Adolescence,* 5.4 (Fall 1985): 411–426; "Remaking Growing Up: Nineteenth-Century America," *Histoire sociale/Social History,* 24 (1991): 35–59; and the reader *Growing Up in America: Historical Experience* (Detroit: Wayne State University Press, 1987).

1. Growing Up in History

1. Telling examples, cited in the preface, include studies by Arlene Skolnick, Joel Best, Ian Hacking, D. Kelly Weisberg, Bruce Bellingham, and Viviana Zelizer; the "rise and fall" and "end of childhood/children" literatures; and the critical literature on Ariès. More generally, see previously cited works by Ludmilla Jordanova, Geoffrey Scarre, Jan Kociumbas, and Hugh Cunningham. See also Margaret Pelling, "Child Health as a Social Value in Early Modern England," *Social History of Medicine,* 1 (1988): 135–164. Michel Foucault's work is also generally relevant here.

2. Major examples, cited in the preface, include works by John Sommerville, John Demos, Lloyd DeMause, and Philippe Ariès among historians, and among contemporary commentators, Neil Postman, Marie Winn, Joshua Meyrowitz, and Vance Packard.

3. See W. Norton Grubb and Marvin Lazerson, *Broken Promises: How Americans Fail Their Children* (New York: Basic Books, 1982). Other important work includes studies by Bruce Bellingham (cited in the preface), which attend closely to discourse and rhetoric. Among histories, on abuse, see Linda Gordon, *Heroes of Their Own Lives: The Politics and History of Family Violence* (New York: Viking, 1987).

4. Among many sources see, for children, Arlene Skolnick, "The Limits of Childhood: Conceptions of Child Development and Social Context," *Law and Contemporary Problems,* 39 (1975): 38–77. For "myths" of adolescence, see Aaron H. Esman, *Adolescence and Culture* (New York: Columbia University Press, 1990); Joseph Adelson, *Inventing Adolescence: The Political Psychology of Everyday Schooling* (New Brunswick, N.J.: Transaction, 1986).

5. Among the works already cited, see those by Jenny Kitzinger, Joel Best, Ian Hacking, D. Kelly Weisberg, and John Demos.

6. Edmund Morgan, *The Puritan Family* (1944; rpt., New York: Harper and

Row, 1966), is the best source. See also John Demos, *A Little Common-wealth: Family Life in Plymouth Colony* (New York: Oxford University Press, 1970).

7. Linda Pollock, *Forgotten Children: Parent-Child Relations from 1500 to 1900* (Cambridge: Cambridge University Press, 1983); see also Barbara Hanawalt, *The Ties That Bound: Peasant Families in Medieval England* (New York: Oxford University Press, 1986); Shulamith Shahar, *Childhood in the Middle Ages* (London: Routledge, 1990), among others, including Mark Golden, *Children and Childhood in Classical Athens* (Baltimore: Johns Hopkins University Press, 1990); and Thomas Wiedemann, *Adults and Children in the Roman Empire* (New Haven: Yale University Press, 1989).

8. On love, see Peter Laslett, *Family Life and Illicit Love in Earlier Generations* (Cambridge: Cambridge University Press, 1977); Jean-Louis Flandrin, *Families in Former Times* (Cambridge: Cambridge University Press, 1978). On labor, see Hugh Cunningham, "The Employment and Unemployment of Children in England, c. 1680–1851," *Past and Present*, 126 (1990): 115–150; Jordanova, "Conceptualizing." On mortality, see Lloyd Bonfield, Richard Smith, and Keith Wrightson, eds., *The World We Have Gained: Essays Presented to Peter Laslett* (Oxford: Blackwell, 1986); and Samuel H. Preston and Michael R. Haines, *Fatal Years: Child Mortality in Late Nineteenth-Century America* (Princeton: Princeton University Press, 1991). On leaving home, see especially Michael Mitterauer, "Servants and Youth," *Continuity and Change*, 5 (1990): 11–38; and essays by Richard Wall, "The Age at Leaving Home," *Journal of Family History*, 3 (1978): 181–202; "Leaving Home and the Process of Household Formation in Preindustrial England," *Continuity and Change*, 2 (1987): 77–101; and "Leaving Home and Living Alone: An Historical Perspective," *Population Studies*, 43 (1989): 369–389.

9. In addition to works previously cited, see Daniel Blake Smith, "Autonomy and Affection: Parents and Children in Eighteenth-Century Chesapeake Families," *Psychohistory Review*, 6 (1977): 32–51, among a very uneven literature.

10. See Viviana Zelizer, *Pricing the Priceless Child: The Changing Social Value of Children* (New York: Basic Books, 1985).

11. See also Carl Degler, *At Odds: Women and the Family in America* (New York: Oxford University Press, 1980); John D'Emilio and Estelle Freedman, *Intimate Matters: A History of Sexuality in America* (New York: Harper and Row, 1988); John Gillis, *For Better, For Worse: British Marriages, 1600 to the Present* (New York: Oxford University Press, 1985).

12. See, among the large but sometimes unreliable literature, Bonfield et al., *World We Have Gained*; Preston and Haines, *Fatal Years*; E. A. Wrigley and R. S. Schofield, *Population History of England, 1541–1871: A Reconstruction* (Cambridge, Mass.: Harvard University Press, 1981); and the many essays on American history by Daniel Scott Smith and Maris Vinovskis. In *The Kindness of Strangers: The Abandonment of Children in Western Europe from Late Antiquity to the Renaissance* (New York: Pantheon, 1988), John Boswell offers some original perspectives.

13. See Keith Thomas, "Age and Authority in Early Modern England," *Proceedings of the British Academy,* 62 (1976): 205–248, among the relevant literature.

14. See Cunningham, "Employment" and *Children;* Jordanova, "Conceptualizing."

15. See, for example, Peter Laslett, *The World We Have Lost: England before the Industrial Era,* 3d ed. rev. (New York: Scribners, 1984); Morgan, *Puritan Family.*

16. A developing literature on migration in early modern Europe, some of which attends to life course mobility, some of it focused on apprentices, includes Wall, "Age," and "Leaving Home"; and Mitterauer, "Servants"; Peter Clark and David Souden, eds., *Migration and Society in Early Modern England* (London: Hutchinson, 1987); A. L. Beier, *Masterless Men: The Vagrancy Problem in England, 1560–1640* (London: Methuen, 1985); Ann Kussmaul, *Servants in Husbandry in Early Modern England* (Cambridge: Cambridge University Press, 1981); Leslie Page Moch, *Moving Europeans: Migration in Western Europe since 1650* (Bloomington: Indiana University Press, 1992).

17. For surveys, see Joseph M. Hawes and N. Ray Hiner, eds., *American Childhood: A Research Guide and Historical Handbook* (Westport, Conn.: Greenwood, 1985), and *Children in Historical and Comparative Perspective: An International Handbook and Research Guide* (Westport, Conn.: Greenwood, 1991); Harvey J. Graff, ed., *Growing Up in America: Historical Experiences* (Detroit: Wayne State University Press, 1987), and "The History of Childhood and Youth: Beyond Infancy?," *History of Education Quarterly,* 26 (1986): 95–109; Harry Hendrick, "The History of Childhood and Youth," *Social History,* 9 (1984): 87–96; Pollock, *Forgotten Children.*

18. Good examples of these differences include work previously cited, by Bruce Bellingham, Carolyn Steedman, Ludmilla Jordanova, and Hugh Cunningham; see also Christine Stansell, "Women, Children and the Uses of the Streets: Class and Gender Conflicts in New York City, 1850–1860," *Feminist Studies,* 8 (1982): 309–335; Joan Jacobs Brumberg, "Chlorotic Girls, 1870–1920: A Historical Perspective on Female Adolescence," *Child Development,* 53 (1982): 1468–77; Carolyn Steedman, *Landscape for a Good Woman: A Study of Two Lives* (London: Routledge, 1987).

19. For girls and young women, examples include Joseph Kett, *Rites of Passage: Adolescence in America, 1790 to the Present* (New York: Basic Books, 1977); Carroll Smith-Rosenberg, "Puberty to Menopause: The Cycle of Femininity in Nineteenth-Century America," *Feminist Studies,* 1 (1973): 58–72. For a different view, see Brumberg, "Chlorotic Girls"; Jane H. Hunter, "Inscribing the Self in the Heart of the Family: Diaries and Girlhood in Late-Victorian America," *American Quarterly,* 44 (1992): 51–81. Both Brumberg and Hunter are at work on book-length studies of female growing up.

20. Although I do not pursue the topic here, "missing paths" might be sketched in part from a combination of secondary sources such as accessible personal, folkloric, or literary materials and letters for African, Asian, Hispanic, and

Native American young people and some immigrant groups. The need for new research on all missing paths is great.

21. Among important examples, see Skolnick, "The Limits"; Denise Riley, *War in the Nursery: Theories of the Child and Mother* (London: Virago, 1983). A critical historical literature on child and adolescent psychology, psychologists and advice literature, and psychologists' relationships with both parents and children is developing. See Margo Horn, *Before It's Too Late: The Child Guidance Movement in the United States, 1922–1945* (Philadelphia: Temple University Press, 1989); Theresa R. Richardson, *The Century of the Child: The Mental Hygiene Movement and Social Policy in the United States and Canada* (Albany: SUNY Press, 1989); Julia Wrigley, "Do Young Children Need Intellectual Stimulations? Experts' Advice to Parents, 1900–1985," *History of Education Quarterly,* 29 (1989): 41–75; Alison Clarke-Stewart, "Popular Primers for Parents," *American Psychologist,* 33 (1978): 359–369; Nancy Pottishman Weiss, "The Mother-Child Dyad Revisited: Perceptions of Mothers and Children in Twentieth-Century Child-Rearing Manuals," *Journal of Social Issues,* 34 (1978): 29–45.

22. See, for example, Norman Kiell, *The Universal Experience of Adolescence* (1964; rpt., Boston: Beacon, 1967); see also Pollock, *Forgotten Children.* Contrast with cited works by Arlene Skolnick, Joseph Adelson, Aaron Esman, Elizabeth Douvan and Adelson, *The Adolescent Experience* (New York: Wiley, 1966), and many historical works.

23. These trends parallel neatly those regarding *mentalité* in cultural history. See, by J. M. Tanner, "Sequence, Tempo, and Individual Variation in the Growth and Development of Boys and Girls Aged Twelve to Sixteen," *Daedalus,* 100 (Fall 1971): 907–931; *Growth at Adolescence,* 2d ed. (Oxford: Blackwell, 1962); and "Growing Up," *Scientific American,* 229 (1973): 34–43. See also Laslett, *Family Life;* Pollock, *Forgotten Children;* the massive comparative historical study of changes in mortality, height, weight, and nutrition directed by Robert Fogel and Roderick Floud; Richard Steckel's research on slaves in the American South; Vern Bullough's studies of age at menarche; and Herbert Moller, "Voice Change in Human Biological Development," *Journal of Interdisciplinary History,* 16 (1985): 239–253, and "The Accelerated Development of Youth: Beard Growth as a Biological Marker," *Comparative Studies in Society and History,* 29 (1987): 748–762. The *Journal of Interdisciplinary History* has published several special issues relevant to these subjects.

24. For one introduction, see Pollock, *Forgotten Children;* see also Peter Smith, "Biological, Psychological, and Historical Aspects of Reproduction and Child-Care," in *Animal Models and Human Behaviour,* ed. G. Davey (London: John Wiley, 1983); Martin Richard and Paul Light, eds., *Children of Social Worlds* (Cambridge, Mass.: Harvard University Press, 1986); Martin Richard, ed., *The Integration of a Child into a Social World* (Cambridge: Cambridge University Press, 1974).

25. Boswell, *The Kindness of Strangers,* pp. 26, 25–26, 27–33, 35–36.

26. Among the literature, see Jay Mechling, "Advice to Historians on Advice to Mothers," *Journal of Social History,* 9 (1975): 44–63; Daniel Calhoun, *The Intelligence of a People* (Princeton: Princeton University Press, 1973); and see works in note 21.

27. For the early modern period, see, in addition to Ariès and his critics, Keith Thomas, "Authority and Age," and "Children in Early Modern England," in *Children and Their Books,* ed. Gillian Avery and Julia Briggs (Oxford: Oxford University Press, 1989), pp. 45–77; for the more modern era, see Kett, *Rites,* and Chudacoff, *How Old Are You?,* among an uneven literature.

28. Boswell ironically risks committing the same fallacies for which he rightly criticizes Ariès and others. His sense of normative succession from stage to stage risks reifying narrow social psychologies. See Skolnick, "Limits," among the literature.

29. Boswell, *Kindness,* pp. 35–36.

30. See Michael Mitterauer and Reinhard Sieder, *The European Family: Patriarchy to Partnership from the Middle Ages to the Present,* trans. Karla Oosterveen and Manfred Hörzinger (Oxford: Blackwell, 1982); and Michael Mitterauer, *A History of Youth,* trans. Graeme Dunphey (Oxford: Blackwell, 1992). Compare with Lutz Berkner, "The Stem Family and the Developmental Cycle of the Peasant Household: An Eighteenth-Century Austrian Example," *American Historical Review,* 77 (1973), or Hanawalt, *Ties That Bound.*

31. Jenny Kitzinger, "Defending Innocence: Ideologies of Childhood," *Feminist Review,* 28 (1988): 79–80. See, among the literature, Joel Best, *Threatened Children: Rhetoric and Concern about Child-Victims* (Chicago: University of Chicago Press, 1990); Ian Hacking, "The Making and Molding of Child Abuse," *Critical Inquiry,* 17 (1991): 253–288; D. Kelly Weisberg, "The 'Discovery' of Sexual Abuse: Experts' Role in Legal Policy Formation," *University of California at Davis Law Review,* 18 (1984): 1–57; Arlene Skolnick, "Limits."

32. See the work of Paul Willis, *Learning to Labour* (Westmead: Saxon House, 1977); also John Hagan, "Destiny and Drift: Subcultural Preferences, Status Attainments, and the Risks and Rewards of Youth," *American Sociological Review,* 56 (1991): 567–582, on class and juvenile delinquency. Other works speak more directly to female offenders.

33. On myths of modern adolescence, see previously cited works by Aaron Esman, Joseph Adelson, Elizabeth Douvan, Ira Schwartz. For partial histories, see Joseph Kett, *Rites;* John Gillis, *Youth in History: Tradition and Change in European Age Relations, 1770–Present,* rev. ed. (New York: Academic Press, 1981); John Modell, *Into One's Own: From Youth to Adulthood in the United States, 1920–1975* (Berkeley: University of California Press, 1989); Hugh Cunningham, *Children of the Poor;* John Springhill, *Coming of Age: Adolescence in Britain, 1860–1960* (Dublin: Gill and Macmillan, 1986); James Gilbert, *A Cycle of Outrage: America's Reaction to the Juvenile Delinquent in the 1950s* (New York: Oxford University Press, 1986); William Graebner, *Coming of Age in Buffalo: Youth and Authority in the Postwar Era* (Philadelphia: Temple University Press, 1988).

34. Richard N. Coe, *When the Grass Was Taller: Autobiography and the Experience of Growing Up* (New Haven: Yale University Press, 1984), p. 109 and passim; Patricia Meyer Spacks, *The Adolescent Idea: Myths of Youth and the Adult Imagination* (New York: Basic Books, 1981).

35. See Jerome Kagan and Howard Moss, *Birth to Maturity: A Study in Psychological Development* (1962; rpt., New Haven: Yale University Press, 1983); Chad Gordon, "Social Characteristics of Early Adolescence," *Daedalus*, 100 (1971): 931–960.

36. Ludmilla Jordanova, "Fantasy and History in the Study of Childhood," *Free Association*, 2 (1985): 111. See also, by Christopher Lasch, *Haven in a Heartless World* (New York: Basic Books, 1977); *The Culture of Narcissism* (New York: Norton, 1978); and the response he stimulated.

37. Douglas W. Maynard, "On the Functions of Social Conflict among Children," *American Sociological Review*, 50 (1985): 207–223.

38. Valerie Walkerdine, "On the Regulation of Speaking and Silence," in *Language, Gender, and Childhood,* ed. Carolyn Steedman, Cathy Urwin, and Valerie Walkerdine (London: Routledge and Kegan Paul, 1985), p. 229.

39. Race properly forms a trinity of elemental historical social forces and structures with class and gender. For reasons discussed in Chapter 1, race is only occasionally a subject of this book.

40. Mihaly Csikszentmihalyi and Reed Larsen, *Being Adolescent: Conflict and Growth in the Teenage Years* (New York: Basic Books, 1984). More broadly, see Jerome Kagan and Howard Moss, *Birth to Maturity;* Michael Cole and Sylvia Scribner, *Culture and Thought* (New York: Wiley, 1974); Richard Shweder and Robert Levine, eds., *Culture Theory: Essays on Mind, Self, and Emotion* (Cambridge: Cambridge University Press, 1984); Richard Shweder, *Thinking through Cultures* (Cambridge, Mass.: Harvard University Press, 1991); Barbara Rogoff and Jean Lave, eds., *Everyday Cognition* (Cambridge, Mass.: Harvard University Press, 1984); Robert Sternberg and Richard Wagner, eds., *Practical Intelligence* (Cambridge: Cambridge University Press, 1986); Glen Elder, "Families and Lives: Some Developments in Life-Course Studies," *Journal of Family History*, 12 (1987): 179–199; Marlis Buchmann, *The Script of Life in Modern Society: Entry into Adulthood in a Changing World* (Chicago: University of Chicago Press, 1989); Paul Baltes and Orville G. Brim, eds., *Life-Span Development and Behavior* (New York: Academic Press, 1979); Martin Kohli and John W. Meyer, eds., "Social Structure and Social Construction of Life Stages," *Human Development*, 29 (1986): 145–180; Aage Sorenson, Franz Weinert, and Lonnie Sherrod, eds., *Human Development and the Life Course: Multidisciplinary Perspectives* (Hillsdale, N.J.: Lawrence Erlbaum Associates, 1986).

41. Csikszentmihalyi and Larsen, *Being Adolescent,* p. 4.

42. Ibid., pp. 11–12, 167, 12.

43. Anne Foner, "Age Stratification and the Changing Family," in *Turning Points: Historical and Sociological Essays on the Family,* ed. John Demos and Sarane Spence Boocock (Chicago: University of Chicago Press, 1978), p. S347.

44. Ibid., p. S349.

45. Ibid., pp. S349, 350.
46. See Abigail J. Stewart, "The Course of Individual Adaptation to Life Changes," *Journal of Personality and Social Psychology,* 42 (1982): 1100–13; Abigail J. Stewart and Joseph M. Healey, Jr., "Linking Individual Development and Social Changes," *American Psychologist,* 44 (1989): 30–42.
47. Kirsten Drotner, *English Children and Their Magazines, 1751–1945* (New Haven: Yale University Press, 1988), p. 4.
48. See Mary P. Ryan, *Cradle of the Middle Class: The Family in Oneida County, New York, 1790–1865* (Cambridge: Cambridge University Press, 1981); on English middle-class formation, see Leonore Davidoff and Catherine Hall, *Family Fortunes: Men and Women of the English Middle Class, 1780–1850* (London: Hutchinson, 1987).
49. Drotner, *English Children,* pp. 45, 47. See also Cunningham, *Children;* Steedman, Urwin, and Walkerdine, *Language;* Ryan, *Cradle.*
50. Compare Drotner's formulation in *English Children* with Jan Radway, *Reading the Romance: Women, Patriarchy, and Popular Literature* (Chapel Hill: University of North Carolina Press, 1984), and with studies of Victorian and Edwardian English girls, including Joan Burstyn, *Victorian Education and the Ideal of Womanhood* (London: Croom Helm, 1980); Deborah Gorham, *The Victorian Girl and the Feminine Ideal* (Bloomington: Indiana University Press, 1982); Judith Rowbotham, *Good Girls Make Good Wives: Guidance for Girls in Victorian Fiction* (Oxford: Blackwell, 1989); Felicity Hunt, ed., *Lessons for Life: The Schooling of Girls and Women, 1850–1950* (Oxford: Blackwell, 1987); Carol Dyhouse, *Girls Growing Up in Late Victorian and Edwardian England* (London: Routledge and Kegan Paul, 1981).
51. Drotner, *English Children,* p. 83 and passim.
52. Ibid., p. 135 and passim.
53. Among an important and growing literature, see Christine Stansell, *City of Women: Sex and Class in New York, 1789–1860* (New York: Knopf, 1986). For an argument that different cultural groups have different forms of competence, see John Ogbu, "Origins of Human Competence: A Cultural-Ecological Approach," *Child Development,* 52 (1981): 413–429; see also Shweder, *Thinking through Cultures;* Shweder and Levine, *Culture Theory.*
54. Buchmann, *Script of Life,* pp. 69–70. See also John Modell, Frank F. Furstenberg, and Theodore Hershberg, "Social Change and Transitions to Adulthood in Historical Perspective," *Journal of Family History,* 1 (1976): 7–33; Modell, *Into One's Own;* Glen Elder, "Families and Lives," among his essays; John S. Clausen, "Adolescent Competence and the Shaping of the Life Course," *American Journal of Sociology,* 96 (1991): 805–842; and the life course literature previously cited.
55. Buchmann, *Script of Life,* p. 77. Compare with Modell, *Into One's Own;* Modell, Furstenberg, and Hershberg, "Social Change"; see also Chapter 6.
56. Francis Ianni, *The Search for Structure: A Report on American Youth Today* (New York: Free Press, 1989), p. 7. On early adolescence, see Tanner, "Sequence, Tempo." There are parallels for childhood; see, for example, Baltes and Brim, *Life-Span Development;* Matilda White-Riley et al., *Aging and*

Society, 3 vols. (New York: Russell Sage Foundation, 1968–1972); John Bongaarts, Thomas K. Burch, and Kenneth W. Wachter, eds., *Family Demography: Methods and Their Applications* (Oxford: Oxford University Press, 1987). Among "stage" notions, Stuart T. Hause with Sally I. Powers and Gil G. Noam, in *Adolescents and Their Families: Pathos of Ego Development* (New York: Free Press, 1991), posit as ego stages profound arrest, steady conformist, progressive, accelerated, moratorium, and regressive. From a very different basis, Ruth Sidel, in *On Her Own: Growing Up in the Shadow of the American Dream* (New York: Viking, 1990), proposes for contemporary girls paths she titles "New American Dreamers," "Neotraditionalists," and "Outsiders." See Clausen, "Adolescent Competence"; Ellen Greenberger and Laurence Steinberg, *When Teenagers Work: The Psychological and Social Costs of Adolescents* (New York: Basic Books, 1986).

57. Ianni, *Search,* p. 15. See also the classic sociological studies of communities from Middletown to Elmtown and River City, the West End, and Crestwood Heights. They are rich sources of description.

58. Ianni, *Search,* p. 19.

59. Tamara K. Hareven, *Family Time and Industrial Time: Family and Work in a New England Industrial Community* (Cambridge: Cambridge University Press, 1982); Hareven, ed., *Transitions: The Family and the Life Course in Historical Perspective* (New York: Academic Press, 1978); Elder, "Adolescence"; "Families and Lives"; "Family History and the Life Course," in Hareven, *Transitions,* pp. 17–64; and "History and the Family: The Discovery of Complexity," *Journal of Family History,* 6 (1981): 489–519; also Demos and Boocock, *Turning Points,* among a growing literature.

60. See Baltes and Brim, *Life-Span Development and Behavior;* John Clausen, *The Life Course* (Englewood Cliffs, N.J.: Prentice Hall, 1986); David Featherman, "Life-Span Perspectives in Social Science Research," in *Life Span Development and Behavior,* ed. Paul Baltes (New York: Academic Press, 1983), 5:1–57. See also Anne Foner, "Ascribed and Achieved Bases of Stratification," *Annual Review of Sociology,* 5 (1979): 219–242; Dennis Hogan, *Transitions and Social Change: The Early Lives of American Men* (New York: Academic Press, 1981); Dennis Hogan and Nan Marie Astone, "The Transition to Adulthood," *Annual Review of Sociology,* 12 (1986): 109–130. Major historical studies have been conducted by Hareven, Glen Elder, John Modell, and Avery Guest et al. See now Glen Elder, John Modell, and Ross Parke, eds., *Children in Time and Place* (New York: Cambridge University Press, 1993).

61. On age, generation, and the like, see, for example, Riley, "Aging, Social Change, and the Power of Ideas," *Daedalus,* 107 (1978): 39–52, or the anthologies and collective works edited by Riley and/or David Kertzer.

62. Glen Elder, "Introduction," in Hareven, *Transitions,* pp. 21–22; emphasis added.

63. David Featherman, "Life-Span Perspectives in Social Science Research," in Baltes, *Life-Span Development and Behavior,* 5:1; emphasis added.

64. For example, Charlotte Hohn writes, "A typology of a maximum of 40 and

a minimum of 12 life courses is suggested"; see "The Family Life Cycle: Needed Extensions of the Concept," in Bongaarts, Burch, and Wachter, *Family Demography.* See also Gaynor Cohen, ed., *Social Change and the Life Course* (London: Tavistock, 1987).

65. Buchmann, *Script of Life,* p. 2 and passim.

66. Summary information on this database appears in the appendix. This appendix also discusses research strategy and design. The collection encompasses manuscript and printed materials, unpublished and published, predominantly archival with some items donated or loaned in response to a letter of solicitation published in the *New York Review of Books.* Lack of comparable data and missing variables from source to source across the collection preclude sophisticated numerical analysis (which I had hoped to conduct at least in small part when I created a dBaseIII+ database for the collection). Nevertheless, the average values by time and sex, as the appendix shows, fall well within the expected ranges.

67. Some historians and other students of the young do explore the nineteenth century. But by and large, despite other contributions, they tend to follow the usual view in considering youth in the twentieth century a separate period. See, for example, the previously cited collections edited by Joseph Hawes and N. Ray Hiner, and also the work of, among others, Joseph Kett and John Demos. Modern social science takes this historical tendency to a fault in its overattention to the present or very recent past. For an anthology that tries to right the balance, see my *Growing Up in America: Historical Experiences* (Detroit: Wayne State University Press, 1987). On G. Stanley Hall, see especially Dorothy Ross, *G. Stanley Hall* (Chicago: University of Chicago Press, 1972).

68. In this book, with only a few qualifications, the story begins with eighteenth-century America. There is an important European, English, and North American background that is much more than a prehistory. Despite the undoubted importance of that history, this work lacks the space to treat its complexity.

69. On age awareness, see Howard Chudacoff, *How Old Are You?*; Kett, *Rites.* See also, among major interpretations, Michael B. Katz *The People of Hamilton, Canada West: Family and Class in a Mid-Nineteenth-Century City* (Cambridge, Mass.: Harvard University Press, 1975); Michael B. Katz, Michael Doucet, and Mark Stern, *The Social Organization of Early Industrial Capitalism* (Cambridge, Mass.: Harvard University Press, 1982).

70. See the important criticisms by Joan W. Scott, "The Evidence of Experience," *Critical Inquiry,* 17 (1991): 773–792. Scott's concern lies with "difference" in ways that overlap but also diverge from mine in this book. Among her most trenchant observations is: "Questions about the constructed nature of experience, about how subjects are constituted as different in the first place, about how one's vision is structured—about language (or discourse) and history—are left aside. The evidence of experience then becomes evidence for the fact of difference, rather than a way of exploring how difference is established, how it operates, how and in what ways it constitutes subjects who see and act in the world" (p. 777).

71. William Sewell, Jr., "How Classes Are Made: Critical Reflections on E. P. Thompson's Theory of Working-Class Formation," in *E. P. Thompson: Critical Perspectives,* ed. Harvey J. Kaye and Keith McClelland (Philadelphia: Temple University Press, 1990), p. 64 and passim. See also Scott, "Evidence."

72. Sewell, "How Classes Are Made" p. 64; see also Scott, "Evidence," p. 797 and passim. Scott advocates "working" with "experience": "This entails focussing on processes of identity production, insisting on the discursive nature of 'experience' and on the politics of its construction. Experience is at once always already an interpretation *and* something that needs to be interpreted. What counts as experience is neither self-evident nor straightforward; it is always contested, and always therefore political. The study of experience, therefore, must call into question its originary status in historical explanation" (p. 797).

73. Consult the appendix for further information on the research design and the collection of primary sources. In "Using First-Person Sources in Social and Cultural History," *Historical Methods,* 27 (1994): 87–92, I present a critical bibliography on first-person sources and a list of other major studies based on first-person testimonial sources. I refer interested readers there.

74. For a select bibliography of critical works on autobiography and other first-person writing, see ibid. Especially useful is recent work from feminist perspectives. See, for example, "Autobiography and Biography: Special Issue," *Gender and History,* 2 (Spring 1990); Susan Groag Bell and Marilyn Yalom, eds., *Revealing Lives: Autobiography, Biography, and Gender* (Albany: SUNY Press, 1990); Mary Jean Corbett, *Representing Femininity: Middle-Class Subjectivity in Victorian and Edwardian Women's Autobiographies* (New York: Oxford University Press, 1992); Margo Culley, ed., *American Women's Autobiography: Fea(s)ts of Memory* (Madison: University of Wisconsin Press, 1992); Regenia Gagnier, "Social Atoms: Working-Class Autobiography, Subjectivity, and Gender," *Victorian Studies,* 30 (1987): 335–364, and *Subjectivities: A History of Self-Representation in Britain, 1832–1920* (New York: Oxford University Press, 1991); Personal Narratives Group, ed., *Interpreting Women's Lives: Feminist Theory and Personal Narratives* (Bloomington: Indiana University Press, 1989).

75. On language, in addition to my "Using First-Person Sources" and the sources cited in note 74, see, for example, M. J. Maynes, "Adolescent Sexuality and Social Identity in French and German Lower-Class Autobiography," *Journal of Family History,* 17 (1992): 397–418, and "The Contours of Childhood: Demography, Strategy, and Mythology of Childhood in French and German Lower-Class Autobiographies," in *The European Experience of Declining Fertility,* ed. Louise Tilly, John Gillis, and David Levine (Cambridge, Mass.: Blackwell, 1992), pp. 101–124; Steven Mintz, *A Prison of Expectations: The Family in Victorian Culture* (New York: New York University Press, 1983); Steven M. Stowe, *Intimacy and Power in the Old South; Ritual in the Lives of the Planters* (Baltimore: Johns Hopkins University Press, 1987); and articles in *Feminist Studies* and *Journal of American History.* In the chapters

based on first-person sources, I indicate whenever possible at what points in the life course the accounts were created. Obviously there is no vantage point without bias. Not attempted systematically in this book but nonetheless an important task is a historical examination of the rhetoric or discourse of growing up. See, on these and related issues, previously cited works by Bruce Bellingham, Jane Hunter, Jan Kociumbas, Ludmilla Jordanova, Carolyn Steedman, and Hugh Cunningham; and Howard Chudacoff, *How Old Are You?*

76. See the bibliographies in Graff, "Using First-Person Sources." I also recognize the limits of a focus on literary texts and their problems for social and cultural history, a large subject in itself. For key points, see the special section of *Social Science History,* 16.3 (Fall 1992), ed. William H. Sewell, Jr., with essays by George Steinmetz and M. J. Maynes; see also M. J. Maynes, "Adolescent Sexuality."

77. The critical literature in oral history is useful here. Some of it is cited in my "Using First-Person Sources."

78. See Daniel Bertaux, ed., *Biography and Society: The Life History Approach in the Social Sciences* (Beverly Hills: Sage, 1981); Paul Thompson, ed., *Our Common History: The Transformation of Europe* (London: Pluto Press, 1982); Michael Frisch, *A Shared Authority* (Albany: SUNY Press, 1990); William H. Sewell, Jr., ed., "Narrative Analysis in Social Science History," *Social Science History,* 16, 3 (Fall 1992); 16, 4 (Winter 1993).

79. Nicole Gagnon, "On the Analysis of Life Accounts," in Bertaux, *Biography and Society,* pp. 53, 55.

80. Steedman, *Landscape for a Good Woman,* is a superb example; see also citations in my "Using Personal Sources."

81. In recent years historians, along with literary critics, philosophers, and some social scientists, have become deeply interested in how "meaning" is made and communicated. From a large and rich body of writing, see, among many others, works by Hayden White, Dominic LaCapra, Carlo Ginzburg, Natalie Zemon Davis, Clifford Geertz, George Marcus, James Clifford, Lynn Hunt, and Joan Scott.

82. These include innovative scholarship by Paul Thompson on Edwardian English society and on fishing people, Thea Thompson on Edwardian children, David Vincent on the English working class, Jeanne Peterson and others on English families and women, Lee Chambers-Schiller on unmarried American women, Carroll Smith-Rosenberg on middle-class girls and women, Ellen K. Rothman on courting couples, Steven Stowe on antebellum southerners, Anthony Rotundo on middle-class boys and men, and a number of studies of immigrants and workers. Noteworthy ongoing projects, including oral histories, include M. J. Maynes's study of French and German working-class autobiographers, Neil Sutherland's oral history of Canadian children in the twentieth century, Paul Thompson's Essex University Edwardian England project, and others. See also my "Using First-Person Sources."

83. Tim Keegan, *Facing the Storm: Portraits of Black Lives in Rural South Africa* (Athens: Ohio University Press, 1988), p. 151.

2. First Steps in the Eighteenth Century

1. For an introduction to issues and questions concerning this period, see, for example, Keith Thomas, "Children in Early Modern England," in *Children and Their Books: A Celebration of the Work of Iona and Peter Opie,* ed. Gillian Avery and Julia Briggs (Oxford: Oxford University Press, 1989), pp. 41–77. See also notes to the preface and Chapter 1.

2. Recent interpretations of this era include James Henretta, "The Transition to Capitalism in America," in *The Transformation of Early American History,* ed. James Henretta, Michael Kammen, and Stanley N. Katz (New York: Knopf, 1991), pp. 218–238; Daniel Vickers, "Competency and Competition: Economic Culture in Early America," *William and Mary Quarterly,* 47 (1990): 3–29; Allan Kulikoff, "The Transition to Capitalism in Rural America," *William and Mary Quarterly,* 46 (1989): 120–144; Gregory Nobles, "Breaking into the Backcountry: New Approaches to the Early American Frontier, 1750–1800," *William and Mary Quarterly,* 46 (1989): 641–670.

3. Henretta, "Transition," pp. 220–221.

4. Vickers, "Competency," p. 12.

5. Kulikoff, "Transition," pp. 137–138.

6. Henretta, "Transition," p. 223; Vickers, "Competency."

7. Vickers, "Competency," p. 28.

8. See, for an example of early death, "Diary of a Little Colonial Girl [Sally Cary Fairfax, 1771–72]," *Virginia Historical Magazine,* 11 (1903–4): 212–214. For a northern example, see Alice Morse Earle, ed., *Diary of Anna Green Winslow. A Boston School Girl of 1771* (Boston: Houghton Mifflin, 1894).

9. Important studies that offer numerical data on mortality include Samuel Preston and Michael Haines, *Fatal Years: Child Mortality in Late Nineteenth-Century America* (Princeton: Princeton University Press, 1991); Daniel Scott Smith, "The Estimates of Early American Historical Demographers: Two Steps Forward, One Step Back, What Steps in the Future?" *Historical Methods,* 12 (1979): 24–38; Robert William Fogel, "Nutrition and the Decline in Mortality since 1700: Some Preliminary Findings," in *Long-Term Trends in American Economic Growth,* ed. Stanley L. Engerman and Robert E. Gallman (Chicago: University of Chicago Press, 1986), pp. 439–555; Maris A. Vinovskis, *Fertility in Massachusetts from the Revolution to the Civil War* (New York: Academic Press, 1981); Darrett B. Rutman and Anita H. Rutman, *A Place in Time: Middlesex County, Virginia, 1650–1750* (New York: Norton, 1984); Lorena S. Walsh and Russell R. Menard, "Death in the Chesapeake: Two Life Tables for Men in Early Colonial Maryland," *Maryland Historical Magazine,* 49 (1974): 211–227; Susan E. Klepp, "Fragmented Knowledge: Questions in Regional Demographic History," *Proceedings of the American Philosophical Society,* 133 (1989). On possible impacts of high mortality on child rearing, see Daniel Blake Smith, "Mortality and Family in the Colonial Chesapeake," *Journal of Interdisciplinary History,* 8

(1978): 403–427; Maris A. Vinovskis, "Angels' Heads and Weeping Willows: Death in Early America," *Proceedings of the American Antiquarian Society,* 86 (1976): 273–302.

10. A literature of fake early salvations also existed. Irene Brown and Richard Brown, University of Connecticut, told me about this genre at a 1989 seminar at the American Antiquarian Society. See also Joanna Bowen Gillespie, "'The Clear Leadings of Providence': Pious Memoirs and the Problems of Self-Realization for Women in the Early Nineteenth Century," *Journal of the Early Republic,* 5 (1985): 197–221, among the literature.

11. See Chapter 1 for discussion of the problem of "missing paths."

12. Among historians of women and gender these issues are debated instructively. See the pages of *Journal of Women's History* and *Gender and History,* as well as, in *Feminist Studies,* Iris Berger, Elsa Barkley Brown, and Nancy A. Hewitt, "Symposium: Intersections and Collision Courses: Women, Blacks, and Workers Confront Gender, Race, and Class," 18 (1992): 283–327; Linda K. Kerber, "Forum: Separate Spheres, Female Worlds, Woman's Place: The Rhetoric of History," *Journal of American History,* 75 (1988): 9–39; Linda Kerber et al., "Beyond Roles, Beyond Spheres: Thinking about Gender in the Early Republic," *William and Mary Quarterly,* 46 (1989): 565–585.

13. See, on these experiences, Joseph Kett, "Adolescence and Youth in Nineteenth-Century America," *Journal of Interdisciplinary History,* 2 (1971): 283–298; "Growing Up in Rural New England, 1800–1840," in *Anonymous Americans,* ed. Tamara K. Hareven (Englewood Cliffs, N.J.: Prentice Hall, 1971), pp. 1–16; *Rites of Passage: Adolescence in America, 1790 to the Present* (New York: Basic Books, 1977).

14. See Joseph Kett, "Curing the Disease of Precocity," in *Turning Points: Historical and Sociological Essays on the Family,* ed. John Demos and Sarane Boocock (Chicago: University of Chicago Press, 1978), S183–211.

15. See, on spinsters, Lee Virginia Chambers-Schiller, *Liberty, a Better Husband: Single Women in America. The Generation of 1780–1840* (New Haven: Yale University Press, 1984).

16. See, for example, for overviews, Mary Beth Norton, "The Evolution of White Women's Experience in Early America," *American Historical Review,* 89 (1984): 593–619; Nancy Cott, *The Bonds of Womanhood: "Women's Sphere" in New England, 1785–1835* (New Haven: Yale University Press, 1977).

17. Recent literature on increasing commercialism in this period is rich if preliminary. See James A. Henretta, "Families and Farms: *Mentalité* in Pre-Industrial America," *William and Mary Quarterly,* 35 (1979): 3–32; James Lemon, "Comment," and James Henretta, "Reply," ibid.: 688–700; James Lemon, "Early Americans and Their Social Environment," *Journal of Historical Geography,* 6 (1980): 115–131; Michael B. Katz, Michael Doucet, and Mark Stern, *The Social Organization of Early Industrial Capitalism* (Cambridge, Mass.: Harvard University Press, 1982); Mary P. Ryan, *Cradle of the Middle Class: The Family in Oneida County, New York, 1790–1865* (Cambridge: Cambridge University Press, 1981); Sean Wilentz, *Chants Democratic: New York City and the Rise of the American Working Class, 1788–*

1850 (New York: Oxford University Press, 1984); Steven Hahn and Jonathan Prude, eds., *The Countryside in the Age of Capitalist Transformation* (Chapel Hill: University of North Carolina Press, 1985); Steven Innes, ed., *Work and Labor in Early America* (Chapel Hill: University of North Carolina Press, 1988).

18. On the transformation of dependency, semidependency or semiautonomy, and autonomy in growing up, see Michael B. Katz, *The People of Hamilton, Canada West: Family and Class in a Mid-Nineteenth-Century City* (Cambridge, Mass.: Harvard University Press, 1975); Katz et al., *Social Organization; Kett, Rites;* Harvey J. Graff, "Patterns of Adolescence and Child Dependency in the Mid-Nineteenth-Century City," *History of Education Quarterly,* 13 (1973): 129–143; idem, "Early Adolescence in Antebellum America: The Remaking of Growing Up," *Journal of Early Adolescence,* 5 (1985): 411–427; idem, "Remaking Growing Up: Nineteenth-Century America," *Histoire sociale/Social History,* 24 (1991): 35–59.

19. Samuel West, Memoirs, 1807, Mss., American Antiquarian Society; subsequent citations appear in the text.

20. On families and child rearing, see Edmund Morgan, *The Puritan Family* (New York: Harper, 1965); Peter G. Slater, *Children in the New England Mind: In Death and Life* (Hamden, Conn.: Archon, 1977); Daniel Calhoun, *The Intelligence of a People* (Princeton: Princeton University Press, 1973); Philip Greven, Jr., *The Protestant Temperament* (New York: Knopf, 1977); Margaret J. M. Ezell, "John Locke's Images of Childhood," *Eighteenth-Century Studies,* 17 (1983–84): 139–155; E. Anthony Rotundo, *American Manhood* (New York: Basic Books, 1993); Robert L. Griswold, *Fatherhood in America* (New York: Basic Books, 1993).

21. In addition to works cited in note 20, see Bernard Wishy, *The Child and the Republic: The Dawn of Modern American Child Nurture* (Philadelphia: University of Pennsylvania Press, 1968); Ryan, *Cradle;* William McLoughlin, "Evangelical Child-Rearing in the Age of Jackson: Francis Wayland's Views on When and How to Subdue the Willfulness of Children," *Journal of Social History,* 9 (1975): 21–43; Charles Strickland, "A Transcendentalist Father: The Child-Rearing Practices of Bronson Alcott," *Perspectives in American History,* 3 (1969): 5–73. See also Jay Mechling, "Advice to Historians on Advice to Mothers," *Journal of Social History,* 9 (1975): 44–63.

22. On colonial colleges, see James Axtell, *The School upon a Hill: Education and Society in Colonial New England* (New Haven: Yale University Press, 1974); Lawrence Cremin, *American Education: The Colonial Experience* (New York: Harper and Row, 1970). Compare with David Allmendinger, *Paupers and Scholars: The Transformation of Student Life in Nineteenth-Century New England* (New York: St. Martins, 1975); Colin Burke, *American Collegiate Populations* (New York: New York University Press, 1982).

23. For an especially negative reaction to the common practice of temporary teaching, see Stephen Bemis, Papers, 1796–1813, January 1, 1797, American Antiquarian Society.

24. Alexander Graydon, *Memoirs of a Life, Chiefly Passed in Pennsylvania,*

Within the Last Sixty Years (Harrisburg: John Wyeth, 1811) (Newberry Library); subsequent citations appear in the text.

25. For another example of traditional career choices, see "Diary of Edward Hooker, 1803–1806," American Historical Association, *Annual Report,* 1 (1896): 824–929.

26. See Daniel Scott Smith, "Parental Power and Marriage Patterns: An Analysis of Historical Trends in Hingham, Massachusetts," *Journal of Marriage and the Family,* 35 (1973): 419–428; Peter D. Hall, *The Organization of American Culture: Institutions, Elites, and the Origins of American Nationality* (New York: New York University Press, 1982); Ronald Story, *The Forging of an Aristocracy: Harvard and Boston's Upper Class* (Middletown, Conn.: Wesleyan University Press, 1980); Edward Pessen, *Riches, Class, and Power before the Civil War* (Lexington, Mass.: D. C. Heath, 1973); William H. Pease and Jane H. Pease, *The Web of Progress: Private Values and Public Styles in Boston and Charleston, 1828–1842* (New York: Oxford University Press, 1985); Frederick Jaher, *The Urban Establishment* (Urbana: University of Illinois Press, 1982); and see E. Digby Baltzell's studies of Philadelphia and Boston.

27. See Greven's genteel mode of child-rearing in *Protestant Temperament.* Barry Levy, *Quakers and the American Family* (New York: Oxford University Press, 1988), offers interesting contrasts.

28. Lucille Griffith, ed., "English Education for Virginia Youths: Some Eighteenth-Century Ambler Family Letters," *Virginia Magazine of History and Biography,* 69 (1961): 8–26. Women of this class are discussed later in this chapter.

29. Compare with Ellen D. Larned, ed., "Yale Boys of the Last Century: The Journal of Elijah Backus Junior, at Yale College, from Jan ye first to Dec 31, 1777," *Connecticut Quarterly,* 1 (1895): 355–361. For a more prosaic teenage example, see Jonathan Hayward, "Diary (1800–1808)," *Danvers Historical Society Collections,* 2 (1915): 53–58.

30. See, for example, *Autobiography of Deacon John Thompson of Mercer, Maine, with Genealogical Notes of his Descendants.* Compiled by His Grandson Josiah M. Thompson in the Year 1920 (Farmington, Maine: Franklin Journal) (Newberry Library). Thompson's autobiography is presented in the form of letters.

31. James P. Collins, *Autobiography of a Revolutionary Soldier, Revised and Prepared by John M. Roberts, Esq.* (Clinton, La.: Feliciana Democrat Print, 1859)(Newberry Library); subsequent citations appear in the text. Neither Collins nor others who served while young during the Revolution, or many during the Civil War, considered their paths uniquely shaped by that experience. See, for example, *Elijah Fisher's Journal While in the War for Independence and Continued Two Years after He Came to Maine, 1775–1784* (Augusta: Press of Badger and Manley, 1880) (American Antiquarian Society).

32. On marriage, see Ellen K. Rothman, *Hands and Heart: A History of Court-*

ship in America (New York: Basic Books, 1984); for Canada, see Peter Ward, *Courtship, Love, and Marriage in Nineteenth-Century English Canada* (Montreal: McGill-Queens University Press, 1990), among a growing literature.

33. Ephraim Bacon, *Autobiography; A Narrative of the Principal Incidents in the Life of Ephraim Bacon* (Des Moines: N. W. Mills and Co., 1957); subsequent citations appear in the text.

34. Compare with Thompson, *Autobiography.*

35. Compare again with *Elijah Fisher's Journal.*

36. Ephraim Abbott, "Autobiography," 1779–1827, Mss. Papers, 1801–1904, American Antiquarian Society.

37. On schools in this period and region, see Cremin, *American Education;* Michael B. Katz, *The Irony of Early School Reform* (Cambridge, Mass.: Harvard University Press, 1968); idem, *Reconstructing American Education* (Cambridge, Mass.: Harvard University Press, 1987); Carl F. Kaestle and Maris Vinovskis, *Education and Social Change in Nineteenth-Century Massachusetts* (Cambridge: Cambridge University Press, 1980); Carl F. Kaestle, *Pillars of the Republic: Common Schools and American Society, 1780–1860* (New York: Hill and Wang, 1983).

38. Allmendinger, *Paupers;* Burke, *American Collegiate.* See also Donald Scott, *From Office to Profession* (Philadelphia: University of Pennsylvania Press, 1978).

39. On student life, see Steven J. Novak, *The Rights of Youth: American Colleges and Student Revolt, 1798–1815* (Cambridge, Mass.: Harvard University Press, 1977); James McLachlan, "The *Choice of Hercules:* American Student Societies in the Early Nineteenth Century," in *The University in Society,* vol. 2., ed. Lawrence Stone (Princeton: Princeton University Press, 1974), pp. 449–494; idem, "The American College in the Nineteenth Century: Toward a Reappraisal," *Teachers College Record,* 80 (1978); Kett, *Rites;* Allmendinger, *Paupers.*

40. On the courtship, see Rothman, *Hands and Hearts,* pp. 17–22.

41. On ages of leaving home, see Chapter 1.

42. On these patterns of growing up, see Kett, *Rites;* Calhoun, *Intelligence;* Ryan, *Cradle;* Joyce Appleby, "New Cultural Heroes in the Early National Period," in *The Culture of the Market: Historical Essays,* ed. Thomas L. Haskell and Richard F. Teichgraeber (Cambridge: Cambridge University Press, 1993), pp. 163–188; on careers, see Daniel Calhoun, *Professional Lives in America* (Cambridge, Mass.: Harvard University Press, 1965); on commerce, see Alan Horlick, *Country Boys and Merchant Princes: The Social Control of Young Men in New York* (Lewisburg, Pa.: Bucknell University Press, 1975); on the ministry, see Donald Scott, *From Office to Profession* (Philadelphia: University of Pennsylvania Press, 1978); on teachers, see Paul Mattingly, *The Classless Profession* (New York: New York University Press, 1975). On migration and mobility, Stephan Thernstrom, *Poverty and Progress* (Cambridge, Mass.: Harvard University Press, 1964), stimulated many studies; see, for example, Douglas Jones, *Village and Seaport* (Hanover,

N.H.: University Presses of New England, 1981); Katz et al., *Social Organization.*

43. "Diary of Archelaus Putnam of New Mills," *Danvers Historical Society Collections,* 4 (1916): 51–72; 5 (1917): 43–69; 6 (1918): 11–29.

44. "Journal of Ephraim Bateman," *Vineland Historical Magazine,* 13 (1928): 55–64, 80–89; 14 (1929): 106–114, 127–135, 154–162, 174–182; 15 (1930): 210–227, 238–246; subsequent citations appear in the text.

45. Charles D. Drake, ed., *Pioneer Life in Kentucky. A Series of Reminiscential Letters from Daniel Drake, M.D., of Cincinnati, to His Children* (Cincinnati: Robert Clarke & Co., 1870); subsequent citations appear in the text. See also Edward D. Mansfield, *Memoirs of the Life and Services of Daniel Drake, M.D., Physician, Professor, and Author; with Notices of the Early Settlement of Cincinnati and Some of Its Pioneer Citizens* (Cincinnati: Applegate and Co., 1855); Richard Wade, *The Urban Frontier* (New York: Oxford University Press, 1960), as well as more recent literature on Cincinnati, including Daniel Aaron's pioneering dissertation, "Cincinnati, Queen City of the West, 1819–1838" (Harvard University, 1940), published in 1992 by Ohio State University Press. The role of published recollections, reminscences, memoirs, letters, and so on in the cultural process of myth making merits direct study.

46. See Linda Kerber, *Women of the Republic: Intellect and Ideology in Revolutionary America* (Chapel Hill: University of North Carolina Press, 1980); Ruth Bloch, "American Feminine Ideals in Transition: The Rise of the Moral Mother, 1785–1815," *Feminist Studies,* 4 (1978): 101–126. For new work, see Jan Lewis, "Motherhood in the Construction of the Male Citizen in the United States, 1750–1850," in *Constructions of the Self,* ed. George Levine (New Brunswick, N.J.: Rutgers University Press, 1992), pp. 143–163, among her studies.

47. James E. Cronin, ed., *The Diary of Elihu Hubbard Smith (1771–1798)* (Philadelphia: American Philosophical Society, 1973); subsequent citations appear in the text.

48. For an interesting contrast, see "Diary of Alexander Anderson," *Old New York,* 1 (1889): 46–55, 85–93, 197–204, 233–253; 2 (1890): 84–105, 184–192, 217–226, 289–301, 428–436.

49. Douglas Adair, ed., "The Autobiography of the Reverend Devereux Jarrat, 1732–1763," *William and Mary Quarterly,* 9 (1952): 346–396; subsequent citations appear in the text. See also Rhys Isaac, *The Transformation of Virginia* (Chapel Hill: University of North Carolina Press, 1980); Harry S. Stout, "Religion, Communications, and the Ideological Origins of the American Revolution," *William and Mary Quarterly,* 34 (1977): 519–541. For young women, see Nancy Cott, "Young Women in the Second Great Awakening in New England," *Feminist Studies,* 3 (1975): 15–19; Ryan, *Cradle;* Greven, *Protestant Temperament;* Randolph Roth, *The Democratic Dilemma: Religion, Reform, and the Social Order in the Connecticut River Valley of Vermont, 1791–1850* (Cambridge: Cambridge University Press, 1987).

50. W. P. Strickland, ed., *Autobiography of Peter Cartwright, the Backwoods Preacher* (New York: Carlton and Porter, 1856) (Newberry Library); subsequent citations appear in the text.

51. For another example of religiosity's influence on growing up and work relations, see "John Baldwin's Diary; or Journal of Time," *Friend's Miscellany,* 5 (1834): 249–269.

52. See, by Elizabeth Kowaleski-Wallace, *Their Father's Daughters: Hannah More, Maria Edgeworth, and Patriarchal Complicity* (Oxford: Oxford University Press, 1991), and "Milton's Daughters: The Education of Eighteenth-Century Women Writers," *Feminist Studies,* 12 (1986): 275–293, on eighteenth-century England; for the United States, see previously cited works by Ruth Bloch, Linda Kerber, Jan Lewis, and Mary Beth Norton.

53. See, for example, Carroll Smith-Rosenberg, "Puberty to Menopause: The Cycle of Femininity in Nineteenth-Century America," in *Clio's Consciousness Raised,* ed. Mary Hartman and Lois Banner (New York: Harper and Row, 1974), pp. 23–37. See Mary Beth Norton's review of Kett, *Rites,* in *Reviews in American History,* 6 (1978): 171–177; also Joseph Hawes, "The Strange History of Female Adolescence in the United States," *Psychohistory Review,* 13 (1985): 51–64.

54. See John Gillis, *For Better, For Worse: British Marriages, 1600 to the Present* (New York: Oxford University Press, 1985). There is no U.S. work like this, but see Rothman, *Hands and Hearts;* Carroll Smith-Rosenberg, *Disorderly Conduct: Visions of Gender in Victorian America* (New York: Knopf, 1985); Carl N. Degler, *At Odds: Women and the Family in America from the Revolution to the Present* (New York: Oxford University Press, 1980); compare with Chambers-Schiller, *Liberty, a Better Husband;* John D'Emilio and Estelle Freedman, *Intimate Matters: A History of Sexuality in America* (New York: Harper and Row, 1988).

55. "Elizabeth Porter Phelps Diary, 1763–1805," *New England Historical and Genealogical Register,* 18–22 (1964–1968): 3–309; subsequent citations appear in the text.

56. "The Journal of Elizabeth Cranch," with an introductory note by Lizzie Norton Mason and James Duncan Phillips, *Essex Institute Historical Collections,* 80 (1944): 1–36; subsequent citations appear in the text.

57. For other marriage paths, see Abigail Gardner, Mrs. Gershom Drew, Jr., "Diary and Reminiscences, 1799–1817," American Antiquarian Society; Louisa Adams Parks, Journal, 1800–1801, American Antiquarian Society.

58. Ruth Henshaw Bascom, Diary, 1789–1846 (1805), American Antiquarian Society. See also Lorena S. Walsh, "'Till Death Do Us Part': Marriage and Family in Seventeenth-Century Maryland," in *The Chesapeake in the Seventeenth Century,* ed. Thad W. Tate and David L. Ammerman (Chapel Hill: University of North Carolina Press, 1979), pp. 126–152.

59. Chambers-Schiller, *Liberty;* Daniel Scott Smith, "Parental Power."

60. Carol F. Karlsen and Laurie Crumpacker, eds., *The Journal of Esther Edwards Burr, 1754–1757* (New Haven: Yale University Press, 1984); Josephine

Fisher, "The Journal of Esther Burr," *New England Quarterly,* 3 (1930): 297–315.

61. See, for example, Karen Lystra, *Searching the Heart: Women, Men, and Romantic Love in Nineteenth-Century America* (New York: Oxford University Press, 1989).

62. Martha (Patty) Rogers, Journal of 1785, Rogers Family Diaries, American Antiquarian Society.

63. The various finding aids to the diary, especially Cathy Davidson's commentary (American Antiquarian Society), are useful.

64. Mary E. Dewey, ed., *Life and Letters of Catharine M. Sedgwick* (New York: Harper and Bros., 1871) (American Antiquarian Society); subsequent citations appear in the text. See Mary Kelley, *Private Woman, Public Stage: Literary Domesticity in Nineteenth-Century America* (New York: Oxford University Press, 1983); Chambers-Schiller, *Liberty;* Cott, *Bonds;* Smith-Rosenberg, *Disorderly.*

65. Sedgwick here reflects the great popular fad of phrenology in the 1840s, not a diagnosis made in her youth. Many young persons seized on phrenology to assist them in determining their future career paths. See John Davies, *Phrenology: Fad and Science* (New Haven: Yale University Press, 1955); Allan Horlick, "Phrenology and the Social Education of Young Men," *History of Education Quarterly,* 11 (1971): 23–38.

66. See Carroll Smith-Rosenberg, "The Female World of Love and Ritual: Relations between Women in Nineteenth-Century America," *Signs,* 1 (1975): 1–29.

67. Instructive cases include those of the Beecher sisters and Louisa May Alcott. See also a wonderful Scottish example, Elizabeth Grant, Lady Strachey, ed., *Memoirs of a Highland Lady. The Autobiography of Elizabeth Grant of Rothiermurchus, Afterwards Mrs. Smith of Baltiboys, 1797–1830* (London: John Murray, 1898) (Newberry Library). Also see Steven Mintz, *A Prison of Expectations: The Family in Victorian Culture* (New York: New York University Press, 1983). For a more traditional early path of a decidedly spoiled but unprecocious girl, see Alice Morse Earle, ed., *Diary of Anna Green Winslow, a Boston School Girl of 1771* (Boston: Houghton Mifflin, 1894). Anna Winslow died at eighteen. See also Sally Ripley, Diary, 1799–1801, 1805–1809, American Antiquarian Society.

68. For connections between work and marriage, see, for southern plantation society, Allie Bayne Windham Webb, ed., *Mistress of Evergreen Plantation: Rachal O'Connor's Legacy of Letters, 1823–1845* (Albany: State University of New York Press); for England, see Adrian Henstock, ed., *The Diary of Abigail Gawthorn, 1751–1810,* Records ser., vol. 36 (Nottingham: Thoroton Society, 1978, 1979). See also Norton, *Liberty's Daughters.*

69. In my research I found no good examples of young female servants for the period, surely prominent if necessarily neglected representatives of this female path. The literature on both women's work and schooling is voluminous and growing. See, for example, Kerber, *Women;* Kathryn Sklar, *Catherine Beecher* (New Haven: Yale University Press, 1973); Claudia Goldin,

Understanding the Gender Gap (New York: Oxford University Press, 1990); Alice Kessler-Harris, *Out to Work* (New York: Oxford University Press, 1982).

70. Elizabeth Bancroft, Diary, 1793–1795, American Antiquarian Society.

71. Rena L. Vassar, ed., "The Life or Biography of Silas Felton Written by Himself," American Antiquarian Society, *Proceedings,* 69 (1959): 119–155; subsequent citations appear in the text. The conclusion about Franklin's "permeation" is also Vassar's. See also Appleby, "New Cultural Heroes."

72. For another case of the Franklinesque path, see Lester Ward Parker, "Diary of a Young Man, 1807–1808," *New England Galaxy,* 7 (1965): 31–42.

73. Edith Davenport Fuller, "Excerpts from the Diary of Timothy Fuller, Jr., an Undergraduate in Harvard College, 1798–1801," Cambridge Historical Society, *Publications,* 11 (1916): 33–53; subsequent citations appear in the text.

74. "A Young Man's Journal of 1800–1813," New Jersey Historical Society, *Proceedings,* 7 (1922): 49–59, 122–134, 211–216, 305–314; 8 (1923): 150–154, 219–225, 313–320; subsequent citations appear in the text. See also Appleby, "New Cultural Heroes."

75. Securing his father's permission was very important. William writes of "asking him in the most formal manner to grant me permission to unite in the solemn contract of marriage with dear Rosaline. This I considered as a son a very indispensable duty. He is a father who does me honor, one whom I hope and reverence" (ibid., p. 318).

76. For another example of the commercial path, see "Journal of William Wait Oliver of Salem, 1802–1803," *Essex Institute Historical Collections,* 81 (1945): 124–137, 227–256, 348–353.

77. John H. Griscom, M.D., comp. *Memoirs of John Griscom, LL.D., Late Professor of Chemistry and Natural Philosophy . . . Compiled from an Autobiography and Other Sources* (New York: Robert Carter and Bros., 1859); subsequent citations appear in the text.

78. Asa Sheldon, *Yankee Drover, Being the Unpretentious Life of Asa Sheldon, Farmer, Trader, and Working Man, 1788–1870* (Boston: Northeastern University Press, 1988); subsequent citations appear in the text.

79. See, among the literature on this transition, Appleby, "New Cultural Heroes"; William Rorabaugh, *The Craft Apprentice: From Franklin to the Machine Age in America* (New York: Oxford University Press, 1986); Bruce Laurie, *Artisans and Workers* (New York: Hill and Wang, 1989); idem, *Working People of Philadelphia* (Philadelphia: Temple University Press, 1980); J. Carroll Moody and Alice Kessler-Harris, eds., *Perspectives on American Labor History: The Problems of Synthesis* (De Kalb: Northern Illinois University Press, 1989), as well as local and regional studies and works on individual crafts and occupations.

80. Among the literature on child rearing, see in particular Calhoun, *Intelligence;* Slater, *Children;* Lewis, "Motherhood"; Alice Ryerson, "Medical Advice on Child Rearing, 1550–1900," *Harvard Educational Review* (1961): 302–323; Nancy Cott, "Notes toward an Interpretation of Antebellum Childrearing," *Psychohistory Review,* 7 (1977–78): 4–20; Bernard Wishy, *The Child and the*

Republic: The Dawn of Modern American Child Nurture (Philadelphia: University of Pennsylvania Press, 1968); Jacqueline Reinier, "Rearing the Republican Child: Attitudes and Practices in Post-Revolutionary Philadelphia," *William and Mary Quarterly,* 39 (1982): 150–163.

3. Hops, Skips, and Jumps into the Nineteenth Century

1. James Henretta and Gregory Nobles, *Evolution and Revolution: American Society, 1600–1820* (Lexington, Mass.: D.C. Heath, 1987), p. 221.
2. For good recent summaries of social change in this period, see Bruce Levine, *Half Slave and Half Free: The Roots of Civil War* (New York: Hill and Wang, 1992); Sean Wilentz, "Society, Politics, and the Market Revolution, 1815–1848," in *The New American History,* ed. Eric Foner (Philadelphia: Temple University Press, 1990), pp. 51–72.
3. Wilentz, "Society," p. 54. See also Michael B. Katz, Michael Doucet, and Mark Stern, *The Social Organization of Early Industrial Capitalism* (Cambridge, Mass.: Harvard University Press, 1982); Steven Hahn and Jonathan Prude, eds., *The Countryside in the Age of Capitalist Transformation* (Chapel Hill: University of North Carolina Press, 1985).
4. Wilentz, "Society," p. 56.
5. Ibid., p. 58.
6. Important studies include, on the working class, Bruce Laurie, *Artisans into Workers* (New York: Hill and Wang, 1990); Christine Stansell, *City of Women: Sex and Class in New York, 1789–1860* (New York: Knopf, 1986); Richard B. Stott, *Workers in the Metropolis: Class, Ethnicity, and Youth in Antebellum New York City* (Ithaca: Cornell University Press, 1990); on immigrants, see among many sources, Charlotte Erikson, *Invisible Immigrants* (Coral Gables: University of Miami Press, 1972); Hasia R. Diner, *Erin's Daughters in America* (Baltimore: Johns Hopkins University Press, 1981); Walter Kamphoefner, Wolfgang Helbich, and Ulrike Sommer, eds., *News from the Land of Freedom: German Immigrants Write Home* (Ithaca: Cornell University Press, 1991). Erickson and Kamphoefner et al. show the uses and limits of family letters for this kind of historical research.
7. Relevant here are the new rural history and studies of the transition to capitalism cited in Chapter 2. See John Mack Faragher, *Sugar Creek: Life on the Illinois Prairie* (New Haven: Yale University Press, 1986); Gerald McFarland, *A Scattered People: An American Family Moves West* (1985; rpt., New York: Penguin, 1987). Hahn and Prude, *Countryside,* is a good place to begin explorations. For urban change, see Elizabeth Blackmar, *Manhattan for Rent, 1785–1850* (Ithaca: Cornell University Press, 1989); Stuart Blumin, *The Emergence of the Middle Class: Social Experience in the American City, 1760–1900* (New York: Cambridge University Press, 1989).
8. See William Rorabaugh, *The Craft Apprentice* (New York: Oxford University Press, 1986). For bibliography, see Blumin, *Emergence;* Laurie, *Artisans.*
9. See Blumin, *Experience.* But for family and growing up, see Joseph Kett,

Rites of Passage: Adolescence in America, 1790 to the Present (New York: Basic Books, 1977); Michael Katz, *The People of Hamilton* (Cambridge, Mass.: Harvard University Press, 1975); Katz et al., *Social Organization;* Mary Ryan, *Cradle of the Middle Class: The Family in Oneida County, New York, 1790–1865* (New York: Cambridge University Press, 1980).

10. See Carroll Smith-Rosenberg's symbolic interpretation of Daniel Boone in *Disorderly Conduct: Visions of Gender in Victorian America* (New York, Knopf, 1985). See also McFarland, *Scattered People,* and Faragher, *Sugar Creek,* as well as works on women in the American West, including Glenda Riley, *The Female Frontier* (Lawrence: University of Kanasas Press, 1988); Julie Roy Jeffrey, *Frontier Women* (New York: Hill and Wang, 1979); Lillian Schlissel, *Women's Diaries of the Western Journey* (New York: Schocken, 1982); Lillian Schlissel et al., *Far from Home: Families of the Western Journey* (New York: Shocken, 1989); Paula Petrick, *No Step Backward: Women and the Family on the Rocky Mountain Mining Frontier, Helena, Montana, 1865–1900* (Helena: Montana Historical Society Press, 1987); Sarah Deutsch, *No Separate Refuge: Culture, Class, and Gender on an Anglo-Hispanic Frontier in the America Southwest, 1880–1940* (New York: Oxford University Press, 1987); Elliott West, "Heathens and Angels: Childhood in the Rocky Mountain Mining Towns," *Western Historical Quarterly,* 14 (1983): 145–164; idem, *Growing Up with the Country: Childhood on the Far Western Frontier* (Albuquerque: University of New Mexico Press, 1989). Urban-oriented studies such as Kett, *Rites,* and my own expectations miss much of the rural view. For Canadian comparisons, see Chad Gaffield, "Children, Schooling, and Family Reproduction in Nineteenth-Century Ontario," *Canadian Historical Review,* 72 (1991): 157–191.

11. See the works of G. Stanley Hall, whose own early experiences of religious conversion influenced his theories about childhood and adolescence.

12. In general, see my "Remaking Growing Up: Nineteenth-Century America," *Histoire sociale/Social History,* 24 (1991): 35–59. Only middle-class paths are discussed in detail here. With little information available about working-class or upper-class growing up, questions about cross-class comparisons must wait, including timing of changes; rural as well as urban developments; and relationships to other social transitions, especially for artisans, apprentices, immigrants, and the rural-born. Key differences within classes also existed; they include, for example, that between "rough" and "respectable" in the working class, lower middle class, and more comfortable middle class, and about peer groups and sociability. Also important, as recent work emphasizes, is discourse on and development of ideas and structures of class, reform, deviance, and institutions. Images that increasingly were based on constructions of the lower or working classes became more and more significant in relation to the new ideals and standards of the middle class. Although it belongs to a later period, a fascinating example is Michael Campbell's unpublished New Haven diary, October 1876–April 30, 1883, 4 vols., Yale University Archives, Sterling Library.

13. This interpretation conflicts with views of a more linear cast, as well as the views of those who argue for homogeneous, standardizing shifts and those who look to urbanization and/or industrialization as root causes. Compare, for example, John Demos's or Joseph Kett's arguments.

14. Compare David Bakan, "Adolescence in America: From Idea to Social Fact," *Daedalus,* 100 (1971), 979–995; Kett, *Rites;* Howard Chudacoff, *How Old Are You? Age Consciousness in American Culture* (Princeton: Princeton University Press, 1989); and John Demos's many articles.

15. New and older elements blended into nineteenth-century romanticization of childhood, resulting in a "new" tradition, a point not always understood by later observers. See "Little Men and Women," *The Child's Friend,* February 7, 1867, pp. 202–208. See also Bernard Wishy, *The Child and the Republic* (Philadelphia: University of Pennsylvania Press, 1968). Literary histories reflect this emphasis even more than cultural or social histories.

16. Amelia L. Hill, "Childhood in 1800," *New England Magazine,* 15 (1896): 406–411, is an interesting example of cultural currents combining.

17. "Diary for the Year 1824, Kept by Moses Porter," Danvers Historical Society, *Historical Collections,* 1 (1913): 31–51; 2 (1914): 54–63; subsequent citations appear in the text.

18. "Diary of Charles Ross, 1861," *Vermont History,* 29 (1961): 65–78; 30 (1962): 85–148; subsequent citations appear in the text. For tradition and lack of awareness of the Civil War's impact on growing up, see John L. Ransom, *John L. Ransom's Diary* (New York: Paul Erickson, 1963). On the Civil War and its impacts more generally, see Gerald Linderman, *Embattled Courage: The Experience of Combat in the American Civil War* (New York: Free Press, 1987).

19. G. Melvin Herndon, "The Unemancipated Antebellum Youth," *Southern Studies,* 23 (1984): 145–154; subsequent citations appear in the text.

20. The words are Herndon's (ibid., p. 154).

21. For a thoroughly nostalgic and romanticized account and defense of growing up on a plantation in the Old South, see John George Clinkscales, *On the Old Plantation: Reminiscences of His Childhood* (New York: Negro Universities Press, 1916).

22. Henry Conklin, *Through "Poverty's Vale": A Hardscrabble Boyhood in Upstate New York, 1832–62,* ed. with intro. by Wendell Tripp (Syracuse: Syracuse University Press, 1974); subsequent citations appear in the text. See also Warren Burton, *The District School As It Was, Scenery-Showing, and Other Writings* (1833; rpt., Boston: T. R. Marvin, 1852).

23. See the editor's introduction; note that Henry was a romantic.

24. Here Henry speaks to new notions of maternal importance in child rearing. This may suggest their wide early diffusion, or it may raise the possibility of Henry's reading later attitudes into his own early history.

25. This was a typical pattern. Compare this family's experience, for example, with the account in McFarland, *Scattered People.*

26. Branson L. Harris, *Some Recollection of My Boyhood* (Indianapolis: Hollenbeck Press, 1908); subsequent citations appear in the text. Elisa W. Keyes, *A*

Reminiscent History of the Village and Town of Lake Mills, Jefferson Country (n.p., n.d.); subsequent citations appear in the text. Compare Branson's community with the Illinois community described in Faragher, *Sugar Creek*.

27. See the classic school stories by Edward Eggleston, *The Hoosier Schoolmaster* (1871; rpt., Bloomington: Indiana University Press, 1984); Warren Burton, *The District School as it Once Was* (1833; rpt., Boston: T.R. Marvin, 1852); Ralph Connor, *Glengarry Schooldays* (1902; rpt., Toronto: McClelland and Stewart, 1968). See also Wayne Fuller, *The Old Country School: The Story of Rural Education in the Middle West* (Chicago: University of Chicago Press, 1982).

28. John Albee, *Confessions of Boyhood* (Boston: Badger, 1910); subsequent citations appear in the text.

29. In addition to Rorabaugh, *Craft Apprentice,* and Hahn and Prude, *Countryside,* on the impacts of economic change, see Thomas Dublin, "Women and Outwork in a Nineteenth-Century New England Town: Fitzwilliam, New Hampshire, 1830–1850," in Hahn and Prude, *Countryside,* pp. 51–70, and "Rural-Urban Migrants in Industrial New England: The Case of Lynn, Massachusetts, in the Mid-Nineteenth Century," *Journal of American History,* 73 (1986): 623–644.

30. Another adventure that accompanied John Albee's commercial education came from spending time with a wandering party of Penobscot Indians who camped for a summer just outside the town. Looking back, Albee recalled the experience in terms suggestive of "recapitulation theory," popularized by the codifier of adolescent psychology G. Stanley Hall: "The boy represents in his growth the different stages of civilization from the savage to the civilized man . . . Some times the average boy typifies the Indian, the cowboy, prize-fighter, pirate." Albee, *Confessions,* p. 201. The "wild man's" appeal to Albee also derived from his covert novel reading: "All these propensities were greatly stimulated by reading at this time the Wandering Jew of Eugene Sue" (ibid., p. 201).

31. On John Todd and his writings, see Kett, *Rites.* On advice literature more generally, see Jay Mechling, "Advice to Historians on Advice to Mothers," *Journal of Social History,* 9 (1975): 44–63; Daniel Calhoun, *The Intelligence of a People* (Princeton: Princeton University Press, 1973).

32. This applies to women as well as men, and persons of all classes and backgrounds. In general, see the now classic accounts of rural and country boy (and girl) ideas and myths in the works of Richard Wohl and Thomas Bender.

33. Francis Bennett, Jr., Diary, January 10, 1852–December 31, 1854, Mss., American Antiquarian Society.

34. On "b'hoys," a style established by young, typically working-class New York youths, see Stott, *Workers in the Metropolis;* Iver Bernstein, *The New York City Draft Riots* (New York: Oxford University Press, 1990); also, Robert Snyder, *The Voice of the City* (New York: Oxford University Press, 1990).

35. On lyceums, see Carl Bode, *The American Lyceum* (New York: Doubleday,

1956); Donald Scott, "The Popular Lecture and the Creation of a Public in Mid-Nineteenth-Century America," *Journal of American History,* 66 (1980): 791–809; idem, "Print and the Public Lecture System, 1840–1860," in *Printing and Society in Early America,* ed. William L. Joyce et al. (Worcester, Mass.: American Antiquarian Society, 1983), pp. 278–299, and his forthcoming book.

36. Charles Oliver Howe, *What I Remember* (Macon, 1928); subsequent citations appear in the text. On kin influence in urban migration and related topics, see Michael Anderson, *Family Structure in Nineteenth-Century Lancashire* (Cambridge: Cambridge University Press, 1972); Clyde Griffen and Sally Griffen, *Natives and Newcomers: The Ordering of Opportunity in Mid-Nineteenth-Century Poughkeepsie* (Cambridge, Mass.: Harvard University Press, 1977); Stuart Blumin, *The Urban Threshold* (Chicago: University of Chicago Press, 1976); Tamara K. Hareven, *Family Time and Industrial Time* (Cambridge: Cambridge University Press, 1982), among the literature.

37. James Lawrence Whittier, Diary, 1830–1831, Mss., American Antiquarian Society.

38. Edward Jenner Carpenter, Journal, 1844–45, Mss., American Antiquarian Society; now published with an introduction by Christopher Clark with the assistance of Donald M. Scott, American Antiquarian Society, *Proceedings,* 98 (1988): 303–394. I thank Scott for providing me with a copy of a typescript transcription. See also the comments on Carpenter in Rorabaugh, *Craft Apprentice.*

39. *The Autobiography of Charles Camden, being a synopsis of main occurrences in his life from August, Eighteen Hundred and Thirty-Four Up to Date May Nineteen Hundred, Written by Himself and Privately Printed and Published After His Death by His Family* (San Francisco, 1916); subsequent citations appear in the text.

40. David Clapp, Journal, 1820–1824, Mss., American Antiquarian Society. On changes in apprenticeship, see Rorabaugh, *Craft Apprentice.*

41. For an apprentice unable to complete his path, see "Extracts from the Diary of Joseph Porter Dwinnell, 1837–1838," Danvers Historical Society, *Collections,* 26 (1938): 23–41. A different route, used by and apparently useful to religious revivalists and promoters, was marked by the sowing of wild oats and endless temptations, but with its subjects finding salvation in the end. For a wonderful if scarcely realistic example, see Allen Richmond, *The First Twenty Years of My Life* (Philadelphia: American Sunday-School Union, 1859). For a more secular example, see George William Curtis, *Trumps: A Novel* (New York: Harper & Bros., 1861); I am grateful to to Paul Mattingly for bringing this source to my attention.

42. Solon J. Buck, "Selections from the Journal of Lucien C. Boynton, 1835–1853," American Antiquarian Society, *Proceedings,* 18 (1933): 329–380.

43. See Marilyn S. Blackwell, "Growing Up Male in the 1830s: Thomas Pickman Tyler (1815–1892) and Tyler Family of Brattleboro," *Vermont History,* 58 (1990); James K. Somerville, "Homesick in Upstate New York: The Saga of Sidney Roby," *New York History,* 72 (1991): 179–196.

44. Samuel Clagett Busey, *A Souvenir with an Autobiographical Sketch of Early Life and Selected Miscellaneous Addresses and Communications* (Washington, D.C., 1896); subsequent citations appear in the text.

45. For another instructive comparison, see Kate Ball Papers, Flora Ball Hopkins and Lucy Hall, compilers, *Autobiography of John Ball* (Grand Rapids, Mich.: Dean-Hicks, 1925). The variety of paths in this particular family is noteworthy.

46. "A Journal of Riley M. Adams," *Vineland Historical Magazine*, 4 (1919): 10–15, 33–36, 56–60, 74–78; 5 (1920): 85–87, 107–110, 127–130, 153–159; subsequent citations appear in the text. See also James McLachlan, *American Boarding Schools: A Historical Study* (New York: Scribners, 1970).

47. Katherine W. Richardson, "Life at Boarding School: The 1843 Letters of William Northey," Essex Institute, *Historical Collections*, 123 (1987): 182–205.

48. Compare Northey's letters with William D. Hoyt, Jr., "A Student's Impression of Newark College 105 Years Ago," *Delaware History*, 2 (1947): 134–137. The student was Matthew Robinson, aged thirteen to fourteen in 1842.

49. "Journal of Cyrus P. Bradley," *Ohio Archaeological and Historical Society Quarterly*, 15 (1906): 207–270.

50. On precocity, see in particular Joseph Kett, "Curing the Disease of Precocity," in *Turning Points*, ed. John Demos and Sarane Boocock (Chicago: University of Chicago Press, 1978), S183–211. See also Carl Kaestle and Maris Vinovskis, *Education and Social Change in Nineteenth-Century Massachusetts* (Cambridge: Cambridge University Press, 1980).

51. Compare Hoyt, "A Student's Impression."

52. Richard Frederick Fuller, "The Younger Generation in 1840, From the Diary of a New England Boy," *Atlantic Monthly*, 136 (1925): 216–224; subsequent citations appear in the text.

53. Only 1 to 2 percent of the youthful antebellum population were enrolled in college. See Colin Burke, *American Collegiate Populations* (New York: New York University Press, 1982); Chudacoff, *How Old*.

54. William Ditto Lewis, ed., "The Diary of a Student at Delaware College, August, 1853, to November, 1854," *Delaware Notes*, 24th ser. (1951): 1–88.

55. For other college experiences in this period, see James C. Mohr, ed., *The Cormany Diaries: A Northern Family in the Civil War* (Pittsburgh: University of Pittsburgh Press, 1982); Ruth Currie McDaniel, "Courtship and Marriage in the Nineteenth Century: Albion and Emma Tougee, a Case Study," *North Carolina Historical Review*, 61 (1984): 185–310.

56. Claude M. Fuess, "An Amherst Graduate of the 1840s," *Amherst Graduates Quarterly*, 23 (1933): 1–10; subsequent citations appear in the text.

57. Compare Fred Nicklason, "The Shaping of Values in Nineteenth-Century Massachusetts: The Case of Henry L. Dawes," *Historical Journal of Massachusetts*, 11 (1983): 35–44.

58. For one example, see Christopher Columbus Cole, Diary, January 12, 1852–July 16, 1854, 2 vols., Mss., Barker Texas History Center, University of Texas at Austin.

59. Joseph Baldwin, Diary, January 1, 1845–June 27, 1854, typescript, Barker Texas History Center, University of Texas at Austin.

60. For another example of long-distance migration and professional achievement, see *Autobiography of John Ball.*

61. Joseph Schafer, ed., *Memoirs of Jeremiah Curtin.* Wisconsin Biography Series, vol. 2 (Madison: State Historical Society of Wisconsin, 1940); subsequent citations appear in the text.

62. For an interesting comparison in rural youth and later professional achievement, see Isaac Phillips Roberts, *The Autobiography of a Farm Boy* (1916; rpt., Ithaca: Cornell University Press, 1946).

63. William H. McIntosh, Autobiography, Mss., Microfilm 345, Newberry Library, p. 1; subsequent citations appear in the text.

64. He did so at an earlier time than either Kett or Chudacoff might expect, given their assumptions about the chronology of changes in age consciousness. To McIntosh "youth" did not denote a vague period ranging from the end of childhood to full adulthood. His usage places this stage much closer to modern notions of adolescence than in the traditional sense of the term.

65. The seminal work here is Natalie Zemon Davis, "The Reasons of Misrule: Youth Groups and Charivaris in Sixteenth-Century France," *Past and Present,* 50 (1971): 41–75; see also John Gillis, *Youth and History,* rev. ed. (New York: Academic Press, 1981).

66. Among a large literature, see first Kett, "Curing the Disease," and *Rites;* on suicide, see Howard Kushner, *Self-Destruction in the Promised Land* (New Brunswick, N.J.: Rutgers University Press, 1989).

67. On the impact of the Civil War on young people, see Linderman, *Embattled Courage.*

68. Harvey Alexander Adams, Diary, Mss., February 18, 1836–January 14, 1853, Barker Texas History Center, University of Texas at Austin; subsequent citations appear in the text.

69. This was likely for good reason; see West, *Growing Up;* Roger Lane, *Violent Death in the City* (Cambridge, Mass.: Harvard University Press, 1979).

70. *Memoirs of Edward Bosqui* (San Francisco, 1904), presumably privately printed (Newberry Library); subsequent citations appear in the text.

71. For two other rural paths, one in the South and the other in New York State, see, respectively, John Banks, *A Short Biographical Sketch of the Undersigned by Himself, 1797–1830* (Columbus, Ga., n.d.), written at age thirty-three; and Yasuo Okada, "The Economic World of a Seneca County Farmer, 1830–1880," *New York History,* 66 (1985): 5–28.

72. For additional examples, see Bayard Still and William Herrmann, eds., "Abner Morse's Diary of Emigrant Travel, 1855–56," *Wisconsin Magazine of History,* 22 (1938): 195–212; "Diary of a Journey to Wisconsin in 1840: Frederick J. Starin," *Wisconsin Magazine of History and Biography,* 6 (1922): 73–94.

73. Earle D. Ross, ed., *Diary of Benjamin F. Gue in Rural New York and Pioneer Iowa, 1847–1856* (Ames: Iowa State University Press, 1962).

74. See also Allen F. Davis, ed., "The Girl He Left Behind: The Letters of Harriet Hutchinson Salisbury," *Vermont History,* 33 (1965): 274–282.

75. John H. Rhea, *Thirty Years in Arkansaw* (Cedar Rapids: Republican Press, 1896); subsequent citations appear in the text.

76. See the literature on religious conversion cited in Chapter 2. For prominent examples of difficult experiences of conversion, see Kathryn Sklar on Catherine Beecher, Charles Strickland on Louisa May Alcott, Steven Mintz on other Victorian authors, Dorothy Ross on G. Stanley Hall. See also Joanna Bowen Gillespie, "'The Clear Leadings of Providence': Pious Memoirs and the Problems of Self-Realization in the Early Nineteenth Century," *Journal of the Early Republic,* 5 (1985): 297–321, among her writings.

77. Ryan, *Cradle,* p. 80 and passim.

78. In addition to his classic *Adolescence: Its Psychology and Its Relations to Physiology, Anthropology, Sociology, Sex, Crime, Religion, and Education,* 2 vols. (New York: Appleton, 1904); see G. Stanley Hall, "Boy Life in a Massachusetts Country Town Forty Years Ago," in *Aspects of Child Life and Education* (Boston: Ginn and Co., 1907), pp. 300–321. See also Dorothy Ross, *G. Stanley Hall: The Psychologist as Prophet* (Chicago: University of Chicago Press, 1972).

79. Hillel Schwartz, "Adolescence and Revivals in Ante-Bellum Boston," *Journal of Religious History,* 8 (1974): 158 and passim. See also Ryan, *Cradle,* and Kett, *Rites,* among the literature.

80. *Memoirs of a Circuit Rider, The Reverend William McKnight,* comp. and ed. Jeanne Temple and Rev. David Miles (Elsie, Michigan: Sun Publishing Co., 1979); subsequent citations appear in the text.

81. See Ann Boylan, "The Role of Conversion in Nineteenth-Century Sunday Schools," *American Studies,* 22 (1979): 35–48; idem, "Sunday Schools and Changing Evangelical Views of Children in the 1820s," *Church History,* 49 (1979): 325–348; idem, *Sunday School: The Formation of an American Institution, 1790–1880* (New Haven: Yale University Press, 1988); for a British comparison, see Thomas W. Laqueur, *Religion and Respectability: Sunday Schools and Working-Class Culture, 1780–1850* (New Haven: Yale University Press, 1976).

82. *The Life of Hosea Smith, A Travelling Minister, Who Was Left Without Father or Mother, Or Any Connexions. Also, An Account of His Sufferings and Cruel Treatment, and His Conviction and Conversion. Also, His Calls into the Ministry* (Providence, 1833); subsequent citations appear in the text. See also Nathan Hatch, *The Democratization of American Christianity* (New Haven: Yale University Press, 1989).

83. Mark A. Strang, ed., *The Diary of James J. Strang* (East Lansing: Michigan State University Press, 1961). Recent histories of Mormons and Mormonism establish more complete contexts for Strang's actions.

84. See Anne M. Boylan, "Growing Up Female in Young America, 1800–1860," in *American Childhood,* ed. Joseph Hawes and N. Ray Hiner (Westport, Conn.: Greewood Press, 1985), pp. 153–184.

85. See Joan Jacobs Brumberg, "Chlorotic Girls, 1870–1920: A Historical Perspective on Female Adolescence," *Child Development*, 53 (1982): 1468–77; idem, *Fasting Girls: The Emergence of Anorexia Nervosa as a Modern Disease* (Cambridge, Mass.: Harvard University Press, 1988); Jane Hunter, "Inscribing the Self in the Heart of the Family: Diaries and Girlhood in Late Victorian America," *American Quarterly*, 44 (1992): 51–81. See also Katherine Dalsimer, *Female Adolescence: Psychoanalytic Reflections on Literature* (New Haven: Yale University Press, 1986).

86. For romanticization and sentimentality, see, for example, Harriet Elizabeth Abbott, *The Little Girl That Once Was I, by Mrs. Francis E. Clark* ["Mother Endeavor" Clark] (Boston: International Society of Christian Endeavor, 1939); Sarah Stuart Robbins, *Old Andover Days: Memoirs of a Puritan Childhood* (Boston: Pilgrim Press, 1908).

87. *Memoirs of Fanny Newell, written by herself and published at her particular request, and the desire of numerous friends*, 2d ed. (1824; rpt., Springfield, Mass.: Merriam, Little, 1832); subsequent citations appear in the text. Some such accounts were fakes, written for their influence and effect, according to Irene Q. Brown in a seminar at the American Antiquarian Society, spring 1989.

88. For an interesting if frivolous account of the influence of wealth and privilege on growing up, see Catherine Elizabeth Havens, *Diary of a Little Girl in Old New York* (New York: Henry Collins, 1919); see also "Lydia Smith's Journal, 1805–1806," Massachusetts Historical Society, *Proceedings*, 48 (1914–15): 508–524.

89. Caroline Clapp Briggs, *Reminiscences and Letters* (Boston: Houghton Mifflin, 1897), p. 1; subsequent citations appear in the text.

90. Caroline Wells Healey Dall, *Alongside, being notes suggested by A New England Boyhood of Doctor Edward Everett Hale* (1900; rpt., New York: Arno Press, 1980); subsequent citations appear in the text. As the title indicates, Dall wrote in explicit response to Hale's *New England Boyhood*.

91. On elite education for girls, see Louise L. Stevenson, "Sarah Porter Educates Useful Ladies, 1847–1900," *Winterthur Portfolio*, 18 (1983): 39–59.

92. Orleana Ellery Walden-Pell, *Recollections of a Long Life* (London: W. P. Griffith, 1896); subsequent citations appear in the text.

93. Elizabeth Duncan Putnam, ed., "Diary of Mrs. Joseph Duncan (Elizabeth Caldwell Smith)," *Illinois State Historical Society Journal*, 21 (1928): 1–91.

94. On women's education to develop their abilities and resources, see Jill Ker Conway, "Perspectives on the History of Women's Education in the United States," *History of Education Quarterly*, 12 (1974); Katherine Sklar, *Catharine Beecher* (New Haven: Yale University Press, 1973), among an important literature.

95. Eleanora Garner Colton, *Memories of Columbus City* (n.p., n.d.); subsequent citations appear in the text. See also Jennie E. Ross, "A Child's Experiences in '49, as Related by Mrs. M. A. Gentry," *Overland Monthly*, 2d ser., 63 (1914): 300–305, 402–408, 505–511.

96. For another typical case of early migration, see Josephine McCurdy Carolina

Smith [Mrs. Charles], *A Sketch of her life written by herself* (1909), March–May 1883, Misc. Mss. B, American Antiquarian Society.

97. Lucy Gilmore Cowles, *Memories* (n.p., n.d.); subsequent citations appear in the text.

98. Mary Ann Hubbard, *Family Memories* ([Chicago?] 1912).

99. Contrast her experience with later urban migrations as presented by Joanne Meyerowitz, *Women Adrift: Independent Wage Earners in Chicago, 1880–1930* (Chicago: University of Chicago Press, 1988); Lisa Fine, *The Souls of the Skyscraper: Female Clerical Workers in Chicago, 1870–1930* (Philadelphia: Temple University Press, 1990).

100. "By Ox-Team to California: Personal Narrative of Nancy A. Hunt," *Overland Monthly* (April 1916): 317–326; subsequent citations appear in the text. See also Ross, "A Child's Experiences in '49"; Ruth Barnes Moynihan, "Children and Young People on the Overland Trail," *Western Historical Quarterly,* 6 (1975): 270–294; West, *Growing Up;* on rural Illinois, see Faragher, *Sugar Creek.*

101. Ottilie Fuchs Goeth, *Memoirs of a Texas Pioneer Grandmother,* trans. with additions by Irma Goeth Guenther (Burnett, Texas: Eakins Press, 1982); subsequent citations appear in the text. My research found few similar sources. Lauren Kattner has written several studies on migrants and their towns in central Texas.

102. Sabrina Ann (Loomis) Hills, *Memories* (Cleveland, 1899); subsequent citations appear in the text.

103. Allen F. Davis, "The Girl He Left Behind: The Letters of Harriet Hutchinson Salisbury," *Vermont History,* 33 (1965): 274–282; subsequent citations appear in the text. See also Mohr, *Cormany Diaries;* McDaniel, "Courtship and Marriage"; Ellen K. Rothman, *Hands and Hearts: A History of Courtship in America* (New York: Basic Books, 1984).

104. See Catherine Clinton, "Equally Their Due: The Education of the Planter Daughter in the Early Republic," *Journal of the Early Republic,* 2 (1982): 39–60; Elizabeth Fox-Genovese, *Within the Plantation Household: Black and White Women of the Old South* (Chapel Hill: University of North Carolina Press, 1988); Steven Stowe, *Intimacy and Power in the Old South* (Baltimore: Johns Hopkins University Press, 1987); idem, "'The *Thing* Not Its Vision': A Woman's Courting and Her Sphere in the Southern Planter Class," *Feminist Studies,* 9 (1983): 113–130.

105. Stowe, "The *Thing*," p. 113.

106. Emily Virginia Semple, *Reminiscences of My Early Life and Relatives at the Request of My Son Henry S. Semple, SJ* (n.p., n.d.); subsequent citations appear in the text. See also Virginia Ingraham Burr, ed., *The Secret Eye: The Journal of Ella Gertrude Clanton Thomas, 1848–1889* (Chapel Hill: University of North Carolina Press, 1990).

107. For a description of a formal wedding ca. 1821, see Anna Quincy Thaxter Parsons, "Journal [of Margaret Carter Wedding], 1821," *Essex Institute Historical Collections,* 87 (1951): 309–332.

108. The recent history of women's work is encapsulated in the literature that

begins with Thomas Dublin, *Women at Work: The Transformation of Work and Community in Lowell, Massachusetts, 1826–1860* (New York: Columbia University Press, 1979), and continues through Mary Blewitt, *Men, Women, and Work: Class, Gender, and Protest in the New England Shoe Industry* (Urbana: University of Illinois Press, 1988). Landmark studies include Alice Kessler-Harris, *Out to Work: A History of Wage-Earning Women in the United States* (New York: Oxford University Press, 1982); Claudia Goldin, *Understanding the Gender Gap: An Economic History of American Women* (New York: Oxford University Press, 1990); Stansell, *City of Women;* Jean Boydston, *Home and Work* (New York: Oxford University Press, 1990); Joan M. Jensen, *Loosening the Bonds: Mid-Atlantic Farm Women, 1750–1850* (New Haven: Yale University Press, 1986).

109. See Stansell, *City of Women;* also the work of Bruce Bellingham, cited earlier; Thomas Bender, *Toward an Urban Vision: Ideas and Institutions in Nineteenth-Century America* (Lexington: University Press of Kentucky, 1975). Richard Wohl's classic work "The 'Country Boy' Myth and Its Place in American Urban Culture," *Perspectives in American History,* 3 (1979): 77–156, is also relevant.

110. Jo Anne Preston, "Learning a Trade in Industrializing New England: The Expedition of Hannah and Mary Adams to Nashua, New Hampshire, 1833–1834," *Historical New Hampshire,* 39 (1984): 24–44; subsequent citations appear in the text. See also idem, "'To Learn Me the Whole of the Trade': Conflict between a Female Apprentice and a Merchant Tailor in Ante-Bellum New England," *Labor History,* 24 (1983): 259–273. See also Jo Anne Preston, "Millgirl Narratives: Representations of Class and Gender in Nineteenth-Century Lowell," *Life Stories/Recits de vie,* 3 (1987): 21–30; Thomas Dublin, "The Mill Letters of Emeline Larcom, 1840–1842," *Essex Institute Historical Collections,* 127 (1991): 211–239, and a novel by Elizabeth Stuart Phelps, *The Silent Partner* (1871; rpt., Old Westbury, N.Y.: Feminist Press, 1983).

111. Compare with Thomas Dublin, "Women and Outwork," "Rural-Urban Migrants," "Women's Work and the Family Economy: Textiles and Palm Leaf Hatmaking in New England, 1830–1850," *Toqueville Review,* 3 (1983): 297–316.

112. The classic study of time discipline is E. P. Thompson, "Time, Work-Discipline, and Industrial Capitalism," *Past and Present,* 50 (1971): 56–97; see also Herbert Gutman, "Work, Culture, and Society in Industrializing America, 1815–1919," *American Historical Review,* 78 (1973): 531–588, among the literature.

113. Jo Anne Preston, who located and reprinted this material, does not indicate if they ever married.

114. Lucy Fletcher Kellogg, "The Diary of, written in 1879 at age of nearly 86," Miscellaneous Mss. K, Box 1, memoir 1879, American Antiquarian Society.

115. Preston, "Millgirl Narratives." See also Nancy Cott's foreword to Lucy Larcom, *A New England Girlhood* (Boston: Northeastern University Press,

1986); Claudia L. Bushman, *"A Good Poor Man's Wife": Being a Chronicle of Harriet Hanson Robinson and Her Family in Nineteenth-Century New England* (Hanover: University Presses of New England, 1981), among the literature.

116. Dublin, *Women at Work,* and the essays that preceded his book.

117. Preston, "Millgirl Narratives."

118. Cott, foreword to Larcom, *New England Girlhood;* see also Bushman, *A Good Poor Man's Wife.*

119. On religion in the mills, see Bushman, *A Good Poor Man's Wife;* Jama Lazerow, "Religion and the New England Mill Girl: A New Perspective on an Old Theme," *New England Quarterly,* 60 (1987): 429–453.

120. For additional information, see Richard M. Bernard and Maris A. Vinovskis, "The Female School Teacher in Ante-Bellum Massachusetts," *Journal of Social History,* 10 (1977): 332–345; Maris A. Vinovskis and Richard M. Bernard, "Beyond Catherine Beecher: Female Education in the Antebellum Period," *Signs,* 3 (1978): 856–869; Sklar, *Beecher;* Conway, "Perspectives"; Anne Firor Scott, "The Ever-Widening Circle: The Diffusion of Feminist Values from the Troy Female Seminary, 1822–1872," *History of Education Quarterly,* 19 (1979): 3–26; David Allmendinger, "Mount Holyoke Students Encounter the Need for Life-Planning, 1837–1850," *History of Education Quarterly,* 19 (1979): 27–46. See also Suzanne L. Bunkers, ed., *The Diary of Caroline Seabury, 1854–1863* (Madison: University of Wisconsin Press, 1991).

121. Susan E. Parsons Brown Forbes [Mrs. Alexander Barclay], Diaries, 1841–1908, Mss., American Antiquarian Society.

122. *The Life and Letters of Mrs. Emily C. Judson,* ed. A. C. Kendrick (New York: Sheldon and Co., 1860); subsequent citations appear in the text. See also Joan J. Brumberg, *Mission for Life: The Judson Family and American Evangelical Culture* (New York: Free Press, 1980); Ryan, *Cradle.*

123. Caroline Barrett White, Mrs. Francis Adams, Papers, 1844–1915, Diary, Mss., American Antiquarian Society.

124. See Carl Kaestle, *Pillars of the Republic: Common Schools and American Society, 1780–1860* (New York: Hill and Wang, 1983); idem, "Social Change, Discipline, and the Common School in Early Nineteenth-Century America," *Journal of Interdisciplinary History,* 9 (1978): 1–17; Harvey J. Graff, *The Literacy Myth: Literacy and Social Structure in the Nineteenth-Century City* (New York: Academic Press, 1979); Alison Prentice and Marjorie Theobald, ed., *Women Who Taught* (Toronto: University of Toronto Press, 1991).

125. "Ellen Parker's Journal," New Hampshire Historical Society, *Collections,* 11 (1915): 130–162. See also Bunkers, *Diary of Caroline Seabury.*

126. One case study that deals with the life cycle aspects of service is Laurence Glasco, "The Life Cycles and Household Structures of American Ethnic Groups: Irish, Germans, and Native-Born Whites in Buffalo, New York, 1855," *Journal of Urban History,* 1 (1975): 339–364; idem, "Migration and Adjustment in the Nineteenth-Century City: Occupation, Property, and Household Structure of Native-Born Whites, Buffalo, New York, 1855," in *Family*

and *Population in Nineteenth-Century America,* ed. Tamara K. Hareven and Maris A. Vinovskis (Princeton: Princeton University Press, 1978), pp. 154–178. See also Stephen Gross, "Domestic Labor as a Life-Course Event: The Effects of Ethnicity in Turn-of-the-Century America," *Social Science History,* 15 (1991): 397–416.

127. Lizzie A. Wilson Goodenough, Diaries, 1865–1903, Mss., American Antiquarian Society.

128. *Memoir of Mary Anna Longstreth by an old pupil* [*Margaret Newlin*] *with a sketch of her work for Hampton by Helen W. Ludlow* (Philadephia: J. B. Lippincott, 1886); subsequent citations appear in the text. For Quaker precedents and paths, see Barry Levy, *Quakers and the American Family* (New York: Oxford University Press, 1988); *Two Quaker Sisters. From the Original Diaries of Elizabeth Buffum Chace and Lucy Buffum Lowell,* with an introduction by Malcolm R. Lovell (New York: Liveright, 1937). See also, for an interesting comparison with a woman who became a teacher later, Bunkers, *Diary of Caroline Seabury.*

129. On women's moral contributions, see also Johanna Bowen Gillespie, "Modesty Canonized: Female Saints in Antebellum Methodist Sunday School Literature," *Historical Reflections,* 10 (1983): 195–220, among her studies; see also the related work of Ann Boylan.

130. R.L.B. [Mrs. Harriet G. Doutney (Storer)], *An Autobiography: being passages from a life now progressing in the city of Boston* (1871); subsequent citations appear in the text.

131. Caroline Cowles Richards [Clarke], *Life in America, 1852–1872, Including the Period of the American Civil War as Told in the Diary of a School-Girl* (1908; rpt., Williamstown, Mass.: Corner House, 1972). See also Virginia Mayberry and Dawn E. Bakken, eds., "The Civil War Home Front: Diary of a Young Girl, 1862–1863," *Indiana Magazine of History,* 87 (1991): 24–78; Linderman, *Embattled Courage.*

132. See Lee Soltow and Edward Stevens, *The Rise of Literacy and the Common School* (Chicago: University of Chicago Press, 1981); Cathy N. Davidson, ed., *Reading in America: Literature and Social History* (Baltimore: Johns Hopkins University Press, 1989); Graff, *Literacy Myth.*

133. Rebecca Ann Lamar, Diary, July 22, 1838–April 7, 1839, Mss., Barker Texas History Center, University of Texas at Austin.

134. Patricia Mercer, Diary, October 13, 1840–September 28, 1841, Mss., Barker Texas History Center, University of Texas at Austin.

135. George W. Robinson, ed., *Journal of Anna May* (Cambridge, Mass., 1941). The editor disguised the name of the diarist.

136. Among the literature, see Carroll Smith-Rosenberg and Charles Rosenberg, "The Female Animal: Medical and Biological Views of Woman and Her Role in Nineteenth-Century America," *Journal of American History,* 60 (1973): 332–356.

137. Hannah Gale, Journal, 1837–38, Mss., Gale Family Papers, 1828–1854, American Antiquarian Society.

138. See Allmendinger, "Mount Holyoke Students Encounter the Need for Life-Planning"; Barbara Miller Solomon, *In the Company of Educated Women* (New Haven: Yale University Press, 1985); Scott, "Ever-Widening Circle"; see also Elizabeth J. Atlee Nichols, Diary, March 25, 1838–May 24, 1839, Mss., Barker Texas History Center, University of Texas at Austin. She was a student at the seminary at Troy.

139. Margaret L. Magnusson, "'Your Affectionate Mary': A Vermont Girl at Mount Holyoke," *Vermont History,* 31 (1963): 181–192; subsequent citations appear in the text.

140. See in particular Rothman, *Hearts;* Lee Schillers-Chamber, *Liberty, A Better Husband. Single Women in America: The Generations of 1780–1840* (New Haven: Yale University Press, 1984); Smith-Rosenberg, *Disorderly Conduct;* Karen Lystra, *Searching the Heart: Women, Men, and Romantic Love in Nineteenth-Century America* (New York: Oxford University Press, 1989); among the literature. See also John Gillis *For Better or Worse: British Marriages, 1600 to the Present* (New York: Oxford University Press, 1985); Kirk Jeffrey, "Marriage, Career, and Feminine Ideology in Nineteenth-Century America," *Feminist Studies,* 2 (1975): 113–130; Ryan, *Cradle;* McDaniel, "Courtship and Marriage."

141. Lizzie Scott Neblett, Diary, March 16–May 1, 1863, Mss., Barker Texas History Center, University of Texas at Austin.

142. For another example of class's influence, see also Eliza Ann Lawton Ninde, Diary, 1861, Mss., American Antiquarian Society.

143. B. and T. C. Hoppin, Account Book, 1813–1817, 1821, Mss., American Antiquarian Society. William Hoppin was later a New York attorney and secretary to the U.S. legation to Great Britain. Given the nature of this record, it is not significant that the boy does not mention his mother. Contrast that omission with the arguments of Steven Mintz, *A Prison of Expectations: The Family in Victorian Culture* (New York: New York University Press, 1983); and my review, "The History of Childhood and Youth: Beyond Infancy?," *History of Education Quarterly,* 26 (1986): 95–109.

144. Samuel Bartlett Parris, Diary, 1817, Mss., American Antiquarian Society.

145. Wilson O. Clough, "A Journal of Village Life in Vermont in 1848," *New England Quarterly,* 1 (1928): 32–40. On precocity, see Kett, "Curing the Disease."

146. See G. Stanley Hall's writings and Dorothy Ross's biography of Hall, cited previously. See also the work of Joseph Kett, Mary Ryan, Michael Katz, and my own work, previously cited, among the literature.

147. For an interesting contrast, see John E. Higgins, "A Connecticut Schoolboy in the 1850s," Connecticut Historical Society, *Bulletin,* 28 (1963): 38–41.

148. Edith Emerson Webster Gregg, "Emerson and His Children: Their Childhood Memories," *Harvard Library Bulletin,* 28 (1980): 407–430; subsequent citations appear in the text.

149. On fathers and sons, see E. Anthony Rotundo, "Boy Culture: Middle-Class Boyhood in Nineteenth-Century America," in *Meanings for Manhood: Con-*

structions of Masculinity in Victorian America, ed. Mark C. Carnes and Clyde Griffen (Chicago: University of Chicago Press, 1990), pp. 15–36; idem, "Romantic Friendship: Male Intimacy and Middle-Class Youth in the Northern United States, 1800–1900," *Journal of Social History,* 23 (1989): 1–26; idem, "Manhood in America: The Northern Middle Class, 1770–1920" (Ph.D. diss., Brandeis University, 1982); idem, *American Manhood* (New York: Basic Books, 1993); and other essays in *Meanings for Manhood.*

150. On children's books in this period, see Ann Macleod, *A Moral Tale: Children's Fiction and American Culture, 1820–1860* (Hamden, Conn.: Archon, 1975); Daniel Rodgers, "Socializing Middle-Class Children: Institutions, Fables, and Work Values in Nineteenth-Century America," *Journal of Social History,* 13 (1980): 354–367, among the literature on children's reading and publications.

151. Edmund Quincy Sewall, Diary, 1840, Mss., American Antiquarian Society.

152. "Diary of the College Life and Times of John B[annan] Douglas," Orwigsburg, Pennsylvania, Yale College Class of 1852, 1849–1853, 2 vols., American Antiquarian Society.

153. This bashfulness with women may support the arguments of historians who see at this point a widening gap between the spheres of men and women. See especially the disagreements between Carroll Smith-Rosenberg and Ellen K. Rothman on gender relations and their meanings. On questions of "separate spheres," see Ellen DuBois et al., "Politics and Culture in Women's History: A Symposium," *Feminist Studies,* 6 (1980): 26–64; Linda K. Kerber, "Separate Spheres, Female Worlds, Woman's Place: The Rhetoric of Women's History," *Journal of American History,* 75 (1988): 9–39; Linda K. Kerber et al., "Forum: Beyond Roles, Beyond Spheres: Thinking about Gender in the Early Republic," *William and Mary Quarterly,* 46 (1989): 565–585.

154. For an example of different emphasis in child rearing, see Lawrence B. Goodheart, "Child-Rearing, Conscience, and Conversion to Abolitionism: The Example of Elizur Wright, Jr.," *Psychohistory Review,* 12 (1984): 24–33.

155. For a useful British study that reiterates the trans-Atlantic and cross-cultural dimensions of the changing patterns of family and growing up, see Lenore Davidoff and Catherine Hall, *Family Fortunes: Men and Women of the English Middle Class, 1750–1850* (London: Hutchinson, 1987). See also the German immigrant Adolph Hammerschmidt, *Memoirs of Youth,* trans. from German (Elmhurst, Ill., 1975).

156. This imagery is reflected in much of the recent historiography of the American family, from Kirk Jeffrey's or Christopher Lasch's "refuges" and "havens," to Mary Ryan's "cradle," Sam Bass Warner, Jr.'s, Kenneth Jackson's, Joel Tarr's, and Margaret Marsh's suburbs, and Gwendolyn Wright's and Clifford Clark's houses.

157. C. S. Parker, "A New Hampshire Courtship in 1826," *Historical New Hampshire,* 4 (1947): 4–18. See also George Anderson, S.J., "The Civil War Courtship of Richard Mortimer William and Rose Anderson of Rockville," *Maryland Historical Magazine,* 80 (1985): 119–138. Highly relevant to useful

interpretations are John Kasson, "Civility and Rudeness: Urban Etiquette and the Bourgeois Social Order in Nineteenth-Century America," *Prospects,* 9 (1984): 143–167; idem, *Rudeness and Civility* (New York: Hill and Wang, 1990); Karen Haltunen, *Confidence Men, Painted Women* (New Haven: Yale University Press, 1982); Rothman, *Hearts;* Lystra, *Searching.*

158. See Kett, *Rites,* among his other writings; Bernard Farber, *Guardians of Virtue: Salem Families in 1800* (New York: Basic Books, 1972). Compare with examples in Chapters 2 and 4; and see the previously cited works by William and Jane Pease, James McLachlan, Ronald Story, Pessen, Peter Hall, Fredric Jaher, and E. Digby Baltzell.

159. William H. Pease and Jane H. Pease, "Paternal Dilemmas: Education, Property, and Patrician Persistence in Jacksonian Boston," *New England Quarterly,* 53 (1980).

160. Stephen Salisbury III, Diaries, 1848, 1850, 1852–1856, Mss., American Antiquarian Society. It is fitting that much of the first draft of this book was written in the American Antiquarian Society, Worcester, which was among the Salisbury family's interests.

161. On Harvard in this era, see especially the work of Ronald Story and Peter Hall.

162. Joseph Hodges Choate, *The Boyhood and Youth of Joseph Hodges Choate* (New York: Privately printed at Scribners, 1917). His reminiscences were dictated while he was ill in 1914.

163. Pease and Pease, "Paternal Dilemmas," p. 167.

4. Paving the Paths in the Nineteenth Century

1. Richard L. McCormick, "Public Life in Industrial America, 1877–1917," in *The New American History,* ed. Eric Foner (Philadelphia: Temple University Press, 1990), p. 93. See also Robert Wiebe, *The Search for Order, 1877–1920* (New York: Hill and Wang, 1967); Nell Irwin Painter, *Standing at Armageddon: The United States, 1877–1919* (New York: Norton, 1987).

2. McCormick, "Public Life," p. 94.

3. Ibid., pp. 95, 103.

4. On myth, ideology, and perception regarding young persons, see Norton Grubb and Marvin Lazerson, *Broken Promises: How Americans Fail Their Children* (New York: Basic Books, 1982); Viviana Zelizer, *Pricing the Priceless Child* (New York: Basic Books, 1986); R. Richard Wohl, "The 'Country Boy' Myth and Its Place in American Urban Culture: The Nineteenth-Century Contribution," *Perspectives in American History,* 3 (1979): 75–156; Thomas Bender, *Toward an Urban Vision* (Lexington: University of Kentucky Press, 1975); also see the work of Bruce Bellingham and Christine Stansell, cited earlier.

5. Myla Jean Martin, ed., *Memoirs of Columbus B(oyd) Campbell,* 1958, Typescript, Ayer Collection, Newberry Library, Chicago; subsequent citations appear in the text. On rural life around 1850, see the well-known

anthologies of essays on the Old Northwest and rural New England, especially Steven Hahn and Jonathan Prude, eds., *The Countryside in the Age of
Capitalist Transformation* (Chapel Hill: University of North Carolina Press,
1985); and John M. Faragher's books, previously cited. On Reconstruction,
see especially Eric Foner, *Reconstruction: America's Unfinished Revolution,
1863–1877* (New York: Harper and Row, 1988). Also for the South in
general, see Edward Ayers, *The Promise of the New South* (New York:
Oxford University Press, 1992); Gavin Wright's books on economic history,
*Old South, New South: Revolutions in the Southern Economy Since the Civil
War* (New York: Basic Books, 1986); idem., *The Political Economy of the
Cotton South* (New York: Norton, 1978); Jacqueline Jones, *Labor of Love,
Labor of Sorrow: Black Women, Work, and the Family from Slavery to the
Present* (New York: Basic Books, 1985); idem., *The Dispossessed: America's
Underclasses from the Civil War to the Present* (New York: Basic Books,
1992).
6. On impacts of the Civil War on family life, see citations in note 5. See also
Gerald Lindermann, *Embattled Courage: The Experience of Combat in the
American Civil War* (New York: Free Press, 1987); Catherine Clinton and
Nina Silber, eds., *Divided Houses: Gender and the Civil War* (New York:
Oxford University Press, 1992).
7. Dwight L. Smith, "Antebellum Boyhood: The School Days of Samuel E.
Tillman," *Tennessee Historical Quarterly,* 46 (1986): 148–156; idem, "An
Antebellum Boyhood: Samuel Escue Tillman on a Middle Tennessee Planta-
tion," ibid., 47 (1988): 3–9; subsequent citations appear in the text. These
are excerpts from Tillman's manuscript autobiography at the U.S. Military
Academy, West Point.
8. Marjory Barnum Hinman, ed., *Diary of a Binghampton Boy in the 1860s,
from the Diaries of Morris Treadwell* (Windsor, N.Y.: Published by the
Editor, 1982).
9. See Howard Chudacoff, *How Old Are You? Age Consciousness in American
Culture* (Princeton: Princeton University Press, 1989).
10. See Carroll Smith-Rosenberg, *Disorderly Conduct: Visions of Gender in
Victorian America* (New York: Knopf, 1985), on the symbolism of Daniel
Boone and related matters. See also E. Anthony Rotundo, *American Manhood: Transformations in Masculinity from the Revolution to the Present*
(New York: Basic Books, 1993), and related work.
11. See the classic account of frontier schooling in Edward Eggleston, *The Hoosier Schoolmaster* (1871; rpt., Bloomington: Indiana University Press, 1984).
12. Examples of transitional paths of growing up from rural, small-town, and
southern foundations cover a wide range of experiences, although some
features are common. The "Buckeye boyhood" of Henry Venable and G.
Stanley Hall's romantic, nostalgic retrospective of "boy life" in New England
underscore the point. Both reveal how easy it was to reweave the facts of
one's early life course into a celebration of good, old-fashioned, innocent
notions of growing up. Henry Venable, *A Buckeye Boyhood* (Robert Clarke,

1911); G. Stanley Hall, "Boy Life in a Massachusetts Country Town Forty Years Ago," in *Aspects of Child Life and Education* (Boston: Ginn and Co., 1907), pp. 300–321.

13. For criticism of small-town life, see Hall, "Boy Life," p. 320 and passim. For the young and urban life, among many relevant works see especially Bruce Bellingham's work cited previously; Michael B. Katz, *Poverty and Policy in American History* (New York: Academic Press, 1983); idem, *In the Shadow of the Poor House* (New York: Basic Books, 1986).

14. In addition to Elliott West's recent work and previously cited studies of women and families in the West, see Annette Atkins, "The Child's West: A Review Essay," *New Mexico Historical Review,* 65 (1990): 477–490. See also James K. Hastings, "Boyhood in the Trinidad Region," *Colorado Magazine,* 30 (1953): 104–109; Ellison Orr, "Reminiscences of a Pioneer Boy," ed. and intro. Marshall McKusick, *Annals of Iowa,* 40 (1971): 530–560, 593–630; Dorothy M. Johnson, "Helena in the 1870s: Some Exciting Years in the Past of Montana's Capital City as Seen through Teen-Age Eyes [James Upton Sanders]," *Montana,* 12 (1962): 2–14; Jerry S. Wilconx, ed., "A Frontier Boyhood: The Memoirs of David Preston Wilson," *Legacies,* 2 (1990): 4–8.

15. For other telling examples proclaiming "traditions," see Hubert E. Collins, *Warpath and Cattle Trail* (New York: William Morrow, 1928); and James L. Hill, *My First Years as a Boy* (Andover: Andover Press, 1927).

16. Neil Brearley, ed., *The Diary and Narrative of Richard Henry Alexander in a Journey across the Rocky Mountains* (Richmond, British Columbia: Alcuin Society, 1973).

17. James G. Rouse, "The Curtain Call," typescript in possession of Jerold D. Cummins, Arlington, Virginia; subsequent citations appear in the text. Jerold Cummins, Rouse's grandson, generously supplied me with a copy in response to my request published in the *New York Review of Books.*

18. Compare James Rouse's history with the story of the Williams family of Iowa in John Kent Folmar, ed., *"This State of Wonders": The Letters of an Iowa Frontier Family, 1858–1861* (Iowa City: University of Iowa Press, 1986).

19. Thomas Arthur Whitaker, Diary, 1874–1878, Mss., American Antiquarian Society.

20. Victor Lincoln Albjerg, "An Adventure in American Education," typescript, 1970–1971; subsequent citations appear in the text. A copy was generously supplied to me by his daughter Patricia Albjerg Graham of the Harvard Graduate School of Education; I am grateful for this material.

21. On Scandinavian immigrants, see in particular the work of Kristian Hvidt, Hans Norman and Harald Ranblom, Sune Akerman, and Jon Gjerde. More generally, see the works of the immigration historians John Bodnar, Kathleen Conzen, and Ewa Morawska. John Bodnar, *The Transplanted* (Bloomington: Indiana University Press, 1985), is the best survey.

22. See Clinton and Silber, *Divided Houses;* George Rable, *Civil Wars: Women and the Crisis of Southern Nationalism* (Urbana: University of Illinois Press, 1989).

23. Mary Custis Lee deButts, ed., *Growing Up in the 1850s: The Journal of Agnes Lee* (Chapel Hill: Published for the Robert E. Lee Memorial Association by the University of North Carolina Press, 1984).

24. For the education of southern girls, see Catherine Clinton, "Equally Their Due: The Education of the Planter in the Early Republic," *Journal of the Early Republic*, 2 (1982): 39–60; Steven Stowe, "The Not-So-Cloistered Academy: Elite Women's Education and Family Feeling in the Old South," in *Web of Southern Social Relations*, ed. Walter Fraser, R. Frank Saunders, Jr., and Jon L. Wakelyn (Athens: University of Georgia Press, 1985). pp. 90–106; Elizabeth Fox-Genovese, *Within the Plantation Household* (Chapel Hill: University of North Carolina Press, 1988); Christie Anne Farnham, *The Education of the Southern Belle* (New York: New York University Press, 1994).

25. Letitia Pendleton, Journal, 1854–1856, Mss., W. W. Fontaine Collection, Barker Texas History Center, University of Texas at Austin.

26. *The Diary of Ann Browder, 1858–1859, 1866–1867*, researched, transcribed, compiled, and published by Dorothy Sturgis Pruett (Macon, Ga., 1984).

27. Mary D. Robertson, ed., *Lucy Breckinridge of Grove Hill: The Journal of a Virginia Girl, 1862–1864* (Kent, Ohio: Kent State University Press, 1979).

28. How quickly one's memory of growing up in such difficult circumstances can be rewritten is shown by Berenice Morrison-Fuller, "Plantation Life in Missouri" (n.p., n.d.). See Chapter 3 for a male counterpart, John George Clinkscales.

29. On rural women outside the South, see Nancy Grey Osterud, *Bonds of Community: The Lives of Farm Women in Nineteenth-Century New York* (Ithaca, N.Y.: Cornell University Press, 1991); Joan Jensen, *Loosening the Bonds: Mid-Atlantic Farm Women, 1750–1850* (New Haven: Yale University Press, 1986); John M. Faragher, *Sugar Creek: Life on the Illinois Prairie* (New Haven: Yale University Press, 1986); Deborah Fink, *Agrarian Women: Wives and Mothers in Rural Negraska, 1880–1940* (Chapel Hill: University of North Carolina Press, 1992), among the literature.

30. Robert D. Clark, "Ada Harris, Teenager: Oswego County, New York, 1873," *New York History*, 66 (1985): 29–47; subsequent citations appear in the text.

31. Clark writes, "more than romantic, she was a universal teenager, languishing in thoughts of death and sentiments of love" ("Ada Harris," p. 38). This is ahistorical and groundless, as are other of his speculations.

32. Victoria R. Lodge, Diary, 1874–75, 1877, typescript, American Antiquarian Society.

33. Elmira Sexton Newcomb, Diary, 1866–67, Mss., American Antiquarian Society.

34. Examples of this path other than the ones discussed here include Mary E. Bamford, "Child-Life among the California Foot-Hills," *Overland Monthly*, 2d ser., 2 (1883): 56–59; Mabel Stoll Brown, "The Prairie Child," *South Dakota Historical Collections*, 39 (1978): 148–223; Clara Hilderman Ehrlich, "My Childhood on the Prairie," *Colorado Magazine*, 51 (1974): 115–

140; Georgia Burns Hills, "Memories of a Pioneer Childhood," *Colorado Magazine,* 32 (1955): 110–128; Venola Lewis Bivans, ed., "The Diary of Luna E. Warner, a Kansas Teenager of the Early 1870s," *Kansas Historical Quarterly,* 35 (1969): 276–311, 411–441. See also Elliott West's writings, previously cited.

35. For two interesting cases of trans-Atlantic migrations to the American West, see Victoria Jacobs, *Diary of a San Diego Girl—1856,* ed. Sylvia Arden (Santa Monica, Calif.: Norton B. Stern, 1974); Mary Hall Paterson, "I Remember," typescript, generously lent to me by her late granddaughter, Dr. Sally Ramsey of Dallas (to whom this book is dedicated).

36. *Mollie: The Journal of Mollie Dorsey Sanford in Nebraska and Colorado Territories, 1857–1866,* ed. and intro. with notes by Donald F. Danker (Lincoln: University of Nebraska Press, 1959).

37. Marlene Springer and Haskell Springer, eds., *Plains Woman: The Diary of Martha Farnsworth, 1882–1922* (Bloomington: Indiana University Press, 1986).

38. See the introduction, ibid.

39. See Sharon O'Brien, "Tomboyism and Adolescent Conflict: Three Nineteenth-Century Case Studies," in *Woman's Being, Woman's Place: Female Identity and Vocation in American History,* ed. Mary Kelley (Boston: G. K. Hall, 1979), pp. 350–373.

40. *The Autobiography of Mary R. Luster, Springfield, Missouri, Written in Her Eighty-First and Eighty-Second Years* (Springfield, Mo.: Cain Printing Co., 1935); subsequent citations appear in the text.

41. Valuable comparisons to the examples in this section include Folmar, *"This State of Wonders";* Paul Gaston, *Women of Fair Hope,* Mercer University Memorial Lectures, no. 25 (Athens: University of Georgia Press, 1984).

42. Blanche Beal Lowe, "Growing Up in Kansas," *Kansas History,* 8 (1985): 36–53; subsequent citations appear in the text.

43. Mary P. Burke, Diary, 1861, photocopy, Mss., Texas State Library and Archives, Austin.

44. Ella Cole, Diary, October 22, 1883–April 16, 1884, typescript, James Reid Cole Papers, Barker Texas History Center, University of Texas at Austin.

45. See in particular the work of Roberta Park and Allen Guttmann on women in sports. In general, see J. A. Mangan and Roberta J. Park, eds., *From "Fair Sex" to Feminism: Sport and the Socialization of Women in the Industrial and Postindustrial Eras* (London: Cass, 1987).

46. Mabel Montgomery Minter, Diary, 1893, typescript, Texas State Library and Archives, Austin.

47. Tennessee Keys Embree, Diary, July 21–December 28, 1862, typescript, Barker Texas History Center, University of Texas at Austin.

48. Margaret Armstrong Bowie, Diary, August 12, 1872–October 12, 1877, typescript, Barker Texas History Center, University of Texas at Austin.

49. Elizabeth Reed Brent, "Childhood on the Western Frontier," *Oregon Historical Quarterly,* 83 (1982): 117–152; subsequent citations appear in the text. See also Elliott West's works on children in the West, cited previously.

50. See also Elizabeth's accounts of beginning school and of her mother's rigid routine (ibid., passim).

51. For additional information on growing up in the West, see Gerald McFarlin, *A Scattered People: An American Family Moves West* (New York: Penguin, 1985).

52. In addition to works cited earlier, see, for example, Carole Srole, "'Beyond One's Control': Life Course and the Tragedy of Class: Boston, 1800 to 1900," *Journal of Family History,* 11 (1986): 43–54; S. J. Kleinberg, *The Shadow of the Mills: Working-Class Families in Pittsburgh, 1870–1915* (Pittsburgh: University of Pittsburgh Press, 1989); Ileen A. DeVault, *Sons and Daughters of Labor: Class and Clerical Work in Turn-of-the-Century Pittsburgh* (Ithaca, N.Y.: Cornell University Press, 1990); Miriam Cohen, *Workshop to Office: Two Generations of Italian Women in New York City, 1900–1950* (Ithaca: Cornell University Press, 1992); Barbara Brenzel, *Daughters of the State* (Cambridge, Mass.: MIT Press, 1983); Eric C. Schneider, *In the Web of Class: Delinquents and Reformers in Boston, 1810s–1930s* (New York: New York University Press, 1992). Secondary materials offering extensive treatment of individual lives include Ellen C. Lagemann, *A Generation of Women: Education in the Lives of Progressive Reformers* (Cambridge, Mass.: Harvard University Press, 1979), which discusses Grace Dodge (upper class), Maud Nathan and Lillian Wald (middle class), and Leonora O'Reilly and Rose Schneiderman (working class); Paul M. Gaston, *Women of Fair Hope,* which discusses Marietta Johnson (middle class) and Marie Howland (working class); Joyce Antler, *Lucy Sprague Mitchell: The Making of a Modern Woman* (New Haven: Yale University Press, 1987); and the many biographies and autobiographies of Jane Addams. Other accounts include, for the middle class, Marlene Deahl Merrill, ed., *Growing Up in Boston's Gilded Age: The Journal of Alice Stone Blackwell, 1872–1874* (New Haven: Yale University Press, 1990); Mary Ellen Chase, *A Goodly Heritage* (New York: Holt, 1932); for the working class, Hilda Satt Polacheck, *I Came a Stranger: The Story of a Hull-House Girl* (Urbana: University of Illinois Press, 1989); Rose [Gallup] Cohen, *Out of the Shadow* (New York: George Doran, 1918), among numerous relevant works in women's history.

53. On the upper class, see in general previously cited works by Frederic Jaher, James McLachlan, Edward Pessen, Jane Pease and William Pease, Peter Hall, and Ronald Story.

54. *Julia Newberry's Diary,* intro. Margaret Ayer Barnes and Janet Ayer Fairbanks (New York: Norton, 1933). Her father's estate established the Newberry Library, Chicago, after his premature death.

55. On the education of girls in this period, see Louise L. Stevenson, "Sarah Porter Educates Useful Ladies, 1847–1900," *Winterthur Portfolio,* 18 (1983): 39–59. In addition to the works of Jill Conway, James McLachlan, and Barbara Miller Solomon, cited earlier, see Helen Horowitz, *Alma Mater* (New York: Knopf, 1984); idem, *Campus Life* (New York: Knopf, 1987); Lynn Gordon, *Gender and Higher Education in the Progressive Era* (New Haven: Yale University Press, 1990).

56. Adeline Atwater, "The Autobiography of an Extravert / One Woman's Story (by the late Mrs. Henry C. Pynchon)," Mss., Atwater Papers, Newberry Library, Chicago; subsequent citations appear in the text.

57. Compare Atwater (ibid.), for example, with Grace Dodge in Lagemann, *Generation*, and various accounts of Jane Addams. Note also Atwater on her illness and her relationship with her mother.

58. On sexuality in practice as well as expectations and proscriptions, see John D'Emilio and Estelle Friedman, *Intimate Matters: A History of Sexuality in America* (New York: Harper and Row, 1988); John Modell, *Into Their Own: From Youth to Adulthood in the United States, 1920–1975* (Berkeley: University of California Press, 1989); Paula Fass, *The Damned and the Beautiful: American Youth in the 1920s* (New York: Oxford University Press, 1977); Beth Bailey, *From Front Porch to Back Seat: Courtship in Twentieth-Century America* (Baltimore: Johns Hopkins University Press, 1988); see also essays by James McGovern and Daniel Scott Smith, among an uneven literature. See also the comments of Henry Seidel Canby, discussed later in this chapter.

59. In addition to the now classic studies of John Rousmanière, Jill Ker Conway, and Allen Davis, see Kathryn Sklar, "Hull House in the 1890s: Community of Women Reformers," *Signs*, 10 (1985): 658–677; Regina G. Kunzel, *Fallen Women, Problem Girls: Unmarried Mothers and the Professionalization of Social Work, 1890–1945* (New Haven: Yale University Press, 1993). See also Polacheck, *I Came a Stranger*.

60. Etta R[ichards] Harlow, Diary, 1860–61, Mss., American Antiquarian Society.

61. Mariana Thompson, Diary, July 20, 1861–September 22, 1864, Mss., Texas State Library and Archives, Austin.

62. For another schoolgirl diary, see Louisa M. Nichols, Diary, May 11, 1863–June 11, 1864, Mss., Nichols Family Collection, Baker Texas History Center, University of Texas at Austin. For another middle-class girl growing up in a near-frontier setting, see David N. Wetzel, "Childhood in Colorado: A Girl's Life at the Turn of the Century," *Colorado Heritage*, 1–2 (1983): 74–79; the girl died prematurely at age thirteen.

63. These figures are taken from Barbara Miller Solomon, *In the Company of Educated Women* (New Haven: Yale University Press, 1985), 63–64 and passim. See also Smith-Rosenberg, *Disorderly;* and the works of Lynn Gordon, Jill Ker Conway, Ellen Lagemann, and Helen Horowitz, cited earlier, among a rich new literature.

64. Mary Roselle Davis, Diary, January 1–December 31, 1876, photocopy, Barker Texas History Center, University of Texas at Austin.

65. On August 16 she wrote: "After dressing this morning I swept some and cleaned up the parlor and my room I commenced to read 'Sex in Education' by Dr. [Edward] Clark[e]." On Clarke, see, for example, Carroll Smith-Rosenberg and Charles Rosenberg, "The Female Animal: Medical and Biological Views of Woman and Her Role In Nineteenth-Century America," *Journal of American History*, 60 (1973): 332–356, and Joan Jacobs Brum-

berg, "Chlorotic Girls, 1870–1920: A Historical Perspective on Female Adolescence," *Child Development,* 53 (1982): 1468–77, among a growing but uneven literature on nineteenth-century women (and men) and their physicians.

66. Margaret Deland, *Golden Yesterdays* (New York: Harper and Row, 1941); subsequent citations appear in the text. Deland became an author, writing *The Iron Woman, The Awakening of Helena Richie, Old Chester Tales,* and other books.

67. Michael P. Weber and Peter N. Stearns, eds., *The Spencers of Amberson Avenue* (Pittsburgh: University of Pittsburgh Press, 1983); subsequent citations appear in the text. Written as a memento in 1959, this was intended for family members. Ethel Spencer never married. For many years she taught English at the Carnegie Institute of Technology, predecessor of Carnegie-Mellon University.

68. On domestic architecture, see the important work of Gwendolyn Wright, *Moralism and the Model Home* (Chicago: University of Chicago Press, 1980); Clifford Clark, Jr., *The American Family Home* (Chapel Hill: University of North Carolina Press, 1986); Kenneth T. Jackson, *Crabgrass Frontier* (New York: Oxford University Press, 1985); Margaret Marsh, *Suburban Lives* (New Brunswick, N.J.: Rutgers University Press, 1990), among others. See Weber and Stearns, *The Spencers,* passim, for details, genealogies, architectural designs, and family photographs.

69. Note here a feminine perspective. Ethel's brothers might well have had different recollections, had they created such a record (though the fact that they did not perhaps constitutes another salient point).

70. Compare with Annie Dillard's recollections of a half century later in *An American Childhood* (New York: Harper and Row, 1987).

71. See Ethel's tabulation of educational expenses in Weber and Stearns, *Spencers,* pp. 91–92.

72. Especially important is the work conducted by Paul Thompson and the development of the oral history archive at the University of Sussex in England. Thompson has also edited several important collections that highlight cross-European approaches and current research.

73. Although its focus is on a later period, the 1920s and 1930s, Lizabeth Cohen's study of Chicago workers and their world is exemplary; see her essay "Encountering Mass Culture at the Grassroots: The Experience of Chicago Workers in the 1920s," *American Quarterly,* 41 (1989), 6–33; and idem, *Making a New Deal: Industrial Workers in Chicago, 1919–1939* (New York: Cambridge University Press, 1990). See also David Nasaw, *Children of the City* (New York: Doubleday, 1985); Cary Goodman, *Choosing Sides* (New York: Schocken, 1979); Harvey Kantor and David Tyack, eds. *Work, Youth, and Schooling* (Stanford: Stanford University Press, 1982); David Hogan, *Class and Reform: School and Society in Chicago, 1880–1930* (Philadelphia: University of Pennsylvania Press, 1985); Reed Ueda, *Avenues to Adulthood: The Origins of the High School and Social Mobility in an Ameri-*

can Suburb (Cambridge: Cambridge University Press, 1987); Joel Perlmann, *Ethnic Differences: Schooling and Social Structure among the Irish, Italians, Jews, and Blacks in an American City, 1880–1935* (Cambridge: Cambridge University Press, 1988); Dominick Cavallo, *Muscles and Morals* (Philadelphia: University of Pennyslvania Press, 1981); Steven Schlossman, *Love and the American Delinquent* (Chicago: University of Chicago Press, 1977); Ewa Morawska, *For Bread with Butter* (Cambridge: Cambridge University Press, 1985); Kathy Peiss, *Cheap Amusements: Working Women and Leisure in Turn-of-the-Century New York* (Philadelphia: Temple University Press, 1986); Elizabeth Ewen, *Immigrant Women in the Land of Dollars* (New York: Monthly Review Press, 1985); Susan Glenn, *Daughters of the Shtetl* (Ithaca, N.Y.: Cornell University Press, 1990); Cohen, *Workshop;* Sydney Stahl Weinberg, *The World of Our Mothers* (Chapel Hill: University of North Carolina Press, 1988); Neil Cowan and Ruth Schwartz Cowan, *Our Parents' Lives* (New York: Basic Books, 1989).

74. See, for example, among many relevant works, Jacqueline Dowd Hall et al., *Like a Family* (Chapel Hill: University of North Carolina Press, 1987); James Borchert, *Alley Life in Washington* (Urbana: University of Illinois Press, 1980); Theodore Hershberg, ed., *Philadelphia* (New York: Oxford University Press, 1981); James Barrett, *Work and Community in the Jungle* (Urbana: University of Illinois Press, 1987); Robert Slayton, *Back of the Yards* (Chicago: University of Chicago Press, 1986).

75. Lizzie Cora Goodenough, Diaries, vol. 8, 1901, Mss., American Antiquarian Society.

76. Catharine Brody, "A New York Childhood," *American Mercury,* 14 (1928): 57–66; subsequent citations appear in the text. See also the memoirs of Kate Simon, discussed in Chapter 5. Colin Ward, *The Child in the City* (New York: Pantheon, 1977), is a basic text.

77. Compare this account with Nasaw, *Children of the City,* and Goodman, *Choosing Sides,* and memoirs such as Kate Simon's (see Chapter 5), as well as the boys' accounts later in this chapter.

78. This is a response Brody shares with peers such as Anzia Yezierska, Kate Simon, and Mary Antin, whose accounts are discussed elsewhere in this volume.

79. See John Kasson, *Amusing the Million* (New York: Hill and Wang, 1978), on Coney Island and "escapism"; compare with the views of Kathy Peiss in *Cheap Amusements* and Elizabeth Ewen in *Immigrant Women.* The interpretation of popular culture, recreation, and the like is an especially lively and diverse area of scholarly interest with a growing literature. See also Kate Simon's books (cited in Chapter 5) and E. L. Doctorow, *World's Fair* (New York: Random House, 1985).

80. The debates, then and now, often hew to extremes. See, among a large and not always sensible literature, Ward, *The Child in the City.*

81. Mary Antin, *The Promised Land* (1912; rpt., Princeton: Princeton University Press, 1985); subsequent citations appear in the text. On the book's reception

and impact, see Oscar Handlin's foreword. See also Anzia Yezierska, *Bread Givers* (1925; rpt., New York: Persea, 1975); Henry Roth, *Call It Sleep* (1934; rpt., New York: Avon Books, 1964); Michael Gold, *Jews without Money* (1930; rpt., New York: Carroll and Graf, 1984); Abraham Cahan, *The Rise of David Levinsky* (1917; rpt., New York: Harper and Row, 1960). There are comparable accounts by authors from Italian, Slavic, and other immigrant groups. See also Bodnar, *The Transplanted.*

82. In contrast to Handlin, among other readers (see his foreword to Antin, *Promised Land*), I dispute the typicality and representativeness of Antin's narrative as a basis for generalization to many others. She was a gifted writer, and very fortunate in many ways. Regardless, her story remains significant. Her book may be compared usefully with those of Anzia Yezierska, Hilda Polacheck, Kate Simon, and others cited in this volume.

83. On the upper class, see in general previously cited works by Frederic Jaher, James McLachlan, Edward Pessen, Jane Pease and William Pease, Peter Hall, E. Digby Baltzell, and Ronald Story.

84. Granville Howland Norcross, Diaries, 1860–1876, Mss., American Antiquarian Society.

85. On age consciousness, see, among other works, Chudacoff, *How Old Are You?;* Joseph Kett, *Rites of Passage: Adolescence in America, 1790 to the Present* (New York: Basic Books, 1977).

86. Amos Armsby, Pocket Diary, 1853(?), Mss., American Antiquarian Society.

87. Mary Ryan, *Cradle of the Middle Class: The Family in Oneida County, New York, 1790–1865* (Cambridge: Cambridge University Press, 1981); see also Kett, *Rites;* Harvey Graff, "Remaking Growing Up: Nineteenth-Century America," *Histoire sociale/Social History,* 24 (1991): 35–59. Chudacoff, *How Old Are You?*

88. James Ferdinand Fiske, Diaries, 1857–1860, Mss., American Antiquarian Society.

89. The subject of romance has received sustained if contradictory attention in histories of women but is much newer to students of men. See Rotundo, *American Manhood,* among an uneven literature.

90. This is a rare statement from a male. As a rule, women's close friendships had an import seldom seen as necessary for men. See Carroll Smith-Rosenberg, "The Female World of Love and Ritual," *Signs,* 1 (1976): 1–29; Rotundo, *American Manhood.* Working-class relationships may offer a contrast; see, for example, Richard Stott, *Workers in the Metropolis* (Ithaca: Cornell University Press, 1990); for women, see Peiss, *Cheap Amusements.*

91. Benjamin Jerome Sands, Diary, 1882, typescript of excerpts. A copy was generously sent to me in response to a request in the *New York Review of Books* by Sands's daughter Dorothy Sands Beer of Boulder, Colorado. I am grateful to her. Compare with Henry George Stern, *Reminiscences of a Gentle Man, 1887–1979* (privately printed). This material was generously sent to me by his son Richard Stern of the Department of English, University of Chicago, in response to my published request. The account was written

after the author's retirement from dentistry at age seventy-eight in 1965 and was typed by his daughter in 1977.

92. See Zelizer, *Pricing the Priceless Child*, among the relevant literature.

93. Drotner, *English Children and Their Magazines, 1751–1945* (New Haven: Yale University Press, 1988), pp. 4, 45.

94. Stephen F. Littlefield, Diaries, 1888–1891, Mss., American Antiquarian Society.

95. On expectations for and treatment of girls, see the important work of Michael Sedlak, Steven Schlossman, Bruce Bellingham, and Barbara Brenzel, among others previously cited.

96. Henry Blake Fuller Papers, Mss., Newberry Library. For "different" paths, see, for gay men, Claude Hartland, *The Story of a Life* (1901; rpt., San Francisco: Grey Fox, 1985); Richard Hall, *Letter from a Great-Uncle and Other Stories* (San Francisco: Grey Fox, 1985). I thank Richard Hall for calling my attention to these accounts. See also the important survey by John D'Emilio and Estelle Freedman, *Intimate Matters*. Another "different" kind of growing up is described in the unique autobiography of Pierrepont Noyes, *My Father's House: An Oneida Boyhood* (New York: Rinehart & Co., 1937). His father was John Humphrey Noyes, founder of the Oneida Community. Also of interest are the lives of missionaries, both male and female. See, for example, Jane Hunter, *American Women Missionaries in Turn-of-the-Century China* (New Haven: Yale University Press, 1984).

97. For the nineteenth century, see G. Stanley Hall's writings, cited previously; on Hall, see Dorothy Ross, *G. Stanley Hall: The Psychologist as Prophet* (Chicago: University of Chicago Press, 1972); Kett, *Rites*. Hall was only one of a number of proponents of "new" child and adolescent psychologies. Also relevant here are the experiences and reactions to various romantic and revolutionary youth currents and movements during the nineteenth century, including the experiences of 1848.

98. Henry Seidel Canby, *The Age of Confidence: Life in the Nineties* (New York: Farrar & Rinehart, 1934); subsequent citations appear in the text. See also his essay "Sex and Marriage in the Nineties," *Harper's Magazine*, 169 (September 1934): 427–436.

99. For student life, peers, and male-female relations, see Fass, *The Damned and the Beautiful*; Modell, *Into One's Own*; idem, "Dating Becomes the Way of American Youth," in *Essays on the Family and Historical Change*, ed. Leslie Moch and Gary Stark (College Station: Texas A&M University Press for the University of Texas at Arlington, 1983), 91–126; Bailey, *From Front Porch to Back Seat*; David Macleod, *Building Character in the American Boy: The Boy Scouts, YMCA, and Their Forerunners, 1870–1920* (Madison: University of Wisconsin Press, 1983); Reed Ueda, *Avenues to Adulthood: The Origins of the High School and Social Mobility in an American Suburb* (New York: Cambridge University Press, 1987).

100. Ford Dixon, ed., "The Diary of Edwin B. Hancock," *Texana*, 3 (1965), 297–320. Dixon comments that Edwin's diary may have been kept at the request of his parents.

101. Philip Scranton, "A Manufacturer's Apprenticeship: The Journal of Charles Doak, 1902–1906," *Pennsylvania Magazine of History and Biography,* 109 (1985): 59–67; idem, "Learning Manufacture: Education and Shop-Floor Schooling in the Family Firm," *Technology and Culture,* 27 (1986): 40–62.

102. Scranton, "Learning Manufacture," p. 60.

103. Though few sources were located by my research, one excellent case, brought to my attention by Glen Wallach, a Yale University graduate student, is that of Michael Campbell, Diary, October 1876–April 30, 1883, 4 vols., Mss., Sterling Library, Yale University Manuscripts and Archives.

104. See Lizabeth Cohen's exemplary study of Chicago workers and their world, previously cited.

5. The Beat of Different Drummers into the Early Twentieth Century

1. Among the literature on this period, see Michael Anderson, "The Emergence of the Modern Life Cycle in Britain," *Social History,* 10 (1985): 69–87; John Modell and Madeline Goodman, "Historical Perspectives," in *At the Threshold: The Developing Adolescent,* ed. S. Shirley Feldman and Glen R. Elliott (Cambridge, Mass.: Harvard University Press, 1990), pp. 93–122; John Modell, *Into One's Own: From Youth to Adulthood in the United States, 1900–1975* (Berkeley: University of California Press, 1989); John Modell, Frank Furstenberg, and Theodore Hershberg, "Social Change and Transitions to Adulthood in Historical Perspective," *Journal of Family History,* 1 (1976): 7–33; Peter Uhlenberg, "Changing Configurations of the Life Course," in *Transitions: The Family and the Life Course in Historical Perspective,* ed. Tamara K. Hareven (New York: Academic Press, 1978), pp. 65–98; Viviana Zelizer, *Pricing the Priceless Child* (New York: Basic Books, 1986); Joseph Kett, *Rites of Passage: Adolescence in America, 1790 to the Present* (New York: Basic Books, 1979); W. Norton Grubb and Marvin Lazerson, *Broken Promises: How Americans Fail Their Children* (New York: Basic Books, 1982); Michael B. Katz, *In the Shadow of the Poorhouse* (New York: Basic Books, 1986).

2. See, for example, among otherwise careful historians, the work of Joseph Kett and John Gillis. Sociological writings, in particular, reflect this perspective, as do most undergraduate textbooks.

3. In addition to the literature previously cited on young persons, schooling, and social reform, see, for social welfare reform in this period, David Rothman, *Conscience and Convenience: The Asylum and Its Alternatives in Progressive America* (Boston: Little, Brown, 1980); LeRoy Ashby, *Saving the Waifs: Reformers and Dependent Children, 1890–1917* (Philadelphia: Temple University Press, 1984); Jeremy Felt, *Hostages of Fortune: Child Labor Reform in New York State* (Syracuse: Syracuse University Press, 1965); Anthony Platt, *The Child Savers: The Invention of Delinquency* (Chicago: University of Chicago Press, 1969); Ellen Ryerson, *The Best-Laid Plans: American's Juvenile Court Experiment* (New York: Hill and Wang, 1978); Sheila Roth-

man, *Women's Proper Place: A History of Changing Ideals and Practices* (New York: Basic Books, 1978); Susan Tiffin, *In Whose Best Interest? Child Welfare Reform in the Progressive Era* (Westport: Greenwood, 1982); Beverly Stadum, *Poor Women and Their Families: Hard-Working Charity Cases, 1900–1930* (Albany: SUNY Press, 1992); Joseph Hawes, *The Children's Rights Movement* (Boston: Twayne, 1991); Peggy Pascoe, *Relations of Rescue: The Search for Female Moral Authority in the American West, 1874–1939* (New York: Oxford University Press, 1990); Theresa R. Richardson, *The Century of the Child: The Mental Hygiene Movement and Social Policy in the United States and Canada* (Albany: SUNY Press, 1989); Margo Horn, *Before It's Too Late: The Child Guidance Movement in the United States, 1922–1945* (Philadelphia: Temple University Press, 1989); Regina G. Kunzel, *Fallen Women, Problem Girls: Unmarried Mothers and the Professionalization of Social Work, 1890–1945* (New Haven: Yale University Press, 1993); Carol Smart, ed., *Regulating Womanhood: Historical Essays on Marriage, Motherhood, and Sexuality* (London: Routledge, 1992); Roger Cooter, ed., *In the Name of the Child: Health and Welfare, 1800–1940* (London: Routledge, 1992).

4. Race is considered in the more general discussion of the twentieth century in Chapter 6.

5. See Grubb and Lazerson, *Broken Promises;* Robert Bremner, "Other People's Children," *Journal of Social History,* 16 (1983): 83–103; John Hagan, "Destiny and Drift: Subcultural Preferences, Status Attainments, and the Risks and Rewards of Youth," *American Sociological Review,* 56 (1991): 567–582, among an unwieldy literature on deviance and delinquency.

6. David Matza, "Subterranean Traditions of Youth," *Annals of the American Academy of Political and Social Science,* 228 (1961): 102–118; idem, "Position and Behavior Patterns of Youth," in *Handbook of Modern Sociology,* ed. Robert E. L. Faris (Chicago: Rand McNally, 1964), pp. 191–215; and idem with Gresham M. Sykes, "Juvenile Delinquency and Subterranean Values," *American Sociological Review,* 26 (1961): 712–719. Note Matza's early criticisms of James Coleman's influential research. Also note his neglect of gender.

7. Given their chronology, certain lives discussed in Chapter 4 overlap with the material discussed here. They include Victor Albjerg among the men and Adeline Atwater among the women. For interesting later accounts, see Russell Baker, *Growing Up* (New York: New American Library, 1982), and its sequels; also Annie Dillard, *An American Childhood* (New York: Harper and Row, 1987), among others.

8. For reasons I have discussed, we generally lack first-person testimonial reports of African Americans, Asians, Hispanics, immigrants from eastern and southern Europe (other than Jews, who are well represented, and to a lesser extent Italians), and poor and working-class persons who did not participate in one or another form of the legendary "making it in America." Even this relatively recent period remains less well served than one might expect.

9. Ray Binns, "My Diary for 1910," copy of ms. donated in response to my request in the *New York Review of Books* by John Klemme of Farmington Hills, Michigan, whose generosity I gratefully acknowledge. Another rural memoir with some middle-class elements, though a slim account, is "Early Life and Times of Curtis Weeks," typescript, 1984, kindly provided in response to my request by his granddaughter Barbara Wiser of Kenexa, Kansas.

10. Everett Ludley, "The Growing Up Years: Memoirs of Farm and Town Life," *Palimpsest*, 70 (1989): 139–145; subsequent citations appear in the text.

11. Charles H. McKenzie, "Growing Up in Alberta, Parts One, Two, and Three," *Alberta History*, 37.3 (1989): 14–23; 37.4 (1989): 1–16; 38.1 (1990): 25–32; subsequent citations appear in the text.

12. Loren Reid, *Hurry Home Wednesday: Growing Up in a Small Missouri Town, 1905–1921* (Columbia: University of Missouri Press, 1978); idem, *Finally It's Friday: School and Work in Mid-America, 1921–1933* (Columbia: University of Missouri Press, 1981); subsequent citations appear in the text.

13. See Reid, *Hurry Home*, chap. 11, on his schooling.

14. Wilbur Cohen, "Growing Up in Milwaukee: 1913–1934," *Milwaukee History*, 7 (1984): 82–92; subsequent citations appear in the text. There is a large literature on Jewish immigrants, though relatively little of it focuses on midwestern cities.

15. For the various urban types, see Louis Adamic, *Laughing in the Jungle: The Autobiography of an Immigrant in America* (New York: Harper, 1932); Colin Ward, *The Child in the City* (New York: Pantheon, 1977); Daniel Calhoun, "The City as Teacher," *History of Education Quarterly*, 9 (1969): 312–325; idem, *The Intelligence*; David Nasaw, *Children of the City* (New York: Doubleday, 1985); Cary Goodman, *Choosing Sides: Playground and Street Life on the Lower East Side* (New York: Schocken, 1979); Jane Jacobs, *The Death and Life of Great American Cities* (New York: Vintage, 1961); Paul Goodman, *Growing Up Absurd* (New York: Vintage, 1960); and Paul Goodman and Percival Goodman, *Communitas* (New York: Vintage, 1960).

16. See, on the suburbs, the now standard historical works of Sam Bass Warner, Kenneth Jackson, and Margaret Marsh, cited earlier. The meaning of the suburbs and suburbanization remains hotly disputed even today.

17. Harry Roskolenko, *The Time That Was Then: The Lower East Side, 1900–1914: An Intimate Chronicle* (New York: Dial Press, 1971), p. 11; subsequent citations appear in the text. See also previously cited works by Mike Gold, David Levinsky, and Henry Roth; Adamic, *Laughing in the Jungle*.

18. Jere Mangione, *Mount Allegro: A Memoir of Italian American Life* (1942; rpt., New York: Columbia University Press, 1981), is a similar memoir of growing up in the smaller city of Rochester, New York.

19. On the socializing role of religion, see Roskolenko, *The Time*, esp. chap. 11, pp. 165–174.

20. Henry May, *Coming to Terms: A Study in Memory and History* (Berkeley: University of California Press, 1987); subsequent citations appear in the text.

See also, for the upper-middle class, Kenneth Sawyer Goodman, Diary, January 1, 1912–1916, Ms., Goodman Papers, Newberry Library, Chicago.

21. The chapters on high school and college (May, *Coming to Terms*) are especially instructive.

22. For middle-class young persons, see Fass, *Damned;* Modell, *Into One's Own;* idem, "Dating Becomes the Way of American Youth," in *Essays on the Family and Historical Change,* Leslie Page Moch and Gary D. Stark, eds. (College Station: Texas A&M University Press for the University of Texas at Arlington, 1983), pp. 91–126; Beth Bailey, *From Front Porch to Back Seat: Courtship in Twentieth-Century America* (Baltimore: Johns Hopkins University Press, 1988); Ellen K. Rothman, *Hands and Hearts: A History of Courtship in America* (New York: Basic Books, 1984); Reed Ueda, *Avenues to Adulthood: The Origins of the High School and Social Mobility in an American Suburb* (Cambridge: Cambridge University Press, 1987), among the literature.

23. Rosemary O. Joyce, *A Woman's Life: The Life History of a Rural Ohio Grandmother* (Columbus: Ohio State University Press, 1983); subsequent citations appear in the text. This life history is constructed from interviews that began in 1975. Joyce is a folklorist. She discusses her method in the book itself. See also, for rural women, works by John Faragher, Susan Osterud, Joan Jensen, and Deborah Fink, cited earlier, and Alan A. Brookes and Catherine A. Wilson, "'Working Away' from the Farm: The Young Women of North Huron, 1910–1930," *Ontario History,* 77 (1985): 281–300. See also, for urban women, the autobiographies of Mary Ellen Chase, *A Goodly Heritage* (New York: Holt, 1932); Dorothy Day, *From Union Square to Rome* (1938; rpt., Silver Springs, Md.: Preservation of the Faith Press, 1942); Rose [Gallup] Cohen, *Out of the Shadow* (New York: George Doran, 1918); Mary Antin, *The Promised Land: From Plotzk to Boston* (Boston: W. B. Clarke, 1899).

24. Interestingly, the intersection of class with gender is missed completely by the "life historian" Rosemary Joyce in *A Woman's Life.*

25. See, for interesting comparisons with girls growing up in the city, the work of Miriam Cohen, Lisa Fine, Joanne Meyerowitz, Susan Glenn, and Kathy Peiss, previously cited.

26. Kate Simon, *Bronx Primitive: Portraits in a Childhood* (New York: Harper and Row, 1982), and *A Wider World: Portraits in an Adolescence* (New York: Harper and Row, 1986); subsequent citations appear in the text, abbreviated *BP* and *WW,* respectively. Annie Dillard's *An American Childhood* provides nice contrasts with Simon, especially regarding education and family.

27. Compare Kate's experiences with those of Anzia Yezierska later in this chapter and Mary Antin, discussed in Chapter 4, as well as those that emerge from the pages of Irving Howe, *The World of Our Fathers* (New York: Harcourt Brace Jovanovich, 1976); Sydney Stahl Weinberg, *The World of Our Mothers: The Lives of Jewish Immigrant Women* (Chapel Hill: University of North Carolina Press, 1988); Neil M. Cowan and Ruth Schwartz

Cowan, *Our Parents' Lives: The Americanization of Eastern European Jews* (New York: Basic Books, 1989), or even those of Sarah Penfield.

28. On sex, see also Simon, *Wider World,* pp. 175–176.

29. Anzia Yezierska, *Children of Loneliness: Stories of Immigrant Life* (New York: Funk & Wagnalls, 1923); subsequent citations appear in the text. See also her *Bread Givers* (1925; rpt., New York: Persea, 1975); *The Open Cage: An Anzia Yezierska Collection,* ed. Alice Kessler-Harris (New York: Persea, 1979); Thomas J. Ferraro, "'Working Ourselves Up' in America: Anzia Yezierska's *Bread Givers,*" *South Atlantic Quarterly,* 89 (1990): 547–581; idem, *Ethnic Passages* (Chicago: University of Chicago Press, 1993). See also Mary Antin, *The Promised Land* (1912; rpt., Princeton: Princeton University Press, 1958).

6. The Disappearance of Childhood in Our Own Time?

1. The ubiquitousness of such commentary is as wearisome as it is noteworthy. I will not burden this note with a lengthy list of the "doom and gloom" literature. For some recent examples, see Donna Gaines, *Teenage Wasteland: Suburbia's Dead End Kids* (New York: Pantheon, 1991); Sylvia Ann Hewlett, *When the Bough Breaks: The Cost of Neglecting Our Children* (New York: Basic Books, 1991); David A. Hamburg, *Today's Children: Creating a Future for a Generation in Crisis* (New York: Times Books, 1992); "America's Childhood," *Daedalus,* 122 (Winter 1993); Donald J. Hernandez, *America's Children: Resources for Family, Government, and the Economy* (New York: Russell Sage Foundation, 1993).

2. Most of this information comes from Children's Defense Fund, *Children 1990: A Report Card, Briefing Book, and Action Primer,* and *S.O.S. America! A Children's Defense Budget* (Washington, D.C.: Children's Defense Fund, 1990). For a similar approach, see KERA-TV (Dallas), *A Better Child Quiz,* 1991, for which I served as chief adviser. See also Victor R. Fuchs and Diane M. Reklis, "America's Children: Economic Perspectives and Policy Options," *Science,* January 3, 1992, pp. 41–46; June Axinn and Mark Stern, *Dependency and Poverty: Old Problems in a New World* (Lexington, Mass.: Lexington Boooks, 1988); Andrew J. Cherlin, ed., *The Changing American Family and Public Policy* (Washington, D.C.: Urban Institute Press, 1988); Richard R. Nelson and Felicity Skidmore, eds., *American Families and the Economy: The High Costs of Living* (Washington, D.C.: National Academy Press, 1983); John L. Palmer, Timothy Smeeding, and Barbara Boyle Torrey, eds., *The Vulnerable* (Washington, D.C.: Urban Institute Press, 1988); Frank F. Furstenberg, Jr., and Andrew J. Cherlin, *Divided Families: What Happens to Children When Parents Part* (Cambridge, Mass.: Harvard University Press, 1991). It is instructive to compare serious research on the young with "doom and gloom" works by both journalistic and academic writers.

3. There are exceptions such as Alex Kotlowitz, *There Are No Children Here: The Story of Two Boys Growing Up in America* (New York: Doubleday,

1991). Yet that two relatively separate sets of images and promotional machines should develop, one for the poor and minorities and one for other children, speaks volumes about the troubled circumstances of those striving to grow up. See Norton Grubb and Marvin Lazerson, *Broken Promises: How Americans Fail Their Children* (New York: Basic Books, 1982), and works cited in note 2, as well as Marion Wright Edelman, *Families in Peril: An Agenda for Social Change* (Cambridge, Mass.: Harvard University Press, 1986); and Ruth Sidel, *Women and Children Last: The Plight of Poor Women in Affluent America* (New York: Viking, 1986), or her more recent *On Her Own: Growing Up in the Shadow of the American Dream* (New York: Viking, 1990). An important feminist literature is emerging, reflecting major differences within American society and culture.

4. On images, myths, and theories, see Arlene Skolnick, "Limits of Childhood: Conceptions of Child Development and Social Context," *Law and Contemporary Problems*, 39 (1975): 38–77; Denise Riley, *War in the Nursery: Theories of the Child and Mother* (London: Virago, 1983); Alison Clarke-Stewart, "Popular Primers for Parents," *American Psychologist*, 33 (1978): 359–369; William Graebner, "The Unstable World of Benjamin Spock: Social Engineering in a Democratic Culture, 1917–1950," *Journal of American History*, 67 (1980): 612–629; Nancy Pottishman Weiss, "Mother, the Invention of Necessity: Dr. Benjamin Spock's *Baby and Child Care*," *American Quarterly*, 29 (1977): 517–546; idem, "The Mother-Child Dyad Revisited: Perceptions of Mothers and Children in Twentieth-Century Child-Rearing Manuals," *Journal of Social Issues*, 34 (1978): 29–45; Michael Zuckerman, "Dr. Spock: The Confidence Man," in *The Family in History*, ed. Charles Rosenberg (Philadelphia: University of Pennsylvania Press, 1975), pp. 179–207; Eli Zaretsky, "The Place of the Family in the Origins of the Welfare State," in *Re-Thinking the Family: Feminist Perspectives*, ed. Barrie Thorne and Marilyn Yalom (New York: Longman, 1982), pp. 188–224; Eileen Boris and Peter Bardaglio, "The Transformation of Patriarchy: The Historical Role of the State," in *Families, Politics, and Public Policy*, ed. Irene Diamond (New York: Longman, 1983), among a growing literature.

5. Viviana Zelizer, *Pricing the Priceless Child* (New York: Basic Books, 1986). See discussion in preface and Chapter 1, with citations to relevant work by Arlene Skolnick, Aaron Esman, Joseph Adelson, Joel Best, Jenny Kitzinger, and Ian Hacking. There are also problems of "middle-class" standards for others. See Catherine J. Ross, "The Lessons of the Past: Defining and Controlling Child Abuse in the United States," in *Child Abuse: An Agenda for Action*, ed. George Gernber, Catherine J. Ross, and Edward Zigler (New York: Oxford University Press, 1980), pp. 63–81; Grubb and Lazerson, *Broken Promises;* Alan Wolfe, "The Child and the State: A Second Glance," *Contemporary Crises*, 2 (1978): 407–435.

6. Grubb and Lazerson, *Broken Promises*, pp. 78, 89, and passim.

7. Alan Wolfe, "The Child and the State," pp. 407–408. See also Grubb and Lazerson, *Broken Promises;* Edward F. Zigler, Sharon Lynn Kagan, and

Edgar Klugman, eds., *Children, Families, and Government: Perspectives on American Social Policy* (Cambridge: Cambridge University Press, 1983); Joseph M. Hawes, *The Children's Rights Movement* (Boston: Twayne, 1991); Glen H. Elder, Jr., John Modell, and Ross D. Parke, eds., *Children in Time and Place* (Cambridge: Cambridge University Press, 1993); Roberta Wollon, ed., *Children at Risk in America* (Albany: State University of New York Press, 1993).

8. On myth and experience in adolescence, see Elizabeth Douvan and Joseph Adelson, *The Adolescent Experience* (New York: Wiley, 1965); and more recently Aaron Esman, *Adolescence and Culture* (New York: Columbia University Press, 1990). Compare with James S. Coleman's classic books on adolescence and more generally with American sociology of the 1950s.

9. Peter Uhlenberg, "Changing Configurations of the Life Course," in *Transitions: The Family and the Life Course in Historical Perspective*, ed. Tamara K. Hareven (New York: Academic Press, 1978), p. 81. See also Marlis Buchmann, *The Script of Life in Modern Society* (Chicago: University of Chicago Press, 1989), among the contemporary and historical literature on paths of growing up.

10. Uhlenberg "Changing Configurations," p. 73; see also Susan Cotts Watkins, Jane A. Menken, and John Bongaarts, "Demographic Foundations of Family Change," *American Sociological Review,* 52 (1987): 346–358.

11. Uhlenberg, "Changing Configurations," p. 80. Uhlenberg's essay is an excellent example of the power of normative assumptions and demographic determinism. Sensitive studies of African Americans and other minorities, women, and communities repeatedly reflect shifting but persisting inequalities.

12. See pathbreaking cultural studies such as Lisabeth Cohen, *Making a New Deal: Industrial Workers in Chicago, 1919–1939* (New York: Cambridge University Press, 1990); studies of "everyday life" in England and the United States, including Mike Brake, *Comparative Youth Culture* (London: Routledge, 1985); Paul Willis, *Learning to Labour* (Farnsborough: Saxon House, 1977); Liz Heron, ed., *Truth, Dare, or Promise: Girls Growing Up in the Fifties* (London: Virago, 1985); Christine Griffin, *Typical Girls* (London: Routledge, 1985); Stuart Hall and Tony Jefferson, eds., *Resistance through Rituals* (London: Hutchinson, 1977); Henry A. Giroux, Roger Simon, et al., *Popular Culture, Schooling, and Everyday Life* (Amherst, Mass.: Bergin & Garvey, 1989); Wini Breines, *Young, White, and Miserable: Growing Up Female in the Fifties* (Boston: Beacon, 1991); Lilian Rubin, *Worlds of Pain* (New York: Basic Books, 1975); Ann Campbell, *Girls in the Gang* (Oxford: Blackwell, 1985).

13. John Modell, Frank Furstenberg, Jr., and Theodore Hershberg, "Social Change and Transitions to Adulthood in Historical Perspective," *Journal of Family History,* 1 (1976): 8.

14. Ibid., p. 17. And see Buchmann, *Script;* John Modell, *Into One's Own: From Youth to Adulthood in the United States, 1920–1975* (Berkeley: University of California Press, 1989); as well as recent literature on life course and life span studies.

15. Modell et al., "Transitions," p. 22. There have been changes after 1970, including the return of young adults who had earlier left home and a lengthening of time spent in family residence more generally. See Buchmann, *Script;* Sandra Hofferth, "Updating Children's Life Course," *Journal of Marriage and the Family,* 47 (1985): 93–115; Margaret Marini, "Age and Sequencing Norms in the Transition to Adulthood," *Social Forces,* 63 (1984): 229–244; idem, "The Order of Events in the Transition to Adulthood," *Sociology of Education,* 57 (1984): 63–84. On leaving home, the work of Frances Kobrin Goldscheider, Larry Long, and Christabel Young is significant; and see Calvin Goldscheider and Frances Goldscheider, *Leaving Home before Marriage* (Madison: University of Wisconsin Press, 1993); also Gerdt Sundstrom, "A Haven in a Heartless World? Living with Parents in Sweden and the United States, 1880–1982," *Continuity and Change,* 2 (1987): 145–187.

16. Modell et al., "Transitions," p. 25.

17. Ibid., pp. 29, 30–31. See also Modell, *Into One's Own;* Buchmann, *Script;* and recent life course and life span studies. Buchmann sees these relations breaking down; see her comments quoted in Chapter 1 of this volume. Confusion about contemporary trends links the "actors" to their interpreters. Some important data do contradict the doomsayers.

18. Buchmann, *Script,* pp. 69–70; Thomas Held, "Institutionalization and Deinstitutionalization of the Life Course," in "Social Structure and Social Construction of the Life Course," ed. Martin Kohli and John W. Meyer, *Human Development,* 29 (1986): 157–162.

19. Steven Dubnoff's largely unpublished research on "income adequacies" of American families speaks to this point, as does Mark Stern's research on the post–World War II period, Glen Elder's on the Great Depression and after, and Paul Osterman's on youth, work, and families. See Mark Stern, "Poverty and the Life-Cycle, 1940–1960," *Journal of Social History,* 24 (1991): 521–540.

20. On juveniles and employment, see Ellen Greenberger and Lawrence Steinberg, *When Teenagers Work: The Psychological and Social Costs of Adolescent Employment* (New York: Basic Books, 1986). See also James S. Coleman et al., *Youth: Transition to Adulthood,* Report of the Panel on Youth of the President's Science Advisory Committee (Chicago: University of Chicago Press, 1974); Centre for Educational Research and Innovation, *Becoming Adult in a Changing Society* (Paris: OECD, 1985); Paul Osterman, *Getting Started: The Youth Labor Market* (Cambridge, Mass.: MIT Press, 1980); Richard B. Freeman, ed., *The Youth Labor Market Problem,* NBER Conference Report (Chicago: University of Chicago Press, 1982); National Commission on Youth, *The Transition of Youth to Adulthood: A Bridge Too Long* (Boulder: Westview, 1980); Victoria Anne Steinitz and Ellen Rachel Solomon, *Starting Out: Class and Community in the Lives of Working-Class Children* (Philadelphia: Temple University Press, 1986). There is a large if uneven historical literature; it can be sampled in the essays reprinted in Harvey J. Graff, ed., *Growing Up in America: Historical Experiences* (Detroit: Wayne State University Press, 1987), among other sources.

21. Among the literature on government intervention, see especially Grubb and Lazerson, *Broken Promises.*

22. Watkins et al., "Demographic Foundations"; Hernandez, *America's Children.*

23. Data from Sandra L. Hofferth, "Updating Children's Life Course," *Journal of Marriage and the Family,* 47 (1985): 93–115; idem, "Recent Trends in the Living Arrangements of Children: A Cohort Life Table Analysis," in *Family Demography: Methods and Their Application,* ed. John Bongaarts, Thomas K. Burch, and Kenneth W. Wachter (Oxford: Oxford University Press, 1987), pp. 168–188, among her work. See also Hernandez, *America's Children.*

24. See, for example, tables in Michael Gordon, *The American Family* (New York: Random House, 1978), and also studies of divorce such as Lenore Weitzman, *The Divorce Revolution* (New York: Free Press, 1985); Furstenberg and Cherlin, *Divided Families;* Sidel, *Women and Children;* Robert E. Emery, E. Mavis Hetherington, and Lisabeth F. Dilalla, "Divorce, Children, and Social Policy," in *Child Development Research and Social Policy,* 1 (1984): 189–266; Frances K. Goldscheider and Linda J. Waite, *New Families, No Families? The Transformation of the American Home* (Berkeley: University of California Press, 1991); Judith Stacey, *Brave New Families* (New York: Basic Books, 1990); Sanford M. Dornbusch and Myra H. Strober, eds., *Feminism, Children, and the New Families* (New York: Guilford Press, 1988). Compare with Barbara Dafoe Whitehead, "Dan Quayle Was Right," *Atlantic* (April 1993); Valerie Polakow, *Lives on the Edge: Single Mothers and Their Children in the Other America* (Chicago: University of Chicago Press, 1993).

25. Andrew J. Cherlin, *Marriage, Divorce, Remarriage* (Cambridge, Mass.: Harvard University Press, 1981). See also Furstenberg and Cherlin, *Divided Families;* Gerald David Jaynes and Robin M. Williams, eds., *A Common Destiny: Blacks and American Society* (Washington, D.C.: National Academy Press, 1989). On the "underclass," see Christopher Jencks and Paul E. Peterson, eds., *The Urban Underclass* (Washington, D.C.: Brookings Institution, 1991); Michael B. Katz, ed., *The Underclass Debate: The View from History* (Princeton: Princeton University Press, 1992).

26. Andrew Hacker, *Two Nations: Black and White, Separate, Hostile, Unequal* (New York: Scribners, 1992), p. 77; Jaynes and Williams, *Common Destiny;* Jencks and Peterson, *The Urban Underclass.* See also Michael B. Katz, *The Undeserving Poor* (New York: Pantheon, 1989); Rickie Solinger, *Wake Up Little Susie: Single Pregnancy and Race Before Wade v. Roe* (New York: Routledge, 1992).

27. Modell, *Into One's Own,* pp. 58–59 and passim, among the specialized literature.

28. On women, see, among a large literature, Miriam Cohen, *Workshop to Office: Two Generations of Italian Women in New York City, 1900–1950* (Ithaca, N.Y.: Cornell University Press, 1992); Kathy Peiss, *Cheap Amusements: Working Women and Leisure in Turn-of-the-Century New York* (Phila-

delphia: Temple University Press, 1986). On deviance and delinquency, see, for example, Michael W. Sedlak, "Young Women in the City: Adolescence, Deviance, and the Transformation of Educational Policy," *Social Service Review,* 56 (1982): 448–464; Steven L. Schlossman and Stephanie Wallach, "The Crime of Precocious Sexuality," *Harvard Educational Review,* 48 (1978): 65–94.

29. On scouts, the best study deals only with boys; see David Macleod, *Building Character in the American Boy: The Boy Scouts, YMCA, and Their Forerunners, 1870–1920* (Madison: University of Wisconsin Press, 1983). For high schools and peer culture, see Dom Cavallo, "Adolescent Peer Group Morality," *Psychohistory Review,* 6 (1977–78): 88–101; Thomas Gutowski, "Student Initiative and the Origins of the High School Extracurriculum: Chicago, 1880–1915," *History of Education Quarterly,* 28 (1988): 49–72; William Graebner, *Coming of Age in Buffalo: Youth and Authority in the Postwar Era* (Philadelphia: Temple University Press, 1990); Gerald Sorin, *The Nurturing Neighborhood: The Brownsville Boys Club and Jewish Community in Urban America, 1940–1990* (New York: New York University Press, 1990); Joseph E. Illick, *At Liberty: The Story of a Community and a Generation: The Bethlehem, Pennsylvania, High School Class of 1952* (Knoxville: University of Tennessee Press, 1989); Richard M. Ugland, "Viewpoints and Morale of Urban High School Students during World War II—Indianapolis as a Case Study," *Indiana Magazine of History,* 77 (1981): 150–178; Barbara Brenzel, Cathy Roberts-Gersch, and Judith Wittner, "Becoming Social: School Girls and Their Culture between the Two World Wars," *Journal of Early Adolescence,* 5 (1985): 479–488; and especially the classic community studies of Middletown, Elmstown, River City, Crestwood Heights, and the West End. Note the regular class, ethnic, racial, and gender distinctions.

30. Peiss, *Cheap Amusements,* p. 56.

31. David Matza, "Subterranean Traditions of Youth," *Annals of the American Academy of Political and Social Science,* 228 (1961): 102–118; idem, "Position and Behavioral Patterns of Youth," in *Handbook of Modern Sociology,* ed. R. E. L. Faris (Chicago: Rand McNally, 1964), pp. 191–216. See also David Matza and Gresham Sykes, "Juvenile Delinquency and Subterranean Values," *American Sociological Review,* 26 (1961): 712–719; also indictments of "myths of adolescence" from the 1950s and 1960s, including Douvan and Adelson, *Adolescent Experience;* William A. Westling and Frederick Elkin, "The Protective Environment and Adolescent Socialization," *Social Forces,* 35 (1956): 243–249; idem, "The Myth of Adolescent Culture," *American Sociological Review,* 20 (1955): 680–684. See also Joseph Adelson, *Inventing Adolescence* (New Brunswick, N.J.: Transaction, 1986); Esman, *Adolescence.* Compare to the work of James Coleman, or even to Erik Erikson. See John Hagan, "Destiny and Drift: Subcultural Preferences, Status Attainments, and the Risks and Rewards of Youth," *American Sociological Review,* 56 (1991): 567–582. For women, see the now classic Judith M. Bardwick and Elizabeth Douvan, "Ambivalence: The Socialization of Women," in

Women in Sexist Society: Studies in Power and Powerlessness, ed. Vivian Gornick and Barbara K. Moran (New York: Basic Books, 1971), pp. 225–241; see also Sidel, *On Her Own.* Carol Gilligan's writings and the feminist response to them are also relevant here.

32. Modell, *Into One's Own,* pp. 169–170.

33. From about 1968 on, scholars divide pro and con, increasingly con on the impact of the events and the legacies of the 1960s. For one synoptic view, see Mary Ryan and Richard Busacca, "Beyond the Family Crisis," *democracy,* 2 (1982): 79–92. See also the classic writings of Kenneth Keniston, Paul Goodman, Edgar Z. Friedenberg, and now Richard Flacks.

34. Ryan and Busacca, "Beyond the Family Crisis," p. 90. See also Arlene Skolnick, *Embattled Paradise: The American Family in an Age of Uncertainty* (New York: Basic Books, 1991); Paul C. Light, *Baby Boomers* (New York: Norton, 1988); Katherine S. Newman, *Declining Fortunes* (New York: Basic Books, 1993); Jack Whalen and Richard Flacks, *Beyond the Barricades: The Sixties Generation Grows Up* (Philadelphia: Temple University Press, 1989); Richard Flacks, *Making History: The American Left and the American Mind* (New York: Columbia University Press, 1988).

35. Douvan and Adelson, *The Adolescent Experience.* See also John R. Seeley, R. Alexander Sims, and E. W. Loosley, *Crestwood Heights: A Study of the Culture of Suburban Life* (Toronto: University of Toronto Press, 1956), among other studies.

36. Adelson, *Inventing,* p. 137. It is useful to take Grubb and Lazerson's *Broken Promises* as a context for framing and interpreting Adelson's cavlier reference to adult society. At the least, he needs to take seriously the roles of class, gender, and race in constructions and representations of the young.

37. Kenneth Keniston, *The Uncommitted: Alienated Youth in American Society* (New York: Harcourt, Brace, 1960); idem, *Young Radicals: Notes on Committed Youth* (New York: Harcourt, Brace, 1968); idem, *Youth and Dissent* (New York: Harcourt, Brace, 1971); Edgar Z. Friedenberg, *The Vanishing Adolescent* (New York: Dell, 1959); idem, *Coming of Age in America* (New York: Random House, 1963); Paul Goodman, *Growing Up Absurd* (New York: Random House, 1959); idem, *Compulsory Mis-Education and The Community of Scholars* (New York: Vintage, 1965); James Coleman, *The Adolescent Society: The Social Life of the Teenager and Its Impact on Education* (New York: Free Press, 1961).

38. Brake, *Comparative Youth Culture,* pp. 7–8. See also Paul Willis's studies; Griffen, *Typical Girls;* Herbert Gans, *The Urban Villagers* (New York: Free Press, 1962); Michael Moffatt, *Coming of Age in New Jersey: College and American Culture* (New Brunswick, N.J.: Rutgers University Press, 1989); Terry Williams and William Kornblum, *Growing Up Poor* (Lexington, Mass.: Lexington Books, 1985); Harriet Pipes McAdoo, ed., *Black Families* (Newbury Park, Calif.: Sage Publications, 1988); Jay MacLeod, *Ain't No Makin' It: Leveled Aspirations in a Low-Income Neighborhood* (Boulder, Colo.: Westview, 1987); Carol Stack, *All Our Kin: Strategies for Survival in a Black*

Community (New York: Harper and Row, 1974), for comparisons, among the literature.

39. Brake, *Comparative Youth Culture*, p. 24.

40. Light, *Baby Boomers*, is a good summary and guide. See also Newman, *Declining Fortunes*. For Richard Easterlin, see his *Birth and Fortune: The Impact of Numbers on Personal Welfare* (New York: Basic Books, 1980).

41. Packard is perhaps the worst offender, but he has rivals. Typically these pessimistic works are marked by (1) the sense that at some undefined and romanticized time prior to the present children were superior to those growing up today (parents too); (2) consequent images of the decline of children, parents, families; (3) a sense of difference derived from notions of children's uniqueness, innocence, vulnerability, incompetence; (4) a sense that that uniqueness is in great danger of being lost, and with it children as we have known them; (5) claims that today's young are singular, homogeneous, and simple; (6) a sense of great changes today, especially as a result of technology that damages and threatens the young—and a collateral sense of a "new era" causing children to grow up too fast while preventing some adults from growing up at all. All these claims suffer from certain general problems: (1) lack of evidence; (2) notions of a fall from a mythical golden age; (3) presumptions of near-total homogeneity among the young; (4) assumptions about the nature and needs of children constituting a version of "invented" or "constructed" children. See also Riley, *War in the Nursery*; Carolyn Steedman, Cathy Urwin, and Valerie Walkerdine, eds., *Language, Gender, and Childhood* (London: Routledge, 1985).

42. Andrew J. Cherlin, "The Changing American Family and Public Policy," in Cherlin, *Changing American Family*, p. 8.

43. For the economic conditions of children, see Palmer et al., *The Vulnerable*; Frank Levy's work on families and the economy; publications of the Children's Defense Fund, Carnegie Council, Ford Foundation; National Academy of Science, *American Families and the Economy*; Axxin and Stern, *Dependency and Poverty*; Dornbusch and Strober, eds., *Feminism, Children, and the New Families*; Rochelle Lefkowitz and Ann Withorn, eds. *For Crying Out Loud: Women and Poverty in the United States* (New York: Pilgrim Press, 1986), among other studies.

44. Cherlin, "American Family," p. 9; Furstenberg and Cherlin, *Divided Families*; Weitzman, *Divorce Revolution*; compare with Hernandez, *America's Children*, or Hamburg, *Today's Children*.

45. Cherlin, "American Family," p. 10; see also Furstenberg and Cherlin, *Divided Families*.

46. Nicholas Zill and Carolyn C. Rogers, "Recent Trends in the Well-Being of Children in the United States and Their Implications for Public Policy," in Cherlin, *Changing American Family*, p. 41.

47. Zill and Rogers, "Recent Trends," pp. 71–72.

48. Ibid., p. 72.

49. Ibid., p. 79.

50. For these and other trends, see, for example, James A. Sweet and Larry L. Bumpass, *American Families and Households* (New York: Russell Sage Foundation, 1987); Goldscheider and DaVanzo, *New Families, No Families?*; Goldscheider and Goldschieder, *Leaving Home*; Dennis P. Hogan, *Transitions and Social Change: The Early Lives of American Men* (New York: Academic Press, 1981), Susan Cotts Watkins et al., "Demographic Foundations."

51. See, among the literature, Greenberger and Steinberg, *When Teenagers Work*; Steinitz and Solomon, *Starting Out*; Willis, *Learning to Labor*; W. Norton Grubb, "The Bandwagon Once More: Vocational Preparation for High-Tech Occupations," *Harvard Educational Review,* 54 (1984): 429–451; Henry M. Levin, "Youth Unemployment and Its Educational Consequences," *Educational Evaluation and Policy Analysis,* 5 (1983): 231–247; Albert Rees, "An Essay on Youth Joblessness," *Journal of Economic Literature,* 24 (1986): 613–628; James S. Coleman et al., *Youth: Transition to Adulthood*; James S. Coleman and Torsten Husen, *Becoming Adult in a Changing Society* (Paris: OECD, 1985), among a broad literature.

52. David Hamburg, *Today's Children*, p. 9–10. Among related studies, see Fred M. Hechinger, *Fateful Choices: Healthy Youth for the 21st Century* (New York: Hill and Wang, 1992), among others.

Acknowledgments

No scholarly study reaches completion without a cast of contributors; certainly none of my books has done so. In these pages I acknowledge with gratitude only those whose assistance registers in my notes and memories. No doubt there are others. All of them, I hope, know the significance of their part and the depth of my thanks. Without them or the funding agencies listed here, this work would have remained on the drafting table.

For financial support, I thank the American Antiquarian Society for a Peterson Fellowship, which I was unable to accept when offered but whose work I accomplished a year later; the Newberry Library for a short-term fellowship that eased a period of research in residence; and the University of Texas at Dallas for the support of a graduate research assistant in the earliest stage of the project. Award of a senior American Antiquarian Society–National Endowment for the Humanities Fellowship in 1989 greatly facilitated completion of research and writing on much of a first draft. During the summers of 1991 and 1992 the Spencer Foundation encouraged and speeded the final drafting, revisions, and manuscript preparation with the award of two invaluable grants from their imaginative Small Grants Program. The University of Texas at Dallas through Dean Michael Simpson provided funds to defray the cost of indexing.

Librarians and staff at several research centers made the primary research into hundreds of first-person sources a pleasure. Most of the original materials on which this study rests are found at the American Antiquarian Society (AAS), Worcester, Massachusetts; The Newberry Library, Chicago; and the Barker Texas History Center, University of Texas at Austin and State of Texas Archives, Austin. I am also grateful for permission to quote from or cite materials held by these institutions. Through Vickie Bullock's interlibrary loans, the University of Texas at Dallas's McDermott Library was also helpful. A great many persons at these institutions responded to my queries, found materials for me, gave aid and encouragement, and not only met my demands with good cheer and fine service but also rewarded me with their interest in the project. At AAS, among many who deserve acknowledgment, I thank Sid Berger, Joanne Chaison, Marie Lamoureau, Richard Knowlton, Joyce Tracey, Barbara Simmons, Laura Wasowicz, Dennis Laurie, and Marc McCorison. Also supportive were Sheila McAvey, John Hench, Diane Schoen, Frances Bernard, Carol Ann Patterson, Nancy Tivenan, and Don Shrader. The personal interest of long-time friend and teacher and then AAS president Jill Conway was a special treat. Other fellows and students made a long nine months alone in Worcester an easier passage than it might have been. Sid Berger and his peas, along with Michele Cloonen and Aaron Berger, were more important than I think they know. Nearby in Cambridge, Johanna Drucker added her interest and support. Beyond the call of sharing was Vicki Graff's willingness, if sometimes a bit begrudging, to do the bulk of the traveling. She knows best the strains and the (sometimes delayed) rewards of those months.

At the Newberry, Dick Brown was as usual a gracious host. I also thank Jan Reiff, for so long my best friend in Chicagoland. In the library, especially helpful (as always) were Diana Haskell and John Aubrey. In the city I was fed, questioned, and supported by Sue Hirsch, Lew Erenberg, Harriet Lightman, and George Huppert, among many friends and colleagues in my second city and longtime research base. In Austin, Johanna Drucker also provided a place to stay, and the Barker Center and State Archives staffs were exceptionally helpful in allowing me to accomplish a great deal within a short stay.

Graduate students at the University of Texas at Dallas helped in one capacity or another, though seldom for direct reward. Jill Milling served as a stimulating graduate research assistant at the project's beginning; Patricia Hill, Lauren Kattner, Steve Hamlin, and Pat Meador assisted in a variety of ways. The many students who participated in my graduate seminars and Interdisciplinary Studies courses on growing up in America rewarded me with their numbers, reactions, questions, demands for clarity, delight in the subject, and tolerance for a history prof. running roughshod through the disciplines and the ages. They allowed me to try out many notions and formulations with good cheer and occasional rude noises. And, most of the time, they liked my choice of movies.

Other audiences honored me with their attention and questions. Working with producer Rob Tranchin on several original programs for the Dallas public television station KERA during PBS's eighteen-month-long Family Project was a special treat and an encouraging experience of rare relevance for a historian.

Several Dallas-area audiences joined those at the American Antiquarian Society, Social Science History Association, Library History Seminar, Simon Fraser University, Universities of Linkoping and Stockholm in Sweden (for which I thank especially Bengt Sandin of Tema, Linkoping), and University of Adelaide in Australia (I thank Ian Davey). Early versions of some of the arguments and materials in this volume appeared in a special historical issue of the *Journal of Early Adolescence* in 1985, *History of Education Quarterly* in 1986, *Histoire sociale/Social History* in 1991, and my anthology *Growing Up in America: Historical Experiences* (Wayne State University Press, 1987). Their editors, especially my friends Paul Mattingly, Bob Mandel, and Chad Gaffield, helped with their critiques and demands for revision.

Far too many other friends and colleagues than I can list here supported, critiqued, prodded, shared, and stimulated. In addition to those I have already named, the tip of this tall structure must include Michael Katz, Jerry Soliday, Roger Schofield, Peter Laslett, Dan Calhoun, Jim Turner, Jerry Zaslove, M. J. Maynes, Leslie Moch, Ellen Dwyer, and Chad Gaffield.

At Harvard University Press, Aïda Donald and Jennifer Snodgrass made the book in this form, true to my conception, possible by aiding its revision. Aïda's enthusiasm, faith, support, and appreciation are rare in my publishing experience. Excellent work by Amanda Heller, Donna Bouvier, and Elizabeth Suttell improved the manuscript and eased the transition into print.

Last but never least, as they know best, are Harrison and Vicki Graff: occasional obstacles, sometimes distractions, always fonts of prodding, pride, and love.

Index